Introduction to
Physical Anthropology

FIFTH EDITION

Introduction to Physical Anthropology

HARRY NELSON

Emeritus
Department of Anthropology
Foothill College
Los Altos, California

ROBERT JURMAIN

Department of Anthropology
San Jose State University
San Jose, California

West Publishing Company
St. Paul   New York   Los Angeles   San Francisco

Library of Congress Cataloging-in-Publication Data

Nelson, Harry.
    Introduction to physical anthropology / Harry Nelson, Robert Jurmain. — 5th ed.
        p.   cm.
    Includes bibliographical references.
    Includes index.
    ISBN 0–314–80906–6
    1. Physical anthropology.   I. Jurmain, Robert.   II. Title.
    [DNLM.   1. Anthropology, Physical.   GN 60 N427i]
GN60.N44   1991
573—dc20
DNLM/DLC
for Library of Congress   91–147
                                                 CIP

Design: Janet Bollow
Copy editor: Stuart Kenter
Illustrations: Brenda Booth, Barbara Barnett, Joseph Fay, Sue Sellars, Evanell Towne
Cover: Painting by Christa Kieffer
Composition: Janet Hansen, Alphatype

Credits

Chapter 1: Fig. 1-2 Public Relations, San Francisco State University; Figs. 1-3, 1-4 Harry Nelson; Fig. 1-5 Robert Jurmain; Fig. 1-7 Diana L. Davis, University of Oklahoma; Fig. 1-8 Wayne Fogle

Chapter 2: Figs. 2-1, 2-4, 2-6, 2-7, 2-8, 2-10, p. 24 The American Museum of Natural History; Fig. 2-5 Bancroft Library, University of California, Berkeley; Fig. 2-11 Library, New York Academy of Medicine; Fig. 2-12(a), (b) M.W.F. Tweedie/Photo Researchers, Inc.

Chapter 3: p. 48 Harvard University; p. 49 Institute of Orthomolecular Medicine.

Chapter 4: Fig. 4-2 The American Museum of Natural History; Figs. 4-4, 4-5 David Frayer; p. 98 Courtesy of *Annual Reviews of Genetics.*

Chapter 5: Fig. 5-1 Courtesy of D. E. Schreiber, IBM Research Laboratory, San Jose; Fig. 5-4 From: A. E. Mourant, et al., *The Distribution of the Human Blood Groups and Other Polymorphisms*, Oxford University Press, © 1976. By permission of the publisher; p. 139 From Edward Novitski, *Human Ge-*

netics, Macmillan Publishing Co., Inc., © 1977. Reprinted with permission of the publisher; Fig. 5-5 From: A. E. Mourant, et al., *The Distribution of the Human Blood Groups and Other Polymorphisms*, Oxford University Press, © 1976. By permission of the publisher.

Chapter 6: p. 157 From C. S. Coon and E. E. Hunt, *The Living Races of Man* © 1965 Alfred A. Knopf, Inc.; Fig. 6-4 Richard Ingraham; p. 165 Reprinted with peermission from *Man in the Andes: A Multidisciplinary Study of High-Altitude Quechia*, edited by Baker and Little © 1976 by Dowden, Hutchinson & Ross, Inc., Stroudsburg, Pa.; Fig. 6-6 P. Grant/UNICEF; Figs. 6-7, 6-8, 6-11 Wide World.

Chapter 7: Fig. 7-1 Courtesy of R. Heglar, photo by H. Nelson; Fig. 7-2 New York Academy of Medicine; Fig. 7-3 H. Nelson.

Chapter 8: p. 215 Courtesy of Biological Sciences Curriculum Study. Permission to use this figure does not constitute an endorsement; Fig. 8-10 The American Museum of Natural History; Fig. 8-17 Courtesy of Biological Sciences Curriculum Study. Permission to use this figure does not constitute an endorsement; Fig. 8-18 San Diego Zoo; Fig. 8-19 New York Zoological Society Photo; Fig. 8-20 Adapted from *Life: An Introduction to Biology* by Simpson, Pittendrigh, and Tiffany. Copyright © 1957 by Harcourt Brace Jovanovich, Inc. Redrawn by permission of the publishers. Redrawn from Romer, *The Vertebrate Body*, W. B. Saunders.

Chapter 9: p. 231 © National Geographic Society, Courtesy of Dian Fossey; p. 233, Figs. 1 and 2 Redrawn with permission of Quadrangle/The New York Times Book Co. from *The Antecedents of Man* by W. E. Le Gros Clark. Also redrawn by permission of Edinburgh University Press, Edinburgh, Scotland. Fig. 9-4 San Diego Zoo; Fig. 9-7, 9-8 Fred Jacobs; Fig. 9-10 R. Jurmain; Fig. 9-12 R. D. Schmidt/San Diego Zoo; Fig. 9-14, 9-15 San Diego Zoo; Fig. 9-16 H. Nelson; Fig. 9-18 R. Jurmain; Fig. 9-19 Phyllis Dolhinow Fig. 9-20 H. Nelson; Fig. 9-24 R. Jurmain; Fig. 9-25(a) Jill Matsumoto/Jim Anderson, (b) R. Jurmain; Fig. 9-27, 9-28(a), (b) Jill Matsumoto/Jim Anderson.

Chapter 10: Fig. 10-1 Fred Jacobs; Fig. 10-2, 10-3 Phyllis Dolhinow; Fig. 10-4 Jean DeRousseau; Fig. 10-5 Phyllis Dolhinow; Fig. 10-6 John Oates; Fig. 10-7(a) Phyllis Dolhinow, (b), (c) H. Nelson, (d) Jill Matsumoto/Jim Anderson; Fig. 10-8(a) Ron Garrison/San Diego Zoo, (b) H. Nelson; Fig. 10-9(a), (b) H. Nelson; Fig. 10-10 Harry Harlow, University of Wisconsin Primate Laboratory; Fig. 10-11 Hans Kummer; Fig. 10-12 Phyllis Dolhinow Fig. 10-13 (left) Masao Kawaki, (right) Porter Zoo, Brownsville, Texas; p. 294 Wide World.

Chapter 11: p. 300 David Bygott © National Geographic Society; Fig. 11-1 T. W. Ransom; Fig. 11-2 H. Nelson; Figs. 11-3(a), (b), (c), 11-4, 11-5 Phyllis Dolhinow; Fig. 11-6(a)–(g) Jill Matsumoto/Jim Anderson; Figs. 11-7, 11-8 Baron Hugo van Lawick © National Geographic Society; p. 317 Wide World; Fig. 11-10(a) Geza Teleki, (b) Phyllis Dolhinow; p. 324(a), (b), (c), p. 325 Phillis Dolinow; Fig. 11-12 Beatrice Gardner; Figs. 11-13, 11-14, 11-15 From George Schaller, *The Serengeti Lion*. University of Chicago Press, © 1972 by the University of Chicago; Figs. 11-17, 11-18, 11-19, 11-20 Jon Yellen.

Chapter 12: Fig. 12-4 Redrawn with permission of Quadrangle/The New York Times Book Co. from *The Antecedents of Man* by W. E. Le Gros Clark. Also redrawn by permission of Edinburgh University Press, Edinburgh,

(continued following Index)

Contents

CHAPTER 3

Biological Basis of Life   45

CHAPTER 4

Genetics and Evolution   77

CHAPTER 5

Evolution in Modern Populations 113

CHAPTER 6

Human Adaptability: Meeting the Challenge of the Environment   149

CHAPTER 7

Human Diversity   183

ISSUE
Perception of Race   184

CHAPTER 8

Evolutionary Record   207

ISSUE
A Cosmic Calendar   208

CHAPTER 9

Living Primates   229

ISSUE
Can the Mountain Gorilla Be Saved?   230

CHAPTER 10

Primate Behavior 259

CHAPTER 13

Paleoanthropology 377

CHAPTER 14

Plio-Pleistocene Hominids 407

CHAPTER 15

Plio-Pleistocene Hominids: Organization and Interpretation 445

ISSUE
Man the Hunter; Woman the Gatherer 446

CHAPTER 16

Homo Erectus 461

ISSUE
Seeking the Peking Bones 462

CHAPTER 17

Homo Sapiens   501

Preface
to
Instructors

Physical anthropology, in the past several years, has seen a remarkable increase in new discoveries, data, and interpretations. In this fifth edition of our text, we have—as mentioned in our prior prefaces—continued our efforts to keep up to date with this burgeoning branch of anthropology.

Besides updating the text, we have retained the well-received pedagogical devices of the previous editions—to help the broad mix of students enrolled in introductory physical anthropology classes. We believe these aids will assist in understanding unfamiliar subject matter. For example, the writing style is geared to the level of students, and a running glossary in the page margins defines difficult or unfamiliar terms, often spelled out phonetically. We have added a few maps. We believe maps help students to fix in their minds the sites and events discussed in the text. Frequent charts, tables, and photographs are used to aid in visualizing and organizing text material.

We believe this approach is effective for students who plan to major in anthropology, as well as for those who do not.

Also retained are the three appendices from the previous edition, including an atlas of primate skeletal anatomy; an illustrated discussion of forensic anthropology; and a brief discussion of the possibilities of a career in physical anthropology, as well as a brief review of several research institutions that fund anthropological research. We hope this last appendix may help guide students in their career choice.

Several new "Issue" sections appear in this edition: "Genethics," (Chapter 4) as the title suggests, looks at the ethical problems raised by the rapid growth of gene manipulation, especially in health and industry. In "Science or Sacrilege," Chapter 6, we discuss the ethical issues involved in the study of human skeletal remains, especially as it pertains to the "reburial" issue in the United States. In Chapter 7 the new Issue asks students to think about their "Perception of Race."

A new feature of the text, "Contemporary Studies of Biocultural Evolution," consists of four short surveys of four societies: !Kung San, Central African Pygmies, Yanomamö, and Solomon Islanders. We believe this may give students a look at several different kinds of current anthropological research from a biocultural evolutionary point of view.

Our reviewers have been very helpful with their advice and suggestions, which we have seriously considered and adopted wherever possible. We appreciated constructive crituques and helpful comments from:

David W. Frayer, University of Kansas

Kim R. Hill, University of Michigan

Barbara Hornum, Drexel University

Rene Peron, Santa Rosa Junior College

Mark G. Plew, Boise State University

James Provinzano, University of Wisconsin, Oshkosh

David L. Schutzer, Los Angeles Pierce College

D. Gentry Steele, Texas A & M University

Norman Sullivan, Marquette University

For their generosity in providing photographs for this edition, we are especially grateful to Phyllis Dolhinow, Milford Wolpoff, Fred Smith, C. K. Brain, Desmond Clark, Ellen Ingmanson, J. J. Hublin, Alan Hughes, John Oates, C. B. Stringer, Philip Tobias, Bernard Vandermeersch, Xinzhi Wu, the National Museums of Kenya, David Frayer, Tim White, Günter Braüer, and Alan Walker.

The authors wish to express their appreciation to Clyde Perlee, our editor and Denise Simon, Executive Editor at West Educational Publishing; Janet Bollow, the text designer; Stuart Kenter, copy editor; Janet Hansen, compositor; Loring Brace, Lynn Kilgore, William Kimble, Fred Smith for their assistance and advice; Desmond Clark and Birute Galdikas for their notes on Glynn Isaac and Dian Fossey; John Oates for his material on primate conservation; Ben Singer for his critique and assistance with pertinent current material, and Sandy Nelson for her help with proofing and indexing; and, finally, to all our students who have helped us see physical anthropology more broadly.

Harry Nelson
Robert Jurmain

Preface
to
Students

We are physical anthropologists. In this text, we introduce you to our discipline, the study of human evolution.

Evolution is a biological process and must therefore be understood from a biological perspective. Accordingly, the early chapters acquaint you with several broad principles of the evolutionary process, as well as with genetics and cell biology.

Unavoidably, a scientific discipline like ours uses many terms which students feel compelled to memorize, and on which instructors feel equally compelled to test. For some of you—particularly those with little or no high school biology—understanding these terms may take some extra effort. Thus, to aid you in learning the basics of physical anthropology, we have set off and clearly defined many of the more important terms and concepts. Studying these (even memorizing them) will help you understand the fundamentals of physical anthropology.

Following the suggestion of students, a further study aid has been incorporated into recent editions. Those boxes that are tinted are, for the most part, somewhat extraneous items concerning the history of discoveries, famous personalities, and so on. They are included for your interest, but it is unlikely you would be responsible for such material on exams. On the other hand, those boxes that are not tinted are more integral to the text and may, in fact, be included as exam material. For further clarification concerning specific items, consult your instructor.

Those of you who have had advanced high school or even college biology courses may find that you are already familiar with much of the introductory material. We suggest that you review this material so that, along with others exposed to it for the first time, you will leave the text with a basic understanding of evolution and how it has affected our ancestors and continues to act on our species.

As a scientific discipline, physical anthropology is an ongoing pursuit of knowledge. Throughout the world today, research projects continue and data accumulate at a fantastic rate. We have made this text as "up-to-date" as possible; however, there will doubtless be new information known by the time you read this book. New data may produce new hypotheses. In any case, your basic understanding should not necessarily be about the minute details of human evolution, but rather about the principles involved in the interpretation of our evolution.

For example, discoveries of a vast new array of 8 to 10 million-year-old fossils have caused dramatic revisions of our ideas concerning this stage of evolution. A partial skull found in Pakistan (during the 1979–1980 field season) and discussed in print in 1982 has had particularly important impact. As another example, a beautifully preserved 2.4 million-year-old skull was found in northern Kenya in

1985. This important new find has caused considerable reevaluation of schemes of human evolution and thus creates differences from earlier editions of this text.

We have modernized this edition considerably, expanding the relevant portions in Chapters 12, 14 and elsewhere. In addition, the complex materials in Chapters 16 and 17 have been updated, condensed, and clarified. Still, no book can be completely up-to-date. As a case in point, further discoveries of related fossil material to the Pakistani skull just mentioned have recently come to light in China—in fact, up to 1,000 new specimens! Unfortunately, almost none of these new fossils have been described. Some preliminary findings (not yet published) suggest that these Chinese fossils are quite different from those in Pakistan (data not discussed in this edition). Thus, further revisions of our text are, no doubt, on the way.

New discoveries are always just around the corner. As members of an educated public, you will be able to understand and perhaps even participate in the development of a more complete comprehension of *Homo sapiens*, the animal, as well as *Homo sapiens*, the human being.

Robert Jurmain
Harry Nelson

FIFTH EDITION

Introduction to Physical Anthropology

Introduction

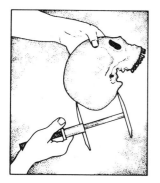

Contents

Fact, Fantasy, and Anthropology

At the beginning of each chapter throughout this book you will find brief discussions of an assortment of contemporary issues. Some of these—for example, the existence and implications of such phenomena as Bigfoot, extraterrestrials, and frozen Neandertals—may seem too bizarre to be discussed in a scholarly textbook. However, scientists and scholars cannot make these issues disappear by ignoring them. Someone in the scientific community must deal with them, hopefully in a rational way. This task often falls to the physical anthropologist.

Since the public is concerned about these topics, we shall address them. You may not always agree with our conclusions (you may notice, by the way, that our own personal biases occasionally emerge), but to induce you to agree or disagree with us is not the point. What you should do is think seriously and rationally about these issues. In light of all the bizarre and ridiculous claims floating around today in pseudoscientific guise, you will do best by adopting the cautious "show me" approach attributed to inhabitants of Missouri. Without hard evidence, no distinction may be made between fiction, fantasy, and fact. Judge for yourself!

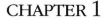

CHAPTER 1

What Is Anthropology?

Anthropology is a scientific approach to the study of human beings, past and present (and even future). It encompasses the study of all human behavior—for example, the building of shelters, the care of children, farming, hunting, religious ritual, speech, and much more. The field of anthropology also incorporates concepts such as economics, kinship, life after death, relationships, social status, and so forth. Such activities and concepts are often the concern of *cultural anthropology, archeology,* and *linguisitics.*

Physical anthropology, on the other hand, is concerned with the physical or biological aspects of human beings. Professionals in this sphere investigate such areas as our ancestry and ancestors, genes and their effect on humans, nonhuman **primates** and their relation to humans, and the evolutionary processes involved in our physical development.

Anthropology, therefore, is a **holistic** science, with the entire gamut of humankind as the focus of study. Other disciplines that deal with people—sociology, psychology, economics, political science, history, and others—tend to specialize in single aspects of human activity. Economists, for example, study the production, distribution, and consumption of goods; market systems; and systems of exchange; but they would rarely consider the effect of religion or kinship on the economic system. Anthropology, however, takes a broader, holistic approach and considers the findings of all academic fields pertaining to humans; in fact, anything associated with humankind is considered within the scope of our discipline.

The wide scope of anthropology is reflected in the two broad categories of anthropology—cultural and physical—which are further divided into subdisciplines, as we see in Fig. 1-1.

The focus of cultural anthropology is **culture**, which has been defined in many ways. It is unnecessary, at this point, to explore the concept of culture in depth, and a traditional definition of the term will serve to suffice for the purposes of our general discussion: "Culture is the socially transmitted knowledge shared by some groups of people" (Peoples and Bailey, 1988, p. 19). (Also see the definition of culture that appears in the marginal glossary on this page.) It is important, however, to note that culture is based on the premise that knowledge is transmitted *socially*, not biologically.

Physical anthropology, in contrast, is genetically based, and *its* focus is on the features we inherit through our genes.

In order to understand the human condition, anthropologists believe it necessary to investigate human biological *and* cultural behavior. Since we are both animal and human, such a broad perspective—what is known as a **biocultural approach**—makes sense. Examining only cultural behavior fails to consider our biological capabilities and limitations, and concentrating on our biology omits the single most important attribute of humans: culture.

Anthropology   anthropos: man
logos: science study of

Primates   (pry´-mates)
The order of mammals to which humans, apes, monkeys, and prosimians belong. All life forms are arranged in a number of divisions. These divisions (e.g., *class, order, family, species*) include groups of animals or plants.

Holism   Viewing the whole in terms of an integrated system; cultural and ecological systems as wholes.

Culture   The set of rules, standards, and norms shared by members of a society; transmitted by learning, and responsible for the behavior of those members.

Biocultural   A combination of the biological, cultural, and ecological. An approach to the study of human evolution and behavior that stresses the influence of each of these three clusters and their reciprocating effects on one another.

ANTHROPOLOGY	

Physical Anthropology
    Human evolution (macroevolution)
        Paleoanthropology
            Comparative anatomy
        Primatology
    Human variation (microevolution)
        Human genetics
        Population genetics
            Human diversity (race)
        Human osteology
	Cultural Anthropology
	    Sociocultural anthropology
	    Archeology
	    Linguistics
	            or
	Behavioral Anthropology
	    Cultural anthropology
	    Archeology
	    Linguistics

This biocultural approach to the study of human beings makes anthropology a unique discipline. As a social science, cultural anthropology is the study of culture—that broad area of learned behavior that humans have developed as their basic strategy for survival. As a biological science, physical anthropology is the study of the biological aspects of humans. Combining the biological and social aspects, we have a comprehensive view of the animal *Homo sapiens*, which we call human.

What Is Physical Anthropology?

As we indicated, anthropology may be divided into cultural and physical approaches to the study of human beings. Whereas it is possible to emphasize one or the other, it is impossible to separate completely the subject matter of these two branches.

In order to understand the physical human being, we must of necessity consider the special way of life of this organism. Unlike all other creatures in the animal kingdom, we human beings have developed a strategy of adaptation—obtaining food, producing the next generation, protecting the group against enemies and the elements, developing concepts of life's meaning—that we call *culture*, which serves as a mediator between society and the environment. In order to serve this function, culture must be learned by humans, as contrasted to the direct comprehension of the environment by other animals. All animals, especially mammals, are capable of learning, and nonhuman primates are very good at this. The learning ability of the great apes (gorillas, orangutans, chimpanzees) is now well recognized; nevertheless, no other mammal is as dependent on learning as are humans. While possessing a biologically based capacity for culture, we humans must learn behavior anew every generation. We must learn what, when, where, and with whom to obtain food, eat, marry, associate, etc. We must learn what is right and wrong, what to wear and not wear, what weapons and utensils to use and when, and how to relate to parents, cousins, and friends. All of this learning process comes under the heading of culture.

Culture, then, is the accumulation of knowledge, rules, standards, skills, and mental sets that humans utilize in order to survive; that is to say, adapt to the envi-

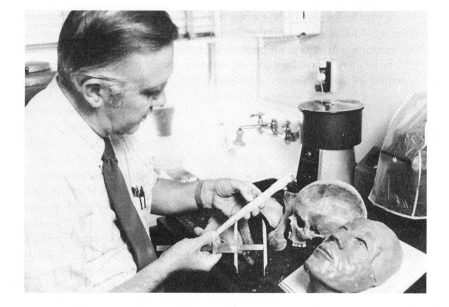

FIGURE 1-2   Physical anthropologist in his lab.

ronments in which they live. One cannot imagine humans today surviving without culture. Indeed, such a case is very likely impossible. Obtaining and preparing food, coping with severe climatic conditions, trying to understand the world around us, cooperating with others—all of these normal and daily activities require cultural solutions. Our bodies alone are not adequate for the task of living. We must have material items to help us acquire what we need and ideas to help us communicate with one another.

Cultural anthropology, as we have emphasized, is the comprehensive study of what humans have learned to do, and are doing, in order to survive and adapt. What is the connection between these learned processes and our biological constitution? Was our evolutionary development dependent on culture? Was the development of culture dependent on our biological constitution?

FIGURE 1-3   Humans are biocultural animals who developed culture as an adaptive strategy for survival and thus became human. Note the many items of material culture and social behavior that make the human way possible.

Human variation Physical differences among humans.

Human evolution Physical changes over time leading to anatomically modern human beings.

Osteology (os-tee-ol′-o-jee)
osteon: bone
The study of bones.

Prosimians (pro-sim′-ee-ens)
pro: before
simian: ape or monkey
Common form of Prosimii, a suborder of primates, composed of small primates such as lemurs and tarsiers.

Forensic (from forum)
Pertaining to courts of law. In anthropology, the use of anthropology in questions of law.

In the biocultural view, culture and our biological structure are critically related. Had we not come from primate beginnings, culture would never have developed, and had our ancestors not developed culture, we would not have evolved our present physical form. The two are inextricably related, and if we wish to learn something of physical anthropology, we *must* understand the role culture has played in the process of human evolution.

The human biological structure today is not simply the result of genetic inheritance; the influence of cultural selection factors plays a large role in our biology. The shape of our bodies, as well as the function of most of our internal organs have been impacted by culture. Our large brain did not come about by accident. It is capable of *producing* culture, but its evolutionary growth is a result of the culture it produced. There is a feedback mechanism at work here in which the brain generated the initial development of culture which, in turn, provoked and stimulated the further expansion of the brain. We do not simply invent tools and language and conceive arts and sciences, we are also the product of these events.

With this introduction, let us examine more closely the field of physical anthropology, the concern of this book. Although physical anthropologists are not in complete agreement on precisely what is to be included within their field, they do generally agree that two areas are basic: **human evolution** and **human variation**.

Human evolution, the subject of much of this text, especially Chapters 13 through 17, may be divided into two areas: paleoanthropology and primatology.

Paleoanthropology is the study of the fossil remains of our ancestors. Physical anthropologists, together with archeologists, geologists, and other scientists, have unearthed fossil remains in many parts of the world. With their knowledge of **osteology**, paleoanthropologists examine, measure, and reconstruct these remains, often from mere fragments. This has enabled physical anthropologists to propose possible lines of descent from our ancient ancestors to our present form, *Homo sapiens*.

Primatology, as the word suggests, is the study of nonhuman primates, the group (*order* is the technical term) of the animal kingdom to which humans, apes, monkeys, and **prosimians** belong. The anatomy of nonhuman primates, especially monkeys and apes, has been studied to ascertain the similarities and differences between these primates and humans. This kind of study helps trace the evolutionary relationships of human and nonhuman primates. Because of the remarkable similarities among monkeys, apes, and humans, researchers have been able, through laboratory experiments with monkeys and apes, to learn what effects certain diseases, stresses, and other conditions might have on humans. Work with the rhesus monkey, for example, led to the discovery of the Rh blood factor which, due to incompatibility between mother and fetus, may cause a disease fatal to human infants. Because of the similarity in blood types and physiological responses of chimpanzees and humans, the space program routinely selects chimpanzees for experiments in outer space. Scientists believe that their reactions are very similar to what human reactions would be under the same experimental conditions.

A fascinating area of primate investigation concerns observing primates in their natural habitat as a means of understanding the organism-environment interaction. This kind of investigation, often difficult and dangerous, has been proliferating. Perhaps the best-known field study is Jane Goodall's work with chimpanzees in East Africa, but a number of others have attracted attention: Phyllis Dolhinow's

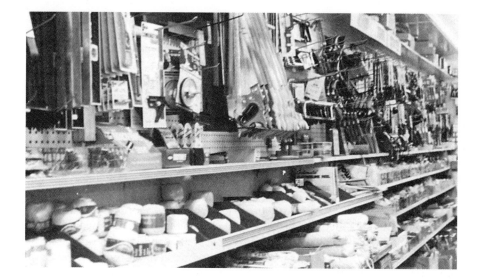

FIGURE 1-4 Early humans possessed a small and simple tool kit. At a modern hardware store, an overwhelming variety of tools, utensils, and weapons is available.

work with langurs in India; Dian Fossey's study of gorillas in Rwanda; Biruté Galdikas' work with orangutans in Borneo; the extensive research on baboons in Africa and macaques at the Japanese Monkey Centers.

These studies have uncovered important patterns of social interactions, such as the relationships between dominant and subordinate males, mothers and offspring, and the young and old. In addition, toolmaking and the ability to learn complex tasks (behaviors until recently hardly believed possible) have also been discovered with surprising frequency among certain species of primates.

Physical anthropologists hope that current, rapidly accumulating data will help trace human evolution from our primate ancestors, as well as aid in understanding the behavior of humans today.

We have been discussing what might be termed *academic anthropology*. There are, however, physical anthropologists who pursue their work outside of (or in addition to) academe in a branch called *applied anthropology*. In this field, the principles and data of anthropology are related to practical situations. Many years ago, for example, physical anthropologists were already applying their knowledge by developing standard sizes for the clothing industry and the military, and more comfortable seats for automobiles and airplanes. Space requirements for industrial workers were also analyzed, and mechanical problems associated with the body, such as the placement of foot pedals and hand controls for machine operators, were studied.

Physical anthropologists sometimes also assist judicial and law enforcement agencies. Practitioners of **forensic anthropology**, as the field is called, may be asked to ascertain the age and sex of a corpse, and how long it has been buried; they may, in some cases, assist the coroner in determining the cause of death. A recent development, part of the remarkable achievement of *biotechnology*, is DNA fingerprinting. The DNA of an individual can be compared with the DNA in a hair, bit of blood, or a drop of semen. If matched, the individual is positively identified by these bits of evidence; if not matched, he or she is thus excluded. There are forensic anthropologists now participating in this work.

Paleopathology (pay'-lee-o-path-ol'-o-jee)
pathos: suffering
The study of ancient diseases.

Microevolution Pertains to minor, gradual changes that may not be observable except over time. (Macroevolution, on the other hand, pertains to great changes in evolutionary history, such as the origin and extinction of species.)

For many years, physical anthropology has had considerable application in the field of medicine. The relationship between body build and disease and the question of whether a particular disease is hereditary or social have been among those investigated by physical anthropologists. Data on diseases have been collected from many countries in an effort to determine what special social conditions might be involved in the causes and cures.

An area of physical anthropology that has been a central focus since the beginnings of the discipline in this country might be termed *skeletal biology*. Over the years, archeologists have excavated thousands of human burials from sites all around the world. As the most durable parts of the human organism, the hard tissues (bones and teeth) may endure for centuries (and, if fossilized, perhaps for millions of years).

As experts in the anatomical structure of these hard tissues, physical anthropologists (here usually called osteologists) can, by using techniques similar to those of forensic anthropologists, often determine the sex and the age-at-death of the individual from which the specimen came. In addition, osteologists can, with the aid of specialized instruments, exactly measure hundreds of different dimensions regarding size and shape variation. Finally, osteologists carefully inspect the skeletal material for indications of such diseases as tuberculosis, healed fractures, arthritis, and rickets. This approach, called **paleopathology**, can inform us not only about the history of human disease, but can also occasionally help elucidate the causes of certain diseases as well.

Human variation (Chapters 5, 6, and 7), the second focus of physical anthropology, examines the differences within and between human populations. Within a population such as the Eskimos* or San,† variation occurs in body shapes and sizes; in anatomical structures, organs, and tissues; and in physiological responses to heat, cold, humidity, and exercise. Physical anthropologists are interested in the environmental and hereditary bases of this diversity and attempt to make evolutionary explanations of it.

As human biologists, physical anthropologists in the field or laboratory collect such data as susceptibility and immunity to disease, the effects of malnutrition, and patterns of human growth. These data may be used by medical scientists, physicians, and government agencies in their efforts to combat disease and improve the health of peoples around the world.

While all human beings belong to the same genus and species (*Homo sapiens*) and can interbreed and produce fertile offspring, there is a wide variation within the species. Physical anthropologists study these variations to learn how humans have biologically and culturally adapted to the stressful conditions of heat, humidity, altitude, working conditions, and other human activities. As evolutionary biologists, anthropologists are interested in **microevolution**, small-scale evolutionary changes (see Microevolution, p. 109). More recently, anthropologists have considered the probability of rapid evolution that produces new species more quickly than small-scale modifications. Such rapid evolutionary change has been called *punctuated equilibrium* (see p. 107).

As comparative human geneticists, physical anthropologists have studied variations among humans and, in the past, have classified the world's population into physical types called races, a practice seldom followed in recent years.

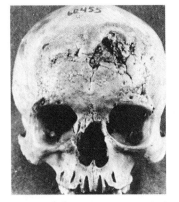

FIGURE 1-5 Paleopathology. The infectious reaction on the frontal part of this twelfth-century Pueblo Indian skull suggests syphilis. Other diseases are also a possibility.

---

*Some Eskimos are now referred to as Inuit.
†San has replaced Bushman as the name of the hunters of the Kalahari Desert, South Africa. See p. 334.

BOX 1-1 **Research in Physical Anthropology***

Behavioral and biogeographical models for the origins of modern humans

Browridge development in anthropoid primates

Behavioral influences on sexual and seasonal variation in skin pigmentation

Evolutionary implications of patterns of male-female bonding

Biological effects of urban migration on Hispanic populations

Hominid evolution in China and Indonesia

Early "Modern" humans from the Levant

Origins of the Polynesians

Paleoenvironment of early *Homo sapiens* in East and Central Africa

Occupation and osteoarthritis: Evidence from some 18th/19th century skeletons

Language, brain, and evolutionary models

Diet, nutritional status, and economic constraints in rural Swazi households

The swing phase of walking in Neanderthals and modern humans

Sex chromosomes and human tooth crown structure

Race: Declining acceptance of the concept in physical and cultural anthropology at universities, colleges, and community colleges

Morphometric analysis of the Mladeč postcranial remains

*A few examples of papers given at a recent meeting of the American Association of Physical Anthropologists.

All the areas of physical anthropology discussed here give only the barest outlines of the fascinating topics investigated by our discipline. In a recent professional meeting of the American Association of Physical Anthropologists, more than 300 academic papers were read, covering a vast array of subjects. Box 1-2 presents a sampling.

Paleoanthropology and Other Disciplines

Searching for ancient human remains—organic and cultural—is the work of *paleoanthropologists* (see Chapter 13). Organic material, such as bones and teeth, is examined and analyzed by physical anthropologists; cultural material, such as tools, weapons, shelters, and so forth, by archeologists.

However, as our discussion suggests, paleoanthropology is quite closely associated with other disciplines. In fact, a paleoanthropologist could not function without cooperation from a host of other scientists. For example, in working out the **phylogeny** of our species, one must have the vital knowledge (as accurately as possible) concerning the dates of fossil remains. To obtain this crucial information, the paleoanthropologist consults the **geochemist** for a **chronometric dating** of the fossils themselves, or of the matrix containing the fossil material.

If these facts are unobtainable, then a **geologist** may be able to give some idea of the dating from an analysis of the rock strata holding the material, and may also

Phylogeny (fy-loj'-en-ee)
phylon: tribe or race
The evolutionary history of a species; evolutionary relationships of organisms; a "family tree."

Geochemistry (jee-o)
ge: earth
The study of the chemical composition of the earth's crust.

Chronometric dating Dating by methods that give time in years, also known as absolute dating (compared with relative dating). It includes radiometric techniques (carbon 14 and potassium-argon) and dendrochronology (tree-ring dating).

Geology The study of the history and structure of the earth, as recorded in rocks.

Hominid   The common term for Hominidae, the family to which humans belong.

Agonistic   agones: ancient Greek contests; therefore, combative
Used by primatologists to describe aggressive, hostile, or threatening behavior.

Taphonomy   (taf-on′-o-mee)
taphe: grave or burial
nomy: rules or laws of
The study of fossil assemblages—especially human and animal bones—to reconstruct human activity.

Paleontology   (pay′-lee-on-tol′-o-jee)
onta: existing things
The study of ancient forms of life based on fossil bones.

Palynology   Identifying ancient plants by examining pollen from archeological sites.

be able to reconstruct the physical landscape of the period in which these ancient creatures were living. Thus, armed with such information, the physical anthropologist may justifiably speculate about the environment of the now-fossilized creatures, how they lived, how they obtained their food, how they used their bodies, and, to some extent, what kind of stone was available for tools.

For purposes of searching for fossils, the actual excavation is usually the responsibility of the archeologist, who studies the material remains—tools, indications of clothing, shelters, fire, etc.—and attempts to reconstruct the culture of that period.

Recently, primatologists have studied single social groups of primates for years, and these longitudinal studies have given them insights into the way of life of **hominid** ancestors. Feeding practices, age and sex relationships, **agonistic** behavior, and other nonhuman primate behavior offer suggestive clues to the transitional period of prehominid to hominid. Paleoanthropologists utilize data from primatologists and archeologists in constructing models for hominid origins (see Chapter 10 for examples of these models).

Also of assistance to paleoanthropologists have been the increasing contributions of a fairly new science, **taphonomy**, defined as "the laws of burial" (Olson, 1980). Taphonomists analyze fossil assemblages and "hope to find the means for reconstructing animals in their community context" (Behrensmeyer, 1980, p. 2). Through their analysis of animal bones found at ancient sites, taphonomists can offer information on: the paleoecology of the early hominid period; the relationship of hominids to the animals they hunted (or scavenged); the possible dates of mammalian bones found in the fossil assemblages; the changes that occur to bones after death, and whether these changes are due to chemical, carnivore, or hominid activity. This information may give paleoanthropologists a better picture of the early hominid environment. It thus extends the ability of paleoanthropologists to understand the behavior, as well as the physical structure, of the hominid remains they discover.

In reconstructing the way of life of our ancient ancestors, one must have certain important knowledge concerning what other animals and plants were living at the same time. Such information would suggest clues to kinds of food eaten, the hunting and gathering techniques, the possible materials for clothing and shelter and, in general, considerable other anthropological data about how these ancient peoples adapted to their environment. For this, the physical anthropologist looks to the **paleontologist** and **palynologist** (who identifies plants by pollen samples taken from the soil) to identify the remains of these materials.

Much of physical anthropology deals with evolution, including physical changes within a species and the transmission of physical characteristics from one generation to the next. Scientists from all the biological sciences have contributed insights to evolutionary theory, and geneticists, in recent years, have greatly expanded their understanding of the processes of biological heredity. This knowledge has been of considerable theoretical assistance to physical anthropologists as they speculate about how the transition from prehuman to human may have occurred.

Since cultural information would shed light on the evolution of the human form, physical anthropologists have currently become increasingly interested in how our early ancestors lived. Necessarily, then, we have come to rely on the findings of those cultural anthropologists who work with less technologically complex societies. Living patterns seen today, such as family structure, division of labor, and hunting techniques, suggest ideas and concepts to physical anthropologists in their reconstructions of the life of early humans and the evolution of physical form.

Similarly, primate anatomy and behavior studies done by zoologists, psychologists, psychiatrists, medical scientists, linguists, and others have contributed to the physical anthropologist's exploration of human evolution.

What Is Human?

Two terms already introduced—"human" and "hominid"—require some clarification. The word hominid comes from *homo*, the Latin word for man:

> From its use in Latin works on logic [and] scholastic language, in the sense "human being" (Oxford English Dictionary).

Whatever its origin, hominid is used by anthropologists as an abbreviated or popular form of **Hominidae**, the animal category to which we belong. Hominid is a useful term since it is neutral, unaffiliated with gender, time, or superiority, and we shall use it extensively in this textbook. Hominidae includes the genus *Australopithecus* (the earliest hominids we know of), who emerged somewhere around 4 mya.* Hominidae also includes the genus *Homo*, with several species (see chart on p. 213 for details). Because **australopithecines**, the early hominids, did not possess all the criteria we assign to humans, especially a complex brain, most anthropologists are reluctant to refer to them as humans.

The concept "human" is more difficult to clarify. What makes human beings unique and thereby different from all other animals is a perplexing and age-old question that has been the subject of religious, philosophical, and sociological inquiry. Human uniqueness is based on two general classes of criteria: biological and behavioral.

From the biological view, the differences between humans and other animals are quantitative. The difficulty is not that we possess physical characteristics lacking in, or radically different from, other animals, but that we possess the same attributes to a greater or lesser degree. To mention only a few: we are larger than most animals, but have less hair; our brain is not the largest in relative or absolute size, but it is very large according to the standards of both these categories. We are not the only animal that is bipedal (birds are, too), but we are the only primates who are so structured—we have a skeleton adapted for standing upright and walking, which leaves the hands free for purposes other than locomotion. All these traits, elaborated and coordinated under the control of a brain capable of abstract thought, give us our remarkable physical uniqueness.

In the behavioral area, human uniqueness is even more noteworthy. Every species, in adapting to its **ecological niche** (econiche), has developed its own distinct behavior, but human uniqueness is revealed in behaviors absent in other animals. For example, our sexual behavior does not include a mating season or **estrus** for females. Or, as another example, most animals build shelters for themselves and eat in ways particular to their species; but among humans, activities like

---

Hominidae From *homo* (man) and the suffix *dae*, indicating the group humans belong to.

Australopithecines (os-tray-lo-pith′-e-seens)
australo: southern
pithecus: ape
The earliest hominids known; located in South and East Africa.

Ecological niche (econiche)
Environment to which a species is totally adapted.

Estrus (also oestrus)
oistros: sting, frenzy
Period of sexual heat of female mammals; receptive period.

---

*The abbreviation mya indicates "million years ago."

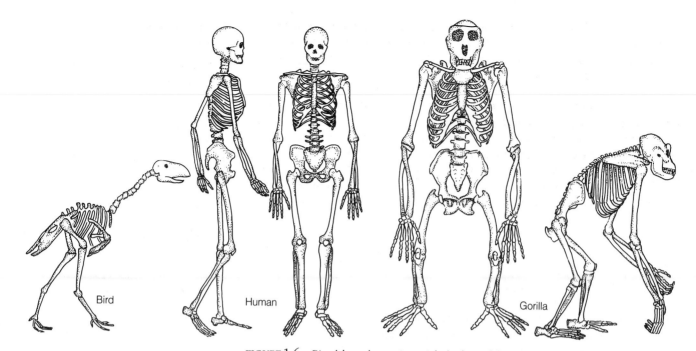

FIGURE 1-6   Bipedal vertebrates. An upright (orthograde) posture with a striding gait evolved from an apelike structure. With striking similarities to humans in skeletal structures, apes (a gorilla in this illustration) are neither bipedal nor orthograde. Note the differences, especially in arms (length), legs (length), feet (arch and big toe), and pelvis (height and width).

Tool   A natural object deliberately modified for utilitarian purposes.

the building of shelters and preparing of food are learned, vary in each society, and can be successfully accomplished only with the assistance of **tools**. Without tools, it is unlikely that any culture could survive.

Our social relationships are not only learned but also vary from society to society. Cultural anthropologists have routinely observed societal differences in marriage, residence, and kinship patterns, in attitudes toward the elderly and the young, and in behavior between the sexes. This diversity is unlike other animal species, where relatively little flexibility occurs in the behavior of individuals. Within species, members of a particular category (such as sex or age) tend to behave similarly. Mammals exhibit more flexibility than other vertebrates, with primates displaying the most of all. Recent observations of the variety of behavior among chimpanzees in the wild, along with the apparent ability of captive chimpanzees to learn sign language in a number of experiments, have astonished scientists. Nevertheless, no troop of chimpanzees displays the degree of variety in behavior found in *any* human society.

One of the most important factors that differentiates humans from other species is our ability to communicate symbolically and orally through language, an activity that, as far as we know, is specific to humans. Chimpanzee achievements with sign language (discussed in Chapter 11) are truly remarkable. Even when these intelligent apes occasionally sign to other chimps, such a display in no way compares to the crucial reliance humans place on symbolic communication. Furthermore, what chimpanzees or any other animals achieve with *human assistance* is quite different from what humans, as a species, develop by themselves.

What then is "human"? There may well be as many definitions as there are human beings! We suggest, however, that a sound explanation of the term be based on the two criteria previously mentioned: first, a body structured for standing upright and walking on two legs (**bipedalism**), thus leaving the arms free for functions other than locomotion; second, a complex brain that provides the abilities for abstract thought, symbolic communication, and the development of culture as a way of life. The term "human," then, is not synonymous with hominid. Early hominids (Australopithecines) possessed only one of these criteria—bipedal locomotion. Although *H. erectus* is included, anthropologists usually reserve the human designation for *Homo sapiens*. With this dual emphasis on biology and culture, our definition once again underlines the biocultural view of human evolution.

Bipedalism (bipedality) (by-pee′-dal-ism)
bi: two
ped: feet
Walking on two feet as among hominids and some other animals.

Empirical (em-pir′-i-kal)
empirikos: experienced
Derived from or depending on experience or experiment.

Hypothesis Unproved theory. A theory is a statement with some confirmation.

Cosmology kosmos: world
The study of the creation of the universe and the laws that govern it.

World view A literal translation from the German *Weltanschauung* (Welt: world; anschauung: view).
A personal or group philosophy explaining history; a way of looking at the world.

The Scientific Approach

Physical anthropology is a scientific discipline and, more precisely, a *biological science*. Physical anthropologists, therefore, employ an **empirical**/scientific approach to understanding the universe.

What do we mean by "scientific"? The scientific approach is still very much surrounded by popular misunderstanding. First of all, scientists do *not* seek to disprove religious doctrine but, rather, attempt to understand the universe through direct *observation*, generating **hypotheses** to explain these observations, and then continually testing their results against further information. As new evidence accumulates, hypotheses are modified.

Strict theologians, on the other hand, understand the universe through faith, not through physical evidence. The written documents of the Eastern and Western religions reveal the universe through the direct word of an all-knowing spiritual power. Such a **cosmology** is intended to explain systematically and completely the nature of the universe, our planet, and ourselves. Since the Truth is known absolutely, there is little room for argument. In the furthest extension of this world view, it is not even necessary or desirable to gather further information about our universe.

In the last 400 to 500 years, however, a different **world view** has come to predominate in the Western world. This view entails what we have called the "empirical/scientific approach." Since theological and scientific approaches consist of entirely different ways of understanding the universe, no reasonable means exist for arguing one versus the other. We simply start with alternate assumptions: either we understand the universe by divine revelation, or we comprehend it by observation. In the former, we can find absolute Truth (large "T"); in the latter, we merely make the most reasonable hypotheses, and in a sense, know only relative truth (small "t"). All of our understanding, religious and scientific, is based on *some* kind of theory.

Because scientists must theorize does not mean, however, that we cannot come to grips with the physical universe and the organisms within it. Scientific theories are only as good as their capacity to explain comprehensively natural and experimental observations, both those already gathered and those that may be made in the future. Some hypotheses, "theories," or "laws" are powerful explanatory

FIGURE 1-7   Observation is a scientific
approach.

ciples, indeed: that the sun is the center of the solar system with the earth rotating
around it; that our universe is not fixed but in constant motion; that heredity is
transmitted from one generation to the next by cells, not blood, to name a few. Organic evolution (discussed in the next chapter) is also a theory; but like those just
noted, it has tremendous explanatory value, and has been *confirmed* by millions
of independent observations.

Must science and religion conflict? Certainly not. It is possible for scientists to
believe in some form of supernatural doctrine and, at the same time, accept evolution as a fact. Unfortunately, science in our society today has become a kind of religion for many people. We often think of scientific principles as unalterable
dogma based on faith. However, from an empirical point of view, our understanding of the universe is never absolute; it is gained by human beings slowly piecing
together bits of evidence gathered through observations that explain the universe.
We certainly do not know everything. But we do know enormously more than we
did a century, a decade, or even a year ago. Every day our data increase, and, consequently, our understanding increases as well. This book attempts to tell the
dramatic and continually unfolding story of human evolution.

Summary

Anthropology is the study of human beings and their primate ancestors. It is a
holistic science divided into two main branches: cultural and physical. Cultural an-

thropology is the study of what humans have learned to do in order to adapt to their environment; physical anthropology, the study of humans as animals, is mainly concerned with human variation and human evolution.

Specialized fields within physical anthropology include comparative human genetics, growth and development, paleoanthropology, human osteology, and primatology. Some physical anthropologists have specialized in applied anthropology, forensic anthropology, and paleopathology. For assistance in their research physical anthropologists work closely with a variety of biological, social, and physical scientists.

Two terms of similar meaning—hominid and human—have been defined. "Hominid," the more inclusive term, embraces australopithecines, which the term "human" does not. Human includes those hominids who display the phenomenon of a complex brain capable of abstract thought, symbolic communication, and culture.

Physical anthropologists, in order to understand the universe, employ an empirical/scientific approach, one based on observation and physical evidence. This method of understanding is opposed to a religionist approach, which is based on faith. Since these are alternative ways of comprehending the universe, there is no necessary conflict between them.

Questions for Review

1. What is meant by "holistic," and why is anthropology a holistic science?
2. Explain the biocultural approach in anthropology.
3. What are the two main branches of anthropology?
4. What are the two main areas of physical anthropology?
5. How do other disciplines assist physical anthropological research?
6. What are the fields of specialization within physical anthropology?
7. How does the concept "hominid" differ from the concept "human"?
8. In what ways are humans unique from other animals?
9. What role does culture play in human uniqueness?
10. Explain why there is no necessary conflict between the scientific and religionist approach to understanding the universe.
11. How do you think culture affects human evolution?

Suggested Further Reading

Benedict, Ruth. *Patterns of Culture*, Boston: Houghton Mifflin, 1934.
    A cultural anthropology classic. Highly recommended for background to the meaning of culture.
Boyd, Robert and Peter J. Richardson. *Culture and the Evolutionary Process*, Chicago: University of Chicago Press, 1985.
    A new look at genes and culture, but not easy going.
Eiseley, Loren. *The Immense Journey*, New York: Random House, 1957.
    This book is also cited in Chapter 2, but it is recommended here as an extended view of human evolution, the main concern of our textbook. Eiseley is well known for his literary and almost mystical style of writing, and *The Immense Journey* has enjoyed much success among college students.

Haviland, Wm. A. *Cultural Anthropology* (4th Ed.), New York: Holt, Rinehart and Winston, 1983.

The second chapter of this textbook offers a useful discussion of the concept of culture.

Hunter, David E. K. and Phillip Whitten. *Anthropology*. Boston: Little, Brown and Company, 1985.

A collection of articles written by specialists in the various fields of anthropology. The articles are written for the general reader.

Johnson, Francis E. and Henry Selby. *Anthropology: The Biocultural View*, Dubuque: Wm. C. Brown Co., 1978.

Another introductory textbook in both physical and cultural anthropology. The coverage in physical anthropology is greater and the approach more dynamic than in many other general anthropology texts.

Napier, John. *Monkeys Without Tails: The Story of Man's Evolution*, New York: Taplinger, 1976.

A light, witty, and brief review of human evolution. The reading is pleasant and the book recommended as an overview of physical anthropology.

Peoples, James and Garrick Bailey. *Humanity*. St. Paul: West Publishing Co., 1988.

This recently published textbook is an excellent source for students interested in the areas covered by cultural anthropology.

Darwin and the Principles of Evolution

Contents

Evolution on Trial

That it shall be unlawful for any teacher in any of the universities, normals and all other public schools of the State . . . to teach any theory that denies the story of the Divine Creation of man as taught in the Bible, and to teach instead that man has descended from a lower order of animals (Section 1 of the Butler Act, March 21, 1925, State of Tennessee).

In May, 1925, several leading citizens from Dayton, Tennessee (population 1,800), were sitting around Doc Robinson's drug store, the town's social center, discussing various and sundry topics of great import. To settle an argument, they sent for John T. Scopes, a local high school coach and teacher of algebra, physics, and chemistry. Scopes came over from his tennis game not realizing that he was about to enter the most dramatic period of his life, one he would never forget.

One of the men, a local businessman, said, "John, we've been arguing, and I said that nobody could teach biology without teaching evolution."

"That's right," said Scopes, and showed them the biology textbook that had been adopted by the State of Tennessee.

"Then, you've been violating the law," Doc Robinson said.

Although he did not teach biology, Scopes had, one day in April, substituted for the principal, who did. Technically, therefore, it could be said that he had taught biology and had thus violated the newly passed law.

As the discussion continued, and it became clear that Scopes felt strongly on the matter of academic freedom, Robinson asked him whether he would stand for a test case. Scopes said he would, whereupon Robinson called the *Chattanooga*

News and reported, "This is F. E. Robinson in Dayton. I'm chairman of the school board here. We've just arrested a man for teaching evolution." The man who had been "arrested" finished his soft drink and returned to his tennis game. (Writing forty years later in 1967, Scopes suggested that the trial was deliberately planned by Dayton businessmen to put that town on the map and bring in business, which is precisely what happened.)

The "arrest" made front page news across the country. William Jennings Bryan—three times Democratic nominee for President, Secretary of State under Woodrow Wilson, famous for his Cross of Gold speech at the Democratic convention of 1896, and acknowledged leader of the crusade against Darwinism—offered his services to the prosecution as the representative of the World's Christian Fundamentals Association.

With Bryan's entry into the fray, Clarence Darrow, nationally known labor and criminal lawyer, offered his services to the defense without fee or expense. The American Civil Liberties Union was in charge of the case for the defense and provided other well-known lawyers: John Randolph Neal, Arthur Garfield Hayes, and Dudley Field Malone.

In the weeks before the trial, the town of Dayton took on the atmosphere of a circus. The trial was referred to as "the monkey business." Merchants used monkey motifs in their advertising: little cotton apes were featured in store windows; pins that read "Your Old Man's a Monkey" could be purchased; and at Doc Robinson's drug store, a monkey fizz was available for refreshment from the summer heat. Hot dog stands, lemonade peddlers, booths selling books on biology or reli-

gion, and Bryan's truck, equipped with a loudspeaker touting Florida real estate, all added spice and noise to the carnival.

The trial began on Friday, July 10, 1925, with Judge John T. Raulston on the bench, and ended on Tuesday, July 21. It was clear from the start that Scopes would be convicted. The court, strongly religious, consistently favored the prosecution and forbade the testimony of expert defense witnesses—scientists—who were prepared to prove that evolution was a valid scientific concept. The prosecution insisted that the trial was not about the validity of evolution but that the real issue was simply whether or not Scopes had violated the law.

There were magnificent speeches. On Monday, July 13, in his support of the motion to quash the indictment against Scopes, Darrow displayed his famous forensic ability, and the crowded courthouse hung on every word. If the teaching of evolution is outlawed, he argued, then:

After a while, Your Honor, it is the setting of man against man and creed against creed until with flying banners and beating drums we are marching backward to the glorious age of the sixteenth century when bigots lighted faggots to burn the men who dared to bring any intelligence and enlightenment and culture to the human mind.

On Thursday, Bryan stood up to speak against the admissibility of scientific testimony. The crowd had been waiting for this moment, but they were to be disappointed. Bryan was an old man, not the man he once was; the fire was missing. H. L. Mencken, the acidulous reporter from the *Baltimore Sun*, attended the trial and wrote:

*His . . . speech was a grotesque perfor-
mance and downright touching in its
imbecility. Its climax came when he
launched into a furious denunciation of
the doctrine that man is a mammal. It
seemed a sheer impossibility that any
literate man should stand up in public
and discharge any such nonsense. Yet the
poor old fellow did it. . . . To call man
mammal, it appeared, was to flout the
revelation of God (Tompkins, 1965,
p. 48).*

Malone replied to Bryan, his former
superior officer at the State Department,
and his eloquence carried the day even
among the spectators who fully supported
Bryan. Bryan himself recognized this
when he told Malone afterwards, "Dudley,
that was the greatest speech I have ever
heard."

The climax of the trial came on Monday afternoon, July 20, when the defense called Bryan as an expert witness on
the Bible. The prosecutors immediately
jumped to their feet protesting, aware of
the danger inherent in the questions that
might be asked and the answers that might
be given. However, Bryan himself insisted
on testifying, perhaps because he felt
compelled to defend the Bible and "show
up" the evolutionists. It was an opportunity not to be missed.

Darrow's strategy was to question
Bryan about his literal interpretation of
the Bible. The Bible, Bryan held, was true,
every word of it, every comma. Every
miracle recorded in the Bible actually
happened. And it was on these points that
Darrow broke Bryan, made him appear
foolish, unthinking, and even a "traitor" to
the cause of fundamentalism. At one point
Darrow asked, "Do you think the earth
was made in six days?"

"Not in six days of twenty-four hours,"
Bryan replied.

The crowd gasped at this heresy. The
Bible read six days, and a day was obviously twenty-four hours. What was Bryan
thinking of? Toward the end of the afternoon Darrow brought up the Bible story
of Adam and Eve and the serpent. Had
God punished the serpent by making him
crawl on his belly? Bryan said he believed
that. Then, Darrow asked, "Have you any
idea how the snake went before that
time?"

"No, sir."

"Do you know whether he walked on
his tail or not?"

"No, sir, I have no way to know."

The crowd laughed and Bryan's hands
nervously trembled and his lips quiv-
ered.*

The trial ended the next day. The jury
(excused for most of the trial) was called
back and charged to decide whether
Scopes had violated the law; no other
question was to be considered. The jury
took but a short time and returned with
their verdict—guilty! Judge Raulston
fined Scopes $100 and the trial closed.

The case was appealed to the Tennessee Supreme Court, which handed down
its decision on January 15, 1927. The Court
upheld the Butler Act and also recommended that the State drop the indictment
against Scopes on the technicality that the
judge had imposed the fine, instead of the
jury, as Tennessee law required. The
Court thus made it impossible to appeal
the case before the United States Supreme
Court.

_____

*A diabetic and in ill health, Bryan died on Sun-
day, July 26, five days after the trial ended.

Update
In the sixty years since the Scopes trial, religious fundamentalists have not ceased
their attempts to remove the teaching of
evolution from the public schools of the
nation. Known as "creationists" because
they explain the existence of the universe,
energy, and life as a result of sudden creation, they are determined either to eliminate the teaching of evolution or to introduce anti-evolutionary subject matter.
Creationists have insisted that "creation-
science" is just as much science as what
they term "evolution science." Therefore,
they claim, in the interest of fair play, a
balanced view should be offered to students—if evolution is taught as science,
then creationism should also be taught as
science.

Now, state legislation that had man-
dated the inclusion of "creation-science"
in the curriculum of public schools (Ar-
kansas, Louisiana, Tennessee) has been
declared unconstitutional by federal
courts, including the U.S. Supreme Court.
The unconstitutionality is based essentially on the judgment that "creation-
science" advances a religious point of
view that interferes with the fundamental
principle of the separation of church and
state.

In 1989, the California Department of
Education denied The Institute for Creation Research the right to award post-
graduate degrees in science, because students were not learning the basics of
science. Also in California in 1989, the
state School Board issued a new science
teaching guideline for public schools that
stresses the importance of evolution as
"the organizing principle of biology."

It is expected that textbook publishers,
who have been reluctant to mention the

word "evolution" in their public school texts, will include at least the basics of evolution in their science books for the State of California.

Nevertheless, creationists continue to pursue their goal to introduce their religious point of view in public schools. They also publish material and hold conferences and lectures on creationism. This, of course, is legal, but creationists are free-wheeling in their use of evidence to prove what they preach. An example of their technique may be seen in what might be called "The Dinosaur/Human Caper."

In 1939, fossil hunter Roland T. Bird, working for the American Museum of Natural History, published an article in *Natural History* about some carved giant human and carved dinosaur footprints he had located near Paluxy Creek, Texas. Bird had learned that these footprints were carved by residents of the nearby town of Glen Rose during the 1930s depression in order to earn money from tourists.

A creationist, Clifford Burdick, read the article and decided to find the "human" footprints, which he believed to be genuine. His intent, apparently, was to prove the so-called human footprints were contemporary with the dinosaur footprints. This would then demonstrate that dinosaurs and humans lived at the same time, that all living organisms were created simultaneously, and that the earth was only a few thousand years old.

Burdick explained the enormous size of the "human" footprints by declaring that modern people degenerated from a Golden Age when men were over ten feet tall. They had since withered to an average of less than six feet, and their average life

span reduced to slightly more than 50 years.

Other creationists hurried to Paluxy to unearth more evidence, and they did: the skull of a monkey or child, saber-toothed tiger footprints, chariot tracks, and an ancient hammer—all of these contemporaneous with the dinosaur tracks!

A few years ago a group of scientists, representing anthropology, physics, geology, and paleontology, visited Paluxy Creek to see what was really there. They found the only real item was dinosaur tracks; everything else was fake. The so-called human footprints exhibited none of the features characteristic of human footprints; the hammer turned out to be a nineteenth-century miner's hammer; and the rest was judged equally fraudulent.

Despite the disclosure that the "human" tracks were not actually human (which some creationists have admitted), creationists continue to advertise them as real human tracks, made at the same time dinosaurs roamed the earth. (Science tells us that dinosaurs lived from about 225 mya to about 65 mya. The earliest date for hominids is about 3.75 mya.)

The question is not which is true, creationism or science. The point is that *creationism is not science*. Creationists argue that it is only fair to balance evolution with creation. It would be just as fair to balance a round earth theory with a flat earth theory, or teach that the sun revolves around the earth. Creationism is a religious belief and while people have a right to their beliefs, as a religious statement creationism has no place in the science curriculum of public schools.

To deny students the opportunity to be taught the principles of evolution is to leave them poorly educated and without

a reasonable understanding of what is going on in a world ever more dependent on the findings of science. As Stanford University's well-known biologist Paul Ehrlich wrote:

. . . we live in a world that has evolved, and we evolved in it. An individual who is not at least passingly familiar with the history and mechanisms of evolution on our planet is out of touch with fundamental aspects of his or her humanity. It is a separation from reality that our overcrowded and hard-pressed species can ill afford.

SOURCES FOR ISSUE

Ginger, Ray. *Six Days or Forever?*, Boston: Beacon Press, 1958.

Scopes, John T. and James Presley. *Center of the Storm*, New York: Holt, Rinehart and Winston, 1967.

Tompkins, Jerry R. (ed.). *D-Days at Dayton*, Baton Rouge: Louisiana State University Press, 1965.

SOURCES FOR THE UPDATE

Godfrey, Laurie R. and John R. Cole. "Blunder in Their Footsteps," *Natural History*, August, 1986.

Kuban, Glen J. "Retracking Those Incredible Man Tracks," *Reports*, National Center for Science Education, 9(4), July–August, 1989.

Ehrlich, Paul. "Why Should We Care About Evolution," *Pacific Discovery*, 36(2):15, April–June, 1983.

CHAPTER 2

Introduction

The major result of evolution—that is, the development of new species of plants or animals from an already existing species—was not taken seriously by medieval philosophers. Literal readings of the Bible, especially Genesis, taught that all plants and animals had been created. Nothing in the Bible suggested the creation of new species; ergo, there were not any. Furthermore, the universe was *fixed* at creation and remain unchanged. The idea of evolution, then, not only would have been considered heretical, but "common sense" would have labeled it ridiculous.

Nevertheless, scholars of the fifteenth, sixteenth, and seventeenth centuries demonstrated that the universe was *not* rigidly fixed. The belief that organic beings were similarly not fixed was being entertained, especially in the eighteenth century. Unfortunately, attempts to explain how the process of evolution worked failed until Charles Darwin, in the nineteenth century, succeeded with his theory of natural selection.

Our understanding of evolution today is based essentially on Darwin's work as well as contributions made in the twentieth century, especially from the field of genetics. Although our focus throughout this text is *human* evolution, in this chapter we discuss general evolutionary principles applicable to all organisms, plant and animal. The evolutionary process is a unified one, and the principles are the same for all life forms, including humans.

We will examine the changes in intellectual thought that led to the theory of natural selection, acclaimed as the most important scientific contribution of the nineteenth century. First, though, let us take a brief look at the man responsible for this theory: Charles Darwin.

Darwin's Life

Charles Darwin (1809–1882) was the son of Dr. Robert and Susannah Darwin and grandson of the eminent Dr. Erasmus Darwin. Charles, one of six children, was thought by his family and by himself to be a "very ordinary boy." As an ordinary boy, he did the usual things (collecting shells, stamps, coins) and, at school, he displayed no special inclination for scholarship.

Because he showed little interest in, or aptitude for, anything particular (with the possible exception of science), Dr. Darwin decided that Charles should study medicine at Edinburgh. After two years, Charles conceded medicine was not for him, and instead turned to hunting and fishing, which he thoroughly enjoyed. His father complained that Charles was only interested in "shooting, dogs and rat-catching."

For sons who had no discernible academic leanings, parents could, as a last refuge, turn them to the church. Although indifferent to religion, Charles dutifully

FIGURE 2-1   Charles Darwin (at age 32).

FIGURE 2-2   Examples of some of Darwin's finches. Note the similarities and differences in beak structure.

took up residence at Christ's College, Cambridge, in 1828, at the age of 19. While ostensibly enrolled in theology, Charles became interested in what we today call natural science. He became a constant companion of the Reverend John Stevens Henslow, professor of botany, and often joined his classes in their botanical excursions.

Darwin was graduated in 1831, at the age of 22, not with a distinguished record, but one good enough to satisfy his family, and he could look forward to a serene future as a country cleric. However, that was not to be, for something happened that summer that Darwin referred to as "the most important event of my life."

He received a letter from his friend, Professor Henslow, informing him that he had recommended Darwin as the best-qualified person he knew for the position of naturalist on a scientific expedition that would circle the globe. (See Box 2-1.) Darwin was willing, even eager, for this opportunity to combine travel with the pursuit of botany, zoology, and geology, but his father objected and Charles regretfully declined. However, Charles found a champion in his uncle, Josiah Wedgewood, who persuaded Charles' father that the voyage would be desirable and Dr. Darwin reluctantly gave his consent. With mixed feelings of elation and trepidation, Charles set sail on board the H.M.S. *Beagle*, December 27, 1831, on a voyage where attacks of seasickness would place him in his hammock for days on end. Having begun the voyage as a clergyman (at least such had been his intent) with hobbies of zoology, botany, and geology, Darwin found, within a short time, that his true calling was natural science. Through his industrious and diligent work of collecting, arranging, and dissecting specimens, Darwin matured from an amateur observer into a professional naturalist.

Darwin went aboard the *Beagle* not as an evolutionist but as a believer in the fixity of species. His observations, however, quickly raised evolutionary suspicions in his mind. As early as 1832, for example, he noted in his diary that a snake with rudimentary hind limbs marked "the passage by which Nature joins the lizards to the snakes." He came across fossils of ancient giant animals that looked, except for size, very much like living forms in the same vicinity, and wondered whether the fossils were the ancestors of those forms. He observed that the Andean Mountain Range constituted a natural barrier to life and, as might be expected according to geologists, flora and fauna on opposite sides of the range differed.

The stopover at the Galápagos Islands (see Fig. 2-3b) profoundly impressed Darwin. He noted that the flora and fauna of South America were very similar—yet dissimilar—to those of the Galápagos. Even more surprising, the inhabitants of the various islands differed slightly. The thirteen kinds of finches resembled one another in the structure of their beaks, body forms, and plumage, and yet each constituted a separate species (but only one species existed on the mainland) despite the fact that few geographic differences existed among the islands. What, he asked himself, could cause this modification if the physical geography and climate were not responsible? These observations, and the questions they raised, caused Darwin to wonder whether the theory of fixity of species was a valid one after all.

This abbreviated account of Darwin and his research on the *Beagle* does not do justice to the significant role the voyage played in Darwin's intellectual growth. He returned to England on board the *Beagle* on October 2, 1836, just short of five years from the date he sailed, a more mature and serious scientist.

In 1842, Darwin wrote a short summary of his views on natural selection and revised it in 1844. The 1844 sketch was surprisingly similar to the argument he pre-

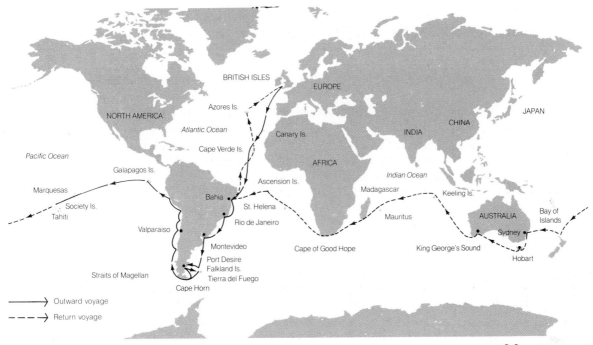

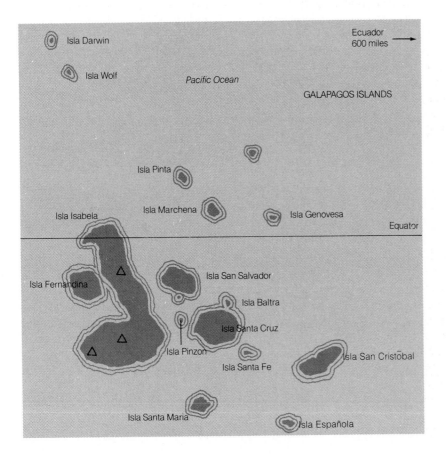

FIGURE 2-3a   The route of the H.M.S. *Beagle*.

FIGURE 2-3b   The Galápagos Islands. Finches (because of their variety) and tortoises (because each island was inhabited by its own variety) influenced Darwin's thinking about evolution.

BOX 2-1 **Darwin: Naturalist or Companion?**

Robert Fitzroy, Captain of the *Beagle*.

Was Darwin invited to sail aboard the H.M.S. *Beagle* as a naturalist or as a companion to **Captain Fitzroy**?* Since Darwin had been recommended as a naturalist, and had acted in that capacity throughout the *Beagle*'s five-year voyage (during which he developed ideas that ultimately led to his concept of natural selection), the answer has always seemed obvious.

However, the well-known contemporary naturalist Dr. Stephen Jay Gould has suggested that Darwin was invited to be Fitzroy's companion, and that the position of naturalist was an enticement to that end. The reasons, says Gould, were that a captain in the British navy was not

---

*The captain's name is spelled variously as Fitz-Roy, FitzRoy, and Fitzroy.

permitted to speak to members of his crew except on ship's business; that Fitzroy was aware of the awful loneliness of a captain who had to dine by himself in his own cabin; and that he, Fitzroy, was not too stable. Therefore, someone to share his cabin, meals, and conversation was absolutely mandatory. For this, Fitzroy required someone of the proper social rank—a gentleman—and in order to persuade such a person, the captain offered the position of naturalist.

The interesting and important aspect of this, according to Gould, is that Darwin's view of evolution may have grown out of the strained relationship that developed between the two men. They argued on several subjects: slavery, for one; God and nature, for another. Fitzroy's dogmatic assertions about the universe, suggests Gould, acted as the catalyst that drove Darwin to an opposite view, leading to "an evolutionary theory based on chance variation and natural selection by a largely external environment: a rigidly materialistic (and basically atheistic) version of evolution."

Today it is difficult to know why Fitzroy wanted a naturalist on board. He has been described as "a public spirited and zealous officer." Since the purpose of the *Beagle*'s voyage was entirely scientific, it is certainly possible that Fitzroy may have been serious in his search for a naturalist who might also—as a subordinate function —serve as companion.

Darwin's correspondence to his friend and professor Dr. Henslow (who first recommended him for the position), and to his father, seems to leave no doubt about why he thought he was sailing: to work as a naturalist. Darwin was aware that he was expected to be a companion to Captain Fitzroy (Henslow mentioned it in his letter to Darwin), but this function must have impressed him very little. He never referred to it in his correspondence.

sented fifteen years later in *The Origin of Species*, but Darwin did not feel he had sufficient data to support his views, and he continued his research.

Time passed. In 1855, an article by Alfred Russel Wallace on the succession of species impressed Darwin because it supported his views on species' mutability. Darwin was not disturbed at this time by the possibility that the publication of his own theory might be anticipated. Darwin had been encouraged by his close friends, especially Lyell (see p. 36) and Hooker (a well-known botanist) to publish his "theory," but he declined because he felt there was much more evidence to collect. His friends cautioned him that someone else might publish before he did, and, indeed, his friends' warning was realized in June, 1858, when Wallace sent Darwin his paper on natural selection.

Alfred Russel Wallace (1823–1913) was born in a small English village into a family of modest means. He went to work at 14 and, without any special talent, moved from one job to the next. He became interested in collecting, and joined an expedition to the Amazon in 1848, at the age of 25. After four happy years of collecting specimens in South America, Wallace returned to England and two years later, in 1854, he sailed to the Malayan Archipelago to continue his study and collection of bird and insect specimens. He remained there eight years, collected 125,660 specimens, and often thought about the problem of the succession of species.

In 1858, on the island of Ternate, just off the coast of the Celebes Islands,* Wallace was in bed suffering from one of his periodic attacks of fever. Suddenly, the solution to the problem he had so long thought about flashed through his mind. Recalling the phrase, "the positive checks to increase," from Malthus' *Essay* (p. 37), he immediately realized that this phenomenon could apply to animals as well as to human beings. If there were no checks, the earth would quickly be overrun by the most prolific breeders. Why, then, did some species of plants or animals perish while others survived? The answer came at once: the best adapted survived; the less well adapted perished. Wallace at once set his thoughts down on paper and sent Darwin his essay, "On the Tendency of Varieties to Depart Indefinitely from the Original Type" (Löwenberg, 1959).

When Darwin read Wallace's paper he was thoroughly depressed. He wrote Lyell, "Your words have come true with a vengeance—that I should be forestalled" (F. Darwin, 1950, p. 199). With the publication of Wallace's paper, Wallace would be given credit for a theory that Darwin felt belonged to him, since he had thought of it at least twenty years before. What to do? Darwin considered publishing a resume of his own work but wondered whether it would be honorable to do so. He told Lyell, "I would far rather burn my whole book, than that he [Wallace] or any other man should think I have behaved in a paltry spirit" (F. Darwin, 1950, p. 201). After much indecision, Darwin finally decided to let his close friends, Lyell and Joseph Hooker, devise a formula that would be fair to both Wallace and himself.

This difficult task was achieved by his friends, who decided that joint papers by Wallace and Darwin would be read before a meeting of the Linnaean Society. The Society agreed, and the papers were read on the evening of July 1, 1858, with Darwin ill in bed and Wallace in the Far East. What is remarkable is that the papers did not create a furor at the meeting, since most members of the Society disagreed with the concepts of natural selection.

FIGURE 2-4   Alfred Russel Wallace.

---

*Now known as *Sulawesi*.

The solution to the problem of Wallace's paper pleased Darwin, and Wallace was delighted that he had been so fairly treated. After the presentation of the two papers, the trustees of the Linnaean Society brought urgent pressure on Darwin to publish as speedily as possible a full account of his "theory." Darwin returned to his work with exemplary energy and, within a year, in 1859, had completed and published his great work, *The Origin of Species*.†

With publication, the storm broke, and has not abated even to this day. While there was much praise for the book from many quarters, the gist of opinion was negative. Scientific opinion gradually came to Darwin's support, assisted especially by Darwin's able friend, Thomas Huxley (known as "Darwin's bulldog"), who for years wrote and spoke in favor of natural selection. The riddle of species was now explained: species were not fixed, but mutable; they evolved from other species through the mechanism of natural selection. Science was never to be the same again.

Darwin's Theory of Evolution

Darwin did not originate the idea of evolution, which had been suggested (or at least hinted at) 200 years previously—and much longer, if we include Greek thought of 2000 years ago. Darwin's grandfather, Erasmus Darwin, had written in defense of evolution before Charles was born, and Lamarck, a French scientist, had drawn up a schema trying to explain how new species were formed. However, his explanation met with unfavorable criticism and, in fact, did not adequately explain how the evolutionary process functioned.

Nor were the basic ideas used by Darwin completely of his own invention. Struggle for existence, extinction of species, variation, adaptation—these were all known and discussed for years by many European scientists. Darwin's great contribution was to bring these divergent ideas together and add the key: natural selection.

In his book, *The Origin of Species*, published in 1859, Darwin explained his concept of evolution:

1. All species are capable of producing offspring faster than the food supply increases (see Malthus, p. 37)
2. All living things show variations; no two individuals of a species are exactly alike
3. Because there are more individuals than can possibly survive, there is a fierce struggle for existence and those with a favorable variation in size, strength, running ability, or whatever characteristics are necessary for survival, will possess an advantage over others (see Malthus, p. 37)
4. These favorable variations are inherited and passed on to the next generation
5. Over long periods of geologic time, these successful variations produce great differences that result in new species

---

†The complete title of Darwin's book is *On the Origin of Species by Means of Natural Selection, or the Preservation of Favoured Races in the Struggle for Life*.

Darwin called this process "natural selection." He did not believe in creation by design; that is, that life forms were placed on earth by creation, that variation in plants and animals was part of a grand divine design, or that the inorganic and the organic could be viewed as a progression from inferior to superior types, with humans at the top.

The Path to Natural Selection

THE GREAT CHAIN OF BEING

Darwin did not arrive at natural selection—his solution to the process of evolution—without assistance. When we look at the intellectual climate of Europe of the Middle Ages, we find that Christianity was associated with certain views of the universe. Since the time of Ptolemy, a Greco-Egyptian mathematician, geographer, and astronomer of the second century A.D., the earth was considered to be fixed at the center of a universe of spheres that revolved with perfect regularity around it. Not only was the inorganic world fixed and unchanging, but the organic world was believed to be equally static. It was believed that all species of the earth had been created (according to Genesis of the Old Testament) on a progression from the simplest living forms to the most complex—humans. This progression was not evolutionary; that is, one species did not lead to or evolve into the next. The forms and sequence were fixed, each creature forever linked to the next in a great chain of beings. No new ones had appeared since creation, and none had disappeared.

This progression was, in fact, known as the Great Chain of Being (see Box 2-2), and the plan of the entire universe was seen as the Grand Design, that is, God's Design. The limbs of men and animals seemed designed to meet the purpose for which they are required. The wings of birds, eyes, etc., all of these structures were interpreted as neatly fitting the functions they performed. It was considered to be a deliberate plan of the Grand Designer. The "Grand Designer" concept was supported by what is known as "argument from design," which was stated by John Ray, one of the leading naturalists of the sixteenth century. Following is a shortened version in somewhat modern English:

> If works of art, designed for a certain purpose, infer the existence of an intelligent Architect or Engineer, then why should not Nature, which transcends human art, infer the existence of an Omnipotent and Allwise Creator?

Furthermore, the Grand Designer had completed all his work in quite a short time, since creation was dated at 4004 B.C. by Archbishop James Ussher (1581–1656), an Irish prelate and scholar, who worked out the date by analyzing the "begat" chapter of Genesis.

Until these concepts of fixity and time were changed, it would be very unlikely that the idea of natural selection could even be conceived. What, then, upset the medieval belief in a rigid universe of planets, stars, plants, and animals? What scientific philosophy would, within the following 150 years, strike a death blow to the whole medieval system of thought? How would the scientific method as we know it today develop and, especially with Newton and Galileo in the seventeenth century, demonstrate a moving, not unchanging, universe?

BOX 2-2

The Great Chain of Being

Originating from ideas of Plato and Aristotle, the Chain of Being was a world view widespread in Europe especially during the seventeenth and eighteenth centuries. This philosophy held that the earth, even the universe, was "full"; that is, everything that was possible, existed. Also, the universe was composed of an infinite and continuous series of forms, each one *grading* into the next, arranged in an hierarchical sequence from the simplest kind of existence to the perfection of God.

Thus, there were superior and inferior beings, and perhaps more important (for evolutionary concepts), a being's step in this linear sequence was fixed, could not be altered and, since the earth was "full," i.e., complete, nothing new (like species) could be added. Gradation did not suggest that a superior being evolved from the next lower one; rather, a being was created forever set and unchangeable in its position in the chain of beings. Since God created the chain, change was inconceivable, for this would challenge God's perfection.

While such beliefs were prominently and widely believed, the concept of a closed and static system was under attack by various scientists and philosophers. It would only become a matter of time before outspoken supporters of evolution would make their ideas known.

The Scientific Revolution

The change might be said to begin in the sixteenth century when Copernicus (latinized from Kopernik), a Polish cleric and astronomer, wrote a treatise on the system conceived by Ptolemy. In it, he noted that earth, rotating on its axis, revolved around a fixed sun, not vice versa.

This heresy attracted little attention at the time, but it was picked up almost a century later by the German astrologer/astronomer Johannes Kepler. Kepler, like Copernicus, was interested in motion, and formulated three laws of planetary motion that influenced later scientists.

In Italy, Galileo, a contemporary of Kepler, reintroduced Copernicus' heliocentric (sun-centered) theory. Although this brought him into conflict with the Church, the notion that the sun revolved around a fixed earth that was the center of the universe was no longer taken seriously by most scientists. Galileo was one of the first scientists to use experiments as an integral part of his science along with mathematical analysis. Galileo was largely responsible for making the basic laws of motion a general feature of seventeenth century science.

The seventeenth century was a beehive of scientific activity, a unique time of exceptional men with remarkable insights whose thinking ended almost two thousand years of dependence on the Aristotelian view of the universe and set on course the methodology of modern science. Francis Bacon emphasized both the use of the inductive method and the need for experiment with careful, detailed observation. René Descarte contributed a new method of mathematics and also established a mechanical philosophy, "which sought to explain the properties and actions of bodies in terms of the parts of which they are composed" (Cohen, 1985, p. 154). In other words, bodies were to be explained in terms of their material composition; the *purpose* of an object or being could no longer be used scientifically as an explanation of its form or behavior.

Probably the greatest of the seventeenth century thinkers was Isaac Newton, the English physicist. His achievements included the reorganization of the calculus, the application of mathematics to physics and astronomy, the formulation of three laws of motion, the creation of the field of optics (theory of light and color), and perhaps his most important contribution, the law of universal gravity.

Scientists of the sixteenth and especially the seventeenth centuries developed methods and theories that revolutionized scientific thought and produced the foundation of modern science. They gave the intellectual milieu of their era a definite naturalistic basis. While still a significant factor in scientific thinking, God was being viewed increasingly as a superfluous factor in a more naturalistic view of the universe. It was becoming possible to investigate the stars, planets, animals, and plants without reference to the supernatural. Nature was seen as a mechanism, functioning according to certain physical laws, and it was these laws that scientists were to seek.

The work of naturalists of that period reflected a modern biological approach. They collected, classified, described; they upset ancient notions and exploded old fables. Like other scientists, they adopted the mechanical model of nature to explain organic function. And yet the notion lingered that a vital principle was necessary to understand the works of nature, which ultimately depended on God's design. God was not considered dead, and many scientists could believe in a mechanistic universe and still insist that a First Cause initiated the entire system. It was a confusing time in scientific thought; science was moving toward a secular approach, but was not quite ready to move all the way.

Nevertheless, the erosion of the concept of God as the center of scientific and philosophic thought continued into the eighteenth century. For some thinkers, known as materialists, nature was the sole reality. They challenged the argument from design, and for them

> Everything we see in the world must be a chance product of the ceaseless activity of material nature, including the various living species and man himself. Fixed species . . . represented vestiges of the old creationist myth . . . (Bowler, 1989, p. 77)

Although materialists were seen as radicals, the trend of scientific thought continued in the direction of secularism. Inevitably, it turned toward the study of humankind, and human nature became the center of science. As Alexander Pope wrote in his famous couplet of the 1730s,

> Know then thyself, presume not God to scan;
> The proper study of Mankind is Man.

The eighteenth century, then, was a less religious time in Europe than the seventeenth century. Reason overshadowed revelation in the early half of the eighteenth century, although the argument from design was still defended, and support for it continued well into the nineteenth century. The *watch*, signifying the order that reigned in the universe, argued the existence of the watch*maker*.

Also retained by many scientists was the insistence on stasis as it applied to life forms. The stars, the sun, the planets, and the earth might move, but life remained as it was created—no new species; no extinctions.

It is ironic, perhaps, that Christian belief—that the order and design of the universe could be interpreted by rational minds—led to Darwin and natural selection. We have remarked that in the seventeenth century there appeared to be an overwhelming thrust by philosopher/scientists toward examining nature in all its

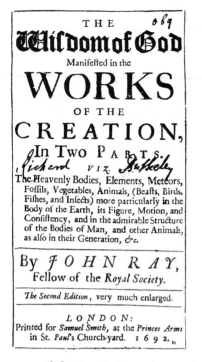

FIGURE 2-5 An early (sixteenth-century) version of the Argument from Design.

FIGURE 2-6 Linnaeus.

aspects. Studying natural relationships diligently was not an irreverant exercise, but a human duty, since such study would demonstrate the majesty and glory of God. This conviction continued through the next two centuries and drove many men to search out the mysteries of nature. It was this same conviction and drive that not only led to Darwin but to the modern concept of a secular science as well. "It is surely one of the curious paradoxes of history that science, which professionally has little to do with faith, owes its origins to an act of faith that the universe can be rationally interpreted, and that science today is sustained by that assumption" (Eiseley, 1958, p. 62).

Although scientists of the seventeenth century remained religiously oriented, their observations and experiments provoked notions of the universe that were new, exciting, and challenging. This emphasis led eighteenth-century thinkers to a more secularist view of the universe. For some scientists, it led to a complete rejection of religion as a factor in the operation of the physical universe. Darwin, in the nineteenth century, was heir to the thinking and ideas of these naturalist/philosophers. At Cambridge, Darwin associated with professors (all churchmen) who were anti-evolutionists, but the radical change in the intellectual climate of the seventeenth century enabled scientists of the century following to think about the universe in a manner that made the idea of evolution possible, and paved the way for Darwin.

LINNAEUS

However, the course to evolution was not an easy one. The notion of the fixity of species certainly held sway among the public, as well as most scientists. One such scientist, and one of the leading naturalists of his day, was **Carolus Linnaeus** who believed that "There are just as many species as there were created in the beginning," and again, "There is no such thing as a new species" (quoted in Singer, 1959, 379–380). He thought of nature as a system of unchangeable substances, "a continuum from algae to humans." He agreed with the notion of a "chain of being" (see Box 2-2), that all life forms were linked together in one great chain, and each species was fixed and unchangeable.

The son of a Lutheran pastor, Linnaeus (1707–1778) was born at Roeshult, Sweden. He is best known for developing a classification system for plants and animals, first published in 1835, which he called *Systema Naturae*. Linnaeus isolated those particular physical traits that best characterized a particular group of organisms. In plants, for instance, he used blossoms; in insects, wings; and in fish, scales. He even included humans in his classification of animals, thus defying the then-contemporary thought that humans, made in God's image, should be considered separately and outside the animal kingdom.

Linnaeus' scheme was well received throughout Europe, and, when applied to collections in museums and botanical gardens, it worked. He then proceeded to assign names to the animals and plants. Linnaeus used the simple but effective idea of assigning two Latin names to each organism. The first word would be the generic term—the genus—for the organism and the second word, the specific term—the species. Thus, the two words together would become a unit internationally recognized as the name for that particular form. This system of binomial (or binominal) nomenclature was widely accepted and is still used today.

We are concerned not so much with the problems and solutions that resulted in Linnaeus' *Systema Naturae* as we are in his ideas about evolution, which reflected the scientific thought of his time. Linnaeus saw nature as a "rationally ordained system of means and ends"; that is, every living thing is created perfectly adapted to the environment in which it lives, making further change unnecessary. Although some scientists by this time had abandoned the age-old notion that nature was fixed, Linnaeus still adhered to the idea that species, once divinely created, had never changed, and "to study nature diligently" meant assigning to every living thing its proper name. He is supposed to have said, "What is a botanist? Simply a person who can give the right names" (Lindroth, 1983, p. 24).

It was a fundamental belief of Linnaeus, as it was of his contemporaries, that species were immutable; therefore, there could be no new species, yet

> . . . with the years Linnaeus began to weaken in his belief that no new species could emerge . . . and in his old age worked out a theory, partly imaginary, according to which the multiplicity of organisms had arisen through hybridization among a limited number of original forms. But this did not mean turning his back on the past. The species, as much as ever, were fixed units, and in themselves just as sharply delimited as before (Lindroth, 1983, p. 24).

However, there were other voices, especially in France, raised loud and clear in favor of a universe based on change, and much more to the point, of the relationship between similar forms based on descent from a common ancestor.

FIGURE 2-7   Buffon.

BUFFON

The leading advocate of this point of view was Georges Louis Leclerc, who came from an old noble family in Burgundy and was later raised to the rank of Count, under the name of Buffon, by Louis XV. **Buffon** (1707–1788), as he is known, was born the same year as Linnaeus. He knew of his contemporary and disagreed with him on most points. Buffon's volumes of *Natural History* were best sellers that influenced the leading scholars of Europe. His writings made natural science popular drawing-room conversation, in which he himself excelled with sly wit. Talking one day with his female visitors, he said, "Nothing stands still. Everything moves. Even the seed of man does so, otherwise it would never reach its goal. May I show it to you under the microscope?" (Wendt, 1963, p. 83).

Buffon suggested ideas that would not be accepted for another generation of scientists. He recognized the dynamic relationship of environment and nature. He was convinced that different species could develop from a common ancestor that divided into two or more groups through migration to different areas of the world. Each group was then influenced by local climatic conditions and gradually changed form. This was very close to what Darwin was to say in the next century, but Buffon rejected transformism; that is, the change of one species into another species.

However, Buffon believed in the mutability of nature and developed a scheme for the evolution of earth similar to the theories of presentday geology. This led him to project a much older earth, some 76,000 years, (in private, he said millions of years) than the 4004 B.C. of Bishop Ussher would have it. Buffon also insisted on the separation of theology and science.

In contrast to Linnaeus' static "rationally ordained system of means and ends," Buffon emphasized the variety and minute gradations of nature, which he explained in terms of "a system of laws, elements and forces." Thus, nature could be seen as functioning by natural means rather than through a divine mind. Buffon considered it important to see life as a dynamic system of processes instead of a static pattern of structure. He felt that the true aim of natural history was to discover and understand these processes, not simply to classify their result. Buffon "did more than any one else to habituate the mind of his time to a vastly (though not yet sufficiently) enlarged time-scale in connection with the history of organic nature, a necessary prerequisite to the establishment of transformation" (Lovejoy, 1959, pp. 111–112).

> Curiously enough, as his work proceeded, Buffon managed . . . at least to mention every significant ingredient which was to be incorporated into Darwin's great synthesis of 1859. He did not, however, quite manage to put these factors together (Eiseley, 1958, p. 39).

The contrast between the thinking of Linnaeus and that of Buffon reflects not merely the old and the new, but also the response of many scientists and clergymen to the publication of Darwin's *Origin*. Although Linnaeus appeared to have modified his views about new species late in life, the concept of immutability of species continued to be the dominant theme among most scientists. Darwin was familiar with the writings of Buffon, which helped make a belief in evolution acceptable. With the voluminous publications of Buffon and others, it is not at all surprising that when we arrive at the latter portion of the eighteenth century, the ideas of mutability of species and the possibility of unlimited organic change were well known throughout Europe. This doctrine of organic change was not widely accepted, but at least it was being discussed at length in intellectual circles.

ERASMUS DARWIN

FIGURE 2-8   Erasmus Darwin.

In this enlightened era of the popularization of science (which saw the beginnings of archeology and the recognition that fossil bones belonged to species of animals since perished), we must take notice of a most interesting figure who saw clearly the force of evolutionary ideas. Charles Darwin was well aware of the writings of this man, his grandfather, **Erasmus Darwin** (1731–1802), who was a country physician, poet, and versatile scientist. More than fifty years before his grandson was to startle the world with his views on natural selection, Erasmus had expressed such ideas as "evolution by natural and sexual selection, protective adaptation, inheritance of acquired characteristics, and even the evolution of mankind" (Francoeur, 1965, p. 68). In fact, one biographer wrote of Erasmus Darwin, "the theory of natural selection was the only cardinal one in the evolution system on which Erasmus Darwin did not actually forestall his more famous and greater namesake" (Clodd, 1897, p. 114).

Although Charles Darwin had read his grandfather's writings, it is not possible to say what influence these had on his views. Erasmus had not solved the problem of the evolutionary process, but it is likely that his discussion of evolution made it easier for Charles to approach it.

During the eighteenth century, Erasmus Darwin wrote about and believed in evolution, but was never able to explain the process. He came close but, as Buffon before him and Lamarck afterwards, he relied on the concept of acquired characteristics to indicate how species were transformed: " 'All animals undergo perpetual transformations; which are in part produced by their own exertions . . . and many of these acquired forms or propensities are transmitted to their posterity' "

(E. Darwin, quoted in Singer, 1959, p. 505). However, neither Buffon nor E. Darwin codified their beliefs into a comprehensive system. The first European scientist to do this was Jean Baptiste Pierre Antoine de Monet de **Lamarck** (1744–1829).

LAMARCK

Lamarck, unlike his predecessors, was the first major proponent of the idea of organic evolution. Erasmus Darwin, and quite a few others during this time, believed in the transmutation or transformation of one species to another, but Lamarck organized his views into a system that attempted to explain how it all happened.

His theory of organic development, or evolution, consisted of three points:

1. The spontaneous generation of the simplest forms of life (see Box 2-3)
2. The evolution from simple to complex forms (see Box 2-3)
3. The influence of "circumstances" (environment) that hinder the natural tendency toward complexity (Burkhardt, 1984, p. xxiii)

Lamarck also provided a method for the origin of *new* species based on the laws of *use and disuse* of organs.

> *First Law:* The more frequent and continuous use of any organ gradually strengthens, develops, and enlarges that organ; while the permanent disuse of any organ imperceptibly weakens and deteriorates it until it finally disappears.

> *Second Law:* All the acquisitions or losses wrought by nature through the *influence of the environment* are preserved by reproduction (Lamarck, Zoological Philosophy, 1809, 1984, p. 113).

Thus, the permanent disuse of an organ, arising from a change of habits, causes the disappearance and even the extinction of that organ; conversely, the frequent use of any organ, when confirmed by habit, leads to its development. Applying this to humans, Lamarck suggested that

> . . . if some race of **quadrumanous** animals were to lose the habit of climbing trees and grasping the branches with its feet; and if the individuals of this race were forced for a series of generations to use their feet only for walking, there is no doubt that these quadrumanous animals would at length be transformed into **bimanous**, [animals] and that the thumbs on their feet would cease to be separated from the other digits . . .

> Furthermore, if the individuals of which I speak were impelled by the desire to command a large and distant view, and hence endeavoured to stand upright, and continually adopted that habit from generation to generation, there is again no doubt that their feet would gradually acquire a shape suitable for supporting them in an erect attitude; that their legs would acquire calves, and that these animals would then not be able to walk on their hands and feet together, except with difficulty (ibid, p. 170)*

FIGURE 2-9   Lamarck.

Lamarck considered wish, desire, will, and needs as ways in which change could be motivated; more important, however, were the animal's habits, which could effectively initiate change through the movements of invisible fluids, especially heat and electricity. Little by little, as habits altered the fluids' pathways, the body's form would change.

---

*These two paragraphs have been abridged to make the citation shorter and, we hope, clearer.

According to Lamarck, then, when the environment changes, there is an alteration in the needs (wishes, desires) of animals that necessitate new activities (habits). The animal is then required to use some of its organs more frequently, or to make use of entirely new organs developed by the fluids. The altered organs or the new ones will then be passed on through heredity to the next generation and, in time, a new species will arise, apparently more complex.

Unfortunately, neither spontaneous generation, a trend toward complexity, or the actions of fluids, as Lamarck described them, are supported by adequate evidence. Also, his notion of the inheritance of acquired traits cannot be scientifically supported. In fairness, it should be mentioned that the belief in the theory of acquired characteristics, as Lamarck's system is known, was so widespread in the scientific community of his day, that Lamarck did not feel a need to prove it.

It is interesting to note that Charles Darwin, who used natural selection as the mechanism for evolution, also used, at times, the belief that acquired characteristics could be inherited. In fact, there are biologists today who believe that under certain conditions, such as virus-induced mutations, a case could be made for the inheritance of certain acquired alterations.

Lamarck developed a detailed system to account for the acquisition of new traits, how they could be transmitted, and how the environment dynamically interacted with organic forms. He brought together vast quantities of materials to support his evolutionary ideas, carrying them beyond those of Buffon. Ernst Heinrich Haeckel, a well-known scientist of the late nineteenth century, said that to Lamarck "will always belong the immortal glory of having for the first time worked out the Theory of Descent as an independent scientific theory of the first order, and as the philosophical foundation of the whole science of Biology" (Clodd, 1897, p. 115). Lamarck was Darwin's only genuine scientific precursor and the world of science, especially biology, owes him a great debt.

Nevertheless, his system was not accepted and today we know that Darwin's *natural selection* explains evolution and inheritance much more adequately. Lamarck, we may say, popularized the idea of evolution, but there remained vehement opposition to the notion that species may change and develop into new species. The outstanding opponent of evolution at this time was one of the best known scientists of his day. He was not only a contemporary of Lamarck, but a man to whom Lamarck had given a position at the Jardin des Plantes, the institution where Buffon had worked for so many years. This was **Georges Cuvier** (1769–1832), who was to become famous as the "Pope of Bones," the father of zoology, paleontology, and comparative anatomy.

CUVIER

Our interest in Cuvier resides mainly in his criticism, often nasty,* of Lamarck's views on evolution. Cuvier never grasped, as Lamarck did, the dynamic concept of nature, and insisted upon the fixity of species. By this time, most scientists thought it quite obvious that new species of animals and plants had come into existence,

---

*Especially in his *Eloge* (address in honor of the deceased) at the time of Lamarck's death. (See Lamarck, 1809, 1984.)

Spontaneous Generation

That life can be generated from nonlife was believed by many people, including scientists, during Lamarck's lifetime and long before that. Lamarck wrote that life is spontaneously generated when the subtle fluids, introduced by Nature into the mass of a small gelatinous or mucilaginous body, enlarge the spaces within it and transform them into cells. This cellular tissue now possessed life where it did not previously exist.

In Lamarck's words: *Nature, by means of heat, light, electricity and moisture, forms direct or spontaneous generations at that extremity [at the very beginning] of each kingdom of living bodies, where the simplest of these bodies are found.*

From Simple to Complex Forms

Lamarck believed, as many others did, that in life forms there was a tendency toward complexity, that nature works toward perfection; that is, the more complex, the more perfect. Lamarck proposed a "Power of Life," a natural force originating in the environment that worked with the "subtle fluids," to produce more complex organs which would, in time, produce more complex forms, which in time would produce more, and so on, and so on . . .

and if Cuvier was to successfully counteract the growing interest in evolution, he had to offer an alternative explanation about how new species could appear. He did so by proposing a theory of *catastrophism*.

This theory was based on the assumption of a series of violent and sudden catastrophes.* These catastrophes were produced by natural, not divine,† means, such as the formation of the Alps, and were responsible for ending each major geographical sequence (see geologic table, p. 220). All creatures living in those parts of the world where "revolutions" or catastrophes took place were destroyed. Then, after things settled down, these areas were restocked with new forms, different from those previously living there. These new forms came from neighboring areas unaffected by the catastrophes or by new creations. Cuvier's representation thus avoided the idea of evolution to explain the appearance of new forms.

Cuvier, one of the most brilliant scientists of his time, was a confirmed antievolutionist who believed, like Linnaeus, that "to name, to classify, and to describe was the beginning and end of science" (Greene, 1959, p. 174). Did his antievolutionist views retard the development of evolutionary ideas? As we have seen, they did not affect Lamarck, who developed his evolutionary scheme despite Cuvier.

However, Cuvier may have unknowingly helped Darwin. In their classification systems, both Linnaeus and Lamarck divided the Animal Kingdom into two divisions: vertebrates and invertebrates. Cuvier changed this scheme, using four separate divisions, each with its particular anatomical and physiological characteristics adapted to its own environment. This approach had the effect of eroding the belief in the linear scheme of life as indicated in the Great Chain of Being. Doubt in the

FIGURE 2-10   Cuvier.

*A recent school of thought suggests that evolution can occur with sudden and rapid change. This idea (quite different from catastrophism) is known as "punctuated equilibrium" and is discussed on p. 107.

†Cuvier's catastrophism had no religious basis, and he was careful to separate his religious beliefs from his scientific work. Creationists mistakenly use Cuvier's views to support their position.

Great Chain suggested that mutability of species was possible and thus made Darwin's views more palatable. As Oldroyd suggests (1980, p. 43), "the route from Linnaeus to Darwin lay through the anti-evolutionist Cuvier, as much as the evolutionist Lamarck."

Cuvier's influence on Darwin was indirect, since his ideas did not impact specifically on matters discussed by Darwin. Still, it may have made it easier for Darwin to argue (and others to accept) the notion that the Chain of Being concept was inadequate. On the other hand, Cuvier's catastrophism was of no help to Darwin; it is quite likely that, early in his thinking, Darwin rejected catastrophism because of the influence of Lyell, the period's most influential opponent of Cuvier's view.

LYELL

Charles Lyell (1797–1875) was a lawyer by training and geologist by choice. When Darwin returned to England in 1836, he became Lyell's close friend and confidant, a relationship that was to last a lifetime despite differences on a number of intellectual points.

Lyell's important contribution to science was his popular three-volume work, *Principles of Geology* (1830–1833), in which he rejected the catastrophism of Cuvier. Lyell reaffirmed the principle of **uniformitarianism**; that is, no forces had been active in the past history of the earth that are not also working today—an idea introduced into European thought in 1785 by James Hutton. Lyell showed, through the process of uniformitarianism, that the earth's crust was formed via a series of slow and gradual changes. Mountains, rivers, valleys, lakes, deserts, and coastlines were not the sudden result of cataclysms, but rather the result of purely natural forces, such as erosion by land, water, frost, ice, and rain. These forces, which could be seen operating in the present, could (assuming sufficient time) have caused all geological events of the past.

When he embarked on the *Beagle*, Darwin was more interested in geology than in any other science. In 1832, while in South America, Darwin received the second volume of Lyell's *Principles* (Professor Henslow had presented Darwin with the first volume just before the *Beagle* sailed, but cautioned Darwin not to believe everything Lyell had written). Lyell's work immediately struck a responsive chord as Darwin observed the mountains, rocks, and coastline of South America. From Lyell, Darwin learned first of all about the development of the earth's crust, the environmental conditions that, through the struggle for existence, could modify living forms, and, secondly, about the immense age of the earth, far beyond Archbishop Ussher's 4004 B.C.

Two important points in Darwin's explanation of evolution are the struggle for existence and descent with modification. The principle of struggle for existence was basic to Darwin's evolutionary theory, and this he credits to Lyell, though the idea was not original with him. Descent with modification Darwin saw as a slow and gradual process and, for this to work, time would be necessary. Lyell believed the earth was extremely old, on the order of hundreds or thousands of million years, thus giving Darwin a dimension of time that would have made the gradual process of evolution possible.

Shortly after his return to England, Darwin opened his first notebook in July, 1837. He planned to collect evidence on the subject of the gradual modification of species since, as he said ". . . the subject haunted me" (F. Darwin, 1950, p. 15). As

FIGURE 2-11   Lyell.

he worked, he came to realize that "selection was the keystone of man's success in making useful races of animals and plants. But how selection could be applied to organisms living in a state of nature remained for some time a mystery to me" (F. Darwin, 1950, p. 53). The mystery was solved for Darwin in October, 1838, fifteen months after he had begun his systematic enquiry, when he happened "to read for amusement" Malthus' essay on the principle of population.

MALTHUS

Thomas Robert Malthus (1766–1834) was an English clergyman, political economist, and devotee of the natural sciences. His work was to become a standard consulted by politicians dealing with population problems and a source of inspiration to both Charles Darwin and Alfred Wallace in their separate discoveries of the principle of natural selection.

In his *Essay*, Malthus pointed out that if human population growth is unrestrained by natural causes, it will double every twenty-five years, but that the capacity for food production increases only in a straight arithmetic progression. In nature, Malthus noted, this impulse to multiply was *checked by the struggle for existence*, but humans had to apply artificial restraints. Malthus emphasized two facts: the infinite fertility of humankind, and the limited size and resources of the earth.

Upon reading this, Darwin wrote:

> . . . it at once struck me that under these circumstances favourable variations would tend to be preserved, and unfavourable ones to be destroyed. The result of this would be the formation of a new species. *Here then I had at last got a theory by which to work* (F. Darwin, 1950, pp. 53–54). (Emphasis added.)

While Darwin had already realized that selection was the key to evolution, it was due to Malthus that he saw *how* selection in nature could be explained. In the struggle for existence, those *individuals* with favorable variations would survive; those with unfavorable variations would not. The significance here is that Darwin was thinking in terms of individuals (not species) that interact with one another. This was quite different from the nineteenth-century philosophy prevalent in Europe since the time of Plato. It was the significance of individuals in the struggle for existence that led Darwin to his concept of natural selection.

Before Darwin, scientists (Linnaeus and Lyell, for example) thought of species as an entity that could not change, and, if species changed, they were not species. It was species that were at the basis of the discussions of plants and animals. Individuals within the species did not appear to be significant and, therefore, it was difficult for many scientists to imagine how change could occur. Darwin, as we have pointed out, saw that variation of individuals could explain how selection occurred. Favorable variations were "selected" by nature for survival; unfavorable ones eliminated (Malthus, of course, believed God did the selecting, not nature). Thus, "Population thinkers stress the uniqueness of everything in the organic world. What is important for them is the individual, not the type. They emphasize that every individual in sexually reproducing species is uniquely different from all others. . . . There is no 'typical' individual, . . ." (Mayr, 1982, p. 46).

This emphasis on the uniqueness of the individual (the variation that occurs in all populations—that a population is a group of interacting individuals and not a type) led Darwin to natural selection as the mechanism that made evolution work.

Natural selection *operates on individuals*, favorably or unfavorably, but it is *the population that evolves*. As pointed out on p. 104, the unit of natural selection is the individual; the unit of evolution is the population.

Darwin's Evidence

By 1859, Darwin had accumulated a tremendous amount of data. In addition to the thousands of observations made during his five-year voyage on the *Beagle*, Darwin read voluminously in geology, paleontology, and related disciplines, and meticulously collected observations on domesticated plants and animals. Darwin had originally planned to detail all this information in a huge multivolume treatise. But when Wallace forced his hand, Darwin—in *Origin*—summarized his conclusions in what he modestly called an "abstract."

DOMESTICATED PLANTS AND ANIMALS

Through what Darwin called "unconscious selection" (what today is called "artificial selection"), animal and plant breeders had greatly modified varieties of domestic species during historic times. Darwin believed such observations provided strong support for the process of natural selection, and was particularly impressed with pigeons (which he had studied and bred for years):

> Altogether at least a score of pigeons might be chosen, which if shown to an ornithologist, and he were told that they were wild birds, would certainly, I think, be ranked by him as well-defined species. Moreover, I do not believe that any ornithologist would place the English carrier, the short-faced tumbler, the runt, the barb, pouter, and fantail in the same genus; more especially as in each of these breeds several truly-inherited sub-breeds, or species as he might have called them, could be shown him.
>
> Great as the differences are between the breeds of pigeons, I am fully convinced that the common opinion of naturalists is correct, namely, that all have descended from the rock-pigeon (*Columbia livia*) including under this term several geographical races or sub-species, which differ from each other in the most trifling respects (Darwin, 1859, pp. 22–23).

GEOGRAPHIC DISTRIBUTION OF LIFE FORMS

Darwin drew widely upon his experience from the *Beagle* voyage, as well as an intimate knowledge of the flora and fauna of his native England, to argue further for the role of natural selection:

> Isolation, also, is an important element in the process of natural selection. In a confined or isolated area, if not very large, the organic and inorganic conditions of life will generally be in a great degree uniform; so that natural selection will tend to modify all the individuals of a varying species throughout the area in the same manner in relation to the same conditions. Intercrosses, also, with the individuals of the same species, which otherwise would have inhabited the surrounding and differently circumstanced districts, will be prevented (Darwin, 1859, p. 104).

THE GEOLOGICAL AND PALEONTOLOGICAL RECORD

Darwin clearly understood that the major verification for his theory of slow and gradual evolutionary modification must come from fossil evidence embedded within the earth's strata. He also recognized that the paleontological record could never be complete (much less, of course, was known about this record at that time). Even given these limitations, Darwin's perceptive use of paleontological examples strengthened his argument and provided a great stimulus for future research:

> We can understand how it is that all the forms of life, ancient and recent, make together one grand system; for all are connected by generation. We can understand, from the continued tendency to divergence of character, why the more ancient a form is, the more it generally differs from those now living. Why ancient and extinct forms often tend to fill up gaps between existing forms, sometimes blending two groups previously classed as distinct into one; but more commonly only bringing them a little closer together. The more ancient a form is, the more often, apparently, it displays characters in some degree intermediate between groups now distinct; for the more ancient a form is, the more nearly it will be related to, and consequently resemble, the common progenitor of groups since become widely divergent (Darwin, 1859, pp. 344–345).

COMPARATIVE ANATOMY

A basic element of biological interpretation in Darwin's time (as well as our own) involves anatomical comparison. How do we know whether two living forms are really related to each other, or to whom a fossil form is related?

> We have seen that the members of the same class, independently of their habits of life, resemble each other in the general plan of their organisation. This resemblance is often expressed by the term "unity of type," or by saying that the several parts and organs in the different species of the class are homologous. The whole subject is included under the general name of Morphology. This is the most interesting department of natural history, and may be said to be its very soul. What can be more curious than that the hand of a man, formed for grasping, that of a mole for digging, the leg of the horse, the paddle of the porpoise, and the wing of the bat, should all be constructed on the same pattern, and should include the same bones, in the same relative positions? (Darwin, 1859, p. 434).

EMBRYOLOGY

It has long been known that the immature stages organisms pass through during development can give important clues concerning evolutionary relationships—a fact that did not escape Darwin's attention.

> The embryos, also, of distinct animals within the same class are often strikingly similar; a better proof of this cannot be given, than a circumstance mentioned by Agassiz, namely, that having forgotten to ticket the embryo of some vertebrate animal he cannot now tell whether it be that of a mammal, bird, or reptile. The vermiform larvae of moths, flies, beetles, &c., resemble each other much more closely than do the mature insects (Darwin, 1859, p. 439).

VESTIGIAL ORGANS

A final line of evidence presented by Darwin concerned those "rudimentary, atrophied, or aborted" organs that had no apparent function. If life had not evolved, what possible "Design" could explain their presence?

> Rudimentary organs may be compared with the letters in a word, still retained in the spelling, but become useless in the pronunciation, but which serve as a clue in seeking

Adaptation An evolutionary shift in a population in response to environmental change; the result of natural selection.

for its derivation. On the view of descent with modification, we may conclude that the existence of organs in a rudimentary, imperfect, and useless condition, or quite aborted, far from presenting a strange difficulty, as they assuredly do on the ordinary doctrine of creation, might even have been anticipated, and can be accounted for by the laws of inheritance (Darwin, 1859, pp. 455–456).

Natural Selection in Action

A modern example of natural selection can be shown through research on the process in operation. The best historically documented case of natural selection acting in modern populations deals with changes in pigmentation among peppered moths near Manchester, England. Before the nineteenth century, the common variety of moth was a mottled gray color that provided extremely effective camouflage against lichen-covered tree trunks. Also present, though in much lower frequency, was a dark variety of moth. While resting on such trees, the dark, uncamouflaged moths against the light tree trunks were more visible to birds and were therefore eaten more often. Thus, in the end, they produced fewer offspring than the light, camouflaged moths. Yet, in fifty years, by the end of the nineteenth century, the common gray, camouflaged form had been almost completely replaced by the black variety.

What had brought about this rapid change? The answer lies in the rapidly changing environment of industrialized nineteenth-century England. Pollutants released in the area settled on trees, killing the lichen and turning the bark a dark color. Moths living in the area continued to rest on trees, but the gray (or light) variety was increasingly conspicuous as the trees became darker. Consequently, they began to be preyed upon more frequently by birds and contributed fewer genes to the next generation.

In the twentieth century, increasing control of pollutants has allowed some forested areas to return to their lighter, preindustrial conditions with lichen growing again on the trees. As would be expected, in these areas the black variety is now being supplanted by the gray.

The substance that produces pigmentation is called *melanin*, and the evolutionary shift in the peppered moth, as well as in many other moth species, is termed *industrial melanism*. Such an evolutionary shift in response to environmental change is called **adaptation**.

This example provides numerous insights into the mechanism of evolutionary change by natural selection:

1. A trait must be inherited to have importance in natural selection. A characteristic that is not hereditary (such as a change in hair pigmentation brought about by dye) will not be passed on to succeeding generations. In moths, pigmentation is a demonstrated hereditary trait.
2. Natural selection cannot occur without variation in inherited characteristics. If all the moths had initially been gray (you will recall some dark forms were present) and the trees became darker, the survival and reproduction of all moths may have been so low that the population would have become extinct. Such an event is not unusual in evolution and, without variation, would nearly always occur. *Selection can only work with variation already present*.
3. "Fitness" is a relative measure that will change as the environment changes. Fitness is simply reproductive success. In the initial stage, the gray moth was the

most-fit variety, but as the environment changed, the black moth became more fit, and a further change reversed the adaptive pattern. It should be obvious that statements regarding the "most-fit" life form mean nothing without reference to specific environments.

The example of peppered moths shows how different death rates influence natural selection, for moths that die early tend to leave fewer offspring. But mortality is not the entire picture. Another important aspect of natural selection is fertility, for an animal that gives birth to more young would pass its genes on at a faster rate than those who bear fewer offspring. However, fertility is not the whole picture either, for the crucial element is the number of young raised successfully to the point where they reproduce themselves. We may state this simply as *differential net reproductive success*. The way this mechanism works can be demonstrated through another example.

In a common variety of small birds called swifts, data show that giving birth to more offspring does not necessarily guarantee that more young will be successfully raised. The number of eggs hatched in a breeding season is a measure of fertility. The number of birds that mature and are eventually able to leave the nest is a measure of net reproductive success, or offspring successfully raised. The following tabulation shows the correlation between the number of eggs hatched (fertility) and the number of young that leave the nest (reproductive success) averaged over four breeding seasons (Lack, 1966).

NUMBER OF EGGS HATCHED (FERTILITY)	2 EGGS	3 EGGS	4 EGGS
Average number of young raised (reproductive success)	1.92	2.54	1.76
Sample size	72	20	16

As the tabulation shows, the most efficient fertility number is three eggs, for that yields the highest reproductive success. Raising two is less beneficial to the parents since the *end result* is not as successful as with three eggs. Trying to raise more than three young is actually detrimental, since the parents may not be able to provide adequate nourishment for any of the offspring. An offspring that dies before reaching reproductive age is, in evolutionary terms, an equivalent of never having been born in the first place. Actually, such a result may be an evolutionary minus to the parents, for this offspring will drain their resources and may inhibit their ability to raise other offspring, thereby lowering their reproductive success even further. Selection will favor those genetic traits that yield the maximum net reproductive success. If the number of eggs laid* is a genetic trait in birds (and it seems to be), natural selection in swifts should act to favor the laying of three eggs as opposed to two or four.

Darwin's Failures

Darwin argued eloquently for the notion of evolution in general and the role of natural selection in particular, but he did not entirely comprehend inheritance and the mechanism maintaining variation.

FIGURE 2-12 Variation in the peppered moth. In (*a*), the dark form is more visible to bird predators on the light (unpolluted) trees. In (*b*), the light form is more visible: trees are darker due to pollution.

---

*The number of eggs hatched is directly related to the number of eggs laid.

As we have seen, natural selection acts on *variation* within species. Neither Darwin, nor anyone else in the nineteenth century, understood the source of all this variation. Consequently, Darwin speculated about variation arising from "use"—an idea similar to Lamarck's. Darwin, however, was not as dogmatic in his views as Lamarck, and most emphatically argued against inner "needs" or "effort." Darwin had to confess that when it came to explaining variation, he simply did not know.

> Our ignorance of the laws of variation is profound. Not in one case out of a hundred can we pretend to assign any reason why this or that part differs, more or less, from the same part in the parents. But whenever we have the means of instituting a comparison, the same laws appear to have acted in producing the lesser differences between varieties of the same species, and the greater differences between species of the same genus. The external conditions of life, as climate and food, &c., seem to have induced some slight modifications. Habit in producing constitutional differences, and use in strengthening, and disuse in weakening and diminishing organs, seem to have been more potent in their effects (Darwin, 1859, pp. 167–168).

In addition to his inability to explain the origins of variation, Darwin also did not completely understand the mechanism by which parents transmitted traits to offspring. Almost without exception, nineteenth-century scholars were confused about the laws of heredity, and the popular consensus was that inheritance was *blending* by nature. In other words, offspring were always expected to express intermediate traits as a result of a blending of their parents' contributions. Given this view, we can see why the actual nature of genes was thus unimaginable. Without any viable alternatives, Darwin accepted this popular misconception. As it turned out, a contemporary of Darwin had systematically worked out the rules of heredity. However, the work of this obscure Augustinian monk, Gregor Mendel (whom you shall meet in Chapter 4), was not recognized until the beginning of the twentieth century.

Summary

The concept of evolution as we know it today is directly traceable to developments in intellectual thought in Western Europe over the last 300 years. In particular, the contributions of Linnaeus, Lamarck, Buffon, Lyell, and Malthus all had significant impact upon Darwin. The year 1859 marks a watershed in evolutionary theory for, in that year, the publication of Darwin's *The Origin of Species* crystallized the evolutionary process (particularly the crucial role of natural selection) and, for the first time, thrust evolutionary theory into the consciousness of the common person. Debates both inside and outside the sciences continued for several decades (and in some corners persist today), but the theory of evolution irrevocably changed the tide of intellectual thought. Gradually Darwin's formulation of the evolutionary process became accepted almost universally by scientists as the very foundation of all the biological sciences, physical anthropology included. In this, the twentieth century, contributions from genetics allow us to demonstrate the mechanics of evolution in a way unknown to Darwin and his contemporaries.

Natural selection is the central determining factor influencing the long-term direction of evolutionary change. How natural selection works can best be explained as differential reproductive success, meaning, in other words, how successful individuals are in leaving offspring to succeeding generations.

Questions for Review

1. Trace the history of evolutionary ideas from Copernicus to the time of Darwin.
2. In what ways do Linnaeus and Buffon differ in their approach to the concept of evolution?
3. What are the bases of Lamarck's theory of acquired characteristics? Why is this theory unacceptable?
4. What was Lamarck's contribution to nineteenth-century evolutionary ideas?
5. Explain Cuvier's catastrophism.
6. What did Malthus and Lyell contribute to Darwin's thinking on evolution?
7. What is the significance of Darwin's population approach?
8. What major areas of evidence did Darwin use to strengthen his argument concerning evolution?
9. How did Darwin's explanation of the source of variation compare with that of Lamarck?
10. What hereditary mechanism did Darwin utilize to explain transmission of traits from parents to offspring?
11. What is meant by adaptation? Illustrate through the example of industrial melanism.
12. Why have Darwin's views on the origin of species been accepted, while Lamarck's views have not?

Suggested Further Reading

There is what is called a Darwin industry, with hundreds (or more) of books written about Darwin, natural selection, his life and times, his family, his grandfather, his influence on other scientists and other scientists on him, and the effects of natural selection on philosophy, religion, economics, and politics. And new books are constantly being published. The following are only a few. For those who wish to read more, the industry awaits.

Barash, David. *Sociobiology and Behavior* (2nd Ed.), New York: Elsevier, 1982.
   A sociobiological survey of the ways natural selection causes behavior to evolve. Many interesting examples from the field of behavior (ethology) are included. While this book is clearly slanted toward a sociobiological orientation, the explanations of how natural selection operates are clear and concise.

Bowler, Peter J. *Evolution: The History of an Idea*, Berkeley: University of California Press, Rev. ed., 1989.
   Bowler, a science historian, has written an excellent account of evolution—what it is and what led up to it. He also covers Darwin and Darwinism. Highly recommended. If you are looking for a bibliography on evolution and Darwin, try the 57 pages in this book.

Darwin, Charles. *Voyage of the Beagle*, New York: Doubleday, 1962.
   Darwin's own account of his historic five-year journey as naturalist on board the *Beagle*. Highly recommended for its insight into Darwin's changing views toward evolution.

———. *On the Origin of Species*, New York: Mentor Books, 1958.
   A book to be read by all students of evolution. This is considered to be one of the most influential books written in the nineteenth century.

———. *The Illustrated Origin of Species*, New York: Hill and Wang, 1979.
   Abridged and introduced by Richard E. Leakey. A handsomely illustrated version of Darwin's 6th edition, with excellent running commentary. This version is often reworded from Darwin's original text. Such abridgement may occasionally aid readability, but the reader should refer to Darwin's original for a more accurate historical document.

Dawkins, Richard. *The Blind Watchmaker*, Essex (England): Harlow, 1986.

The concept of a world created by design was a common belief of the Middle Ages and prevalent in the nineteenth century. Anything as complex as the universe, it was argued, could not have happened by chance but deliberately; i.e., by design, just as the complicated works of a watch was designed. Dawkins explains how natural selection replaced design in science.

Eiseley, Loren. *Darwin's Century*, Garden City, N.Y.: Doubleday and Co., Inc., 1958; Anchor Books (paper), 1961.

Eiseley, a physical anthropologist, analyzes, discusses, and interprets the writings of well-known and not so well-known scholars of the eighteenth and nineteenth centuries. The book is well written in Eiseley's elegant style.

————. *The Immense Journey*, New York: Random House, 1958, 1961.

A fascinating story of evolution told by Eiseley who became well known for his writings on nature. Every student should read this most interesting book.

————. *The Firmament of Time*, Philadelphia: University of Pennsylvania Press, 1960.

This is a history of science written in Eisley's readable style. He traces the development of thought that led to Darwinian evolution. Highly recommended and available in most public libraries.

Futuyma, Douglas J. *Science on Trial*, New York: Pantheon Books, 1983.

Futuyma (who has subtitled this book "The Case for Evolution") presents a clear and readable discussion of evolution, as well as the fallacies of creationism. Recommended for beginning students.

Gillespie, Neal C. *Charles Darwin and the Problem of Creation*, Chicago: University of Chicago Press, 1979.

Intellectual thought of the last century from a philosophical point of view. One of the questions the author attempts to answer is why Darwin pursued so assiduously the idea of natural selection. For the more serious student.

Godfrey, Laurie R. (ed.). *Scientists Confront Creationism*, New York: W. W. Norton & Co., Inc., 1983.

This work contains an introduction by Richard Lewontin and articles by fifteen different scientists—anthropologists, geologists, astronomers, biochemists, etc.—who refute creationist arguments. For a well-rounded view of the weaknesses of the creationist viewpoint, this book is excellent.

Huxley, Julian and H.B.D. Kettlewell. *Charles Darwin and His World*, New York: The Viking Press, 1965.

An interesting biography of Darwin by Julian Huxley, noted biologist and grandson of T. H. Huxley, Darwin's most powerful supporter; also by Bernard Kettlewell, well-known geneticist. Many excellent illustrations.

Irvine, William. *Apes, Angels and Victorians*, New York: McGraw-Hill Book Co., 1955.

A readable story of Darwin, Huxley, and evolution. It is told in detail, with skill and imagination.

Keynes, Richard Darwin. *The Beagle Record*, New York: Cambridge University Press, 1979.

A splendidly illustrated book worthwhile for the beautiful drawings and photographs alone. Selections from Darwin's journal. Highly recommended.

Löwenberg, Bert James. *Darwin, Wallace, and the Theory of Natural Selection*, Cambridge: Arlington Books, 1959.

A brief review of the developments leading to Darwin's and Wallace's concept of natural selection. Interesting and dramatic story.

Miller, Jonathan and Borin Van Loon. *Darwin for Beginners*, New York: Pantheon Books, 1982.

An amusing account of Darwin, natural selection, and evolution, or, as the authors say, "The Strange Case of Charles Darwin and Evolution." There are many drawings in cartoon style; nevertheless, evolution is well discussed, and students without a background in Darwin and evolution are encouraged to read this small book.

Rose, Michael. *The Darwinian Revolution*, Chicago: University of Chicago Press, 1979.
A historian discusses the intellectual climate of Darwin's time and its influence on Darwin's study of evolution. For the more serious student.

Simpson, G. G. *The Book of Darwin*. New York: Simon & Schuster, Inc. (Washington Square Press), 1982.
A small book, paperback, in which one of the twentieth century's foremost paleontologists has brought together a number of Darwin's papers with his comments and remarks. An excellent introduction to Darwin, his life, his work, and his writings as seen by Dr. Simpson. Readable and recommended for students.

Stebbins, G. Ledyard. *Processes of Evolution* (2nd Ed.), Englewood Cliffs: Prentice-Hall, Inc., 1971.
A straightforward discussion of the modern, synthetic theory of evolution. Very well organized and presented with many excellent illustrations. Highly recommended for the beginning or moderately advanced student.

Stone, Irving. *The Origin: A Biographical Novel of Charles Darwin*, Garden City, N.Y.: Doubleday and Co., 1980.
Although a somewhat fictional account, this massive work gives a detailed background of Darwin's childhood, education, family life, scientific experiences, and personal concerns. Written by a leading historical biographer, this book is entertaining.

Biological Basis of Life

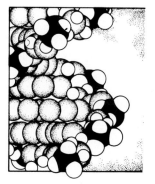

Contents

The Race to Discover the Genetic Code

At Cambridge University's Cavendish Laboratory, from 1951 to 1953, a brash young American scientist from Chicago, **James D. Watson**, and a garrulous Englishman from Northampton, **Francis H. C. Crick**, worked more or less together (with the assistance of English physicist Maurice Wilkins and others) to solve the puzzle of DNA structure.

Watson should have been hard at work in Copenhagen learning chemistry to help him in his postdoctoral biological research, and Crick, already at Cambridge, should have been busily engaged researching hemoglobin crystals for his Ph.D. Neither should have been involved in DNA research, but, as a matter of fact, both men were very much involved, and they hoped not only to discover the structure of DNA and win a Nobel Prize, but to beat **Linus Pauling** who, they were quite sure, was close to success on the same project at California Institute of Technology.

But Pauling was not as close to success as Crick and Watson believed. In November, 1951, Pauling started working on a triple helix and thought he succeeded, "although the structure was described as 'an extraordinarily tight one, with little opportunity for change in positions of the atoms'" (Pauling, 1974). A copy of the paper on his experiment was sent to Crick and Watson, who had themselves built an unsuccessful triple helix model a year ear-

James Watson and Francis Crick.

lier. They had considered their model a failure, and, after reading Pauling's paper (and catching an error in basic chemistry), knew his to be a failure also.

As Watson tells the story, he knew that Pauling was wrong, and that the earlier model he and Crick had constructed was also wrong, and now he was stumped. It was not until Wilkins showed him an X-ray diffraction photograph of DNA (taken by Cavendish scientist Rosalind Franklin)* early in 1953, that Watson thought he saw a bit of light. The X-ray indicated that a helix was the correct structure, which he had been sure of anyway, and, further, that a 2-chain model—a double helix rather than a triple helix—might possibly be the answer. Watson and Crick deliberately kept the X-ray photograph from Pauling, since they feared that if he saw the X-ray, he would solve the problem before they did.

Watson designed a 2-chain metal helical model of DNA for experimental purposes to be built by the Cavendish Labora-

*Rosalind Franklin, working on DNA at King's College, London, at the same time Crick and Watson were working on it at Cambridge, seems to have discovered the DNA double helix before Crick and Watson. In fact, it wasn't until Watson saw a diffraction X-Ray taken by Franklin, that he recognized the significance of a double helix. (See Ann Sayre, *Rosalind Franklin and DNA*, Suggested Further Reading, end of chapter.)

Linus Pauling.

tory. The key to the mystery occurred abruptly to Watson while he was impatiently waiting for the Lab machine shop to complete the model. He had cut accurate representations of the four bases from stiff cardboard and was shifting them around trying out various pairing possibilities when:

Suddenly I became aware that an adenine-thymine pair held together by two hydrogen bonds was identical in shape to a guanine-cytosine pair held together by at least two hydrogen bonds. All the hydrogen bonds seemed to form

naturally; no fudging was required to make the two types of base pairs identical in shape (Watson, 1968, p. 194).

The enigma of the basic DNA structure was solved and the race won. In 1962, the Nobel Prize for Medicine and Physiology was awarded to Crick, Watson, and Wilkins.

Actually, Watson and Crick need not have worried about Pauling's beating them to the DNA solution since Pauling did not consider this research a race (Pauling, personal communication); however, Pauling does believe there was a chance, had he seen the X-ray photograph,

. . . that I would have thought of the Watson-Crick structure during the next few weeks. . . . Nevertheless, I myself think that the chance is rather small that I would have thought of the double helix in 1952, before Watson and Crick made their great discovery (Pauling, 1974, p. 771).

SOURCES

Olby, Robert. *The Path to the Double Helix*, Seattle: University of Washington Press, 1974.

Pauling, Linus. "Molecular Basis of Biological Specificity," *Nature*, 248 (no. 5451):769, 771, April 26, 1974.

Watson, James D. *The Double Helix*, New York: Atheneum, 1968.

Somatic cells   soma: body
Cells that do not divide by meiosis and do not become gametes.

Sex cells   Cells that divide by meiosis and become gametes.

Nucleus   A body, present in most types of cells, containing chromosomes.

Chromosome   chrome: color
soma: body
Threadlike, gene-containing body found in the nucleus.

Introduction

In the preceding chapter, evolution was discussed from a conceptual point of view, but the mechanics of evolution—how hereditary characteristics are actually passed on from one generation to the next—were not included in that generalized presentation. In the body, what physiological processes operate to produce and distribute variation and enable natural selection to function? In this chapter, we shall examine the specifics, beginning with the nature of the cell, since that is where, in a sense, the evolutionary process begins. The basic evolutionary process applies to all forms of life—to plants as well as to animals; however, our interest is mainly humankind, and cells and genetics will be discussed for the most part from the point of view of human beings. Nevertheless, we should keep in mind that the cell is basic to all forms of life, and that cellular characteristics (such as genes, chromosomes, and DNA) are found in the cells of all complex organisms, but the DNA messages differ. Certain messages produce tomatoes, others roses, and still others human beings. We should remember that the process of heredity is essentially similar in all species. Heredity, as we deal with it here, refers simply to the passage of genetic information from the cells of one generation to those of another.

The Cell

SOMATIC AND SEX CELLS

Basically, two kinds of cells are directly involved with heredity: **somatic cells** and **sex cells**. The body is composed of various kinds of specialized tissues (blood, liver, muscle, skin, nerve) consisting of billions of somatic cells continually being manufactured to replace those that have died. Indeed, one estimate has it that the cells of the human body are replaced every seven years.

Sex cells are similar to somatic cells but play no part in the structural composition of the body. They originate in the testes of males and ovaries of females, and their only function is to transmit life and hereditary information from parents to offspring.

In all organisms, except bacteria and blue-green algae, the focal point of heredity is the **nucleus**, usually located in the center of the cell and separated from the cytoplasm by a thin nuclear membrane. Within the nucleus are two nucleic acids central to understanding the hereditary process: ribonucleic acid (RNA) and deoxyribonucleic acid (DNA).

Chromosomes   In the higher-organism cells possessing nuclei, the genetic material (DNA) is usually found in a loose, unwound state called *chromatin*. This

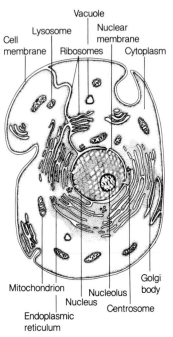

FIGURE 3-1   Generalized diagram of a cell.

Vacuole
Lysosome   Nuclear
Cell   membrane
membrane   Ribosomes   Cytoplasm

DNA

Mitochondrion   Golgi
                Nucleolus   body
       Nucleus
Endoplasmic   Centrosome
reticulum

BOX 3-1   **The Nucleus**

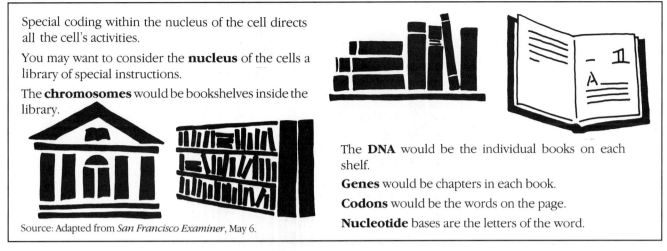

Special coding within the nucleus of the cell directs all the cell's activities.

You may want to consider the **nucleus** of the cells a library of special instructions.

The **chromosomes** would be bookshelves inside the library.

The **DNA** would be the individual books on each shelf.

Genes would be chapters in each book.

Codons would be the words on the page.

Nucleotide bases are the letters of the word.

Source: Adapted from *San Francisco Examiner*, May 6.

---

material, which consists of exceedingly long, thin molecules, is crammed into a very small space. Geneticists estimate that as much as six feet of DNA is packed into the nucleus of each of our somatic cells. This would be the equivalent of stuffing several thousand feet of extremely fine thread into a thimble. This DNA material is normally active during the life cycle of the cell, most of which is spent in various metabolic activities and not in the process of dividing.

However, when the cell does begin to divide, a difficulty arises. All this somewhat jumbled genetic material is first replicated, making two versions of the DNA. Since one (and only one) version is to be transmitted to each daughter cell, the problem, more specifically, is one of packaging and organization. In order to efficiently divide and transmit the genetic material, the DNA is condensed into much more compact packages called *chromosomes*.

Chromosomes—meaning "colored bodies"—were given their name in the last century because they took up certain vegetable dyes and were visible under a light microscope. It is important to remember that chromosomes are visible *only* when a cell is entering active division, and this condensed structure basically serves as a packaging vehicle to distribute the genetic material to the next generation of cells.

When chromosomes can be seen, their structure may be depicted as two arms joined by a **centromere** (Fig. 3-2). The number of chromosomes in different plant and animal species varies, but normally all the members of a single species possess the same number of chromosomes (46 for humans).

The 46 chromosomes normally found in the somatic cells of all human beings are more accurately considered as 23 pairs, since there are two sets of 23 different chromosomes (Fig. 3-3). One set comes from the father (P, for paternal) and one from the mother (M, for maternal). Thus, one-half of a person's heredity derives from each parent. The first 22 pairs of chromosomes are known as *autosomes*; the 23rd pair (or *sex chromosomes*) is known alphabetically as XX or XY. (A female carries two X chromosomes and a male one X and one Y.)

Centromere   centro: central
mere: part
That part of the chromosome to which spindle fibers are attached during mitosis and meiosis.

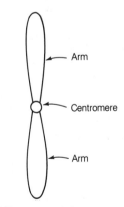

FIGURE 3-2   A normal chromosome.

BOX 3-2 **Genetic Engineering**

Genetic engineering refers mainly to the manipulation of genes in order to alter the genetic structure of a DNA sequence. These manipulation techniques are barely over twenty years old, but the improvements in the techniques and the results obtained by this engineering have been so startling, they would have been considered fantasy fifty years ago. In a way, we could say that humans employed a kind of genetic engineering ages ago—when liquor was first fermented, bread baked, and animals and plants hybridized to develop improved stock.

That genetic engineering has come of age can be seen in the following statistics: In 1989, biotechnology sales totaled over $1.2 billion, and will top $40 billion by the year 2000.

Tools used in the genetic engineering trade include enzymes that can snip a DNA sequence as neatly as a scissors; enzymes that can repair the DNA breaks; and short DNA sequences that are not on chromosomes.

Restriction enzymes slice DNA strands at a particular base sequence. More than 300 restriction enzymes are now known so that DNA can be cut at over 300 different places. Restriction enzymes are taken from *bacterial* species and can apparently be used on any kind of DNA.

Repair enzymes, known as *ligases*, are capable of bonding broken segments of DNA. They are used in conjunction with restriction enzymes by bonding DNA that has been spliced.

Plasmids, found in bacteria, are small circular sets of genes not connected to chromosomes. They are very useful in the process of altering the genetic structure and recombining genes to produce a different protein.

Although complex to undertake, the engineering technique can be simply described: plasmid genes are separated by a restriction enzyme; the target gene is altered, removed, or a foreign gene inserted; the break is then repaired by ligases; and the altered plasmid is either transferred to another bacterium where it can be cloned many times for experimental purposes, or else is transferred to an individual who needs the recombined genes. Scientists are using engineering techniques in university and industrial genetic labs to produce human-manufactured genes for a wide variety of uses, especially in the areas of human disease therapy and the improvement of plants and animals for the human diet. The following paragraphs convey achievements in genetic engineering already accomplished and expected to be completed in perhaps the next few years.

In May, 1989, a terminally ill cancer patient was infused with his own white blood cells carrying a foreign gene genetically engineered in a mouse. The white cells were tracked as they searched for tumors. Researchers believe this technique could lead to treatment for sickle-cell anemia and other inherited diseases.

Researchers reported they can swap one form of a gene for another in mice and breed the engineered animals through several generations. This gene-switching method presents unlimited possibilities for analyzing genes that cause cancer, immune deficiencies, and hereditary disorders such as cystic fibrosis and muscular dystrophy.

In June, 1990, a researcher at the University of Tennessee reported that eight children with muscular dystrophy received a myoblast transfer (transplant of healthy muscle cells). The children showed improvements in muscle function and structure.

Engineered bacteria protects corn plants by produc-

Mitosis (my-toe'-sis)
mit: thread
osis: process or state
Somatic cell division producing two daughter cells identical to the parental cell.

Chromosomes play their role during division of both somatic and sex cells. We can better understand these functions as we follow chromosome behavior during somatic cell division (*mitosis*) and sex cell division (*meiosis*) in the following sections.

Cell Division: Mitosis

The nature of most cells is to divide. Since division of the two kinds of cells differs, let us first take the less complex somatic cell division, called **mitosis**.

BOX 3-2

ing a protein that paralyzes the digestive system of certain insects and caterpillars. This could make for cheaper popcorn.

Researchers reduced the production of an enzyme that was responsible for fruit softening. Engineered tomatoes won't soften or bruise so quickly and can be left on the vine until they ripen.

A University of California, Davis, researcher inserted engineered bacteria genes into walnut trees. The trees will produce their own insecticide to kill nut-hungry caterpillars.

The human growth hormone, now being manufactured, is used to restore a potential midget (who lacks the pituitary growth hormone) to normal height.

A recent study (of only twelve men) found that the synthetic human growth hormone boosts muscle mass and skin thickness in (some) men over 60. Even more interesting is the suggestion that it may reduce aging, since some of the tested men appeared to look younger.

Genetic engineers are developing techniques to coax plants into producing latex, the raw material of rubber.

Researchers, working in "insectaries," believe they can alter genes in certain mosquitoes in such a way that will prevent them from transmitting their disease. This could ultimately render all mosquitoes harmless.

The gene for cystic fibrosis (affected individuals usually die before age 30) was identified in 1989. Prenatal screening will be capable of identifying carriers.

Removing a patient's natural tumor-fighting cells, strengthening them in the laboratory and putting them back into the patient's body has produced the best results to date in patients with advanced melanoma, a form of skin cancer that is almost always fatal.

University of Utah researchers have developed a new genetic engineering technique to selectively modify or replace defective genes. This may facilitate efforts to treat human diseases by replacing abnormal genes.

Bacteria eat oil. At the 1989 Exxon oil spill, a French fertilizer that stimulates the growth of bacteria with an appetite for hydrocarbons was sprayed on the Prince William Sound beaches. Within 15 days these beaches showed dramatic improvement.

We may be seeing blue roses in a few years. A biotech company in Davis, California, is planning to transfer genes from blue flowers to roses. They also plan to keep roses fresher longer by blocking the gene that produces ethylene, the gas that causes flower petals to lose color and wither.

Possibilities for the future:

- Giving sick cells life-saving instructions that are delivered by a specially engineered gene placed into the chromosome.
- Informing a diabetic's cell to make insulin; or a hemophilic's cell to make a complex protein that helps blood to clot.
- Providing an HIV (AIDS virus)-infected cell with the command to self destruct via a genetically altered virus.
- Using a gene gun based on high-pressure gas to transform cells by shooting genes into them.

Somatic cell division serves several functions. As cells divide, they multiply, thus aiding in the growth of the organism. Cell division is also a means by which old cells are replaced by new ones. What is of interest to us is the part of this process of cell division resulting in the development of two daughter cells identical to the mother cell. In this way, as new body cells are produced they are exactly the same as those they replace, and the body, except for maturation and degeneration, remains essentially the same throughout life.

Mitosis operates in ingenious fashion in order to produce these two identical daughter cells (Fig. 3-4). A cell with 46 chromosomes divides into two daughter cells, each containing the exact number of chromosomes as the mother cell. This is accomplished in the following manner:

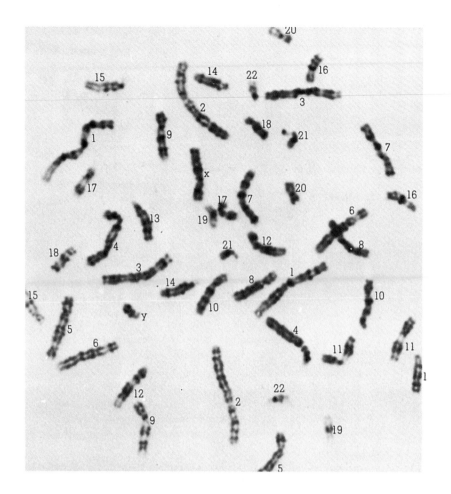

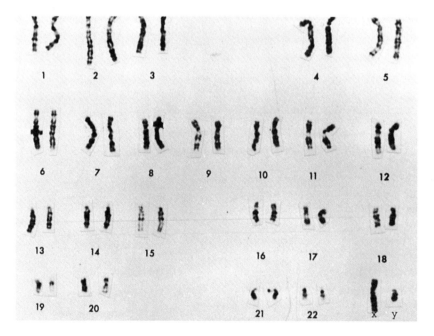

FIGURE 3-3   Human chromosomes; a male **karyotype**. *Upper portion*: Chromosomes as they appear under a microscope. *Lower portion*: Each pair of chromosomes is identified by the size of the arms on each side of the centromere and arranged, by number, from large to small (as well as by bands seen with special stains).

Somatic cell with 46 chromosomes in nucleus

Cell divides; the nucleus of each daughter cell contains 46 chromosomes

FIGURE 3-4   An "ingenious" method of dividing a cell with 46 chromosomes and producing two daughter cells with 46 chromosomes identical to each other and to the mother cell.

At the beginning of the division process, each chromosome duplicates itself, and now consists of two identical strands, or DNA molecules joined by a common centromere (Fig. 3-5). There are now 46 double-stranded chromosomes.

The double-stranded chromosomes position themselves along the equator of the nucleus and, as the cell divides, the centromere splits and the strands, or DNA molecules, separate.

As the cell continues to divide, the DNA molecules move away from each other to opposite ends of the cell. When the cell completes its division, there are two daughter cells, each with a complete set of 46 chromosomes (each with one DNA molecule).

The result of this division is the production of two daughter cells, each identical to the other and to the mother cell. Each daughter cell contains the same 46 chromosomes, exactly the same genetic material as the mother cell.

Cell Division: Meiosis

We have seen how mitosis produces two daughter cells with the same number of chromosomes and genetic material as the mother cell. Sexual reproduction, however, is quite another matter, requiring a specialized division process called **meiosis**, (see Fig. 3-6 for a comparison of mitosis and meiosis).

The meiotic operation also appears simple—the production of cells with 23 chromosomes by the division of a cell of 46 chromosomes. However, it is not merely a matter of dividing 46 by 2, since that could result in cells with a random collection of 23 chromosomes. The goal is to produce cells (called **gametes**) containing one of each of the 23 chromosomes, no more and no less. A normal gamete, following the meiotic process, will have a complete set of 23 chromosomes, one member of each homologous pair (see Figs. 3-3 and 3-7).

The process of reducing the number of chromosomes from 46, the diploid number, to 23, the haploid number, requires two divisions, which are usually referred to as Meiosis I and Meiosis II.

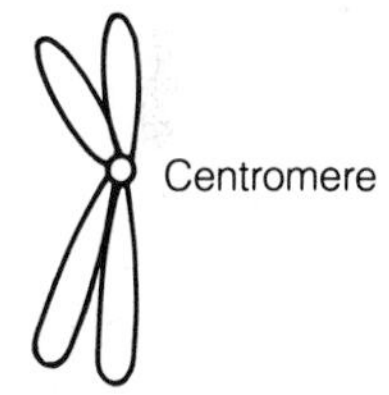

Meiosis I Before first division begins, each chromosome replicates itself, resulting in a cell containing 46 double-stranded chromosomes. Both members (paternal and maternal) of each pair come together, forming a tetrad, and the homologous chromosomes may cross-over, or more accurately, exchange some parts (Fig. 3-9). In this way, sections of original (paternal and maternal) chromosomes are exchanged. Thus, the material in each DNA molecule is reshuffled, and will be passed on in a combination different from either of their parents.

The chromosomes, as tetrads, then line up randomly (in no special order) along the equator of the cell. As the cell divides, the chromosome pairs separate, carrying a mix of maternal and paternal hereditary material into *separate* cells (Fig. 3-9).

When first division ends, each of the two resulting daughter cells contain 23 double-stranded chromosomes.

Meiosis II The second division completes the meiotic process. The double-stranded molecules in each of the two cells again line up in both the cells and the

Meiosis (my-oh′-sis)
meioun: to make smaller
osis: process or state
Reduction division; sex cell division; reduction of a diploid cell, through two divisions, to a haploid (gamete) cell.

Karyotype (care′-ee-o-type)
karyo: nut, kernel
In biology, refers to the nucleus—a description or illustration of the number, size, and shapes of the chromosomes in the cells of an organism.

Gamete A haploid cell (sperm or ovum) that may combine with a haploid cell of the other sex to form a fertilized cell.

Double-stranded

FIGURE 3-5 When a chromosome replicates itself, each unit is a separate DNA molecule, joined together at the centromere.

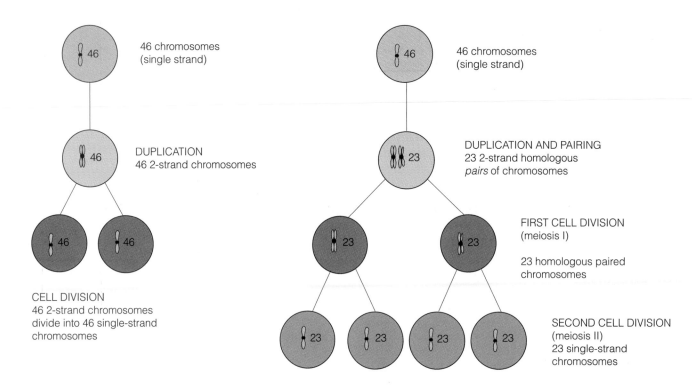

46 chromosomes
(single strand)

DUPLICATION
46 2-strand chromosomes

CELL DIVISION
46 2-strand chromosomes
divide into 46 single-strand
chromosomes

46 chromosomes
(single strand)

DUPLICATION AND PAIRING
23 2-strand homologous
pairs of chromosomes

FIRST CELL DIVISION
(meiosis I)

23 homologous paired
chromosomes

SECOND CELL DIVISION
(meiosis II)
23 single-strand
chromosomes

MITOSIS

Occurs during a *single* cell division

Results in the production of two *diploid* cells

Daughter cells all genetically *identical*

No crossing-over

Chromosomes are *randomly* aligned on the equatorial plane

The two strands of each chromosome separate

Does *not* result in production of gametes

MEIOSIS

Occurs during *two* sequential divisions

Results in the production of four *haploid* cells

Daughter cells *not* all genetically identical

Crossing-over (genetic recombination) occurs

First meiotic division, chromosomes are aligned in *homologous pairs* on the equatorial plane

Of first meiotic division, *whole homologous chromosomes* separate from each other (reduction division); chromosomes separate during the second meiotic division

Does result in the production of gametes

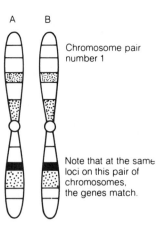

A   B

Chromosome pair
number 1

Note that at the same
loci on this pair of
chromosomes,
the genes match.

FIGURE 3-7   Idealized chromosome form.
Each space represents a locus; 12 are shown
here. Actually, there are thousands of loci on a
chromosome. The figure is a diagrammatic
representation of a pair of chromosomes with
matching genes: an homologous pair.

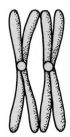

FIGURE 3-8   A tetrad (4 strands).

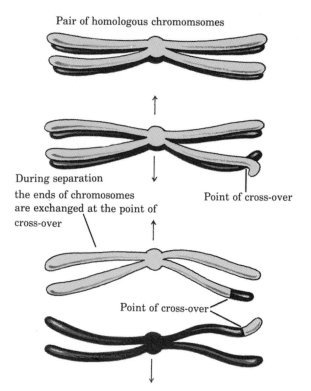

Pair of homologous chromomsomes

During separation
the ends of chromosomes
are exchanged at the point of
cross-over

Point of cross-over

Point of cross-over

FIGURE 3-9   Crossing-over. During Meiosis I homologous
chromosomes pair very tightly. While paired, during the tetrad
stage, corresponding sections of DNA molecules of homologous
chromosomes are exchanged. This event, crossing-over, results
in greater variation among the gametes produced by meiosis and
therefore also among the offspring of sexually reproducing
organisms. (See pp. 61–63 for more on crossing over.)

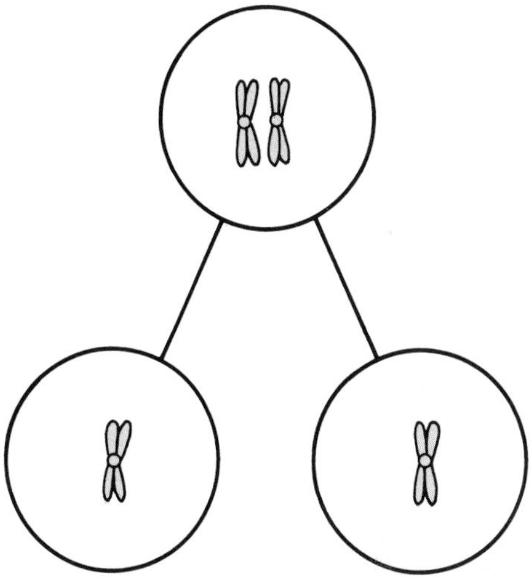

FIGURE 3-10   When the cell divides, the tetrad separates with
one double-stranded chromosome in each of the daughter cells.

strands divide, producing four cells, each with 23 single-stranded chromosomes.
The result of Meiosis I and II is the division of one cell into four, each containing
single-stranded chromosomes (Fig. 3-11).

In males, the newly produced gametes are known as *spermatids* and the process of sperm cell formation is called *spermatogenesis* (Fig. 3-12). Once meiosis is
completed, the spermatids develop tails and become mature sperm cells.

Spermatogenesis determines the sex of the offspring. A male parent carries an
X and Y, a female, XX. When the sperm cells divide in Meiosis II, two of the four
cells carry an X and two, a Y. Therefore, the chances are about even that the sperm
fertilizing the ovum will carry either an X or a Y. If it is a Y, the offspring will be
male; if an X, female. A female can only transmit an X. (Actually, the chances of a
baby boy are slightly greater, in most populations around 106 boys are born for
every 100 girls.)

Female cell division (oögenesis) differs slightly from spermatogenesis (Fig.
3-12). First division produces one relatively large cell and one very small cell
called a *polar* body. In second division, the polar body divides, producing two
polar bodies (Fig. 3-12); the large cell divides and produces one large cell and one
polar body. Normally, polar bodies are not functional. It should be clear, however,
that in spite of the difference, the purpose of meiosis is the same in both sexes: to
produce functional gametes, carrying hereditary material ready for the fertilization process.

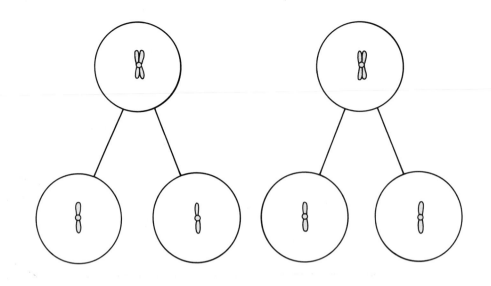

FIGURE 3-11 Second Division. As the two cells divide into four, the double-stranded chromosomes separate, resulting in one single-stranded chromosome in each of the four cells.

FIGURE 3-12 Spermatogenesis and oögenesis.

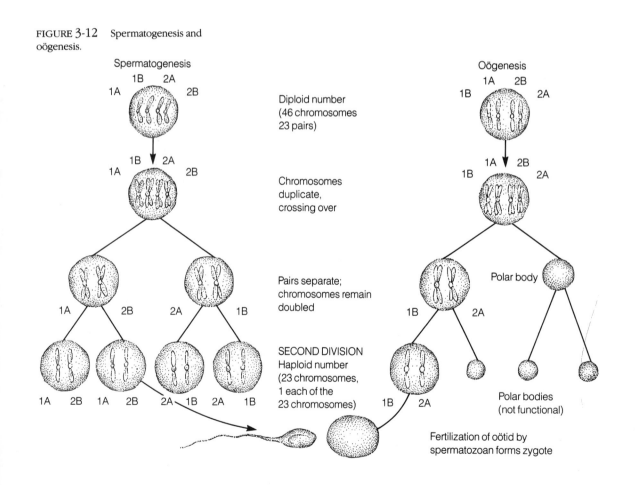

Spermatogenesis

Diploid number (46 chromosomes 23 pairs)

Chromosomes duplicate, crossing over

Pairs separate; chromosomes remain doubled

SECOND DIVISION Haploid number (23 chromosomes, 1 each of the 23 chromosomes)

Oögenesis

Polar body

Polar bodies (not functional)

Fertilization of oötid by spermatozoan forms zygote

BOX 3-3 **Vocabulary: Terms Used in Discussion of Chromosomes**

ALLELE (a-lee′-l) allelon: of one another. An alternative form of a gene located at the same locus (position) on a chromosome.

AUTOSOMES In humans, the first 22 pairs of chromosomes; not sex chromosomes.

CENTROMERE centro: central; mere: part. That part of the chromosome to which spindle fibers are attached during mitosis and meiosis.

CHROMOSOME chrome: color; soma: body. Threadlike, gene-carrying body, consisting of one or two DNA molecules, found in the nucleus.

DIPLOID dipl: double; oid: resembling, similar to. The full set of chromosomes, 46 in humans. Since there are 23 different chromosomes, doubling that makes 46, the diploid number. There are two (a pair) of each kind of chromosome.

GAMETE A haploid cell (sperm or ovum) that may combine with a haploid cell of the other sex to form a fertilized cell.

GENE to be born; beget. That section of DNA that specifies the production of a polypeptide chain; the basic unit of inheritance.

HAPLOID hapl: single, simple; oid: resembling, similar to. Simple here means uncomplicated, the basic number, referring to the 23 different chromosomes found in the gamete after the second division. There is a single representative, not a pair, of each kind of chromosome.

HOMOLOGOUS homo: same; logous: speech, gather. Matching; corresponding. Two chromosomes that carry genes at corresponding locations are called an homologous pair.

HOMOLOGOUS CHROMOSOMES A matched pair of chromosomes.

LOCUS (pl. loci; lo-sigh or lo-see); place. The position of a gene on a chromosome.

OÖCYTE (oh′-oh-site) oö: egg; cyte: cell. Female sex cell; a cell that undergoes meiosis and produces an egg, or ovum.

OÖGENESIS genesis: origin; coming into being. Division process of the female sex cell that produces ova.

OÖTID A haploid cell produced by meiosis and differentiating into an ovum.

OVUM (pl. ova). Egg; female sex cell.

SPERM Male fertilizing fluid; semen.

SPERMATID A haploid cell produced by meiosis and differentiating into a sperm cell.

SPERMATOCYTE (sper-ma′-ta-site). A cell that undergoes meiosis and produces a spermatid. A male sex cell.

TETRAD tetr: four. A structure of four—refers here to the four DNA molecules of a pair of homologous chromosomes—the 4-strand stage.

ZYGOTE yoked. A fertilized cell formed by the union of a male gamete and a female gamete.

Three functions of meiosis have now been discussed: (1) the reduction of the number of chromosomes in a sex cell from 46, the diploid number, to 23, the haploid number; (2) separation of X and Y chromosomes in the male sex cells so that sex determination of the offspring becomes possible; and (3) facilitating the recombination of genetic variation, thus providing alternatives for natural selection.

Recombination

Random Assortment The reshuffling of parental DNA material is known as *recombination*, a very important process that influences heredity and natural selection. Meiosis I provides two methods of recombination: (1) the random arrange-

FIGURE 3-13   At alignment before division, chromosomes assort themselves randomly (but always in homologous pairs). Each different alignment produces a different random assortment of chromosomes in the daughter cells after first division. In the two daughter cells of cell 1, for example, cell 1a carries an X, and cell 1b a Y. Since chromosomes carry genes, the varying combinations of chromosomes result in the recombination of genes. In cell 1a, genes on X chromosomes are combined with those on 1A, 2B, and 9A. In cell 1b, Y is combined with the opposite members of those chromosomes. This particular combination of chromosomes produced by random assortment plus crossing-over is unique. It probably never occurred before and will probably never occur again.

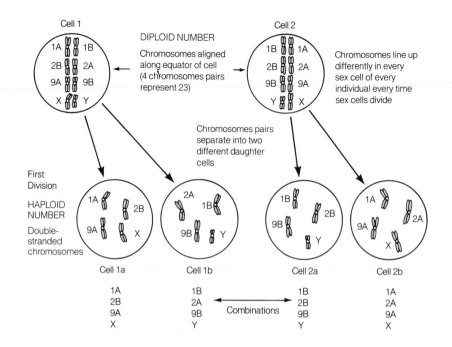

ment of chromosomes; and (2) crossing-over. Both of these events occur before the chromosomes divide.

Figure 3-13 shows two sex cells with alternating positioning of the same chromosomes when they align along the cell's equator. After first division, when the chromosomes have separated, the four daughter cells show four different combinations of genes. Cell 1a, for example, combines chromosomes 1A, 2B, 9A, and X. Cell 1B contains the other members of the pair, 1B, 2A, 9B, and Y.

If cell 2a fertilized the ovum, the combination would be different from the action of 1b. Cell 2a would produce a male; cell 1b, a female, and there would be other differences as well. We can see this more clearly, perhaps, if we look at actual traits in Fig. 3-14. Please note this drawing represents a simplification of the real situation; at the molecular level, heredity is much more complicated than this illustration suggests.

The spermatocyte cell 1 has divided and produced cell 1a and cell 1b with different gene combinations. If cell 1a fertilized the ovum the offspring would be a *female* with O blood type, the *Rb⁻* negative factor, free earlobes, and a nontaster.* If cell 1b were the lucky one, the offspring would be a *male* with *B* blood type, the *Rb⁺* positive factor, free earlobes, and a nontaster.

This may not seem like much variation, but we worked here with just five traits; there are genes for thousands of traits in one cell. Furthermore, since there are 23 pairs of chromosomes instead of just one pair, the number of different possible combinations is staggering. Imagine Fig. 3-14 with cell 1a containing 23 pairs (instead of 4 pairs) of chromosomes all randomly aligned independently of one another. The number of different possible combinations for any given gamete is then about 8 million. This number represents the possibility of only *one* gamete—the sperm, for example. An equal number of possibilities (8 million)

*Not all humans can taste PTC (phenylthicarbamide), a synthetic compound.

exists for the gametes of the other parent, so the possible kinds of different individuals that could result from one human mating is about 70 trillion. The number is mind-boggling. It is more than all the human beings who have ever lived or are ever likely to live.

Another way of looking at this process is to consider that a human male can produce several hundred million sperm a day from puberty until death and, including the effects of crossing-over, the chances are that no two of those sperm will be identical.

Crossing-Over   Another form of recombination is crossing-over, a process that occurs during the tetrad stage of the chromosomes. The chromosomes, arranged in pairs, have duplicated themselves, resulting in four DNA molecules. Before division, sections of the DNA molecule may exchange. Figure 3-15 shows the exchange of corresponding parts of sister molecules. At crossing-over, a section of P² has crossed over with a section of M¹. When crossing-over is completed, a portion of M¹ has become part of P², and P² of M¹.

FIGURE 3-14   A spermatocyte with five traits. When cell 1 divides, the genes are also distributed. The offspring will vary depending on whether cell 1a or cell 1b fertilizes the ovum.

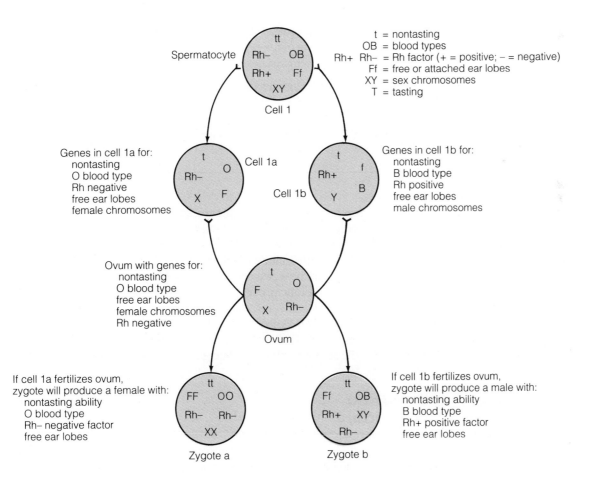

BOX 3-4   Vocabulary: Terms Used in Discussion of DNA

BASE   One of the four chemicals attached to a sugar molecule and a phosphate to make up a nucleotide; in DNA and RNA, a base is always paired with another base.

ADENINE
GUANINE
CYTOSINE
THYMINE
} The four chemical bases. Adenine and thymine are paired; cytosine and guanine are paired.

URACIL   A chemical base found in RNA in the same position as thymine in DNA.

AMINO ACIDS   Small molecules that are the building blocks of protein.

CODON   A triplet sequence of bases on DNA and mRNA.

ANTICODON   A triplet sequence of bases on tRNA.

DNA   Deoxyribonucleic acid; a large molecule composed of adenine, guanine, cytosine, and thymine plus phosphate and sugar; carries the genetic code.

RNA   Ribonucleic acid; slightly different chemically from DNA; found in the nucleus and the cytoplasm.

mRNA   Messenger RNA; carries genetic information from DNA in the nucleus to the ribosomes in the cytoplasm.

tRNA   Transfer RNA; brings an amino acid to match the mRNA bases.

rRNA   Ribosomal RNA; a major constituent of ribosomes.

MOLECULE   Smallest portion of a substance (element or compound) that acts like that substance and is capable of existing independently. Several to many atoms constitute a molecule.

NUCLEOTIDE   A base attached to a sugar and a phosphate group; a subunit of DNA and RNA.

PEPTIDE   A compound of two or more amino acids joined by peptide bonds. Linked peptides form polypeptides which, in turn, join to form proteins.

POLYPEPTIDE   A group of peptides joined together.

PROTEIN   A macromolecule, composed of one or more polypeptide chains of amino acids, responsible for carrying out most of the cell's metabolic activities; also contributes to cell structure.

RIBOSOMES   Small, minute bodies found in the cytoplasm of the cell; composed of rRNA and proteins; site of protein synthesis.

PROTEIN SYNTHESIS   The manufacture of a protein. The process by which amino acids are linked (by a peptide bond) to form a polypeptide chain. The completed chain or chains form a protein.

Figure 3-15 depicts further examples of crossing-over. These illustrate the extent to which an "original" M DNA molecule takes on portions of P, and vice versa.

When we consider the random assortment of chromosomes and crossing-over, we are struck with the truly infinite number of recombination possibilities. And when we add mutation to these, we realize the astonishing potential for variation that occurs during the meiotic process. This process produces the raw material that natural selection acts on.

Interestingly, Darwin, who knew the significance of variation, was unable to explain how it was produced. The answers to this puzzle came only with the modern development of the sciences of biology and genetics.

DNA: Structure

We have seen how heredity is influenced through what might be called mechanical processes. Sex cells divide, chromosomes cross-over, and genes recombine.

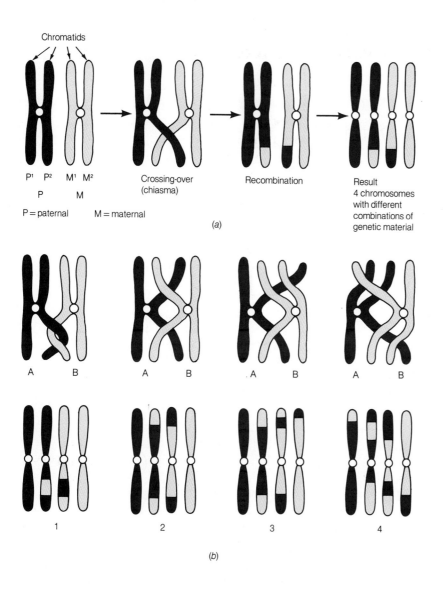

Chromatids

P¹ P² M¹ M²

P   M

P = paternal   M = maternal

Crossing-over
(chiasma)

Recombination

Result
4 chromosomes
with different
combinations of
genetic material

(a)

A   B   A   B   A   B   A   B

1   2   3   4

(b)

FIGURE 3-15 (*a*) Recombination of genes at cross-over. (*b*) Four examples of crossing-over. An infinite number of gene combinations may easily be imagined. The single chromosomes show how the genes contributed by parents may be recombined.

These mechanical processes do not, however, transmit actual characteristics; in fact, parents do not pass on physical traits, they pass on information.

Heredity is transmitted through information chemically coded in deoxyribonucleic acid (DNA), which is usually referred to as the carrier of the genetic code. It may help to think of DNA as a language composed of 64 three-letter words made up of bases and called *triplets* or *codons* (see Fig. 3-21). The structure of DNA is arranged to transcribe (or decode) the message programmed in the codons.

The basic structure of DNA is not difficult to understand if you follow carefully the next few paragraphs and check the diagrams.

DNA is a two-stranded molecule consisting of four chemical bases. The four bases are the **purines** *adenine* (A)* and *guanine* (G), and the **pyrimidines** *cytosine* (C) and *thymine* (T). Each base is bonded to another partner base:

Purines A class of chemical bases—adenine and guanine—in DNA and RNA.

Pyrimidines A class of chemical bases—thymine, cytosine, uracil—found in nucleic acid.

---

*Bases are usually referred to by their letters: A, G, C, T.

FIGURE 3-16 Part of a DNA molecule. The illustration shows the two DNA strands with the sugar and phosphate backbone and the bases extending toward the center.

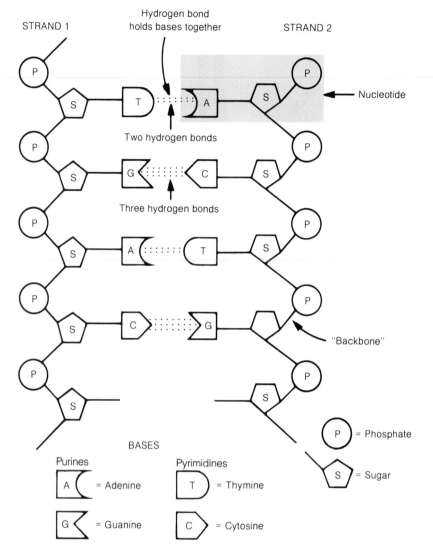

Double helix The structure of DNA composed of a pair of matching helixes.

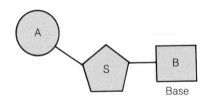

FIGURE 3-17 A nucleotide consisting of a phosphate, sugar, and base.

adenine to thymine and guanine to cytosine (note that a purine must bond with a pyrimidine). Any exception to this pairing rule would be a serious structural error that could lead to vital body defects.

Each base is attached to a phosphate group and a sugar molecule (deoxyribose). As a unit, these three parts—base, phosphate, and sugar—are called a nucleotide (Fig. 3-16). DNA, then, is composed of a double string of nucleotides twisted into a spiral or helix shape. Since it is two-stranded, it is called a **double helix** (Fig. 3-17b).

In Fig. 3-18a, DNA is shown in ladder form to simplify graphically the molecule's structure. The alternating sugars and phosphates represent the sidepieces of the ladder, and the bases, which extend inward and are hydrogen bonded at the center, represent the rungs (Fig. 3-16). Actually, as we have seen, the two strands twist around each other to form a double helix (Fig. 3-18b).

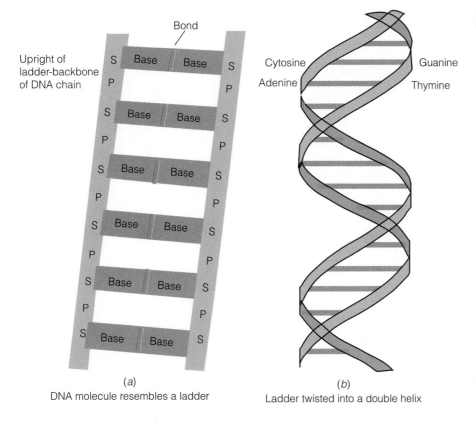

Bond

Upright of
ladder-backbone
of DNA chain

S	Base	Base	S
P			P
S	Base	Base	S
P			P
S	Base	Base	S
P			P
S	Base	Base	S
P			P
S	Base	Base	S
P			P
S	Base	Base	S

Cytosine   Guanine
Adenine   Thymine

(a)
DNA molecule resembles a ladder

(b)
Ladder twisted into a double helix

FIGURE 3-18   (a) DNA molecule resembles a ladder. (b) Ladder twisted into a helix.

The double helix is passed on from one generation of cells to the next by DNA replication (Fig. 3-19). Before division in mitosis the two DNA strands pull apart, a fairly easy task since the hydrogen bond that holds them together is weak. Within the nucleus are free nucleotides that are drawn to their complement (partner) nucleotides on the two separated primary strands. This process continues until all the bases are paired and replication of the primary strands is completed. There are now two identical double helixes (what we called above a double-stranded chromosome) and, as the cell divides, each double helix becomes a part of one or the other daughter cells.

DNA: Process

Before reading the following, review these terms (Box 3-4, p. 62): *mRNA, tRNA, ribosome, codon, anticodon, amino acid, enzyme, polypeptide.*

Transcription   When triggered by an enzyme, DNA—containing the necessary information for a liver, nerve, kidney, or any other kind of cell—unzips and the strands partly unwind. Free-floating RNA nucleotides attach to their complementary DNA bases, and a short strand of RNA is thus formed, using DNA as a template.

FIGURE 3-19   The replication of a DNA molecule. The double helix uncoils and then unzips, separating base pairs. Complementary base pairs are attracted and attach to the exposed nucleotides. When replication is completed, each daughter strand is composed of one strand of the parent DNA and one new strand.

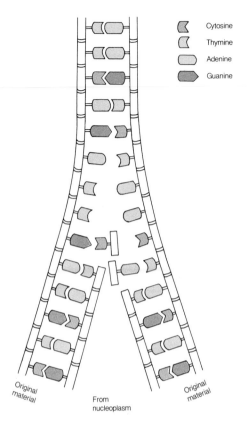

Cytosine
Thymine
Adenine
Guanine

Original material

From nucleoplasm

Original material

The RNA strand is complementary to the DNA, except that *uracil*, a pyrimidine, replaces thymine, which RNA does not possess (Fig. 3-20).

When transcription is completed, the RNA strand departs the nucleus and moves into the cytoplasm of the cell, carrying the genetic information in its sequence of bases. Because RNA is carrying the message, it is known as *messenger RNA* or *mRNA* (Fig. 3-22). Now in the cytoplasm, the mRNA strand attaches to a string of ribosomes, which have been called protein factories.

Translation   A ribosome (or several ribosomes) moves along the mRNA strand "reading" the message, located in the codons (Fig. 3-21). These three-letter codons are symbols for the twenty common amino acids, the building blocks of proteins (see Table 3-1 for a complete listing of DNA and mRNA codons). As the ribosome reads the mRNA, it translates the mRNA codons.

The ribosome translates by attracting another kind of RNA known as *transfer RNA* or *tRNA* (Fig. 3-21). Each tRNA carries a cargo fore and aft. In front is a triplet consisting of three nucleotides called an *anticodon*. The rear cargo is an amino acid, and each tRNA is specific for a particular amino acid.

When the ribosome reads the mRNA codon (Fig. 3-21), say UUU, a tRNA with its complementary AAA anticodon will be attracted to the ribosome-mRNA complex, bringing along its amino acid, phenylalanine. The tRNA molecule plugs into the mRNA codon and then slips away, leaving the amino acid behind. The amino acid joins other amino acids left there by the same process, forming an amino acid chain, and the ribosome moves on. The completed polypeptide chain of amino

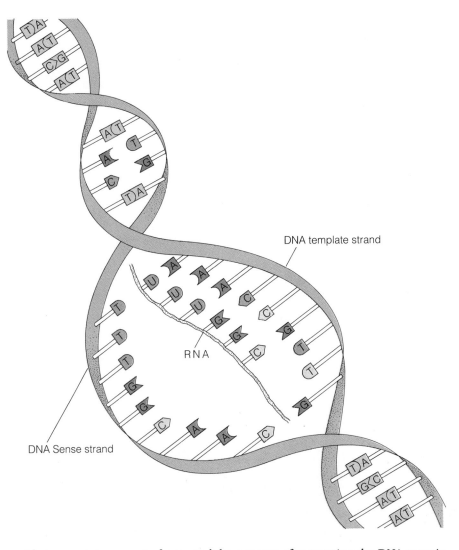

FIGURE 3-20 Transcription. The two DNA strands have unzipped and partly separated. Free nucleotides have been drawn to the template strand and a copy of the DNA strand is being made. Note that the RNA strand will be exactly the same as the DNA sense strand except that uracil (U) replaces thymine (T).

DNA template strand

RNA

DNA Sense strand

acids is a protein or part of one, and the process of converting the DNA genetic code for this particular protein has ended.

Proteins are the basic structural and functional compounds of the cell; they are responsible for carrying out most of the metabolic functions of the cell, as well as for making up most of the cell structure. The structural components of tissue, hormones, enzymes, hemoglobins, etc., are proteins. In turn, the kind of protein that is synthesized depends upon the information that comes from the DNA. The result is that the kind of body the proteins build (pigmentation, blood type, body build, etc.) is largely determined by the sequence of bases found in DNA.

The discovery of the structure of DNA and how it functions (although the entire story is still unknown) resolves a number of questions about heredity. We now know that what children inherit from their parents are not actual traits, such as hair color or stature, but a genetic blueprint—DNA. We also know that the information is stored in the nucleus and, when required, is taken from the nucleus and brought into the cytoplasm of the cell. And we know further that this information is instrumental in building or synthesizing proteins which will, in turn, build and maintain the body according to that information.

TABLE 3-1   **The Genetic Code**

AMINO ACID SYMBOL	AMINO ACID	mRNA CODON	DNA CODON
ALA	ALANINE	GCU, GCC, GCA, GCG	CGA, CGG, CGT, CGC
ARG	ARGININE	CGU, CGC, CGA, CGG, AGA, AGG	GCA, GCG, GCT, GCC, TCT, TCC
ASN	ASPARAGINE	AAU, AAC	TTA, TTG
ASP	ASPARTIC ACID	GAU, GAC	CTA, CTG
CYS	CYSTEINE	UGU, UGC	ACA, ACG
GLN	GLUTAMINE	CAA, CAG	GTT, GTC
GLU	GLUTAMIC ACID	GAA, GAG	CTT, CTC
GLY	GLYCINE	GGU, GGC, GGA, GGG	CCA, CCG, CCT, CCC
HIS	HISTIDINE	CAU, CAC	GTA, GTG
ILE	ISOLEUCINE	AUU, AUC, AUA	TAA, TAG, TAT
LEU	LEUCINE	UUA, UUG, CUU, CUC, CUA, CUG	AAT, AAC, GAA, GAG, GAT, GAC
LYS	LYSINE	AAA, AAG	TTT, TTC
MET	METHIONINE	AUG	TAC
PHE	PHENYLALANINE	UUU, UUC	AAA, AAG
PRO	PROLINE	CCU, CCC, CCA, CCG	GGA, GGG, GGT, GGC
SER	SERINE	UCU, UCC, UCA, UCG, AGU, AGC	AGA, AGG, AGT, AGC, TCA, TCG
THR	THREONINE	ACU, ACC, ACA, ACG	TGA, TGG, TGT, TGC
TRP	TRYPTOPHAN	UGG	ACC
TYR	TYROSINE	UAU, UAC	ATA, ATG
VAL	VALINE	GUU, GUC, GUA, GUG	CAA, CAG, CAT, CAC
Terminating triplets		UAA, UAG, UGA	ATT, ATC, ACT

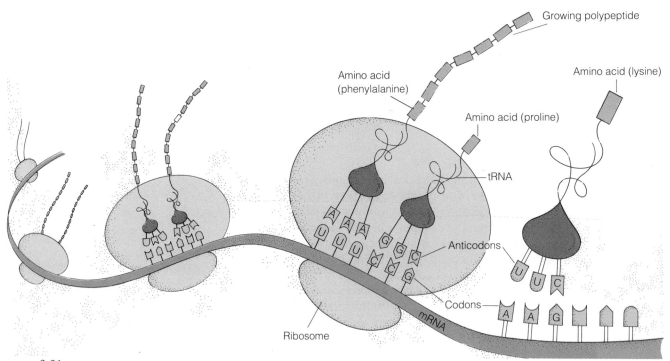

FIGURE 3-21   Translation. Ribosomes move along mRNA strand and attract tRNA molecules with appropriate anticodons. Then tRNA carries amino acid which joins the peptide chain already forming (or begins to form a chain). When the chain is completed, it is a protein, or part of one. Peptide chains have already formed on the left.

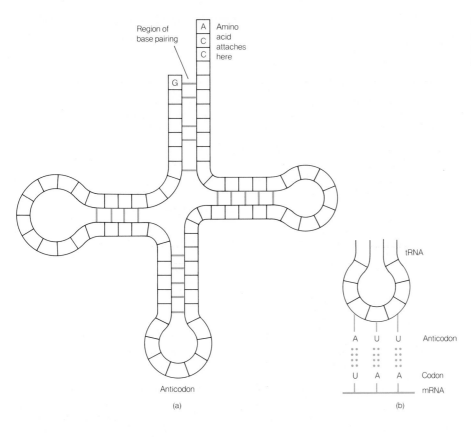

Region of
base pairing

A
C
C

Amino
acid
attaches
here

G

Anticodon

(a)

tRNA

A U U   Anticodon

U A A   Codon

mRNA

(b)

FIGURE 3-22   tRNA. The cloverleaf
molecular configuration of tRNA. (*a*) The open
end attaches to free amino acids. (*b*) The
anticodon loop attaches to a codon on mRNA.

Theory of the Gene

POINT MUTATION

Normal adult hemoglobin is made up of protein chains that are direct products of
gene action. One of these chains, called the *beta chain*, is in turn made up of 146
amino acids. Individuals with **sickle-cell anemia** inherit from *both* their parents
deleterious gene variants (alleles) that produce a different type of hemoglobin. As
a result, these individuals usually have major circulatory disturbances, destruction
of red blood cells, and severe anemia often resulting in early death. Individuals
who inherit this gene from only one of their parents are much less severely affected and usually have a normal life span.

The cause of all these dramatic changes in the individual's health is a seemingly
minute change in the gene that produces hemoglobin. Both normal adult hemoglobin and the sickle-cell variety have 146 amino acids and, of these, 145 are identical. A substitution of only one amino acid (at position #6—see Fig. 3-23) causes
all the problems.

We know, of course, that it is the sequence of bases in the DNA that codes for
the sequence of amino acids in the final protein product. We also know that 3
bases (1 codon) code for one amino acid. Therefore, it takes 438 bases (146 × 3)
to produce the chain of 146 amino acids seen in the adult hemoglobin beta chain.

Sickle-cell anemia   A disease caused by a
mutant form of hemoglobin (when inherited
in double dose).

While DNA replication is highly efficient and accurate, it is not perfect—mistakes can and *do* occur. The difference between normal and sickling hemoglobin, however, concerns a change at only one point in the hemoglobin gene. The first 5 and the last 140 amino acids in the protein chains of both varieties of hemoglobin are identical. Only at position #6 (Fig. 3-23) is there an alteration.

Figure 3-23 shows a possible DNA base sequence and the resulting amino acid products for both normal and sickling hemoglobin. As can be seen, a single base substitution (from CTC to CAC) could result in an altered amino acid sequence (. . . proline—*glutamic acid*—glutamic acid . . . to . . . proline—*valine*—glutamic acid . . .). This, in turn, would alter the properties of the whole protein (hemoglobin), changing its three-dimension structure and resulting in differently shaped red blood cells, oxygen-bonding properties, etc. In other words, the only difference between normal hemoglobin and sickling hemoglobin is a change in *one base* out of the 438 bases that make up the coded portion of this gene. Such an alteration is called a **point mutation** and, in evolution, is probably the most common and most important source of new variation.

Recent research has shown that, within the DNA, there are considerably more nucleotides than just those that are eventually translated into amino acid sequences. In fact, in human DNA (and other organisms with nucleated cells, but *not* bacteria) most genes are fragmented. Between those sections that are eventually coded there are often long intervening sequences called **introns**, which do not contribute information for protein synthesis. For example, for the hemoglobin

FIGURE 3-23 Substitution of one base at position #6 produces a sickling hemoglobin.

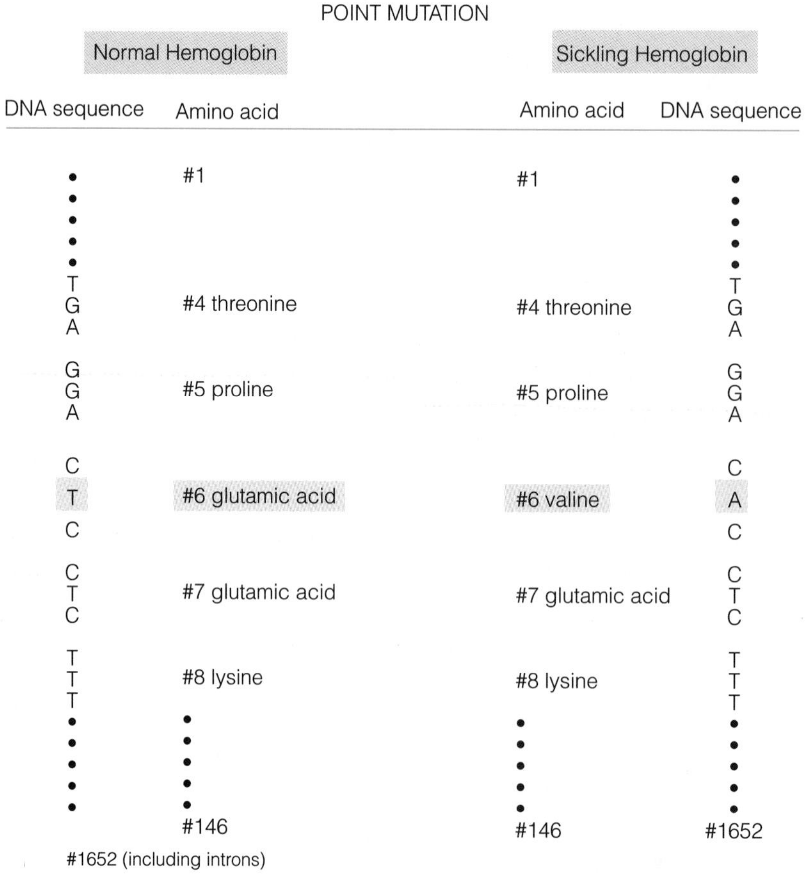

POINT MUTATION

Normal Hemoglobin			Sickling Hemoglobin	
DNA sequence	Amino acid		Amino acid	DNA sequence
• • • • •	#1		#1	• • • • •
T G A	#4 threonine		#4 threonine	T G A
G G A	#5 proline		#5 proline	G G A
C T C	#6 glutamic acid		#6 valine	C A C
C T C	#7 glutamic acid		#7 glutamic acid	C T C
T T T	#8 lysine		#8 lysine	T T T
• • • •	• • • • #146		• • • • #146	• • • • #1652

#1652 (including introns)

beta locus we have seen there is a total of 438 nucleotides that codes for the eventual polypeptide chain. However, when one also counts those sections at the beginning and end of the locus (promoter and termination regions), as well as two long introns, the entire locus is 1,652 nucleotides long.

With recent advances in recombinant DNA technology, it has become possible to sequence the nucleotides within the introns. As a result, a variety of *evolutionary* mechanisms have been brought into clearer focus. For example, comparisons of intron sequences in different populations have indicated that the sickle-cell mutation has probably occurred several different times (that is, mutated in slightly different ways in these groups).

Point mutations probably occur relatively frequently during cell division, but a new mutation will have evolutionary significance only if it is passed on to offspring through the gametes. Once such a new mutation has occurred, its fate in the population will depend on the other evolutionary forces, especially natural selection. Sickle-cell, in fact, is the best-demonstrated example of natural selection acting in human beings, and we will take this point up in considerably more detail in Chapter 5.

DEFINITION OF THE GENE

Although not all biologists agree on the definition, we have defined the gene as that section of DNA—a sequence of codons on the DNA template—responsible for the ultimate synthesis of a specific polypeptide chain of amino acids. To put it another way, a gene is that portion of a DNA molecule that specifies the manufacture (synthesis) of a protein or part of a protein (hemoglobin, say) that will produce, or assist in the production of, one or more physical traits. A gene, then, is not a discrete unit operating in the nucleus of the cell; it is part of a large DNA molecule.

HEREDITY AND ENVIRONMENT

For years scientists, debating societies, philosophers, writers, preachers, and others have debated, often acrimoniously, the question of what is more important: heredity or environment, nature or nurture. The question is whether human beings—physically, behaviorally, and psychically—are the result of their heredity or are fashioned and molded by their environment. Or, if both, which is more influential? Differences of opinion on this subject have been bitter.

The English philosopher John Locke (1632–1704) believed that, at birth, the mind of the human being is a blank slate (*tabula rasa*), and all differences are environmentally produced. On the other hand, the French writer Count Joseph Arthur de Gobineau (1816–1882), notorious for his belief in the inequality of races, held that differences in ability are inherited. The behavioral psychologist J. B. Watson left no doubt of his position:

> Give me a dozen healthy infants, well-formed, and my own specified world to bring them up, and I'll guarantee to take any one at random and train him to become any type of specialist I might select—doctor, lawyer, artist, merchant and yes, even beggar and thief, regardless of the talents, penchants, tendencies, abilities, vocations, and race . . . (Watson, 1924, p. 42).

Genotype The actual genetic makeup of an individual.

Phenotype (phee'-no-type)
phen: showing
The observable or measurable characteristics of an individual as determined by the genotype and the influence of the environment.

To demonstrate whether heredity or environment is the primary factor responsible for human development is very difficult. Genetics teaches that it is not an either-or proposition, since both factors contribute to what we are physically and behaviorally. As biochemist Daniel C. Koshland, Jr. succinctly states it, "In fact the neurobiological evidence indicates that part of the brain is 'hard-wired' in advance of birth and part is designed to be plastic and learn from experience" (1987, p. 1445). From our discussion of genes, we might infer that heredity determines exactly what the nature of a physical trait will be. This circumstance may be so with some genes, but probably not so with most. In the case of the ABO blood system mentioned above, the genes do determine blood type, and, as far as we know, the environment has no effect on the expression of the blood-group genes. If both parents are O, then all their children will be O, regardless of environmental conditions.

Nevertheless, the environment is a powerful factor shaping our lives. For example, parental treatment can be rewarding or devastating, the quality and quantity of education can produce success or failure, an only child develops differently than one with siblings. A slum, ghetto, or posh surroundings; attitudes and behavior toward males/females; the social class structure; a person's job and its milieu, etc.—all influence us.

Furthermore, our culture invokes aphorisms that confirm our statement that genes are not all-decisive: "If at first you don't succeed, try, try again." "God helps those who help themselves." "You can do it if you try." "Success is 10 percent inspiration and 90 percent perspiration." These suggest that a person can succeed regardless of his genes. We do not claim that genes are unimportant in determining what we are. We do insist that nurture is as involved as nature. After all, culture has played a compelling role in human evolution, and culture is acquired, *not* genetic.

At the same time, we must also remember that the capacity for culture is based in the human neurological system ("wired in") and *is* genetic. We believe it is necessary to consider both nature and nurture, in order to take a biocultural approach.

Genotypes and Phenotypes The underlying basis of what we have called heredity in the preceding discussion is known as the **genotype**—"the sum total of the hereditary materials received by an individual from its parents and other ancestors" (Dobzhansky, 1979, p. 32).

An individual's genotype does not change during his or her lifetime—with the exception of some cells in aberrant tissue lines that arise from what are called *somatic mutations*. The consequences may be quite significant for the individual, since experimental work with animals suggests some cancers may well arise from somatic mutations. However, in no case are these somatic mutations passed to offspring. Moreover, for the vast majority of genes in the vast majority of one's cells, we could say the genotype is "fixed" at birth and does not change.

When we observe, probe, or measure people, what we see is their **phenotypes**; for example, a person's skin color, stature, blood type, etc. The phenotype is the *ascertainable* aspect of an organism. Phenotypes, as such, are partly products of the genotype, but, because of their plasticity, *they also* can be modified by the environment. However, other more complex traits, such as stature, weight, personality, or intelligence, are often modified dramatically by the environment. In these cases, a person's phenotype could be said to result from an interaction of the genotype with the environment.

Diet, good or poor, may affect stature and weight; sun exposure may affect skin pigmentation; phenotypes of monozygotic twins, genetically identical individuals, may vary if the twins are raised in different environments. Thus, it is obvious that an individual's phenotype changes continuously from birth to death as glandular and maturation effects occur.

What we are, then, for the most part, is the result of the interaction of hereditary material and environmental conditions. As the well-known geneticist Theodosius Dobzhansky wrote:

> Between the genes . . . and the adult phenotypes [observable characteristics] . . . there intervenes a set of developmental processes, which . . . may be exceedingly long and elaborate. This leaves ample opportunity for the uniform primary action of a gene to yield a variety of manifestations in the developing phenotypes. . . . Which potentialities will in fact be realized in a given individual at a certain stage of his development is decided by the sequence of the environments in which the development takes place (Dobzhansky, 1970, p. 33).

A gene may be perceived as potentiality. What potentiality will actually be realized, after an "exceedingly long and elaborate" developmental process, depends upon the environmental conditions. It is this interaction between biology and environment, nature and nurture, which makes us the kind of individuals we are—physically, behaviorally, and psychically. This interaction also emphasizes the point already made in the first chapter: That humans are biocultural beings.

With this introduction to the biological basis of life in mind, let us now, in the next chapter, examine how the genetic process can be applied to the process of evolution.

Summary

We have dealt with two kinds of cells in this chapter—somatic cells, of which our bodies are composed, and sex cells, which are used only in the transmission of hereditary information.

Somatic cells divide by mitosis, producing two daughter cells identical to each other and to the mother cell. Sex cells divide twice by meiosis and produce four gametes. Meiosis is known as reduction division because the diploid number of chromosomes (46) is reduced to the haploid number (a complete set of 23).

There are 23 pairs of chromosomes in a human cell. Chromosomes with similar loci, of which there are 22 pairs, are called autosomes. The 23rd pair is the sex chromosomes.

Genetic information is contained in the DNA double helix. Information is taken from nucleus to cytoplasm by mRNA. Ribosomes in the cell translate the mRNA message and attract tRNA molecules. The tRNA molecules transport amino acids to the ribosomes, forming a polypeptide chain. A polypeptide chain (or chains) of amino acids is a protein that makes up most of the cell structure and carries out most of the cell's metabolic functions.

During DNA replication errors may occur at one point in a gene sequence. Such an error is a point mutation and could cause considerable harm. Also, within DNA there are nucleotide sequences that do not provide information for protein synthesis. These are called introns, and their precise function is not yet known.

A gene is not a discrete unit but is an orderly sequence of DNA codons that designates a specific chain of amino acids. The equation, one gene equals one polypeptide chain, is sometimes used as a definition of a gene.

Genes do not necessarily determine the precise nature of a physical characteristic. Genes are potentials modified by the environment, and it is the interaction of genes and environmental conditions that produces physical traits.

Questions for Review

1. Name the parts of a cell discussed in the chapter.
2. List the differences between mitosis and meiosis.
3. Name two important functions of meiosis.
4. Why is a pair of homologous chromosomes homologous?
5. What is the difference between a locus and a gene?
6. Why are triplets or codons referred to as "words"?
7. What is the role of chromosomes in sex determination?
8. Define DNA.
9. What different kinds of RNA are there?
10. What is the function of mRNA?
11. What is the function of ribosomes?
12. What is a nucleotide?
13. Name the four bases. Which bases complement each other in DNA?
14. What base is found in DNA but not in RNA?
15. What are the building blocks of a protein?
16. How is a chain of amino acids formed?
17. How are tRNA and mRNA matched?
18. What is the difference between codon and anticodon?
19. What is the difference between diploid and haploid?
20. Why do gametes contain the haploid instead of the diploid number?
21. What is the function of cross-over?
22. What is meant by recombination of genes?
23. How would you answer the question of nature versus nurture?
24. Why is the gene said to be a "potentiality"?
25. Give an example of how the effect of a gene may be modified by the environment.
26. How does phenotype differ from genotype?

Suggested Further Reading

Gribbin, John. *In Search of the Double Helix*, New York: Bantam Books, 1985, 1987.
The author traces the history of biological achievements leading up to the discovery of the double helix. This is not a technical book and the history is filled with interesting personal anecdotes.
Rosenfield, I. et al. *DNA for Beginners*, London: Writers and Readers Publishing Cooperative Ltd., 1983.
An easy method of learning DNA is presented in this book of cartoons. There is a text, explaining probably all you need to know, illustrated with cartoons that make it interesting, useful, and amusing.

Sayre, Ann. *Rosaline Franklin and DNA*, New York: W. W. Norton, 1978.

It could probably be claimed that Franklin discovered the double helix before Watson and Crick. Watson failed to include her contribution in his book, but Ann Sayre does.

Stebbins, G. Ledyard. *Darwin to DNA, Molecules to Humanity*, San Francisco: W. H. Freeman and Co., 1982.

An outstanding biologist, Professor Stebbins reviews evolution (including some genetics) from just about every point of view. This is another book that is written for biology nonmajors.

Stwertka, Eve and Albert. *Genetic Engineering*, New York: An Franklin Watts, 1982.

Genetic engineering has made incredible strides in the past ten years, and discoveries and inventions occur almost every day. For a guide to what genetic engineering is, this serves the purpose very well indeed. It is a small book packed with valuable information that everyone should be interested in.

Watson, James D. *The Double Helix*, New York: Atheneum, 1968.

One of the discoverers of the DNA structure, writes a short, gossipy, personal, and nontechnical account of the story of how he and Crick learned the secret of the double helix.

Yoxen, Edward. *The Gene Business*, New York: Oxford University Press, 1983. (Paperback edition.)

The title suggests the book is about the biotechnology industry, and it is. But there are several excellent chapters on how biotechnology and genetic engineering work. The author also gives a readable explanation of DNA. As an expert on the subject, Professor Yoxen also tells us what we should know about the gene business.

Note: Newspapers, weekly news magazines, popular science journals, and television frequently carry stories on biotechnology and genetic engineering. The above books will help you understand current news accounts and the continuing biological revolution.

Genetics and Evolution

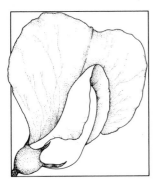

Contents

Genethics*

Genetic engineering (See Box 3-2, Chapter 3) has developed incredibly fast in the past 20 years. Breakthroughs in gene manipulation continue to accumulate; additional disease cures are frequently announced; identification of disease-causing genes is becoming common; public investments in over 1,000 genetic companies have reached into the billions of dollars, and the stock market records the ups and downs of the leading genetic corporations. Biotechnology has become big business, and predictions are that its growth limit is not yet in sight.

In these days of ecological awareness, any new industry is likely to raise ethical questions. Biotechnology, however, is special since one of its main concerns is human disease therapy based on new methods and techniques that disturb many people. A few years ago, critics warned that genetic laboratory and field experiments were dangerous, that bacteria might escape and damage human health and the area's ecology. Fortunately, through the care taken by scientists, no such catastrophes have yet occurred.

It is quite clear that the "biotech" industry is here to stay. It is also clear that ethical questions about the industry are here, if not to stay, then to be resolved. We shall discuss below a few of the problems that concerned people—scientists, members of the clergy, politicians, physicians, and many thoughtful persons—consider troublesome if ethics are not addressed.

1. Right to privacy. Should employers have the right to require a health examination as a prerequisite for employment? To

*The term is taken from the title of a book by Suzuki and Knudtson—see sources at end of chapter.

what extent should a childhood illness be considered a factor in employment? Who should evaluate a medical exam or a medical record?

Questions of this sort have taken on a new significance since biotechnology has discovered so much more about genetic diseases. Is it ethical for people without training in genetics to interpret the genetics of disease? For example, a person with one gene for sickle-cell anemia is fully capable of working. To be a victim of this disease, two genes for the disease are required. Many employers in the past denied employment to anyone with only one gene for the trait because they misunderstood the genetics.

Should your medical record be readily available to employers, insurers, credit bureaus, police, federal and state agencies, lawyers, and so forth? Should you have easy access to your own medical record? Should only a pertinent section of your record be available? "If an insurance company wants medical records to determine whether someone has an asthma condition, and that patient also saw the same doctor for a VD infection five years ago, the insurer gets that information, too" (Norton, 1989, p. 55).

Norton adds that the Medical Information Bureau, a nonprofit association, represents about 800 North American insurance companies. In addition to storing computerized medical data, the Bureau also stores nonmedical information, such as bad driving records or hazardous hobbies, on 13 million North Americans. Should insurance companies have access to this information?

2. New biotech techniques. Biotechnologists are inventing new techniques that have raised questions yet to be set-

tled. There is the Jane vs. John Doe* case of *in vitro* (test tube) fertilization that teems with ethical problems.

Failing many attempts to have children in their nine years of marriage, Jane and John turned to in vitro fertilization. Six attempts failed, and they decided to try a new program. Nine of Jane's ova were inseminated by John, two of them were implanted in Jane without success, and the remaining seven placed in cold storage.

Several months later, John filed for divorce, and shortly thereafter Jane announced her plans for implantation of an embryo. At the divorce trial, each of the parties claimed custody of the embryos. The judge ruled that Jane had the right to custody because "life begins at conception." John has appealed the case, but the appeal has not yet been heard at this writing.

Should Jane proceed with the implantation despite her ex-husband's opposition? Should the judge have based his decision on the concept that life begins at conception, or on the position that embryos are property and should be included as part of the property settlement? Was the judge's decision ethical? If so (or if not) by what criteria? If there is a child, what are John's responsibilities? Privileges?

Update: On appeal the judge decided that the embryos would be held in joint custody. Does this solve any of the ethical questions involved?

3. Medical ethics. Biotechnology's success in identifying genes that cause disease has led to knowledge about diseases that occur late in life, such as Alzheimer's and Huntington's disease. If an adult fam-

*Case is real; names are not.

ily member is found to have a gene for a late-onset disease, it is reasonable that he or she be informed. However, should it be the physician who does the informing? Would this be ethical if the physician is not trained in genetics nor in how to deal with the emotional impact of knowledge the patient must live with for the next twenty or thirty years?

Since the disease is genetic, it is possible other members of the family may also possess the gene. Should they be encouraged to find out whether they also possess the gene, even if they would rather not know? Should the parents insist that the children be tested, or would it be more compassionate to wait until they were, say, eighteen and could decide then? Should the government become involved and insist all family members be tested?

4. Fetal Tissue. Some researchers believe that fetal tissue, (the tissue of aborted fetuses) may prove useful in the treatment of Parkinson's disease and diabetes, for the study of the human immune system, in possible therapy for AIDS, for therapy against other infectious diseases, and for certain bone marrow problems.

Many objections have been made, on moral and ethical grounds, to the use of fetal tissue for research purposes. Medical researchers would argue that, since human organs are transplanted, and blood is transfused from other people, placentas are regularly used for studies in medicine, and fetal tissue itself is discarded as waste since it cannot live on its own, there should be no problem here.

The problem, of course, is abortion. Fetal tissue is derived from aborted fetuses, and it is feared that fetal tissue research will encourage induced abortions. Dr. Daniel E. Koshland, Jr., a biochemist,

points out that "Taking the kidney from a brain-dead victim of an automobile crash has not led scientists to encourage automobile accidents" (1988, p. 1733). The Reagan administration banned funds for fetal tissue research in March, 1988, and the Bush administration (in March, 1990) refused to lift the ban. Meanwhile, research continues in Europe.

In the United States, the ethical issues raised are now familiar: pro-life versus pro-choice, use of human tissue for medical experiments, use of public money when public opinion is divided, and the cost/benefits of saving human lives.

5. Biological weaponry. Poison gas has long been used in warfare, but probably not extensively until World War I, when both sides used several poison gases. It is believed that most industrial nations today have stockpiled biological weapons, ostensibly for defense purposes. Because of the secrecy involved, it is difficult to know for certain whether biological weapons are, in fact, being manufactured and stored. However, with the rapid development of biotechnology in recent years, the possibilities of the secret manufacture of poison weapons cannot be ignored. For example, it has been denied by the Iraqi government, but it is well known that poison gas was used in their conflict with the Kurds of northern Iraq.

There are two basic ethical issues here: (a) the manufacture and storage of biological weaponry and (b) the use of them. Because of government secrecy, citizens may not be aware of the extent or existence of biological weaponry factories. Nevertheless, it is a serious ethical question that many people believe must be dealt with. In 1974, at a meeting of leading molecular

scientists at Asilomar, California, one of the committees addressed the ominous possibility of using recombinant DNA techniques in weapon research. The committee issued this statement:

We believe that perhaps the greatest potential for biohazards involving alteration of microorganisms relates to possible military applications. We believe strongly that construction of genetically altered organisms for any military purpose should be expressly prohibited by international treaty, and we urge that such prohibition be agreed upon as expeditiously as possible. (Cited in Suzuki and Knudtson, p. 229.)

A major international treaty, the Biological Weapons Convention, went into effect in 1975. It was signed by about half the nations of the world, including the United States and the Soviet Union. The treaty has been criticized since it allows biological weapons research (but not production). Also, the sophistication of biotechnology today suggests the treaty be reexamined. (The chapter on this subject in Suzuki and Knudtson is worthwhile reading.)

6. Germ Cell Therapy. At the present time, genetic engineering for humans is confined to body (somatic) cells. If this proves successful—results may be seen within the next few years—would germ (sex) cell therapy be desirable?

If individuals were to be cured by genetic therapy of *body* cells, they could still transmit the disease to their offspring. This procedure would not eliminate the disease, and each generation *ad infinitum* could require treatment. One way to avoid this is to treat the germ cells. Thus, if the germ cells of everyone who possessed a disease-causing gene were altered,* the disease could not be transmitted, and all genetic diseases, in principle, could be completely eliminated.

This idea may sound utopian—a world without genetic diseases! However, majority opinion appears to be dead set against tampering with the germ cell. It is feared that opening this can of worms

_____

*This would require universal testing, another ethical problem, in order to locate defective recessive alleles.

would be more costly than the benefits that might accrue. As more is learned about which genes are responsible for which traits, and as techniques for manipulating and inserting genes improve, we could have the "slippery slope" effect. That is, once germ cell engineering begins, one thing leads to another, and it is soon out of control.

Curing a disease, even eliminating it forever, may not be a danger (but see sickle-cell, p. 69). But suppose it were possible to make people smarter. Those opposed to germ cell therapy ask, Who

decides who gets the gene? They fear scenarios such as societies divided into inherited classes of slaves, laborers, and rulers; undesirables genetically programmed out of existence; a special group playing God. They worry about who would be the regulators of such programs, and who would regulate the regulators? They wonder whether it would even be possible to control germ cell therapy in a democratic society. Would it lead to an Orwellian world, or a medical utopia? Think about it.

CHAPTER 4

Introduction

In Chapter 3, we have seen in some detail how, within the cell, genetic material is organized, packaged, distributed, and passed on to succeeding generations of cells. But when we look at the world of organisms, we see individuals who are in most cases composed of billions of cells, and our focus of organization must be shifted to a different level. In this chapter, we shall investigate the processes that allow us not only to understand, but also to predict, how genes are passed from parent to offspring. This process is the basis of the science of genetics, and its modern beginnings date to Gregor Mendel's work in the 1850s and 1860s.

Early Theories of Inheritance

For ages humans have been interested in the rules of heredity. We can easily imagine the early farmers of 10,000 years ago wondering how tiny grains produced wheat. Already in the fourth century B.C., Theophrastus, a Greek, had carefully studied seed germination and written a book on the subject. Some early Greeks believed that heredity among humans was a question of which sex dominated in the sex act. In the eighteenth century, Linnaeus suggested a two-layer theory, which held that "the outer layer including the vascular system is derived from the father, the inner layer including the nervous system comes from the mother."

An interesting theory dating as far back as Aristotle was developed further in the seventeenth century (E. Gardner, 1965, p. 275). This theory was based on the belief, called *preformation*, that "the development of an organism is no more than the unfolding of that which is already present in miniature (Fig. 4-1). Every organism must therefore contain in its reproductive organs an infinite series representing all of its future descendants." Ovists believed the female possessed this future of the series, and the spermists insisted it was the male.

While there were differences of opinion about the role of sex, and ignorance of the laws of animal heredity, plants were not generally discussed in these terms. That plants lacked sexuality was the conventional wisdom of the day. Not until the end of the seventeenth century was the presence of sex organs in plants demonstrated in the experiments performed in Germany by Rudolph Camerarius.

The notion that plants consisted of male and female parts came as a shock to many people. " 'What man,' exclaimed J. G. Siegesbeck, Professor of Botany at St. Petersburg, 'will ever believe that God Almighty should have introduced such confusion, or rather such shameful whoredom, for the propagation of the reign of plants. Who will instruct young students in such a voluptuous system without scandal?' " (Olby, 1985, pp. 18–19).

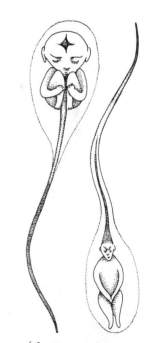

FIGURE 4-1   Some early investigators thought that they could see tiny human embryos within the sperm.

The discovery of sexual reproduction in plants was a notable achievement not simply because it added to our knowledge of plants, but also because it makes possible an experimental approach to plant hybridization. Once begun by Camerarius, crossing hybrids and observing what regularities might occur among the offspring became one of the most popular methods of investigating the laws of heredity.

Hybridization experiments continued in the eighteenth and nineteenth centuries. Hybrids offered an opportunity, it was believed, to work out the rules of heredity. Purebred plants produced purebreds, and there was little to learn about heredity from that kind of experiment. Among the offspring of hybrids, on the other hand, some resembled the parents, but others were quite different. If, in this apparent confusion of offspring, there were regularities of such traits as form, color, or germination patterns, they would serve as clues to the principles of heredity.

Or so it seemed. Many investigators worked on plant hybrids, but the secrets of heredity eluded them. Experimenters demonstrated, for example, that neither sex was entirely responsible for offspring but both parents contributed equally. They also demonstrated that hybrids did not breed true (as Linneaus believed they did), yet the laws of heredity remained undiscovered.

There were several reasons for this failure. The plants used were not the proper ones for the study of heredity—they were genetically too complex for the kind of observations possible at that time. Experimenters did not work with enough plants, or through sufficient generations, to find regularities. And, finally, they did not count the offspring of hybrids; that is, they failed to examine the results of their experiments from a statistical point of view. What the early experimenters saw were offspring in a confusing variety of forms and colors, which they were unable to clarify. Their conclusion was that clarification was impossible, that there probably were no universal laws of heredity.

Thus matters stood, more or less at a standstill as far as the laws of heredity were concerned, until Gregor Mendel solved the riddle in the 1860s.

Mendel's Life

Gregor Mendel (1822–1884), shown in Figure 4-2, was born into a family of peasant farmers, in the small Silesian village of Heinzendorf in what we now call Czechoslovakia. At school, he did so well in his academic studies that his teachers recommended he be transferred to a high school in a nearby town. Within a year, he had moved on to the Gymnasium (an advanced high school) at Troppau where, in 1840, he received a certificate which recognized his "great industry and all-round ability."

To continue his studies, he enrolled in the University Philosophical Institute of Olmutz. Because of lack of funds, Mendel had a difficult time, and his attempts to earn money as a private tutor failed. He wrote of this period of his life (in the third person): "The sorrow over these disappointed hopes and the anxious, sad outlook which the future offered him, affected him so powerfully at that time that he fell sick and was compelled to spend a year with his parents to recover!" (in Olby, 1985, p. 106).

FIGURE 4-2   Gregor Mendel.

FIGURE 4-3 Central Europe during Mendel's lifetime.

In 1841, Mendel returned to the university, and this time succeeded in finding part-time tutorial work, but he worked so hard his health failed again. In 1843, he discussed his future with one of his professors, Friedrich Franz, who suggested a monastery as a place that would provide the quiet kind of life Mendel required. He encouraged Mendel to apply to the monastery at Brünn and recommended him as "a young man of very solid character. In my own branch [physics] he is almost the best" (in Olby, 1985, p. 107). Mendel followed Franz' advice, was admitted as a novice on October 9, 1843, and took the name of Gregor.

Early on, it became clear that Mendel was not temperamentally suited to serve as a parish priest, since he could not witness suffering without falling ill himself. The understanding abbot of the monastery assigned him as a substitute teacher to a high school in a nearby town, and Mendel soon became known as an excellent teacher. He could not be given a permanent appointment because he lacked a teacher's certificate, and for him to obtain this document, he had to take courses at the University of Vienna.

It was at Vienna, where he came into contact with leading professors in botany, physics, and mathematics, that Mendel acquired his scientific education. His studies there helped him in his later experiments, especially in his mathematical approach, which was so different from that of other plant experimenters.

Upon completing his studies at Vienna, Mendel returned to the monastery and resumed his teaching career, as well as his work in the monastery garden. He had been experimenting for some time with the fertilization of flowers, attempting to develop new variations in colors. What impressed Mendel was the "striking regularity with which the same hybrid forms always reappeared when fertilization took place between the same species," which induced him "to follow up the development of the hybrids in their progeny."

Mendel's Experiments

Mendel was well aware that no laws governing the formation and development of hybrids had yet been formulated, and he was also aware that hybridization experiments were very difficult. Nevertheless, he decided to proceed with his experiments and had definite ideas of how to go about it. He pointed out that not one experiment

> had been carried out to such an extent and in such a way as to make it possible to determine the number of different forms under which the offspring of hybrids appear,

FIGURE 4-4   The church next to the monastery at Brünn (as it looks today), where Mendel spent much of his life.

or to arrange these forms with certainty according to their separate generations, or definitely to ascertain their statistical relation (Mendel, 1965, pp. 1–2).

What Mendel decided to do apparently even before he began his experiments on hybrids was: (a) to determine the number of different forms of hybrids produced; (b) to arrange the forms according to generations—F_2, F_3, etc.; and (c) to attempt to evaluate the statistical relations (the proportions) of the various forms.

These three points, wrote the eminent geneticist of the early twentieth century, William Bateson, led to "the whole success of Mendel's work. . . . So far as I know this conception was absolutely new in his day" (Mendel, 1965, p. 2n). They are the basis of modern biological research.

Selection of Plants   Before discussing Mendel's actual experiments and his conclusions, one more point should be considered, for it illustrates Mendel's genius compared to other plant hybridizers. This point concerns the *kind* of plant to be used. "The value and utility of any experiment," Mendel noted in the paper he read at a meeting of the Natural History Society of Brünn in February, 1865, "are determined by the fitness of the material to the purpose for which it is used, and thus in the case before us it cannot be immaterial what plants are subjected to experiment and in what manner such experiments are conducted" (Mendel, 1965, p. 2). He went on to say that the selection of the plant "must be made with all possible care" and two qualifying conditions *must* be met: that the plant (1) possess constant differentiating characters and (2) the hybrids of such plants be protected from foreign pollen.

By constant differentiating characters—a most important point—Mendel meant that the plant must possess two contrasting characters of the same trait. If color were the trait, then the plant should possess two contrasting colors; if stature, then tall and short. These conditions led Mendel to devote his attention to

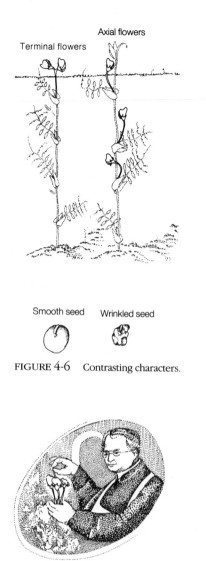

Terminal flowers   Axial flowers

Smooth seed   Wrinkled seed

FIGURE 4-6   Contrasting characters.

FIGURE 4-7   Mendel cross-fertilizing his plants by hand.

legumes, and experiments with several members of this group led him to the genus *Pisum*, the common garden pea.

Clearly, Mendel knew what he was doing from the very beginning. Unlike those who preceded him, he concentrated on the underlying genetic factors, what we today call genes. He proposed to follow the progress of the hybrids through a number of generations, counting the number of different types of hybrid progeny. He would carefully select the kind of plant that possessed the traits he considered necessary for the experiment, contrasting characters and fertility for a number of successive generations. Finally, he planned to use a large number of plants, so that the uniqueness of a small number of seeds would not bias the results.

From several nurserymen, Mendel obtained thirty-four varieties of peas, and, after checking them during a two-year trial, he selected twenty-two varieties for fertilization. Most of them belonged to the species *Pisum sativum*. As already noted, Mendel deliberately planned to use a plant that possessed at least one set of contrasting characters. With luck (insight, more probably), he selected the pea with *seven* characteristics (see Table 4-1). Had this not been the case, it is doubtful his experiments would have succeeded.

THE PEA EXPERIMENTS—P_1 GENERATION

Mendel launched his experiment in the spring of 1856. He divided the garden into sections, one for each of the seven characters of the pea. He placed contrasting characters next to each other so they would be easier to compare. Smooth seeds went next to wrinkled; yellow next to green; tall next to dwarf.

When the plants were ready to blossom, Mendel opened the flower buds of each plant and performed the surgery necessary to prevent the peas from fertilizing themselves in the normal manner. He then proceeded to do the cross-fertilizing himself (Fig. 4-7). Altogether, Mendel made 287 cross-fertilizations on 70 plants and then waited for the plants to mature in what the other monks called "Mendel's pea plantation."

F_1 Generation   The offspring of the P_1 cross (Fig. 4-8*a*) are designated as the F_1 generation, and when the F_1 generation matured, Mendel observed the seeds. They were all smooth (as in Fig. 4-8*a*). He then grew plants from these F_1 smooth

TABLE 4-1   **The Seven Characteristics of the Garden Pea Mendel Selected**

| | CONTRASTING | |
CHARACTERISTICS	*Dominant Traits*	*Recessive Traits*
1. form of the ripe seed	smooth	wrinkled
2. color of seed albumen	yellow	green
3. color of seed coat	gray	white
4. form of ripe pods	inflated	constricted
5. color of unripe pods	green	yellow
6. position of flowers	axial	terminal
7. length of stem	tall	dwarf

seeds and, when the plants matured, allowed them to self-fertilize (Fig. 4-8*b*). Mendel then examined the offspring of the F_1 generation of smooth peas and found that in this generation (F_2) there were both smooth seeds *and* wrinkled seeds (Fig. 4-8*c*). When he carefully counted the numbers of each, they added up to 5,474 smooth seeds and 1,850 wrinkled, a ratio of 2.96 to 1. Among the other traits, the ratios (Table 4-2) were slightly over or under 3:1, and the average ratio of all the seeds of all the traits in the F_2 generation was 3:1 (Fig. 4-8).

Mendel now saw clearly that when F_1 hybrids are bred, three offspring are produced that resemble one P_1 grandparent for every one offspring that resembles the other P_1 grandparent. The character that appeared three times, Mendel called **dominant**, and that which appeared once, **recessive**.

F_2 Generation The experiment continued through another (F_3) generation. The plants of the F_2 generation were allowed to self-fertilize, and once more Mendel carefully counted the results. He found that one-half of the F_2 plants produced smooth and wrinkled seeds at a ratio of 3:1; one-fourth produced only smooth seeds; and one-fourth produced only wrinkled seeds. Since the one-half that produced a 3:1 ratio of smooth to wrinkled seeds behaved in exactly the same way as the F_1 hybrids, Mendel reasoned that these must also be **hybrids**, or **heterozygotes** (Fig. 4-8).

... it is now clear [said Mendel] that the hybrids form seeds having one or the other of the two differentiating characters, and of these one-half develop again the hybrid form, while the other half yield plants which remain constant and receive the dominant or the recessive characters in equal numbers (Mendel, 1965, p. 13).

EXPERIMENT RESULTS—THE RIDDLE SOLVED

Using current terminology, we would say that one-half of the F_2 generation plants must be heterozygous, since they produced a 3:1 ratio just as the F_1 hybrids did. One-fourth of the F_2 plants produced only smooth seeds; therefore, they must be **homozygous** dominant. The remaining one-fourth produced only wrinkled seeds; therefore, they must be homozygous recessive. This led to Mendel's conclusion that the genotypic ratio is 1:2:1 for the F_2 generation:

¼ homozygous dominant
½ heterozygous dominant = 1 : 2 : 1
¼ homozygous recessive   SS : Ss : ss

Dominant A trait determined by a dominant allele. A trait that is visible or measurable and that prevents the appearance of the recessive. The allele for smooth seeds is dominant and when present "prevents" the appearance of wrinkled seeds.

Recessive A trait determined by the recessive allele. A trait is not visible or measurable when paired with the dominant allele. The heterozygote Ss possesses both the dominant and recessive allele, but the wrinkling is not expressed phenotypically. (S = uppercase of first letter of dominant trait; used as symbol for dominant trait. s = lowercase of dominant symbol, used as a symbol for recessive trait.)

Hybrid The progeny resulting from a cross of different parental stock.

Heterozygote A cell or individual that is heterozygous. (A hybrid is heterozygous for a particular trait.) A person who is AO is heterozygous for ABO blood system; an F_1 round pea (Ss) is heterozygous for form.

Heterozygous Having different alleles at a given locus on a pair of homologous chromosomes.

Generation
P_1 The parental generation in which homozygous dominants and recessives are crossed. Parents pure or homozygous for smooth seeds and parents homozygous for wrinkled represent such a parental cross.

F_1 First filial generation. The offspring resulting from a parental cross of homozygotes for different alleles.

F_2 Second filial generation. The offspring resulting from a cross of F_1 individuals (or self-fertilization of F_1 individuals, where this is possible).

Homozygous Having the same allele at a given locus on a pair of homologous chromosomes.

Homozygote A cell or individual that is homozygous. (A purebred is homozygous for a particular trait.) A pea that is SS or ss is a homozygote.

TABLE 4-2 **The Ratios of Mendel's Experiment**

CHARACTERISTICS	NUMBERS OF PEAS		RATIO
1. form of ripe seed	5,474 smooth	1,850 wrinkled	2.96:1
2. color of seed	6,022 yellow	2,001 green	3.01:1
3. color of seed coat	705 gray	224 white	3.15:1
4. form of ripe pods	882 inflated	299 constricted	2.95:1
5. color of unripe pods	428 green	152 yellow	2.82:1
6. position of flowers	651 axial	207 terminal	3.14:1
7. length of stem	787 tall	277 dwarf	2.84:1

FIGURE 4-8 Gregor Mendel's logic.
Mendel concluded: (1) the ½ of F$_2$ plants that
produced a 3:1 ratio of smooth to wrinkled
were the same as the F$_1$ smooths that produced
a 3:1 ratio—therefore ½ of the F$_2$ plants *must
be hybrids* (heterozygous); (2) the ¼ of the F$_2$
plants that produced only smooth seeds must
be homozygous for smooth; (3) the ¼ of the F$_2$
plants that produced only wrinkled must be
homozygous for wrinkled; (4) hybrid forms
yield a genotypic ratio of 1:2:1 (that is,
1:homozygous dominant to 2:heterozygous
dominant to 1:homozygous recessive).

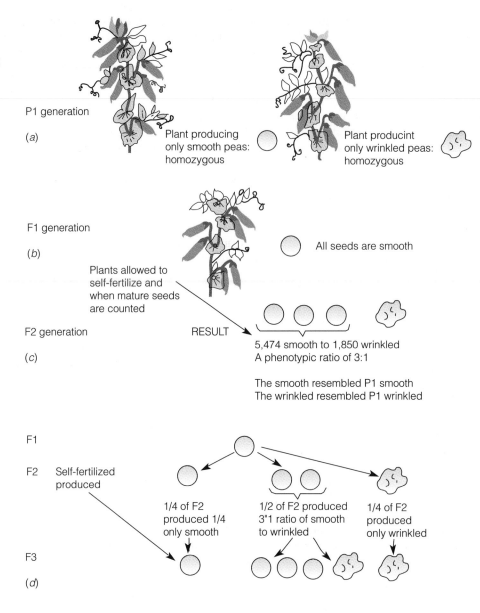

P1 generation

(a)

Plant producing
only smooth peas:
homozygous

Plant producint
only wrinkled peas:
homozygous

F1 generation

(b)

All seeds are smooth

Plants allowed to
self-fertilize and
when mature seeds
are counted

F2 generation   RESULT

(c)

5,474 smooth to 1,850 wrinkled
A phenotypic ratio of 3:1

The smooth resembled P1 smooth
The wrinkled resembled P1 wrinkled

F1

F2   Self-fertilized
        produced

1/4 of F2
produced 1/4
only smooth

1/2 of F2 produced
3"1 ratio of smooth
to wrinkled

1/4 of F2
produced
only wrinkled

F3

(d)

    Mendel continued his experiments through several succeeding generations,
and the results reinforced conclusions already reached. He had succeeded bril-
liantly where others had failed. By carefully selecting the proper experimental
plant, by using a large number of plants, and—perhaps, most importantly—by
carefully counting the numbers and kinds of offspring, Mendel had accomplished
two goals: (1) he clarified the confusion surrounding the reproduction of hybrids;
and (2) he discovered the laws of heredity. For a modest, unknown amateur this
achievement was indeed remarkable.
    We should point out that this method of experimental breeding was simple, but
original and unique. Moreover, the experiments were *deliberately designed to test
a theory*, a new idea in biology (Dunn, 1965, p. 193).

Mendel's Report   After eight years of constant work, Mendel was at long last prepared to report on his findings, and, at the February, 1865, meeting of the Natural History Society of Brünn, Mendel read his paper. Members of the society, familiar with the methodology of more traditional botanists, were confused by his ideas. The next month, when Mendel presented his algebraic equations, the lack of understanding was even greater. The idea that "heredity was the giant shuffling and reshuffling of separate and invisible hereditary factors" was so different from what had been taught that it was probably incomprehensible. When Mendel finished his report, no one rose to ask a question, and the minutes of the society record no discussion.

The society published the monograph Mendel had prepared and copies were sent, as was the custom, to cities throughout Europe, but it attracted no attention. Mendel was disappointed. He was aware of the significance of his work and decided to send his report to one of Europe's outstanding botanists, Karl von Naegeli of Munich. Naegeli obviously failed to understand the experiment and replied in a condescending letter that Mendel's work was "far from being finished." Thus, a second opportunity for science to learn the rules of heredity was lost, not to be rediscovered until 1900.

In 1868, at the age of 46, Mendel was elected abbot of the monastery and, because of heavy administrative duties, he was unable to continue his scientific work. He died January 6, 1884, a beloved figure in the town of Brünn but unknown to the world of science.

Alleles   Alternative forms of the same gene. (In the ABO blood system, A, B, and O are alternative forms found at the same locus. In a population where alternative forms are available at a particular locus, they are called alleles. The gene for smooth seeds and the gene for wrinkled seeds are such alternative forms.)

GENES, CHROMOSOMES, AND MENDEL

With this brief survey, let us now examine more systematically the rules of heredity Mendel discovered. First, it may be useful to summarize pertinent information regarding genes and chromosomes already presented in Chapter 3.

Somatic cells carry two sets of chromosomes to make up a full complement (46 in humans), the diploid number. On a pair of homologous chromosomes there is a number of loci, and at each locus on the pair is genetic material (a segment of DNA—a gene) that affects a particular trait. Thus, in any individual there are two genes for each trait. There may be several loci, by the way, that affect the same trait (stature, say), but, for our purpose, it is sufficient to deal with only one locus at a time. These are called simple or Mendelian traits and follow Mendelian ratios. If at a locus there is genetically coded material, let us say, for smooth seeds or genetically coded material for wrinkled seeds, then these different forms of the gene are known as **alleles**. Alleles are similar, but slightly different, sequences of DNA that control the same trait. Normal hemoglobin and sickling hemoglobin discussed in the preceding chapter are examples of alleles for the same trait. With this review, we return to Mendel's rules.

PRINCIPLE OF SEGREGATION

Dominant and Recessive Cross   In his experiment with peas, Mendel obtained seeds that were homozygous. He tested them by planting to make sure that those intended to produce smooth seeds did so, and those for wrinkled seeds produced only wrinkled. The second step was to cross the plants producing only

FIGURE 4-9   Dominance.

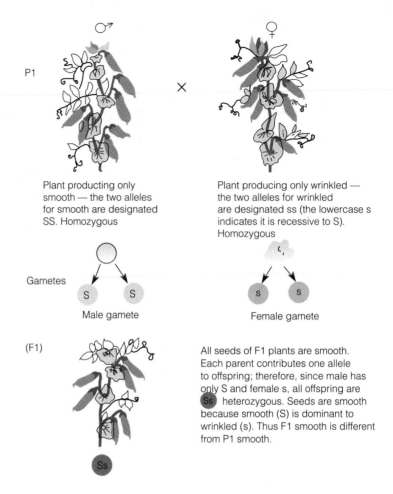

P1

Plant producing only
smooth — the two alleles
for smooth are designated
SS. Homozygous

Plant producing only wrinkled —
the two alleles for wrinkled
are designated ss (the lowercase s
indicates it is recessive to S).
Homozygous

Gametes

S   S

Male gamete

s   s

Female gamete

(F1)

All seeds of F1 plants are smooth.
Each parent contributes one allele
to offspring; therefore, since male has
only S and female s, all offspring are
Ss heterozygous. Seeds are smooth
because smooth (S) is dominant to
wrinkled (s). Thus F1 smooth is different
from P1 smooth.

Ss

smooth seeds with plants producing only wrinkled seeds.* The offspring of this cross were all smooth even though the sex cells of the plant contained an allele for wrinkled (Fig. 4-9). They were all smooth, as we know, because smooth is dominant to wrinkled. Please note that, phenotypically, the seeds are smooth, but, genotypically, both alleles are present, Ss, or heterozygous. The F_1 smooth (Ss) are genotypically different from their P_1 smooth (SS) parent (Fig. 4-9).

How is the difference between the F_1 and P_1 smooth seeds to be explained? Both seeds are phenotypically smooth, but the genotypes are different. Recalling the meiotic process, we know that after cell division a gamete contains one set of chromosomes, the haploid number. Therefore, the gamete contains only one of the alleles for a particular trait. To take Mendel's example, the parent plants each contained two genes for either smoothness or wrinkledness. Because of meiotic division, each parent contributes only one. Since both parents are homozygous— one for smooth and the other for wrinkled—one parent would have to contribute an S allele and the other an s allele (Fig. 4-10).

The offspring in the F_1 generation possess both alleles, the big S from one parent and the small s from the other. Thus, the offspring are hybrid, or heterozygous.

---

*In our discussion, we shall use the smooth and wrinkled traits. Mendel, of course, experimented with all seven traits, and the results in every case were similar.

Heterozygous Cross—3:1 Phenotypic Ratio In the next step of the experiment, Mendel allowed these F_1 heterozygotes to fertilize themselves (pea plants contain both male and female parts). Although fertilization occurs within one plant, the male and female sex cells may be diagrammed thus:

$$Ss \times Ss$$

The result of this self-fertilization, as we have seen, was the production of three smooth seeds for every wrinkled. What happened in the F_1 cross to produce a 3:1 ratio? Bearing in mind what we know of meiosis, homologous chromosomes, and alleles, it is only necessary to add one point, the element of chance.

We know that as a result of meiosis a parent can contribute, at any one time, only one of a pair of chromosomes and therefore only one of two alleles for a trait. In this case, each parent will contribute either S *or* s. There is an even chance that the male S will combine with the female S or with the female s. Similarly, the odds are even that the male s will combine with the female S or s. In other words, there are four, and only four, possible combinations. Each combination has an equal chance, a one out of four (or 25%) chance of occurring (Fig. 4-11).

Since smooth, S, is dominant, a smooth seed must contain at least one gene for smooth, S. In the F_2 generation, Mendel counted three smooth seeds for every wrinkled, which means that three-fourths (or 75%) of the seeds contained at least

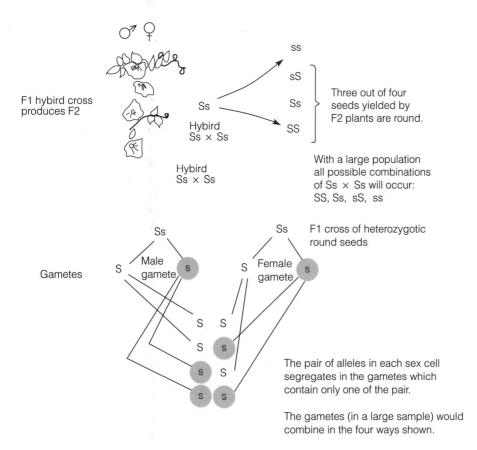

FIGURE 4-10   Segregation of gametes.

F1 hybird cross produces F2

Ss
Hybird
Ss × Ss

Hybird
Ss × Ss

ss
sS
Ss
SS

Three out of four seeds yielded by F2 plants are round.

With a large population all possible combinations of Ss × Ss will occur: SS, Ss, sS, ss

Ss

Ss   F1 cross of heterozygotic round seeds

Gametes

S   Male gamete   s

S   Female gamete   s

S   S
S   s
s   S
s   s

The pair of alleles in each sex cell segregates in the gametes which contain only one of the pair.

The gametes (in a large sample) would combine in the four ways shown.

FIGURE 4-11   Gametic combinations.

Male gamete with S may fertilize female gamete with S   =   SS

Male gamete with S may fertilize female gamete with s   =   Ss

Male gamete with s may fertilize female gamete with S   =   sS

Male gamete with s may fertilize female gamete with s   =   ss

one gene for smooth, S. A glance at Figure 4-10 indicates that this percentage is exactly correct. The fourth combination, ss, does not contain a big S; therefore, that seed cannot be smooth. A seed with two alleles for wrinkled—ss—must be phenotypically wrinkled.

An illustration using heads and tails of two coins might possibly let us see the situation more clearly. Let us say we have a dime and a quarter, both of which are tossed in the air simultaneously. What possible combinations will come up, and what are the chances of these combinations? The possibilities, as we see in Figure 4-12, are two heads, two tails, and one heads and one tails. The latter combination can occur in two ways: quarter heads and dime tails, or dime heads and quarter tails. Thus, there are four possible combinations.

What are the chances of any one of these combinations coming up? Well, if you were to wager on the toss of one coin, you would have a 50% chance of calling the right combination. You have as much chance of winning the bet as your partner. In our illustration, however, you are betting on the simultaneous toss of *two* coins, so the chances of calling the correct combination are cut to 25%, exactly half of the first. Since there are four possible combinations, you have one chance in four of any one combination turning up.

Statistically, that is precisely the situation with the smooth and wrinkled peas, and it was Mendel's insight that perceived this when none of his predecessors had done so. Perhaps it was Mendel's training in mathematics at the university that enabled him to approach his experiments from a statistical point of view.

FIGURE 4-12   Possible combinations of coins. If any two coins are tossed many times, the probability is that each combination would come up the same number of times. Since there are four combinations, each combination will turn up 25% of the time. Or, in other words, there is a 25% chance of any one combination coming up. If you were betting on the toss, which combination would be your best bet? Heads/tails, of course, because there are two ways in which this combination could turn up. Therefore, there is a two out of four, or 50% chance of its success, whereas there is only a 25% chance of two heads or two tails coming up.

Mendel could not have worked the statistics out had he used only a few plants. To flip a coin ten times and expect it to come up heads five times and tails five times is unreasonable. A thousand flips might average 500 heads and 500 tails. Similarly, Mendel was aware, as we have seen, that a large number of plants are required to achieve a complete random assortment. When Mendel counted all the dominant and recessive characters of the seven traits, he found an average **phenotypic ratio** of 2.98 to 1, which he considered to be a 3:1 ratio.

Mendel's explanation for the 3:1 ratio solved the riddle of heredity. He suggested that the characters (alleles) are paired and *segregated* when they are passed on from one generation to the next. That is, the allele on one chromosome does not normally affect the allele at the same locus on the paired chromosome. We might say each allele goes its own way. Therefore, the capital S in the male influences inheritance separately from the influence of the lowercase s, and similarly with the female. (We have seen how this separation operated during meiosis.) This is Mendel's first law, called the **principle of segregation**, which states that alleles, the units of heredity, exist within individuals in pairs. The pairs are segregated during the production of gametes, so that a gamete has only one of each kind.

Interestingly, Mendel was not the first to observe this 3:1 ratio. In 1820, an Englishman named John Goss carried out an experiment very similar to Mendel's, even to the extent of using peas. When the hybrids produced a mixture of dominants and recessives, he merely pointed out the facts but did not count the numbers of each. He failed to see the significance of the ratio of dominants to recessives. Perhaps even more curious is Darwin's experience with snapdragons. Darwin crossed normal and irregular snapdragons and in the F_1 generation all the offspring were normal. When he bred the F_1 normal snapdragons, the offspring were normal to irregular at roughly a 3:1 ratio. Darwin noted the F_1 uniformity and the mixture of the F_2 generation, but the significance of the 3:1 proportion escaped him also (Iltis, 1966, pp. 118–127).

PRINCIPLE OF INDEPENDENT ASSORTMENT

Having solved the problem of the 3:1 ratio, Mendel's next task was to determine whether what he called "the law of development" also applied to a cross of two different traits (a dihybrid cross). For this experiment he used the traits of form, smooth/wrinkled—Ss—and color, yellow/green—Yy. He crossed smooth and wrinkled peas with yellow and green peas, and he found the results were the same as in the first experiment. The proportions in the F_2 generation for color and form of seeds were:

9 smooth and yellow—both traits dominant

3 smooth and green—smooth dominant, green recessive

3 wrinkled and yellow—wrinkled recessive, yellow dominant

1 wrinkled and green—both traits recessive

When the numbers of smooth and wrinkled seeds are totaled, a proportion of 12 smooth to 4 wrinkled, or a 3:1 phenotypic ratio, emerges. When the number of yellow (dominant) and green seeds are totaled, we find 12 yellow to 4 green, also a 3:1 phenotypic ratio.

Phenotypic ratio The ratio of phenotypes, especially from a hybrid cross. Mendel's famous F_1 hybrid cross of peas produced a 3:1 phenotypic ratio.

Principle of segregation Genes occur in pairs. In the production of a gamete, the pair is separated so that each gamete contains only one of the pair.

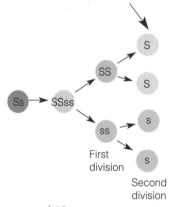

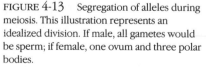

FIGURE 4-13 Segregation of alleles during meiosis. This illustration represents an idealized division. If male, all gametes would be sperm; if female, one ovum and three polar bodies.

FIGURE 4-14 Mendel's principle of
independent assortment.

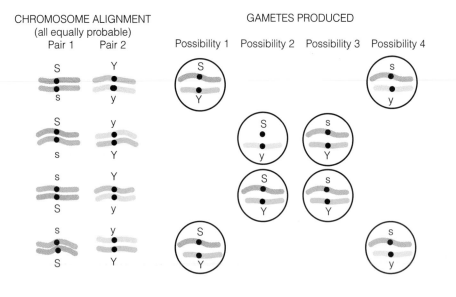

CHROMOSOME ALIGNMENT
(all equally probable)
Pair 1   Pair 2

GAMETES PRODUCED

Possibility 1   Possibility 2   Possibility 3   Possibility 4

Principle of independent assortment
The separation of one pair of genes does not
influence the separation of other pairs of genes.

Conclusion: Gene pairs on one set of homologous chromosomes do not influence the distribution of gene pairs on other chromosomes; they separate independently from one another during meiosis, and are randomly assorted in the gametes.* This phenomenon is known as Mendel's second law, the **principle of independent assortment** (Figs. 4-14, 4-16).

Random Assortment   Mendel was not aware of the precise cellular mechanism that caused this random assortment of one trait with respect to another.
However, a brief glance at our earlier discussion of meiosis (p. 59) quickly solves
the mystery. As you will recall, when homologous pairs of chromosomes align
along the equator of a cell, the relative positions of one homologous pair are independent of all other pairs.

Simply stated, this is the process of *random assortment*. The independent assortment of traits observed by Mendel is the direct result of the random assortment of chromosomes that respectively carry those traits.

Figure 4-16 shows two pairs of chromosomes in an F_1 (heterozygous) pea
plant, each containing one of the two traits discussed above (color of seed, shape
of seed). As can be seen, the way the chromosomes align during meiosis directly
affects the combination of alleles in the resulting gametes, which, in turn, combine to produce individuals exhibiting the phenotypic ratios of observed traits
(smooth and yellow, smooth and green, etc.).

Possible Alignments   There are four equally possible ways the chromosomes
can align, and four different kinds of gametes that can be produced in this manner
in each parent. This recombination of genes—by random assortment of chromosomes—leads to all the combinations of traits we observe in different individuals
in the next generation.

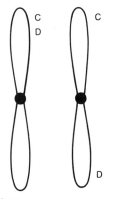

FIGURE 4-15   Crossing-over in chromosomes. Genes are more likely to cross-over and
recombine when they are far apart (right) than
when they are close together (left).

_____

*Actually, not all the characteristics chosen by Mendel are governed by loci on different chromosomes,
but most gene-pairs do assort randomly.

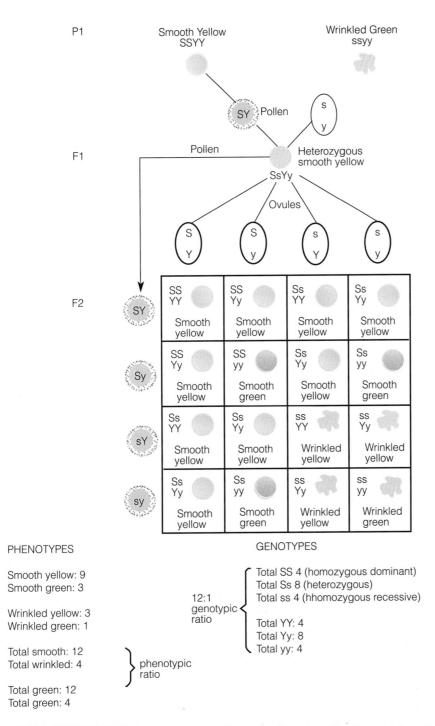

P1

Smooth Yellow
SSYY

Wrinkled Green
ssyy

SY Pollen

s
y

F1

Pollen

Heterozygous
smooth yellow

SsYy

Ovules

S
Y

S
y

s
Y

s
y

F2

SY

| SS YY Smooth yellow | SS Yy Smooth yellow | Ss YY Smooth yellow | Ss Yy Smooth yellow |

Sy

| SS Yy Smooth yellow | SS yy Smooth green | Ss Yy Smooth yellow | Ss yy Smooth green |

sY

| Ss YY Smooth yellow | Ss Yy Smooth yellow | ss YY Wrinkled yellow | ss Yy Wrinkled yellow |

sy

| Ss Yy Smooth yellow | Ss yy Smooth green | ss Yy Wrinkled yellow | ss yy Wrinkled green |

FIGURE 4-16   Dihybrid cross; principle of independent assortment. Shape (smooth and wrinkled) has no effect on color (yellow and green). The phenotypic ratios for both shape and color are 3:1, as in the cross of a single trait. Similarly, the genotypic ratio—1:2:1—is the same for both traits.

PHENOTYPES

Smooth yellow: 9
Smooth green: 3

Wrinkled yellow: 3
Wrinkled green: 1

Total smooth: 12
Total wrinkled: 4 } phenotypic ratio

Total green: 12
Total green: 4

GENOTYPES

12:1 genotypic ratio {
Total SS 4 (homozygous dominant)
Total Ss 8 (heterozygous)
Total ss 4 (hhomozygous recessive)

Total YY: 4
Total Yy: 8
Total yy: 4

If Mendel had used just *any* two traits for recombination, the phenotypic ratios would quite possibly not have conformed to those expected by independent assortment (9:3:3:1). The ratio came out as he predicted, because the traits Mendel chose to observe were carried on different chromosomes (see footnote, p. 94). Had the two traits *both* been carried on the *same* chromosome, the alleles for the two traits would not have assorted independently but would have been transmitted together.

An exception may be produced by the process of crossing-over (see p. 61). Even if carried on the same chromosome, genes can and usually do cross-over independently of each other *if* they are not located too closely together. In this case, all four possible recombinations of alleles (CD, Cd, cD, cd) may be produced, and the expected ratios of independent assortment (9:3:3:1) may be approached (Fig. 4-15). This phenomenon explains why most of Mendel's traits appeared to assort independently.

Genotypic Ratio Going one step further, Mendel also demonstrated that the genotypic ratio for form and color remained the same as it did in his first experiment with the contrasting characters of only one trait. The ratio of homozygous dominant, SS, to heterozygous, Ss, to homozygous recessive, ss, is 1:2:1. (The entire process from the parental generation to the F_2 generation is shown schematically in Fig. 4-16.) The proportions for color, YY, Yy, yy, are of course the same, 1:2:1.

In summary, Mendel demonstrated, and cellular biology has confirmed, that there are regularities or laws of heredity. The laws may be explained in the following manner:

1. Each individual possesses two alleles for a particular trait.
2. During meiosis, the two alleles from each parent segregate into different gametes (principle of segregation). This means that a parent contributes only one of the two alleles to an offspring.
3. If each parent contributes a different allele for a particular trait (such as S or s), a hybrid (heterozygote) results.
4. When the two heterozygotes are crossed, or self-fertilized, there is an even chance that each of the two alleles from one parent will combine with each of the two alleles from the other parent. A male Ss and a female Ss can combine in four ways: SS, Ss, sS, ss. (In a large population, the result of such a hybrid cross would produce 25% SS, 25% Ss, 25% sS, and 25% ss. If we combine the two Ss, then the genotypic ratio would be 25% SS, 50% Ss, 25% ss, or 1:2:1.)
5. When two traits are crossed, each pair assorts independently of the other (principle of independent assortment).

The concept of two alleles for each trait—that the two alleles segregate independently of one another, that a parent contributes one of the two, that alleles from parents enter into all possible combinations with each other, that alleles during meiosis segregate into separate gametes—all of these made sense of what appeared to be unintelligible confusion in the process of heredity.

Professor L. C. Dunn has nicely summed up Mendel's contribution:

> . . . his work has served as a kind of constructional keystone upon which subsequent developments of genetics have rested. The discovery of the statistical unit of heredity has turned out to be the spearhead of a changing conception of living matter which has penetrated and illuminated all of the major questions of biology (Dunn, 1965, p. 197).

It would be pleasing to report that Mendel's experiments and conclusions were swiftly accepted by an eager community of scientists that immediately applied his conclusions to the development of genetic research. Unfortunately, the case was otherwise. Mendel's methods were ahead of his time. It was not until 1900, thirty-five years after he read his paper before the Natural History Society of Brünn, that three geneticists—Hugo de Vries in Holland, Erich von Tschermak in Austria, and

Carl Correns in Germany—working independently of one another, discovered for themselves the laws Mendel had already formulated. Genetics had lost thirty-five years.

Modern Theory of Evolution

Following the rediscovery of Mendel's work in 1900, attention quickly turned to the study of genetics in animals, particularly humans. In 1902, Archibald Garrod identified the pattern of incidence in a metabolic disorder called *alkaptonuria* as a clear example of Mendelian inheritance in humans. Since that time the catalog of human traits known to operate in simple Mendelian fashion has grown steadily. Recent advances in biochemical techniques have greatly aided this research; the list now includes almost 5,000 such traits (McKusick, 1990). In addition, great advances have been made in chromosome mapping, and approximately 1,500 have been at least provisionally pinpointed to specific human chromosomes (McKusick, 1990).

By the beginning of the twentieth century, the essential foundations for evolutionary theory had already been developed. Darwin and Wallace had articulated the key principle of natural selection forty years earlier, and the rediscovery of Mendelian genetics contributed the other major component—a mechanism for inheritance. We might expect that these two basic contributions would have been joined rather quickly into a consistent theory of evolution. However, such was not the case. For the first thirty years of this century, geneticists (working with experimental animals, such as fruit flies) emphasized sharp contrasts within particular characteristics of organisms. As such, evolution was seen as a process of fairly large radical "jumps," and this "mutationist" view came to be seen as an alternative to the "selectionist" tradition.

A *synthesis* of these two views was not achieved until the mid-1930s, and we owe much of our current view of the evolutionary process to this intellectual development. (See Box 4-1.)

THE MODERN SYNTHESIS

Biologists working on mathematical models of evolutionary change in the late 1920s and early 1930s came to realize that genetic and selective processes were not opposing themes, but that a comprehensive explanation of organic evolution required *both*. Small new changes in the genetic material—transmitted from parent to offspring by strict Mendelian principles—are, in fact, the fuel for natural selection. The two major foundations of the biological sciences had thus been brought together in what Julian Huxley termed the "modern synthesis."

From such a "modern" (that is, the middle of the twentieth century onwards) perspective we define evolution as a two-stage process:

1. Production and redistribution of **variation** (inherited differences between individuals).
2. **Natural selection** acts on this variation (inherited differences, or variation, among individuals differentially affect their ability to reproduce successfully).

BOX 4-1

Development of Modern Evolutionary Theory

Our modern understanding of the evolutionary process came about through contributions of biologists in the United States, Great Britain, and the Soviet Union.

While "mutationists" were arguing with "selectionists" about the single primary mechanism in evolution, several population geneticists began to realize that both small genetic changes and natural selection were necessary ingredients in the evolutionary formula.

These population geneticists were largely concerned with mathematical reconstructions of evolution—in particular, measuring those small accumulations of genetic changes in populations over just a few generations. Central figures in these early theoretical developments included Ronald Fisher and J.B.S. Haldane in Great Britain, Sewall Wright in the United States, and Sergei Chetverikov in the Soviet Union.

While the work of these scientists often produced brilliant insights (see particularly Fisher's *The Genetical Theory of Natural Selection*, 1930), their conclusions were largely unknown to most evolutionary biologists, especially in North America. It remained, therefore, for an individual to transcend these two worlds: the mathematical jargon of the population geneticists and the general constructs of theoretical evolutionary biologists. The scientist who performed this task (and to whom we owe the most credit as the first true synthesizer) was Theodosius Dobzhansky. In his *Genetics and the Origin of Species* (1937), Dobzhansky skillfully integrated the mathematics of population genetics with overall evolutionary theory. His insights then became the basis for a period of tremendous activity in evolutionary thinking that directly led to major contributions by George Gaylord Simpson (who brought paleontology into the synthesis), Ernst Mayr,* and others. In fact, the "Modern

Theodosius Dobzhansky.

Synthesis" produced by these scientists stood basically unchallenged for an entire generation as *the* explanation of the evolutionary process. In recent years, however, some aspects of this theory have been brought under serious question. (See the section "Recent Challenges to the Modern Synthesis," this chapter.)

---

*For an interesting discussion of the intellectual developments concerning the formulation of modern evolutionary theory, see Ernst Mayr and William B. Provine (eds.), *The Evolutionary Synthesis*, Cambridge, Mass.: Harvard University Press, 1980.

Population Within a species, a community of individuals where mates are usually found.

Darwin saw evolution as the gradual unfolding of new varieties of life from previous forms over long periods of time. This depiction is what most of us think of as "evolution," and it is indeed the end result of the evolutionary process. But these long-term effects can only come about by the accumulation of many small evolutionary changes occurring every generation. In order to understand how the process of evolution works, we must necessarily study these short-term events. Darwin attempted this kind of study in his breeding experiments, but because the science of genetics was still in its infancy, he was not able to comprehend fully the mechanics of evolutionary change. Today, we study in various organisms (including humans) evolutionary changes occurring between generations, and are able to demonstrate how evolution works. From such a modern genetics perspective, we define evolution as *a change in allele frequency from one generation to the next*.

Allele frequencies are numerical indicators of the genetic makeup of an interbreeding group of individuals known as a **population**. (We will return to this topic in more detail in Chapter 5.) Here, let us illustrate the way allele frequencies change (that is, how evolution occurs) through a simplified example. First of all, we must look at a physical trait that is inherited, in this case human blood type. The best known of the human blood-type traits is ABO. There are, however, many similar blood-type systems controlled by different genes, which determine genetically transmitted properties of the red blood cells.

An inherited trait, such as human blood type, may be of slightly different form in different individuals. As mentioned, we call the variant genes that underlie these different forms of an inherited trait, alleles. The best-known blood-type alleles are A, B, and O. These different expressions of inherited traits are the results of genetic variation within a population.

Let us assume that your present class represents a population, an interbreeding group of individuals, and that we have ascertained the blood type of each member for the ABO trait. To be a population, individuals in your class must choose mates more often from *within* the group than from outside it. Of course, the individuals in your class will not meet this requirement, but for this example's sake we will make the assumption that they do. The proportions of each of the A, B, and O alleles are the allele frequencies for this trait. For example, suppose we find that the proportion of alleles in your class (population) is as follows:* A = .50; B = .40; 0 = .10.

Since the frequencies for combinations of these genes represent only proportions of a total, it is obvious that allele frequencies can refer only to whole groups of individuals; that is, populations. Individuals do not have an allele frequency, they have either A, B, or O (or a combination of these). Nor can individuals change alleles. From conception onward, the genetic composition of an individual is fixed. If you start out with blood type A, you will remain type A. Therefore, an individual cannot evolve: Only a group of individuals—a population—can evolve over time.

What happens when a population evolves? Evolution is not an unusual or a mysterious process. In fact, it is incredibly commonplace, and may occur between

---

*This simplified example shows frequencies for the various gene combinations, what are called genotypes. The way allele frequencies are calculated will be shown in Chapter 5.

Microevolution Small, short-term changes occurring over just a few generations.

Macroevolution Large changes produced only after many generations.

Mutation An alteration in the genetic material (a change in the base sequence of DNA).

Migration Movement of genes between populations.

every generation for every group of organisms in the world, including humans. Assume we measure the allele combination frequencies for the ABO blood trait twenty-five years later in the children of our classroom population and find the following: A = .30; B = .40; O = .30.

We can see that the relative proportions have changed: A has decreased, O has increased, while B has remained the same in frequency. Such a simple, apparently minor, change is what we call evolution. Over the short run of just a few generations, such changes in inherited traits may be only very small, but if further continued and elaborated, the results can and do produce spectacular kinds of adaptation and whole new varieties of life.

Whether we are talking about such short-term effects as our classroom population from one generation to the next, which is sometimes called **microevolution**, or the long-term effects through fossil history, sometimes called **macroevolution**, the basic evolutionary mechanisms are similar. As we will discuss below, however, they are not necessarily identical.

The question may be asked: How do allele frequencies change? Or, to put it another way, what causes evolution? The modern theory of evolution isolates general factors that can produce alterations in allele frequencies. As we have noted, evolution is a two-stage process. Genetic variation must first be produced and distributed before it can be acted upon by natural selection.

FACTORS THAT PRODUCE AND REDISTRIBUTE VARIATION

Mutation An actual alteration in genetic material is called **mutation**. A genetic locus may take one of several alternative forms, which we have defined as alleles (A, B, or O, for example). If one allele changes to another—that is, if the gene itself is altered—a mutation has occurred. As we have seen, a mutation is a molecular alteration—a change in the base sequence of DNA. For such changes to have evolutionary significance, they must occur in the sex cells, which are passed between generations. Evolution is a change in allele frequencies *between* generations. If mutations do not occur in sex cells (either the egg or sperm), they will not be passed to the next generation, and no evolutionary change can result. If, however, a genetic change does occur in the sperm or egg of one of the individuals in our classroom (A mutates to X, for instance) the offspring's blood type also will be altered, causing a change in allele frequencies of that generation. Evolution would have occurred by mutation. For a discussion of chromosomal and other types of disorders, see Issue, Chapter 6, pp. 150–152.

Actually, it would be rare to see evolution occurring by mutation *alone*. Mutation rates for any given trait are quite low, and, thus, their effects would rarely be seen in such a small population as our class. In larger populations mutations might be observed (one individual in 10,000, say), but would, by themselves, have very little impact on shifting allele frequencies. However, when mutation is coupled with natural selection, evolutionary changes are quite possible.

Mutation is the basic creative force in evolution, and in fact is the only way to produce "new" variation. Its key role in the production of variation represents the first stage of the evolutionary process. Darwin was not aware of the nature of mutation. Only in the twentieth century, with the spectacular development of molecular biology, have the secrets of genetic structure been revealed.

Migration The movement of genes from one population to another is called **migration**. If all individuals in our classroom population do not choose their mates from within the group, significant changes in allele frequencies could occur. For example, if four of the people who were type A married and settled outside the population, and four new individuals who were type O moved in and interbred with classroom individuals, the allele frequencies would be altered. If a change in allele frequency does take place, evolution will have occurred, this time by migration.

In humans, social rules, more than any other factor, determine mating patterns, and cultural anthropologists must work closely with physical anthropologists in order to isolate and measure this aspect of evolutionary change.

Genetic Drift   The random factor in evolution is called **genetic drift**, and is due primarily to sampling phenomena (that is, the size of the population). Since evolution occurs in populations, it is directly tied not only to the nature of the initial allele freqencies of the population, but to the size of the group as well. If, in our parent population of, say, 100 individuals, two type O individuals had been killed in an auto accident before completing reproduction, their genes would have been removed from the population. The frequency of the O allele would have been reduced in the next generation, and evolution would have occurred. In this case, with only 100 individuals in the population, the change due to the accident would have altered the O frequency in a noticeable way. If, however, our initial population had been very large (10,000 people), then the effect of removing a few individuals would be very small indeed. In fact, in a population of large size, random effects, such as traffic accidents, would be balanced out by the equal probabilities of such events affecting all the other individuals with different genetic combinations (i.e., different genotypes). As you can see, evolutionary change due to genetic drift is directly and inversely related to population size. To put it simply, the smaller the population, the larger the effect of genetic drift.

When considering genetic drift, we must remember that the genetic makeup of individuals is in no way related to the chance happenings that affect their lives. When applied to our example, this fact means that the genetic makeup of individuals has absolutely nothing to do with their being involved in automobile accidents. This is what is meant by a random event and why this factor is usually called *random genetic drift*. If, for example, a person had died in an auto accident caused by hereditary poor eyesight, such an event would not be genetic drift. If the individual, because of some such hereditary trait, dies early and produces fewer offspring than other individuals, this is not random genetic drift, it is natural selection.

Recombination   Since in any sexually reproducing species both parents contribute genes to offspring, the genetic information is inevitably reshuffled every generation. Such recombination does not in itself change allele frequencies (i.e., cause evolution). However, it does produce the whole array of genetic combinations, which natural selection can then act upon. In fact, we have shown how the reshuffling of chromosomes during meiosis can produce literally trillions of gene combinations, making every human being genetically unique.

NATURAL SELECTION ACTS ON VARIATION

The evolutionary factors just discussed—mutation, migration, genetic drift, and recombination—interact to produce variation and to distribute genes within and between populations. But there is no long-term *direction* to any of these factors.

Genetic drift   Evolutionary changes produced by random factors.

BOX 4-2

Models of Natural Selection

Directional Selection

As environmental pressures change gradually, selection pressures should also shift. If the environmental pressure is directional, selection should also be directional (see Fig. 1). For example, in the last one million years, there have been long periods of gradual cooling in the earth's climate. One means of coping with cold among mammals has been increase in body size (see p. 161). If we assume animals, such as mammoths, are descendants from smaller ancestors, how did they gradually get bigger? The answer lies in understanding natural selection.

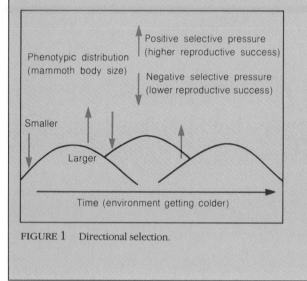

FIGURE 1   Directional selection.

Those animals with genotypes for larger overall size perhaps resisted cold better, lived longer, mated more often, cared better for their young, and so forth. In any case, the result was that they reproduced more successfully than other (smaller) individuals. Gradually, then, allele frequencies shifted. As the climate continued to grow progressively colder, allele frequencies also continued to shift, and average mammoth size gradually increased.

Stabilizing Selection

If, on the other hand, environments remain relatively stable, there should be selection for those genotypes already established within an "adaptive plateau" (see Fig. 2). In other words, those phenotypes (which are influenced by genotypes) in the center of the populational distribution ("modal" varieties) should have higher reproductive success, and those at either extreme will be selected against (as long as the environment remains stable).

If we again choose size as a characteristic, we can note that some varieties of turtle have changed little in millions of years. In any given generation, the environment of turtles has not changed much from that of previous generations. Therefore, the "optimal" phenotype is probably an average-sized turtle, and those much larger or much smaller should be selected against.

Adaptation   Genetic changes in response to selection (environmental) factors.

What then does enable populations to adapt to changing environments? The answer is, of course, natural selection—the process so well elucidated by Darwin more than 125 years ago. Given that there is genetic variation among individuals within a population, some of these variations *may* influence reproductive success (numbers of offspring successfully raised). If, as a result of genetic variation, some individuals contribute more offspring to succeeding generations, this is natural selection. In fact, we have defined natural selection as *differential net reproductive success* (see p. 41).

How then do populations adapt? A result of natural selection is a change in allele frequency relative to specific environmental factors. If the environment changes, then the selection pressures change as well. Such a functional shift in allele frequencies is what we mean by **adaptation**. If there are long-term environmental changes in a consistent direction, then allele frequencies should also shift gradually each generation. If sustained for many generations, the results may be quite dramatic. (See Box 4-2.)

BOX 4-2

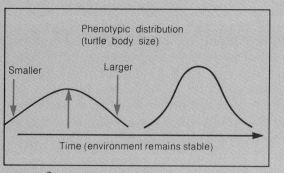

FIGURE 2   Stabilizing selection.

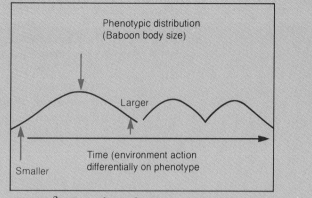

FIGURE 3   Diversifying selection.

Diversifying Selection

In this type of selection, phenotypic variants at *both* extremes are favored, and those in the center of the distribution (closer to the mean) are selected against. For example, in the case of baboon size relative to predation pressure, it may be advantageous to be small (less conspicuous) or very large (for active defense).

Over time, such selection pressure would act to create a twin-peak (bimodal) phenotypic distribution as shown in Figure 3.

In fact, such a process would not have long-term effects in a *fully* reproductive population, since individuals of all sizes would be mating with each other, thus producing individuals of intermediate body size. In order for the diversifying selection pressures to be maintained, some degree of *reproductive isolation* between segments of the population would be required. Another possibility is that phenotypic variation can be partitioned and maintained by other genetic differences—sex, for example. In fact, baboons do differ markedly in size, with males averaging about twice the size of females.

The Unit of Selection   Selection acts on the individual. It is individuals who reproduce or do not reproduce and who continually attempt to maximize their own reproductive success. Thus, statements such as "The group was undergoing selection in order to survive" have no meaning. *The individual, not the group, is the unit of selection.* If the total reproductive success of all members of a population continuously falls below replacement value (where more individuals die than are born in a generation), the population will become extinct. Individuals will attempt to maximize their own reproductive success even in the face of such impending extinction.

Overpopulation is the result of individuals maximizing their reproductive success. Even if such behavior means the whole group will perish, no special evolutionary mechanisms exist to keep individuals from reproducing at their greatest capacity. Of course, humans have the potential to manipulate their numbers, and the entire world now faces the problem of controlling an exploding population. Evolution, therefore, has no built-in mechanism to guard against extinction. Indeed, extinction is actually the rule—not the exception—in evolution. Of all the species that have ever lived on earth, it is estimated that less than .1% (one-tenth of one percent) are now currently living; the remaining 99.9% met their almost inevitable evolutionary fate.

The Unit of Evolution While selection acts on the individual, changes in allele frequency occur *between* generations for an entire population; that is, an interbreeding group of organisms. The net result of all individuals' reproductive success (natural selection)—in addition to the possible effects of mutation, migration, and genetic drift—will affect the entire population. *The population, then, is the unit of evolution*, and it is the population that changes (as measured by allele frequencies) from generation to generation.

EVOLUTION AT THE SPECIES LEVEL

A **species** is defined as a group of interbreeding organisms that are *reproductively isolated* and, therefore, cannot successfully interbreed with other groups (species). The capacity to reproduce is the critical factor in defining species. Theoretically, one can test whether two kinds of organisms are members of different species by observing their reproductive behavior under natural conditions (who mates with whom), and by observing the results (are the offspring fertile?).

Actually, a species is composed of subunits that are the breeding communities we have called populations. All members of a species can potentially interbreed, and some degree of interbreeding (migration) is theoretically possible between all populations of that species.

The net result of all the forces of evolution (mutation, migration, genetic drift, and natural selection) acting on all populations determines the fate of the species as a whole. If sustained over a long period of time, gradual changes in allele frequencies between member populations can eventually lead to sufficient genetic differences, so that fertile reproduction is no longer possible. We then may recognize a new form of life having arisen from one species "splitting" and producing new species, a process called **speciation**. (See Box 4-3.) This level of evolutionary change was the one described by Darwin and Wallace. If, on the other hand, total reproductive success is so low that all, or even most, populations become extinct, the whole species will be doomed and will disappear from the earth forever. The gross interference of natural habitats by modern industrial society has pushed numerous "endangered species" to this crucial juncture.

Recent Challenges to the Modern Synthesis

In the last two decades, serious reexamination has stimulated ongoing debate concerning some aspects of modern evolutionary theory.

NEUTRAL MUTATIONS

One of the premises postulated by traditional evolutionists is that natural selection is the major factor explaining most of the variation found in contemporary or-

BOX 4-3 Speciation

According to the biological species concept (Mayr, 1970), the way new species are first produced involves some form of isolation. Picture a single species of some organism (baboons, say) composed of several populations distributed over a wide geographic area. Gene exchange (migration) will be limited if a geographic barrier, such as a river, lake, ocean, or mountain range, separates these populations. This extremely important form of isolating mechanism is called *geographic isolation*.

Now, if one population (A) is separated from another population (B) by a mountain range, individual baboons of A will not be able to mate with baboons from B. As time passes (several generations), genetic differences will accumulate in both populations. If group size is small, we can predict that drift will cause allele frequency changes in both population A and population B. Since drift is *random* in nature, we would not expect the effects to be the same. Thus, the two populations would begin to diverge.

As long as gene exchange is limited, the populations can only become more divergent with time. Moreover, further genetic difference would be expected if the baboon groups are occupying somewhat different habitats. (Ecological conditions usually do vary from one area to another within a species' range.) These additional genetic differences would arise through the process of natural selection. Certain individuals in population A may be most reproductively fit in their own environment, but may be less fit in the environment occupied by population B. Consequently, allele frequencies will change, and the pattern will be dissimilar in the two populations.

Again, as time passes, and perhaps as environments change further, the populations will become still more divergent. Indeed, more often than not, the most isolated populations are the most peripheral, are usually coping with the harshest environments, and are thus experiencing the strongest selection pressures.

With the cumulative effects of drift and natural selection acting over many generations, the result will be two populations which—even if they were to come back into geographic contact—could no longer interbreed fertilely.

More than just geographic isolation would now apply; there may, for instance, be behavioral differences interfering with courtship—what we call *behavioral isolation*. There may even be sufficient differences in body size and proportions to make copulation physiologically impossible.

Using our *biological* definition of species, we now would recognize two distinct species, where initially only one existed.

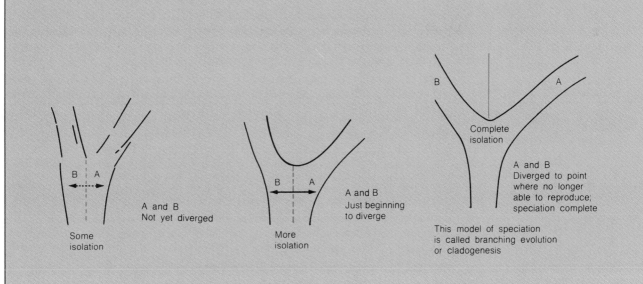

B | A
A and B
Not yet diverged

Some isolation

B | A
A and B
Just beginning to diverge

More isolation

B   A
Complete isolation

A and B
Diverged to point where no longer able to reproduce; speciation complete

This model of speciation is called branching evolution or cladogenesis

ganisms. There is general agreement that significant aspects of variation are channeled by selection, thus leading to adaptation. But is all (or even most) of the "genetic baggage" that a species carries understandable strictly in terms of natural selection? Some scientists believe it is not. Pointing to the vast amount of variation seen in all organisms (28% of all human genes are estimated to exhibit significant population variation), these researchers argue that *much* of variation seen in natural populations is due to neutral mutations and chance factors (i.e., genetic drift).

A major aspect of this argument is that many mutations are neutral; in other words, they have no impact on reproductive success in any conceivable environment. We know, of course, that there is considerable redundancy in the DNA code, so that many point mutations will not alter the amino acid sequence whatsoever. In such a case, the phenotype is not affected at all, and selection cannot act on what it cannot see. Or as King and Jukes have put it, "Natural selection is the editor, rather than the composer of the genetic message" (King and Jukes, 1969, p. 788). These researchers, however, go far beyond postulating strictly synonymous mutations as neutral—they claim a large majority of other genetic changes are completely neutral to selective action, and are established in populations by random genetic drift.

This controversy has not yet been completely resolved. There is a vast store of genetic variation in all interbreeding populations. Certainly, both selection and drift have contributed, but what has been the primary architect? The consensus among most evolutionary biologists still is that natural selection is the most significant factor in explaining evolutionary change. Moreover, the action of selection is the explanation of the "fit" between an organism and its environment, the relationship that so intrigued Darwin.

MODES OF EVOLUTIONARY CHANGE

The modern synthesis primarily explains those allele frequency changes seen over just a few generations—what is called *microevolution*. Until recently, the general consensus among evolutionary biologists was that these microevolutionary mechanisms could be translated directly into large-scale evolutionary changes—what is called *macroevolution*, or transspecific evolution. These major evolutionary events involve the appearance of new species (i.e., speciation) as well as even broader more encompassing groups of organisms. A smooth gradation of changes was postulated to run directly from microevolution into macroevolution. A representative view was expressed by a leading synthesist, Ernst Mayr:

> The proponents of the synthetic theory maintain that all evolution is due to the accumulation of small genetic changes, guided by natural selection, and that transspecific evolution is nothing but an extrapolation and magnification of the events that take place within populations and species (Mayr, 1970, p. 351).

In the last decade, however, this view has been seriously challenged. Many theorists now believe that macroevolution cannot be explained *solely* in terms of accumulated microevolutionary changes. Many current researchers are now convinced that macroevolution is only partly understandable through microevolutionary models, as stated by two proponents of this revised view:

> We recognize that the within-population concept of adaptation via natural selection is a viable hypothesis accounting for the deterministic part of much genetic, behavioral,

and morphological change in evolution. However, we strongly disagree that a smooth extrapolation of within-population (microevolutionary) processes is a logical or effective integration of such within-population mechanisms with among-species phenomena (macroevolution) (Eldredge and Cracraft, 1980).

Gradualism vs. Punctuationalism The traditional view of evolution has emphasized that change accumulates gradually in evolving lineages—the idea of "phyletic gradualism." Accordingly, the complete fossil record of an evolving group (if it could be recovered) would display a series of forms with finely graded transitional differences between each ancestor and its descendant. The fact that such transitional forms are only rarely found is attributed to the incompleteness of the fossil record, or, as Darwin called it, "a history of the world, imperfectly kept, and written in changing dialect."

For more than a century, this perspective dominated evolutionary biology. Paleontologists searched diligently to find evidence of these gradual changes. So strong was this notion of gradualism that when little evidence was found to support it, researchers assumed there must be something wrong with their data—either their geological beds were inadequately dated or the paleontological record was yet too incomplete to allow a firm conclusion. Rarely did anyone suspect that the premise of gradualism itself might be flawed.

In the last fifteen years, some evolutionary biologists have called this notion into serious question. The evolutionary mechanisms operating on species over the long run are often not continuously gradual. In a great many cases, species persist for thousands of generations basically unchanged. Then, rather suddenly—at least in evolutionary terms—a "spurt" of speciation occurs. This nongradual process of long stasis and quick spurts has been termed **punctuated equilibrium** (Gould and Eldredge, 1977).

From a comprehensive survey of well-documented and long-ranging fossil series (including especially marine invertebrates), paleontologists Stephen Gould and Niles Eldredge conclude that:

> Most species during their evolutionary history, either do not change in any appreciable way, or else they fluctuate mildly in morphology, with no apparent change in any direction. Phyletic gradualism is very rare and too slow, in any case, to produce the major events of evolution. Evolutionary trends are not the product of slow, directional transformation within lineages; they represent the differential success of certain species . . . speciation may be random with respect to the direction of a trend (Gould and Eldredge, 1977, p. 115).

What the punctuationalists are disputing concerns the "tempo" and "mode" of evolutionary change commonly understood since Darwin's time. Rather than a slow steady tempo, this new view postulates long periods of no change interspersed only occasionally by sudden bursts. From this observation, punctuationalists concluded that the mode of evolution, too, must be different from that suggested by classical Darwinists. Rather than gradual accumulation of small changes within a single lineage, advocates of punctuated equilibrium believe an additional evolutionary mechanism is required to push the process along. Accordingly, *speciation* (see Box 4-3) is seen to be the major influence in bringing about rapid evolutionary change. Given numerous small population isolates and corresponding opportunities for random genetic drift, speciation events could occur in a sudden flurry—a whole array of new, fairly isolated and small incipient species would then possess a great deal of evolutionary potential. Of these, probably only a small minority would survive—through a "higher" evolutionary process sometimes called *species selection.*

How well does the paleontological record agree with this new theory? Indeed, for some organisms a tremendous amount of fossil data shows long periods of stasis punctuated by occasional quite rapid changes (the transformation taking perhaps on the order of 10,000 to 50,000 years). Intermediate forms are rare, not because the record is so poor, but because the speciation events and longevity of these transitional species were so short we should not expect to find them very often.

The best supporting evidence for punctuated equilibrium has come from the fossilized remains of a variety of invertebrates, the paleontological specialty of both Gould and Eldredge. How well, then, does the human fossil record fit a punctuationalist model? Gould and Eldredge (1977, p. 115) believe "the record of human evolution seems to provide a particularly good example." When it comes to the evolution of our family, other researchers, however, are still not as convinced. Many believe punctuationalism is not all that apparent in the human evolutionary record and, alternatively, that gradualism fits the facts better (Cronin et al., 1981). Others (e.g., Tobias, 1983) believe human evolution displays periods of both punctuated *and* gradualistic changes.

It would be unreasonable to expect a single mode of evolutionary change to characterize all lineages at all times. Clearly, the rigid Darwinian belief that evolutionary change must *always* be gradual in nature is improbable. Abundant evidence shows that, in some evolutionary lines, this has not been the case. Punctuated equilibrium with change brought about by rapid speciation is another mode that now must be considered. However, this mechanism also should not be overly generalized to include all evolutionary change; indeed, such a view reflects the ongoing debate within paleontology (Hoffman, 1989). Regarding human evolution, specifically, it is still not clear which of the two models (gradualism or punctuationalism)—or a combination of the two—provides the best approximation. As we will be discussing in great detail later in this text (Chapters 14–17), speciation was probably never very common within our particular evolutionary line since the time we diverged from other primates. As such, our lineage may not be typical, and is thus not a good example on which to base general theories of evolutionary change.

Microevolution and Macroevolution　As we have seen, allele frequencies over the span of a few generations seem to change in gradual fashion. Thus, microevolution, as conceived within the modern synthesis, conforms to the gradualistic model.

We have also seen that long-term changes (i.e., macroevolution) are not always gradual in nature; in fact, in many evolutionary lineages, the rate of change is manifestly sporadic. Are, then, microevolution and macroevolution really quite different phenomena?

While the mechanisms of microevolution and macroevolution may be partially "decoupled," that is not to say that they are unrelated. In fact, speciation can be understood as the result of accumulated genetic changes, particularly when facilitated by geographic isolation. This does not imply that the process is always gradual. Indeed, since processes affecting isolating mechanisms (for instance, mountain building, formation of island chains, etc.) are themselves irregular, we should expect speciation rates to vary as well. Species, once they have formed, are real entities. Categories of higher rank (genera, families, and so on) are merely human abstractions; they do not exist in nature. Populations evolve; species may eventually diverge and, once distinct, can only become more genetically separate. All the rest of evolutionary change is basically an extension of this process.

Review, Genetics and Evolutionary Factors

Starting in Chapter 2 with a discussion of natural selection, we proceeded in Chapter 3 to show the molecular and cellular bases of heredity, and to illustrate in this chapter how such genetic information is passed from individuals in one generation to those in the next. It may seem that these different levels, molecular, cellular, individual, and populational, are different aspects of evolution, but they are all related and highly integrated in a way that can eventually produce evolutionary change. A step-by-step example will make this clear.

In our earlier discussion of sickle-cell hemoglobin (see p. 69), you will recall that the actual genetic information was coded in the sequence of bases in the DNA molecule. We started out with a situation where everyone in the population has the same hemoglobin type; therefore, initially no variation for this trait exists, and without some source of new variation evolution is not possible. How does this gene change? We have seen that a substitution of a single base in the DNA sequence can alter the code significantly enough to alter the protein product and ultimately the whole phenotype of the individual. Imagine that, several generations ago, just such an "accident" occurred in a single individual. For this mutated gene to be passed on to succeeding offspring, the gametes must carry the alteration. Any new mutation, therefore, must be transmitted during sex cell formation.

TABLE 4-3   **Levels of Organization in the Evolutionary Process**

EVOLUTIONARY FACTOR	LEVEL	EVOLUTIONARY PROCESS	SCIENCE	TECHNIQUE OF STUDY
Mutation	DNA	Storage of genetic information; ability to replicate; influences phenotype by production of proteins	Molecular biology	Biochemistry, electron microscopy, recombinant DNA
Mutation	Chromosomes	A vehicle for packaging and transmitting genetic material (DNA)	Cytogenetics	Light, electron microscope
Recombination (sex cells only)	Cell	The basic unit of life that contains the chromosomes and divides for growth and for production of sex cells	Cytogenetics	Light, electron microscope
Natural selection	Organism	The unit, composed of cells, which reproduces and which we observe for phenotypic traits	Genetics	Visual, biochemical
Drift, migration	Population	A group of interbreeding organisms. We look at changes in allele frequencies between generations; it is the population that evolves	Population genetics	Statistical

Once the mutation has occurred in the DNA, it will be packaged into chromosomes, and these chromosomes in turn will assort during meiosis to be passed to offspring. The results of this process are seen by looking at phenotypes (traits) in individuals, and the mode of inheritance is described simply by Mendel's principle of segregation. In other words, if our initial individual has a mutation in only one paired allele on a set of homologous chromosomes, there will be a 50% chance of passing this chromosome (with the new mutation) to an offspring.

Thus far, we have seen what a gene is, how it can change, and how it is passed on to offspring. But what does all this activity have to do with *evolution*? To repeat an earlier definition, evolution is a change in allele frequency in a *population* from one generation to the next. The key point here is that we are now looking at a whole group of individuals, a population, and it is the population that will or will not change over time.

We know whether allele frequencies have changed in a population where sickle-cell hemoglobin is found by ascertaining the percentage of individuals with the sickling allele (Hb^S) versus those with the normal allele (Hb^A). If the relative proportions of these alleles alter with time, evolution has occurred. In addition to discovering that evolution has occurred, it is important to know why. Several possibilities arise. First, we know that the only way the new allele Hb^S could have arisen is by mutation, and we have shown how this process might happen in a single individual. This change, however, is not yet really an evolutionary one, for in a relatively large population the alteration of one individual's genes will not significantly alter allele frequencies of the entire population. Somehow, this new allele must *spread* in the population.

One way this could happen is in a small population where mutations in one of just a few individuals and their offspring may indeed alter the overall frequency quite quickly. This case would be representative of genetic drift. As discussed above, drift acts in small populations where random factors may cause significant changes in allele frequency. Due to small population size, there is not likely to be a balance of factors affecting individual survival, reproduction, etc. Consequently, some alleles may be completely removed from the population, while others may become established as the only allele present at that particular locus (and are said to be "fixed" in the population).

In the course of human evolution, drift may have played a significant role at times, but long-term evolutionary trends could only have been sustained by *natural selection*. The way this has worked in the past and still operates today (as in sickle-cell) is through differential reproduction. That is, individuals who carry a particular allele or combination of alleles produce more offspring. By producing more offspring than other individuals with alternative alleles, such individuals cause the frequency of the new allele in the population to increase slowly in proportion from generation to generation. When this process is compounded over hundreds of generations for numerous genes, the result is significant evolutionary change.

Summary

We have now come full circle. We started our discussions of evolution (Chapter 2) talking about populations and, indeed, this is where evolution occurs. But populations are made up of individual organisms, organisms are made up of cells, cells contain chromosomes, and chromosomes are composed of DNA. Understanding the actual mechanics of the evolutionary process comes *only* from considering all these various levels of organization.

Questions for Review

1. Explain why botanists before Mendel failed to solve the problem of heredity.
2. How was Mendel's approach to the study of heredity different from those of his predecessors?
3. Why did the pea plant suit Mendel's experimental model?
4. What is the significance of contrasting characters?
5. What are the differences between P_1 and F_1 crosses?
6. Explain the principle of segregation.
7. Explain the principle of independent assortment.
8. How do these principles help us to understand evolution?
9. How is a mutation—a change in the DNA genetic code—transmitted into an actual physical change? Use sickle-cell hemoglobin as an example.
10. What are the major elements of the modern synthesis? What earlier dispute did the modern synthesis resolve?
11. Discuss two recent challenges to the modern synthetic theory of evolution.
12. Assume a mutation occurs in a small human population. What does this mutation have to do with evolution? In other words, how might allele frequencies be changed?

Suggested Further Reading

Many of the reading suggestions for Chapter 3 are recommended for this chapter as well.

Bodmer, W. F. and L. L. Cavalli-Sforza. *Genetics, Evolution, and Man*, San Francisco: W. H. Freeman & Co., 1976.
An excellent authoritative discussion of the hereditary mechanism and specific genetic traits seen in human populations. With its emphasis on medical genetics, this work is a superb source for premedical students.

Cavalli-Sforza, L. L. *Elements of Human Genetics* (2nd Ed.), Menlo Park, Ca.: W. A. Benjamin, Inc., 1977.
A relatively simplified discussion of genetics that should be useful for an introductory student who wishes to refer to an expanded discussion of genetics. Recommended especially for students with little or no background in biology.

Cummings, Michael R. *Human Heredity* (2nd Ed.), St. Paul: West Publishing Co., 1991.
An up-to-date and understandable text on human genetics. Well-illustrated, this book includes excellent information on controversial social applications of genetic knowledge.

Dunn, Leslie C. and Th. Dobzhansky. *Heredity, Race and Society*, New York: Mentor Books, 1953.
Although somewhat dated, this work is still a classic for the subjects mentioned in the title. The book is written in layman's language and aimed at the beginning student. (Try a used book store if otherwise unavailable.)

Eldredge, Niles and Joel Cracraft. *Phylogenetic Patterns and the Evolutionary Process*, New York: Columbia University Press, 1980.

A straightforward introduction to cladistic analysis in evolution written in a nontechnical fashion. Also included is a thought-provoking discussion of microevolution and macroevolution.

Hartl, Daniel L. *Human Genetics*, New York: Harper and Row, 1983.

An excellent, up-to-date textbook on human genetics, primarily for premedical courses. Detailed and well written. Recommended for advanced students.

Scheinfeld, Amram. *The Basic Facts of Human Heredity*, New York: Washington Square Press, Inc., 1961.

Written in simple language, this book provides excellent background for students lacking knowledge in biology or genetics. In addition to basic genetics, there is also material on "racial" characteristics such as pigment, hair-form, etc.

Sciulli, Paul W. *Introduction to Mendelian Genetics and Gene Action*, Minneapolis: Burgess Publishing Co., 1978.

This short paperback (sixty-three pages) is intended as a supplement for students who feel their background in genetics is inadequate. The bulk of the book deals with Mendel's laws and molecular genetics.

CHAPTER 5

Evolution in Modern Populations

Contents

Science or Sacrilege?

You can tell from even cursory thumbing through this textbook that the study of human skeletons is a central component of physical anthropology (see, especially, the appendices). Indeed, in the United States, the founding of physical anthropology early in this century was largely based upon human skeletal biology. The founders of American physical anthropology included most notably Aleš Hrdlička and Ernest A. Hooton, both of whom were experts in the study of human skeletons.

Still today, human skeletal biology is a primary focus for physical anthropologists. In recent years, 20 percent of submissions to the *American Journal of Physical Anthropology* have included articles dealing with human skeletal biology, the largest percentage for any subdiscipline of the field (Ubelaker, 1989).

Physical anthropologists are keenly interested in human biology, both past and present; but for populations no longer living, the most *direct* biological evidence we have is from preserved body parts, most especially those calcified, "hard," tissues—bones and teeth. We thus can learn about changes in body size and proportions and reveal epidemiological patterns and the histories of a variety of significant human diseases. Preserved skeletons also offer direct clues regarding diet and nutritional problems, as well as how past cultures adjusted to the myriad demands of their environments. Additionally, skeletal biologists are interested in sorting out the "biological distance" (i.e., population relationships) of past groups. Finally, modern skeletons are crucial in developing techniques for legal identification of recently deceased individuals (see Appendix B) and for comparing the very ancient remains of early humans (found as mineralized hard tissues; that is, fossils) with physical conditions seen today. Only in this way can we hope to understand how we as a species compare with earlier members of our lineage and ultimately how we came into existence in the first place.

For all these reasons and more, as physical anthropologists we have been and continue to be highly interested in the study of human skeletons. Yet, recently in the United States (as well as in some other countries) strong concerns have been voiced regarding this research, at least as it pertains to certain groups. In North America, especially, deeply felt objections have come from American Indians who regard the permanent curation and ongoing study of remains of their ancestors as a sacrilege and thus incompatible with proper religious respect for these dead individuals. After all, these individuals who make up skeletal collections did not give permission to be removed from their "final" resting places, to say nothing of being placed on shelves in museums or university laboratories.

Many American Indians have understandably been deeply disturbed about such moral issues for some time. In 1989, these concerns received great impetus from Congressional action, which was aimed at the Smithsonian Institution. The end result is that large segments of the human skeletal *and* artifactual collections are to be returned to descendants for reburial. (Note: the Smithsonian has the largest and most important collection of human skeletal remains in the United States; in fact, probably in the whole world!) At about the same time some universities (Stanford, for example) and a few state legislatures took action along similar lines.

Should *all* American Indian remains be returned for reburial to those descendants who can be identified? Beyond the deep moral convictions of many Native Americans, such a view is now supported by many federal and state legislatures, museum professionals, and academics. It is felt that continued retention of Indian remains is a further manifestation of past racist policies that saw the near obliteration of native Indian culture. And, it is true, the majority of human skeletal remains housed in United States' museums and universities are those of Native Americans. Yet, there are also thousands of other skeletons from many other groups (ancient and modern). Moreover, medical schools throughout the nation maintain teaching collections of thousands more human skeletons. If it is immoral to keep skeletons of one group, why not of all groups?

We might also point out that Native Americans, who insist on the return of bones and artifacts, are removing the sources that are used for reconstructing their culture before the arrival of Europeans. Archeologists and cultural anthropologists have learned a great deal about Indian pre-Columbian history. It seems ironic that Indians themselves are responsible for compromising, and ultimately eliminating, research into the life of their ancestors.

Anthropologists are not racists. We study human beings in order to understand the human condition. As scientists, our results belong to all humanity. To return a large proportion of irreplaceable information to the ground—where it will quickly disintegrate—will not only rob current researchers of the opportunity for study, but will also sacrifice all future research for later generations of scientists as well. Furthermore, as a self-perfecting intellectual pursuit, science always attempts to improve results—with new perspectives, new techniques, even entirely new questions. Who is to say what new information can be obtained 50 or 100 years

from now, information potentially important to all, including American Indians?

Can some compromise be reached? Justifiable moral concerns regarding religious respect (especially fragile for oppressed minority groups) and scientific ideals are *both* crucially important to our cultural ethic. We therefore *must* find a compromise. Time, however, is running out.

SOURCES

Buikstra, J. E. and C. C. Gordon. The Study and Restudy of Human Skeletal Series: The Importance of Long-term Curation. In: A. Cantwell et al., (eds.), *The Research Potential of Anthropological Museum Collection.* Annals of the New York Academy of Sciences 376(1981):449–465.

Ubelaker, D. H. and L. G. Grant. *Human Skeletal Remains: Preservation or Reburial? Yearbook of Physical Anthropology* 32(1989):249–287.

CHAPTER 5

Introduction

Microevolutionary Small-scale evolutionary changes (shifts in allele frequency) that can occur over the span of just a few generations and can, therefore, be seen in living populations.

Macroevolutionary Large-scale evolutionary changes that require many hundreds of generations and can, therefore, usually only be seen paleontologically (that is, in the fossil record).

The process of evolution acts on all species, including *Homo sapiens*. In modern populations, recombination and mutation continue to produce variation, the fuel for natural selection. Can we then see these ongoing evolutionary processes at work in human populations?

Today we find only one species of hominid represented by more than 5 billion individuals widely scattered over most of the earth. However, the distribution is by no means even, since both geographical and social factors influence where people live, how many individuals collect to form a group, and who mates with whom. Moreover, there are obvious visible physical differences as well as numerous biochemically detectable variations among groups of modern human beings. How do we explain these differences?

The branch of physical anthropology dealing with modern human variation is centrally concerned with answering such questions in *evolutionary* terms. As discussed throughout this text, physical anthropology is the study of human evolution, not just in the past but the present as well.

Human populations continue to be influenced by the forces of evolution, continue to adapt to their biocultural environments, and thus continue to evolve. Investigating the dynamic processes that mold our species is the domain of **microevolutionary** studies. From such work we not only develop a fuller understanding of why *Homo sapiens* varies from area to area (as well as from individual to individual), but we also can more fully comprehend how *Homo sapiens* came to be in the first place.

The following chapters tell the tale of a long succession of hominid fossils, but these are simply luckily preserved bits and pieces of earlier populations who were subject to the same dynamic evolutionary processes influencing humankind today. Over the space of several tens of thousands or millions of years small microevolutionary changes can be modified into **macroevolutionary** ones. Given the process of punctuated equilibrium (see pp. 107–108), macroevolutionary changes do not necessarily translate *completely* from microevolutionary events.

In this chapter we will discuss some of the ways modern human beings vary from one another as well as the evolutionary interpretations of this variation. Bear in mind that the continuing saga of humankind evolving is but the most recent chapter in a very long tale indeed.

The Population

The unit of evolutionary change is the *population*, which we defined in Chapter 4 as a group of interbreeding individuals. More precisely, the population is the group within which one is most likely to find a mate. As such, a population is a genetic unit marked by a degree of genetic relatedness and sharing in a common **gene pool**. In theory, this concept is not particularly difficult. Picture a kind of giant blender into which every generation's genes are mixed (by recombination). What comes out in the next generation is a direct product of the genes going into the pool, which in turn is a direct result of who is mating with whom.

In practice, however, isolating and describing actual human populations is a sticky business. The largest population of *Homo sapiens* that could be described is the entire species, all of whose members are at least potentially capable of interbreeding (but are incapable of interbreeding, fertilely, with members of other species). Our species is thus a *genetically closed system* (human/nonhuman hybrids are not known). The problem arises not in describing who potentially can interbreed, but in isolating exactly the patterns of those individuals who are doing so.

Factors that determine mate choice are geographical, ecological, and social. If individuals are isolated into groups in an Alpine village or on an island in the middle of the Pacific, there is not much possibility of finding a mate outside the immediate vicinity. Such **breeding isolates** are fairly easily defined and are a favorite target of microevolutionary studies. Geography plays a dominant role within these isolates through influencing the range of available mates. But even within these limits cultural prescriptions can still play a powerful part in deciding who is most proper among those potentially available.

Since social factors usually play such a crucial role in human mating patterns, a cultural anthropologist is an invaluable aid to population studies in helping to decipher what is going on in the complex world of real human beings. Additional complexity (sometimes found in other cultures) is introduced when biological and social paternity are defined differently. Moreover, the physical anthropologist must always be aware of the possibility of illegitimacy; whereas marriage patterns are useful indicators, what we are ultimately after is the pattern of actual matings.

Smaller human population segments within the species are defined as groups with relative degrees of **endogamy** (marrying/mating within the group). They are not, however, totally closed systems. Migration often occurs between groups, and individuals may choose mates from distant localities. The advent of modern means of rapid transportation has greatly accelerated **exogamy** (marrying/mating outside the group), a process which always has characterized human society to some degree.

It is obvious that most humans today are not clearly members of specific breeding populations as they would be in breeding isolates. Inhabitants of large cities may seem to be members of a single population, but actually within the city borders social, ethnic, and religious boundaries crosscut in a complex fashion to form smaller population groupings. In addition to being members of these highly open local population segments, we are simultaneously members of overlapping gradations of larger populations—the immediate geographical region (a metropolitan area or perhaps a whole state), a region of the country, the whole nation, the Western world, and ultimately again, the whole species.

In all this confusion how do anthropologists locate a population? Since most humans today live in densely inhabited, socially complex areas, a population must be isolated arbitrarily. Usually the population is defined with a particular research goal in mind.

For example, the Jewish inhabitants of New York City form a *partially* closed population defined by socioreligious affiliation—an example of religious en-

Gene pool The total complement of genes in a population.

Breeding isolates Populations geographically (and/or socially) separate and, therefore, easy to define.

Endogamy Mating within a social unit.

Exogamy Mating outside a social unit.

Hardy-Weinberg equilibrium The mathematical relationship expressing—under ideal conditions—the predicted distribution of genes in populations; the central theorem of population genetics.

dogamy. Certainly, considerable migration occurs both in and out of this group, and degree of genetic relatedness is therefore probably not all that significant. However, for some purposes it is useful to treat this group as a population. The incidence of Tay-Sachs disease (see p. 132) is known to be considerably higher in descendants of Eastern European Jewish populations than in other groups. In order to ascertain the frequency of this tragic disease in New York City and to target prevention programs, it is useful to contrast parents of Jewish and non-Jewish heritage. In addition, studies of changes in allele frequency (evolution) in this or any other population can be facilitated in the same manner. Of course, the definition of this population does not refer directly to the socioreligious makeup of this group, but only to a degree of shared relationship dating back to earlier generations in Eastern Europe. For that matter, the whole Jewish "population" could be broken down further into smaller populations, those with Eastern European ancestry and all others. In fact, this has been done, and Jewish descendants of non-Eastern European populations have about the same low incidence of Tay-Sachs disease as that of the overall United States population.

Several other social/ethnic subpopulations are treated in this manner for particular microevolutionary studies. Please remember that none of these populations is a completely closed system and, indeed, most of them are quite open.

Population Genetics

Once the microevolutionist has isolated a specific human population, the next step is to ascertain what evolutionary forces, if any, are operating on this group. In order to determine whether evolution is taking place, we measure allele frequencies for specific traits and compare the observed frequencies with a set predicted by a mathematical model: the **Hardy-Weinberg equilibrium** equation. This model provides us with a baseline set of evolutionary expectations under *known* conditions.

More precisely, Hardy-Weinberg equilibrium postulates a set of conditions where *no* evolution occurs. In other words, none of the forces of evolution is acting, and all genes have an equal chance of recombining in each generation (that is, random mating of individuals):

1. The *population* is assumed to be *very large* (therefore no sampling error—*no random genetic drift*)
2. *No mutation* (no new alleles are added by molecular alterations within gametes)
3. *No migration* (no new alleles added by influx from outside our target population)
4. *No selection* (alleles have no differential advantage relative to reproductive success)
5. *Random mating* (panmixia—no bias in who mates with whom; any female is assumed to have an equal chance of mating with any male)

If all these conditions are satisfied, allele frequencies will not change (that is, no evolution will take place) and a permanent equilibrium will be maintained as long as these conditions prevail. An evolutionary "barometer" is thus provided which may be used as a standard against which actual circumstances are compared. Similar to the way a typical barometer is standardized under known temperature and altitude conditions, the Hardy-Weinberg equilibrium is standardized under known evolutionary conditions.

The relationship of the allele frequencies in populations to Mendelian genotypic proportions is a straightforward extension of simple Mendelian genetics. In fact, in 1903, soon after the rediscovery of Mendel's work, the American geneticist and animal breeder W. E. Castle developed a model showing the relationship of genes to populations. However, Castle felt the results were so obvious that he did not take the trouble to state unequivocally the conditions for genetic equilibrium nor did he actively push for acceptance of his views.

However, within just five years the English mathematician G. H. Hardy (1877–1947) and the German physician W. Weinberg (1862–1937) independently reached the same conclusion, and their formulation eventually won wide acceptance. The mathematical relationship of allele and genotype frequencies in populations is therefore usually called the Hardy-Weinberg formula or "law."

Interestingly, we note once again that the science of genetics was advancing intellectually along a broad international front. At the turn of the century three scientists in three different countries discovered Mendel's initial contribution and realized its implications. Within just another eight years the application of these principles to populations was again independently reached in three separate countries, and the discipline of population genetics was born.

Under the idealized conditions of Hardy-Weinberg equilibrium no new alleles are added and no alleles removed from the population. Morever, every allele for a given locus has an equal chance of combining with any other allele at that locus within the gene pool.

The simplest situation applicable to a microevolutionary study is a genetic trait that follows a simple Mendelian pattern and has only two alleles (A, a). As you recall from earlier discussions, there are then only three possible genotypes: AA, Aa, aa. Proportions of these genotypes (AA:Aa:aa) are a function of the allele frequencies themselves (percentage of A; percentage of a). In order to provide uniformity for all genetic loci, a standard notation is employed to refer to these frequencies:

Frequency of first allele (A) = p (p = frequence of the dominant allele—
if there is dominance)

Frequency of second allele (a) = q (q = frequence of the recessive allele)

Since in this case there are only two alleles, their combined total frequency must represent all possibilities. In other words:

$$p \quad + \quad q \quad = 1 \text{ (unity; that is, 100\% of alleles in the gene pool)}$$

(Proportion   (Proportion
of A alleles)   of a alleles)

To ascertain the expected proportions of genotypes, we simply compute the chances of the alleles combining with one another into all possible combinations. Remember, they all have an equal chance of combining and no new alleles are being added.

These probabilities are a direct function of the frequency of the two alleles. The chances of all possible combinations occurring randomly can be simply shown as:

$$
\begin{array}{r}
p + q \\
\times \quad p + q \\
\hline
pq + q^2 \\
p^2 + \quad pq \\
\hline
p^2 + 2pq + q^2
\end{array}
$$

(mathematically, this is known as a binomial expansion)

What we have just calculated is simply:

ALLELE COMBINATION	GENOTYPE PRODUCED	EXPECTED PROPORTION IN POPULATION
Chances of:		
A combining with A	AA	$p \times p = p^2$
Chances of:		
A combining with a	Aa	$p \times q$
a combining with A	aA	$p \times q = 2pq$
Chances of:		
a combining with a	aa	$q \times q = q^2$
Proportions of		
genotypes AA: Aa:	aa	
p^2 $2pq$	q^2	

where p = frequency of dominant allele and q = frequency of recessive allele in a population.

CALCULATING ALLELE FREQUENCIES: AN EXAMPLE

How microevolutionists use the Hardy-Weinberg formula is best demonstrated through an example. Let us return to the classroom "population" we discussed in Chapter 4 (and now assume it consists of 100 individuals). Now that you are aware of the precise definition of a breeding population you can see that a classroom group does not meet the key prerequisite of social and/or geographic isolation. But once again let us assume that it does and thus represents a good biological population.

In addition, we will use the MN blood group locus as the gene to be measured. This gene produces a blood group antigen—similar to ABO—located on red blood cells. We therefore can fairly quickly ascertain everyone's phenotype by taking blood samples and observing reactions with specially prepared antisera. From the phenotypes we can then directly calculate the allele frequencies. So let us proceed.

All 100 individuals are tested and the results are shown in Box 5-1. Although the match between observed and expected frequencies is not perfect, it is close enough statistically to satisfy equilibrium conditions. Since our population is not a large one, sampling may easily account for the small observed deviations. Our population is therefore probably in equilibrium (that is, it is not evolving). At the minimum, what we can say scientifically is that we cannot reject the *null hypothesis* (a statement of equilibrium in this case).

Genetic screening Testing programs to ascertain individuals with genetic diseases or carriers of deleterious genes.

Evolution in Modern Populations

DEVIATIONS FROM HARDY-WEINBERG EXPECTATIONS

Our small population is seemingly in evolutionary equilibrium, but in many modern human populations we can find examples where this is not the case. In other words, we can discover populations that are evolving.

What causes evolution in human populations? Evolution operates in our species through the same factors as in any other species: mutation, migration, genetic drift, and natural selection. In addition, nonrandom mating—while it does not change allele frequencies by itself—may contribute to the conditions for evolutionary change.

MUTATION

Mutation is one way that new alleles can be introduced into a population. Effects on any given gene should be minor, however, since mutation rates at a single locus are quite low (estimated at about 100 per million gametes per generation). In fact, because mutation occurs so infrequently at any particular locus it would rarely have any significant effect on Hardy-Weinberg equilibrium comparisons. Certainly, mutations occur every generation, but unless we sample a huge number of subjects we are unlikely to detect any effects.

However, because we each have many genes (estimated between 100,000 and 2.5 million), we all possess numerous mutations that have appeared over recent generations. Most of these are not expressed in the phenotypes and are "hidden" as recessive alleles. (See Chapter 4 for a discussion of the mechanics of inheritance for such traits.) This situation is fortunate because most mutations are likely to be harmful, just as any random altering would mess up a finely tuned machine. One of the more common variant alleles (which probably arose by a mutation) found in white American populations produces a genetic disease called PKU (phenylketonuria). When a recessive allele is inherited in double dose, it leads to a metabolic block in the conversion of the amino acid phenylalanine into the amino acid tyrosine. As a result, phenylalanine accumulates and eventually leads to severe mental retardation. It is estimated that about 500 babies per year are born in the United States with this disease and another 1,000 individuals appear with the mutation in heterozygous and therefore unexpressed form.

Fortunately, this disease can be effectively treated if diagnosed early and the infant is placed on a special diet. As of 1976, thirty-seven states required a compulsory test of all newborns for PKU. Such testing is part of a **genetic screening** program which in many states has been extended to include several other genetic diseases. In addition, subcommittees within the United States Congress have considered adoption of a national genetic screening program requiring mandatory testing of newborns for PKU and other inherited diseases.

Another fairly common variant allele leads to what is called *familial hypercholesterolemia*. Here, however, individuals can be affected when they carry the allele in *single* dose (that is, a dominant allele). (See p. 87 for a discussion of dominance.) In individuals who carry this allele the risk of coronary disease is five

BOX 5-1 **Calculating Allele Frequencies in a Hypothetical Population**

OBSERVED DATA:

Genotype	Number of Individuals*	Percentage	Number of Alleles M	N
MM	40	(40%)	80	
MN	40	(40%)	40	40
NN	20	(20%)		40
Totals	100	(100%)	120 + 80 = 200	
		Proportion:	.6 + .4 = 1	

OBSERVED ALLELE FREQUENCIES:

$M = .6(p)$ $p + q$ should $= 1$ (and they do)
$N = .4(q)$

Expected Frequencies   What are the predicted genotype proportions if genetic equilibrium (no evolution) applies to our population? We simply apply the Hardy-Weinberg formula: $p^2 + 2pq + q^2$

$$p^2 = (.6) \times (.6) = .36$$
$$2pq = 2(.6)(.4) = 2(.24) = .48$$
$$q^2 = (.4) \times (.4) = .16$$

Total   1.00

There are only three possible genotypes (MM:MN:NN) so the total of the relative proportions should equal 1.00; as you can see, they do.

How do these expected frequencies compare with the observed frequencies in our population?

	EXPECTED FREQUENCY	OBSERVED FREQUENCY
MM	.36	.40
MN	.48	.40
NN	.16	.20

*Please note: The whole purpose of using the Hardy-Weinberg equilibrium is to make these kinds of comparisons between observed and expected frequencies. Each individual has two alleles; thus a person who is MM contributes two M alleles to the total gene pool. A person who is MN contributes one M and one N. One hundred individuals, then, have 200 alleles for the MN locus.

times that of the general population (Kane et al., 1981). In fact, for untreated heterozygotes, males often display cardiovascular problems before age 50, and females before they reach 60. Those unfortunate individuals who inherit the defective allele in double dose usually develop severe problems in childhood, and death commonly occurs before age 20.

This genetic condition is particularly significant, as it occurs frequently: $\frac{1}{500}$ individuals have the heterozygous condition and $\frac{1}{3,500}$ display the more severe homozygous affliction. The situation, however, is not hopeless. Drug therapy is making progress in alleviating some of the potentially disastrous effects.

Another kind of mutation that affects several loci simultaneously is caused by chromosomal rearrangements. These result mainly from mistakes during meiosis when chromosomes come apart, attach incorrectly, and lose pieces, or when distribution to the gametes is unequal (producing sperm or egg cells with too many or too few chromosomes).

Some chromosomal aberrations are probably quite common. Because they are so deleterious, most of them remain undetected as very early and unnoticed spontaneous abortions. Lerner and Libby estimate that between 25 and 50% of all **spontaneous abortions**—totaling several hundred thousand per year in the United States—are due to chromosomal rearrangements (1976, p. 285).

NONRANDOM MATING

Although sexual recombination does not itself alter *allele frequencies*, any consistent bias in mating patterns can alter the *genotypic proportions*. By affecting the combination frequencies of genotypes, nonrandom mating causes deviations from Hardy-Weinberg expectations of the proportions: p^2, $2pq$, and q^2. It, therefore, sets the stage for action of other evolutionary factors, particularly natural selection.

One such variety of nonrandom mating is called **positive assortative mating**, and occurs when individuals of like phenotype mate more often than expected by random mating predictions. Because individuals with like phenotypes are also similar to some degree in genotypes as well, the result of positive assortative mating increases the amount of homozygosity in the population and reduces heterozygosity (p^2 and q^2 greater than expected; $2pq$ less than expected).

The most consistent mating biases documented in the United States deal with stature and IQ. Of course both these traits are influenced by environment as well as heredity (see pp. 200–201), and observed correlations also reflect socioeconomic status (generating like environments). Eye color in a Swedish population and hair color in a Lapp group have shown significant degrees of correlation among married couples. Moreover, several studies in the United States and Britain have shown significant correlations for several other phenotypic traits (see Table 5-1).

The other side of the coin of positive assortative mating is **negative assortative mating** or mating with an individual who is phenotypically dissimilar. Theoretically, if this occurs more than expected by random mating predictions, it should increase the amount of heterozygosity in the population while correspondingly reducing homozygosity. Curt Stern (1973) suggested that red-headed persons marry each other less often than would be expected, but this has not been substantiated; nor has any other instance of negative assortative mating been conclusively demonstrated in human populations.

A third type of nonrandom mating in humans that can disrupt expected genotype proportions occurs when relatives mate more often than expected. Called **inbreeding** or consanguinity, such mating will increase the amount of homozygosity, since relatives who share close ancestors will more than likely also share similar genes.

All societies have some sort of incest taboo banning matings between very close blood relatives such as parent/child or brother/sister. Therefore, such matings usually occur less frequently than predicted under random mating conditions (which postulates that these matings, like all others, have a certain probability of occurring).

Spontaneous abortion Occurs naturally and is not induced by artificial means. Geneticists now suspect a large proportion, perhaps a majority, of conceptions end this way.

Positive assortative mating A type of nonrandom mating in which individuals of like phenotype mate more often than predicted under random mating conditions.

Negative assortative mating A type of nonrandom mating in which individuals of unlike phenotype mate more often than predicted under random mating conditions.

Inbreeding A type of nonrandom mating in which relatives mate more often than predicted under random mating conditions.

TABLE 5-1 **Positive Correlations between Husbands and Wives in the United States and Britain**

IQ	.47
Ear lobe length*	.40
Waist circumference	.38
Stature	.28
Hip circumference	.22
Weight	.21
Neck circumference	.20

*This is not to say that prospective mates go around measuring or even paying particular attention to each other's ear lobes. Correlation for this trait may be residual of assortative mating for overall size or for certain head dimensions. It also may mean absolutely nothing. If one measures enough traits, statistically some will appear associated strictly on the basis of chance.

Source: Lerner and Libby, 1976, p. 369.

Whether incest is prohibited strictly by social proscriptions or whether biological factors also interact to condition against such behavior has long been a topic of heated debate among anthropologists. For numerous social, economic, and ecological reasons exogamy is an advantageous strategy for hunting-gathering bands. Moreover, selective pressures may also play a part, since highly inbred offspring have a greater chance of expressing a genetic disorder and thereby lowering their reproductive fitness. In addition, inbreeding reduces variability among offspring thereby also potentially reducing reproductive success (Murray, 1980). In this regard, an interesting note is that incest avoidance is widespread among vertebrates (Parker, 1976). Moreover, detailed studies of free-ranging chimpanzees indicate they avoid incestuous matings within their family group (Goodall, 1968b), and savanna baboon males consistently establish themselves, and then mate, within groups other than the one in which they were reared (Packer, 1979). Apparently, both biological factors (in common with other primates) and uniquely human cultural factors have interacted during hominid evolution to produce this universal behavior pattern among contemporary societies.

Conversely, in certain societies inbreeding among fairly close relations such as cousins is actively encouraged or is unavoidable due to the small number of potential mates available. A famous case of the latter situation occurred on Pitcairn Island among descendants of the mutineers of the *Bounty* and their Tahitian wives. Only a small founding population (23 or 24) initially settled this tiny island, and this group was still further reduced by intragroup violence. As a result, young men and women of the ensuing generations usually chose spouses with whom they shared several common ancestors. On Pitcairn there was no choice but to partake in considerable inbreeding.

On the other hand, there are some areas where, although inbreeding is avoidable, it is still actively encouraged. In some parts of Japan, among certain social classes, first cousin marriages make up almost 10% of all marriages, and in the Andhra Pradesh area of India, among certain castes, uncle/niece unions also make up about 10% of marriages.

It must be kept in mind, however, that such considerable inbreeding is the exception rather than the rule among human populations. In fact, most groups seem to work very hard at maintaining exogamy, actively promoting exchange of marriage partners between groups. For example, many polar Eskimo groups live in small geographically separate isolates. Despite this, through socially established rules, very little inbreeding occurs.

As a general rule, then, most human populations do not inbreed if they can at all help it. A measure of the relative degree of inbreeding, the inbreeding coefficient (see Box 5-2), reveals no exceedingly high values for any human group so far studied. The highest inbreeding coefficient yet observed is among Samaritans of Israel and Jordan, a small socially isolated religious sect today consisting of only about 350 individuals. This group has an average inbreeding coefficient of .04, which is between the average for first and second cousin matings. The vast majority of human groups, however, are characterized by values of less than .001.

Inbreeding has important medical consequences in addition to its influence on genetic equilibrium. When relatives mate, their offspring have increased probability of inheriting an allele in homozygous dose. Many potentially deleterious genes normally "masked" in heterozygous carriers may be expressed in offspring of consanguineous matings and thereby "exposed" to the action of natural selection. Among offspring of first cousin matings in the United States the risk of con-

BOX 5-2 **Inbreeding Coefficients**

Inbreeding coefficient (F) measures the increased chance of inheriting an allele in double dose (homozygous) from a common ancestor. For an entire population, estimates are for the average amount of inbreeding ($\propto$).

Values of 0 = no inbreeding—mates unrelated
Values of 1.0 = total inbreeding—on average mating with identical twin (all members of population are genetically identical)

Values of .50 = on the average mating between parent-child
Values of .25 = on the average mating with full sibling
Values of .063 = on the average mating with first cousin
Values of .016 = on the average mating with second cousin

genital disorders is 2.3 times greater than it is for the overall population. Matings between especially close relatives—incest—often lead to multiple congenital defects.

MIGRATION (GENE FLOW)

A factor more significant than nonrandom mating in human evolutionary history is *migration* (also known as *gene flow*), the exchange of alleles between populations. Population movements (particularly in the last 500 years) have reached enormous proportions, and few breeding isolates remain. It should not, however, be assumed that significant population movements did not occur prior to modern times. Our hunting and gathering ancestors probably lived in small groups which were both mobile and flexible in membership. Early farmers also were probably highly mobile, moving from area to area as the land wore out. Intensive, highly sedentary agricultural communities came later, but even then significant migration was still possible. From the Near East, one of the early farming centers, populations spread very gradually in a "creeping occupation of Europe, India, and northern and eastern Africa" (Bodmer and Cavalli-Sforza, 1976, p. 563).

Migration between populations has been a consistent feature of hominid evolution since the first dispersal of our genus, and helps explain why speciation has not occurred in human evolution for at least the last million years. Of course, migration patterns are a manifestation of human cultural behavior, once again emphasizing the essential biocultural nature of human evolution.

An interesting application of how migration influences microevolutionary changes in modern human populations is seen in the admixture of parental groups among American blacks over the last three centuries. Blacks in the United States are largely of West African descent, but there has also been considerable influx of alleles from European stock. By measuring allele frequencies for specific genetic loci (for example, Rh and Duffy blood groups—discussed subsequently) we can estimate the amount of migration: European alleles → Afro-American gene pool. By using different methods, migration rate (or the percentage of gene flow from one population into another) estimates have varied considerably, but one of the most comprehensive studies has suggested for northern cities a figure close to 20% (22% in Oakland, California, but much lower in the deep South: 4% in Charleston, South Carolina, and 11% in rural Georgia).

It would be a misconception to think that migration can occur only through such large-scale movements of whole groups. In fact, significant alterations in genotype frequencies can come about through long-term patterns of mate selection. If exchange of mates were consistently in one direction over a long period of time, ultimately genotype frequencies would be altered. Due to demographic, economic, and social pressures, individuals must often choose mates from outside the immediate vicinity. For example, exogamy rates (percent marrying outside village or parish) for English villages were 40% in the early seventeenth century, increasing to about 64% in the last fifty years.

Transportation factors play a crucial role in determining the potential radius for finding mates. Limited to walking or use of the horse, transportation ranges were restricted to around 10 miles. With the advent and spread of railway transportation into the rural areas of England in the nineteenth century, a dramatic increase in mean marital distance* (20–30 miles) is seen. Today, highly efficient mechanized forms of transportation make the potential radius of mate choice worldwide, but actual patterns are obviously somewhat more restricted. For example, data from Ann Arbor, Michigan, indicate marital distance of about 160 miles, which obviously includes a tremendous number of potential marriage partners.

GENETIC DRIFT

As discussed earlier, random genetic drift is the chance factor in evolution and is hence tied to population size. More important than overall population size, drift is directly related to the size of the *effective breeding population*, those individuals actually producing offspring. Since other individuals are not contributing to the gene pool of the next generation, they are not considered. Thus, the effective breeding population is usually considerably smaller than the overall population, usually representing about one-third of the total.

An example of a particular kind of drift seen in modern populations is called the **founder effect**, or after its formulator, the *Sewall Wright effect*. Founder effect operates when only an exceedingly small group of individuals contributes genes to the next generation, a kind of genetic bottleneck. This phenomenon can occur when a small migrant band of "founders" colonizes a new and separate area away from the parent group. Small founding populations may also be left as remnants when famine, plague, or war ravage a normally larger group. Actually, each generation is the founder of all succeeding generations in any population.

The cases of founder effect producing noticeable microevolutionary changes are necessarily in small groups. For example, several small and isolated Alpine villages have unusually high frequencies of albinism, and an island in the South Atlantic, Tristan da Cunha, has unusually high frequencies of an hereditary eye disorder. First settled in 1817 by one Scottish family, this isolated island's native inhabitants include only descendants of this one family and a few other individuals, such as shipwrecked sailors. All in all, only about two dozen individuals consti-

---

*The average distance between husband's and wife's birthplaces.

tuted the founding population of this island. In 1961, the 294 inhabitants were evacuated because of an impending volcanic eruption and removed to England. Extensive medical tests were performed, which revealed four individuals with the very rare recessive disease, retinitis pigmentosa. The frequency for the allele causing this disease was abnormally high in this population* and a considerable portion of the group were no doubt carriers.

How did this circumstance come about? Apparently, just by chance, one of the initial founders carried the gene in heterozygous form and later passed it on to offspring who through inbreeding occasionally produced affected individuals. Since so few individuals founded this population, the fact that one carried the allele for this disease made a disproportionate contribution to succeeding generations (Bodmer and Cavalli-Sforza, 1976).

Genetic drift has probably played an important role in human evolution, influencing genetic changes in small isolated groups. From studies of recent hunter-gatherers in Australia the range of potential mates is limited to the linguistic tribe usually consisting of around 500 members. Hence, the effective breeding population is less than 170, allowing for significant effects of genetic drift, particularly if drought, disease, etc., should reduce the population even further.

Much insight concerning the evolutionary factors that have acted in the past can be gained by understanding how such factors continue to operate on human populations today. In small populations like Pitcairn or Tristan da Cunha, drift plays a major evolutionary role. Fairly sudden fluctuations in allele frequency can and do occur owing to the small population size. Likewise, throughout a good deal of human evolution (at least the last 4–5 my†) hominids probably lived in small groups, and drift, therefore, would have had significant impact.

Joseph Birdsell, a physical anthropologist who has worked extensively in Australia, has postulated general models for human evolution from his Australian data. He suggests population size during most of the Pleistocene was comparable to the 500 "magic number" seen in Australia. Moreover, when agriculturists became sedentary and isolated in small villages, the effects of drift may have been even greater. Indications of such a phenomenon are still operative in Melanesia, where individuals often spend their entire lives within just a few miles of their birthplace.

While drift has been a factor in human evolution from the start, the effects have been irregular and nondirectional (for drift is *random* in nature). Certainly the pace of evolution could have been accelerated if many small populations became isolated and thus subject to drift. However, by producing populations with varying evolutionary potential, drift only provides fodder for the truly directional force of evolution, natural selection.

NATURAL SELECTION

Over the long run of evolution in hominids or any other organism, the most important factor influencing the direction of evolutionary change is natural selection.

---

*See if you can calculate the allele frequencies and the expected percent of carriers in the population. Hint: $q^2 = 4/294$.

†my is an abbreviation for million years.

TABLE 5-2 Sickle-Cell Terminology

Sickle-cell allele in single dose:

$Hb^A Hb^S$ = carrier, called the sickle-cell trait (not much affected; functions normally in most environments)

Sickle-cell allele in double dose:

$Hb^S Hb^S$ = sickle-cell disease or sicklemia (very severe effects, usually lethal)

Controlled observations on several experimental animals and natural populations of quickly reproducing organisms such as bacteria, fruit flies, and moths (industrial melanism, for example—see Chapter 2) have repeatedly demonstrated how differential reproductive success eventually leads to adaptive shifts.

Human beings are neither quickly reproducing nor are they amenable to controlled laboratory manipulations. Therefore, unambiguous examples of natural selection in action among contemporary human populations are extremely difficult to demonstrate.

The best documented case deals with the *sickle-cell trait*, which, as discussed earlier, is the result of a point mutation within the gene producing the hemoglobin beta chain. If inherited in double dose, this gene causes severe problems of anemia, circulatory disturbances, and usually early death. (See Table 5-2.) Even with aggressive medical intervention, life expectancy in the United States today is less than twenty years for victims of sickle-cell anemia. Worldwide, sickle-cell anemia causes an estimated 100,000 deaths per year, and in the United States an estimated 40,000–50,000 individuals, mostly of African descent, suffer from this disease.

With such obviously harmful effects it is surprising to find the sickle-cell allele (Hb^S) so frequent in some populations. The highest allele frequencies are found in western and central African populations, reaching levels close to 20%; values are also moderately high in some Greek and Asiatic Indian populations. How do

FIGURE 5-1   A clinal map of the sickle-cell allele distribution in the Old World.

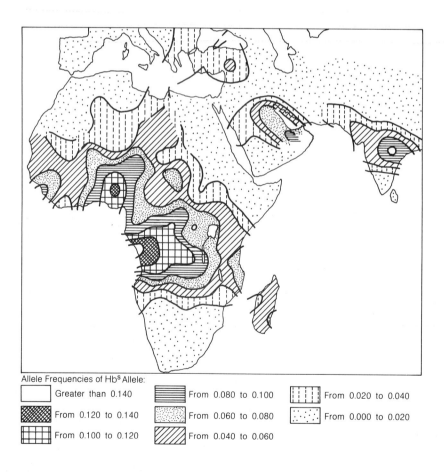

Allele Frequencies of Hb^S Allele:

Greater than 0.140	From 0.080 to 0.100	From 0.020 to 0.040
From 0.120 to 0.140	From 0.060 to 0.080	From 0.000 to 0.020
From 0.100 to 0.120	From 0.040 to 0.060	

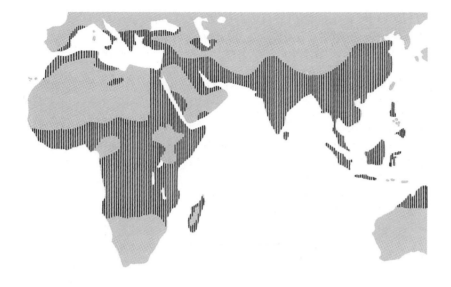

FIGURE 5-2   Malaria distribution in the Old World.

we explain such a phenomenon? Obviously the allele originated from a point mutation, but why did it spread?

The answer lies in yet another kind of disease producing enormous selective pressure. In those areas of the world where Hb^s is found in unusually high frequencies, *falciparium malaria* is also found (see Fig. 5-2). Caused by a protozoan parasite (*Plasmodium*), this debilitating infectious disease is transmitted to humans by mosquitoes. In areas that are endemically affected, many individuals suffer sharp declines in reproductive success due to high infant mortality or lowered vitality as adults.

Such a geographic correlation between malarial incidence and sickle-cell distribution is an indirect suggestion of a biological relationship. More positive evidence comes from experimental work done by the British biologist A. C. Allison. Volunteers from the Luo population of East Africa with known genotypes were injected with malaria-causing agents. After a short time the results showed that heterozygous carriers were much more resistant to malarial infection compared to homozygous "normals." (Hb^{A}Hb^A: 15 injected—14 had malarial parasites; Hb^{A}Hb^S: 15 injected—only 2 had malarial parasites.) Carriers (people with the sickle-cell trait) resist malarial infection because their red blood cells provide a less adequate environment for the *Plasmodium* parasite. Approximately 40% of a carrier's hemoglobin is Hb^s; some of their red blood cells should therefore show tendencies to sickle. Under normal circumstances only about 5% would be expected to sickle, but when infected by the parasite this is greatly increased. The presence of the parasite apparently stimulates greater sickling, disrupting the cell membrane, releasing intracellular potassium and thereby killing the host cell (*and* the parasite—before it can reproduce itself) (Friedman and Trager, 1981).

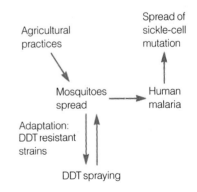

The sickle-cell allele apparently has not always been an important genetic factor in human populations. In fact, human cultural modification of environments provided the initial stimulus. Before agriculture humans rarely, if ever, lived close to mosquito breeding areas. With the development and spread to Africa of slash-and-burn agricultural practices, perhaps in just the last two thousand years, penetration and clearing of tropical rain forests occurred. As a result, open stagnant

BOX 5-3 **Other Genetic Traits Possibly Associated with Malaria**

In many parts of the world malaria has been an extremely important selective factor over the last several thousand years. Sickle-cell is probably only one of several inherited traits that have spread because they provide resistance. It must be noted, however, that none of these other traits has been documented as well as sickle-cell nor has there been conclusive experimental evidence comparable to the work of A. C. Allison. Concordance between higher incidence of these genetic traits with geographic areas exhibiting high malarial infection provides *indirect* evidence of possible association in the following:

1. Hemoglobin C—allele of the same gene producing Hb^A and Hb^S; distributed in Africa mainly in the west but a few pockets of high incidence in the south. Hb^C is found in many populations where Hb^S is also present. Possibly this allele provides resistance to another strain of malaria and *both* alleles occur in populations exposed to multiple varieties of malaria (Weiss and Mann, 1981).

2. Thalassemia—a general term for several inherited disorders. Rather than a defect in the hemoglobin molecule itself, thalassemias involve a block in hemoglobin production (absence of, or deficient production of, the alpha or beta globin molecules). There are probably a variety of genetic mechanisms (mutations) that can lead to thalassemia, including point mutations, deletions, and disruption of gene regulation. For example, one variety of thalassemia (β^+) is caused by inadequate production of mRNA; consequently, protein synthesis of the beta hemoglobin chain is disrupted. The most harmful expression of this disease syndrome is seen in homozygous dose, producing severe anemia. In heterozygous dose there are little, if any, harmful effects. Geographic evidence suggests a possible connection between thalassemia and malaria—with the highest frequencies of the disease found among populations around the Mediterranean. The severe form of beta-thalassemia (in homozygous dose called *Cooley's anemia*) affects as many as 1% of newborns in some parts of southern Europe. Tentative experimental evidence suggests that in heterozygous dose thalassemia—like sickle-cell—provides an inadequate environment for malarial infestation and proliferation (Friedman and Trager, 1981).

3. G-6-PD—glucose-6-phosphate dehydrogenase—an enzyme in red blood cells; individuals with a genetically caused deficiency do not produce this enzyme. The gene for this trait is on the X-chromosome (that is, X-linked), and some populations are up to 60% deficient (Bodmer and Cavalli-Sforza, 1976). First discovered by adverse reactions with severe anemia when individuals were given certain antimalarial drugs, anemia can also result from exposure to some foods (fava beans, for example). Distribution is again correlated with malarial areas, but apparently different alleles cause the deficiency in southern Europe from those in sub-Saharan Africa. At the biochemical level G-6-PD deficiency may act like thalassemia, producing a cellular environment not conducive to malarial infection. When exposed to certain drugs or foods (particularly fava beans), individuals with G-6-PD deficiency may have a severe anemic reaction. It is possible, however, that heterozygous carriers may actually increase malarial resistance by eating such foods—potentially an extremely important biocultural interaction (Friedman and Trager, 1981).

pools provided fertile mosquito breeding areas in close proximity to human settlements.

Malaria, for the first time, now struck human populations with its full impact, and as a selective force it was powerful indeed. No doubt, humans attempted to adjust culturally to these circumstances, and numerous biological adaptations also probably came into play. The sickle-cell trait is one of these, and the experimental evidence just cited demonstrates its biological value as a malarial resistant. However, there is a definite cost involved with such an adaptation. While carriers have more malarial resistance and presumably higher reproductive success, some of their offspring will be lost through the genetic disease, sickle-cell anemia. So there is a counterbalancing of selective forces with an advantage for carriers *only* in malarial environments.

Following World War II extensive DDT sprayings by the World Health Organization began systematically to wipe out mosquito breeding areas in the tropics. As would be expected, malaria decreased sharply, and also as expected Hb^S frequencies were apparently on the decline. The intertwined story of human cultural practices, mosquitoes, malarial parasites, and the sickle-cell trait is still not finished. Thirty years of DDT spraying killed many mosquitoes, but selection is acting on these insect populations also. Due to the tremendous amount of genetic diversity among insects as well as their short generation span, several DDT-resistant strains have arisen and spread over the last few years. As a result, malaria is again on the upswing, with several hundred thousand new cases reported in India, Africa, and Central America.

Recent advances in recombinant DNA technology have provided evidence suggesting the sickle-cell mutation arose independently in different parts of the world. The appearance of the sickle-cell mutation in West Africa was apparently of different origin from that in other parts of Africa or in Asia (Kan and Dozy, 1980).

A genetic trait like sickle-cell that provides a reproductive advantage in certain circumstances is a clear example of natural selection in action among human populations. The precise evolutionary mechanism in the sickle-cell example is usually called a **balanced polymorphism**.

A genetic trait is called a polymorphism "when two or more alleles at a given genetic locus occur with appreciable frequencies in a population" (Bodmer and Cavalli-Sforza, 1976, p. 308). How much is "appreciable" is a fairly arbitrary judgment, but is usually placed at around 1%. In other words, if a population is sampled for a particular genetic trait and frequencies of more than one allele are higher than 1%, the trait is polymorphic.

The limit of 1% is an attempt to control for mutation effects, which should always be adding new alleles much less frequently than our 1% level (for example, mutation rates are probably more like $\frac{1}{10,000}$—or lower). So when a trait like sickle-cell is found in some populations in frequencies approaching 10%, this is clearly polymorphic. It is higher than can be accounted for by mutation *alone* and thus demands a fuller evolutionary explanation. In this case, the additional mechanism is natural selection.

This brings us back to the other part of the term, balanced polymorphism. By "balanced," we are referring to the interaction of selection pressures operating in malarial environments. Some individuals (mainly Hb^{A}Hb^A) will be removed by the infectious disease malaria and some (Hb^{S}Hb^S) will be eliminated by the inherited disease, sickle-cell anemia. Those with the highest fitness (that is, reproductive success) are the heterozygotes (Hb^{A}Hb^S), but what alleles do they carry? Obviously they are passing *both* Hb^A and Hb^S alleles to offspring, and that explains why both alleles are maintained in the population—at least as long as malaria continues to be a selective factor.

Balanced polymorphism The maintenance of two or more alleles in a population due to a selective advantage of the heterozygote.

Interaction of Evolutionary Forces

Human populations usually evolve not simply through the action of single evolutionary agents, but by a complex interplay of several forces. For example, the partially isolated population comprised of people of Eastern European Jewish descent previously discussed illustrates these processes. Tay-Sachs disease, a lethal degenerative disease of the nervous system, is caused by a mutant recessive allele. In descendants of Eastern European Jews the incidence of this disease is more than 100 times more frequent at $\frac{1}{4,000}$ ($q \cong .0158$) compared to only $\frac{1}{500,000}$ ($q = .0014$) for the general United States population. Interestingly, a clinically identical disease is also found in high frequency among some French-Canadian groups, but caused here by a different mutation (Myerovitz and Hogikyan, 1986).

Where did this allele come from, and why is it so much more frequent in some populations, particularly considering its deleterious effects in the homozygote? Apparently, it first arose as a simple mutation and possibly spread initially through random genetic drift factors, such as founder effects in small migratory populations fleeing the persecutions of the Crusades six to seven centuries ago. Another possibility is that the allele spread because of some selective advantage of the heterozygote (that is, a balanced polymorphism), and some very tentative data suggest a possible greater resistance to pulmonary tuberculosis.

In any case, effects of nonrandom mating today certainly increase the likelihood of this allele being expressed in its lethal homozygous form. In fairly small socially isolated groups, individuals who mate may well share some fairly recent common ancestors. By inbreeding they have more chance of passing on the deleterious allele in double dose to an offspring.

What has probably happened with Tay-Sachs is an interaction of evolutionary factors. Mutation was the starting point, and further spread probably occurred through the combined effects of genetic drift and nonrandom mating. Moreover, possible intermittent selection effects to yet unknown factors in particular environments may also have acted to alter allele frequencies. A form of selection still obviously operates against the homozygous recessive, an inevitably lethal condition by age 5.

We can see that evolution in modern populations is a complex phenomenon. Simple models like the Hardy-Weinberg equilibrium give us a means of measuring the overall evolutionary effects, but are not really sufficient in sorting out the specific factors involved.

Human Polymorphisms

Human geneticists study some human polymorphisms because, as we have seen in cases like sickle-cell and Tay-Sachs, these traits can be expressed as tragic, deadly diseases.

Other genetic polymorphisms are also medically important due to incompatibilities and clinical complications during pregnancies or following transfusions and organ transplants. In addition, there are several other genetic polymorphisms (mainly studied through biochemical analysis) that are interesting because they vary significantly from one human population to another. As we have seen, a genetic trait can be a polymorphism *only* if more than one allele exists in appreciable frequency. Therefore, new alleles must have somehow increased in frequency from initially very low mutation rates to those recognizable as "appreciable." In other words, some *additional* evolutionary factor must have been at work. Clearly, then, the understanding of human genetic polymorphisms demands evolutionary explanations. As students of human evolution, physical anthropologists use these polymorphisms as their principal tool to both measure and understand the dynamics of evolution in modern populations.

In particular, they employ *simple* genetic polymorphisms whose genetic mechanisms are known. Such *complex traits* as stature, IQ, etc. (see pp. 153–155) are no doubt partly genetic, but we do not know which or even how many alleles are involved. On the other hand, simple polymorphisms are controlled by one genetic locus, and the different alleles are directly ascertainable at the phenotypic level.

By employing such simple polymorphisms, and by comparing allele frequencies in different human populations, we can reconstruct the evolutionary events that relate these groups with one another.

Polymorphisms Found in Human Blood

In addition to the hemoglobin and other polymorphisms possibly related to malaria, there are a great many other polymorphisms known in human blood. Because samples can be easily obtained and transported, blood has long been the favorite tissue for studying human polymorphisms. Consequently, we know a good deal concerning a wide variety of polymorphisms in red blood cells, white blood cells, and in the blood serum. Other tissues are probably just as variable, but as you will see, most of our current information concerns traits found in human blood.

RED BLOOD CELL ANTIGEN SYSTEMS

ABO   With the first use of transfusions as a medical practice around the turn of the century, serious problems were immediately recognized. Some patients had severe reactions, such as agglutination (clumping) of their blood cells, kidney failure, and even death. Very soon after transfusions became common, the underlying cause of these incompatibilities was shown by Karl Landsteiner, in 1900, to be due to a genetic trait. This trait, called the ABO blood group system, is expressed phenotypically in individuals as antigens* located on the surface of their red blood cells. The blood group (that is, what antigens a person has) is directly determined by his/her genotype for the ABO locus. The complications sometimes resulting from transfusions are due to *antigen-antibody* reactions. In a manner still largely a mystery, the body can recognize foreign antigens (proteins) and combat their invasion by producing specific antibodies that deactivate the foreign substances. Such an *immune response* is normally beneficial, for it is the basis of fighting infections caused by a foreign bacteria or virus. (See pp. 170–172.)

Usually antibodies are produced "on the spot" when foreign antigens are introduced. However, in the case of ABO, naturally occurring antibodies are already present in the blood serum at birth. Actually, no antibodies are probably "natural," although they may be (as in ABO) stimulated early in fetal life. The genotypes, phenotypes, and antibody reactions in the ABO system are shown in Table 5-3.

---

*Antigens are large macromolecules, usually proteins, which react specifically with antibodies.

TABLE 5-3 **The ABO Blood Group System**

INDIVIDUAL'S GENOTYPE	PHENOTYPE (BLOOD GROUP)	ANTIBODIES IN SERUM	CLUMPING* WILL OCCUR WHEN EXPOSED (E.G., THROUGH TRANSFUSION) TO THE FOLLOWING KINDS OF BLOOD:
OO	O	anti-A and anti-B	A, B, AB
AA AO }	A	anti-B	B, AB
BB BO }	B	anti-A	A, AB
AB	AB	neither	none

*In ABO antigen-antibody reactions, clumping, or agglutination, of cells occurs with some destruction of cells. In other immune responses, such as Rh, more complete destruction of cells takes place.

Cline A distribution of allele frequencies over space. Actually, the depiction of frequencies by connecting lines of equal frequency (an isopleth), as in temperature indicators on a weather map. See Figures 5-1, 5-4, and 5-5 for examples.

The ABO system is most interesting from an anthropological perspective because the frequencies of the three alleles (A, B, O) vary tremendously among human populations. As the distribution maps indicate (see Fig. 5-4), A or B is only rarely found in frequencies greater than 50%; usually frequencies for these two alleles are considerably below this figure. Most human groups, however, are polymorphic for all three alleles. Occasionally, as in native South American Indians, frequencies of O reach 100%, and this allele is said to be "fixed" in this population. Indeed, in most native New World populations, O is at least 80% and is usually considerably higher. Unusually high frequencies of O are also found in northern Australia, and some islands off the coast show frequencies of 90% and higher. Since these frequencies are considerably greater than for presumably closely related mainland populations, founder effect is probably the evolutionary agent responsible.

In general, the lowest values for O found in the world are in eastern Europe and central Asia.

As you might expect, frequencies for A and B can only be relatively higher where O tends to be lower. Generally, B is the rarest of the three alleles and, except for Eskimos, it is completely absent in the pre-Columbian New World. Moreover, the allele has apparently been introduced into Australia only in recent times.

The B allele reaches its highest peak in Eurasia, where its distribution is the inverse of O. Values up to 20% and occasionally slightly higher are found in a broad area in central Asia, western Siberia, and central Mongolia. The highest reported frequencies for B are found in the Himalaya area, reaching a peak of 25–30%.

Generally, the frequency of B declines gradually in populations the further westward they are in Eurasia. Such a gradual distribution of allele frequencies over space is a good example of what is called a **cline**.

The A allele has two interesting peaks, one among Blackfoot Indians and surrounding groups in North America and the other distributed over almost the entire Australian continent. With frequencies greater than 50%, the Blackfoot display the highest frequencies of A anywhere in the world. Certainly they are divergent from other North American groups, who all have very high frequencies of O (and,

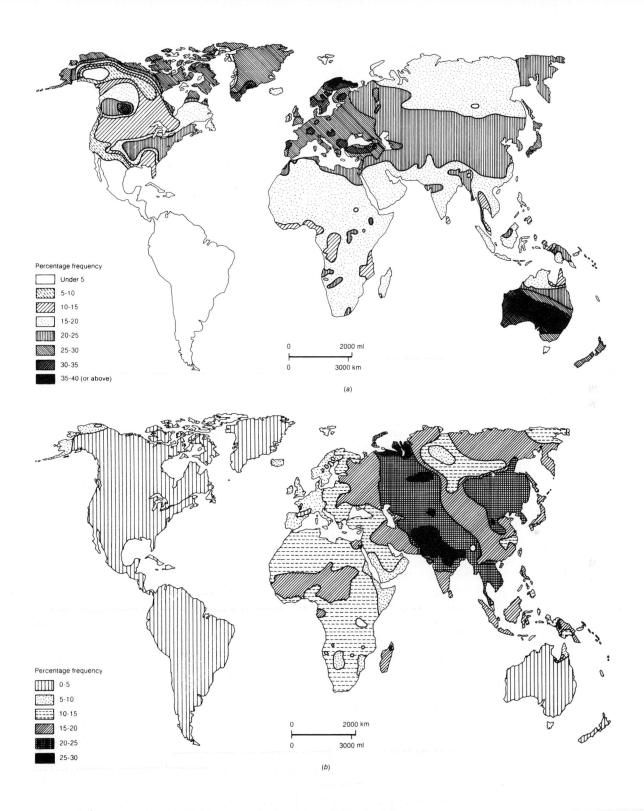

Percentage frequency

	Under 5
	5-10
	10-15
	15-20
	20-25
	25-30
	30-35
	35-40 (or above)

0   2000 ml

0   3000 km

(a)

Percentage frequency

	0-5
	5-10
	10-15
	15-20
	20-25
	25-30

0   2000 km

0   3000 ml

(b)

FIGURE 5-4   (a) ABO blood group system. Distribution of the A allele in the indigenous populations of the world. (b) ABO blood group system. Distribution of the B allele in the indigenous populations of the world. (After Mourant et al., 1976.)

therefore, low frequencies of A). How did A increase so much among this one tribe and its close neighbors compared to surrounding populations? Possibly drift (founder effect) is the answer, possibly some unknown selective factor. No one knows.

In Australia, except for the northern part, frequencies of A are generally high—particularly in central Australia, where frequencies are 40% or higher. One tribe has especially high frequencies of A (53%), significantly higher than any surrounding group. Once again, is founder effect responsible? Over the rest of Australia, A frequencies are fairly even in distribution and are gradually decreasing as populations become further removed from the center of the continent.

We must point out that distributions of alleles for a single genetic trait like ABO do not conclusively demonstrate genetic relationships between populations. For example, the North American Blackfoot and central Australian Mandjiljara have similar frequencies of A, but are obviously not closely related. On the other hand, in South Africa, San have lower B frequencies than Hottentots with whom they share fairly close genetic ties. In order to understand *patterns* of population relationships, it is absolutely necessary to consider allele frequency distributions for several traits simultaneously.

Why do frequencies of the ABO alleles vary so much in different populations? In some cases, as with the islands off northern Australia and perhaps with the Blackfoot, drift may be the key factor. However, the clinal distribution of alleles (as B in Eurasia; A in Australia) indicates selection may also be playing an important role, for the regularity in the frequency distributions is thought to mirror gradual changes in environments.

If, in fact, selection is operating, what are the specific factors involved? Unfortunately, unlike sickle-cell, there is not as yet any proven association between ABO frequencies and *any* selective agent (such as various diseases, etc.) There are, however, some suggestive clues. For example, A individuals have significantly more stomach cancer and pernicious anemia, while O individuals have more gastric and duodenal ulcers (Vogel, 1970). Such chronic diseases as these are not that common; indeed, they probably do not affect reproductive success very much, since they occur so late in life.

On the other hand, infectious diseases (as already shown for malaria) are potentially selective factors of enormous significance. Some interesting clinal association between ABO frequencies and incidence of smallpox, tuberculosis, syphilis, bubonic plague, and leprosy have been suggested. Moreover, it has also been suggested that O individuals are more attractive to mosquitoes and are thus bitten more often than A, B, or AB individuals (Wood et al., 1972). Here, too, could be an important contributing factor for infectious disease, since many—malaria, yellow fever, typhus, etc.—are transmitted by insects (Brues, 1977). As yet none of these associations is well substantiated. Consequently, the evolutionary factors influencing the distribution of ABO alleles are still largely a mystery.

Rh Another group of antigens found on red blood cells is called the *Rh system*, named after rhesus monkeys that initially provided the source of red blood cells to make antiserum. Discovered in 1940 by Wiener and Landsteiner (a full forty years after the latter's discovery of ABO!), this antiserum was then tested in a large sample of white Americans, in which 85% reacted positively.

The individuals showing such a positive agglutination reaction are usually called Rh positive (Rh^+) and those whose blood does not agglutinate with the antiserum are called Rh negative (Rh^-). These standardized designations refer to an apparently simple two-allele system with DD and Dd as Rh^+ and the recessive dd as Rh^-.

Clinically, the Rh factor—like ABO—can also lead to serious complications. However, the greatest problem is not so much incompatibilities following transfusions as those between a mother and her developing fetus. (See Box 5-4.) For most significant medical applications, Rh^+ compared to Rh^- is accounted for by the three genotypes noted above (DD, Dd, dd). However, the actual genetics of the Rh system are a good deal more complex than explained by just two alleles at one locus. The famous English population geneticist Sir R. A. Fisher suggested that the Rh system is actually three closely linked loci with at least two alleles each (C and c, D and d, E and e).

The fact that the various antigens of the Rh system occur much more frequently only in a few combinations is of great interest to anthropologists. Of all the possible combinations in Fisher's three-locus system (eight of them), only three are commonly found. These eight combinations are called **haplotypes**, and their standard designations according to Fisher, with the common ones in boldface, are:

CDE   **CDe**   **cDE**   cDe   **cde**   Cde   cdE   CdE

The precise genetics of the Rh system remain a mystery. An alternative hypothesis to Fisher's three-locus system was suggested by Weiner and postulates one locus with at least eight alleles.

In either hypothesis there are numerous *possible* gene combinations; what is interesting is that only a minority of these are actually found in human populations. In a very large Swedish study (sample greater than 8,000) nine combinations (out of forty-five possibilities when haplotypes from *both* parents are considered) were found in frequencies exceeding 1% (Heiken and Rasmuson, 1966).

The distribution of the various allele combinations within the Rh system (which may be pictured as large genes) varies considerably among human populations. Generally Rh^- (d) is quite high in European groups, averaging around 40%. Of those Europeans who are Rh^-, the vast majority (more than 95%) have the haplotype, cde. African populations also have a fair amount of polymorphism at the D locus, with frequencies of Rh^- centering around 25%. American Indians and Australians, on the other hand, are almost 100% Rh^+.

An evolutionary explanation is demanded to account for this polymorphism. Why is Rh^- so high only in certain populations, particularly those in Europe? Due to mother-fetus incompatibilities (see Box 5-4) heterozygotes (Dd) should be selected against. Theoretically then, whichever allele starts out in a population with a lower frequency should be gradually selected out. In all human populations except the Basques of the Pyrenees mountain area between Spain and France (where d = 53%), Rh^- is lower in frequency than Rh^+. In all these populations, then, Rh^- theoretically should gradually be eliminated. Apparently, in European and African populations, this phenomenon has not happened. We are not sure why this case should be so, but a possible, totally unconfirmed, suggestion is that the Dd heterozygote has some sort of reproductive advantage later in life (another balanced polymorphism?).

Haplotype   A group of alleles from closely linked loci on the same chromosome.

BOX 5-4

Mother-Fetus Incompatibilities

A mother-fetus incompatibility occurs when the system of the mother is immunized by cells from a fetus and forms antibodies which then raise problems for that fetus, or future ones.

For the Rh trait, complications occur only when the mother is Rh⁻ (dd) and the father Rh⁺ (DD or Dd). Actually, the other loci (C, E) can also cause incompatibilities, but 95% of the problems are due to the D locus.

European populations are the most polymorphic for Rh, and around 13% of all matings are at risk. Not all those at risk, however, run into problems. Only about 6% of those potentially in danger have any complications. With new preventative treatment this figure can be expected to decline even further.

The problem of incompatibility arises only if the mother is Rh⁻ and her fetus is Rh⁺. Usually there are no serious effects in the first pregnancy, for the mother's system has not been immunized. Transfer along the placental boundary does not generally include blood cells, except in the case of rupture. Ruptures, however, do occur normally at birth so that fetal blood gets into the mother's system, stimulating the production of antibodies. Such antibodies do not occur naturally as in the ABO system, but they are produced "on the spot" quite quickly. About 70% of all Rh⁻ people have the capability of producing significant amounts of these antibodies, and it requires only one drop of Rh⁺ blood to stimulate the process!

When the next pregnancy occurs, transfer of the antibodies from the mother's system takes place across the placental boundary into the fetus. Here is the real problem: The anti-Rh⁺ antibodies react with the fetal blood,

causing cell destruction. Consequently, the fetus will be born with a severe malady called *hemolytic disease of the newborn*, which produces severe anemia with accompanying "oxygen starvation." Because of the lack of oxygen, such newborns are sometimes called "blue babies." In recent decades, doctors, prepared in advance for such complications, administered massive transfusions and often saved the infant. However, previous to modern medical treatment this disease was probably nearly always fatal. Such incompatibilities were thus fairly common in polymorphic populations and should have exerted a powerful selection pressure.

Quite recently physicians have sought to prevent incompatibilities by administering serum containing anti-Rh⁺ antibodies to women at risk after their first birth. These antibodies quickly destroy any fetal red blood cells as they enter the mother's circulation thereby preventing her from forming her own antibodies. Since the serum given the mother is a passive form of immunization (to her), it will shortly leave her bloodstream. She, therefore, does not produce any long-acting antibodies, and the quite low risk of first pregnancies should not be increased in the future.

It should also be mentioned that mother-fetus incompatibilities result from ABO as well. However, these are considerably rarer than Rh complications, with less than 0.1% of newborns affected. It is possible, though, that some ABO incompatibilities go undetected due to early fetal death.

A very interesting relationship appears to exist between Rh and ABO incompatibilities. Surprisingly, if the

OTHER RED BLOOD CELL ANTIGEN SYSTEMS

MN   The pattern of inheritance of the MN blood group that we have referred to a number of times is very straightforward and is thus a favorite tool in population genetics research. There are three genotypes—MM, MN, NN—all clearly ascertainable at the phenotypic level using antisera obtained from rabbits. Clinically, no observable complications arise due to transfusions or mother-fetus incompatibilities; the MN system is anthropologically important because of its variable distribution among human populations.

Almost all human populations are polymorphic (that is, having both M and N in "appreciable" frequencies), but the relative frequency of the two alleles varies tremendously. In some areas of Australia, M is as low as 2% contrasted with many

BOX 5-4

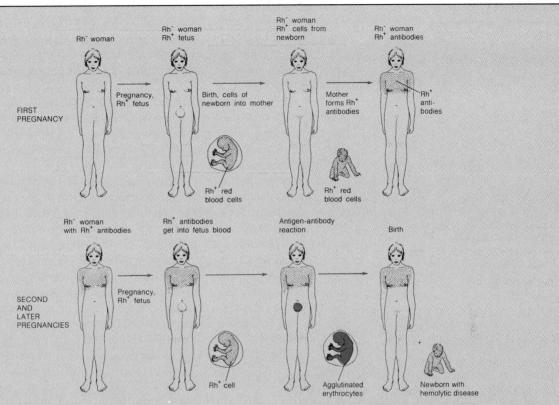

FIGURE 1   Rh incompatibility and hemolytic disease of the newborn. The series of events during first and later pregnancies. (After Novitski, 1977.)

fetus is *both* ABO and Rh incompatible with the mother, the effects are less than if the incompatibility were for only one trait. ABO incompatibility seems to buffer the potentially very serious effects of Rh immunization. How this occurs is still unknown, but possibly the naturally occurring anti-A and/or anti-B antibodies coat and inactivate incoming cells, thus preventing them from stimulating the Rh immune response in the mother's system.

areas of the New World, where frequencies exceed 90%, even 100% in some areas. The allele M is also found in quite high frequency in Arabia, Siberia, and portions of Southeast Asia.

In addition to ABO, Rh, and MN, there are several other polymorphic red blood cell antigen systems. While not clinically significant like ABO or Rh, many of these are important for anthropological studies of population variation. Table 5-4 lists the currently known major antigen systems of human red blood cells.

POLYMORPHISMS IN WHITE BLOOD CELLS

An important polymorphic trait called the HLA system has been discovered on some white blood cells (lymphocytes). Of great medical importance, HLA affects

TABLE 5-4   **Other Blood Group Systems Used in Human Microevolutionary Studies**

MAJOR SYSTEMS	NUMBER OF KNOWN ANTIGENS
P	3
Lutheran	2
Kell-Cellano	5
Lewis	2
Duffy	2
Kidd	2
Diego	1
Auberger	1
Xg (sex-linked)	1
Dombrock	1
Stolzfus	1

Source: Lerner and Libby, 1976, p. 354.

FIGURE 5-5   MN blood group system. Distribution of the M allele in the indigenous populations of the world. (After Mourant et al., 1976.)

histocompatibility or recognition and rejection of foreign tissues—the reason skin grafts and organ transplants are usually rejected. Genetically, the HLA system is exceedingly complex, and researchers are still discovering further subtleties within it. There are at least seven closely linked loci on chromosome number six, making up the HLA system. Taken together, there are already well over 100 antigens known within the system, with a potential of at least 30,000,000 different genotypes (Williams, 1985). By far, this is the most polymorphic of any known human genetic system.

The component loci of the HLA system function together as a kind of "supergene." In addition to the components of the HLA loci themselves, many other components affecting immune response are known to exist in the same region of chromosome number six. Altogether, the whole system is called the *major histocompatibility complex* (MHC). (See pp. 170–171.)

Since this system has only recently been discovered, the geographic distribution of the various alleles is not yet well known. Some interesting patterns, however, are apparent. For example, Lapps, Sardinians, and Basques show deviations in frequencies of HLA alleles from other European populations, paralleling evidence for ABO, Rh, and MN. In addition, many areas in New Guinea and Australia are quite divergent, possibly suggesting the effects of drift. It is imperative, however, that care be taken in postulating genetic relatedness from restricted polymorphic information. Otherwise, such obviously ridiculous links as some of those proposed from HLA data (for example, Tibetans and Australian aborigines; Eskimos with some New Guineans) would obscure the evolutionary process in human populations (Livingstone, 1980). Since HLA is involved in the superfine detection and deactivation of foreign antigens, selection relative to infectious dis-

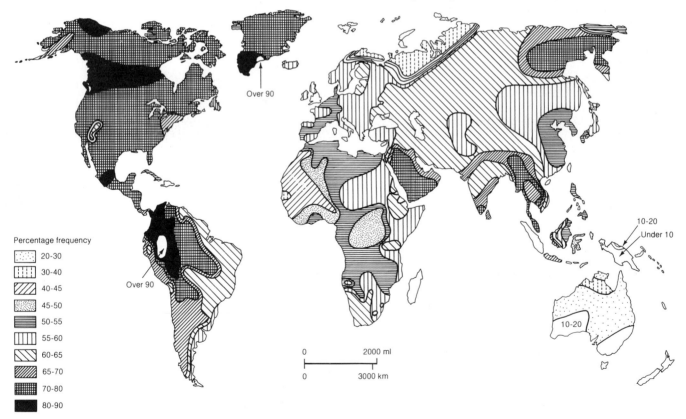

Percentage frequency
- 20-30
- 30-40
- 40-45
- 45-50
- 50-55
- 55-60
- 60-65
- 65-70
- 70-80
- 80-90

Over 90
Over 90
10-20
Under 10
10-20

0   2000 ml
0   3000 km

eases (particularly those caused by viruses) may also play a significant role in the distribution of HLA alleles.

Evidence is still exceedingly tentative, but some HLA antigens are apparently associated with susceptibility to certain diseases. A disease of the spine called ankylosing spondylitis, the disease multiple sclerosis, and some varieties of hay fever may all result from individuals developing an autoimmune response to their own HLA antigens.

POLYMORPHISMS IN THE BLOOD SERUM

In addition to those found on the red and white blood cells, polymorphisms have also been discovered in the blood serum. The most important of these are the *immunoglobulins* and *haptoglobins*. Immunoglobulins are themselves antibody molecules made of long chains, which apparently have the capacity to change in response to foreign antigens. The best known of the immunoglobulins is called the *Gm system*, composed of several closely linked loci. Alleles for these loci are combined into haplotypes, which are of anthropological interest because of their variable occurrence among human populations. As has been demonstrated for ABO and HLA, the Gm system perhaps acts as part of the human immune response system and may therefore be distributed relative to particular infectious diseases.

Haptoglobins are serum proteins whose function is to bind with free hemoglobin and transport it to a site where it will be recycled. Haptoglobins are apparently determined by one locus with two common alleles (Hp^1, Hp^2), whose geographic distribution varies considerably. Frequencies of Hp^1 as low as .12 are found among Swedish gypsies, while frequencies as high as .90 are known in parts of Nigeria.

Miscellaneous Polymorphisms

TASTERS AND NONTASTERS

An interesting genetically controlled variation in human populations was discovered by accident in 1931. When the artificially synthesized chemical phenylthiocarbamide (PTC) was dropped in a laboratory, some researchers were able to smell it, while others could not. It was later established that there is a dichotomy in human populations between individuals who can and cannot taste PTC (although tasters vary considerably in sensitivity). The pattern of inheritance appears to follow that of a simple Mendelian trait, with TT and Tt being the tasters and tt the nontasters. In most populations, a majority of individuals are tasters, but the frequency of nontasters varies considerably from as low as 5% in sub-Saharan Africa to as high as 40% in India.

It is an interesting fact that other primates show the PTC polymorphism, suggesting this trait is a long-standing one. What is its function? Obviously selection pressures were not operating in primate evolution relative to a synthesized substance. PTC-tasting variability, then, is probably an expression of a gene coding for taste discrimination for some naturally occurring substance(s). Chemically,

PTC is similar to substances found in plants of the mustard family (cabbage, brussels sprouts, etc.), which, if overconsumed, can cause thyroid problems. Perhaps a selective mechanism allowing avoidance of these plants explains this mysterious polymorphism.

In any case, it is easy to postulate that genetically conditioned tasting variability among human populations could be an important adaptation. High taste discrimination could be of great selective advantage particularly to children who, uninitiated into the dietary rules of the group, may easily pick up and eat poisonous wild plants. The fact that tasting ability appears to vary with age may well indicate the importance of taste discrimination in early childhood.

EARWAX

Another puzzling human polymorphism is the genetic variability seen in earwax, or cerumen. Earwax is found in human groups in two basic varieties: (1) yellow, sticky, with a good deal of lipids (fats and fatlike substances); and (2) gray, dry, with less lipids.

Cerumen variation appears to be inherited as a simple Mendelian trait with two alleles (dry=homozygous recessive). Interestingly, frequencies of the two varieties of earwax vary considerably among human populations. In European populations, about 90% of the individuals have the sticky variety, while in northern China only about 4% are of this type.

How do we explain these differences? What selection pressures would act directly on earwax are difficult to imagine. Perhaps earwax variation is an incidental expression of a gene controlling something more adaptively significant. Production of earwax is apparently related to secretion in other glands, particularly the axillary glands under the arms. Odors produced by these glands may have importance for sexual behavior, as recent studies in nonhuman primates suggest. Moreover, human males produce characteristically different scents from females. It might be added that other animals also recognize differences in human scents, as shown by the particular aversion of Southeast Asian water buffaloes to the smell of Europeans.

Human Polymorphisms: Anthropological Applications

All the patterns of variation in the diverse traits we have discussed may seem somewhat confusing. In fact, without the aid of computer technology it is difficult to gain a clear view of what is going on. More than looking at just one trait at a time, anthropologists seek to understand the *pattern* of several polymorphisms simultaneously. From an analysis of these patterns we hope to reconstruct the evolutionary events and population histories that have shaped the development of human variation observable today. In a sense, we are looking for the family tree of *Homo sapiens*.

With the assistance of computer analysis, we can construct trees, or **clado-grams**, such as the one shown in Figure 5-6 based on fifteen different genetic polymorphisms (including ABO, MN, Rh, Gm, and HLA). The logic behind such a reconstruction is based on the assumption that populations more closely related

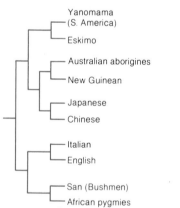

FIGURE 5-6   Cladogram. A "tree" of relationships among human populations derived from statistical analyses of fifteen human polymorphisms. (After Bodmer and Cavalli-Sforza, 1976.)

Yanomama (S. America)
Eskimo
Australian aborigines
New Guinean
Japanese
Chinese
Italian
English
San (Bushmen)
African pygmies

should be more similar in allele frequencies. Many traits must be used together, since drift may cause wide and nonsystematic deviations in the pattern of only a few loci.

Anthropological studies of modern evolution seek to make these kinds of reconstructions, but even abundant allele frequency data do not provide clearcut solutions. The form of the tree varies considerably depending on which loci are employed. A vast variety of possible interpretations can be drawn from the same data. As a population geneticist has stated, "Phylogenetic trees are like flower arrangements: it is enough that they are pretty, without asking that they are meaningful" (N. E. Morton, quoted in Livingstone, 1980, p. 33). Still, such an approach is extremely helpful and provides an alternative to the traditional "racial" studies of the history of human populations (see Chapter 7).

Genetic Coadaptation

Throughout this chapter we have discussed evolutionary factors, such as selection and drift acting on single genetic loci. This device is a convenient way to picture evolution, but in natural populations the situation is not so simple. Genes are not floating around as isolated entities, but are "packaged" into individuals who are composites of many (perhaps 100,000?) loci. Selection acts not on the genetic locus itself, but on the whole individual—the combined product of genes and environment.

Moreover, genes interact complexly with one another so that the allele frequency values observed in populations are more intricate than simple totals would indicate. Such interaction at the genotypic level is called **coadaptation**. The kinds of interactions are not simply additive because some genes are better "mixers" than others. For example, ABO and Rh appear to mix well, since incompatibility for both traits is less harmful than for one. (See p. 139.)

From the view of selection, the crucial bottom line is the most fit *total* genotype, and factors influencing this composite are complex and multiple. Consequently, simple evolutionary models cannot cope with such complexity, and computer-generated multivariate ("many variables") simulations are required.

However, for the purposes of demonstration and to gain a basic understanding of the evolutionary process, it is still beneficial to conceptualize evolution as acting on single genes. We can then use relatively simple models, such as the Hardy-Weinberg formula, to ascertain crude approximations of evolutionary changes in populations.

Understanding Human Polymorphisms: What Makes Evolution Tick

From the discussion of numerous human polymorphisms in this chapter (Table 5-5), you may begin to feel there is a great deal of variability in human populations. Indeed there is. Research thus far has but scratched the surface of the vast store of genetic variation in our species. A random sample of various proteins indicates that approximately 28% of all loci in humans are polymorphic, and similar results

Cladogram (tree diagram) A diagrammatic presentation of population relationships using several genetic traits simultaneously.

Coadaptation Interaction of genes to produce phenotypes which selection then acts upon.

TABLE 5-5   **Human Polymorphisms of Anthropological Interest**

In the Blood

Red blood cells:
Hemoglobins (hemoglobin beta chain: Hb^A, Hb^S, Hb^C)
G-6-PD and several other enzymes
Thalassemia loci (suppress production of hemoglobin)

Antigen systems:
ABO
Rh
MN
Others (Kell, Diego, Duffy, for example)

White blood cells:
HLA system (part of the major histocompatibility complex, MHC)

Blood serum:
Immunoglobulins (Gm, for example)
Haptoglobins

Miscellaneous Polymorphisms
PTC tasting
Cerumen (earwax)

in other animals suggest such a tremendous store of variation is typical. Where did all this variation come from?

Obviously any new allele must first be introduced through a mutation. But to be polymorphic this allele *must* somehow spread; in other words, allele frequencies must increase well above low mutation rates.

There are several possible explanations of the ways genes have spread in human populations. One possibility that comes to mind immediately concerns balancing selection, as demonstrated so well by the sickle-cell trait. Such a balanced polymorphism fully explains why more than one allele is maintained in relatively high frequency. This mechanism has also been suggested for other human polymorphisms such as ABO, MN, HLA, and so forth, but *none* of these has yet been demonstrated.

Whereas it is true that we rarely know how selection pressures directly influence human variation, we certainly can see the gross effects of natural selection at work. You will recall that selection is defined as "differential reproductive success." Clearly, not all humans reproduce equally, and some of the reasons causing these disparities are genetic. Put quite simply, this is natural selection.

Even in our medically sophisticated culture, many individuals never pass on their genes. Of all the zygotes conceived in the United States currently, it is estimated that the great majority never make it to reproduction. Based on very rough approximations, it is believed that approximately 50% are lost before birth, 3% are stillborn, 2% die shortly after birth, and another 3% die before maturity. Of those who survive into adulthood, approximately 20% never marry (and presumably do not mate) and 10% of those who marry are childless (Damon, 1977, p. 111). The cumulative result is that perhaps only about 10–15% of all zygotes conceived ever reproduce! Without modern medicine, the incidence of stillbirths and infant deaths would be considerably higher (see Fig. 5-7).

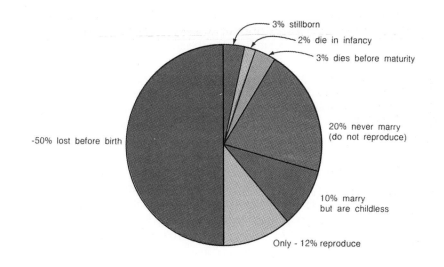

FIGURE 5-7   Natural selection today. Perhaps only about 15% of all zygotes conceived ever reproduce.

Reproductive rates in human populations are influenced by several complex factors, some biological/ecological, others cultural. Some populations, particularly in "open" environments, have shown high fertility rates, increasing extremely quickly in size. For example, the offspring of the *Bounty* mutineers and Tahitian women on Pitcairn Island increased fourfold in just forty years (Shapiro, 1936). The peopling of the New World may also have involved rapid expansion of an initially fairly small group.

The highest fertility rate known in recent human groups was recorded in the 1930s for Hutterites, an isolated religious sect living in the United States. The *average* number of children born per Hutterite woman was an incredible 10.4. Given the cooperative social structure of this group, sound medical treatment, and so on, this probably represents close to the maximum potential for human groups.

Fertility rates for the overall United States population are much lower, and social factors within the last century have seen them drop significantly further. In the middle of the nineteenth century, the average number of children per woman was somewhat over 5; in the period 1960 to 1964 this figure had fallen to approximately 3.5. Since the 1960s, fertility rates in the United States have shown an even steeper decline. Figures for 1973 indicate a rate of only 1.9, a full 45% drop from a decade before (Damon, 1977).

Obviously, social pressures of an urbanized, technological society have a great deal to do with this decline, but there may be a biological component as well. Are reduced fertility rates partly the product of altered selection pressures in crowded urban environments?

Selection pressures may go a long way toward explaining human polymorphisms, but they do not completely account for all the observed variation. Another significant factor, particularly in small populations, is *genetic drift*. Drift explains the spread of alleles due strictly to chance factors. As we discussed in Chapter 4, many biologists today argue for a primary role for random drift in the development of human variation and thereby dispute the role of selection (see, for example, King and Jukes, 1969).

In all probability, *both* natural selection and genetic drift acted significantly as factors influencing the spread of alleles in human populations. Selection certainly acts on alleles causing severe inherited disorders such as sickle-cell anemia, Tay-

Sachs, and cystic fibrosis. These are all very deleterious, causing early death. Therefore, the allele causing these diseases should gradually be reduced in frequency (or never have spread initially) in the absence of some special balancing mechanism.

Moreover, selection pressures no doubt also relate to such infectious diseases as malaria, smallpox, typhoid, and plague, which either kill or debilitate much larger numbers of people than the inherited disorders noted in the preceding paragraph. If there are genes that lead to some form of protection (those that build up immunity, for instance) from these infectious diseases, they should spread in human populations. Keep in mind that exposure of human populations to most infectious diseases is greatly influenced by cultural factors, such as settlement patterns, population size, and prevailing standards of sanitation. (See pp. 169–170.)

Drift too has been significant, particularly when small human populations become isolated—either socially or geographically. During most of human prehistory, hunting-gathering subsistence groups were probably fairly small, but their available range of mates was expanded considerably due to group exogamy and mobility. Drift may have played its most decisive role in early agricultural times when human groups were not only small but sedentary as well.

Today, facilitated by mechanized transportation, migration is breaking down genetic isolates throughout the world. As human groups become less and less isolated, we can expect the evolutionary effects of genetic drift to decrease. That does not mean our species has stopped evolving. On the contrary, our ever-increasing disruption of the earth's ecosystem, our overcrowded cities, our synthesized and often inadequate diets, and the manifold psychological stresses of complex society are all causing new kinds of selection pressures. The question is therefore not whether our species is still evolving, but in which direction, how rapidly, and is it evolving rapidly enough to prevent extinction?

Summary

Physical anthropologists study evolution in human populations using the perspective of *population genetics*. In order to apply the principles of this perspective, we first must isolate actual human *populations*. As we have seen, in geographically and/or socially isolated situations, this process is relatively straightforward, but, in complex societies, it becomes quite arbitrary.

Once populations are defined, we can apply evolutionary models, such as the Hardy-Weinberg formula, to ascertain whether changes in allele frequency (that is, evolution) are occurring. In human populations, allele frequencies change through one or a combination of the four forces of evolution: mutaton, migration, random genetic drift, and natural selection.

The kinds of genetic traits measured in population genetics studies are called *polymorphisms*, traits with more than one allele in appreciable frequency. Some of these traits, particularly the *sickle-cell trait*, have a direct relation to potent selection pressures due to malaria.

In addition to hemoglobin, there are many other polymorphisms found in human blood that are of interest to anthropologists. On the red blood cells are several antigen systems, the most important of which are ABO, Rh, and MN. There are also polymorphisms on the white blood cells (HLA, for instance) and in the blood serum. Finally, two other rather puzzling polymorphisms—PTC-tasting and cerumen (earwax)—are also of anthropological significance.

All these traits vary considerably among modern human populations and thus demand evolutionary explanations. Such explanations are, however, necessarily complex and must account for interaction of genes (*coadaptation*) and interaction of evolutionary forces. For example, mutation is the usual starting point, but further spread of alleles must involve some combination of natural selection, drift, and migration.

We seek to understand human variation, but such an understanding is grounded in basic knowledge of the processes of human evolution.

Questions for Review

1. Why is it so important to study human *populations* in order to understand human evolution?
2. Why is it difficult to isolate actual populations?
3. Under what conditions does the Hardy-Weinberg equilibrium model hold true? If a deviation from expected frequencies is found, what does that suggest?
4. What is nonrandom mating? Cite some suspected examples for human populations and explain how each will affect Hardy-Weinberg predictions.
5. What is meant by migration? Give examples of how migration has affected human evolution.
6. What is genetic drift and why are examples of drift in human populations usually found in small groups?
7. What is a polymorphism? Why are polymorphisms used in evolutionary studies?
8. How does the distribution of the sickle-cell trait indicate the action of natural selection? Describe the specific evolutionary mechanics involved in this "balanced polymorphism."
9. Why are so many polymorphisms known in human blood? Give several examples and discuss why they are of evolutionary interest.
10. Give a detailed account for a hypothetical human population: (a) How a mutant allele might arise; and (b) how it might then spread.

Suggested Further Reading

Two other introductory physical anthropology texts cover the topics of this chapter in somewhat more depth, but at approximately the same level of difficulty.

Birdsell, Joseph. *Human Evolution* (3rd Ed.), Boston: Houghton Mifflin Co., 1981.
    Excellent review of human microevolution drawing particularly on the author's wide experience in Australia. (See Chaps. 14 through 16, especially.)
Weiss, Mark L. and Alan E. Mann. *Human Biology and Behavior* (3rd Ed.), Boston: Little, Brown, and Co., 1981.
    An up-to-date look at human biology from the perspective of human evolution with a strong emphasis on biocultural factors. (See Chaps. 8 through 12.)

Other, more specialized works:

Bodmer, W. F. and L. L. Cavalli-Sforza. *Genetics, Evolution, and Man*, San Francisco: W. H. Freeman & Co., 1976.

This work emphasizes medical genetics. Written by two leading population geneticists, discussions of this topic are authoritative and up-to-date.

Brues, Alice. *People and Races*, Prospect Heights, Il: Waveland Press, 1977; reissued, 1990.

A clearly written summary of topics in human variation, emphasizing easily visible phenotypic traits.

Cavalli-Sforza, L. L. and W. F. Bodmer. *The Genetics of Human Populations*, San Francisco: W. H. Freeman & Co., 1971.

The most authoritative synthesis of human population genetics. This highly technical work is recommended only for those students wishing to explore the detailed mathematics of population genetics.

Cummings, Michael R. *Human Heredity* (2nd Ed.), St. Paul: West Publishing Co., 1991.

An excellent, up-to-date, and easy to understand introduction to human genetics. (See particularly Chapters 14–16 on Polygenic Inheritance, Genes in Populations, and Human Diversity and Evolution.)

Damon, Albert. *Human Biology and Ecology,* New York: W. W. Norton and Company, 1977.

A straightforward approach to understanding human variation, adaptations, and disease from an evolutionary point of view. This work also contains a good review of population genetics.

Garn, Stanley. *Human Races* (3rd Ed.), Springfield, Ill.: Charles C. Thomas, Inc., 1971.

Although concentrating primarily on patterns of geographic variation, this book is an excellent reference for discussions of the various polymorphisms discussed in this chapter.

Underwood, Jane. *Biocultural Interactions and Human Variation*, Dubuque, Iowa: Wm. C. Brown Co., 1975.

Brief but excellent introduction into how evolution is measured in human populations, particularly estimating the effects of natural selection. Especially helpful are the discussions of dietary adaptations and the influence of disease.

Human Adaptability: Meeting the Challenge of the Environment

Contents

Babies by Choice
and Not by Chance*

About 12 million Americans have disabilities attributable to heredity, and such traits account for approximately one-third of admissions to pediatric wards. The estimates for 1980 suggested that out of 3.5 million newborns in the United States, 96,075 would be afflicted with genetic disorders: 19,075 with chromosomal abnormalities; 35,000 with deleterious Mendelian traits; and 42,000 with multifactorial disorders (Miles, 1980).

Dramatic advances in human genetics, medicine, and the law now allow the detection of certain carriers of recessive mutations and chromosomal aberrations, prenatal diagnosis by amniocentesis, and safe, selective abortion to alleviate the personal and social burdens of the abovementioned hereditary disorders. The U.S. Supreme Court decision in *Roe* vs. *Wade* (1973) stipulates that a woman's right to privacy has precedence over the life of any embryo or fetus that is incapable of independent existence outside the womb. Consequently, in the United States, abortion is permitted in the first six months of a pregnancy.

Prenatal diagnosis becomes feasible after the sixteenth week of pregnancy when the uterus has enlarged above the pubic bone (allowing a needle to penetrate the abdominal wall and uterus) and there is sufficient amniotic fluid to withdraw 10 to 20 milliliters in a syringe without endangering the fetus. This procedure is termed *amniocentesis*.

*This Issue was contributed by Richard L. Ingraham, Ph.D., Professor of Biology, San Jose State University, San Jose, California.

Certain diagnostic tests can be made directly on the fluid, but the tests for most metabolic errors and the analysis of chromosomes require that fetal cells be cultured for a few weeks to obtain a large enough population for making karyotype preparations and biochemical assays. Waiting for results can be disconcerting for participating couples since abortion is a more difficult procedure medically and psychologically the longer it is delayed. However, amniocentesis has proven to be "safe, highly reliable, and extremely accurate" (Golbus et al., 1979). At present, any identifiable chromosomal anomaly and well over 100 metabolic disorders can be ascertained *in utero*. A test result indicating the fetus is free from a suspected disorder allays the anxiety of those couples with a high risk of producing defective offspring. A recent government study indicates that prenatal diagnosis has led to a 10% increase in the childbearing of such couples.

Down's syndrome (sometimes called "mongolism"—a disorder caused by the presence of an extra chromosome number 21) increases in frequency with advanced maternal age. The risk of a woman bearing an affected baby is 1 out of 1,923 at 20 years and 1 out of 32 at 45 years. About one-half of all Down's infants are born to women 35 years or older. Although such children may be cheerful and affectionate, their mental handicap (usually severe mental retardation as well as physical disorders) and continued dependency can disrupt normal family life and make them a financial burden upon society. Since modern medicine has increased the life span of those affected with Down's syn-

drome, it is quite possible that an affected person will outlive his or her parents.

Inasmuch as the care of the 50,000 Down's individuals in the United States costs families and society about $250 million annually, some states have passed legislation that encourages the expansion of prenatal diagnostic services to reduce the incidence of such traits. Considering the pluralistic character of American society and the social, ethical, and legal issues raised by advances in human genetics, controversy cannot be avoided. The current foment spilling over into state and federal legislatures as well as into the courts only serves to emphasize this point.

Regardless of parental age, couples carrying recessive mutations for hereditary disease (for example, Tay-Sachs disease, hemophilia, and thalassemia major) and/or structural aberrations of chromosomes constitute a second group seeking prenatal diagnoses. Neural tube defects, involving the brain and spinal cord, may result in neonatal death, mental retardation, and paralysis. In Great Britain, neural tube defects are the most common of serious congenital malformations. Evidence suggests a multifactorial cause for this malady. The presence of abnormally high levels of a particular protein in the maternal blood serum (as well as in the amniotic fluid) is a good indication that the neural tube has not closed properly. Visual evidence of malformation can be corroborated by ultrasound techniques that use the same equipment employed to ascertain the position of the fetus in the womb prior to making a transabdominal tap by amniocentesis. Some families have an unusually high occurrence of chromosomal aberrations perhaps caused by a translocated chromosome. In fact, the probability that normal carriers of such translocated chromosomes will have affected offspring may be as high as one in three.

The analysis of chromosomal problems utilizes a now fairly standard technique; thus, most major hospitals provide such karyotyping service. However, detecting metabolic errors (most of which are individually rare) requires a multiplicity of sophisticated procedures that differ among traits. Not every research laboratory can suitably handle such complex diagnoses.

A method of prenatal diagnosis that can be performed as early as 10 weeks after conception has become available in the last few years. Known as *chorionic villi sampling*, the method involves the insertion of a plastic catheter (tube) through the cervix of the uterus. Chorionic tissue, consisting of rapidly dividing fetal cells, is then removed for subsequent chromosomal and biochemical studies. It is often possible to obtain diagnostic information from chorionic cells within a day—instead of after a wait of several weeks. Consequently, a pregnancy that is diagnosed by this technique to have a major genetic problem can (at the discretion of parents and physician) be more safely terminated within the medically suggested period of the first trimester.

Since technical problems associated with chorionic villi sampling are greater than they are for amniocentesis, this newly developed technique is still only available at a few medical centers. Even though more general adoption of the

THE AMNIOCENTESIS PROCEDURE, STEP BY STEP

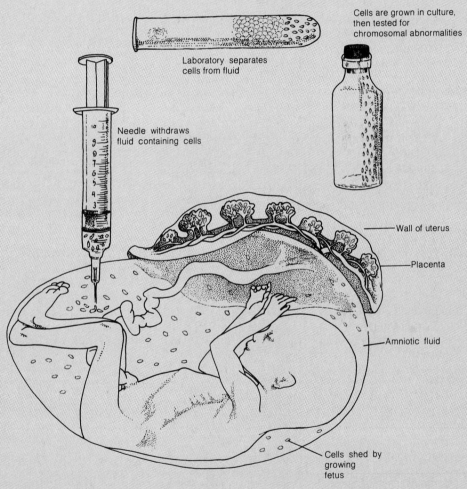

Laboratory separates cells from fluid

Cells are grown in culture, then tested for chromosomal abnormalities

Needle withdraws fluid containing cells

Wall of uterus

Placenta

Amniotic fluid

Cells shed by growing fetus

method would lead to a decline in the number of amniocentesis tests performed, amniocentesis itself will still be used for certain diagnostic purposes, such as ascertaining neural tube defects, a pro-

cedure that requires a sample of amniotic fluid.

Even more sophisticated techniques are on the drawing board. For example, a significant "fall-out" from genetic engineering research that utilizes recombinant DNA has allowed accurate diagnosis of a number of deleterious genetic traits. Such techniques have already made it possible to ascertain several medically important mutations (including sickle-cell and cystic fibrosis), and are but a portent of the extraordinary array of tests that will be available in the future. You are especially encouraged to look into some of the recent summaries on the following Recent Publications list.

SOURCES:

"Cutting the Risk of Childbirth after 35," *Consumer Reports*, May 1979, pp. 302–306.

Emery, A.E.H. (ed.). *Antenatal Diagnosis of Genetic Disease*, Baltimore: The Williams and Wilkins Co., 1973.

"First-Trimester Prenatal Diagnostic Method Becoming Available in U.S.," Medical News, *Journal of the American Medical Association*, 250(Sept. 9, 1983):1249–1250.

Golbus, M. S., et al., "Prenatal Genetic Diagnosis in 3000 Amniocenteses," *New England Journal of Medicine*, 300(Jan. 25, 1979):157–163.

Harris, H. *Prenatal Diagnosis and Selective Abortion*, Cambridge, Mass.: Harvard University Press, 1975.

Miles, J. H. "Medical Genetics: Impact and Strategy," *Stadler Genetics Symposia*, 12(1980): 33–41.

"Recombinant DNA Methods for Prenatal Diagnosis," *Annals of Internal Medicine*, 99(Nov. 1983):718–719.

Recent Publications:

Duster, Troy. *Backdoor to Eugenics*, New York: Routledge, 1990.

Filkins, Karen and Joseph F. Russo (eds.). *Human Prenatal Diagnosis*, 2nd ed., New York: Marcel Dekker, Inc., 1990.

Holtzman, Neil. *Proceed with Caution—Predicting Genetic Risks in the Recombinant DNA Era*, Baltimore: Johns Hopkins University Press, 1988.

CHAPTER 6

Introduction

In the previous chapter, we discussed several specific genetic traits that are known to vary among human populations. Some of these, particularly sickle-cell hemoglobin, are probably directly related to selection pressures. Most human variation, however, cannot yet be conclusively tied to any specific selection factor.

In this chapter, we will take up possible adaptive responses in human populations to more general kinds of selection pressures. For example, are there genetic differences in human populations allowing adaptation to heat stress, cold stress, high altitude, ultraviolet radiation, or specific dietary factors? Moreover, have the conditions of modern technological society presented new selection pressures such as crowding, artificial radiation, and noise?

Again, we must emphasize that demonstrating direct effects of natural selection on humans is extremely difficult. So many variables have to be considered simultaneously that clearly proven associations between specific phenotypes and specific environments are not usually possible. Rigorous experimental controls, practical for studies of other organisms, are not feasible for humans. Moreover, adaptations to general kinds of ecological conditions of heat, light, altitude, etc., are made through numerous complex physiological changes. Such adaptations involve several **polygenic** traits, none of which has a clearly understood hereditary basis.

Many different human populations today live under arduous environmental conditions. Some live in scalding temperatures averaging above 100°F in the summer and others survive through frigid winter months averaging −50°F. Still others exist all year long at altitudes above 15,000 feet. In all these cases, the groups living under these severe environmental stresses have made adjustments, both behavioral and physiological. Without the human nervous system which in turn produces culture (which *is* humankind's ecological niche), none of these demanding environments could ever have been conquered. If culture is the dominant means of human adaptation, are there also biological changes in populations that have been subjected for several generations to severe stresses?

Certainly, general climatic/ecological conditions exert strong selection pressures, and human populations do show differences in their average physiological responses to certain environmental conditions. The question then becomes: *Are these populations more adapted through natural selection (differential success of certain genotypes), or are they just showing a physiological adjustment capacity common to all humans?*

Polygenic   poly: many
genic: genes
Traits controlled by several loci; for example, stature, weight, skin color. Also called complex traits.

Complex Traits

All the genetic traits discussed in the previous chapter (Chapter 5) were examples of simple, one-locus (Mendelian) mechanisms. On the other hand, traits such as

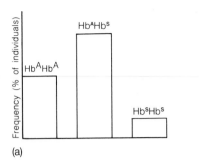

(a)

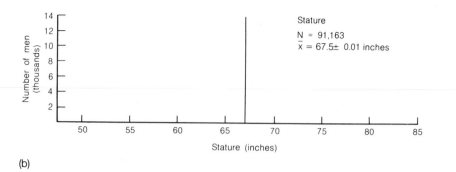

(b)

FIGURE 6-1   Distribution of phenotypes. (*a*) Distribution of phenotypes for adult hemoglobin (beta chain). Example: population living in malarial area. (*b*) Distribution of stature. The data shown are from a population of over 90,000 English military recruits (1939). The mean ($\bar{X}$) is shown by the solid line. Data from Martin, Physique of Young Adult Males, HMSO, 1949.

stature, weight, IQ, body proportions, skin color (that is, all the traits discussed in this chapter except that for lactose production) are controlled by several genetic loci and are thus termed polygenic traits. For those simple traits the distribution of phenotypes is discontinuous with no overlap. For example, the gene for hemoglobin (beta chain) in some populations has two alleles (Hb^A, Hb^S) that combine to produce three and *only* three genotypes. These genotypes are in turn reflected in the phenotypes, so for a population we can ascertain the phenotypes of all individuals in a completely clearcut fashion.* (See Fig. 6-1.)

As can be seen, no overlap exists between phenotypes; in other words, they are discontinuous. All individuals are specifically one of the three phenotypes, and there is an observable *qualitative* difference in their hemoglobin.

On the other hand, polygenic traits are influenced by several loci, each perhaps with several alleles. The possible number of genotypes and corresponding phenotypes is therefore very large, and the gradation between them appears to overlap. In addition, the differences between individual phenotypes is further obscured by environmental influence which, in traits like weight (due to excess food, dieting, starvation, etc.) or IQ (due to early schooling, family size, etc.), can greatly affect phenotypic expression. Because the relationship between the actual genotype and the eventual phenotypic expression in polygenic traits is so complexly determined, phenotypic variation can only be handled in a statistical manner. Contrary to simple traits, their distribution appears *continuous* with only *quantitative* phenotypic differences observable.

Since both genetic and environmental variability influence the expression of polygenic traits, it is often an interesting venture to try to partition this variation. As we have noted before, such an undertaking raises the age-old nature/nurture argument.

For domestic animals or crops, such a study can provide important economic information. For example, if a dairy farmer wants to improve the milk yield of his cows, should he invest his capital in better food or in upgrading his stock (buying a prize bull or sperm for artificial insemination)? Such a question can be answered by a *heritability* study, which will partition the variance between genetic and environmental components of this polygenic trait (milk yield in cows). In animals the methodology is fairly straightforward, where controls are possible such as de-

---

*In this case Hb^A and Hb^S are codominant (i.e., *both* alleles are expressed in the heterozygote), so there is no difficulty in directly relating the observed phenotypes to their underlying genotypes. However, in traits where there is *dominance*, it may be difficult or impossible to differentiate all the genotypes (in other words, AA and Aa would *appear*—at least as far as we can tell—phenotypically identical).

liberately randomizing environments or breeding in genetic homogeneity (accomplished in laboratory animals through successive close inbreeding).

However, humans present a much stickier problem, since we cannot artificially manipulate human beings in laboratories. We must therefore attack the genetic/environmental issue somewhat indirectly. Human heritability studies are accomplished through comparative studies of twins: **monozygotic** and **dizygotic**. From such investigations we can obtain crude approximations of genetic vs. environmental influence on the variance of polygenic traits in human groups (samples). However, many complexities remain that are difficult or impossible to control. For example, twins are not necessarily representative of whole populations, and even more significantly, studies done on one population under special environmental conditions do not apply to other populations.

The tremendous public furor over the genetic environmental contributions to IQ and variability in scores among human groups dramatizes many of the problems in our still very crude attempts at understanding polygenic inheritance in human beings. (See p. 201.)

Monozygotic   mono: one
zygote: fertilized egg
Twins derived from one zygote, genetically identical. Differences between the twins are caused solely by the environment.

Dizygotic   di: two
zygote: fertilized egg
Twins derived from two zygotes, genetically related the same as any full siblings, and differences between them are caused both by the environment and genetic variation.

Biological adaptation   Genetic changes within populations in response to selection (environmental) pressure; usually takes many generations.

Adaptation and Acclimatization

The way in which humans and other organisms meet the challenges of the environment is through a general process called *adaptation*. This term has a wide variety of meanings, and in its broadest connotation can refer to any changes (genetic, environmental, physiological, or behavioral) by which organisms surmount the challenges to life (Lasker, 1969). In fact, archeologists and cultural anthropologists often refer to *cultural* adaptive responses of human societies, such as those dealing with the adjustments resulting from technological innovation.

Among physical anthropologists and other human biologists, however, a more restricted definition of **biological adaptation** is usually implied. From this perspective, adaptation is viewed as an *evolutionary* process and, even more precisely, as the result of natural selection. Consequently, biological adaptation applies only to whole populations.

In terms of natural selection, individual organisms cannot adapt; they just produce offspring as well as they can under the circumstances. Biological adaptation occurs only *between* generations as the result of differential reproductive success among all the individuals of the population. Biological adaptations, then, *must* have a genetic basis. As environments change so do selection pressures and so also does the reproductive success of various genotypes. Groups of organisms can respond adaptively to changing environmental conditions only over the span of several generations. In quickly reproducing organisms, demonstrated by the adaptation of mosquito populations to DDT, this may appear rapid. However, for slowly reproducing organisms, such as *Homo sapiens*, at least a few thousand years are required for significant adaptive shifts. For example, the spread of the sickle-cell allele in the human populations of the western and central portions of Africa took at least 2,000 years and perhaps considerably longer (8,000–10,000 years?).

On the other hand, all *individual* organisms can respond to environmental changes by physiological adjustments, displaying their phenotypic plasticity.

Acclimatization Physiological response within individuals to environmental pressure; usually takes a few weeks to a few months.

Called **acclimatization**, such responses can occur relatively quickly as in the physiological changes induced by high altitude stress.

For this reason, some college football teams playing the Air Force Academy in Colorado Springs (elevation 6,008 ft.) like to arrive a day or two early to allow some time for some short-term physiological responses to occur. The same was true of athletes training for the 1968 Olympic Games in Mexico City (elevation 7,347 ft.), who began training months earlier at high-altitude locations to permit a more long-term physiological acclimatization.

Light/Solar Radiation and Skin Color

One kind of environmental stress that varies considerably over the earth (and therefore differentially affects human populations) is the amount of solar radiation.

In response to this kind of environmental stress, the body uses a mechanism that alters the skin pigment. Actually, the color of the skin is influenced by three pigments: (1) carotene (yellow) derived from foods such as sweet potatoes and carrots, but not really important in determining skin color—the other two pigments are much more significant; (2) hemoglobin (red) in the red blood cells; and (3) melanin, a biochemically complex compound produced in the basal layers of the epidermis and secreted by specialized cells called *melanocytes*. Populations differ in skin color not so much because of the number of melanocytes, but in the way these cells are bunched and in the size and number of the melanin granules produced.

Of these pigments, only melanin absorbs ultraviolet light (the end of the spectrum causing radiation), so only melanin can protect against the really harmful effects of solar radiation. One potentially and extremely hazardous result of overexposure to ultraviolet (u-v) solar radiation is skin cancer. An immediate way the body can respond is to increase the production of melanin granules, causing what we call a "tan." All human populations can tan in response to exposure to u-v light, but the effects are obviously more noticeable in those who are more fair-skinned.

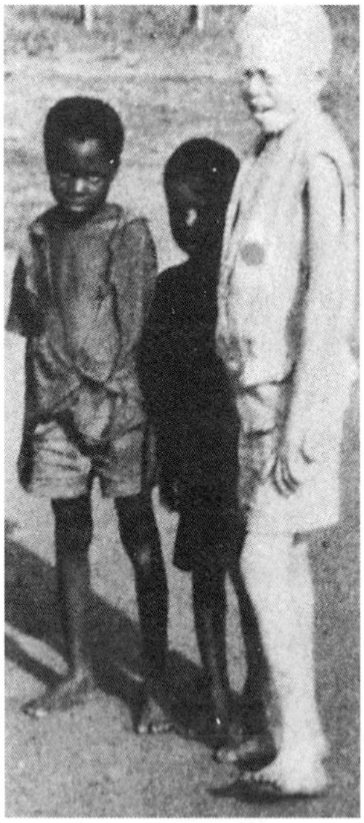

FIGURE 6-2 An African albino. (From *Genetics, Evolution, and Man* by W. H. Bodmer and L. L. Cavalli-Sforza. W. H. Freeman and Company. Copyright © 1976.)

Individuals with albinism (Fig. 6-2), a rare inherited condition found in all human populations, produce no melanin, cannot tan, and in tropical populations often develop skin cancer early in life. For that matter, there is considerable variation in skin cancer incidence in the United States depending on the intensity of u-v light. Among United States whites, rates of skin cancer are five times higher in Texas than in Massachusetts (Damon, 1977, p. 216).

In the United States today, skin cancer afflicts people mostly late in life—after reproduction is completed; its role as a potent selective agent could thus be questioned. However, in considering the potentially harmful effects of u-v radiation from an *evolutionary* perspective, three points must be kept in mind: (1) Early on, hominids lived mostly in the tropics, where u-v radiation is more intense than in temperate areas like the United States; (2) unlike modern urban dwellers, most earlier hominids spent the majority of time outside; and (3) they wore little or no clothing. As we will see below, however, adoption of clothing in temperate climes may have played a role in influencing depigmentation. Thus, it is reasonable to consider protection against skin cancer and severe sunburn as *potentially* important selective factors influencing the evolution of dark pigmentation.

Another physiological effect caused by sunlight, particularly u-v radiation, is the stimulation in the human body of the production of vitamin D, necessary for normal bone growth and maintenance. Individuals with insufficient vitamin D often develop such growth defects as rickets. Presumably, it would be harmful, particularly to children, to be too dark-skinned in areas where sunlight is low.

Dr. Peter Post has suggested an additional factor that may help explain the distribution of skin color. Epidemiological data from the Korean War (such as more frostbite occurring in black soldiers) as well as experimental evidence led Post to the conclusion that light skin is less susceptible to cold injury. Therefore, in northern latitudes—which not only get less u-v radiation but are also colder than tropical areas—light skin may provide protection against cold injury (Post et al., 1975).

So far we have established that: (1) solar radiation exerts potentially harmful environmental stress if too much is absorbed (possibly leading to skin cancer) or if too little is absorbed (leading to insufficient vitamin D production and/or cold injury); and (2) individual human beings can respond by tanning to increased amounts of u-v light.

The important question remains: Do populations that have long resided under widely varying u-v conditions show *biological adaptations* in skin color?

For a long time, data on skin color were inconsistent, but recent application of reflectance spectrophotometry has removed some of the earlier problems. Such observations of human skin color have shown that average readings vary considerably with latitude and, presumably, amount of u-v light. (See map, Fig. 6-3.) This association is, of course, inconclusive; we still do not know for certain the specific selection factors involved. As we noted above, hypothetically, dark skin in areas with high u-v light protects against skin cancer.

FIGURE 6-3 Distribution of skin color among the indigenous populations of the world. (After Coon and Hunt, 1965.)

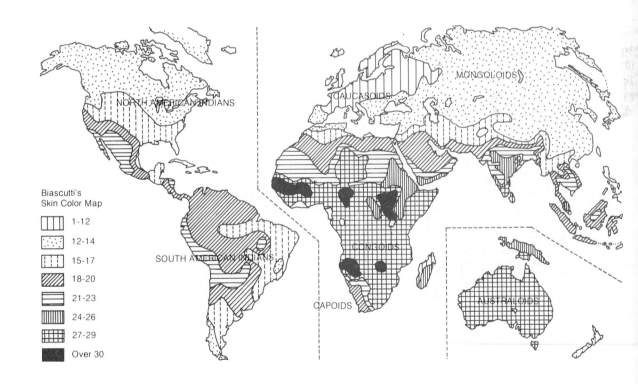

Biascutti's
Skin Color Map

1-12
12-14
15-17
18-20
21-23
24-26
27-29
Over 30

Why skin on the average is dark in some areas may therefore be reasonably explained if we *assume* that sunburn, skin cancer, or some other unknown consequence of overexposure to sunlight is an important selection factor. But then why, on the average, are some populations light-skinned? The popular hypothesis here runs as follows: In northern areas, dark skin would be selected against since it would cause underproduction of vitamin D, thereby resulting in growth defects (leading to lower reproductive success).

Another theory explaining why some humans have light skin has been proposed by anthropologists Loring Brace and Ashley Montagu (1977). As with the vitamin D hypothesis, the assumption here is that humans originated in the tropics, where darkly pigmented skin was a selective advantage. According to Brace and Montagu, permanent habitation of extreme northern temperate zones occurred only within the last 100,000 years and was partly made possible by the cultural innovation of warm clothing. Once humans in these northerly areas began to wear full-body clothing, the selective advantage of dark skin was no longer in force; thus, through random mutation and genetic drift (with no selective mechanism opposing it), depigmentation eventually took place.

All this conjecture concerning skin color as an adaptation to differential amounts of solar radiation remains open to question. No proven association exists, and the only tentative supporting evidence is the rough correlation with latitude. But even here some notable exceptions occur. In the New World, there is tremendous latitude variation encompassing almost the full range of u-v conditions; but, among native populations, only minor differences in skin color exist.

The smaller degree of geographic skin color variation in the New World may be explained by (1) the amount of time involved; and (2) the rates of evolutionary change postulated for skin color adaptations. In fact, computer simulations of evolutionary rates for skin pigmentation (Livingstone, 1969) suggest that as many as 30,000 years would be required to produce the magnitude of color variation seen in the Old World. If we further assume that New World population distribution (at least into the tropics) occurred in the last 10,000 to 20,000 years, we should not necessarily *expect* extremely marked pigmentation variation. Of course, the possibility also exists that New World populations have evolved some novel biological mechanism for coping with the effects of u-v light.

The Thermal Environment

Homo sapiens is found in a great variety of habitats, with thermal environments differing from exceedingly hot deserts to the frigid tundra of the Arctic circle. Human groups live through the winter in areas as cold as eastern Siberia, where January temperatures *average* an incredible −63°F. Such extreme environmental conditions place the human body under great stress.

COLD STRESS

The way the human body copes with cold stress is mostly through those physiological adjustments we have termed acclimatization. Perhaps there are some differences between populations in the rate such adjustments occur, but the ability to adjust gradually to cold is a general capacity of all human beings.

The manner of studying human reaction to cold involves either controlled laboratory observations, such as taking skin temperatures of appendages immersed in cold water, or such overall tolerance measurements as the sleeping bag test. This latter method is a testimony to the dedication and foolhardiness of physical anthropologists. Using standardized sleeping bags, experimenters sleep out in the open and contrast the amount of sleep, comfort, and shivering between themselves and natives. Many a researcher has spent long, cold nights with chattering teeth and shivering body!

In addition, inferential support for populational adjustment to cold stress has been obtained through the distributional method. In this kind of study, data are gathered from several populations on such physical characteristics as stature and nose shape and are then checked for any correspondence with environmental factors (for example, mean annual temperature, humidity).

From such observations, several mechanisms of physiological acclimatization to cold have been demonstrated in different human populations (after Damon, 1977, p. 222):

1. Redistribution of heat to extremities (shown in the Quechua of South America and Lapps of Scandinavia)
2. Overall metabolic rate increased (shown in Eskimos and Alacaluf of Tierra del Fuego—the high protein diet of Eskimos is an important contributing factor among this group)
3. Insulation acclimatization yielding cooler skin surface temperatures, but maintaining internal ones (shown in central Australians and Kalahari San). Such a physiological response may have originated in tropical areas where no real danger of frostbite prevails. However, in northern latitudes, it would be highly maladaptive, and physiological responses have apparently been modified (Steegman, 1975).

It is remarkable how well these physiological changes will eventually buffer the effects of cold. For example, Australian aborigines sleep in the nude with no covering in temperatures close to freezing! In sleeping bag tests in Scandinavia, Norwegian students gradually acclimatized and could sleep although they continued to shiver. An involuntary response, shivering is controlled by the hypothalamus mediated by cold receptors in the skin. By increasing the body's heat production up to three times that of resting temperatures, shivering is an effective response to cold.

Carleton Coon and his associates proposed a cold stress hypothesis to explain facial shape variation among human populations (Coon et al., 1950). Since genetic shifts are seen here to have occurred as the result of evolution, this type of change would be an adaptation (not acclimatization, as in the adjustments discussed above). It is postulated that cold stress selective factors (particularly frostbite) have favored wider (less sharp) noses and larger, more protrusive cheekbones, thus accounting for the evolution of the "Asian face." However, experimental evidence (Steegman, 1970) appears to contradict this hypothesis. In fact, facial temperatures were colder in those individuals with more protrusive cheekbones. Moreover, no consistent correlations exist between temperature and nose shape, although the latter does appear to be influenced by humidity (see the following section).

All the means of tolerating cold stress just discussed are physiological responses seen to some degree in all populations, and not merely those most subject to cold conditions. While mechanisms of physiological response to cold may

Axillae Armpits.

vary somewhat among human groups, as yet we cannot conclusively demonstrate any clear biological adaptations specific to certain populations.

HEAT AND HUMIDITY

While populations living in extremely cold climates face the problem of conserving heat, those groups living in hot environments face the opposite challenge, how to dissipate excess heat. In fact, the human body can adjust more easily to heat load than it can to extreme cold. Thus, cold is usually considered more of a serious threat to life than heat, unless the latter is accompanied by a lack of water. This greater tolerance of heat as opposed to cold might well reflect the tropical origins of our lineage.

Whereas body build, skin pigmentation (which protects against solar radiation), and the circulation of more blood close to the skin surface are all factors that help the human body adjust to heat stress, the most efficient means for humans is sweating. By cooling the surface of the skin, sweating causes heat to radiate to the surrounding air. In desert climates, individuals can lose up to one quart of water per hour; however, if such rates of water loss go unchecked, dangerous tissue dehydration and sodium loss will result. At maximum sweating capacity, the body can lose its entire sodium pool in just three hours—ultimately leading to death (Hanna and Brown, 1979).

The capacity to dissipate heat by sweating is seen in all populations to an almost equal degree. Interestingly, the average number of sweat glands does not vary among human populations. Each of us has approximately 1.6 million sweat (eccrine) glands. In addition, in the **axillae** and groin areas, apocrine glands are found; these, however, are not really involved in heat regulation but are more likely olfactory in nature (scent cues, particularly for sexual attraction?). While humans are not unique for the number or size of their eccrine glands, these are remarkable for their high secretory level. "*Homo sapiens* has the greatest sweating capacity for a given surface area for any known animal" (Newman, 1970).

When introduced into very hot areas, humans acclimatize quite rapidly, the process taking just a few days. Such plasticity seems to characterize all human populations, and no heat adaptations have been found that differentiate one human group from others. "Indeed, the similarity in response of all acclimatized peoples is remarkable" (Hanna and Brown, 1979, p. 179). This physiological adjustment is accomplished through a faster response and increased output of the sweat glands (directed by the thyroid) and a general decrease in the pulse rate and heart output. Again, is it possible that such a rapid and efficient capacity to adjust to heat stress reflects our tropical hominid origins?

More than just temperature, rapid physiological adjustment is also dependent on humidity. All populations seem to be able to adjust quickly to hot, wet climates, but acclimatization to hot, dry areas takes longer. The most consistent data suggesting a connection between physical response and humidity concern nose shape (Weiner, 1954). Populations living in colder areas (where absolute humidity is lower) have narrower noses. Similarly, in deserts (where absolute humidity is also low), narrow noses also are the rule. The physiological explanation is not yet completely understood, but a narrow nose may act as a more efficient humidifier (Steegman, 1975). Such changes in nose shape would obviously be significantly influenced by genetic shifts; that is, this explanation emphasizes adaptation rather than acclimatization.

Clearly, all humans have inherited a genetically based plasticity to deal with heat stress. In this context, it may be said that we have been adapted for adaptability. Even given such a flexible physiological capacity there are limitations (such as the one just discussed concerning severe sodium loss). Consequently, humans also adjust to hot climates through a variety of cultural means (Hanna and Brown, 1983). Among the Tuareg people of the Sahara, clothing is worn loosely, thereby allowing sweat to evaporate and additionally providing an insulating layer of air next to the skin. Physical activities are usually performed during the cooler hours, and individuals stay in the shade whenever possible. In the Sahara, the air is hot and dry with solar radiation intense, posing the dual problems of excessive water loss and sunburn. On the other hand, in tropical humid rainforests, such as those occupied by the Semai of Malaya, the reverse is true—sweat evaporation is much slower. Accordingly, these people wear few clothes.

Likewise, human adjustments to cold also are mostly cultural in nature. As we will see later in the text, our ancestors long ago invaded temperate latitudes, and there is little doubt that it was primarily cultural innovation that allowed such a migration in the first place. Evidence of consistent use of fire is at least 500,000 years old. Artificial structures are also exceedingly ancient. Windbreaks may have been constructed in Africa almost 2 million years ago, and by 200,000 years ago more sophisticated structures were being erected in Europe.

There is little direct evidence for the earliest use of clothing. Long before garments were sewn, loose untailored skins, furs, etc., were certainly utilized. Archeological evidence of needles suggests the advent of sewn clothing by at least 35,000 years ago (Chard, 1975). After this, as Brace and Montagu have suggested (see p. 158), *permanent* habitation of really cold areas became possible.

As we see, humans cope with environmental challenges by a *combination* of both biological and cultural strategies, which again underlines the essential biocultural nature of human existence.

Another feature of human physiological response to the thermal environment that has received considerable attention concerns body proportions. Data on heat-related deaths among World War II soldiers in the deserts of North Africa indicate excess quantities of fat or muscle are a hindrance in such an environment. A linear body build is apparently the most advantageous and is reflected in many groups who have been subject to heat stress for a long time: Arabs, Nilotic Africans (Watusi, Nuer, Dinka, etc.), and central Australians.

BODY SIZE AND SHAPE

Indeed, there seems to be a general relationship between climate and body size/ shape within warm-blooded species (that is, both mammals and birds). In general, within a species, body size (weight) increases proportionately as distance from the equator increases. In humans, this relationship holds up fairly well, but there are numerous exceptions. For example, Polynesians basking in the sunny climes of the South Pacific are tall and heavy, whereas Scandinavian Lapps are short and slender.

Presumably, body size and proportion are strongly influenced by genetic mechanisms; thus, shifts in these dimensions should come about primarily as the result of adaptation. Yet, physiological response (that is, acclimatization) may also be playing an important role here. Body weight and limb length are both phenotypically plastic, with significant environmental influence upon them (Hanna and

Brown, 1983). Even first generation migrants to tropical areas (American children reared in Brazil) show different body proportions (more linear than would be expected). Obviously, this response occurs too quickly to be explained by genetic adaptation. The body during development is being influenced by environmental factors, such as heat, which in turn influences blood flow which, in turn, might well affect the differential growth of bone and other tissues.

Nevertheless, some general principles applicable to body size/shape variation seen in other warm-blooded species seem also to apply broadly to *Homo sapiens*:

1. *Bergmann's Rule* involves the relationship of body mass to surface area. As weight (mass) increases, the relative amount of surface area decreases proportionately. Therefore, large size with relatively less surface area for heat loss is an adaptation for more efficient heat maintenance. It is interesting to note that cold-adapted fauna during glacial peaks of the Pleistocene are generally larger than their modern descendants. Moreover, humans are almost certainly less robust than our ancestors during much of the last 1 million years. In humans today, there is also some correspondence of size with climate, since peoples living farther from the equator tend to be larger. Eskimos, who are stocky in physique, are one good example.
2. *Allen's Rule* involves the shape of the body, particularly the appendages. In colder climates, appendages should be short, thereby reducing the amount of surface area. In humans, this is seen as shorter arms and legs, but in other animals, tails, ears, or beaks may be affected.

Considerable data gathered from several human populations generally conform to the above rules. In colder environments, body sizes are larger with broader, longer chests and shorter arms (Roberts, 1973). These relationships pertain most clearly to indigenous New World populations, but they do not apply to the populational distribution of body size and shape found in Africa (Hiernaux, 1968).

Another complication in attempting to apply these rules to humans is that of acclimatization. An individual's body size may reflect much more about short-term physiological adjustment to ecological/dietary conditions than about long-term biological adaptation. For example, an extensive study of more than 15,000 white males in the United States revealed as large a correspondence in body size and temperature (based on the State in which one was born) as that seen for indigenous North American populations (Newman and Munro, 1955). Since this entire group represented recent migrants from generally the same region (Europe), biological adaptation was ruled out (too little time). Acclimatization, therefore, was responsible for the tendency for larger males to predominate in colder parts of the United States. Colder weather may be a direct causative factor, stimulating more physical activity and appetite.

Body size and shape variation among relatively ancient human populations may also be influenced by cultural factors. Alice Brues in an article titled "The Spearman and the Archer" suggested that different body builds are better suited for use of different weapons (Brues, 1959). According to Brues, the most efficient body build for spear use is long and slender, but for using a bow the body should be short with thick muscles. Hypothetically, as bow technology spread several thousand years ago selection pressures would have shifted favoring a shorter, stockier build. A potential complication here is that most populations that use bows *also* use spears.

A similar scenario to the one above has been recently proposed by David Frayer (1980). In this theory, body size among our ancestors also changed as a result of cultural variables, but here the key was a shift in size of game animals. From 35,000 to 10,000 years ago, larger, more aggressive game was hunted less and less as our ancestors gradually adopted a more sedentary way of life. Thus, according to this view, the males (who, presumably, were doing most of the big game hunting) gradually became smaller, while female body size remained approximately the same. While biocultural factors have assuredly influenced human body size, these imaginative suggestions still remain unproven.

High-Altitude Stress

Today perhaps as many as 25 million people live at altitudes above 10,000 ft. In Tibet, permanent settlements exist above 15,000 ft., and in the Andes they can be found at 17,500 ft. (with daily trips to mines at 19,000 ft.)!

At such high altitudes, multiple stresses act on the human body creating several physiological problems. Most pervasive is the low barometric pressure creating low oxygen pressure in inspired air. Consequently, oxygen diffuses less quickly into the lung membranes and less oxygen eventually reaches the body's tissues. All these problems become particularly critical during any kind of exercise.

High altitude, however, also involves cold stress. In Tibet, winter temperatures plunge to as low as $-27°F$. In addition, populations living in such environments must also cope with low humidity, high winds, high solar radiation, a limited nutritional base (generally poor agricultural land), and rough terrain.

Initially, human beings respond to high-altitude stress (primarily low oxygen pressure) through short-term compensation, but eventually a more permanent acclimatization develops. When freshly introduced into high altitude environments, we react by breathing faster and deeper. Gradually, our systems adjust so that respiration rates are permanently increased and the number of red blood cells is also increased. In the Peruvian Andes (from which our most comprehensive data come), natives have up to 30% more red blood cells than populations at sea level. Such an adjustment allows the blood to carry more oxygen. The right ventricle of the heart may also increase in size, pumping more blood to the lungs. Also, there are probably adjustments in the body tissues to function at lowered oxygen tension.

With the increased physiological demands of pregnancy, hypoxia (oxygen deficiency) could be expected to have negative effects on fertility. However, the data here are somewhat conflicting. A recent comparative study of Himalayan populations suggests that there is no evidence to support the popular conception that high-altitude stress reduces fertility (Goldstein et al., 1983). In fact, as this study points out, confounding cultural attitudes (such as those affecting the exposure of females to intercourse) must be considered.

On the other hand, high infant mortality has been reported for several groups living at high altitude, most of the problems resulting from respiratory infections. Many of these infant deaths are attributable to the generally poor health care available, but once infants contract bronchitis, tuberculosis, etc., the low oxygen pressure, no doubt, causes further complications. Even in areas with good health care, infant mortality resulting from respiratory problems is greater at high altitudes.

For example, in Colorado, infant deaths were nearly twice as common in areas above 8,200 ft. (2,500 m) as at lower elevations (Moore and Regensteiner, 1983).

Other physiological adjustments displayed by highland Andean peoples include lower birth weights, but relatively larger placentas—probably supplying more oxygen to the developing fetus. In addition, slower rates of maturation with delayed sexual maturity may provide more time to grow in an oxygen-poor and nutritionally deprived environment.

Most of the adjustments humans exhibit in response to high-altitude stress can be accounted for by physiological plasticity (acclimatization). However, some effects of natural selection may well cause differential spread of genotypes more adapted to high altitudes.

How do we sort out the possible effects due to adaptation from those due to acclimatization? Once again we are faced with a complex nature/nurture phenomenon and, once again, for humans the answers are far from clear. Laboratory tests may tell us something of the range of variation of human responses, and observations of other animals may tell us something about general physiological plasticity. However, for human populations, so complexly intertwined in a web of environmental/cultural/genetic factors, we require a special methodology. One helpful technique is called the *migrant model*, which compares genetically related populations living under very different environmental conditions. For example, investigations of lung function were done on the Aymara (highland natives) of northern Chile and compared with data from non-Aymara (Spanish) and a group termed "mixed" (Mueller et al., 1979). Upward migrants as well as downward migrants were contrasted with nonmigrants, controlling for age, sex, stature, ethnicity, occupation, and permanence (age at migration and length of stay). Even with all these controls, confounding factors obscure results from such cross-sectional studies. Long-term physiological data collected periodically from the same individuals (longitudinal studies) are therefore also necessary to help untangle the web of genetic, physiological, ecological, and cultural variables.

High-altitude inhabitants may also meet the rigorous demands of their environment through nutritional adaptations. Some evidence points to differences among high-altitude populations in food utilization, particularly fat metabolism. Their typically low fat/low protein/high carbohydrate diet may possibly be a cultural adaptation to living under high-altitude conditions. In addition, alcohol consumption and coca leaf chewing have also been suggested as cultural adjustments to high-altitude stress (particularly, cold). Alcohol facilitates vasodilation, making the skin surface feel warmer. Over the short run, alcohol consumption can thus increase comfort levels. If extended over long periods, however, it can be dangerous, causing greater heat loss and further contributing to possible frostbite.

Coca leaves contain cocaine and may also act to warm surface temperatures. Native chewers claim coca helps alleviate the symptoms of hunger, thirst, fatigue, cold, and pain. Controlled studies show, however, that when consumed in small amounts (as is typical), coca chewing has no observed effect on metabolism or work performance.

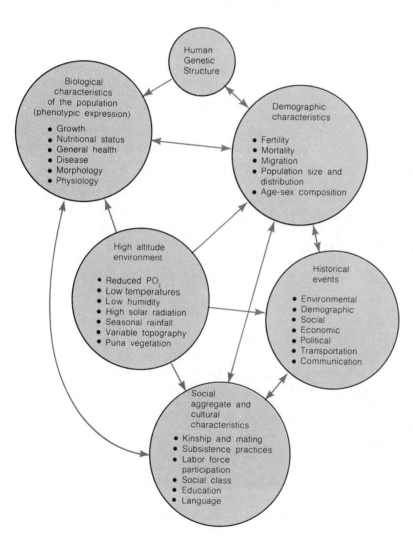

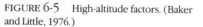

FIGURE 6-5   High-altitude factors. (Baker and Little, 1976.)

Dietary Adaptations

Nutritional behavior has long been a central element in human evolution. For at least the last 1 million years, meat has been an extremely important element in human diets; evidence from modern hunter-gatherers suggests perhaps only about one-third of all calories come from meat, but it still provides a crucial qualitative contribution in the form of essential amino acids. Adult humans can get by on a strictly vegetarian diet, but only with considerable effort. The increased demands of pregnancy, lactation, or disease make a wholly vegetarian diet even more marginal. For an infant, the protein sources from mother's milk are essential for normal development.

Beginning around 10,000 years ago, the agricultural revolution wrought a profound ecological impact on human evolution. Domestication of crops provided a larger and more geographically concentrated food resource, permitting both permanent settlements and population expansion, which in turn greatly increased the spread of infectious diseases in human populations.

Moreover, dietary habits shifted profoundly. The varied ecological base characteristic of hunter-gatherers gave way to the generally much more restrictive diets of settled agriculturists. Relying primarily on a few or perhaps just one staple crop, such diets can be exceedingly narrow, giving way easily to malnutrition. Did such massive shifts in human diets bring about any behavioral changes? Perhaps. Some recent evidence has suggested a possible relationship between a low calorie/high carbohydrate diet and increased aggressiveness (Bolton, 1973). When combined with intense physical activity, such diets lead to chronic lowering of blood sugar levels (hypoglycemia), which in turn may be reflected as behavioral alterations.

Such a diet is characteristic of the physically active Qolla Indians of the Andean Highlands. From a limited data base (one village of 1,200 individuals documented over about 15 years), the Qolla have been depicted as unusually aggressive on the basis of an apparently quite high homicide rate (Bolton, 1984). This is a position, however, that has not gone unchallenged (see Lewellen, 1981). In order to determine how characteristically aggressive the entire Qolla cultural group is, as well as the precise degree of their nutritional/metabolic difficulties, will require further research. In any case, many biologists and anthropologists believe there is sufficient data at hand at least to *suspect* a link between diet and behavior.

NO MILK, PLEASE!

Probably the best-known genetic adaptation to dietary factors is shown by the population distribution of the ability in adults to digest cow's milk. A main ingredient in milk is the sugar *lactose*, which the body normally breaks down by an enzyme called *lactase*.

In all human populations, infants and young children can digest milk, an obvious necessity to any young mammal. However, in many populations the gene coding for lactase production "switches off" by about four years of age. If too much milk is ingested, it ferments in the large intestine leading to diarrhea and severe gastrointestinal upset. Among many African and Asian populations—a majority of humankind today—most individuals are *intolerant* of milk (see Table 6-1). Contrary to popular advertising, every body does *not* need milk, at least not as adults.

TABLE 6-1 **Frequencies of Lactose Intolerance**

POPULATION GROUP	PERCENT
U.S. whites	2–19
Finnish	18
Swiss	12
Swedish	4
U.S. blacks	70–77
Ibos	99
Bantu	90
Fulani	22
Thais	99
U.S. Orientals	95–100
Australian aborigines	85

Source: Lerner and Libby, 1976, p. 327.

In fact, for millions of human beings, milk consumption leads to severe discomfort.

Unfortunately, this fact had been overlooked by United States foreign aid personnel who naively shipped huge quantities of powdered milk to Asia and Africa. Occasionally, a good deal of sickness resulted, but more usually the natives simply avoided drinking the milk. Some of it even ended up being used as whitewash!

Quite apparently, lactose intolerance is a hereditary trait, but the pattern of inheritance is not yet clearly established. Some familial data suggest that the trait operates as a simple dominant or, perhaps, is more complicated with three alleles.

The environment also plays a role in expression of the trait (that is, whether a person will show milk intolerance) since intestinal bacteria can somewhat buffer the adverse effects. Because these bacteria will increase with previous exposure to smaller quantities of milk, some acclimatized tolerance can be acquired even in individuals who are genetically lactase-deficient.

Why do such differences occur in lactose tolerance among human populations? Throughout the Stone Age (i.e., prior to 10,000 years ago*), no milk was generally available after weaning in hunting-gathering societies. Perhaps, in such circumstances, continued action of an unnecessary enzyme might get in the way of digesting other foods. Therefore, there *may* be a selective advantage for the gene, coding for lactase production, to switch off. The question then can be asked: Why can some adults (a majority in many populations) tolerate milk? The distribution of lactose-tolerant populations is very interesting, revealing the probable influence of cultural factors on this trait.

European groups, who are generally lactose-tolerant, are partially descended from groups of the Middle East. Often economically dependent on pastoralism, these groups raised cows, goats, etc., and no doubt drank considerable milk. Strong selection pressures would act in such a *cultural* environment to shift allele frequencies in the direction of more lactose tolerance. Modern European descendants of these populations apparently retain this ancient ability.

Even more informative is the distribution of lactose tolerance in Africa. For example, groups such as the Fulani and Tutsi, who have been pastoralists probably for thousands of years, have much lower rates of lactose intolerance than nonpastoralists. Former hunters and gatherers, such as the Ibo and Yoruba, are as much as 99% lactose-intolerant. (See Table 6-1.) More recently, these groups have abandoned their former subsistence pattern. They do not raise cattle, however, since they have settled in areas infested with tsetse flies.

As we have seen, the geographic distribution of lactose tolerance is related to a history of cultural dependence upon milk products. There are, however, some populations that culturally rely on dairying but are not characterized by high levels of lactose tolerance. It has been suggested that such populations have traditionally consumed their milk produce as cheese and other derivatives in which the lactose has been metabolized through bacterial action (Durham, 1981). In fact, peoples can be generally divided into lactose absorbers and nonabsorbers. Because lactose acts biochemically in a similar fashion to vitamin D (facilitating the absorption of calcium), we should expect the frequency of lactose absorption to increase directly with increasing distance from the equator—a prediction generally supported by the data (Durham, 1981).

---

*Years ago will be abbreviated throughout as ya.

Undernutrition A diet insufficient in quantity (calories) to support normal health.

Malnutrition A diet insufficient in quality (i.e., lacking in some essential component) to support normal health.

The interaction of human cultural environments and changes in lactose tolerance in human populations is a clear example of biocultural evolution. In the last few thousand years, cultural factors have produced specific evolutionary changes in human groups.

Cultural factors no doubt have influenced the course of human evolution for at least the last three million years (probably much longer), and today they are of paramount importance.

MALNUTRITION

While the agricultural revolution brought about a restricted dietary base, most groups were probably able to supplement their diets adequately by hunting small mammals, raising domesticated animals, and so on. However, today the crush of billions of humans almost completely dependent on cereal grains has drastically altered the situation, so that millions face undernutrition, malnutrition, and even starvation.

By **undernutrition** we refer to an inadequate quantity of food. In other words, not enough calories are consumed to support normal health. Exactly what constitutes an "adequate" diet is difficult to ascertain, and estimates of minimum requirements vary widely—body size and activity level are important considerations.

Given these uncertainties there are no precise data on how many human beings are today undernourished, but estimates vary between 16 and 63% of the world's population.

Malnutrition refers to inadequacy of some key element in the diet, such as proteins, minerals, or vitamins. In underdeveloped countries, protein malnutrition is the most common variety, and probably one-fourth to one-third of individuals in the underdeveloped world are protein deficient (M. Newman, 1975). The hallmark of severe protein malnutrition is a generalized disease called *kwashiorkor*, showing typical symptoms of tissue swelling, anemia, loss of hair, and apathy. A related syndrome called *marasmus* is caused by the combined effects of protein *and* calorie deficiency.

More than causing discomfort, malnutrition greatly affects reproduction and infant survival. Malnourished mothers have more difficult labor, more premature births, more children born with birth defects, higher prenatal mortality, and generally lower birth weights of newborns. Given all these potential physiological difficulties, it is surprising that overall *fertility* among malnourished mothers is not disrupted more than it is. Moderate chronic malnutrition (unless it becomes exceedingly severe, approaching starvation) has only a small effect on the number of live births (Bongaarts, 1980).

MALNUTRITION AND DEVELOPMENT

Children born to malnourished mothers are already at a disadvantage: They are smaller and behind in most aspects of physical development. After birth, if malnourished conditions persist, such children fall further behind due to their mothers' generally poor lactation (the milk quantity may be cut by as much as one-half).

FIGURE 6-6   Kwashiorkor. Bangladesh.

Growth processes often slow down greatly when environmental insults are severe (malnutrition and/or disease). Later on, a period of accelerated growth (called the "catch-up period") can make up some of the deficit. However, there are some critical periods in which growth in certain tissues is normally very rapid. If a severe interruption occurs during one of these periods, the individual may never catch up completely. For example, severe malnutrition during the last trimester of fetal life or during the first year of infancy can have marked effects on brain development. Children who had died from complications accompanying severe malnutrition and were subsequently autopsied showed reduced brain size and weight, as well as fewer numbers of brain cells (Frisancho, 1978).

Researchers estimate that in some countries one-half of all newborns die before the age of 5. Of the estimated 60 million deaths per year worldwide, perhaps as many as 20 million are due to dietary deprivation (Dumont and Rosier, 1969). Not all of these people "starve to death," but most die as a result of weakened resistance to a whole set of infectious and gastrointestinal diseases.

Infectious disease, in particular, seems to act in a feedback relationship with malnutrition. Inadequate nutrition can interrupt the normal functioning of the immune response system by reducing the number of active cells or antibodies available (see below). "In summary, a vicious cycle between malnutrition, infection, and immunodeficiencies is established, further intensifying malnutrition, facilitating new infection or permitting existing infection to become more severe" (Frisancho, 1978, p. 181).

Disease and Human Adaptation

Without question, one of the primary challenges to survival faced by all humans is that of disease. Diseases vary tremendously in their causes and their consequent effects on human health. For example, diseases may originate from any one, or a combination of, the following factors: hereditary (e.g., cystic fibrosis, sickle-cell anemia); metabolic (vitamin deficiencies, such as rickets); degenerative (e.g., heart disease); cell malignancy (e.g., many varieties of cancer); or infections (e.g., malaria).

Human disease does not only result from a complex set of physiological causes—cultural factors are also a crucial element. Settlement patterns and architectural style greatly influence the spread of disease-carrying pathogens (e.g., viruses and bacteria). In New Hebrides the typical Melanesian house is not only designed to be "ghost-tight" but also air-tight thereby greatly facilitating the spread of respiratory diseases among the occupants (Weiner, 1977). Settlement patterns and population density are also most important. Before urbanization (with its large permanent settlements) became characteristic (5,000–10,000 ya), airborne infections (influenza, common cold, measles, smallpox) were of less significance; in moderately small communities, there is insufficient quantity and variety of contacts among individuals to perpetuate these diseases (Weiner, 1977).

Domestication of animals also brought the risk of disease. Of course, the development of domesticated animal varieties initially was itself a culturally directed process. Mediating cultural factors further influencing disease are: which animals are kept; in how close proximity; and what (if any) sanitary practices are followed.

Major histocompatibility complex (MHC) The large genetic complex (located in humans on chromosome #6) that plays a central part in immune response—recognition of foreign antigens and production of specialized cells to deactivate them.

In the Arctic, for example, pathogens (tapeworm, rabies) carried by domestic dogs can be significant factors affecting human health.

Ritual, too, can be a contributing factor to the spread of disease. In Yemen, schistosomiasis (a fluke worm infection) is sometimes spread through communal use of ceremonial pools, and the kuru viral infection was spread in some New Guinea highland groups by ritual cannibalism of the brains of one's dead relatives.

Finally, major ecological modifications usually have marked impacts on disease. As we discussed in Chapter 5, the spread of slash-and-burn agriculture cleared previously forested areas, created more stagnant pools, and consequently greatly stimulated mosquito breeding—a crucial vector in the spread of malaria. Likewise, unsanitary crowded urban conditions contribute to an increase in the rat population size, and these animals also act as a vector in exposing humans to a host of infectious diseases. The best known of these diseases is bubonic plague, which in the thirteenth century "Black Death" epidemic is estimated to have killed one-third the population of Europe.

For thousands of years, the interaction of biology and culture has produced fertile conditions for some diseases while limiting the spread of others. The great twentieth-century advances in controlling many infectious diseases have not, of course, eliminated human disease, but have simply shifted the focus. As average life span increased, degenerative syndromes, such as coronary artery disease, have become much more prevalent. Such crucial cultural factors as diet and psychological stress also have contributed to this increase.

INFECTIOUS DISEASE

Those diseases, however, which have had the most dramatic and long-lasting impact on human populations are infectious in nature. We have seen the potent effect of malaria and the consequent spread of the sickle-cell allele (see pp. 128–131). Several other hereditary traits have also been suggested as possible biological mechanisms providing resistance against malarial infection (e.g., thalassemias, G-6-PD, and some alleles of the Duffy blood group system) (Livingstone, 1980).

Infection refers to the introduction into the body of foreign organic matter; these may include microbes (viruses, bacteria, protozoa), fungi, or even entire multicellular organisms (e.g., worms). Each of us is equipped with a genetically programmed defense apparatus—called the *immune system*—which discriminates such foreign invaders from our own cells and attempts to isolate and deactivate them.

The Immune System The immune system is made up of several components, the primary one of which includes several linked loci on chromosome number 6. In addition to the seven HLA loci (see p. 139), there are nearby a large number of additional loci. These code for specific proteins (antigens) characteristic of various cell populations that are integral parts of the immune system. The entire genetic region as a whole (HLA and associated regions) in humans is called the **major histocompatibility complex**.

What stimulates the immune system are antigens—the introduction into the body of proteins perceived as different from self. Actually, our bodies can recognize *any* foreign molecule, even nourishing ones that originate in other organisms. The only way to incorporate these vital nutritive materials is to have them first pass through the digestive tract where they are broken down by enzymes and then absorbed through the intestinal walls as amino acids.

Other foreign antigens that enter the body via the respiratory tract or through breaks in the skin surface elicit an immune response. It is this ability to recognize any foreign cell that causes a reaction in blood transfusions of unmatched type (see p. 133). Since red blood cells lack nuclei, blood matches are relatively easy to make. Most other tissues, however, contain nucleated cells, and proper matches are much more difficult to obtain, as in kidney or liver transplants.

Occasionally, the immune system fails to distinguish truly foreign materials from self, and one's own cells are attacked. Such a reaction is termed an *autoimmune response*. Medical research has recently implicated such a process as an important contributory agent in several human diseases: a severe form of spinal arthritis (ankylosing spondylitis); rheumatoid arthritis; and (as recent compelling evidence suggests) multiple sclerosis.

The cells that control the immune response are a variety of white blood cells called *lymphocytes*, which are small, spherical cells, usually found in the blood, spleen, and lymph system. Lymphocytes can arise either directly from bone marrow (called B-cells), or may mature within the thymus gland (called T-cells). Both these B-cells and T-cells are essential for an efficient immune response. B-cells have receptor areas on their surface that, when stimulated by a foreign antigen, cause the cells to differentiate into plasma cells. These plasma cells can in turn produce antibodies (immunoglobulins), complex protein arrangements that can deactivate a foreign antigen (by physically attaching to it). Humans possess several different loci that contribute to assembling these antibodies. It is estimated that, at birth, each of us potentially can recognize up to one million different foreign antigens and can quickly assemble appropriate antibodies—without question a marvelously flexible system.

Once antibodies have been produced, the system has a capacity to "remember." If later exposure should occur, the antibodies can then be produced much faster. It is this mechanism that provides for **immunity** and explains why mild early exposure environmentally or through a vaccine provides later resistance.

In addition to the antibody production of B-cells, T-cells contribute to immune response in a complex fashion. Since the action of T-cells can (though not always) be a direct cell process, their role is usually referred to as the *cell-mediated response*. There are several populations of T-cells, each characterized by different antigenic properties. Some directly attack and destroy foreign cells (T-effectors); others send molecular messages to B-cells, stimulating antibody production (T-helpers); still others act to switch off the helper activity and terminate the immune response (T-suppressors).

Immune response can thus be seen as a complex system with the capacity to make specific antibodies against foreign antigens and to recognize and deactivate cells containing such foreign materials. Moreover, considerable flexibility is provided in that once the response is begun, it can be halted.

Another related function of the immune system is its ability to recognize and destroy our own cells that have gone awry. In this way, early cancerous cells are normally contained. Since cell mutations or viruses can often cause highly irregular cell development, we would be overwhelmed with cancerous tissues if we had no regulatory mechanism. In fact, some forms of cancer probably develop due to a failure in the immune system.

Immunity An organism's ability to recognize and deactivate foreign antigens very quickly as a consequence of earlier (mild) exposure (for example, through vaccination).

The immune system has been adapted in a wide variety of vertebrates; an apparatus similar to that of humans has been discovered in the mouse, pig, rabbit, rhesus monkey, and chimpanzee (Amos and Kostyu, 1980). We and other organisms are constantly exposed to possible danger by a variety of foreign antigens (e.g., insect or snake venom). Most especially, however, the immune system has evolved to protect against infection by microbes. Natural selection has thus endowed the entire human species with a finely tuned defense mechanism.

Although every individual has a unique tissue type and consequently varies in some genetic components of the immune system, it remains to be determined whether *populations* differ in their immune response to specific diseases. The history of plague, measles, smallpox, influenza, and other diseases suggests that natural selection could well have acted differentially on human populations. The questions remain: What diseases have average populational differences in immune response? What ecological/evolutionary factors brought them into being? How might individuals be ascertained for risk to specific diseases? What kinds of therapeutic intervention may mitigate or even prevent the development of a variety of human diseases? One of the great frontiers of medical and evolutionary research concerns the attempt to answer these questions.

AIDS   In the last few years, the general public has come to hear a good deal about the immune system as a result of the catastrophic AIDS epidemic. As most of you know, AIDS is an abbreviation for Acquired Immune Deficiency Syndrome. This name indicates that the major problem (a severely compromised immune system) is *acquired*—i.e., the condition is caught during one's lifetime. We have known for a while now of inherited problems that disturb immune function, and many of you have seen pictures of children so-affected living within sterile bubbles. While tragic in their ramifications, these genetically caused syndromes are exceedingly rare, affecting only a handful of individuals. AIDS, however, is acquired as a viral infection that can devastate one's natural immunity. It thus has the potential to spread widely in human populations—obviously a major concern to us all (and, undoubtedly, a terrifying prospect for some).

The magnitude of the problem is truly catastrophic in its dimensions. As a result, a tremendous amount of research energy is being devoted to AIDS—in the laboratory, the clinic, and in the field, where epidemiological data are gathered. It is virtually impossible to give a completely up-to-date account of this disease, as our data change constantly. At this writing, we are able to make some reasonably firm statements concerning cause and some general predictions of future trends.

First of all, AIDS is known to be caused by a virus, one called a *retrovirus*. Differing nomenclature has been used (HTLV-III, LAV, ARV), but a recent consensus of an international committee has agreed to designate the AIDS virus as HIV (Human Immunodeficiency Virus). Viruses may store their genetic information as DNA (e.g., the herpes family) or as RNA (e.g., polio, smallpox, influenza, measles). As a type of RNA virus, HIV functions as a *retrovirus*, and it is able to convert genetic structure into DNA, which can then be permanently incorporated into our own DNA. The viral genes thus become part of the genetic structure of host cells, take over the machinery of certain of these cells, and produce more viral particles, even to the point of killing some of these cells. A chronic infection results—potentially for the lifetime of the individual (even if it does not kill).

Another terribly complicated aspect of retroviruses is that they are exceedingly variable and subject to rapid mutation. In other words, it may not be possible to develop a *single* vaccine effective against all strains of the AIDS-causing virus.

Individuals are exposed to the virus through exchange of bodily fluids—most notably blood and/or semen. While in the United States AIDS has predominantly affected homosexual men and intravenous drug users, it is anticipated that, in the next few years, it will spread among the heterosexual community as well. Indeed, AIDS is already widespread in central and eastern Africa, where it is primarily a heterosexual disease (Quinn et al., 1986).

The virus thus enters a human through direct and intimate contact with bodily fluids from someone carrying the virus. Once infected, individuals make antibodies to the HIV virus. Currently used screening tests check for seropositivity, that is, presence of these antibodies in the blood.

Not everyone exposed to the virus will necessarily develop the disease called AIDS. Current estimates, which vary widely, suggest that anywhere from 25 to 65% of those exposed eventually develop the disease. Indeed, some experts believe that given enough time, *everyone* exposed will in time develop AIDS. What, then, exactly is AIDS? First of all, AIDS is characterized by an immune system that is severely compromised. The virus appears to attack certain white blood cells critical in immune response (T-helper cells), and its multiplication leads to the death of such cells but not necessarily other types of host cells (such as macrophages and neurons). Also, with AIDS, the regulation of the production of antibodies that normally would protect a person against other infections runs amok, leading to the synthesis of nonfunctional antibodies. Basically, the entire immune system becomes dysfunctional. As a result, an individual is unable to ward off ubiquitous infectious agents that are innocuous to a normal person. These *opportunistic infections* (most especially a cancer of endothelial cells called *Kaposi's sarcoma* and a form of pneumonia) are what then kill the individual. At present, treatment has proven sadly ineffective, and, once the immune system fails, the disease is always lethal.

We reiterate, however, that not everyone who has been exposed to the virus will necessarily get AIDS. That is not to downplay its significance. Through 1989, more than 116,000 Americans were diagnosed as having AIDS—with more than 68,000 recorded deaths.

There are no precise estimates of how many Americans *already* have been exposed, but best guesses place the figure between 1 and 1.5 million. Given the rate of AIDS involvement from exposed individuals, it is conservatively estimated that, by 1991, about 200,000 victims will have this currently incurable disease. Just considering the direct medical costs in the United States, the financial burden will be staggering (estimated at 8 to 16 billion dollars per year by 1991) (Barnes, 1986).

Until breakthroughs emerge, little help will be available for the potential one-quarter million affected Americans in the next five years. Worldwide, during this same period, hundreds of thousands more could get AIDS with most, if not all, dying from the disease.

Some hope does exist: An effective vaccine (useful for those not yet exposed) does seem a reasonable expectation. Especially with breakthroughs in recombinant DNA technology, it has been possible to sequence most of the envelope proteins of the HIV virus—probably the best avenue to realizing an effective vaccine. Yet, the problems are enormous, and most experts do not foresee a safe and effective product generally available for at least five years (and probably longer).

A further moral problem exists regarding the *testing* of any new vaccine. Human volunteer subjects could be used, but the ethics of doing so are most debatable. Many researchers believe the best animal model on which to test is the chimpanzee. Nowhere near a sufficient number of chimpanzees now in captivity are available for such testing. It thus might mean decimating most (if not all) of the still free-ranging populations to solve the human problem of AIDS. Will such a circumstance prove necessary? And, if so, is it worth such a price?

The Hazards of Modern Life

The specter of tens of millions dying annually because of dietary deprivation or tens of thousands dying from AIDS are but two of the many hazards humanity has created for itself. The cultural pace set by technological, urbanized humankind is radically altering our environments and presumably selection pressures as well. As yet, however, the specific adaptive responses are unknown.

ARTIFICIAL RADIATION

One of the potential perils receiving wide public attention is the danger of human-made radiation. We are all constantly subjected to natural forms of radiation (called background sources) as we are bombarded by cosmic rays from above and from below by radiation-emitting elements in the earth's crust (radium and thorium, for instance).

Worldwide, there is considerable variation in the amount of such background radiation (particularly correlated with altitude), but a typical natural dose for an individual (that is, a "whole body") over a thirty-year period is on the order of 3,000 to 5,000 mrems.*

We are concerned with radiation hazards because of their potentially harmful biological effects. In particular, radiation is a known cause of mutation (changes in DNA sequence).

Estimating possible genetic damages of increased radiation involves considerable guess work, but the dangers are alarming. If there were an approximate tenfold increase in annual background radiation (from 500 to 5,000 mrems, say) by artificial sources (nuclear weapons, medical sources, nuclear power plants/waste), an estimated 50,000 new cases of inherited disease would appear worldwide in the first generation alone. Eventually the effects would translate into as many as 500,000 additional cases every generation. (See Box 6-1.)

SOURCES OF ARTIFICIAL RADIATION

Nuclear Weapons   Most of the evidence concerning the effects of nuclear explosions on humans comes from long-term studies of the survivors of Hiroshima and Nagasaki and their descendants.

Comparative studies conducted initially by the Atomic Bomb Casualty Commission and later by the Radiation Effects Research Foundation surprisingly have not demonstrated any proven association among survivors' offspring for congenital defects, stillbirth rate, newborn mortality, or childhood mortality. Among those

---

*Radiation is measured in absorption units. A rem (radiation equivalent for man) is a unit expressing the biological effects of a standard dose (one roentgen) of radiation; 1,000 mrems = 1 rem.

BOX 6-1   **Artificial Radiation**

Dosage effects of radiation tend to accumulate through time, so that several small doses can eventually have biologically harmful ramifications. However, a single large dose will probably do more damage than several small ones, where cells at least have some opportunity for repair.

Accidental exposure to very large doses of radiation at one time will cause severe radiation sickness that especially affects areas of rapidly forming cells, such as the gastrointestinal tract, skin, and blood-forming marrow. A very large single dose of radiation usually causes irreparable damage and can be lethal. The long-term effects of smaller radiation exposure are not well known, but experimental evidence suggests increased incidence of cataracts (scarring of the cornea of the eye), increased frequency of several varieties of cancer, and accelerated aging (Gerson, 1977).

RADIATION EXPOSURE LEVELS*

Lethal dose (would kill 50% of population)	400,000 mrems/single dose**
Maximum permissible to an individual without clearly harmful effects	500 mrems/year
Exposure from background sources	120 mrems/year
Exposure from medical sources	70 mrems/year

*Extrapolated from experimental evidence and observations on humans who have been exposed.

**Note: A lethal dose is extremely large compared to dosages normally incurred.

who were themselves directly exposed to the explosion (including *in utero*) there is an increase in chromosomal abnormalities. Since these usually cause death or sterility, they are not generally passed on to the next generation. For those who were severely exposed, there is also a sharp increase in overall mortality rates. It would seem that the effects of radiation exposure of the magnitude of Hiroshima and Nagasaki cause severe biological effects in the first generation, but surprisingly few in future generations (Schull, et al., 1981). However, long-term

FIGURE 6-7   Hiroshima, several months after the atomic bomb was dropped in August, 1945.

effects may initially appear "masked" as recessive mutations that will express themselves as lethals somewhere down the road. We may well see some of these biological costs as the studies of the Japanese descendants continue. Much concern also surrounds the possible dangers of atmospheric nuclear testing. Prior to 1963, the United States and the Soviet Union exploded several large devices in the atmosphere. The total radiation produced, however, was not an important mutagenic factor, for a dosage less than 1% of background radiation was generated.

Medical Sources   From medical practice, the major source of biologically harmful radiation exposure is X-rays, particularly if the gonads are exposed. As a diagnostic tool, X-rays are extremely helpful, but great caution must be used—particularly in individuals who have not completed reproduction. Even more hazardous is the X-ray exposure of a developing fetus, for an early somatic mutation may be ramified into major abnormalities.

Radiation is also used for therapeutic purposes in the treatment of some cancers. Such exposure, however, applies only to a tiny fraction of the population, and these few individuals are usually critically ill before exposure. Given the dire circumstance there is often little choice, but harmful side effects are significant. While the treatment is designed to slow down the progress of a lethal tumor, it can stimulate the onset of other cancers (in skin, thyroid, and bone, for example).

Nuclear Power Plants   Hazards from conventional nuclear power plants can potentially come from either release of radioactive elements in the fission process or release from waste material. Barring a major accident, the kinds of materials *likely* to escape from a nuclear power plant are not exceedingly radioactive. On

FIGURE 6-8   Chernobyl.

the other hand, a major failure (that is, a "meltdown") of the plant's radioactive core could be catastrophic.

The most serious accident yet to occur at a nuclear power plant took place at Chernobyl in the Soviet Ukraine on April 26, 1986. As a result of human error and a test procedure gone terribly wrong, the reactor building exploded, releasing large amounts of radioactive isotopes into the atmosphere (*Nature*, 1986). The resulting fire further damaged the reactor core (leading to at least a partial meltdown), burned for several days, and released substantially more radioactivity.

Spreading from the Ukraine, the radioactive cloud passed over Eastern Europe, Scandanavia, and eventually reached England on May 2 (ApSimon and Wilson, 1986). The fallout came down on Europe mostly as a result of rainfall carrying the radioactive material. By the time the "cloud" had reached the Western Hemisphere, it had dissipated to such an extent as to prove of no significant danger.

How much harm was done, however, in Europe? Most immediately, at least 31 deaths have been reported by Soviet authorities—primarily due to severe radiation suffered by plant workers and firemen in the immediate vicinity. The long-term impacts are not yet fully understood. On the basis of Soviet estimates of radioactive release, some experts place the eventual cost at approximately 4,000 additional cancer deaths over the next 30 years (i.e., above and beyond what would have occurred without the accident) (*Nature*, 1986).

In the United States, the most serious nuclear plant accident occurred at the Three Mile Island facility near Harrisburg, Pennsylvania, on March 28, 1979. Due to mechanical failure and human error, the plant's cooling system failed to operate correctly, causing the nuclear reactor's fuel core to overheat, and bringing the plant dangerously close to a meltdown. In addition, a large (1,000 cubic foot) bubble of explosive hydrogen gas formed within the reactor building, and this potentially dangerous situation was only brought under control after five days.

Waste material (as a direct product of uranium fission) from nuclear power plants can be highly radioactive and must be disposed of with extreme caution. Usually, such material is buried in special underground facilities hopefully far from dense population centers and active geological faults.

Careful monitoring around nuclear power plants has thus far shown little radiation pollution—well within minimum safety limits; potential dangers persist, however. The possibility of a major leak at a plant or waste site due to carelessness, sabotage, or earthquake continues to cause much apprehension.

CHEMICALS AND MUTATIONS

Today, more significant than radiation as a mutagenic agent is the wide variety of synthesized chemicals we eat, breathe, and with which we come into physical contact. We might be startled to learn that few of these exotic chemicals so widely used in business, agriculture, food processing, and the drug industry have received adequate enough systematic testing to measure their mutagenic danger accurately.

A clarification of terms is required. Researchers use three different but somewhat overlapping terms for agents that negatively affect health/cell function. **Mutagen** (or mutagenic) refers to an agent that actually alters the genetic material (DNA) of a cell. A mutagen can affect somatic cells or gametic cells. A **carcinogen** (carcinogenic) simply means any agent that promotes cancer (many carcinogens

Mutagen An agent that mutates (alters the DNA of a cell).

Carcinogen An agent that promotes cancer (often a mutagen as well).

Teratogen An agent that disrupts development.

will also be mutagens of somatic cells). Finally, a **teratogen** (teratogenic) is an agent that in any way disrupts *in utero* development, potentially leading to a birth defect. Likewise, such factors may also be mutagenic.

Not only those chemicals produced by human innovation have mutagenic effects; some of those formed naturally also have striking mutagenic properties. For example, aflatoxin—a substance formed from mold on peanuts and other organic substances—is one of the strongest mutagens known. In addition, in laboratory animals, numerous other chemicals found in common foods have been shown to be mutagenic and/or carcinogenic. Among those foods containing such possible harmful substances are black pepper, mushrooms, celery, parsley, figs, and cocoa powder (i.e., chocolate) (Ames, 1983).

We often read of experimental evidence (on lab animals) pointing to possible harmful effects of cyclamates, saccharin, Alar, and so forth. After some public furor and industry protests, these substances are usually removed from the market—not so much because we understand their effects on humans, but because we fear their possibilities.

Cyclamate is apparently not a mutagen itself, but it can be converted into a substance that is. Caffeine may also increase the likelihood of mutation by interfering with DNA repair. In all these cases, however, the direct evidence obtained from laboratory organisms is still unclear when extrapolated to human beings.

CROWDING

Another human problem realized only since the advent of agricultural settlements is crowding. Today, the stresses of humanity pressing against humanity are becoming ever more apparent throughout most of the inhabited world.

Crowding is defined as a problem primarily in terms of population density—in other words, the numbers of people per unit area. Population densities alone, however, do not measure the human stress involved. More relevant here is the *quality* of life possible, which in turn is dependent on technological sophistication, architectural design, and prevailing cultural values.

What is most significant in determining whether an individual feels crowded is his/her microenvironment, or what is sometimes called "personal space." In some urban areas of the United States and many parts of the underdeveloped world, several families crowd into housing units designed for single families. The amount of personal space per individual is thus reduced to just a few dozen square feet. Experimental data support this aspect of immediate space, since the strongest density-dependent correlations with social pathologies concern the number of people per room (Altman, 1978).

How much space is required for individuals to feel comfortable and function normally depends on the individual and the situation. In addition to actual physical space, other important aspects include: cleanliness, heat, odor, ventilation, whether individuals can be mobile within the space provided, whether they are in the crowded conditions voluntarily or not, and most importantly, how long they are required to stay in such conditions (ranging from a few minutes to a lifetime). Individual tolerance of crowded conditions and ability to adjust to altered quantity and quality of social interactions also show marked variation.

While there are no *absolute* measures of minimum space requirements, a general standard of 38 sq. ft. per person has been recommended for United States

FIGURE 6-9 Hong Kong. A side alley packed with humanity.

penal institutions. If this is taken as a rough standard, the following extremely crowded conditions come into sharper focus:

	SQ. FT./PERSON
Crowded disco	10
Nineteenth-century London slum	9
Nazi concentration camp at Belsen	3
New York subway at rush hour	2
Black Hole of Calcutta	2

As humans pack themselves in ever larger numbers into smaller areas, what effects can we expect? Numerous experimental studies have shown serious behavioral disturbances among overcrowded animals. Moreover, there are also physiological alterations, such as increased production of steroids. The exact functions of these substances are still unclear, but they seem to be secreted in generally stressful situations.

Observations of overcrowding in animals either in the laboratory (rats, mice) or in natural populations (among deer and lemmings, for example) indicate three major kinds of behavioral and reproductive abnormalities (Damon, 1977):

1. Disruption of reproduction, ovulation, sperm function, mating, nest building, lactation
2. Increase in incidence of abortions, stillbirths, infant mortality
3. Increase in aggression, particularly by males

The direct pathological associations of overcrowding in animals, however, are still far from clear. If growth is slow in mice populations, they generally will adjust, showing no more mortality than a control group. Moreover, definite associations of disease incidence and overcrowding are also not clearly established. Sometimes animals (normally social) have higher incidences of disease when they are isolated; other animals show more disease symptoms when crowded.

What does all this experimental evidence from animals mean for humans? Very few studies have been done on crowding using human data, but as yet no clearly harmful associations of overcrowding have been demonstrated.

We must reemphasize that the concept of crowding is not strictly a biological one but has important cultural connotations as well. In fact, most researchers consider "crowding" as primarily a psychological subjective state. Typically, some sort of stress is implied. This is believed to be derived from individual perceptions of too little physical and/or psychological space (social overload theory) or from feelings of loss of personal control over interpersonal interactions ("thwarting" theory).

In many cultures close physical contact with other humans is seen as highly desirable, whereas in others it is avoided. For example, the !Kung San* of the Kalahari Desert live in an environment with vast open space. In fact, their overall population density (approximately one person per ten square miles) is among the lowest in the world (Draper, 1973). However, San deliberately arrange their living space—huts in tight circles with few physical barriers—in order to provide maximum interpersonal contact. A possible explanation of this kind of behavior is that it is a cultural means of coping with the cold during the long, chilly Kalahari nights. Indeed, this arrangement creates the equivalent effect of thirty people living in a single room! The !Kung do not have to live closely together but clearly pre-

---

*The mark ! indicates a clicking sound in the pronunciation of Kung San.

fer to do so. How we then perceive their personal environment (as overcrowded or not) depends largely on what cultural definition we apply.

NOISE

One by-product of crowding in urban, heavily industrialized areas is noise. The largest contributor to noise pollution is made by mechanical devices. We are all constantly bombarded by the sounds of planes, buses, cars, construction equipment, and even music.

An obvious physical effect of excessive noise (high amplitude) is a deterioration of hearing ability. Urban dwellers on the average perform less well on hearing tests than rural folk. Such loss of hearing is seen particularly in airline workers, construction personnel, and rock band members. Just two hours in a disco can adversely affect one's hearing—even permanently! Noise-induced hearing loss may be quite common. Two different studies estimate the number of individuals in the United States suffering from such hearing loss at between 4.5 and 5 million people (Bugliarello et al., 1976).

Clearly, extremely high levels of noise produce harmful effects, but what about moderate noise levels? Some evidence suggests such pollution can lead to a loss of sleep and reduced concentration (Damon, 1977). We all have experienced such noise levels (for example, with traffic or construction equipment) and obviously considerable adaptability is possible. Particularly if the noise is steady and predictable, we can learn to "phase it out." But are we really able to ignore it completely? Some extremely tentative data suggest that continuous noise pollution may produce harmful consequences in humans. For example, in the area around a London airport, admissions to mental hospitals are significantly higher than in less noisy areas (Damon, 1977).

In recognition of the harmful effects of noise pollution around airports, a California Superior Court decision in 1970 awarded $740,000 to 549 property owners around Los Angeles International Airport for "loss of full enjoyment of their property" (Anthrop, 1973). Debate concerning noise pollution from jet aircraft peaked in the early 1970s over the proposed development of a commercial supersonic transport (SST). Eventually, the U.S. Senate withdrew federal support for an American SST; the English/French-built supersonic *Concorde* began operation in the mid-1970s, but has been allowed only restricted access to a few United States airports.

Summary

In this chapter, we have investigated human responses to a variety of environmental stresses: solar radiation, heat, cold, high altitude, malnutrition, disease, artificial radiation, crowding, and noise. We have seen that in most cases individual humans make physiological adjustments to such environmental stress—what we have termed *acclimatization*.

We have also posed the question of adaptation: Do human populations vary in the proportions of genotypes in response to general ecological stress? The answer to this last query is still open, since it necessitates a demonstration of specific selection pressures affecting differential reproductive success—a most tricky task for human data!

While still unproven, we may reasonably postulate that variable conditions of solar radiation, the thermal environment, nutrition, disease, and altitude have led to differential success of genotypes influencing body size/shape, skin pigmentation, the immune response system, and so forth.

We may also, with some reason, postulate that cultural environments of the technological, urban, overcrowded twentieth century are also acting to shift selection pressures. The real question is: How?

Questions for Review

1. What are the differences between adaptation and acclimatization? Illustrate through the example of high altitude adjustments.
2. Under what conditions might light skin color be adaptive? Under what conditions might dark skin color be adaptive?
3. What physiological adjustments do humans show in coping with cold stress?
4. What physiological adjustments do humans show in coping with heat stress?
5. What does body size and shape have to do with climate adaptation?
6. How do humans cope with high altitude stress (both physiologically and culturally)?
7. Give an explanation for the distribution of lactose intolerance among the world's populations.
8. How might malnutrition cause changes in selection pressures? Describe what kinds of data would *test* for such changes.
9. Discuss how human disease is influenced by an interaction of biocultural factors.
10. A foreign antigen has just entered your body. Discuss how your body recognizes it as foreign and deals with it.
11. What causes AIDS? Of those exposed to the virus, who actually gets AIDS?
12. What are the various possible sources of artificial radiation? Why is there so much concern over radiation pollution?
13. Discuss how crowding and noise *might* affect selection pressures.

Suggested Further Reading

Anthropological Aspects of Pigmentation. *American Journal of Physical Anthropology*, **43**:387–443, November 1975.
  A collection of seven articles providing an historical perspective and current hypotheses concerning the nature and evolution of human skin pigmentation.
Baker, Paul T., and Michael A. Little (eds.). *Man in the Andes*, Stroudsburg, Penn.: Dowden, Hutchinson, & Ross, Inc., 1976.
  This book is the report of seventeen scientists involved in the multidisciplinary study of highland Quechua Indians (part of the International Biological Program). The most thorough and systematic study of human adaptation/adaptability yet attempted, this work includes information on ecological conditions, physiological responses, diet, disease, and demographic patterns.
Bier, O. G., W. D. da Silva, D. Götze, and I. Mota. *Fundamentals of Immunology*, New York: Springer-Verlag, 1981.
  An introduction to the complex and rapidly advancing field of immunology. Although this work is aimed at introductory students (in biology and medicine), the technical details of this complex field are still imposing.

Bodley, John H. *Anthropology and Contemporary Human Problems*, Menlo Park, Ca.: Cummings Publishing Co., 1976.

A thorough review of the world's nutritional crisis and the related problem of overconsumption. Written from an evolutionary, cross-cultural perspective, this work makes extreme efforts to show the relevance of anthropology to contemporary problems.

Damon, Albert (ed.). *Physiological Anthropology*, New York: Oxford University Press, 1975.

A superior set of articles with clear authoritative reviews of environmental stress resulting from solar radiation, heat (and humidity), cold, high altitude, malnutrition, disease, and noise. Every article is well written, and this work is highly recommended for any initial study of human adaptability.

————. *Human Biology and Ecology*, New York: W. W. Norton and Company, 1977.

A look at contemporary issues in human biology. Includes a good review of general evolutionary processes and excellent discussion of crowding, noise, and artificial radiation (the latter in a chapter by Donald F. Gerson).

Harrison, G. A., J. M. Tanner, D. Pilbeam, and P. T. Baker. *Human Biology* (3rd Ed.), New York: Oxford University Press, 1988.

Written by leading human biologists, this work contains authoritative discussions of human evolution, genetics, population genetics, growth and development, and ecology. Particularly relevant to topics relating to human adaptability is the section by P. T. Baker on human ecology.

Roberts, D. F. *Climate and Human Variability* (2nd Ed.) (An Addison-Wesley Module in Anthropology, No. 34), Reading, Mass.: Addison-Wesley, 1978.

Written by one of the leading authorities on human adaptability, this short discussion pulls together much of the current knowledge in this field, particularly relating to associations of body build and climatic factors. Also included is a good summary of skin pigmentation and climatic variables. Highly recommended for introductory students.

Stini, William A. *Ecology and Human Adaptation*, Dubuque, Iowa: Wm. C. Brown Company, 1975.

A short but authoritative review of selective processes acting on human populations. Particularly recommended is the discussion of high-altitude stress.

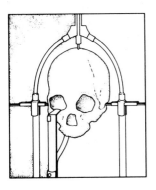

Human Diversity

Contents

Perception of Race

The racial discrimination suffered by Blacks, Latins, Asians, and other ethnic groups comprise one of the most troublesome and persistent social problems in the United States.* Bigotry itself has a long history in America. Many immigrants from southern and eastern Europe, for example—the Irish, Italians, Jews, and Poles—have all, at one time or another, been victims of prejudice. It is ironic that members of such groups often turn around and discriminate against others.

Many legislative attempts by both federal and state governments to end bigotry have failed. Such actions as the destroying or defacing of church or synagogue property, or burning crosses on lawns, may bring court action against the vandals, if they are caught, but the racially motivated hatred continues. Part of the problem may be due to the errors of an earlier generation of scientists who did not fully understand the genetics of heredity and thus supported the notion that there are superior and inferior races, a belief that is still tenaciously held by much of the general public. Many other reasons for bigotry abound, such as scapegoating, a false sense of patriotism, and the invalid belief

*Racial discrimination, of course, is not confined to the United States—all nations experience similar problems with varying ethnic groups.

that hereditary traits are carried in the blood passed from parents to children.

In this chapter, we discuss attitudes toward race, racial classifications, IQ and intelligence, and racism. Obviously, these topics are related, and a common theme runs through all of them: Heredity is responsible for personality traits, character, ability, morality, and intelligence.

The question "Are these attributes inherited or are they acquired from the environment?" is no longer an issue, since almost all scientists concerned with the problem are satisfied that research findings are clear on the subject. Both heredity *and* environment influence behavior. There have been attempts to determine the percentage of each, but opinion varies. To be sure, individuals are certainly subject to the influences of family genes, but they are also influenced by school, church, and peers. And nowadays there are certain to be effects from movies, radio, and especially television. To what degree do each of these factors shape attitudes? It is not yet possible to say.

As scientists continue their research, perhaps their future findings may be more helpful. However, the importance of the problem cannot be overemphasized—explosive racial incidents occur with entirely too much frequency in our society.

If you wonder where you stand on the issue of race, ask yourself what your posi-

tions are on the following statements (adapted from Barzun, 1937, 1965, p. 12ff). Answer each statement *True* or *False*, then check your score below.

1. Humankind consists of permanent types that are recognizable by physical features inherited by blood and that permit distinctions to be made between "pure" and "mixed" races.
2. Mental and moral behavior of humans is related to physical structure; knowing the structure, or the racial label associated with that structure, provides a satisfactory understanding of the behavior.
3. Individual personality, ideas, and capacities, as well as national culture, politics, and morals, are produced by social entities such as race, nation, class, and family. The connection between the group and the spiritual "product" is obvious without further discussion.

YOUR SCORE:

■ If you answered *False* for each statement, give yourself full points.
■ If you answered *True* for any statement, please read this chapter carefully. Scientific evidence *does not support* any of these assertions. On the contrary, the evidence overwhelmingly demonstrates their falsity.

CHAPTER 7

Introduction

We examined human variation in Chapters 5 and 6 from an adaptive point of view, in which physical differences among populations were explained largely in terms of selection pressures leading to possible adaptive responses.

This emphasis on selection and adaptation is a recent approach to human variation. In the past, scholars busied themselves constructing racial typologies, seeking the origin of races, and attributing to races a variety of personality traits.

In this chapter, we shall briefly trace the history of the scholarly and scientific approaches to human diversity. We shall question the value of racial typologies and the concept of race itself. We shall also examine the relationship—if any—between human diversity and behavior. And we will examine the question, Is intelligence, as reflected in IQ test achievements, the result of heredity or environment, or the interaction of both?

The Concept of Race

As early as 1350 B.C., Egyptians recognized physical differences of populations by using four colors to distinguish various groups: red for Egyptian, yellow for those to the east, white for people from the north, and black for Africans to the south (Gossett, 1963, p. 4). Greeks, more than two thousands years ago, placed non-Greeks in an outsider category of barbarians, and Romans, somewhat later, identified themselves simply as Roman citizens; all others were alien. It has probably been a very old custom, long before the Greeks, to separate one's own group from all others, a practice that continues to this day.

However, it was only in fairly recent times that outsiders were categorized as inferior, and according to a recent history of race (Stepan, 1982), this was due to the European slave trade (outlawed in Britain in 1803 and on the continent in 1833) and the practice of slavery in North America (outlawed in the United States in 1865). In Greek and Roman times, slaves were mainly war captives who were physically similar to their masters. The slave trade dealt with people—mostly from West Africa—that the Europeans knew very little about, and who were markedly different in physical appearance from themselves. Furthermore, Europeans considered the Africans' technology primitive and their morals backward. To the Europeans, dark Africans were not "civilized" which, apparently, made them acceptable as slaves.

During the fifteenth, sixteenth, and seventeenth centuries, explorers returning from their travels to newly discovered lands brought back stories of strange, dark-skinned people—from Australia, the Americas, Africa, and various areas of Asia. That there were so many populations in the world so different from Europeans raised many religious, moral, and scientific questions. Did these people belong to

Monogenists Term applied to those who believe that all races derived from a single pair (Adam and Eve).

Polygenists Term applied to those who believe in a multiple origin of races.

Anthropometry anthropos: man
metric: measure
Measurement of the human body.

the same species as Europeans? Were all peoples in the world descendants of the originally created pair, Adam and Eve, or were there later creations of non-Europeans who were of different species? Was it possible for Europeans and out-siders to interbreed and produce fertile and healthy offspring? Was their mental capacity comparable to Europeans? Could all humans live in all climates, or were certain people restricted to a specific environment? What purposes did racial traits serve? Did color of skin and head shape contribute to character and morality?

Europeans were both upset and tantalized by these questions, and scientists felt obligated to find answers. For more than 100 years, scientists had been investigat-ing the questions that the concept of race had raised. These questions, which im-pinged on Christian beliefs and standards of morality, were being clearly voiced late in the eighteenth century (some of them much earlier), and two schools of thought, known as **monogenism** and **polygenism**, devised responses. The monogenist view, that all races were descended from a single, original pair—Adam and Eve—was a position that required an explanation of the diversity found around the world. Insisting on the plasticity of the human physical structure, monogenists contended that climate, environment, and local conditions modified the original race, resulting in separate races. (Buffon made a similar suggestion in the preceding century.) Some monogenists saw races as "degenerative" modifica-tions that could be reversed under favorable conditions.

The polygenists, on the other hand, argued that races did not descend from a single, original pair, but from a number of pairs. Also, they saw such a wide gap in the physical, mental, and moral attributes between themselves and other races that they were sure these outsiders belonged to different species. Other poly-genists were dissatisfied with the concept of species and resorted to using the word *type*, instead. However, they believed there had been "pure" races in the past which, through intermixture, migration, and conquest, were modified to their present condition. Nor did polygenists accept the monogenist notion of plasticity of physical traits, and they rejected the proposition that climate and environment were modifying instruments.

Although most scientists were monogenists in the early years of the nineteenth century, by 1850 polygenism was gaining favor. Anthropologists, taking the poly-genist view of the stability of physical traits, began measuring the skull (regarded as a stable, unchanging organ) in order to determine racial differences. In this methodology, the skull was selected because it housed the brain. (Conventional wisdom of the times held that there was a direct correlation between size and shape of the brain and intelligence and morality.)

This view encouraged taking and recording skeletal measurements, especially of the skull. Such cranial measurements had already been developed in the eighteenth century by Johann Friedrich Blumenbach, a German anatomist who saw skulls as suitable for the study of race differences. On the basis of his study, Blumenbach divided humans into five races (see p. 190), but he believed in the unity of humankind. He did not find the huge differences between races later enunciated by the polygenists. He wrote that

> a single primeval 'Caucasian' had 'degenerated' in two directions under the influence of environment—on the one hand, through the American toward the Mongolian; on the other, through the Malayan toward the Ethiopian (Stocking, 1988, p. 5).

This new science of measurement, called **anthropometry**, became the *sine qua non* of physical anthropological methodology in the nineteenth century and the first half of the twentieth. The measurements were mainly, though not entirely, of the skull.

In 1842, Anders Retzius, a Swedish anatomist, believed he had discovered a true scientific basis for racial classification: the shape of the head. Called the *cephalic index*, this technique focused on the ratio of the breadth of the skull to its length. Retzius used the cephalic index to divide Europe into two types: long-headed or **dolichocephalic** and broad-headed or **brachycephalic**. This system led to futile, but heated and nationalistic,* wrangling on whether dolichocephalics were superior to brachycephalics, or vice versa.

Anthropometry was enthusiastically promoted by Paul Broca, a French neurosurgeon and physical anthropologist who staunchly supported polygenism. In 1859, he founded The Anthropological Society of Paris, the first anthropological organization in Europe. He also located the center in the brain essential for articulate speech (known as Broca's area) and originated methods of classifying hair and skin color.

Broca was also a resourceful and ingenious inventor of instruments for measuring. He devised craniometers and other gadgetry in order to search for statistical relationship in measurements of the skull. Scientists proceeded on cranial measurements with enthusiastic zeal, and the peak of anthropometry may have been reached in 1900, when A. von Torok took 5,000 measurements on a single skull (Barzun, 1965, p. 117).

In contrast to polygenists, the monogenists, in the early 1800s, took the view that all humans belong to the same species and are equal in the eyes of God. By midcentury, however, the concept of racial egalitarianism was being replaced by a hierarchical view of races, an interesting return to the discarded Great Chain of Being philosophy. Even monogenists, who believed that all humankind belonged to one species, accepted what appeared to most Europeans as an obvious, empirical truism: Europeans were superior to all other peoples and, among Europeans, northern, light-skinned Europeans were superior to southern, darker Europeans. Races were ranked essentially on a scale based on color (along with size and shape of heads), with Africans at the bottom. The rationale for the low ranking of Africans appeared to be based primarily on their history as slaves and the very dark skin pigmentation.

Although it might seem strange today,† **phrenology** played a significant role in relating brain shape to intelligence. Phrenologists claimed that the mind was a compound of distinct, innate, and fixed faculties, and each faculty, possessing a unique function, had its locus in different areas of the brain, popularly believed to be detectable by bumps on the head! They maintained that human behavior was the result of the structure and functions of the mind, and these were fixed by heredity. From this point of view, it was easy to conclude that groups, endowed with different brain structures, were biologically committed to play different societal roles.

One phrenologist observed that the uniformity of nature, by the laws of propagation, "stamps an impress of brotherhood upon each particular race, and gives a

Dolichocephalic   dolicho: narrow
cephal: head
Narrow or long-headed; a skull in which the width is less than 75 percent of the length.

Brachycephalic   brachy: short, broad
Broad-headed; a skull in which the width is 80 percent or more of the length.

Phrenology   phreno: heart, mind
The study of the shape of the skull to determine mental faculties, personality, and character traits.

---

*Northern Europeans tended to be dolichocephalic; southern Europeans (including the French and many Germans), brachycephalic.

†Then again it might not. Considering contemporary movies and television, the strange cults and sects that thrive today, and the popularity of astrology and reincarnation, phrenology in retrospect seems quite a conservative philosophy.

Eugenics The "science" that attempts to improve the race through breeding.

corresponding resemblance in character among all the individuals distinguished from the character of all other races, and therefore essentially national" (Combe, cited in Stephan, 1982, p. 25). In other words, biology and national character are linked to race.

By mid-nineteenth century, phrenology was on the wane, but its influence lingered. The phrenologist axiom—that individual function must correspond with different parts of the brain—was widely accepted. It provided for the conviction that some measurement—cranial capacity, facial angle, cephalic index, brain size, or brain weight—would truly indicate innate ability and thus justify the formation of a hierarchy of races.

Another unfortunate approach to race was taken by Francis Galton, cousin to Darwin, and "a polymath" who "contributed significantly . . . to psychology, biology, and anthropology" (Stocking, 1968, p. 167). Galton created, with others, the science of "biometrics," the mathematical study of evolution. Like Morton (see p. 189) and Linnaeus before him, he associated behavioral and personal traits with race. Influenced by Darwin's *Origin*, Galton was concerned that civilized society was being weakened by the failure of natural selection to eliminate the unfit and inferior members (Greene, 1981, p. 107).* He wrote and lectured on the necessity of race improvement and suggested governmental regulation of marriage and family size, an approach he named **eugenics**.

Eugenics is based on the premise that intelligence, morality, and behavioral characteristics are inherited. This view, boasting a long history, was accepted by the general public and scientists alike. Apparently, it is easily believed, or difficult not to believe, since it seems to be empirically obvious. However, no one has ever found a gene that controls personality, morals, or behavior in general (we shall discuss intelligence shortly). It is not surprising, therefore, that eugenics "caught on." Eugenic societies were founded in both Europe and the New World, with many biologists and anthropologists as members.

The popularity of eugenics flourished on both sides of the Atlantic until the 1930s, when environment was shown to be a significant factor in behavior. Eugenics is now generally discredited, but in Germany, after World War I, it took an abhorrent turn. The idea of pure race was extolled as a means of re-establishing a strong and prosperous state, and eugenics was seen as scientific justification for purging the German population of the "unfit." Many of Germany's anthropologists accepted this interpretation (known as *Rassenhygiene* or racial hygiene) and continued to support it during the Nazi period (Proctor, 1988, p. 143), when it served as justification for condemning millions of people to death.

Although eugenics was already under critical attack in the 1930s, some anthropologists remained attached to the idea. Earnest Hooton, for years the leading physical anthropologist teaching at a major university (Harvard), took a eugenic stance in his reflection on race and behavior in the second edition of his textbook, *Up from the Apes*, published in 1946:

> It is a conviction of many a physical anthropologist, many biologists, and some psychologists that human behavior in general cannot be substantially improved unless individual human organisms are bettered in quality, either by eliminating the degenerate, inferior, and chronically diseased, or by applying the science of human

---

*Greene suggests that Darwin also held this belief. Scholars, however, are divided about Darwin on this point.

genetics actually to breed stocks that are individually superior animals. The social problems of man will never be solved by merely tinkering with human institutions and trying to temper the blasts of environment to hereditarily shorn lambs (Hooton, 1931, 1946, pp. 663–664).

Scientists in the United States were also interested in the general topic of race. Books and articles were published in response to questions similar to those raised in Europe. As early as 1787, the Rev. Dr. Samuel Stanhope Smith, professor of moral philosophy at the College of New Jersey (Princeton) and later its president, took the monogenist position in his *Essay on the Causes of the Variety of Complexion and Figure in the Human Species*.

In his book, Smith promoted the concept of the unity of the human species and vigorously opposed the idea of several distinct human species. He declared the notion that racial crossing produced infertile offspring and contradicted God's purpose. (See Stanton, 1960, for more on Smith's views). He attributed color to the effect of climate and, anticipating Darwin, suggested that human adaptability to different environments explained the differences among the various populations.

There was a good deal of unscientific discussion about Africans, skin color, and human origins in the United States during this period. It was not until Dr. Samuel George Morton's publication of *Crania Americana* in 1839 that we find, in America, the quality of scientific investigation equivalent to that being pursued in Europe.

Morton, a Philadelphian, was a physician, professor of anatomy at Pennsylvania Medical College and (publishing articles on anatomy, medicine, vertebrate paleontology, geology, and craniology) a well-known scientist. Becoming interested in crania in the 1820s, Morton started collecting skulls from all over the world, especially those of North American Indians, leading to his work conducted in 1839. His study consisted of measurements similar to the Europeans' but he added a new technique for measuring cranial capacity. He would fill a skull with white pepper seeds (later changed to BB lead shot), and then poured the seeds back into a cylinder, which displayed the volume in cubic inches. This method continued to be used by anthropologists for many years.

In his *Crania Americana*, Morton assumed the standard polygenist position that climate did not effect changes in race. He based his reasoning on the fact that his measurements demonstrated that bony structure remained unaffected by climate.

Although Morton developed a careful system of measuring skulls, his work had little influence on American anthropology. The reasons may be, as Brace has suggested, that in his principal work Morton added a chapter on phrenology (by Combe, an avid phrenologist) and "because those who claimed to be his disciples, after his early death in 1851, used his name and his work to try to justify the institution of slavery in the American South" (Brace, 1982, p. 18).

A constant theme of biological determinism ran through scientific research after 1850; namely, that heredity determined intelligence, behavior, and a host of other attributes. In order to demonstrate that there were, in fact, racial differences, body measurements were necessary, especially of the skull. As we mentioned, such measurements supported a racial hierarchy, with Europeans at the top and Africans at the bottom. Measurements were also used to type populations into races, the number of which varied wildly (See Box 7-1 for a few examples).

BOX 7-1 Racial Classifications

LINNAEUS, 1758

Homo europaeus
Homo asiaticus
Homo afer
Homo americanus

BUFFON, 1749

Lapland
Tartar
Southern Asiatic
European
American

BLUMENBACH, 1781

Caucasian
Mongolian
Malay
Ethiopian
American

SAINT HILAIRE, 1861

Caucasian	(Caucasian, Alleghenian)
Mongolian	(Hyperborean, Malay, American, Mongolian, Paraborean, Australian)
Ethiopian	(Kaffir, Ethiopian, Negro, Melanesian)
Hottentot	(Hottentot)

THOMAS H. HUXLEY, 1870

Negroid	(Bushman, Negro, Papuan)
Australoid	(Australians, Dravidians, Ethiopian)
Mongoloid	(Mongol, Polynesian, American Eskimo, Malay)
Xanthochroid	(Xanthochroid of Northern Europe, Melanochroid of Southern Europe, Melanochroid of Asia—Arabs, Afghans, Hindus, etc.)

J. DENIKER, 1900

Types	*Examples*
Wooly hair, broad nose:	Bushman, Negrito, Negro, Melanesian
Curly or wavy hair:	Ethiopian, Australian, Dravidian, Assyroid
Wavy brown or black hair, dark eyes:	Indo-Afghan, Arab or Semite, Berber, Littoral-European, Ibero-insular, Western European, Adriatic
Fair, wavy or straight hair, light eyes:	Northern European, Eastern European
Straight or wavy hair, dark, black eyes:	Ainu, Polynesian, Indonesian, South American
Straight hair:	Northern American, Central American, Patagonian, Eskimo, Lapp, Ugrian, Turkish, Mongol

E. A. HOOTON, 1946

Primary Race	*Primary Subrace*	*Composite Race**	*Composite Subrace**	*Residual Mixed Types**
White	Mediterranean	Australian	Armenoid	Nordic-Alpine
	Ainu	Indo-Dravidian	Dinaric	Nordic-Mediterranean
	Keltic	Polynesian		
	Nordic			
	Alpine			
	East Baltic			

*Example of categories, not to be read across.

190   CHAPTER 7   HUMAN DIVERSITY

BOX 7-1

| Negroid | African Negro
Nilotic Negro
Negrito | Bushman-
Hottentot |
| Mongoloid | Classic
Mongoloid
Arctic Mongoloid | Indonesian-
Mongoloid
American Indian |

Secondary Subrace

Malay-Mongoloid
Indonesian

STANLEY M. GARN, 1965

Geographical Races: "A collection of race populations, separated from other such collections by major geographical barriers" (p. 14).

Amerindian
Polynesian
Micronesian
Melanesian-Papuan
Australian
Asiatic
Indian
European
African

Local Races: "A breeding population adapted to local selection pressures and maintained by either natural or social barriers to gene interchange" (p. 16).

Northwest European   These are examples of local races; there are many, many more.
Northeast European
Alpine
Mediterranean
East African
Bantu
Tibetan
North Chinese
Extreme Mongoloid
Hindu

Micro-Races: Not well defined but apparently refers to neighborhoods within a city or a city itself since "marriage or mating, is a mathematical function of distance. With millions of potential mates, the male ordinarily chooses one near at hand" (p. 19).

With the publication of Darwin's *Origin of Species* in 1859, there was some attempt to take evolutionary principles into consideration for racial classifications. But the emphasis on typology continued in the racial types suggested by Deniker in 1900 and Hooton as late as 1946 (Box 7-1).

The division of the earth's human population into races was the concern of many physical anthropologists during this period. The assumption that pure races existed (some time in the past) was presumed, as was the responsibility of anthropologists to define them. To support such a position, it was necessary to believe that races had not basically changed from whatever they were at their time of origin. That is, those physical traits that did not adapt to environmental conditions could be used for racial classification; those that did adapt, could not. There was, therefore, constant effort to locate *nonadaptive* traits.

The search for nonadaptive traits to serve as a basis for the classification of racial types centered on the cephalic index, although hair form, eye form, and prominence of the nose were also judged nonadaptive. W. Z. Ripley, in *Races of Europe* (1899) summarized much of the research of European scientists. Relying heavily on headform as a basis for his racial classification, Ripley divided Europeans into three types. Not everyone agreed with the emphasis on head measurement, and Franz Boas, early in this century, criticized Ripley for "treating the cephalic index as the 'primary principle of classification'" (Stocking, 1968, p. 181).

In 1909, Boas, professor of anthropology at Columbia University working on behalf of the U.S. Immigration Commission, conducted what has become a classical study of European immigrants. He took various body measurements of immigrant parents and their children, totaling almost 18,000 persons. Among other results, Boas found that headform was not stable. In some immigrant groups, the heads of the children were longer than those of their parents; in other groups, broader. This was the first time the stability of headform had been tested in this way. It was clear that headform was indeed influenced by the environment and therefore could no longer be considered nonadaptive. However, Boas' evidence had little immediate effect on the stubbornly held notions of race.

Concerning the widely held belief that racial intermixture reduced fertility, Boas found that "half-breed" women, among North American Indians, bore more children than women of "pure" stock, and their children were taller. In fact, his data indicated that intermixture had a favorable effect.

Two aspects of race remained the principal study of physical anthropology for the first half of the twentieth century: (a) racial classification and (b) race and behavior. Typing people and placing them into divisions called races has not proved a satisfactory enterprise in anthropology, which is evident in the many and conflicting typological classifications anthropologists have created.

Typology presents problems not readily resolved. How many divisions are there? Estimates range from as few as 3 to more than 300. There are primary divisions, major subdivisions, minor subdivisions, composite subdivisions, and so on. What is the significance of these divisions of divisions, and what is their reality? Do they represent actual living populations, or merely ideal types? What criteria are used to separate one type from another, one subdivision from another? Is one trait more important than another? Skin pigmentation, for example, is the trait most people would consider as the basic classificatory criterion; should it carry more weight than, say, head shape, nose shape, body build, or stature? If so (or if not), why? For example, in his racial classification of 1900, Deniker typed northern Europeans as tall with wavy, reddish hair, reddish white skin, and dolichocephalic skulls. What, then, shall we do with a northern European answering this description whose brother is short, not tall, with straight rather than wavy hair, and a darkish rather than reddish white skin?

Finally, typologies tell us little if anything of human evolution. Classification, Washburn noted, is useful if we are concerned with anatomical, genetic, and structural differences between people, "but it is useful under no other circumstances, as far as I can see" (Washburn, 1963, p. 527).

Physical anthropology began to turn away from racial classification after World War I. There was some questioning of the concept of race and eugenics, the stability of racial traits, and the assumption that racial traits were adaptively neutral in evolution. Attitudes toward race were affected by the unscientific and bigoted views of Nazi racial philosophy. Also, the synthesis of Mendelian genetics and Darwin evolution in the 1930s (see Modern Synthesis, p. 97) affected all the evolutionary sciences, and physical anthropologists began, at least systematically, to apply evolutionary principles to their study of human evolution.

Attitudes toward race and the study of race changed more rapidly after World War II. Racial classification was not of much concern to younger anthropologists, who were more interested in developing theories that could be tested. More emphasis was placed on analysis, and field work was gaining attention. Physical anthropology diversified as paleoanthropology and primatology became significant subdivisions of the discipline. Dental anthropology, nutritional anthropology, and paleopathology gave anthropologists an even broader research base. Today, racial classification and racial problems seem to be of more interest to psychologists and sociologists.

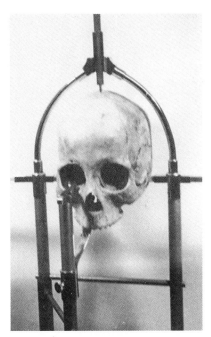

FIGURE 7-1   Craniometer.

Definitions of Race

To understand the difficulties the concept of race presents, it may help to review briefly the process of speciation (p. 105). Species is defined as "a group of interbreeding organisms that are reproductively isolated from other such groups" (p. 104), and biologists are agreed that species is an evolutionary unit. The definition of race is more elusive, and race is not an evolutionary unit, but an arbitrary one. We see this more clearly with the process of speciation.

As the populations within a species diverge, especially between isolated groups, differences arise. When the differences become detectable, taxonomists may classify the populations as races or subspecies. With continued isolation and divergence, the groups are known as *incipient species* (or biological races), on their way to becoming species. However, the traits that characterize differences tend to be arbitrary.

The division of the populations of any species into biological "races" tends to be arbitrary to some degree, but when it comes to human races, the situation is a quagmire. The populations of *H. sapiens* are not on their way to becoming separate species, and the reasons for this are quite clear. Human groups have been isolated in the past but never long enough to speciate. Taking their culture with them when they migrate, humans are not entirely dependent on environment. Consequently, they exchange genes with the people they meet, and this gene exchange has kept humans interfertile and members of the same species. As communication and the means of transportation improved, and as more efficient technology de-

FIGURE 7-2   Rudolf Virchow.

veloped, humans became even more independent of the environment, and the chance of speciation has become remote.

Perhaps the basic problem in defining race is to decide on the criteria. As we see from the examples on pages 190–191, these are arbitrary. The following definition demonstrates the dilemma: A race is ". . . a division of a species which differs from other divisions by the frequency with which certain hereditary traits appear among its members" (Brues, 1977, p. 1). Which hereditary traits? How are they selected? On what basis? Do the same traits apply in all cases? There is no agreement on the answers. Besides, no group classified as a race differs in all its traits from another race. If we cannot agree on racial criteria, then defining race and classifying populations into racial groups appears impossible.

Although we question the value of the racial concept, it may be instructive to list definitions of race, which may delineate even further the reasons why anthropologists are dissatisfied with the concept.

Rudolf Virchow (1896) also saw races as varieties originating from two factors, heredity and environment: ". . . there can be no doubt that *races are nothing more than hereditary variations* . . . we must derive races also from the influence of external causes, and we may define them as *acquired deviations from the original type*" (cited in Count, 1950, p. 193).

As time went on, anthropologists emphasized phenotypic traits as important in racial analysis. In 1926, Hooton offered the following definition:

> A race is a great division of mankind, the members of which, though individually varying, are characterized as a group by a certain combination of morphological and metrical features, principally non-adaptive, which have been derived from their common descent.

In addition to emphasizing visible phenotypic traits (morphological features), Hooten included measurements of the body that had occupied so much of anthropological research in the latter half of the nineteenth century. He also made an attempt to construct a more precise definition by restricting it to traits that were presumably nonadaptive—since he considered these the most objective racial markers. Implicit in this approach is the belief that races do not change over time, that if it were possible somehow to find traits unaffected by the environment, true or pure races could be determined (see p. 192).

We now know the search for nonadaptive traits is a pointless quest, that most visible phenotypes are the result of the dynamic interaction of several genes *and* the environment. As population genetics became important in biological research, the concept of population became part of the definition. In 1950, Boyd defined race "as a population which differs significantly from other human populations in regard to the frequency of one or more genes it possesses" (Boyd, 1950, p. 207). Livingstone objects to the simplistic use of gene frequencies as a criterion for race, since such a position implies that each population—which probably differs in the frequency of some gene from other populations—would be a separate race (Livingstone, 1964, p. 49).

One of the most recent modifications of the definition of race adds the concept of a *breeding*, or Mendelian, population (Garn, 1969). Livingstone again objects since the concept of breeding population may be difficult to apply. For example, Garn calls Mediterranean a local race (see Box 7-1) that ranges from Tangier to the Dardanelles and includes the Arabian Peninsula. However, this is a very unlikely breeding population, containing, as it does, wide differences in such factors as so-

FIGURE 7-3   E. A. Hooton.

cial class, religion, economy, and philosophy. Very few Christians interbreed with Muslims, or Arab Beduins with, say, Italian farmers.

The foregoing definitions of race and comments are not intended to discourage or confuse. The plain fact is that a great deal of confusion abounds among anthropologists, geneticists, and other researchers concerned with the concept of race. That there are physical differences among human beings is an obvious fact requiring no discussion. No one will mistake an indigenous resident of China for a European or African. But the matter is not that simple.

Topinard, writing almost 100 years ago, already recognized the problems still being discussed today:

> Races exist; it is undeniable; our intelligence comprehends them; our minds see them; our labors separate them out. . . *But nowhere can we put our fingers upon them* (emphasis ours, cited by Scheidt, 1924, p. 389).

To confuse the matter of race definition even further, the term "race," as it is popularly used, is more a sociocultural than biological concept. That is, a group of people may be designated as a race regardless of their genetic traits. Thus, children of mixed black and white parents are considered black, though genetically they are as much "white" as "black." Often designated as races are ethnic groups (Germans, French, Russians, etc.), religious groups (Muslims, Buddhists, Jews, etc.), political groups (communists, fascists). This also adds to the confusion. In wartime, when emotions run high, all manner of vices, based on "racial" traits, are attributed to the enemy (e.g., the Germans and Japanese in World War II and the Vietnamese in the Vietnam War).

What, then, are we to do about the concept of race? Is race a reality? Is a breeding population a race? Are races geographic isolates? Is it even possible to study races? Is the word "race" so loaded with misconception, misunderstanding, fallacy, prejudice, and bigotry that the term itself should be changed and its study limited? Or is Dunn more perceptive when he suggests, "It seems better to define and explain its use, and to free it from its bad and false meaning, than to give up the problem by excluding the word" (Dunn, 1951, p. 12).

As a concept, the validity and utility of race is declining among anthropologists. A survey taken in 1984 and 1985 disclosed anthropology as a house divided against itself on the race matter. Asked to respond to the statement, "There are biological races within the species *Homo sapiens*," 31% of cultural anthropologists agreed compared to 50% for physical anthropologists; 52 and 42%, respectively, disagreed (Lieberman et al., 1989, p. 67).

We have already noted that typological divisions of humankind, which once occupied so much anthropological effort, are now passé. As we have indicated, there are too many problems in the construction of racial typologies, and, once a typology is developed, the nagging question remains: So what?

In their conclusion, the authors of the above survey recommend disposing of the concept of race:

> In view of the variation in support of the race concept [among anthropologists], it is possible that as a starting point the public can be brought to recognize that this concept no longer enjoys scientific consensus. It will be necessary at the same time to communicate to other scientists that the concept does not have a firm base in theory or data as applied to the human species. . . . "Race," conceptual child of the colonial era, remains a sterile idea, while variation, gradation, or cline is a useful approach for future anthropological research and teaching about human hereditary traits (ibid, p. 72).

Many anthropologists consider the study of the distribution of single traits to be more rewarding (than the concept of race) from an evolutionary theory point of view, which is in essence the clinal approach to human diversity.

Clinal Distribution: One Genetic Trait

A relatively recent approach* to human variation is *clinal distribution*. Just as temperatures are plotted on a weather map by means of isotherms that join points with the same temperature, so also may gene frequencies be plotted. Thus, the distribution of a particular trait is indicated on a map by zones, known as clines (Fig. 7-4). This description simply reveals the variation of that trait over a geographic area, and by itself implies no explanation, racial or otherwise. Nor does such a distribution lead to racial typologies. A clinal distribution calls for an *evolutionary explanation* of the variation: Why does the frequency of allele B, in our figure, vary as we move from east to west across Europe? Evolutionary theory—mutation, genetic drift, natural selection, migration—is one way in which clinal variation may be explained.

*J. S. Huxley introduced the clinal concept, as it applied to plants, in 1938.

FIGURE 7-4   A cline frequency of the B allele. This computer-generated map shows the frequency of the B allele of the ABO blood-group system. Note the higher frequencies in Asia and the gradual decreasing frequencies as the clines move into Europe. (Courtesy of P. E. Schreiber, IBM Research Laboratory, San Jose, California.)

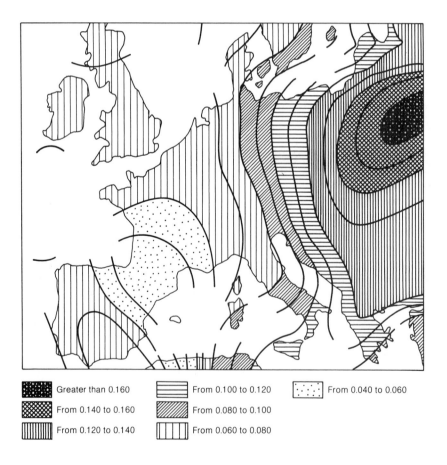

Greater than 0.160 From 0.100 to 0.120 From 0.040 to 0.060
From 0.140 to 0.160 From 0.080 to 0.100
From 0.120 to 0.140 From 0.060 to 0.080

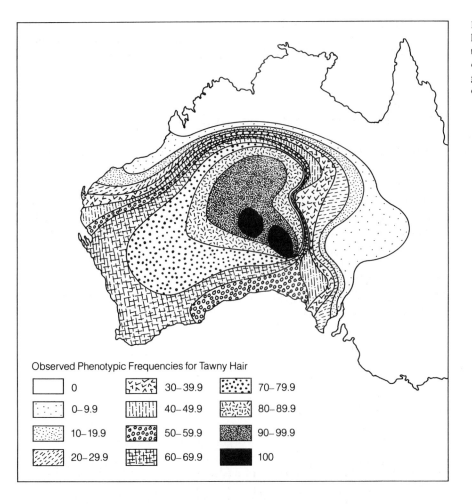

FIGURE 7-5   Phenotypic distribution, tawny hair in Australia. Note the concentration of tawny hair in the center of distribution which can be traced by clines in a decreasing gradient. This pattern can thus be viewed on an evolutionary and genetic basis.

Observed Phenotypic Frequencies for Tawny Hair

0	30–39.9	70–79.9
0–9.9	40–49.9	80–89.9
10–19.9	50–59.9	90–99.9
20–29.9	60–69.9	100

Human variation is perceived quite differently when approached from a clinal point of view. No attempt is made to construct a typology of traits, but rather to apply the principles of evolution. Is the variation of allele frequency due to the advantage of one allele over another? Has there been migration to or from the clinal area that may have altered the gene frequency, or perhaps an accident known genetically as drift? An advantage of a clinal study is that allele and trait frequencies can be graphically represented as they are in Figures 7-4 and 7-5. They suggest "migratory patterns and other aspects of population history" and "observed clinal variation in a trait is particularly amenable to explanation by mathematical methods of population genetics. In this sense, there is probably no superior method by which the evolutionary mechanisms responsible for interpopulation variation in single traits can be identified" (Bennett, 1979, pp. 357–358).

An example of an evolutionary clinal approach may be seen in Dr. Joseph Birdsell's discussion of the distribution of tawny hair he found in his fieldwork among Australian aborigines. The heaviest distribution of this blond hair is among several tribal groups in the Australian western desert (see Fig. 7-5), and the frequency then declines on a gradient outward from this center, although not uniformly in all directions. Professor Birdsell writes (1981, pp. 352–353):

Multivariate Pattern for several traits.

The evolutionary significance of this clinal distribution seems apparent, even though the exact genetic basis for its inheritance has not yet been unraveled. The trait acts as though it was determined by a single codominant gene. It would appear that somewhere in the central region of high frequency, mutations, and probably repeated mutations, occurred from normal dark brown hair to this depigmented variety. The pattern of distribution indicates that it was favored by selection in some totally unknown fashion. Over considerable periods of time, through gene exchange between adjacent tribes, the new mutant gene prospered and spread outward. It seems unlikely that lightly pigmented hair in childhood should in itself have any selective advantage. Rather, it is much more probable that certain effects of this mutant gene have somehow biochemically heightened the fitness of these Aborigines in their generally desert environment.

Professor Birdsell goes on to point out that one character cannot define a subspecies or race, and that "this example illustrates why races are scientifically undefinable." (Birdsell, p. 352). However, while this example does nothing for the definition of race, it is a good example of microevolution. "This pattern of blondness is a spectacular case of *transient polymorphism*, that is, a polymorphic character changing in time, here reflected as changes in space" (Birdsell, 1981, p. 352). And Birdsell wonders whether, if British colonization had not cut the process short, all Australian aborigines might have become blond-haired.

Multivariate Population Genetics

Whereas clinal studies isolate patterns of genetic variation one trait at a time, **multivariate** studies seek to describe the pattern for several traits simultaneously. Because the statistical manipulations of such analyses are exceedingly complex, high-speed computers have proven an invaluable tool.

An excellent example of this kind of approach to human diversity was undertaken by Harvard population geneticist R. D. Lewontin (1972), and his results are most informative. Lewontin measured the degree of population differences in allele frequencies for seventeen polymorphic traits, including many of those discussed in Chapter 5. In his analysis, Lewontin immediately faced the dilemma: Which groups (populations) should he contrast and how should they be weighted (all equally, or bigger groups like Arabs weighted differently than smaller ones like residents of the island, Tristan da Cunha)? After considerable deliberation, Lewontin decided to break down his sample into seven geographical areas (corresponding to the traditional concept of "major race") and included several (all equally weighted) populations within each. He then calculated how much of the total genetic variability within our species could be accounted for by these population subdivisions. (See Table 7-1.)

Surprisingly, only 6.3% of all variation can be accounted for at the level of major (geographic) race. In other words, close to 94% of human genetic diversity occurs *within* these gigantic groups. The large population units within races (generally corresponding to Garn's local races) account for an average of an additional 8.3%. Amazingly, the traditional concept of race (which isolates large human groups) explains about 15% of human genetic variation, leaving the remaining 85% unaccounted for.

TABLE 7-1   **Inclusive List of All Populations Used in
Lewontin's Population Genetics Study (1972)**

CAUCASIANS

Arabs, Armenians, Austrians, Basques, Belgians, Bulgarians, Czechs, Danes, Dutch, Egyptians, English, Estonians, Finns, French, Georgians, Germans, Greeks, Gypsies, Hungarians, Icelanders, Indians (Hindi-speaking), Italians, Irani, Norwegians, Oriental Jews, Pakistani (Urdu-speakers), Poles, Portuguese, Russians, Spaniards, Swedes, Swiss, Syrians, Tristan da Cunhans, Welsh

BLACK AFRICANS

Abyssinians (Amharas), Bantu, Barundi, Batutsi, Bushmen, Congolese, Ewe, Fulani, Gambians, Ghanaians, Hobe, Hottentot, Hututu, Ibo, Iraqi, Kenyans, Kikuyu, Liberians, Luo, Madagascans, Mozambiquans, Msutu, Nigerians, Pygmies, Senegalese, Shona, Somalis, Sudanese, Tanganyikans, Tutsi, Ugandans, U.S. Blacks, "West Africans," Xosa, Zulu

MONGOLOIDS

Ainu, Bhutanese, Bogobos, Bruneians, Buriats, Chinese, Dyaks, Filipinos, Ghashgai, Indonesians, Japanese, Javanese, Kirghiz, Koreans, Lapps, Malayans, Senoy, Siamese, Taiwanese, Tatars, Thais, Turks

SOUTH ASIAN ABORIGINES

Andamanese, Badagas, Chenchu, Irula, Marathas, Naiars, Oraons, Onge, Tamils, Todas

AMERINDS

Alacaluf, Aleuts, Apache, Atacameños, "Athabascans," Aymara, Bororo, Blackfeet, Bloods, "Brazilian Indians," Chippewa, Caingang, Choco, Coushatta, Cuna, Diegueños, Eskimo, Flathead, Huasteco, Huichol, Ica, Kwakiutl, Labradors, Lacandon, Mapuche, Maya, "Mexican Indians," Navaho, Nez Percé, Paez, Pehuenches, Pueblo, Quechua, Seminole, Shoshone, Toba, Utes, "Venezuelan Indians," Xavante, Yanomama

OCEANIANS

Admiralty Islanders, Caroline Islanders, Easter Islanders, Ellice Islanders, Fijians, Gilbertese, Guamians, Hawaiians, Kapingas, Maori, Marshallese, Melanuans, "Melanesians," "Micronesians," New Britons, New Caledonians, New Hebrideans, Palauans, Papuans, "Polynesians," Saipanese, Samoans, Solomon Islanders, Tongans, Trukese, Yapese

AUSTRALIAN ABORIGINES

Source: Evolutionary Biology, Volume 6, ed. by Dobzhansky et al. (article by R. Lewontin), p. 387. Reprinted with permission of Plenum Publishing Corporation.

The vast majority of genetic differences among human beings is thus explicable in terms of differences from one village to another, from one family to another, and to a very significant degree, from one person to another—even within the same family. Of course, when you recall the vast amount of human polymorphism (discussed in Chapter 5) and the ways this genetic variability is rescrambled during meiosis/sexual reproduction (discussed in Chapter 3), all this individual variation should not be that amazing.

Our superficial visual perceptions tell us race does exist. But the visible phenotypic traits usually used to make racial distinctions (skin color, hair shape, nose shape, etc.) may very well be a highly biased sample, not giving an accurate picture of the actual patterns of *genetic variation*. The polymorphic traits used by Lewontin are a more objective basis for accurate biological comparisons of human groups, and they indicate that the traditional concept of race tells us very little about human variation. Indeed, Lewontin concludes with a ringing condemnation:

> Human racial classification is of no social value and is positively destructive of social and human relations. Since such racial classification is now seen to be of virtually no genetic or taxonomic significance either, no justification can be offered for its continuance (Lewontin, 1972, p. 397).

Not all population geneticists, however, are quite this critical. After all, Lewontin did find that slightly more than 6% of human variation is accounted for in the large geographic segments traditionally called major races. Whereas this is certainly a minority of all variation within *Homo sapiens*, it is not necessarily biologically insignificant. If one feels compelled to continue classifying humankind into large geographic segments, population genetics offers some aid in isolating consistent patterns of geographic variation. One such classification suggests our species can be partitioned into three major geographic groups: Africans, Caucasians, and a heterogeneous group of Easterners, including all aboriginal populations of the Pacific area (Bodmer and Cavalli-Sforza, 1976).

Whereas, to some degree, these three groups form contrasting genetic units, we must remember that the total amount of genetic variation *within* them (from one person to another, one village to another, one tribe to another, etc.) is far more than exists *between* them.

We have thus far discussed race in the abstract, as a concept, but there is a very practical aspect of race that must be considered in our modern world: the association of race and behavior, which we take up in the following section.

Race and Behavior

The fact that people differ has, as we remarked at the beginning of this chapter, long been recognized, at least as far back in recorded history as the ancient Egyptians. Association of personality traits and race has also long been suggested. In his famous taxonomic scheme, Linnaeus (see p. 30), in 1758, classified humans into four groups (Box 7-1). He also assigned behavioral traits to each group: American Indians are choleric; Europeans, sanguine; Asiatics, melancholy; and Africans, phlegmatic.

One hundred years later, personality traits were still being attributed to race by, among others, Count de Gobineau, sometimes called the "Father of Racist Ideology" (Biddiss, 1970). We must point out that a *racial* classification differs from a *racist* one. The former attempts—usually unsuccessfully—to categorize humans into meaningful groups without making distinctions concerning the superiority of one versus another. Racist typologies, on the other hand, explicitly attempt to impute "superior" behavioral characteristics to some races and "inferior" attributes to others. The best known, and most infamous, attempt to label people superior/inferior occurred in Nazi Germany, especially in the 1930s and 1940s. The Nazi solution to the presence of Nazi-defined inferior races was annihilation. It is estimated they murdered, in gas chambers, nine million men, women, and children.

RACE AND INTELLIGENCE

Belief in the relationship between race and personality is popular even today, but there is no evidence that personality or any cultural trait, or any aspect of culture, such as religion or language, is in any way racial. Very likely, most scholars today would agree with this last statement, but there is an area of disagreement still to be reconciled. That area is the question of whether race (a biologically related group) and intelligence are associated. The overwhelming majority of academic opinion (in anthropology, biology, genetics, psychology, and sociology) cannot find valid evidence that relates the two phenomena. There are, however, scientists who *do* believe in the relationship, and perhaps the best-known advocate of the proposition that race (i.e., heritability) is the *causal* factor in intelligence is Professor Arthur R. Jensen. He estimates the heritability of intelligence at about 75% (Jensen, 1980, p. 244).

Jensen, professor of educational psychology at the University of California, Berkeley, believes that intelligence is a correlate of race, that intelligence is inherited, that IQ tests measure intelligence, that racial intelligence differences can be researched from a heritability point of view, that the uncertainty of the heredity-environment problem can be reduced, and that the lower average IQ scores of blacks (about 15 points) are a function of race (Jensen, 1969a).

Jensen's views have been criticized by scientists from various disciplines. In his review and analysis of the literature on testing intelligence, Eckberg (1979, p. 55) is led to seriously question the degree to which the idea of a general intelligence can have usefulness in real-world pursuits. Instead, all the various lines of evidence indicate that behavior is too multiform to be encapsulated under the label of *intelligence*, unless what we intend by intelligence is something quite a bit different from that which is usually intended. Also, many research studies have shown that environment is a vital factor in an IQ test score. Furthermore, there is no consensus among researchers on the extent of environmental influence or how to factor in the many environmental components that affect IQ test scores. Anthropologists Brace and Livingstone (1971, p. 67) suggest that *all* measured differences among major groups of humans may be explained primarily by environmental factors.

Much of the criticism of Jensen's (and other similar) views may be grouped under two headings: (1) inadequacy of the IQ test as a measure of intelligence; and (2) the failure to consider the influence of environment (in a broad sense) on ability and performance.

With the bulk of scientific opinion opposed to heritability as the explanation for racial intelligence, troublesome questions arise regarding the validity of IQ tests as well as the reliability of the monozygotic twin studies. We agree with Professor William Howells (1971, p. 8): "In all honesty, therefore, scientists must decline to see the existence of racial variation in mental ability at this stage."

The Solomon Islands Project—Calculating Biological Distance

The Solomon Islands are an island chain comprising more than 15 islands in the South Pacific located between New Guinea and Fiji (Fig. 1). The Solomon Islands Biomedical Project has carried on systematic research there going back to the 1960s (initial surveys, 1966–1972) and has resampled most of the study populations again in the 1980s (1985–1986).

The island populations are diverse linguistically and culturally as well as genetically. Thus, these groups offer a unique opportunity for systematic, multidisciplinary study of biological relationships (and microevolutionary explanations for these relationships). Accordingly, over the study periods, diverse experts from physical anthropology and other biomedical sciences, linguistics, archeology, and cultural anthropology have been involved in the research.

As Fig. 1 shows, seven different cultural groups have been sampled (in both early and more recent surveys), and these populations are distributed over three different islands. Linguistically, the three groups on Bougainville speak a "non-Austronesian" ("Papuan") language; the three groups on Maleita are Austronesian (formerly called, "Malayo-Polynesian") speakers; and the Ontong Java population speak a Polynesian language. How genetically diverse are these populations, and how well do biological indices correlate with geography and/or linguistics? These have been two of the central questions of the Solomon Islands Project since its earliest stages. In order to obtain relevant data to test for answers to these questions, systematic information was gathered for Mendelian traits (mostly blood group polymorphisms) as well as for polygenic indicators as estimated by comparative dermatoglyphics (fingerprints), anthropometrics (body size and proportions), and ondontometrics (tooth measurements).

The results first of all showed that even within quite small areas (on a single island) there is significant intra- and interpopulation variation (not a surprise, considering Lewontin's similar results discussed earlier—see p. 198). Moreover, microevolutionary factors (especially genetic drift), acting on isolated and mostly *small* populations, contribute even further to interpopulation diversity.

Correlations from one measure of biological distance (e.g., dermatoglyphics) are not always systematic with all other measures. It thus takes several different lines of evidence (including using many genetic polymorphisms) to assemble a clear picture. The cladogram shown in Fig. 2 is the best recent combined approximation of biological distance of the seven populations. As can be seen, the biological distances are closely parallel with both geographic and linguistic relationships. It is exactly these kinds of data that are most crucial in piecing together the microevolutionary background of modern human populations. Such an approach is considered a more practical and more empirical alternative to the more traditional racial studies discussed earlier in this chapter.

SOURCES:

Friedlaender, J. S. "The Solomon Islands Project: An Introduction," *American Journal of Physical Anthropology* 81(1990):459–464.

Friedlaender, J. S., W. W. Howells, and J. G. Rhoads (eds.). *The Solomon Islands Project: A Long-term Study of Health, Human Biology, and Culture*, Oxford: Oxford University Press, 1987.

RACISM

As a subject of inquiry, racism is not usually pursued by physical anthropologists. It may be surprising, therefore, that a discussion of racism is included in a physical anthropology textbook. Although racism, from a holistic and biosocial point of view, is a cultural phenomenon (based on attitudes, values, philosophies, economics, etc.), we believe it is not possible to divorce biological from cultural aspects in the study of humans.

Racism is the belief that one race is superior to another, and is associated with discriminatory acts and attitudes toward the "inferior" race(s). Belief in racism is

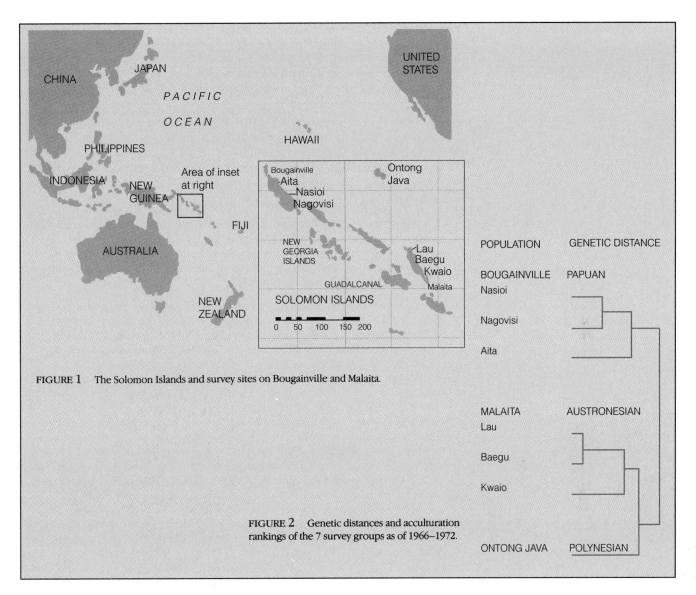

FIGURE 1   The Solomon Islands and survey sites on Bougainville and Malaita.

FIGURE 2   Genetic distances and acculturation rankings of the 7 survey groups as of 1966–1972.

usually based on the alleged inferior mental abilities of a people, and is often extended to the moral and ethical character of the "inferior" race. It is also assumed that mental abilities, ethics, and morals are hereditary.

The belief that a people is genetically inferior may be due to a number of factors, such as conquest, religion, family practices, moral and ethical systems, economic practices, and technology. Economic exploitation by imperialistic powers and competition for jobs, for example, have been suggested as reasons (or justification) for racist attitudes. European and American whites have frequently been singled out as practitioners of racism. However, there is evidence of racism in Japanese behavior toward the Eta (a lower social class in Japan) and the Ainu; in the historic attitude of the Chinese toward Mongols; and among the Bantu of South Africa toward the San (Bushmen).

From a physical anthropological point of view, racism is a cultural phenomenon that has no genetic basis. That one race is mentally or morally superior or inferior to another has yet to be demonstrated. Realistically, it is more likely that the basis of racism is rooted in economic, political, social, and psychological factors. Because it is cultural rather than genetic in character, it is difficult for physical anthropologists to address the problem. No matter what we say about the lack of evidence for mental inferiority and raise doubts about the validity of IQ scores, racism continues in many areas of the world. People point to the "strange," "immoral," and "odious" behavior of other people and assign these characteristics to genetic factors of the "inferior" race.

We end our discussion of race and racism with comments from two prominent scientsts: Theodosius Dobzhansky, a geneticist, and Sherwood Washburn, a physical anthropologist.

> The contention of racists is that cultural achievements of different races are so obviously unlike, their genetic capacities for achievement are just as different. It is, however, a matter of elementary genetics that the capacities of individuals, populations, or races cannot be discovered until they are given an equality of opportunity to demonstrate these capacities . . . (Dobzhansky, 1961, p. 31).

> Whether we consider intelligence, or length of life, or happiness, the genetic potential of a population is only realized in a social system. It is that system which gives life or death to its members, and in so doing changes the gene frequencies. We know of no society which has begun to realize the genetic potential of its members. We are the primitives living by antiquated customs in the midst of scientific progress. Races are products of the past. They are relics of times and conditions which have long ceased to exist.
>
> Racism is equally a relic supported by no phase of modern science. We may not know how to interpret the form of the Mongoloid face, or why Rh is of high incidence in Africa, but we do know the benefits of education and of economic progress. We know the price of discrimination is death, frustration, and hatred. We know that the roots of happiness lie in the biology of the whole species and that the potential of the species can only be realized in a culture, in a social system. It is knowledge and the social system which give life or take it away, and in so doing change the gene frequencies and continue the million-year-old interaction of culture and biology. Human biology finds its realization in a culturally determined way of life, and the infinite variety of genetic combinations can only express themselves efficiently in a free and open society (Washburn, 1963, p. 531).

Summary

This chapter is essentially divided into two parts: (1) the concept of race and (2) race and behavior.

The history of attitudes toward race is traced over several centuries of scientific inquiry in Europe. Scientists attempted to explain the presence of newly discovered peoples outside of Europe according to the biblical account of creation. This led to two schools of thought that used various conjectural explanations, such as separate species, climate and environment, second creations, and unity of mankind.

To deal with all the data, anthropologists and other scientists classified humans into racial groupings based on body (especially skull/head) measurements and degrees of skin pigmentation.

The turning point of physical anthropological thinking about racial classification, as well as attitudes toward race, came in the decade or so before World War I. Since World War II there has been little interest in racial classification; instead, evolutionary principles are applied in research projects.

IQ testing has been a controversial venture, and its validity is in question because environment is not considered in the evaluation of results. Racism is discussed as a cultural phenomenon. It is shown not to be supported by genetic evidence. The very concept of race has come under attack by anthropologists, many of whom believe the concept should be dropped once and for all.

Questions for Review

1. Trace the changes in European attitudes toward race.
2. What causes are suggested for these changes?
3. To what extent do you think these causes, in fact, explain the changes?
4. From a scientific point of view, defend or attack the bases for the historic attitudes toward race.
5. Discuss the monogenist and polygenist positions. Which do you think is correct? Are both correct? Are both incorrect? Explain.
6. What criteria have been used for racial classification?
7. Why is racial typology no longer considered a useful concept in the study of human diversity?
8. Why are anthropologists dissatisfied with the concept of race?
9. Do you think the race concept is valid? Useful? Dangerous? Unscientific? Racist? How do you support your decision?
10. Critique the definitions of race from Virchow to Garn.
11. What is a cline? What is the utility of a clinal distribution?
12. What is the value of multivariate population genetics?
13. What are the problems in correlating personality with race?
14. What are the objections to the use of IQ tests as measures of intelligence?
15. Do you believe there is any validity in the superior/inferior approach to race? Why?

Suggested Further Reading

It is possible to list only a few of the hundreds, perhaps thousands, of books and articles written on the subject of race, and race and intelligence. The books listed here (plus those in references cited) are intended to give some understanding of the seriousness and immensity of academic and popular attempts to cope with the concept of race, the social, political, and economic problems of racism, and the association of race and intelligence.

Although many of the books listed seem out of date, there appears to be little change in the conclusions about race in the writings of the past twenty to thirty years.

Banton, Michael. *Racial Consciousness*, New York: Longman Inc., 1988.
  For those who seek a readable account of race, this is an excellent book by a sociologist. Race and intelligence is not discussed.
Barzun, Jacques. *Race: A Study in Superstition*, New York: Harper and Row, 1965.
  The author, a well-known historian, discusses beliefs about race in the recent past. Very well written and strongly recommended for its enlightened view.

Block, N. J., and Gerald Dworkin (eds.). *The IQ Controversy*, New York: Pantheon Books (Random House), 1976.

Included in this volume are a number of classic articles on intelligence and heredity, some of them quite old (1915) and others more recent. Articles by Jensen and Herrnstein are also included. Most articles are not technical and are easily understood.

Brues, Alice M. *People and Races*, New York: Macmillan Publishing Co., 1977.

An excellent summary of the somewhat more traditional anthropological view of race. Recommended for students who wish more detail than most anthropology textbooks offer.

Gould, Stephen Jay. *The Mismeasure of Man*, New York: W. W. Norton & Co., 1981.

A well-written argument against biological determinism by a respected paleontologist and science historian. Gould points out the fallacies in historic attempts to classify human groups on a superior/inferior basis. He also discusses the problems of testing for intelligence and attacks the belief that intelligence is a single entity. Highly recommended.

Kennedy, Kenneth A. R. *Human Variation in Space and Time*, Dubuque, Iowa: Wm. C. Brown Co., 1976.

A short monograph that includes an historical view of the development of the race concept in Western thought. A good book for the beginning student.

Lawler, James M. *IQ, Heritability and Racism*, New York: International Publishers, 1978.

A fairly thorough review of the IQ controversy. Although definitely biased against heritability as a factor in intelligence, there is valuable information on the background of the development of the notion that heredity is a factor in IQ scores.

Molnar, Stephen. *Human Variation*, Englewood Cliffs, New Jersey: Prentice-Hall, Inc., 1983, 1975.

An excellent survey of human variation and a helpful supplement to this chapter. It is a revised edition of the author's *Races, Types, and Ethnic Groups*.

Montagu, Ashley. *Race, Science and Humanity*, Princeton, N.J.: D. Van Nostrand Co., Inc., 1963.

The author has long been interested in the concept of race and has written abundantly about it. This book is composed of a number of articles he has written on the subject. Recommended for the beginning student.

Osborne, Richard H. (ed.). *The Biological and Social Meaning of Race*, San Francisco: W. H. Freeman and Co., 1971.

A collection of articles written by specialists in the fields of anthropology, genetics, and sociology. For the more advanced student.

Snyderman, Mark, and Stanley Rothman. *The IQ Controversy, the Media and Public Policy*, New Brunswick, N.J.: Transaction Books, 1988.

The authors support IQ measurements; the book is informative and not too difficult for those unfamiliar with the technical aspect of measurements.

Stanton, William. *The Leopard's Spots*, Chicago: The University of Chicago Press, 1960.

This is subtitled, "Scientific attitudes toward race in America. 1815–1859." It is an interesting and often anecdotal account of scientific attitudes which, from where we stand today, are strange and remarkable.

Sternberg, Robert J., and D. K. Detterman (eds.). *What Is Intelligence?*, Norwood, N.J.: Ablex Publishing Corp., 1986.

Twenty-four of the foremost experts in the field of intelligence respond with contemporary viewpoints on the same questions asked in the 1921 symposium on the same question. The book includes two dozen definitions of intelligence.

Yeboah, Samuel Kennedy. *The Ideology of Racism*, London: Hansib Publishing Limited, 1988.

The author presents the case for blacks and includes such topics as discrimination, racism, black intelligence, and contributions of blacks in historical and contemporary times.

Evolutionary Record

Contents

A Cosmic Calendar

How can we possibly conceive of the awesome stretch of time that has been flowing since, scientists inform us, our universe was first formed by the cosmic explosion called the Big Bang 15 billion years ago? In *Dragons of Eden*, Carl Sagan (1977) has condensed this prodigious period into one year he calls "The Cosmic Calendar." There are three parts to the calendar.

1. A pre-December calendar. A list of a few of the significant events in the history of the universe and earth in the first 14 billion years, represented by the 334 days from January 1 through November 30.

2. A month of December calendar. Events of the last 1.25 billion years represented by the month of December.

3. An evening of December 31 calendar. From 10:30 P.M. (the first humans) until midnight (now), which represents the last 2.5 million years.

Examine the calendar and the place of *Homo sapiens* in a time perspective. Modern humans appeared a bit more than a minute before 12:00 midnight. You may feel humble before the immensity of time of our universe, or you may feel proud of the human achievements accomplished in such a brief speck of time.

PRE-DECEMBER DATES

Big Bang	January 1
Origin of the Milky Way Galaxy	May 1
Origin of the solar system	September 9
Formation of the Earth	September 14
Origin of life on Earth	≈September 25
Formation of the oldest rocks known on Earth	October 2
Date of oldest fossils (bacteria and blue-green algae)	October 9
Invention of sex (by microorganisms)	≈November 1
Oldest fossil photosynthetic plants	November 12
Eukaryotes (first cells with nuclei) flourish	November 15

DECEMBER 31

Origin of *Proconsul* and *Ramapithecus*, probable ancestors of apes and men[?]	≈ 1:30 P.M.
First humans	≈10:30 P.M.
Widespread use of stone tools	11:00 P.M.
Domestication of fire by Peking Man*	11:46 P.M.
Beginning of most recent glacial period	11:56 P.M.
Seafarers settle Australia	11:58 P.M.
Extensive cave painting in Europe	11:59 P.M.

Invention of agriculture	11:59:20 P.M.
Neolithic civilization; first cities	11:59:35 P.M.
First dynasties in Sumer, Ebla and Egypt; development of astronomy	11:59:50 P.M.
Invention of the alphabet; Akkadian Empire	11:59:51 P.M.
Hammurabic legal codes in Babylon; Middle Kingdom in Egypt	11:59:52 P.M.
Bronze metallurgy; Mycenaean culture; Trojan War; Olmec culture; invention of the compass	11:59:53 P.M.
Iron metallurgy; first Assyrian Empire; Kingdom of Israel; founding of Carthage by Phoenicia	11:59:54 P.M.
Asokan India; Ch'in Dynasty China; Periclean Athens; birth of Buddha	11:59:55 P.M.
Euclidean geometry; Archimedean physics; Ptolemaic astronomy; Roman Empire; birth of Christ	11:59:56 P.M.
Zero and decimals invented in Indian arithmetic; Rome falls; Moslem conquests	11:59:57 P.M.
Mayan civilization; Sung Dynasty China; Byzantine Empire; Mongol invasion; Crusades	11:59:58 P.M.

*See page 483 for comment on Peking Man's association with fire.

Renaissance in Europe; voyages of discovery from Europe and from Ming Dynasty China; emergence of the experimental method in science

Widespread development of science and technology; emergence of a global culture; acquisition of the means for self-destruction of the human species; first steps in spacecraft planetary exploration and the search for extraterrestrial intelligence

11:59:59 P.M.
Now:
The
first
second
of
New
Year's Day

1 year	=	15,000,000,000 years
1 month	=	1,250,000,000 years
1 day	=	41,000,000 years
1 minute	=	29,000 years
1 second	=	475 years
1 billion years	=	24 days

DECEMBER — COSMIC CALENDAR

SUNDAY	MONDAY	TUESDAY	WEDNESDAY	THURSDAY	FRIDAY	SATURDAY
	Significant oxygen atmosphere begins to develop on Earth.	2	3	4	5 Extensive vulcanism and channel formation on Mars.	6
7	8	9	10	11	12	13
14	15	16	17 Precambrian ends. Paleozoic Era and Cambrian Period begin. Invertebrates flourish.	18 First Oceanic plankton. Trilobites flourish.	19 Ordovician Period. First fish, first vertebrates	20 Silurian Period. First vascular plants. Plants begin colonization of land.
21 Devonian Period begins. First insects. Animals begin colonization of land.	22 First amphibians. First winged insects.	23 Carboniferous Period. First trees. First reptiles	24 Permian Period begins. First dinosaurs.	25 Paleozoic Era ends. Mesozoic Era begins.	26 Triassic Period. First mammals.	27 Jurassic Period. First birds.
28 Cretaceous Period. First flowers. Dinosaurs become extinct.	29 Mesozoic Era ends. Cenozoic Era and Tertiary Period begins. First cetaceans. First primates.	30 Early evolution of frontal lobes in the brains of primates. First hominids. Giant mammals flourish.	31 End of the Pliocene epoch. Quaternary (Pleistocene and Holocene Period. First humans.			

SOURCE

Sagan, Carl. *Dragons of Eden*, New York: Random House, Inc., 1977.

Calendar reprinted by permission of the author and the author's agents, Scott Meredith Literary Agency, Inc., 845 Third Avenue, New York, New York 10022.

CHAPTER 8

Introduction

Metazoa   meta: beyond
zoion: animal
Multicellular animals. A major division of the
Animal Kingdom.

In preceding chapters, we have discussed the mechanics of the evolutionary processes—adaptation and change through natural selection—according to concepts developed by Charles Darwin. We have also discussed the mechanisms of genetics that explain evolutionary changes between generations.

Having already dealt with the *process* of evolution, we shall now consider the *result* of that process. What actually occurred in the evolutionary record of life on earth? What were the adaptations made by living forms, and what physical changes took place in the various organisms that inhabit our globe? What evolutionary changes led to hominids, what other groups do hominids belong to, and what are the origins of these groups? We shall briefly trace invertebrate and vertebrate evolutionary history which, we believe, will help answer these questions, provide a deeper insight into evolutionary processes, and place humankind in a zoological and chronological perspective. (See Box 8-2, p. 216, Box 8-3, p. 217, and Box 8-5, p. 225 for additional views of the evolutionary processes.)

Since this book is about *Homo sapiens*, we can present only in outline the infinite number of events that occurred over the vast period of 3 billion years (and probably more) (Gurin, 1980), the time of life on earth. Let us then begin with the place of humans in evolutionary history.

The Human Place in the Animal Kingdom

The first chapter emphasized that we are both animals and human beings. We intend, throughout the text, to discuss the relationship between both these aspects of humankind, but since we wish to trace our antecedents, we will concern ourselves first with *Homo sapiens*, the organic being.

Humans are zoologically classified as animals because we possess animal characteristics, such as obtaining nourishment (energy) from ingesting other organisms, and not through photosynthesis as most plants do. We are mobile, as most animals are, and our structure and organization is similar to that of other animals. We also have nerves and muscles, both of which are absent in plants.

These criteria—although incomplete—place humans in the Animal Kingdom. (See chart, Fig. 8-3.) As *multi*celled animals within the Animal Kingdom, we belong to the **Metazoa**, a subdivision classified into more than twenty major groups called *phyla* (sing., *phylum*). One of the phyla is Chordata, animals with a spinal cord. Vertebrates, the most numerous of the chordates, are different in certain ways from all other Metazoa. Their primary structural feature, a vertebral column, distinguishes them from invertebrates and gives them their name.

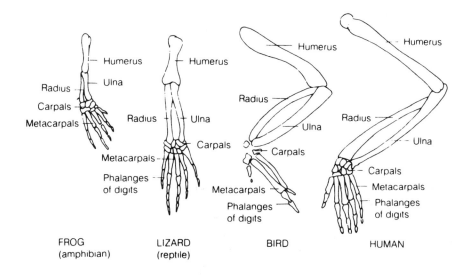

FIGURE 8-1 Homologies. The similarities in the bones of these air-breathing animals can be most easily explained by descent from a common ancestor.

FROG (amphibian)   LIZARD (reptile)   BIRD   HUMAN

TAXONOMY

Before going further, it may be useful to discuss the basis of animal classification. Organisms are classified on the basis of evolutionary relationships, that is, the extent to which one group is related to another through descent from a common ancestor. This is determined mainly by structural similarities based on common descent, called *homologies*. Thus, the bones of the forelimb of air-breathing vertebrates are so similar in arrangement and number (Fig. 8-1) that the simplest and best explanation for the remarkable resemblances (homologies) is that all four kinds of air-breathing vertebrates ultimately derived their forelimb from a common ancestor.

Structures that are *functionally* similar, but without genetic affinity—that is, *not* derived from a common ancestor—are *analogous*. The wing of a butterfly and the wing of a bird are analogous; they perform a similar function, but are without genetic affinity (Fig. 8-2).

Hominids (the group to which humans belong), prosimians, monkeys, and apes are all classified as primates. The reason for this is their teeth, limbs, digits, and other physical characteristics are so similar (homologies) that a common ancestor is the most reasonable explanation.

The system of classification based on homologies is usually attributed to Linnaeus, who successfully instituted the binomial system of naming animals using two terms: genus and species. Humans are known as *Homo sapiens*, the domestic cat as *Felis domesticus* and so on. All the people in the world today belong to one species, *Homo sapiens sapiens*, a form that has existed for about 150,000 years.

Figure 8-3 is a classification chart arranged according to evolutionary relationships. Observe in both Fig. 8-3 and the adjoining chart, Fig. 8-3a, that, the closer the animals resemble one another (the more homologies they share), the smaller the group to which they are assigned. The two species (in Fig. 8-3a), *H. sapiens* and *H. erectus*, belong to the genus *Homo* because they resemble each other more than either of them resembles the other three hominid species, *A. afarensis*, *A. africanus*, and *A. robustus*, which are assigned to the genus *Australopithecus*.

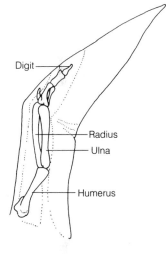

(a)

(b)

FIGURE 8-2 Analogies. The wings of these animals perform the same function, but their structure is quite different. Similar structure may be traced to a common ancestor; similar function represents a similar adaptive response, not necessarily a common ancestor. (*a*) Structure of bird wing; (*b*) butterfly wing.

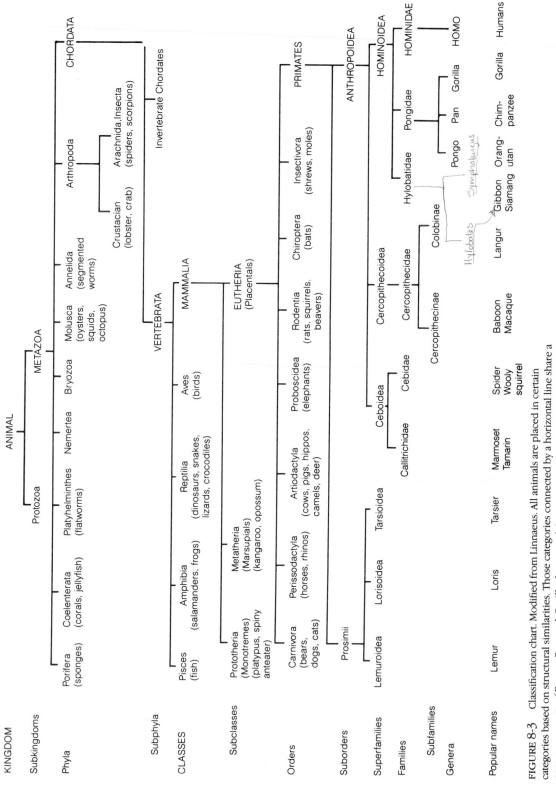

FIGURE 8-3 Classification chart. Modified from Linnaeus. All animals are placed in certain categories based on structural similarities. Those categories connected by a horizontal line share a common ancestor (*Pongo*, *Pan*, and *Gorilla*, for example).

Homo and *Australopithecus* resemble each other more than either one resembles apes and are, therefore, placed in the family Hominidae, whereas apes are placed in Pongidae. Apes and humans resemble each other more than either resembles monkeys and are, therefore, placed in the superfamily Hominoidea, and so forth.

In summary, the more homologies two groups share, usually the more recent their descent from a common ancestor, the closer their evolutionary relationship, and the closer their position on the taxonomic chart.

To place hominids in their proper perspective in nature and to help understand human evolution, we shall glance very briefly at the evolutionary history of the Metazoa.

Early Evolutionary History

Abundant fossil evidence for the Precambrian (see the Geologic Time Scale, Fig. 8-4) is lacking, and what does exist points to different kinds of algae as the domi-

ERA	PERIOD SYSTEMS	Time m.y.a.*	EVENTS
MESOZOIC (Middle Life)	Cretaceous (chalk)	65 136	Appearance of placental and marsupial mammals. Dinosaurs peak and become extinct. First modern birds.
	Jurassic (Jura Mts., France)	190	Great age of dinosaurs—flying and swimming dinosaurs. First toothed birds.
	Triassic (from tripartite division of strata of Germany)	225	Reptiles dominant. First dinosaurs. Egg-laying mammals.
PALEOZOIC (Ancient Life)	Permian	280	Reptilian radiation. Mammal-like reptiles. Many forms die out.
	Carboniferous (abundance of coal)	345	First reptiles. Radiation of amphibia. Modern insects evolve.
	Devonian (Devonshire in England)	395	Age of fish. Amphibians—first air-breathing vertebrates. First forests.
	Silurian (the Silures, an ancient British tribe)	430	Jawed fishes appear. First air-breathing animal—scorpion-like aurypterid. Definite land plants.
	Ordovician (the Ordovices, an ancient British tribe)	500	First fishes. Trilobites still abundant. Graptolites and corals becoming plentiful. Possible land plants.
	Cambrian (Roman name for Wales)	570	Trilobites abundant, also brachiopods, jellyfish, worms, and other invertebrates.
PRECAMBRIAN			

*Million years ago.

FIGURE 8-3a   Classification of Hominoidea.

Kingdom
    Phylum
        Class
            Order
                Family
                    Genus
                        Species

The Linnaean hierarchy of zoological classification. Indentation indicates decreasing inclusiveness of the various levels (Simpson, 1961).

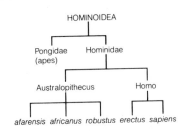

FIGURE 8-4   The periods of the time scale reflect systems of rock strata (layers) and the fossil remains that were prevalent in those systems as shown under "Events." Boundaries between systems reflect those points where rocks and fossil assemblages were in great contrast to those in the strata above and below.

BOX 8-1 **Vocabulary**

ANALOGOUS (ah-nal'-o-gus) Similar in function or appearance but not in origin or development.

HOMOLOGOUS (hom-ol'-o-gus) Structures that are similar in form (or function) in two or more groups of organisms related through descent from a common ancestor.

PHYLUM (fy'-lum; pl. phyla) A primary division of the Animal (or Plant) Kingdom. We belong to Phylum Chordata.

SUBPHYLUM A major division of a phylum, such as Vertebrata.

CLASS A subdivision of subphylum.

SUPERFAMILY A group of closely related families.

FAMILY Members of a family usually inhabit a similar environment; a category which includes genera and species.

GENUS (jee'-nus; pl. genera) A category that groups together closely related species usually inhabiting similar ecological niches.

SPECIES (spee'shies; sing. *and* pl.) A reproductive community; an interbreeding population (or populations) reproductively isolated from other interbreeding populations.

DORSAL (dor'-sull) Back, pertaining to the back of an animal.

VENTRAL (ven'-trull) Toward the belly; the front of an organism (as in humans) or the undersurface of an animal that does not stand erect (as a dog).

ENDOSKELETON (en'-doe-skeleton) An internal bony skeleton, characteristic of vertebrates.

EXOSKELETON (ex'-o-skeleton) A hard, supporting external covering, characteristic of many invertebrates such as ants and lobsters.

TAXONOMY The theoretical study of classification, including its bases, principles, procedures, and rules (Simpson, 1961, p. 11).

FIGURE 8-5   Pangea. Continents at the end of the Paleozoic (*a*) and during much of the Mesozoic (*b*).

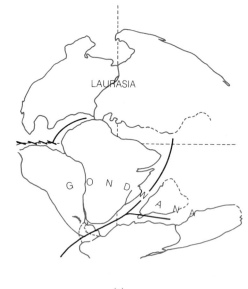

(a)

(b)

nant life form. It is not until the Cambrian (the first period of the Paleozoic) is reached that the rocks contain enough fossils to give a fuller view of the lifeforms in existence at that time.

Beginning with the Paleozoic era, fossils become more abundant. Geologically, the southern continents—South America, Africa, Antarctica, Australia, and India—were closely joined into one mass known as *Gondwanaland*. The northern continents—North America, the island of Greenland, Europe, and Asia—are known as Laurasia; both continents combined are called Pangea (Fig. 8-5.)

During the 345 million years of the Paleozoic, evidence for members of every phylum of animals is present. Evolution continues primarily in water, but land plants appear toward the middle, and land animals toward the end, of the era. Vertebrates evolve fairly early to become successful aquatic animals. Late in the Paleozoic, they invade land habitats.

The fish that left their aquatic home for land habitats were an odd form unlike the main branch of ray-fins (Fig. 8-6b). They are known as lobe-fins because their fins are fleshy and enclose the same basic structure of limb bones found in vertebrates today (Fig. 8-6a). In fact, the form and number of bones of our own limbs can be traced back to lobe-fins of the Paleozoic. It is believed that it was the lobe-finned crossopterygians (Fig. 8-7) that initiated the move from water to land on their fleshy, bone-structured fins. With the change to land habitats and adapting to new ecological conditions, lobe-fins evolved to an amphibian body plan (Fig. 8-8).

As vertebrate evolution continued for millions of years, amphibians diverged into many different forms. (See Adaptive Radiation, Box 8-2.) From one of these amphibian forms, another milestone in vertebrate evolution was reached with the rise of reptiles, the first true land vertebrates. These are known as *stem reptiles*, ancestors of the huge ruling reptiles of the Mesozoic and the line leading to our own group, the mammals.

Incisors Front teeth used for cutting and nipping.

Canines Usually long and pointed teeth used for piercing and grasping.

Cheek teeth Premolars and molars used for chewing and grinding.

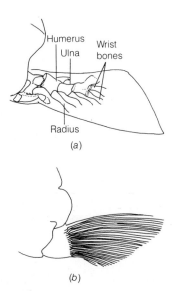

FIGURE 8-6 (*a*) Lobe-fin. The fin is fleshy and contains a bone structure similar to vertebrates. (*b*) Ray-fin. The fin is composed of a web of skin supported by hornlike rays.

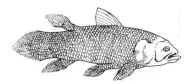

FIGURE 8-7 Crossopterygian. The fish that made the transition to amphibians. Long thought to be extinct. A modern survivor is the coelacanth.

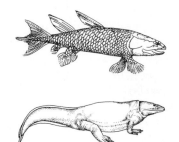

FIGURE 8-8 Early amphibian and lobe-finned fish. These drawings of an early amphibian and a lobe-fin illustrate the similarities of the two forms. Not a great deal of change was required to transform the fish to the air-breathing amphibian.

BOX 8-2   **Evolutionary Processes**

Adaptive Radiation

The potential capacity of an organism to multiply is practically unlimited; its ability to increase its numbers, however, is regulated largely by the available resources of food, shelter, and space. As the size of a population increases, its food, shelter, and space decrease, and the environment will ultimately prove inadequate. Depleted resources engender pressures that will very likely drive some members of the population to seek an environment where competition is considerably reduced and the opportunity for survival and reproductive success increased. This evolutionary tendency to exploit unoccupied habitats may eventually produce an abundance of diverse species.

An instructive example of the evolutionary process known as *adaptive radiation* may be seen in the divergence of the stem reptiles to the profusion of different forms of the late Paleozoic, and especially the Mesozoic. It is a process that has taken place many times in evolutionary history when a new form of life rapidly takes advantage, so to speak, of the many now available ecological niches.

The principle of evolution illustrated by adaptive radiation is fairly simple, but important. It may be stated thus: *When a new form arises, it will diverge into as many variations as two factors allow—(1) its adaptive potential and (2) the adaptive opportunities of the available zones.*

In the case of reptiles, there was little divergence in the very early stages of evolution, when the ancestral type was little more than one among a variety of amphibian water-dwellers. A more efficient kind of egg had already developed and, although it had great adaptive potential, there were few zones to invade. However, once reptiles became fully terrestrial, there was a sudden opening of available zones—ecological niches—accessible to the adaptive potential of the reptilian evolutionary grade.

This new kind of egg provided the primary adaptive ingredient of the reptilian form that freed reptiles from attachment to water; strengthened limbs and skeleton for locomotion on land followed. The adaptive zones for reptiles were not limitless; nevertheless, continents were now open to them with no serious competition from any other animal. The reptiles moved into the many different econiches on land (and to some extent in the air and sea), and as they adapted to these areas, diversified into a large number of species. This spectacular radiation burst with such evolutionary rapidity, it may well be termed an adaptive explosion.

Generalized and Specialized

Another aspect of evolution closely related to that of adaptive radiation involves the transition from *generalized* to *specialized characteristics*. These two terms refer to the adaptive potential of a particular trait: one that is adapted for many functions is termed generalized whereas a trait that is limited to a narrow set of ecological functions is called specialized.

For example, a generalized mammalian limb has five fairly flexible digits adapted for many possible functions (grasping, weight support, digging). In this respect, our hands are still quite generalized. On the other hand (or foot), there have been many structural modifications in our feet suited for the ecologically specialized function of stable weight support.

These terms are also sometimes used when speaking of the adaptive potential of whole organisms. For example, the aye-aye (a curious primate living in Madagascar) is a highly specialized animal structurally adapted in its dentition for an ecologically narrow rodent/woodpecker-like niche—digging out insect larvae with prominent incisors.

The notion of adaptive potential is a relative judgment and can estimate only crudely the likelihood of one form evolving into another form or forms. Adaptive radiation is a related concept, for only a generalized ancestor can provide the flexible evolutionary basis for such rapid diversification. Only a generalized organism with potential for adaptation into varied ecological niches can lead to all the later diversification and specialization of forms into particular ecological niches.

Superior/Inferior, Primitive/Derived

Arthropods* illustrate an important point in understanding the process of evolution. It is not possible to rank organisms as better or worse. Or, if we do, our criteria must be stated. One criterion is biological success, which may be said to depend on the number of species, the number of individuals, the number of adaptations to different kinds of environments and habitats and duration of the phylum. On all these counts, arthropods are superior to vertebrates. Arthropods are

> from ten to a hundred times more numerous than vertebrates in species, incomparably more abundant in individuals, and divergently adapted to an even wider range of environments and habits. They easily hold their own against all the attacks of man and of other animals (Simpson et al., 1957, p. 570).

Evolution is not the process of superior animals triumphing over inferior ones but is, rather, a series of alternative adaptive strategies that have arisen in response to inconstant environments.

In this connection it may be well to add two more terms often used in discussing evolution: *primitive* and *derived*. The same point made with the terms superior/inferior may be applied here if primitive is interpreted as somehow inferior to derived. There are no backward or advanced animals, only animals that have adapted, or extinct forms that have not. Nor can modern forms be considered advanced over fossil forms. Living species have adapted to present environmental conditions; fossil species to the environments of their day.

Sometimes the word "primitive" is used for an early form from which later (called "derived") forms have arisen. Even when terms are carefully defined in this way, their use can be misleading and confusing.

_____
*Arthropoda is a phylum. See chart on p. 212.

The reptilian strategy of adaptation was more successful than the amphibian. Developing a more efficient limb structure, an improved heart, and (perhaps most important) a self-contained, self-protected, and self-feeding egg—the *amniote* egg (Fig. 8-9)—reptiles filled many of the terrestrial econiches.

One of the results of reptilian radiation was a reptilelike mammalian form (or a mammal-like reptilian form) called *therapsids* (Fig. 8-10) that appeared near the end of the Paleozoic. With mammalian traits such as a bony palate separating the oral and nasal cavities, teeth differentiated into **incisors**, **canines**, and **cheek teeth** that were cusped instead of cone-shaped, and limbs arranged in a fore-and-aft position under the body (see Figs. 8-10 and 8-11), therapsids were well on their way to becoming mammals and are, in fact, considered to be the ancestors of mammals.

In the next era, the Mesozoic, climatic conditions were milder. Pangea began to separate, and when the Mesozoic ended, the position of the continents had approached their present locations. Early in the Mesozoic, reptiles became the dominant land animal and reigned supreme until the era ended. Now known as the *Age of Reptiles*, this was the time of the enormous creatures we know as dinosaurs (terrible lizards) that ruled the earth for 150 million years. Their end came, according to one theory, when an asteroid struck the earth. Dust ejected from the enormous crater (over 100 miles across) reached the stratosphere and then spread around the earth. Sunlight was blocked from reaching the earth's surface for about two and a half years, suppressing photosynthesis. Most food chains collapsed, and mass extinctions, including dinosaurs, followed. (For other opinions on dinosaur extinction, see Box 8-4.)

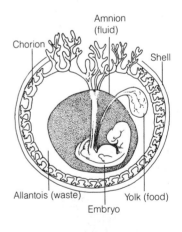

Amniote Egg

FIGURE 8-9   Amniote egg. Generalized diagram of the amniote egg. The embryo is surrounded by the liquid-filled amniotic chamber. The yolk sac contains food, and within the allantois enclosure (which also serves as a waste receptacle), oxygen-carbon dioxide exchange takes place.

FIGURE 8-10 Therapsid. Mammallike reptiles or reptilelike mammals. Mammalian characteristics include heterodont teeth, at least some chewing instead of swallowing whole, probably a coat of hair, and perhaps incipient milk glands. The limbs are more mammalian than reptilian. (Artist's rendition.)

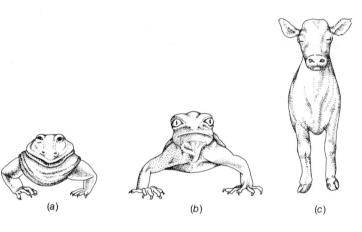

FIGURE 8-11 Evolution of body support in land vertebrates. The figures illustrate changes in land vertebrate limbs: (*a*) amphibian limbs project laterally from the body; (*b*) reptiles, with stronger pectoral and pelvic girdles, are more upright in an intermediate position; (*c*) in mammals, the legs project straight down.

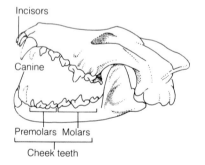

MAMMALIAN
(heterondont)

REPTILIAN (alligator)
(homodont: no differentiation of teeth)

FIGURE 8-12 Reptilian and mammalian teeth.

Reptiles dominated the Mesozoic, but an important event in that era, especially from a human point of view, was the appearance of mammals. Mammals in the Mesozoic were not awe-inspiring giants like dinosaurs (Fig. 8-13), but their turn came in the following era, the Cenozoic, after the extinction of dinosaurs and many other species.

The modern world as we know it—geologically and geographically—assumed its present configuration during the Cenozoic era. Major continental drifting slowed considerably, and interior seas on most continents were reduced. This alteration of the topography may explain the diversity of climates, patterns of seasons, water and wind currents, and the eventual onset of the Pleistocene Ice Ages. We may view life in the Cenozoic as a process of adaptation to the climatic extremes and topographic diversity, a situation for which mammals are well equipped.

The Cenozoic (see Figs. 8-14 and 8-15) is divided into two periods, the **Tertiary** (about 63 million years' duration) and the **Quaternary**, from about 1.8 mya up to and including the present. Because so much evidence of living forms is available from the Cenozoic, the two periods are further subdivided into epochs. The five epochs of the Tertiary are: Paleocene, Eocene, Oligocene, Miocene, and Pliocene. The Quaternary, the final period of the Cenozoic, is divided into two epochs: the Pleistocene, well known for its *ice ages*, and the present epoch, the Holocene, which begins with the melting of the last glaciation.

BOX 8-4 **Extinction**

"The theories that have been propounded (to explain the extinction of dinosaurs) are legion, and one cannot do better than quote Jepsen on this topic: 'Authors, with varying competence, have suggested that the dinosaurs disappeared because the climate deteriorated (became suddenly or slowly too hot or cold or dry or wet), or that the diet did (with too much food or not enough of such substances as fern oil; from poisons in water or plants or ingested minerals; the bankruptcy of calcium or other necessary elements). Other writers have put the blame on disease, parasites, wars, anatomical or metabolic disorders (slipped vertebral discs, malfunctions or imbalance of hormone or endocrine systems, dwindling brain and consequent stupidity, heat sterilization), racial old age, evolutionary drift into senescent overspecialization, changes in the pressure or composition of the atmosphere, poison gases, volcanic dust, excessive oxygen from plants, meteorites, comets, gene pool drainage by little mammalian egg-eaters, overkill capacity by predators, fluctuation of gravitational constants, development of psychotic suicidal factors, entropy, cosmic radiation, shift of Earth's rotational poles, floods, extraction of the moon from the Pacific Basin, drainage of swamp and lake environments, sunspots, God's will, mountain building, raids by little green hunters in flying saucers, lack of even standing room in Noah's Ark, and palaeoweltschmertz' " (Jepsen, in Halstead, 1968, pp. 146–147).

MAMMALS

Tertiary Third part.

Quaternary Fourth.

Arboreal Tree living.

Conditions in the Cenozoic were nearly ideal for mammals. They radiated so rapidly and filled the available econiches so well that the Cenozoic is known as the *Age of Mammals.*

Mesozoic mammals were small animals, about the size of mice, which they resembled in appearance. Since they were so small, and many of the dinosaurs so large, the primitive mammals remained inconspicuous by dwelling in wooded or bushy areas and may have been **arboreal**. They are not what we would consider to be very noble creatures to have as ancestors. Romer (1959) suggests the Mesozoic may be seen as a training period during which mammalian characters

FIGURE 8-13   Mesozoic mammal. A speculative reconstruction of what a Mesozoic mammal might have looked like. Probably no bigger than a kitten, but with mammalian teeth, these animals were capable of attacking small lizards.

FIGURE 8-14   Geologic Time Scale: Cenozoic.

Era	Period	Epoch	Time Years ago	Glacial Sequence Alpine
CENOZOIC	QUATERNARY	HOLOCENE		
		UPPER PLEISTOCENE	10,000 40,000 75,000 100,000 125,000	WÜRM RISS WÜRM
		MIDDLE PLEISTOCENE	175,000 225,000 265,000 300,000 380,000 400,000 430,000 500,000 750,000	RISS MINDEL RISS MINDEL GUNZ- MINDEL GÜNZ
		LOWER PLEISTOCENE	1.8 million	Uncertain Geological Sequences
	TERTIARY	Pliocene	5 million	Hominids (Australopithecines) present
		Miocene	25 million	Hominoidea (apelike creatures) Dryopithecines flourish . . . Probable appearance of hominids
		Oligocene	35 million	Anthropoidea and appearance of Hominoidea
		Eocene	53 million	Prosimians flourish; possible appearance of Anthropoidea
		Paleocene	65 million	Appearance of Prosimii

CENOZOIC

Quaternary
HOLOCENE

PLEISTOCENE

Tertiary
PLIOCENE
MIOCENE
OLIGOCENE
EOCENE
PALEOCENE

FIGURE 8-15   The Cenozoic. The most recent era. The two epochs, Tertiary and Quaternary, and their divisions are shown. (The Precambrian, Paleozoic, and Mesozoic are shown on p. 213.)

were being perfected and wits sharpened. The mammalian radiation of the Cenozoic (65 mya to present) saw the rise of the ancestors of all modern mammals. Mammals replaced reptiles as the dominant terrestrial vertebrate, a position they still retain.

Campbell (1974, p. 39ff) has proposed that the striking radiation of mammals was based on a single adaptive development: the ability for constant lively activity; that is, "the maintenance of a steady level of activity in the face of basic changes in the external environment." This was made possible by four complexes:

1. **homoiothermy**—commonly called warm blood, making activity possible in almost all kinds of climates and weather.
2. **heterodontism**—four different kinds of teeth: incisors, canines, premolars, and molars (Fig. 8-12), that evolved especially for trapping, nipping, chewing, cutting, crushing, and grinding, thus exploiting various kinds of food more effectively. Also, mammals' jaws can effectively break up nuts, seeds, plant material, meat, and other foods for more nutritive value.
3. **reproductive efficiency**—live birth (**viviparity**) makes for greater safety and nourishment of the developing fetus inside the mother. This compares favorably with **oviparity**, in which the egg develops outside the body.
4. **effectance motivation**—a drive, a curiosity, to investigate and explore the environment. This "mammalian play" is actually a means of discovering and learning to interact with the environment.

These complexes explain such mammalian traits as hair/fur, sweat glands, a stronger jaw, and suckling. In addition to these innovations, other distinguishing mammalian traits are an internal eardrum with an external ear flap, a four-chambered heart that generates greater energy, and more efficient limbs for improved locomotion.

Homoiothermy Homo: same
therm: heat
Same temperature.

Heterodontism hetero: different
dont: teeth

Oviparity ovum: egg
parere: to bear

Viviparity vivus: alive
parere: to bear

Monotreme mono: one
treme: a hole

MAMMALIAN SUBCLASSES

At the present time, placental mammals comprise most of the mammalian class; however, there still survive a few **monotremes** (egg-laying mammals) and marsupials (pouched mammals).

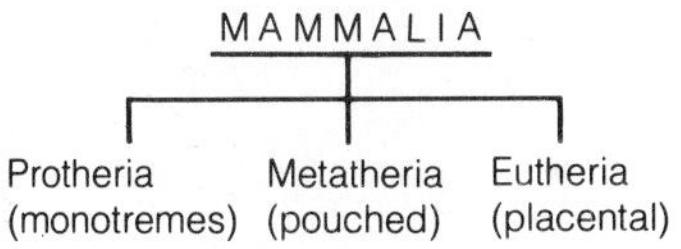

Monotremes (Prototheria) Living in the Australasian region of Australia and New Guinea are two surviving highly specialized egg-laying mammals—the duck-billed platypus (Fig. 8-17) and the spiny anteater (Fig. 8-18). Monotremes are classified as mammals because the young nurse from teatless, mammary glands. However, they are very primitive mammals and, as such, retain a number of reptilian characteristics. Some authorities consider monotremes to be mammal-like reptiles.

MAMMALIA

Protheria (monotremes) Metatheria (pouched) Eutheria (placental)

FIGURE 8-16 Mammalian classification chart.

FIGURE 8-17 The duck-billed platypus. Offspring licking milk from mother's fur.

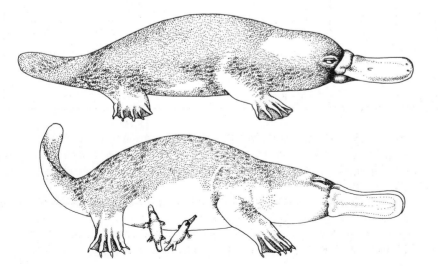

FIGURE 8-18   Spiny anteater, a monotreme.

FIGURE 8-19   Wallaby with infant in pouch, marsupials.

Marsupials (Metatheria)   At the present time, marsupials (Fig. 8-19) are found only in Australia and the New World (opossums), although they were once more widely distributed in North America, South America, and Europe. Their extermination can be laid at the hands (or claws and teeth) of the brainier placental mammals, who won out whenever these two mammals competed. Pouched animals survived in Australia because placental mammals never reached that continent before its separation from other land masses.

Placental Mammals (Eutheria)   One of the outstanding features of placental mammals (**Eutheria**) is the placenta, which gives the subclass its name. This disclike organ furnishes oxygen and nutrients from mother to developing embryo and gets rid of waste products as well. Young are born alive, as are marsupials, but in a much more advanced stage of development.

Among the many other differences distinguishing marsupials and placentals, two stand out. First, placentals possess an expanded brain, which has been suggested as the most important reason for their superiority over the pouched mammals. It may be of interest to briefly review this development.

The evolutionary history of the brain, center of the nervous system, reflects a steady growth in size and complexity as we move from fish to mammals (Fig. 8-20). The diversification of vertebrates depends largely upon the operation of the central nervous system, and the relative success of mammals over reptiles (and perhaps reptiles over amphibians) may be largely due to greater brain efficiency.

Fish reflect the basic vertebrate brain, which is composed of three sections: forebrain, midbrain, and hindbrain, or **cerebellum**. Much of the forebrain is devoted to the sense of smell. The trend in brain evolution has been toward an increase in the forebrain and decrease in the mid- and hindbrain. The amphibian brain is not much modified from that of the fish.

Significant changes appeared in the reptile brain. The **cerebrum** is greatly enlarged, but much of the forebrain is still concerned with smell. A remarkable innovation developed in the reptilian cerebrum. Cerebral hemispheres are coated by a pallium (covering) of neurons; in the reptile, a small portion of the front part of the cerebrum is covered with a new sort of nervous tract called the **neopallium** or **neocortex** (Fig. 8-21). This covering in general is what we know as "gray matter," and while the reptilian neopallium was a feeble beginning, it was a most important one.

FIGURE 8-20   Lateral view of brain. The illustration shows the increase in the cerebral cortex of the brain. The cerebral cortex integrates sensory information and selects responses.

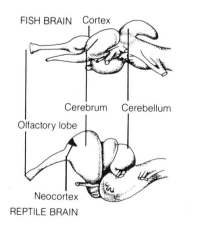

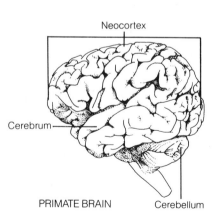

TABLE 8-1 **Mammalian Innovations**
(Distinguishing Mammals from Reptiles)*

INNOVATIONS	COMPLEXES
Warm blood Hair/fur Sweat glands	Homoiothermy
Heterodontism Strong jaw	Mastication and heterodontism
Viviparity Suckling	Reproductive efficiency
Mammalian play	Effectance motivation

*There is some evidence that homoiothermy, fur, and viviparity are more common among animals than once believed.

Eutheria eu: good
therion: beast
All mammals except monotremes and pouched animals.

Cerebellum (sara-bell'-um)
That part of the brain concerned with coordination and balance. In humans, back of and below the cerebrum.

Cerebrum (sar'-a-brum or se-ree'-brum)
Largest part of the human brain; the forebrain and midbrain.

Neopallium neo: new
pallium: cloak

Neocortex neo: new
cortex: bark, covering

In mammals, the neopallium dramatically expanded and spread over the cerebral hemispheres. Central control, formerly in the midbrain, passed almost entirely to the neopallium of the forebrain. The cerebrum increased in size to compose most of the brain and developed convolutions making for an even greater surface area without increasing brain size.

In humans, the growth of this section of the brain reaches its ultimate development, a fact which has made the human brain, in proportion to body weight, one of the largest and most complex of any animal (Passingham, 1982).

The second important difference between placentals and marsupials is *teeth*. These clearly distinguish the two forms and have been used as a basis for classification as well as the reconstruction of mammalian evolutionary history.

FIGURE 8-21   Human brain. In humans the gray matter (cerebral cortex) is highly convoluted, which provides a greater surface for nerve connections and for eight billion brain cells. The cerebral cortex has also greatly expanded to cover most of the brain.

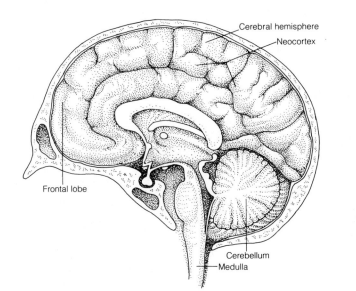

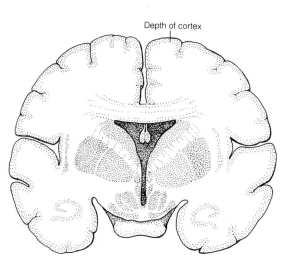

Cerebral hemisphere, Neocortex, Frontal lobe, Cerebellum, Medulla, Depth of cortex

Carnivore   carni: meat
A flesh-eating animal.

Herbivore   herba: grass
A plant-eating animal.

Omnivore   omnis: all
Plant and meat eating.

Artiodactyl   (are-tee-o-dak'-til)
artios: even
daktylos: finger, toe
Even-toed hoof.

Perissodactyl   perissos: odd
Odd-toed hoof.

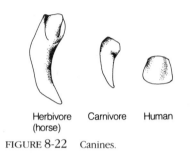

Herbivore   Carnivore   Human
(horse)

FIGURE 8-22   Canines.

FIGURE 8-23   Examples of specialization in herbivorous and carnivorous teeth. There is great variation in the size and shape of the canine in herbivorous animals, and canines are entirely lacking in many species.

The structure of teeth often informs us of their use so that it is fairly easy, for example, to distinguish between the specializations of predator and herbivore teeth. Of all the teeth, it is probably the molars that are the most specialized. They perform the powerful grinding, chewing, and crushing functions, and their structure is closely associated with diet. It is difficult to exaggerate the role of teeth in studying mammalian (and especially for our purposes, primate) evolution. The student is asked to keep this in mind when we look at primate evolution, since in many cases identification, classification, relationships, and chronological placement may be based on the structure of fossil teeth. This is particularly the case for hominids because, quite often, teeth are the only fossil evidence available.

Appearing in placentals of Cretaceous age and still persisting in many modern animals, the basic pattern of placental mammalian teeth is (on each side and in both upper and lower jaws) three incisors, one canine, four premolars, and three molars (see Box 9-2, p. 245). Incisors tend to be pegs or blades—adapted for nipping or cutting food, as can be seen when biting into an apple.

Canines come in a variety of forms. **Carnivore** canines are spikelike and used for stabbing, piercing, and holding. In **herbivores** canines tend to be molarlike with a grinding surface, and among humans, who are **omnivores**, canines are spatulate, similar to incisors and utilized in a similar manner.

Premolars (called "bicuspids" by dentists) are generally complex and used are for crushing and/or grinding (as are molars, which are even more complex).

Placental mammals today are found almost everywhere on earth. With sea mammals such as dolphins and seals, we find them in water, and some placentals, the bats, have taken to the air. But placentals are essentially terrestrial animals and land is where they are found in abundant numbers and species. For example, there are the even-toed ungulates (**artiodactyls**), such as cows, deer, camels, and pigs; odd-toed ungulates (**perissodactyls**), such as the horse and rhino; carnivores, such as the bear, dog, and cat; proboscids, such as elephants; insectivores, such as shrews, moles, and hedgehogs; the incredibly successful rodents, including rats, squirrels, beavers, and gophers; and, of course, the primates, including prosimians, monkeys, apes, and humans.

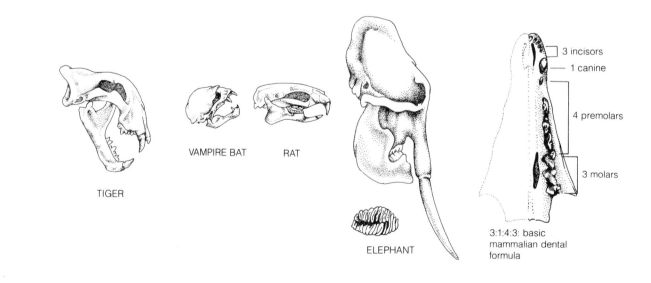

VAMPIRE BAT   RAT

TIGER

ELEPHANT

3 incisors
1 canine
4 premolars
3 molars

3:1:4:3: basic mammalian dental formula

BOX 8-5 **Convergent and Parallel Evolution**

Convergent Evolution

The discussion of marsupials offers an opportunity to present another evolutionary process, *convergent evolution*. We pointed out (in Box 8-2, Evolutionary Processes) that in the early stages of development, there is a tendency for newly evolved forms to become highly diversified when they invade varied environments. The diversification results from the modification of the ancestral type in adapting to new ecological niches.

Convergent evolution—a variation of adaptive radiation—is the process in which two *unrelated* groups of organisms, living in similar but separate environmental conditions, develop a similar appearance and life style. That is, similar environmental demands make for similar phenotypic responses (Mayr, 1970, p. 365). This should not be surprising since the requirements of adapting to a particular environment would require modifications of physical traits. Two similar environments would, therefore, result in similar adaptive characters.

Striking examples of convergence are the pouched mammals of Australia and placental mammals. As we have seen, Australia was isolated from South America before the great placental mammalian radiation of the Cenozoic, and marsupials survived because they were free from the competition of the more efficient placen-

tals. When placental mammals became prominent in the Cenozoic, only a few were able to invade Australia (via island-hopping from Southeast Asia).

Without competition, the pouched mammals spread into the varied environments of the isolated continent. There were marsupials that resembled, to a lesser or greater degree, a wolf, cat, flying squirrel, groundhog, anteater, mole, and mouse. And they occupied ecological niches similar to the placental mammals they resembled (Simpson et al., 1957, p. 470).

The variety of marsupials illustrates adaptive radiation; the resemblance in form due to similarity of econiches illustrates convergent evolution.

Parallel Evolution

A variation of both adaptive radiation and convergent evolution is *parallel evolution*. This process may be illustrated as a kind of tailed U. *Related* forms diverge as in adaptive radiation, responding to different ecological niches. Then, because of the similarity of econiches, the two or more forms respond to similar selection pressures and evolve somewhat similar phenotypes, for example, the New World and Old World monkeys (see further discussion in Chapter 9).

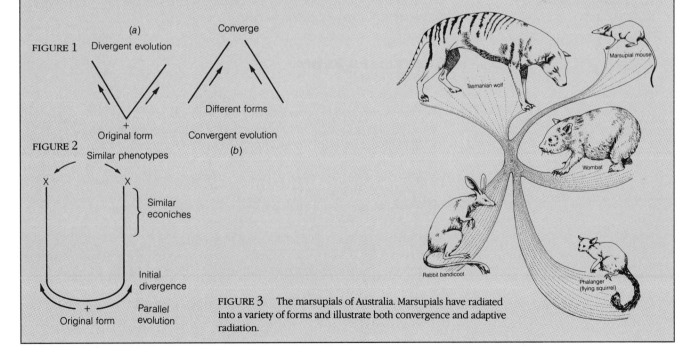

FIGURE 1

(a) Divergent evolution

Converge

Different forms

+
Original form

Convergent evolution
(b)

FIGURE 2

Similar phenotypes

X   X

Similar econiches

Initial divergence

+
Original form

Parallel evolution

FIGURE 3   The marsupials of Australia. Marsupials have radiated into a variety of forms and illustrate both convergence and adaptive radiation.

Tasmanian wolf

Marsupial mouse

Wombat

Rabbit bandicoot

Phalanger (flying squirrel)

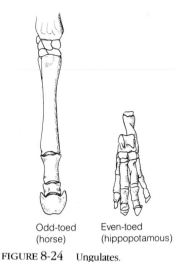

Odd-toed
(horse)

Even-toed
(hippopotamous)

FIGURE 8-24   Ungulates.

Of all these groups the rodents are clearly the most successful of all mammals if number of species and individuals is our criterion. In fact, they outnumber all other species of mammals combined (Romer, 1959, p. 228). Their enormous adaptive flexibility is clearly demonstrated by their ability to cope successfully with humanmade environments.

We have traced the evolution of vertebrates from fish to mammals. Mammals, as we have seen, had come a long way from the small, insignificant, insectivorelike animals of the Mesozoic to the highly diversified and very successful vertebrates of the present. We are now prepared to take up the discussion of our own order, Primates, which, like other mammals, most likely originated as shrewlike animals in the Paleocene (or possibly the late Cretaceous). Very early, they adapted to an arboreal way of life that emphasized vision, an expanded brain, and prehensile digits, as we shall see in the next three chapters.

Summary

In this chapter, we have placed humans in their natural perspective by tracing the development of evolutionary changes of invertebrates and vertebrates. We also placed humans in a temporal perspective by tracing the evolutionary development of lifeforms, especially vertebrates, over the immense time period of Precambrian through Tertiary.

Structural modifications of the evolutionary sequence of vertebrates—from fish to amphibians to reptiles to mammals—were included to give the very long developmental background of the hominid form. This will be continued in the chapter on primate evolution.

The basis for taxonomic classification (why animal X is placed in category Y) and several evolutionary concepts (adaptive radiation, generalized and specialized, and convergent and parallel evolution) were discussed to give a deeper understanding of "how evolution works."

Questions for Review

1. What characteristics place humans in the Animal Kingdom?
2. Distinguish between homologies and analogies.
3. To what groups of the Animal Kingdom do hominids belong?
4. Explain the basis for the arrangement of the classification chart. Give several examples.
5. Outline the evolutionary history of vertebrates during the Paleozoic, Mesozoic, and Cenozoic.
6. What changes occurred in the structure of fish, amphibians, and reptiles that enabled them to adapt to their econiches?
7. Define adaptive radiation and give examples.
8. Explain the evolutionary principle "generalized to specialized." Why is the reverse—"specialized to generalized"—rarely found?
9. Why are therapsids believed to be ancestors of mammals?
10. What characteristics of lobe-fins suggest they are ancestral to amphibia?

11. What "four great complexes" distinguish mammals from reptiles and contributed to mammalian success?
12. Explain the differences between convergent and parallel evolution.
13. Why are placental mammals so much more successful than marsupials?
14. Explain why marsupials are found in Australia.

Suggested Further Reading

Augusta, Josef. *Prehistoric Reptiles and Birds*, London: Paul Hamlyn, 1961.
An excellent book containing beautiful illustrations of fossil reptiles, especially dinosaurs, and birds of the Mesozoic.

Bakker, Robert T. *The Dinosaur Heresies: New Theories Unlocking the Mystery of the Dinosaurs and Their Extinction*, New York: Wm. Morrow, 1986.
Professor Bakker disagrees with the Berkeley asteroid theory as well as with Nemesis. He believes dinosaurs should be classified as reptiles but deserve their own class, one to which birds also belong.

Barnett, Lincoln. *The World We Live In* (Vols. 1, 2), New York: Time, Inc., 1962.
Written for the layman; outstanding drawings and color illustrations of ancient geology and life forms.

Beiser, Arthur. *The Earth* (Life Nature Library), New York: Time, Inc., 1973.
Another in the series of excellent Time-Life books.

Carrington, Richard. *The Mammals* (Life Nature Library), New York: Time, Inc., 1963.
One of the series dealing with various life forms. The text is good and illustrations and photographs are of the high quality found in these publications.

Lewin, Roger. *Thread of Life*, New York: W. W. Norton & Co. (Smithsonian Books), 1982.
A beautifully illustrated book by a well-known scientist presently a writer for *Science* (a weekly journal published by the American Association for the Advancement of Science). Lewin covers the history of the earth and the evolution of animals from "Life Emerges from the Soup" through human evolution. Written in popular style. Highly recommended for students and nonstudents alike.

Ommanney, Francis D. *The Fishes* (Life Nature Library), New York: Time, Inc., 1964.
Another in the Time-Life series. Well worth reading.

Romer, Alfred S. *The Vertebrate Story* (4th Ed.), Chicago: University of Chicago Press, 1959.
A popular account of vertebrate evolution by an outstanding paleontologist. Excellent as a reference book as well as pleasant reading.

Simpson, George G. *The Meaning of Evolution*, New York: Mentor Books, 1951.
One of the best statements on what evolution means.

Simpson, G. G., C. S. Pittendrigh, and L. H. Tiffany. *Life*, New York: Harcourt, Brace & Co., 1957.
A biology textbook that has become a classic. Easy to read, many illustrations, authoritative.

Wilford, John N. *The Riddle of the Dinosaur*, New York: Alfred A. Knopf, 1985.
The book discusses mass extinction with special emphasis on dinosaurs. The author suggests a rather radical view to explain their disappearance and believes dinosaurs are closer to mammals than most paleontologists believe. Interesting and useful, especially to students interested in the Mesozoic monsters.

Wood, Peter, Louis Vaczek, Dora J. Hamblin, and Jonathan N. Leonard. *Life Before Man* (Emergence of Man Series), New York: Time, Inc., 1972.
Like other series published by Time, "Emergence of Man" fits very nicely the fossil hominid section of a physical anthropology course. Material is written for those without a technical background, illustrations are superb, and students are encouraged to examine these books.

Living Primates

Contents

Can the Mountain Gorilla Be Saved?

Today, one species of primate, *Homo sapiens*, dominates our planet. Numbering now 5 billion, we use, alter, and ultimately destroy huge hunks of the world's surface.

In the face of such an onslaught, many of the other species that share our planet are being driven to the brink of extinction. As primates ourselves, we have a special interest in the problem of preserving our primate relatives.

Even before the advent of modern technological society, primates (compared to such groups as rodents or even-toed ungulates) were not abundant. Largely restricted to forested areas in South America, Africa, and South Asia, the primates had—despite their comparative numerical inferiority—achieved a successful adaptation.

Such is no longer the case. In addition to being diminished by the dangers stemming from reduced or completely obliterated habitats, nonhuman primates are also easy prey for local peoples looking for food, hunters looking for scientific (mostly medical) specimens, or for poachers strictly after financial gain.

What does the future hold for these animals? The prospects are not hopeful. The Convention on International Trade in Endangered Species (ratified by the United States in 1973) already lists *all* nonhuman primates as endangered or facing the prospect of soon becoming so. All of the apes—gibbons, orangutans, gorillas, and chimpanzees—are now in the convention's "most endangered" category. (All are also on the United States' endangered species list.)

Among the most imminently endangered of all primates is the mountain gorilla—a subspecies of the largest primate form—now restricted to an exceedingly small area of East Africa (where the borders of Rwanda, Uganda, and Zaire converge).

Mountain gorillas once ranged widely through the densely forested mountain regions bordering the great lakes of East Africa. Foraging in rough terrain, gorilla groups survived for centuries, impervious to any potential predator. In fact, the mountain gorilla was not even known to the Western world until 1903, when it was first reported by a German military expedition.

The mountain gorilla's comparative isolation from humans has been dramatically altered in recent years. It is estimated that today there are only about 400 mountain gorillas left in the wild. In the last twenty years alone, their numbers have been reduced by nearly one-half.

Most of the deaths (perhaps as many as two-thirds) are at the hands of poachers. Gorillas are prized specimens for trophy hunters; consequently, they are often shot with high-powered rifles, after which they are decapitated, their hands cut off, and these grisly remains sold for trophies.

Gorillas also are victims of poachers in a more accidental fashion. Traps and snares are set by poachers primarily to capture antelope and buffalo, which can be sold as meat. Mountain gorillas who live in the same area step into these traps and, even if they manage to escape, usually die later from infected wounds.

Why is such reckless exploitation allowed? The answer is that, legally, it is not. Throughout the world illegal poaching of endangered species is banned, and most countries prohibit imports of products derived from such animals. Enforcement, however, is another matter. Due to political instability and periodic warfare in East Africa, central governments have been at a loss to stop the killing. In Zaire and Uganda most of the mountain gorillas are now gone. Rwanda continues to struggle

Digit, an adult male gorilla; found after poachers had decapitated him and cut off his hands. (This graphic photo, which has appeared in prior editions of this book, has brought strong responses from both students and instructors. We include it at the specific request of the late Dian Fossey, who provided the photograph.)

with the problem, but the choices are not always easy. Among the most over-crowded and undernourished popula-

tions in Africa, Rwandans are hard-pressed to find adequate sources of animal protein. Local populations conse-

quently feel compelled to trap antelope and buffalo and, in the process, gorillas as well.

Despite wide publicity of the gorilla's plight in the Western world and a large influx of money from concerned conservationists, the slaughter goes on. Is there then any hope for saving the mountain gorilla? Perhaps—but time is growing dangerously short. As Dian Fossey, the late leading field researcher of these primates, ominously warned, "The mountain gorilla may become an animal which was discovered and driven extinct—in the same century."

The tragic story of Dian Fossey's work with the mountain gorilla reached a terrible climax when, on Christmas Eve 1985, she was brutally murdered at her research station in Rwanda. Following her wishes, she was buried next to her beloved Digit and the other gorillas for whom she had given so much.

SOURCES:

Fossey, Dian. "The Imperiled Mountain Gorilla," *National Geographic*, **159**:501–523, April, 1981.

Fossey, Dian. *Gorillas in the Mist*, Boston: Houghton-Mifflin Co., 1983.

Introduction

Evolutionary trends General structural and behavioral traits that are commonly shared by a related group of organisms.

Postorbital bar The bony element that closes in the outside of the eye orbit—a characteristic of primates.

We have seen in Chapter 8 that we are a certain kind of placental mammal, a primate. This order of rather diverse animals is characterized by a set of evolutionary trends that sets it apart from other mammals. In this chapter, we will discuss what characteristics link us to our primate cousins, and we will explore some of the fascinating and unique adaptations that the nonhuman primates display. (Numerous physical characteristics, especially those relating to the skeleton, are discussed in this chapter. For a detailed comparison of human and nonhuman skeletons, see Appendix A.)

Primate Evolutionary Trends

Structurally, primates are not easily distinguished as a group chiefly because of the fact that, as an order, we and our close relatives have remained quite *generalized*. Unlike the specialized dentition of rodents or the specialized limbs with great reduction of digits found in artiodactyls (cows, deer, camels, pigs), primates are characterized by their *lack* of extreme structural specializations.

For this reason, it is difficult to point to a single anatomical feature that can be applied exclusively and universally to the primates. Some primate anatomists, however, do suggest derived characteristics of the primate cranium, especially the region around the earhole (Szalay and Delson, 1979). (See Box 9-1.) At a more general level, there is a group of **evolutionary trends** (Clark, 1971) which, to a greater or lesser degree, characterize the entire order. Keep in mind, these are a set of *general* tendencies and are not equally expressed in all primates. Indeed, this situation is one that we would expect in such a diverse group of generalized animals. In addition, trends are not synonymous with *progress*. In evolutionary terms, we are using "trend" only to reflect a series of shared common characteristics (i.e., general homologies).

Following is a list of those evolutionary trends that tend to set the primates apart from other mammals. A common evolutionary history with similar adaptations to common environmental challenges is reflected in the limbs and locomotion; teeth and diet; and in the senses, brain, and behavior of the animals that make up the order.

A. *Limbs and Locomotion*

　1. *Retention of five digits* in the hands and feet—*pentadactyly*. As in primitive mammals, this characteristic is found in all primates, though some show marked reduction of the thumb (e.g., spider monkeys, langurs) or the second digit (e.g, lorises). In no case is reduction as extreme as that seen in such animals as cows or horses.

BOX 9-1 **Primate Cranial Anatomy**

Several significant anatomical features of primate skulls help us distinguish primates from other mammals. Continuing the mammalian trend of increasing brain development, primates go even further as shown by their well-expanded brain boxes. In addition, the primate trend of increased dependence on vision is shown by the generally large eye sockets; less emphasis on smell is shown in the reduced snout; the shift to using hands for grasping (instead of using the front teeth for this purpose) is revealed in the dentition; and the tendency towards more upright posture is indicated by the relationship of the head to the spinal column.

Some of the specific anatomic details seen in all modern and most fossil primate crania are:

1. Eye sockets are enclosed circumferentially by a complete ring of bone, compared to other placental mammals where the ring is incomplete (no **postorbital bar**). This bony arrangement provides protection for the eyes.

2. The entrance into the skull for the spinal column, the *foramen magnum* (Latin: "big hole") on the base of the skull, faces more downwards instead of backwards as it does in other completely quadrupedal mammals. The position of the *foramen magnum* indicates the direction of the spinal column and is related to the posturing and balancing of the head on the trunk.

3. The face of primates is reduced (snout shortened) with the axis at the base of the skull bending, thus pulling the face more underneath the brain box. This arrangement now provides a greater vertical distance in the movable lower jaw from the point of pivot (P) to the plane of the teeth (T) allowing more biomechanical action for up-and-down crushing, grinding, etc., instead of just simple back-and-forth tearing and gnashing.

4. The ear region containing the middle ear ossicles is completely encircled by a bony encasement (bulla) whose floor is derived from a particular segment of the temporal bone. Most primate paleontologists consider this feature and the formation of a postorbital bar as the structurally best diagnostic characteristics of the primate order.

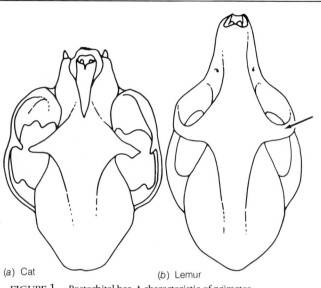

(a) Cat　　　　　(b) Lemur

FIGURE 1　Postorbital bar. A characteristic of primates.

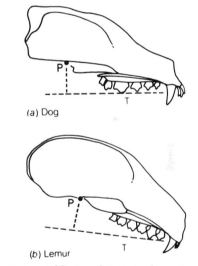

(a) Dog

(b) Lemur

FIGURE 2　Basi-cranial flexion relative to tooth row. In primates, the skull base is more flexed, elevating the point of pivot (P) further above the tooth row and thereby increasing the force of chewing. (© 1959 by W. E. Le Gros Clark.)

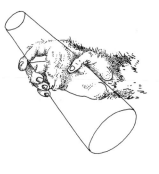

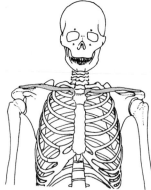

FIGURE 9-1   Primate (macaque) hand.

FIGURE 9-2   Position of the clavicle in the human skeleton.

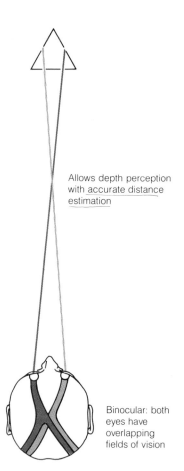

Allows depth perception with accurate distance estimation

Binocular: both eyes have overlapping fields of vision

Stereoscopic: optic nerve transmissions from each eye are relayed to *both* sides of the brain

FIGURE 9-3   Binocular, stereoscopic vision. Fields of vision overlap and sensory information from each eye is relayed to both sides of the brain.

2. *Nails instead of claws.* A consistent characteristic on at least some digits of all contemporary primates. Unlike rodents or cats, most primates must climb by wrapping their hands and feet around branches and holding on by grasping. This grasping function is further aided by the presence of tactile pads at the ends of digits.

3. *Flexible hands and feet* with a good deal of **prehensility** (grasping ability). This feature is associated directly with the lack of claws and retention of five digits.

4. A *tendency toward erectness* (particularly in the upper body). Shown to some degree in all primates, this tendency is variously associated with sitting, leaping, standing, and, occasionally, walking.

5. *Retention of the clavicle* (collarbone). Seen in all primates. The clavicle has been lost in many other quadrupedal mammals. In primates, the clavicle allows for more flexibility of the shoulder joint.

B. *Teeth and Diet*

6. A *generalized dental pattern*, particularly in the back teeth (molars). Characteristic of primates, such a pattern contrasts with the highly specialized molars seen in herbivores.

7. A *lack of specialization in diet.* This attribute is usually correlated with a lack of specialization in teeth. In other words, primates can generally be described as *omnivorous.*

C. *Senses, Brain, and Behavior*

8. A *reduction of the snout* and the proportionate reduction of the smell (olfactory) areas of the brain. Seen in all contemporary primates, but baboons show a secondary (coming later) increase of a *dental* muzzle.

9. An *increased emphasis on vision* with elaboration of visual areas of the brain. A trend related to the decreased dependence on smell. Binocular and stereoscopic vision is a further elaboration wherein visual fields of the two eyes overlap, transmitting both images to the brain, thus allowing depth perception. Except for some specialized nocturnal forms, color vision is most likely present in all primates.

10. *Expansion and increasing complexity of the brain.* A general trend among placental mammals and one especially true of primates. This expansion is most evident in the visual and association areas of the neopallium and to some degree in the motor cortex and cerebellum. (See p. 222.)

11. *A more efficient means of fetal nourishment,* as well as *longer periods of gestation (with single births the norm), infancy,* and extension of the whole life span.

12. *A greater dependency on highly flexible learned behavior* is correlated with longer periods of infant and child dependency. As a result of both these trends, parental investment in each offspring is increased so that although fewer young are born, they receive more efficient rearing.

13. *Adult males often associate permanently with the group.* A behavioral trait rarely seen in other mammals, but widespread among the primates.

Prehensility   Adapted for grasping.

Arboreal   Adapted to life in the trees.

Adaptive niche   The whole way of life of an organism: where it lives, what it eats, how it gets food, and so forth.

Substrate   The surface on which an animal moves or rests.

Nocturnal   Active at night.

Diurnal   Active during daylight hours.

The Arboreal Adaptation

The single most important factor influencing the evolutionary divergence of primates (with elaboration of all the trends just noted) was the adaptation to **arboreal** living. While other placental mammals were going about their business adapting to grasslands, subterranean or even marine environments, primates found their **adaptive niche** in the trees. Indeed, some other mammals also were adapting to arboreal living, but primates found their home (and food) mainly in the tree tops and at the ends of terminal branches. This environment—with its myriad challenges and opportunities—was the one in which our ancestors established themselves as a unique kind of animal.

Primates became primates *because* of their adaptation to arboreal living. We can see this process at work in their reliance upon vision for survival (as opposed to their depending chiefly on a sense of smell). In a complex environment with uncertain footholds, acute vision with depth perception is a necessity. Climbing can be accomplished by either digging in with claws or grasping around branches with prehensile hands and feet. Primates adopted the latter strategy, which allowed a means of progressing on the narrowest and most tenuous of **substrates**. Thus, we also see in primates pentadactyly, prehensility, and flattened nails. In addition, the varied foods found in an arboreal environment (such as fruits, leaves, berries, gums, flowers, insects, small mammals) led to the primate omnivorous adaptation and, hence, to retention of a generalized dentition.

Finally, the long life span, increased intelligence, and more elaborated social system are primate solutions to coping with the manifold complexities of their arboreal habitat (that is, such factors as varied and seasonal food resources; and potential predators from above, below, and in the trees). This crucial development of increased behavioral flexibility may have been further stimulated by a shift from **nocturnal** (nighttime) to **diurnal** (daytime) activity patterns (Jerison, 1973).

A recent critique of the traditional arboreal explanation for the origin of primate structure has been proposed by Matt Cartmill (1972, 1974) of Duke University. Cartmill points out that the most significant primate trends—close-set eyes, grasping extremities, and reduced claws—may *not* have arisen from adaptive advantages in an arboreal environment.

Homology Similarities between organisms based on common evolutionary descent.

According to this alternative theory, ancient primates may have first adapted to living in bushy forest undergrowth and only the lowest branches of the forest canopy. All these traits would have been well-suited for an animal that foraged for fruits and insects. Particularly in searching for insects, early primates are thought to have relied heavily on vision, and this theory is hence called the *visual predation hypothesis*.

The close-set eyes would have allowed these primates to judge accurately the distance from their prey without moving their heads, similar to the hunting manner of cats and owls. The regression of the olfactory sense is then viewed as a necessary result of the eye orbits coming closer together. Grasping extremities may have initially been an adaptation for pursuing insects along very narrow supports (like twigs) in the forest undergrowth. Feet, as well as hands, would be prehensile to allow the animal to maintain support while snaring its prey with both hands.

The visual predation hypothesis is as internally consistent and as likely an explanation for the early evolution of primates as the arboreal theory. In fact—given the fossil record and the morphology typical of many contemporary prosimians— it may be a better explanation for the functional developments among the *earliest* primates. In particular, the small body size and insectivorous diet seen in several living prosimians and a similar adaptation inferred from the fossilized remains of many very early primates are consistent with the visual predation hypothesis.

The visual predation ("bug snatching") hypothesis and the arboreal theory are not mutually exclusive explanations. The complex of primate characteristics could have begun in nonarboreal settings, but would have become even more adaptive once the bug snatching was done *in the trees*.

At some point, in fact, the primates did take to the trees in earnest, and that is where the vast majority still live today. Whereas the basic primate structural complexes may have been initially adapted for visual predation, they became ideally suited for the arboreal adaptation that followed. We would say then that primates were "preadapted" for arboreal living.

The Living Primates

When we apply the set of evolutionary trends under discussion here, we are able to classify a remarkable array of living forms as members of the same mammalian order, the Primates. We and our primate cousins, you will recall, share these characteristics due to **homology**. In other words, primates are part of a single evolutionary radiation, and the traits we all share derive from a common evolutionary descent. Please note, however, that "homologies" can be indicators of *primitive* relationships rather than more *derived* features (see p. 217). In this sense, characteristics such as pentadactyly and retention of the clavicle serve to provide only general evolutionary evidence.

PRIMATE CLASSIFICATION

While controversy on some minor points still exists, the living primates are commonly categorized into subgroupings (based on increasingly similar evolutionary relationships) in the following manner:

```
ORDER    Primates
  SUBORDER    Prosimii
    SUPERFAMILY    Lemuroidea (lemurs of Madagascar)
    SUPERFAMILY    Lorisoidea (loris, bushbaby)
    SUPERFAMILY    Tarsiioidea (tarsier)
  SUBORDER    Anthropoidea
    SUPERFAMILY    Ceboidea (New World monkeys; e.g., spider monkey,
                     howler monkey, capuchin)
    SUPERFAMILY    Cercopithecoidea (Old World monkeys; e.g., baboon,
                     macaque, langur)
    SUPERFAMILY    Hominoidea
      FAMILY    Hylobatidae (gibbons)
      FAMILY    Pongidae
        GENUS    Pan (chimp)
        GENUS    Gorilla
        GENUS    Pongo (orangutan)
      FAMILY    Hominidae
        GENUS    Homo (human)
```

For nearly fifty years, primatologists have been most frequently using this scheme, which dates most notably from George Gaylord Simpson's classification of mammals in 1945. But more recent evidence has demonstrated a few major flaws in this framework, especially flaws that relate to the positioning of the tarsier and the great apes/humans. For this reason, several alternative (and evolutionarily more accurate) classifications have been proposed (for an example, see Table 9-1).

Nevertheless, one lingering problem involves the standardized use of terminology. For example, some scholars (ourselves included) use "hominid" in the *restricted* sense; that is, to refer to humans and our immediate ancestors. Conversely (as shown in Table 9-1), other researchers broaden the family to include humans and all the great apes. As discussed later in this chapter (p. 254), the most important links are among the *African large-bodied hominoids* on the one hand (humans, chimps, gorillas) and the single surviving *Asian large-bodied hominoid* (the orang) on the other.

In order to keep terminology clear, we continue to use the traditional classification, but will point out its limitations where appropriate. This same dilemma has been similarly resolved by other researchers in recent years (Fleagle, 1988, Smuts et al., 1987).

Grades of Primate Evolution

In terms of size, structure, and behavior, contemporary primates certainly represent a varied group of animals. What is even more remarkable about the living primates is that they still display in some form all the major grades of evolution that primates have passed through over the last 70 million years.

An evolutionary grade is, in Mayr's terms, "A group of animals similar in level of organization" (Mayr, 1970). We do not use the term, as some evolutionary biologists have done, to imply a strict commonality of evolutionary descent and/or

TABLE 9-1   Alternative Classification of Living Primates—Based upon Biochemical Data (after Dene et al., 1976)

Order Primates
  Semiorder Strepsirhini
    Suborder Lemuriformes
      Superfamily Lemuroidea
        Family Lemuridae
          Genus *Lemur*   common lemur
        Family Lepilemuridae
          Genus *Lepilemur*   sportive lemur
        Family Indriidae
          Genus *Propithecus*   sifaka
      Superfamily Cheirogaleoidea
        Family Cheirogaleidae
          Genus *Microcebus*   mouse lemur
          Cheirogaleus   dwarf lemur
      Superfamily Daubentonioidea
        Family Daubentoniidae
          Genus *Daubentonia*   aye-aye
    Suborder Lorisiformes
      Superfamily Lorisoidea
        Family Galagidae
          Subfamily Galaginae
            Genus *Galago*   bushbaby
        Family Lorisidae
          Genus *Nycticebus*   slow loris
          Loris   slender loris
        Family Perodicticidae
          Subfamily Perodicticinae
            Genus *Perodicticus*   potto
            Arctocebus   angwantibo
  Semiorder Haplorhini
    Suborder Tarsioiidea
      Family Tarsiidae
        Genus *Tarsius*   tarsier

    Suborder Anthropoidea
      Infraorder Platyrrhini   New World monkeys
        Superfamily Ceboidea
          Family Cebidae
            Genus *Ateles*   spider monkey
            Logothrix   woolly monkey
            Alouatta   howler monkey
            Saguinus   tamarin
            Aotus   night monkey
            Callicebus   titi
            Chiropotes   saki
            Cebus   capuchin
            Saimiri   squirrel monkey
    Infraorder Catarrhini
      Superfamily Cercopithecoidea
        Family Cercopithecidae
          Subfamily Colobinae
            Genus *Colobus*   guereza
            Presbytis   langur
            Pygathrix   douc langur
            Nasalis   proboscis monkey
          Subfamily Cercopithecinae
            Genus *Macaca*   macaque
            Papio   baboon
            Theropithecus   gelada
            Mandrillus   drill
            Cercocebus   mangabey
            Erythrocebus   patas
            Cercopithecus   guenon
      Superfamily Hominoidea
        Family Hylobatidae
          Subfamily Hylobatinae
            Genus *Hylobates*   gibbon
            Symphalangus   siamang
        Family Hominidae
          Subfamily Ponginae
            Genus *Pongo*   orangutan
          Subfamily Homininae
            Genus *Gorilla*   gorilla
            Pan   chimpanzee
            Homo

an equivalent adaptive response (suggesting selection above the species level). In fact, such processes are not now believed to be accurate depictions of macroevolution (Eldredge and Cracraft, 1980). (See p. 108.)

You should also note that the concept of grade does not imply any inferiority or superiority. Grades only reflect different stages of organizational levels seen during primate evolution—from more primitive to more derived. (See p. 217.)

GRADE I: TREE SHREWS (PRIMITIVE MAMMALIAN GRADE; NOT A TRUE PRIMATE)

Tree shrews are an enigma to the taxonomist. In classifying the natural world into the higher taxonomic categories of family, order, etc., we are attempting to simplify and hopefully make sense out of the complex organic continuum that evolution has produced. Indeed, the categories are *created by us* for us. They are symbolic devices typical of the human mind's capacity to "impose arbitrary form on the environment." A tree shrew could not care less whether it is classified as a primate, an insectivore (another order of placental mammals), or a whale.

It is often readily apparent that similar structural and behavioral characteristics of contemporary life forms reflect their shared evolutionary ancestry (for example, lemurs and lorises both as prosimians; humans and apes both as hominoids). There are, however, many organisms that do not fit neatly into *any* of our categories.

The tree shrew is such an animal. Some investigators, impressed by several structural similarities, regard tree shrews as primates (Simpson, 1945; Clark, 1971). However, most current researchers (Simons, 1972; Buettner-Janusch, 1973) view the primatelike characteristics of tree shrews as merely reflections of their primitive mammalian heritage. As another popular alternative, tree shrews have often been placed among the insectivores, where they do not really fit either. As a final act of taxonomic desperation, then, most experts now place tree shrews within their own order of placental mammals (Luckett, 1980a).

Given that tree shrews are an order unto themselves, what are their closest relatives among the placentals? Morphological and some biochemical data (see pp. 254–257) suggest that tree shrews, flying lemurs, and primates form an evolutionary "cluster" and could be included together within a common superorder (Cronin and Sarich, 1980; Luckett, 1980). However, other biochemical techniques suggest the tree shrew/flying lemur/primate cluster is not a natural grouping, and that tree shrews, in fact, find their nearest mammalian affinities with bats (Dene et al., 1980) or even rabbits (Goodman et al., 1983). What makes tree shrews intriguing and relevant to a discussion of primate evolution is that their overall anatomical structure and level of adaptation are probably very similar to the earliest primates of 70 mya.

Today, tree shrews live in Southeast Asia, extending from India to the islands of Indonesia. They are all generally small, squirrellike animals and may not be recognized initially as primatelike in appearance. First, they have long, projecting snouts, and their eyes do not face forward (see Fig. 9-4). Second—even more unprimatelike—they have claws (not nails) on *all* their digits. Finally, their social behavior is most unlike primates in their "absentee" system of mothering. (On the other hand, their tendency toward grasping definitely parallels the well-developed grasping features of the primates.) It is no wonder that the tree shrews look **primitive**, since they are not much altered from the probable general appearance and adaptive level of very early placental mammals. Since the primate adaptive radiation goes back to the roots of the placental mammal radiation at the beginning of the Cenozoic (*circa* 65 mya), living tree shrews provide an excellent structural model for the earliest primates as well as for generalized placental mammals.

Primitive In evolutionary terms, an organism or a characteristic of an organism that is closer to an evolutionary divergence than a later (more derived) one.

FIGURE 9-4   Tree shrew.

GRADE II: LEMURS AND LORISES

Lemurs are found today only on the island of Madagascar and adjacent islands off the east coast of Africa. They probably reached their island sanctuary several million years ago and were able to diversify into the many ecological niches offered on this large island of 227,000 square miles. As the *only* primates on the island, lemurs were able to survive. In continental areas, most of their prosimian cousins perished. Thus, these surviving forms represent a kind of "living fossil," preserving an evolutionary grade that has long since vanished elsewhere.

Lemurs, however, are not uniform. Some are nocturnal, others diurnal; some are completely arboreal, others are more terrestrial. In fact, the range of forms and habitats occupied before recent human interference (in the last few hundred years) reveals a remarkable evolutionary display. One unusual lemur (called the aye-aye), still living in Madagascar, suggests a rodentlike adaptation; another

FIGURE 9-5   The grades of primate evolution.

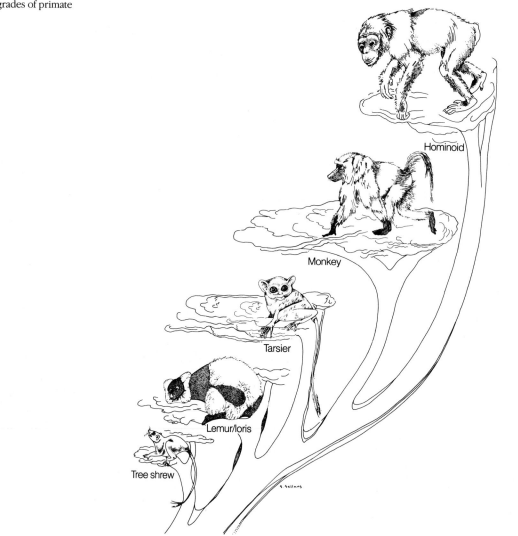

Hominoid

Monkey

Tarsier

Lemur/loris

Tree shrew

(indri) resembles a small monkey; and, finally, an incredible beast with extremely short hind limbs (*Megaladapis*, now extinct) weighed more than 300 pounds (Fleagle, 1988).

Some forms like the aye-aye are socially solitary, whereas others primarily associate in large permanent groups (the ring-tailed lemur). All these forms evolved in the relative sanctuary that Madagascar provided. This kind of evolution, characterized by rapid diversification and expansion into varied ecological niches, is another beautiful example of **adaptive radiation**.

Adaptive radiation   The diversification and expansion of a lifeform into a number of niches.

Lorises, very similar to lemurs, were able to survive in *continental* areas by adopting a nocturnal activity pattern at a time when most other prosimians became extinct. In this way, they were (and are) able to avoid competition with their primate descendants, the monkeys, as well as another group—including many highly successful arboreal, diurnal forms—the rodents.

Today, the geographic range of lorises is confined to tropical areas in Africa and Southeast Asia. Their nocturnal adaptation is immediately revealed structurally by their greatly enlarged eyes. Usually quite small animals, they have elongated hindlimbs, providing an adaptation for leaping and hopping. Socially, most lorises are solitary, but in some species, the individuals sleep in pairs or in larger groups.

Both lemurs and lorises represent the same general adaptive level. They both have good grasping and climbing abilities and have fairly well-developed vision that is not completely stereoscopic. They all have nails on at least one of their digits (the aye-aye has a nail only on the big toe). Most of the other varieties have only one clawed digit (on the second toe). This digit is used for grooming and is called the toilet digit. Lemurs and lorises also have prolonged life spans as compared to other small mammals, averaging about fourteen years for the lorises and nineteen years for the lemurs.

However, lorises and lemurs still show many characteristics suggesting their relatively closer relationship to early placental mammals than is true for the anthropoids (monkeys, apes, and humans). For example, their faces for the most part are still quite snouty, with a markedly projecting nose. As this feature would suggest, they still rely a great deal on the olfactory sense, and some lemurs have developed specialized scent glands for the purpose of leaving "smell" messages. Dependence on olfactory cues is also shown by the naked area of moist skin— *rhinarium*—on the nose. This area is used to conduct scent efficiently. Suggestive also of their early primate ancestry are their expressionless faces, large mobile ears, seasonal breeding in most species, and a generally unelaborated pattern of social behavior. Finally, there are some unusual specialized aspects in their dentition, particularly the projecting lower incisors and canines forming a structure used for grooming and hence called a dental comb.

FIGURE 9-6   Distribution of modern lemurs.

GRADE III: THE TARSIER

A once widespread prosimian form, the living tarsier is today limited to one genus (*Tarsius*) and is confined to island areas in Southeast Asia. This tiny animal (about the size of a small kitten) has avoided competition in much the same way as the lorises—by adapting to a nocturnal niche. The large forward-placed eyes which dominate the face strikingly reveal this adaptation. Another unusual feature shown by the tarsier is a greatly elongated ankle joint (tarsus), which gives the animal its name and allows it to leap great distances.

FIGURE 9-7   Ring-tailed lemur.

FIGURE 9-8   Sifakas in native habitat in Madagascar.

Like lemurs and lorises, tarsiers are traditionally classified as prosimians, as revealed by their small body size, large ears, unfused lower jaw (mandible), toilet digits on toes, and unelaborated social behavior (in some species). However, they exhibit several physical characteristics similar to anthropoids, placing them at a different organizational level than lemurs and lorises. Indeed, like the tree shrew, tarsiers present somewhat of a taxonomic dilemma. Today, most primatologists, pointing to the numerous physical characteristics that tarsiers share with anthropoids (which are seen as derived states), classify tarsiers closer to anthropoids than to prosimians. Moreover, biochemically, tarsiers are more closely related to anthropoids than to lemurs or lorises (Dene et al., 1976). However, chromosomally tarsiers are unique among primates. In order to accommodate this revised

FIGURE 9-9   Distribution of modern lorises and galagos.

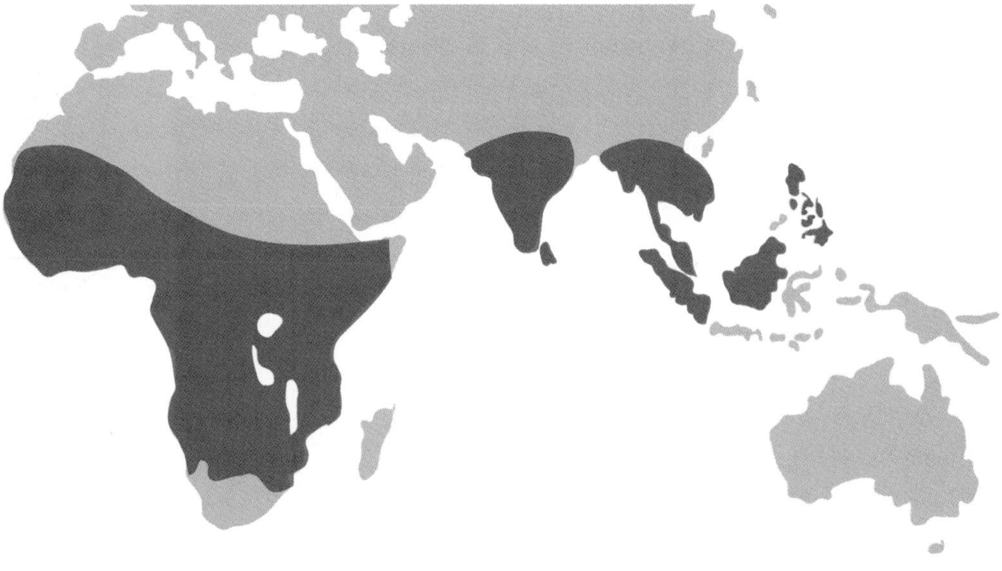

view, classification schemes and classificatory labels have been changed. For example, the suborder that includes lemurs and lorises is termed the **Strepsirhini** (moist-nosed), while tarsiers, monkeys, apes, and humans are included within another suborder, the **Haplorhini** (hairy-lipped) (Szalay and Delson, 1979). Another means of accomplishing the same goal is to retain the traditional subordinal nomenclature but to distinguish lemurs and lorises from tarsiers, monkeys, apes, and humans at a level above suborder (i.e., semiorder—see Table 9-1) (Dene et al, 1976).

As we indicated above, tarsiers show many similarities to anthropoids. Contrasted to those of other prosimians, tarsier eye orbits are almost completely closed *in back* by bone in the manner of the anthropoids. (Lorises and lemurs are "primitive" in this respect, having an opening between the orbit and the cranial vault, or brainbox.) You will recall that all primates have orbits that are completely encircled by bone *on the outside*. In addition, tarsier skulls are more rounded and their snouts less projecting than those of other prosimians, a situation partially explained by their small size and huge eyes. Another anthropoidlike feature is their lack of a rhinarium and a more flexible upper lip, a structure allowing for more facial expression. Finally, the bony ear canal of the tarsier is also more like anthropoids than that of prosimians.

In addition to those features already pointed out, several other characteristics exist that tend to distinguish monkeys, apes, and humans from the "lower" primates. These are:

1. Generally larger body size
2. Larger brain size (in absolute terms and relative to body weight)
3. More rounded skull (seen to some degree in tarsiers also)
4. Eyes completely in front of skull, full stereoscopic vision
5. Complete back wall to eye orbit (also seen in tarsiers)
6. No rhinarium (also seen in tarsiers)
7. Fused mandible
8. More complex social systems
9. More parental care; often by males as well as females
10. More mutual grooming

GRADE IV: MONKEYS

The monkey grade of evolution is today the most varied group of primates (see Table 9-2). Of the 185 or so living species of primates, approximately 70% (about 130 species) are classified as monkeys. These are divided into two groups separated by geographical area (New World and Old World), as well as several million years of separate evolutionary history.

New World Monkeys The New World monkeys (Ceboidea) exhibit a wide range of size, diet, and ecological adaptation. In size, they vary from the tiny (about twelve ounces) marmosets (family: Callitrichidae) to the twenty-pound howler monkey, a member of the family Atelidae (see Table 9-3). New World monkeys are almost exclusively arboreal and will usually come to the ground only to cross spaces in order to gain access to other trees. Although confined to tree environments, New World monkeys can be found in a wide range of arboreal habitats

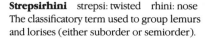

Strepsirhini strepsi: twisted rhini: nose
The classificatory term used to group lemurs and lorises (either suborder or semiorder).

Haplorhini haplo: simple rhini: nose
The classificatory term used to group tarsiers with monkeys, apes, and humans (either suborder or semiorder).

FIGURE 9-10   Galago or "bushbaby."

FIGURE 9-11   Distribution of modern tarsiers.

FIGURE 9-12   Tarsier. Note the huge eyes.

Dental formula The arrangement of teeth showing the number of each type (incisors, canines, premolars, and molars).

Quadrupedal Using all four limbs relatively equally while moving.

TABLE 9-2 **Numbers of Groups of Living Primates**

GROUP	GENERA	SPECIES
Lemur	12	28
Loris	5	11
Tarsier	1	3
New World monkey	16	52
Old World monkey	16	78
Hominoids	6	14
Total	56	186

Source: Data abstracted from A. Jolly, 1985, pp. 6–11.

TABLE 9-3 **New World Monkey Classification**

SUPERFAMILY	Ceboidea
FAMILY	Callitrichidae (marmosets and tamarins)
FAMILY	Cebidae (squirrel monkey, owl monkey, capuchin)
FAMILY	Atelidae (wooly monkey, howler monkey, spider monkey)

FIGURE 9-13 Distribution of modern New World monkeys.

throughout most forested areas in southern Mexico, Central America, and South America.

Nose shape is one of the characteristics distinguishing New World monkeys from those found in the Old World. New World forms have broad, widely flaring noses with a thick nasal septum, with nostrils facing outward. Conversely, Old World monkeys have narrower noses with a thinner nasal septum, and the nostrils face downward. This difference in nose form has given rise to the terms *platyr-rhine* (flat-nosed) and *catarrhine* (down-nosed), the latter referring to *all* Old World anthropoids (Old World monkeys, apes, and humans). Another characteristic of New World monkeys is seen in their dentition, which has retained three premolars. All Old World anthropoids have only two (see Box 9-2). Another feature found only in the New World, though not in all forms, is the development of a prehensile (grasping) tail that can be used like a fifth limb.

FIGURE 9-14 A pair of golden marmosets.

FIGURE 9-15 Howler monkey with infant.

BOX 9-2   **Tale of the Teeth**

Extremely important for interpreting the relationships of *both* living and fossil forms are the number and kinds of teeth present. There are four different kinds of teeth found in a generalized placental mammal, and primates have almost universally retained all four types: incisors, canines, premolars, and molars. A shorthand device for showing the number of each kind of tooth is called a **dental formula**. This formula indicates the teeth in one-quarter of the mouth (since the arrangement of teeth is symmetrical and usually the same in upper and lower jaws). For example, the dental formula in New World monkeys for cebids is 2-1-3-3 (2 incisors, 1 canine, 3 premolars, and 3 molars in each quarter of the mouth—a total of 36 teeth); and 2-1-3-2 in marmosets. The formula in *all* Old World monkeys, apes, and humans is normally 2-1-2-3—a total of 32 teeth. Most lemur and loris dental formulae are 2-1-3-3 (total of 36), but the highly specialized aye-aye shows (for a primate) remarkable reduction in numbers of teeth

$$\frac{1\text{-}0\text{-}1\text{-}3^*}{1\text{-}0\text{-}0\text{-}3}$$

for a total of only 18 teeth.

Relative dental formulae are extremely useful indicators of phyletic relationships because they are normally under tight genotypic control. In other words, environmental influence will usually not alter the tooth formula. In making studies of primate dental phenotypes, we are quite certain, therefore, that our comparisons are based on structural homologies. Thus, similarities in structure (relative numbers of teeth) can be used as indicators of evolutionary similarity.

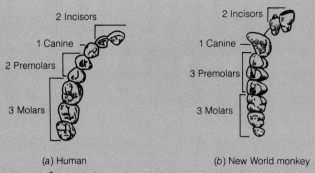

(a) Human   (b) New World monkey

FIGURE 1   Dental formulae. The number of each kind of tooth is given for one-quarter of the mouth.

Dental evidence is extremely important in the interpretation of fossils, since teeth—the hardest component of the body—are the most commonly fossilized part and comprise the vast majority of fossil primate discoveries. In addition, cusp pattern and functional wear can be used to help reconstruct dietary behavior in fossil animals. The identification of diet is of central importance in any attempt to reconstruct the nature of the ecological niche, and ultimately the whole way of life of a fossil form.

---

*When the formula differs in the lower jaw from that of the upper jaw, both are shown. For example, the tarsier has one less incisor in each half of its lower jaw than it does in its upper jaw:

$$\frac{2\text{-}1\text{-}3\text{-}3}{1\text{-}1\text{-}3\text{-}3.}$$

In locomotion, all New World forms are basically **quadrupedal**, but some forms (for example, the spider monkey, or the howler monkey) are able to perform considerable arm-swinging suspensory locomotion (see Box 9-3).

Old World Monkeys   After humans, Old World monkeys (Cercopithecoidea) are the most widely distributed of all living primates. They are seen throughout sub-Saharan Africa and southern Asia, ranging from tropical jungle habitats to semiarid desert and even to seasonally snow-covered areas in northern Japan.

The classification of Old World monkeys reveals how the same root with different endings designates the various levels (taxonomic categories) in a formal classification:

FIGURE 9-16   A New World monkey prehensile tail. Shown here in a spider monkey.

SUPERFAMILY	Cercopithecoidea (sur-ko-pith-e-koid'-ee-uh)	oidea = superfamily
FAMILY	Cercopithecidae (sur-ko-pith-ee'-si-dee)	idae = family
SUBFAMILY	Cercopithecinae (sur-ko-pith-ee'-si-nee)	inae = subfamily
	Colobinae (kol-o-bine'-ee)	
GENUS	Colobus (kol'-o-bus)	genus endings are variable, but -us is common

The same dental formula, 2-1-2-3 (2 incisors, 1 canine, 2 premolars, 3 molars) found in apes and humans also characterizes Old World monkeys. They are all quadrupedal and mainly arboreal, although some (baboons, for example) are adapted primarily to life on the ground. Whether in trees or on the ground, these monkeys spend a good deal of time sleeping, feeding, and grooming while sitting with their upper bodies held erect. Associated with this universal sitting posture are usually areas of hardened skin on their rear ends called *ischial callosities* that serve as sitting pads. Old World monkeys have a good deal of manual dexterity and most have well-developed tails that are never prehensile (in adults), as is true of many New World forms; the tail, however, does serve a purpose in such functions as communication and balance.

FIGURE 9-17   Distribution of modern Old World monkeys.

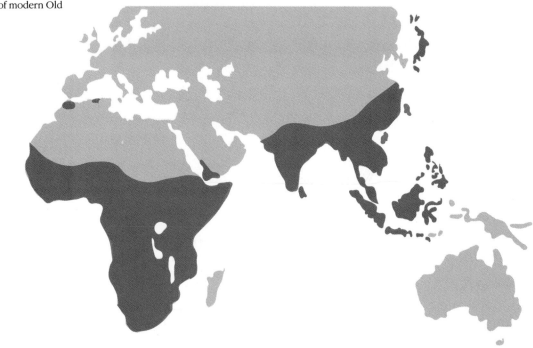

Within the entire group of Old World monkeys (superfamily: Cercopithecoidea), there is only one taxonomically recognized family, Cercopithecidae. Within this family there are in turn two subfamilies, the cercopithecines and the colobines. The former are found mainly in Africa, but some forms (the macaques) are widely distributed in southern Asia. The colobines are found mainly in Asia, but the colobus (kol'-o-bus) monkey (from which the group is named) is widely distributed in tropical Africa.

The cercopithecines are the more generalized of the two subfamilies, showing a more omnivorous dietary adaptation and distinctive cheek pouches for carrying food. The colobines, on the other hand, are more limited dietarily, specializing more on mature leaves, a behavior that has led to their designation as "leaf-eating monkeys." As a result of this behavior, structural adaptations for digestion of cellulose (a usually indigestible plant substance) have arisen. These adaptations are reflected in the high crowned molars, sacculated (divided) stomachs, and elongated intestines.

The most common forms of cercopithecines include the highly diversified, mostly arboreal guenons (genus: *Cercopithecus*); the slightly larger but still arboreal mangabeys (genus: *Cercocebus*); and the more terrestrial macaques (genus: *Macaca*), baboons—both savanna and hamadryas (genus: *Papio*), forest baboon (genus: *Mandrillus*), and the gelada baboon (genus: *Theropithecus*)—as well as the patas monkey (genus: *Erythrocebus*).

The colobus monkey of Africa (genus: *Colobus*) and the various forms of Asian langurs (genus: *Presbytis, Rhinopithecus*, etc.) and the proboscis monkey of Borneo (genus: *Nasalis*) make up the colobine subfamily.

Locomotory behavior among Old World monkeys includes arboreal quadrupedalism in the guenons and mangabeys, arm-swinging and acrobatic leaping in many of the colobines, and terrestrial quadrupedalism in the baboons, macaques, and patas monkey. In the baboons particularly, adaptation to ground living has

FIGURE 9-18   A patas monkey with infant.

FIGURE 9-19   A toque macaque with infant (nursing).

FIGURE 9-20   Black-and-white colobus monkeys.

BOX 9-3   **Tale of the Limbs**

Besides teeth (and diet), the other major functional complex most useful in describing both extant (living) and extinct primates relates to the structure of the limbs and the form of locomotion.

A meaningful functional description of locomotion among contemporary primates should include position of the body, which limbs are used, the manner and frequency they are employed, and the nature of the substrate (such as wide tree branch, narrow branch, flat ground). By understanding the locomotory behavior of contemporary primates we can analyze their respective limb structures and form meaningful *structural-functional correlations*. With such a perspective, we can then interpret fossil primates and reconstruct their probable locomotory behavior.

A common locomotory classification of contemporary primates with their typical structural correlations is shown below (after Napier and Napier, 1967):

CATEGORY	DESCRIPTION OF BEHAVIOR	STRUCTURAL CORRELATES	EXAMPLES
A. Vertical clinging and leaping	leaping in trees with propulsion from hindlimbs, clinging with forelimbs for vertical support	elongated hindlimbs, particularly ankle area, upper body held semi-erect	tarsier
B. Quadrupedalism	using all limbs relatively equally; body horizontal	front- and hindlimbs relatively equal length; spine flexible	
1. Slow climbing	slow, cautious climbing; often associated with capturing insects	widely abducted (spread) thumb, reduction of second digit	potto, slow loris
2. Branch running and walking	walking or running on tops of branches, also leaping	generalized quadruped; limbs equal sized; spine flexible	ringtailed lemur, all marmosets, squirrel monkey, guenons
3. Ground running and walking	quadrupedal walking and running on ground, also tree climbing	all limbs elongated, body size usually larger than strictly arboreal species	baboons, most macaques, patas monkey
4. New World "semibrachiation"	usually quadrupedal, some arm-swinging beneath branches with use of prehensile tail; little or no leaping	forelimbs elongated; fingers often curved, thumb reduced	howler monkey, spider monkey
5. Old World "semibrachiation"	usually quadrupedal with arm-swinging and often considerable acrobatic leaping from branch to branch	forelimbs elongated; fingers often curved, thumb reduced	colobines (colobus, langurs)
C. Ape locomotion			
1. True brachiation	acrobatic swinging arm-over-arm along (under) same branch, associated with feeding on small terminal branches	small body size, greatly elongated forelimb, curved fingers, shoulder joint oriented upward, upper body held fairly erect; spine not flexible	gibbon, siamang

BOX 9-3

2. Quadrumanual climbing	slow deliberate climbing using all four limbs for grasping	large body size, hip joint flexible like shoulder, upper body held erect, spine not flexible	orang
3. Knuckle-walking	on ground semiquadrupedal, but hands supported on knuckles; while in trees considerable arm-swinging	large body size, elongated fore-limbs; stable wrist joint; upper body held erect; spine shortened and inflexible	chimp, gorilla
D. Bipedalism	strictly terrestrial, standing, striding, running upright; weight alternately on single hindlimb	medium-large body size; hind-limb elongated; pelvis altered for support and muscular leverage; feet altered for stable support with little flexibility, toes shortened; upper body completely erect; head balanced on spine; spine shortened and inflexible	human*

It is important to remember that the above classification is a *simple* one, intended to give a sense of the range of locomotory behaviors among the primates. However, if not viewed carefully, it can obscure the diversity of locomotory behavior within a species; indeed, that displayed by a single animal.

Some species are, of course, less varied than others in terms of their typical locomotory repertoire. For example, baboons are easily classified as "quadrupeds," as this is mostly what they do. Likewise, humans are "bipeds," since this is pretty much exclusively what we do. Nevertheless, many primate species are quite diverse in how (and where) they move about. David Pilbeam (1986, p. 298) has summarized some of the most salient features of the locomotory behavior of several species, three examples of which are listed below:

		TERRESTRIAL				ARBOREAL				
	Terrestrial/ arboreal	*Biped*	*Quadruped walk/run*	*Knuckle walk*	*Knuckle walk*	*Quadruped walk/run*	*Leap sway*	*Quadruped climb*	*Arm-swing brachiate*	*Biped*
Baboon	50/50	2	48	—	—	25	20	5	—	—
Orang	—/100	—	—	—	—	13	15	51	21	—
Chimp	50/50	2	—	48	3	11	6	15	10	5

(Figures are relative percentage of behavior. Note especially the marked behavioral diversity of the chimp.)

*True bipedalism among the primates is an adaptation *only* of modern humans and our hominid ancestors. Thus, the structural correlates associated with this functional complex are crucial in determining the status of our possible ancestors.

Estrous cycle Hormonally initiated physiological changes in female primates—associated with ovulation.

Parallel evolution The process where two life forms (that are initially related) become physically more similar through time due to adaptation to similar environments.

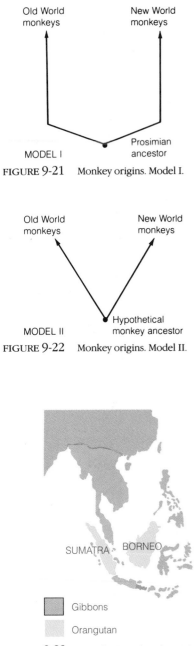

FIGURE 9-21 Monkey origins. Model I.

MODEL I

Old World monkeys

New World monkeys

Prosimian ancestor

MODEL II

Old World monkeys

New World monkeys

Hypothetical monkey ancestor

FIGURE 9-22 Monkey origins. Model II.

SUMATRA BORNEO

◼ Gibbons

Orangutan

FIGURE 9-23 Distribution of modern Asian apes.

given rise to larger body size, especially in males. Such a marked difference in body form between males and females of a species is called *sexual dimorphism*. Another striking difference in baboons is canine size, which is much larger in males.

In addition, many Old World monkey females (especially baboons and many macaques) exhibit pronounced external changes, such as swelling and coloration of the genitalia, associated with the **estrous cycle**—a hormonally initiated period of sexual receptivity in female mammals correlated with ovulation.

Because of their general hardiness even under extremely trying circumstances, Old World monkeys (particularly the versatile macaques) have been the preferred laboratory subjects for both biomedical and behavioral experiments. Indeed, much of what we know about the effect of infant and child deprivation has been learned from the Harlows' well-known experiments with rhesus macaques at the University of Wisconsin (Harlow, 1959). (See p. 276.)

However, recent stronger enforcement limiting monkey exportation by the Indian government has made acquisition of rhesus macaques much more difficult and more expensive. Consequently, laboratory researchers routinely use smaller (and also very hardy) New World varieties, especially squirrel monkeys and cebus monkeys. Despite what would now appear as large free-ranging populations, many conservationists are concerned for their future given the huge demands (thousands of animals per year) that such exploitation places upon these species.

Monkeys, Old and New World: A Striking Case of Parallel Evolution We have mentioned several differences between monkeys in the Old World compared to those in the New World. However, the striking fact remains that they are *all* monkeys. By this statement, we mean that they all are adapted to a similar (primarily arboreal) way of life. With the exception of the South American night monkey (*Aotus*), they are diurnal and all are social, usually fairly omnivorous, and quadrupedal, though with variations of this general locomotory pattern (see Box 9-3).

These similarities are all the more striking when we consider that Old and New World monkeys have gone their separate evolutionary paths for tens of millions of years. In fact, a noted primatologist, Dr. E. L. Simons (1969), suggests the split may have occurred more than 50 mya. Both forms of monkey would then have evolved independently from separate prosimian ancestors. The current consensus among researchers, however, disputes this claim (Hoffstetter, 1972; Ciochon and Chiarelli, 1980) and postulates both Old and New World monkeys arose in Africa from a common monkey ancestor and later reached South America by rafting over. (Note: South America and Africa were considerably closer together earlier in the Cenozoic. In addition, migration over water barriers may have been facilitated by "island hopping" over a chain of volcanic islands.)

In either case, what is most remarkable is that the two forms of monkey have not diverged more than they have—given the time depth of separate evolutionary history in the two hemispheres. What we see today in the diverse arboreal adaptations of monkeys is then a result of **parallel evolution** (see p. 225). Similar ecological selective forces, mainly in tropical arboreal environments, led to structural evolution in different but parallel directions. The result is that the same grade of primate we today recognize as "monkey" evolved in both New and Old Worlds.

The superfamily Hominoidea includes "lesser" apes (gibbons and siamangs), great apes (orangutans, gorillas, chimpanzees), and humans. Classifying humans with the apes is not an arbitrary device, for it indicates our close structural similarities, as well as shared evolutionary history. This close similarity was noted by Tyson at the end of the seventeenth century and was forcefully restated by Huxley and Darwin in the nineteenth century. As this classification indicates, we and the apes are more closely related to each other than *either* is to an Old World monkey. In fact, many primatologists feel that the relationship between humans and great apes is so close that they are often grouped within a single family (Dene et al., 1976; Szalay and Delson, 1979). (See Table 9-1.)

The structural similarities we share with the apes are numerous but most importantly include absence of a tail, generally large body size, shortened deep trunk, stable spine, and the position and musculature of the shoulder joint (the latter adapted particularly for suspensory locomotion).

The Gibbon and Siamang   The gibbon and closely related siamang (**Hylobatidae**) are today found in the southeastern tropical areas of Asia. These animals are the smallest of the apes, with a long, slender body weighing only about 13 pounds in the gibbon and about 25 pounds in the larger siamang.

The most distinctive structural feature of the hylobatids is related to their functional adaptation for **brachiation**. Consequently, they have extremely long arms, long, permanently curved fingers, and powerful shoulder muscles. This highly specialized locomotory adaptation may be related to feeding behavior while hanging beneath branches.

The Orangutan   The orang (genus: *Pongo*) is found today only in heavily forested areas on the Indonesian islands of Borneo and Sumatra. Due to poaching by humans in the past and the continuing commercial encroachment on its habitats, the orang faces imminent extinction. Such a loss would be tragic on several counts, especially because little is currently known of these mysterious red giants of the forest. Orangs are slow, cautious climbers whose whole locomotory behavior can best be described as a **quadrumanual** adaptation—a tendency to use all four limbs for grasping and support. They are large animals with pronounced sexual dimorphism (males weigh about 180 pounds and females less than half that). Orangs were thought to be exclusively arboreal, but more recent evidence (Galdikas, 1979) suggests they (especially males) occasionally come to the ground to traverse fairly long distances and even occasionally visit caves.

The Gorilla   The largest of all living primates, the gorilla (family: Pongidae; genus: *Gorilla*) today is confined to forested areas in West Africa and the great lakes area of East Africa. This species exhibits marked sexual dimorphism, with males weighing up to 400 pounds in the wild and females around 200 pounds. Due to their very large adult weight, gorillas are almost completely terrestrial, adopting a semiquadrupedal (knuckle-walking) posture on the ground. Their forelimbs are elongated, though not so much as in gibbons, their upper bodies are normally held semierect, and their arms possess considerable mobility. Consequently, there are numerous structural modifications: a flattened (front-to-

Hylobatidae   (Hy-lo-bat´-i-dee)

Brachiation   Arm-over-arm suspensory locomotion beneath branches.

Quadrumanual   quadru: four
manual: hand
Using all four limbs for grasping during locomotion.

FIGURE 9-24   Siamang.

(a)

(b)

FIGURE 9-25   (a) Male orangutan; (b) orangutan climbing quadrumanously.

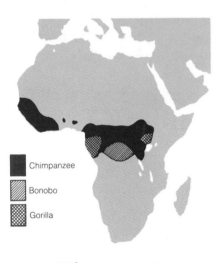

Chimpanzee

Bonobo

Gorilla

FIGURE 9-26   Distribution of modern African apes.

back) and broadened (side-to-side) chest; a shortened, more stable spine (compared to quadrupedal monkeys); longer clavicles; and flexible, powerful shoulders. The wrist joint is also modified to support the considerable weight of the upper body during knuckle-walking. In addition, gorillas have brains more complexly organized than monkeys or gibbons, thus allowing for more learned behavior. Once considered a wild and savage beast, the gorilla has been shown by field studies to be a shy, usually gentle vegetarian (Schaller, 1963; Fossey, 1970). Recent reports, however, have shown that—like many other primates—gorillas fairly frequently attack and kill other members of their species, particularly infants (Fossey, 1981).

The Chimpanzee   Probably the best known and most loved of all the nonhuman primates is the chimpanzee (family: Pongidae; genus: *Pan*). Often misunderstood because of their displays within zoos and carnival sideshows, the chimps' true nature did not come to light until long hours of fieldwork in their natural environments provided a reliable picture. Chimps are found today in equatorial Africa stretching in a broad belt from the Atlantic Ocean in the west to Lake Tanganyika in the east.

There are actually two species of chimpanzee: the "common" chimpanzee (*Pan troglodytes*) and the bonobo or pygmy chimp (*Pan paniscus*). The bonobo is smaller than most common chimps (though some *P. troglodytes* are almost as small as the bonobo) with several intriguing differences in social behavior as well. Today, the bonobo's range is extremely restricted. It is found only in Central Zaire, where it is in great danger of extinction.

Chimpanzees are in many ways structurally quite similar to gorillas, with corresponding limb proportions and thorax (chest) shape as well as specific features

FIGURE 9-27   A male lowland gorilla.

(a)

(b)

FIGURE 9-28   Chimpanzees. (*a*) male; (*b*) female.

of the upper limb and wrist joint. This similarity is due to the likeness in their mode of locomotion (knuckle-walking) while on the ground. Indeed, many authorities (for example, Tuttle, 1990) consider chimps and gorillas as members of a single genus (*Pan gorilla* for the gorilla; *Pan troglodytes* for the common chimp). However, the ecological adaptations of the chimp and gorilla differ, since chimps spend a great deal of time arm-swinging in the trees and feeding primarily on fruit. Conversely, gorillas are almost exclusively terrestrial vegetarians, consuming such vegetative matter as roots, shoots, and bark.

Like the brain of the gorilla, the chimpanzee brain is highly developed, and the learning capabilities of these animals are well known to visitors to animal shows as well as to scientific investigators.

Humans   Humans (family: Hominidae; genus: *Homo*) belong to the one remaining genus of the superfamily Hominoidea, a genus that today consists of only one species, *Homo sapiens*. Our primate heritage is shown again and again in the structure of our body: our dependence on vision; our lack of reliance on olfactory (smell) cues; and our flexible limbs and grasping hands are all long rooted in our primate, arboreal past. Indeed, among the primates, we show in many ways the most developed set of primate characteristics. For example, the development of our cerebral cortex and reliance on learned behavior with resulting complexity in social behavior are but elaborations of long-established primate trends.

As we will discuss in the next chapter, there are several features of humans and our most immediate ancestors that distinguish us from other primates. However,

Karyotype The characteristic number, size, and pattern of the chromosomes that are distinctive for particular species.

probably the most distinctive, and certainly that most clearly observable in our earliest (hominid) ancestors is our unique manner of locomotion. The striding, bipedal gait with alternating support placed on a single hindlimb has required significant structural modifications in the pelvis and leg. By isolating similar structural modifications in the remains of fossil animals, we are able to distinguish our closely related or direct ancestors.

Primate Chromosomes, Proteins, and DNA

The classification of primates used thus far in this chapter has employed the traditional approach of looking for homologies in morphological traits. However, another relatively new perspective with enormous potential for helping to clarify taxonomic problems compares **karyotypes** (chromosome numbers, shapes, banding patterns), proteins, and even roughly correlates the DNA code itself.

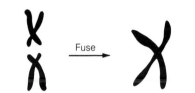

FIGURE 9-29 Fusion of two small chromosomes. This fusion produces one large chromosome (human chromosome number 2?).

The usefulness of this approach is immediately obvious. When we compare outward morphology, such as limb proportions and dental formulae, we are comparing phenotypes, usually far removed from their underlying genetic basis. However, what we are really after in the construction of classification schemes are homologies, traits based on common evolutionary descent. In other words, we want to compare traits that are inherited—those coded directly in the genotype.

Direct protein products of DNA, such as hemoglobin and serum proteins (found in the blood), are excellent indicators of homologies. If two species of primates are systematically similar in their protein structure, we can infer their DNA sequences are also similar. When two species share similar DNA, that means both inherited the same blueprint (with minor revisions) from a common ancestor. Thus, we have *direct* indicators of real homologies. Two primates that superficially resemble one another (some New World and Old World monkeys, for example) may in fact not be closely related at all. Using outward morphology alone may be confusing due to unknown effects from parallel evolution. But such evidence as biochemical data and karyotype comparisons avoids these pitfalls, and indeed shows Old and New World monkeys as genetically (and evolutionarily) quite distinct.

Primatologists utilizing these techniques have, in conjunction with biochemists, in the last few years added considerable insight into our classifications of the primate order. A point worthy of mention: In most cases, biochemical evidence has reaffirmed the taxonomies constructed from comparative morphological studies (thereby supplying an extremely important independent source of data). When contradictions with traditional taxonomies have cropped up, much needed new knowledge has been gained. For example, classifying the orang with the African great apes superficially makes good sense since their outward body structures appear similar. Biochemical evidence, however, shows that both Asian apes (orangs and gibbons) are quite distinct from chimps and gorillas. Since our classifications are designed to reflect evolutionary relationships, they will have to be revised in the future to accord with this new information. (See Table 9-1.)

The way the various chromosomal and biochemical techniques are performed requires considerable technological sophistication, but their applications are straightforward. For example, two species can be compared for karotype. The more closely two species are related, the closer their karyotypes should be. When one looks at the chromosomes of the hominoids, it is readily apparent that humans and the great apes are all quite similar, with gibbons and siamangs having the most distinctive (i.e., derived) pattern (Stanyon and Chiarelli, 1982; Mai, 1983).

Among the large-bodied hominoids, the orang karyotype is the most conservative, with humans and the African apes displaying more derived features. It is interesting to note that the fossil data (which we'll take up in Chapter 13) also now suggests that orangs are probably the most conservative (i.e., primitive) of the large hominoids.

Within the human/gorilla/chimp group there are a tremendous number of similarities of the structural arrangement and banding patterns of almost all the chromosomes. A relatively small number of alterations are required to transform all three living species from a theoretical ancestor (Yunis and Prakash, 1982).

The exact sequence of evolutionary relationships among humans and the African great apes is still in some dispute. Some tentative chromosomal data have suggested that humans and chimps share a more recent ancestry after separating from gorillas (Yunis and Prakash, 1982). A more controlled study, however, with consideration of within-species variation of karyotype (Stanyon and Chiarelli, 1982), has supported the more traditional branching order, where humans and *both* African apes diverge first—followed later by a separation of chimps and gorillas.

Detailed protein structures can be compared, as between chimp and human hemoglobin, by isolating the amino acid sequences. Comparisons between humans and the African great apes for the approximately half dozen proteins analyzed in this manner show striking similarities; they are either identical or show a difference of only one or two amino acids in the entire sequence (as you will recall, the hemoglobin beta chain is 146 amino acids long).

Another method used to contrast proteins in different species is not as precise as a detailed protein analysis but is less time-consuming and less costly. By measuring the strength of reaction to specially prepared antisera, similarities in proteins are calibrated on a relative scale, indicating *antigenic distance*. This approach, developed by Vincent Sarich and Allan Wilson at the University of California, Berkeley, has enabled many more proteins to be compared among a wide variety of different primate species. The results again generally tally favorably with traditional classifications (see Table 9-4).

Moreover, differences in DNA strands themselves can be compared using an elaborate technique called DNA hybridization. Scientists have recently performed some remarkable experiments in which double strands of DNA are artificially separated in two different species and then recombined into a new molecule, a hybrid DNA unlike anything nature ever concocted. The genetic (and evolutionary) similarity of the two species is then calculated by measuring the number of mismatched base pairs along the hybrid sequence (in other words, places where the two sides of the molecule are not complementary: A with T, G with C, etc.).

As in the other techniques discussed above, DNA hybridization has reaffirmed the basic tenets of primate classification. Indeed, better than any of the other approaches, DNA hybridization has shown how close genetically we and the African great apes are. A recent systematic application of this relatively new and fascinating technique (Sibley and Ahlquist, 1984) has shown that humans and chimps are closer genetically than *either* is to the gorilla and, in fact, even closer than two similar species of gibbons. Or, for that matter, humans and chimps are more similar than zebra and horse or goat and sheep. On the basis of these results, it would be

TABLE 9-4 **Biochemically Determined Distances between Humans and Other Animals**

COMPARISON	AMINO ACID DISTANCE	ANTIGENIC DISTANCE	DNA DISTANCE
Human—chimp	0.27	1.0	1.8
Human—gorilla	0.65	0.8	2.3
Human—orang	2.78	2.0	4.9
Human—gibbon	2.38	2.6	4.9
Human—macaque	3.89	3.6	—
Human—spider monkey	8.69	7.6	—
Human—tarsier	—*	8.8	—
Human—loris	11.36	11.2	42.0
Human—tree shrew	—	12.6	—
Primates—other placentals	—	12.11–14.91	—
Placentals—marsupials	—	15.83	—

All these figures are averages drawn from numerous individual comparisons. Each scale should be interpreted not as absolute measures, but only as *relative* ones. In addition, the scalings for each of the three sets of comparisons are independent of one another.

*Line (—) indicates data undetermined.

Source: Data abstracted from Goodman and Lasker, 1975.

entirely consistent to classify human and chimps (perhaps, gorillas as well) within the *same* genus. In other words, we would continue to be called, *Homo sapiens*, while the chimp would be classed as *Homo troglodytes*. Certainly, not everyone is prepared to accept this terminology; nevertheless, it underlines the basic genetic/evolutionary facts.

Finally, the revolution in molecular biology brought about by recombinant DNA research has now made it possible to sequence directly the nucleotides of humans and other organisms (Goodman et al., 1983). As a result—when this new technique has been more widely applied—we should be able to ascertain even more unambiguously the precise genetic/evolutionary relationships among the primates. In addition, these nucleotide sequence data will inform us concerning the frequency of "neutral" mutations and (when calibrated with fossil data) may elucidate whether primate evolution has been more characterized by gradual or punctuated modes of change (see pp. 107–108).

Summary

Primates are an order of placental mammals characterized by their generalized limb structure, dependence on vision, lack of reliance on smell, developed brain (particularly cerebral cortex), and complex social organizations. All these evolutionary trends have developed, or at least have been elaborated, as a direct result of adaptation to an arboreal environment.

In addition to the primitive placental mammal—tree shrew grade (Grade I, not a true primate)—living primates today represent four major grades of evolution that correspond to various stages of primate evolution over the last several million years. These grades are:

I. Lemurs and lorises
II. Tarsiers
III. Monkeys (New World and Old World)
IV. Hominoids (apes and humans)

Traditionally, primatologists made comparisons of anatomy and behavior. In recent years, considerable additional understanding of evolutionary relationships has been contributed by studies of DNA, chromosomes, and gene products.

We are a primate and our ancestors have been primates for at least 70 million years. Only by looking at humans *as primates* can we hope to understand the kind of animal we are and how we came to be this way.

Questions for Review

1. How are primates similar to other placental mammals?
2. Discuss how binocular vision, prehensility, and an expanded cerebral cortex are adaptations for an arboreal niche.
3. What are the various superfamilies of the primate order? To which one do humans belong?
4. Discuss the geographic distribution and ecological adaptations of contemporary prosimians.
5. What are the most important differences between prosimians and anthropoids?
6. How do monkeys in the Old and New Worlds exhibit parallel evolution?
7. How do teeth reflect evolutionary relationships?
8. What are some important relationships between limb structure and locomotion in contemporary primates?
9. In what ways are humans typical primates?
10. How does biochemical evidence give indication of homologies? Why are effects due to parallel evolution more likely to cloud the picture for morphological traits than for biochemical traits?

Suggested Further Reading

Buettner-Janusch, John. *Physical Anthropology: A Perspective*, New York: John Wiley and Sons, 1973.
 Chapters 4–6 (pp. 43–194) offer a superb, in-depth introduction to the anatomy, taxonomy, and biology of nonhuman primates. Written by one of today's leading authorities, this book is highly recommended for those introductory students wishing to delve further into primate studies.
Campbell, Bernard. *Human Evolution*, Chicago: Aldine Publishing Co., 1974.
 A functionally oriented review of primate dentition, locomotor systems, digestion, etc. A truly excellent source for the moderately advanced student.
Eimerl, S., and I. DeVore. *The Primates*, New York: Time, Inc., 1965.
 An excellent introduction to the primates. This beautifully illustrated work is written for the layman with many superior photos of contemporary primates, taken mainly in the wild. The first chapter is a superb summary of primate anatomical characteristics.

Flegle, John. *Primate Adaptation and Evolution*, New York: Academic Press, 1988.

A recent, highly authoritative overview of the primate order. Excellent evolutionary and ecological discussions are included as well as beautiful illustrations. Also highly recommended as background for Chapters 10–12.

Le Gros Clark, W. E. *The Antecedents of Man*, Chicago: Quadrangle Books, 1971.

An advanced analysis of primate anatomy from an evolutionary perspective. Excellent introductory chapters define primite evolutionary trends and survey contemporary forms.

Napier, J. R., and P. H. Napier. *A Handbook of Living Primates*, New York: Academic Press, 1967.

A detailed account summarizing geographical, ecological, and morphological data for fifty-six extant genera. This book also contains an excellent introduction into primate functional anatomy and is the standard reference for classifications of locomotory behavior.

Napier, Prue. *Monkeys and Apes*, New York: Grosset and Dunlap, Inc., 1972.

A Bantam Nature Paperback. An excellent reference for the introductory student. Outstanding illustrations.

Schultz, Adolf. *The Life of Primates*, New York: Universe Books, 1969.

Written by the world's leading authority on comparative primate anatomy, this book provides an excellent introduction to this complex topic. Written at a level comprehensible to introductory students.

Tuttle, Russell H. *Apes of the World. Their Social Behavior, Communication, Mentality, and Ecology,* Park Ridge, N.J.: Noyes Publications, 1986.

A comprehensive review of the anatomy, ecology, and behavior of apes, in comparative and historical perspective. Well written with a superb bibliography.

Watts, Elizabeth. *Biology of the Living Primates*, Dubuque, Iowa: Wm. C. Brown, 1975.

A short nontechnical introduction and summary of living primates. Highly recommended for introductory students.

Primate Behavior

Contents

Primates in the Laboratory

In the Issue for Chapter 9 (p. 230), we discussed the critical problems of continued survival faced by primates in the wild. We will return to this crucial issue later in this chapter. Indeed, the conservation of primates in their natural habitats could be regarded as *the* issue in contemporary primate field studies. As anthropologists have chiefly been the researchers who study primates in the field (see p. 267), it is of central importance to ponder whether, in the next century, any primates will be left to study.

A major drain on wild populations has been their capture for use in medical research laboratories. In the recent past, the numbers have been staggering. For example, in 1968 alone 113,714 were received just in the United States (many more animals were probably trapped, but died en route). Indeed, in the development and testing of polio vaccines, more than one million rhesus monkeys were used!

As a result of this huge drain on their indigenous rhesus monkey populations (coupled with concern for humane treatment), the Indian government has recently moved to severely restrict export. Even though species such as macaques are no longer as readily available, capture of nonhuman primates for laboratories still continues at a rapid level. Now, however, varieties of New World species are the chosen targets (including squirrel monkeys, cebus monkeys, and a variety of marmosets). No accurate estimates of numbers captured are available, but for the labs in the United States, Europe, and Japan there are surely tens of thousands of animals seized every year.

Some progress is being made, however. The figure just cited (for 1968) was prior to the United States' ratification of the Convention in the Trade of Endangered Species (CITIES) in 1973. In 1984, for example, the number of imported animals had declined dramatically to 13,148 (Mittermeir and Cheney, 1987).

Given this steady loss of wild animals—in addition to the other problems faced by free-ranging nonhuman primates (especially habitat destruction; see p. 291)—it is obvious that continued use of *any* species cannot be long sustained. Recognizing this fact, federal research agencies in the United States have sought to establish breeding colonies in North America. However, up to now, the annual supply of captive-born animals falls far short of the numbers required (less than 10% of the primates needed).

A more basic ethical question remains: Even if we could supply all the nonhuman primates sought by laboratories, is all the proposed research really necessary? And, if so, how should the animals be treated in these facilities?

Much of the use of animals (primates and other species as well) is not within state-of-the-art or life-saving contexts. Indeed, the pharmaceutical industry has used many primates to test a host of "elective" therapies and even a variety of cosmetic products. It must be noted, however, that several of the larger cosmetic firms have entirely eliminated the use of laboratory animals in the last two years.

The answers are not easy, and we do not wish to advocate an overly strident position. *Some* research is obviously essential for human well-being. But we do ask that what is considered "essential" be appraised more critically than has been done in the past. Recent years have brought some progress along these lines. For instance, all who seek to use animals for research, and are applying for funds through the National Science Foundation, are now required to provide a rationale. Moreover, researchers are specifically requested to consider *alternatives* to the use of live animals.

Those primates who find their way into most research facilities face a very unhappy future. Because they are easier to capture and maintain, young animals have frequently been used. We know that immature primates (human and nonhuman) require intimate physical contact and care from their mothers. For monkeys, this period of crucial dependency lasts two to four years, and, in great apes, it can extend for eight years. In addition, as highly social animals, primates grow up in an environment rich in social stimuli from age-mates and other members of the social group (a situation also demonstrated as essential for normal psychological development—see p. 277).

Nevertheless, young primates are frequently removed from their mothers and peers, and are maintained in complete isolation. Often in painfully small cages, in darkness and solitude, these animals live out their lives. Sometimes imprisonment is for a short term. For other experiments, though, particularly those involving infectious diseases, such as hepatitis or AIDS, confinement may extend for years, or even decades. In such a deprived environment, captive primates display a variety of abnormal behaviors, such as pacing constantly about their cage, pulling out their hair, biting themselves, or incessantly rocking back-and-forth. Humans in similar circumstances who display quite similar behavioral abnormalities are usually termed "severely disturbed" or "insane."

In response to these conditions, a variety of legislative measures have been considered by the U.S. Congress and by numerous state legislatures as well. In Congress, several bills have included language specifying "procedures to insure that animal pain and distress is minimized" and, in the case of primates, to consider "the psychological well-being of the animals."

In the United States, the leading financial sponsor of research utilizing nonhuman primates is the National Institutes of Health (NIH). In the past few years they have more intensively consulted with those primatologists (most notably, Jane Goodall) who can provide them with better information regarding the social needs of primates.

Assuming some research will continue, what can be done? First of all, the issue of minimal cage size can be addressed. A research lab outside Washington, D.C., recently was found to house two young chimpanzees together in a cage 24 inches by 24 inches by 22 inches. Here, there was not even enough room to stand up, much less move about! Secondly, except where isolation is absolutely necessary for experimental purposes, primates should be kept in a *social* environment. For example, a lab in

Europe has instituted measures so that the primate lab subjects are daily brought together in a common area, allowed to interact and play. And, finally, those individuals charged with the responsibility for care of captive animals can be recruited partly on the basis of awareness and compassion. Moreover, their training can be much more specifically oriented toward learning about the psycho-social requirements of their charges.

All of this will not be done easily. In addition, it will cost more money than current funds provide. Most importantly, however, public awareness must first be heightened.

CHAPTER 10

Introduction

How can we better understand human behavior? Solely observing an urbanized industrialized society such as ours will not tell us very much of our hominid heritage. After all, we have been urbanized for only a few thousand years, and the industrial revolution is merely a few centuries old, barely a flicker in evolutionary time. Consequently, to understand what behavioral components may have shaped our evolution, we need a perspective broader than that which our own culture supplies. Since little is known about early hominid behavior, we study the behavior of contemporary animals adapted to environments similar to those of early hominids in the hope of gaining insight into early hominid evolution.

In this chapter, we place nonhuman primate behavior in the context of its possible relationship to human behavior; that is, we address the question: Does the study of nonhuman primates serve as a window on (or model for) human behavior? Or are nonhuman primates so different in behavior from hominids that the uniqueness of the latter derives little from the former?

Behavior and Human Origins

What does it mean to be human? There are several *physical* characteristics, such as adaptations for bipedal locomotion and enlarged brain, that characterize humans and—to varying extents—our hominid ancestors. But from a strictly structural point of view, we are not really that unique compared to other primates, especially when compared with the great apes. In patterns of dentition, bone development, muscle structure, and so forth, we and the other hominoids are very similar, reflecting a fairly recent shared ancestry. (Probably no more than 7 or 8 million years (my) at most separate us from the African great apes.) Indeed, in the non-repeated portions of DNA, humans and chimpanzees are 98% identical. So what, precisely, is it that distinguishes the human animal?*

Quite clearly, it is behavioral attributes that most dramatically set humans apart. Human culture is our strategy for coping with life's challenges. No other primate even comes close to the human ability to modify environments. Communication through symbolic language is yet another uniquely human characteristic (see pp. 326–328 for a discussion of "language" in great apes). In addition, several other features differentiate humans from the majority of other primates. These are summarized below, but keep in mind that any one of the following may be found in one or another primate species. While all of these are part of human behavior,

---

*"Our species is unique because, in only 35,000 years or so, we have revolutionized the face of the Earth. We have created entirely new environments for ourselves, have changed the lives of animals, and have the power to threaten the existence of life on our planet" (Passingham, 1982, p. 21).

there is no other primate species of which this may be said. For example, humans are bipedal; however, apes occasionally walk bipedally, but not regularly. All primates learn, as do all mammals, but none learn nearly as much as humans, and so forth.

Humans are bipedal.

Humans live in permanent bisexual social groups with males often bonded to females.

Humans have large brains relative to body weight and are capable of *complex* learning.

Partly as a consequence of neurological reorganization, humans make *highly advanced* use of symbolic language.

Also related to neurological developments and bipedality, *cultural* response has become the *central* hominid adaptive strategy.

Humans obtain food through some male/female division of labor; moreover, food is actively transported back to a base camp (home) for purposes of sharing.

There is a relaxation of the estrous cycle and concealed ovulation in humans, so that females can be sexually receptive throughout the year.

These traits are fairly characteristic of all modern humans. Moreover, much of this behavioral complex is thought to be a good *baseline* for the early stages of hominid emergence. In fact, behavioral reconstructions are often central to theories explaining how hominids came to be hominids in the first place.

A recent comprehensive reconstruction of the factors influencing human origins has been proposed by C. Owen Lovejoy (1981).* The Lovejoy model attempts to integrate the behavioral and structural modifications that prevailed during the earliest stages of hominid emergence (10–5 mya). A "prime mover," according to Lovejoy, was the selective advantage of increased male parental investment.

Lovejoy sees ecological strategies of early hominids based on some *division of labor*, where males and females exploited slightly different resources. This pattern was elaborated further as males ranged farther away (particularly in search of high-quality foods, such as meat), while females remained closer to a central rendezvous point, which eventually became a base camp. With females staying closer to a fixed base, they would avoid carrying their infants long distances, thus reducing infant mortality. While females are thought to have ranged closer to camp, gathering wild plant foods and perhaps small mammals, they alone presumably could not provide sufficient subsistence for themselves and several young. The solution, Lovejoy believes, lay in male provisioning—bringing food back to the base camp for purposes of sharing. This key aspect concerning active transport of food to a central point in order to be shared is not seen in any other primate. The same idea had also been put forth by Glynn Isaac (1976, 1978) as a significant influence on early human emergence.

With males investing more, females could raise more young than would otherwise be the case. Thus, birth spacing could be reduced, and hominid males and

---

*Lovejoy's model is given simply as one of a number of scholarly suggestions of human origins. Many anthropologists disagree with this interpretation and organization of the data. The authors do not necessarily agree with Lovejoy's point of view.

Social behavior Exhibiting gregariousness, sociability. The behavior of animals that live together in, and interact as, a group consisting of adults and young of both sexes.

Polygyny (po-lyj′-y-nee)
poly: much, many
gyn: female
One male and two or more females in a mating relationship.

females behaving in this way would consequently increase their reproductive success.

Several males returning to the females at the base camp might encourage male-male competition, but this could possibly be diffused by the development of one-to-one male/female bonding; i.e., a monogamous relationship (an idea championed by Desmond Morris, 1967).

Bipedality* (probably the first major distinction of hominids) would have evolved because the male carrying food to his female would have to do so bipedally. Bipedality in the female would be adaptive because she could carry an infant in one arm, and provision herself with the other.

For this system to work, it would be necessary for the male to carry food to his female throughout the year. He would have to be permanently attracted to her, not just at the time of estrus. This could be arranged through the development of permanent features on the female's body, such as hair, skin, shape, and prominent breasts, which would permanently attract the male and keep him interested the year-round (also proposed by Morris). According to Lovejoy's model, distinctive human traits, such as bipedality, pair bonding, food sharing, and sexual and reproductive behavior, are thus explained.

The Lovejoy model proposes a comprehensive and internally consistent explanation of human origins. However, it is not a scientific theory, since it cannot be framed into testable hypotheses. More appropriately, Lovejoy's assertions (just as those of others before him—Desmond Morris, Robert Ardrey, and so forth) could be termed a *scenario*, a speculative reconstruction. Since **social behavior** does not fossilize (except for some tantalizing hints—see Chapter 13), it is unlikely that we will be able to fully reconstruct the details of early hominid biosocial evolution. If anything, the physical evidence of the early hominids themselves (Chapter 14) suggests that some of the central premises in Lovejoy's scenario are probably wrong.

However, the Lovejoy model is extremely useful in highlighting some of the major differences between humans and other primates. Sometime during the course of human evolution, the complex of features discussed in this scenario did emerge. We mainly disagree with Lovejoy, though, concerning the *sequence* and *timing* of these behavioral modifications. Unlike Lovejoy, we do not believe it likely (or even probable) that very early hominids were paired monogamously. The other developments—bipedalism, increased meat exploitation, food sharing, and greater parental investment (by males, too, but indirectly)—could very well all have proceeded in a **polygynously** mating, early hominid society similar to the vast majority of living primates.

Nonhuman Primates

Modern African apes and humans last shared an ancestor in common somewhere between 8–5 mya according to most experts. Researchers believe that ape behavior has changed since then, but not nearly as much as the behavior of

---

*There are other explanations for the origin of bipedality. Tanner, for example, suggests that bipedality may have been the result of sexual selection, a theme developed by Darwin. Females may have been attracted to males who exhibited bipedalism. Obvious visual cues, such as male genitalia, "could have attracted female attention and action" (1981, pp. 165–166).

FIGURE 10-1   These baboons have adapted quadrupedally to a terrestrial savanna life.

hominids, who developed culture as their strategy of adaptation. Therefore, if we are interested in what hominid behavior might have been like before culture became a significant factor, and if we wish to know what behaviors may have led hominids to become dependent on culture, we may find clues in the behavior of our closest relatives, the nonhuman primates.

The social behavior of nonhuman primates may be viewed as a simplified model of human behavior. The shorter life span of nonhuman primates allows us to follow their behavior through developmental stages with more ease than a similar study of human behavior would provide. As intimated, nonhuman primate behavior provides clues to, or suggests ideas about, what early hominid behavior may have been like. This approach emphasizes correlating particular social structures of given animals with attributes of their habitats, since all living organisms must adapt to their environment (Figs. 10-1 and 10-2). Such observations may offer hints to the environmental pressures involved and may ultimately lead to comprehending the factors that led to human emergence (see pp. 262–264).

Studies of nonhuman primates also assist with present human behavioral problems. Humans are *not* monkeys or apes, of course, but similarities do exist. For example, the way human infants learn to love and bond to mother and then family is reflected in the infant behavior patterns of monkeys and apes. It is, after all, possible that "The more we can learn about the evolutionary history and adaptations of other primate forms, the more we will know about the processes which shaped our own species" (Lancaster, 1975, p. 5).

Species of primates are numerous, and their behavior varies a good deal. Nevertheless, there are characteristics common to most, if not all, primates. Most primates live in tropical or semitropical regions, but a few, such as the Japanese

FIGURE 10-2 Chimpanzee family, a long-term cohesive unit. These individuals associate often throughout their lives (see Chapter 11).

Diurnal Active during the day.

Crepuscular (kre-pus´-kew-ler) creper: dark, dusty Active at twilight or dawn.

Nocturnal Active at night.

macaque and some langurs, have adapted to cold weather. Although they vary, primates are mainly **diurnal**, a few are **crepuscular** and others, especially among prosimians, are **nocturnal**. Relatively few nonhuman primates are terrestrial—savanna baboons and gorillas are the best known; most others are arboreal. Intelligence, a difficult concept to define, is another characteristic common to primates, and it is generally conceded that all primates are more intelligent than most, if not all, other mammals.

Living in social groups (see Box 10-1) is one of the major characteristics of primates, who solve their major adaptive problems within this social context. For other animals, "mating, feeding, sleeping, growth of the individual, and protection from pedators are usually matters for the solitary individual to solve, but for . . . primates they are most often performed in a social context" (Lancaster, 1975, p. 12).

Many different patterns of social groupings exist among the primates. Typically, the primate social group includes members of all ages and of both sexes, a composition that does not vary significantly during the annual cycle. This situation differs from that of most mammals, whose adult males and females associate only during the breeding season, and whose young of either sex do not usually remain with the adults after reaching puberty.

Because they remain together over a long period of time, members of the specific primate group learn to know each other. They learn—as they must—how to respond to a variety of actions that may be threatening, cooperative, or indifferent. In such social groups, individuals must be able to evaluate a situation before acting. Evolutionarily speaking, this would have placed selective pressure on social intelligence which, in turn, would select for brains that could assess such situations and store the information. One of the results of such selection would be the evolution of proportionately larger and more complex brains, especially in the higher primates.

BOX 10-1

Types of Nonhuman Primate Social Groups*

1. *One-male*. A single adult male, several adult females, and their offspring. This is the commonest primate mating structure, in which only one male actively breeds (Jolly, 1985). Usually formed by a male or males joining a kin group of females. Females usually form the permanent nucleus of the group. Examples: guenons, orangs, gorillas, some pottos, some spider monkeys, patas.

2. *Multimale*. Several adult males, several adult females, and their young. Several of the males reproduce. The presence of several males in the group may lead to tension and to a dominance hierarchy. Examples: some lemurs, macaques, mangabeys, savanna baboons, vervets, squirrel monkeys, spider monkeys, chimpanzees.

3. *Family, or monogamous*. A mated pair and their young. Usually arboreal, minimal sexual dimorphism, frequently territorial. Adults usually do not tolerate other adults of the same sex. Not found among great apes, and least common of the breeding structures among nonhuman primates. Examples: gibbons, indris, titis, sakis, owl monkeys, pottos.

---

*These are called breeding groups by Jolly and permanent groupings by Napier and Napier. There are also other groupings, such as foraging groups, hunting groups, all female or male groups, and so on. Like humans, nonhuman primates do not always maintain one kind of group; single male groups may sometimes form multimale groups and vice versa. The gelada and hamadryas baboons, for example, are listed here as one-male groups but "form herds of 100 or more at night when they move towards the safety of the steep cliffs where they sleep" (Napier and Napier, 1985, p. 61). Also variability is seen in other forms, for example, red colobus monkeys (see p. 272).

SOURCE

Jolly, 1985; Napier and Napier, 1985.

Primate Field Studies

While other disciplines, such as psychology and zoology, have long been concerned with nonhuman primates, the study of these animals in their *natural habitats* has primarily become a focus of anthropology. Early work—that done before World War II—was especially stimulated through the influence of the American psychologist Robert Yerkes, who in the late 1920s and 1930s sent students out to the field to study gorillas, chimpanzees, and howler monkeys. It was the last of these studies by Clarence Ray Carpenter (along with his work on gibbons) that stands out particularly as a hallmark of early primate field investigations.

American anthropologists became vitally involved somewhat later—the 1950s—following the lead established by Sherwood Washburn who, with his colleague, Irven DeVore, carried out a pioneering study of savanna baboons in the late 1950s. At about the same time, Phyllis Dolhinow was researching langurs in India and George Schaller was collecting data on mountain gorillas in Africa. And, of course, there is the famous research that Jane Goodall began with chimpanzees in 1960 (see p. 317). In addition, primate studies were also being pursued in the 1950s by Japanese anthropologists, who actively began their long-term study of Japanese macaques in 1952 (see p. 324). They have since extended their fieldwork to include numerous other species elsewhere in Asia and Africa.

The key aspect of these field studies is that they attempt to collect and synthesize information on **free-ranging** animals. That is, the animals are in their "natural" settings in which they travel, feed, mate, and so forth without severe constraints imposed by humans.

Free-ranging Applied to animals living in their natural habitat.

Artificially provisioned   Food is made available to primates by humans.

Socioecology   The study of primates and their habitats; specifically, attempts to find patterns of relationship between the environment and primate social behavior.

Several points, however, must be kept in mind. Free-ranging does not necessarily imply that these animals remain uninfluenced by human activities. It is highly unlikely that there is a single group of nonhuman primates anywhere in the world that has not experienced some human interference. Indeed, the incredibly rapid destruction of tropical rainforests (see pp. 291–295) now threatens the very existence of most primates. Moreover, while "free-ranging" implies that animals move about on their own volition to find food, in several cases (Japanese macaque studies, Jane Goodall's work at Gombe Stream) the animals have been **artificially provisioned** by the observers. This means, of course, that some of their food comes from other than normal or natural sources. We would also expect that the different levels of provisioning employed would affect the free-ranging behavior of the animals in foraging and other activities.

Why, then, is artificial provisioning practiced? The answer relates to the difficulties involved in following free-ranging primates. As discussed in Chapter 9, most species of nonhuman primates live in the tropical rainforests of the Americas, Africa, and Asia. Dense foliage and ground cover severely inhibit the movement of observers as they attempt to follow their study animals. Perhaps even worse, these animals are usually high up in the forest canopy, obscured from vision, and are often moving rapidly. Then there are almost invariably numerous individuals in a social group who can be expected to exhibit highly individualistic behaviors. The problem: How does one recognize individuals under such field conditions? In fact, individuals frequently cannot be recognized accurately, so that the best that can be accomplished is to record the sex and age of the animals. Some provisioning of the study animals draws them into the open, where they can be observed and recognized.

Because of these problems, the most systematic information thus far collected on free-ranging animals comes from species that spend considerable time on the

FIGURE 10-3   Black-and-white colobus monkeys high up in the forest canopy. Can you spot the animals? Imagine trying to recognize them as individuals!

ground (including langurs, gorillas, chimps) and most especially those species that travel and feed frequently in open (i.e., mostly treeless) country (for example, macaques, baboons, vervet monkeys, patas monkeys). Note that the selection and emphasis on certain species in this and the next chapter reflect this research bias.

Another research tack pursued by some anthropologists involves studying primates not in their natural habitats but rather in large provisioned colonies, where at least some movement, group dynamics, etc. are possible. Probably the best example of this type of research is the long-term study of rhesus macaques conducted on Cayo Santiago Island off the coast of Puerto Rico. First established in 1938, the island population now totals close to 1,000 individuals (Richard, 1985).

Despite significant gaps in our knowledge about many aspects of primate behavior, we nevertheless presently have field data on more than 100 nonhuman primate species. The information from this fascinating and rapidly advancing discipline of primatology forms the remainder of this chapter.

FIGURE 10-4 Rhesus monkeys. Part of the large colony on Cayo Santiago Island.

The Ecology of Nonhuman Primates

For those anthropologists who study free-ranging primates, the key considerations have always been (1) to characterize the nature of the animals' environments and (2) to hypothesize how these environments shape primate social behavior.

Early on, researchers routinely recorded the types of food eaten, the distances traveled to get to food/water/sleeping sites, the size of groups, the composition of groups, and so on. In the 1970s, an emerging perspective called **socioecology** grew out of this approach and looked at such factors as the following regarding the possible effects on primate social groups:

1. Quantity and quality of different kinds of food (caloric value, digestive energy required, net value to the animals)
2. Activity patterns: Are the animals nocturnal or diurnal?
3. Distribution of food resources (widely spread or tightly packed?)
4. Distribution of water
5. Distribution of predators
6. Distribution of sleeping sites

A great deal of enthusiasm resulted from this approach and led to new research directions as well as attempts to synthesize the information in order to discern broad patterns for the entire order. Initially, schemes were relatively simple and attempted to show very broad aspects of ecological/behavioral correlations (Crook and Gartlan, 1966; Crook, 1970; Eisenberg et al., 1972). Rather quickly, as more data accumulated, it became obvious that primates in the wild displayed considerably more variability of social behavior than these simple schemes could accommodate.

As a result, more sophisticated approaches have evolved (Clutton-Brock and Harvey, 1977; Richard, 1985). Primatologists now view ecology, behavior, and biology as complexly interdependent. In addition to the general ecological factors listed above, primatologists must also consider an animal's body size, relative brain size, metabolism, reproductive physiology, the distribution of food resources into "food patches," and the nutritional value of foods and how they are selected and processed. (See Fleagle, 1988, for a good discussion of these factors.)

FIGURE 10-5 Rhesus monkeys in India. These "urban" monkeys have adapted well to new environmental challenges—reflecting the behavioral flexibility characteristic of many primates.

Moreover, the variability exhibited between closely related species (and even *within* the same species) in ecological adaptations must be understood. Also, the way primates relate to their overall surrounding biological communities, especially to other species of primates, must be described. Indeed, it is a common phenomenon for many prosimian and monkey species to travel, and to socially relate over long periods with other primate species. Do they eat different foods? How do they efficiently subdivide their habitat? These questions, too, must be addressed. Lastly, it is of interest to study why primates select certain foods and avoid others. What is the nutritional value of insects, fruits, leaves, nuts, gums, small mammals, etc., that are available to them? What toxins exist in certain plant foods that could do harm? Thus, as a central focus of ecology, let us turn to the diets of nonhuman primates.

WHAT DO PRIMATES EAT?

Certainly a basic way any animal relates to its environment concerns the foods it finds and eats. We mentioned in Chapter 9 that primates are omnivorous, implying they eat many plant and animal foods. But as Alison Richard has pointed out (1985, p. 167), omnivory is rarely carefully defined—and, as such, does not constitute a particularly useful concept.

It is more productive, then, to describe in some detail what primates actually eat. Of course, most primate species do in fact have quite diversified diets. For example, macaques (e.g., Japanese macaques, rhesus macaques), like most primates, are primarily vegetarians. Yet, when we consider ground cover accumulation of snow (which is an important seasonal factor for some macaques), we can see that very different foods may be exploited. Consequently, in the winter, rhesus macaques in highland Pakistan eat tough plant leaves (oak), pine needles, pine gum, and herb roots. At other times of the year, they eat flower blossoms, fruits, grasses, and seeds (Richard, 1985). This is perhaps an extreme case (for most primates do not live in such seasonal environments, and foods are thus more consistently available). And, in fact, most species do concentrate on a particular combination of food sources. Special terminology has been devised to describe the type of diet as characterized by the most predominant type of food:

1. Insectivore—primarily eats insects
2. Folivore—primarily eats leaves
3. Frugivore—primarily eats fruits
4. Gramnivore—primarily eats seeds
5. Gumnivore—primarily eats gums

Characterizing particular primate species according to this scheme is frequently difficult; yet, some species are easier to classify than others. Chimps in all parts of their range where they have been observed eat primarily fruits (i.e., they are primarily frugivorous). On the other hand, olive baboons (one variety of savanna baboons) show dietary diversity in different areas of their range. In one area of Kenya, they eat primarily grass blades and seeds, but little fruit. In Ethiopia, however, they spend almost half their time eating fruit. Although there are certainly differences in the environment between the two regions, it has been suggested that the dietary differences may also relate to differences in food-harvesting techniques (Richard, 1985). Indeed, such differences in local *traditions* can dramatically influence primate behavior, a point to which we will return in the next chapter.

ENVIRONMENT AND SOCIAL BEHAVIOR

In the remainder of this chapter and in the chapter following, we will discuss various aspects of nonhuman primate social behavior. An ecological focus can, in many ways, be utilized to illuminate much of primate behavior (see Jolly, 1985, and Richard, 1985, for excellent discussions of this perspective). Here, we cannot adequately discuss all the ways primatologists use ecological, behavioral, and biological data. Nor can we completely summarize the huge amount of information that has accumulated in recent years. What is important, however, is to get a sense of how this approach is used currently by primatologists; hence, we will discuss a comprehensive example of such primate ecological research.

Five Monkey Species in the Kibale Forest, Uganda   One of the most detailed and controlled studies of primate socioecology has been undertaken in the Kibale Forest of western Uganda (Struhsaker and Leyland, 1979). The five species thus far studied in detail are all varieties of Old World monkeys and include black-and-white colobus (*Colobus guereza*), red colobus (*Colobus badius*), mangabey (*Cercocebus albigena*), blue monkey (*Cercopithecus mitus*), and the redtail monkey (*Cercopithecus ascanius*). In addition to these five Old World monkey species, there are also in the Kibale Forest two other monkey species (*Ceropithecus* and the "savanna baboon"), as well as the potto, two species of galago, and the chimpanzee (for a discussion of the latter, see Ghiglieri, 1984). Indeed, there are eleven different species of nonhuman primates at Kibale and together they display the greatest number of total individuals and highest primate biomass for any site yet described (Waser, 1988). Comparisons are facilitated in this study because all species were sampled using similar methodologies. This avoids the pitfall of making comparisons between highly variable research strategies, a problem usually unavoidable in making cross-species comparisons. Moreover, the research at Kibale is important because this region is probably the least disturbed habitat where primates have been studied long-term.

While sympatric, numerous fascinating differences exist among the five species. Body weights vary considerably (3–4 kg for redtails and up to 7–10 kg for the mangabey and colobus species). Diet also differs at a gross level, with the two colobus species eating primarily leaves (i.e., they are folivorous) and the other three species showing more dietary diversity: concentration on fruits supplemented by insects.

At the same time, several aspects of social organization varied among the five species. For example, the red colobus and mangabey had several adult males in the group, while only one fully adult male was typically present in the other species. Furthermore, all five species occasionally had solitary males moving independently of the bisexual groups, but bachelor groups (consisting solely of adult and subadult males) did not typically form (as has been observed in other primates, such as langurs and gelada baboons). Even among the multimale bisexual groups there is a marked difference. In mangabeys, the females are the permanent core of the group (with males transferring out), while in red colobus, it is the females who transfer (with the males remaining the long-term residents). (Struh-

FIGURE 10-6   Kibale Forest habitat, Uganda.

saker and Leyland, 1987.) Indeed, there is so much variability that Struhsaker and Leyland could find little correlation between social organization and gross feeding ecology.

More detailed analysis of feeding patterns showed even further differences. For instance, while both colobus species eat mostly leaves, they still exploit different resources. (Black-and-white colobus eat considerably mature leaf blades, some high in protein; red colobus, on the other hand, eat a wider variety of leaves, but usually not mature ones, as well as fruits and shoots.) Perhaps correlated with these dietary differences are the observations that black-and-white colobus spend less time feeding but more time resting and, in contrast, red colobus range further and live in higher density (i.e., higher biomass). In addition, some species show dramatic variability from month to month. Among redtail monkeys, the proportion of fruit in the monthly diet varies from as low as 13% to as much as 81% (Richard, 1985).

Ecological patterns and social ramifications are unquestionably most complicated. In the same forest at Kibale, the closely related species black-and-white colobus and red colobus show marked differences in social organization. Yet in another area (the Tana River Forest of Kenya), red colobus have only one-male groups (like black-and-white at Kibale) and *both* males and females transfer (unlike either colobus species at Kibale) (Richard, 1985). The distinct impression one gathers from attempts to find correlations is that most primate species are exceedingly flexible, a fact that makes generalizing an extremely tentative undertaking at best.

Still, the highly controlled nature of the Kibale study makes some comparisons and provisional generalizations such as the following possible:

1. The omnivores (mangabeys, redtails, blues) locomoted more than the folivores (the two colobus)

2. Among the omnivores there is an inverse relationship of body size and group size; also among the omnivores, there is a direct relationship of body size with home range (area exploited, see p. 302)

3. Omnivores were spatially more spread than folivores

4. Female sexual swelling (see p. 250) was obvious only in those species (red colobus and mangabeys) that lived in multimale groups

5. Feeding, spacing, group residency, dispersal, and reproductive strategies may be very different for males and females of the same species. These considerations have become a central focus of ecological and sociobiological research (see p. 289).

Because of the complexity of the social relationships among primates, long-term studies are absolutely necessary. As Struhsaker and Leyland conclude from their studies at Kibale, "Meaningful data on group dynamics and probable degree of genetic relatedness among the members can only be collected by observing groups for at least half the adult life span, which for most Old World monkeys means a period of five to six years" (1979, p. 222). Alison Richard (1985) is even more conservative in generalizing about long-term ecological patterns. She suggests such patterns should be observed at least as long as the periodicity of cycles of critical resources. For Old World monkeys, then, as much as ten generations might be required—a total of up to eighty years of study!

Clearly, the kinds of data now emerging from primate ecological research (and its manifold social and biological connections) pose tremendous interest and opportunities for primatologists. However, the challenges involved in collecting such data are equally great.

Social Behavior

Since primates solve their major adaptive problems in a social context, we might expect that they participate in a number of activities to reinforce the integrity of the group for purposes of holding it together. The better known of these activities are described in the sections that follow.

ASPECTS OF SOCIAL BEHAVIOR

Grooming Almost all primates groom one another. **Grooming** occurs in other animal species, but social grooming is a unique primate activity and plays an important role in the life of most primates. It is hygienic since it removes ectoparasites, dead skin, and debris from the skin and fur, but it is much more than that. It has been called a social lubricant because it eases the interaction between male/female and higher/lower rank, where there is a possibility of friction. It has also been called "the social cement of primates from lemur to chimpanzee" (Jolly, 1984, p. 207) since it helps in maintaining the organization of the group. Grooming is often reciprocal with roles interchanged—the groomer may become the groomee, a process resulting in the establishment of friendly social relations among the animals in the group.

Grooming Cleaning through the hair and fur.

(a)

(b)

(c)

(d)

FIGURE 10-7   Grooming primates.
(a) vervet monkeys; (b) patas monkeys;
(c) black-and-white colobus monkeys;
(d) chimpanzees.

Displays   A wide variety of body movements, vocalizations, olfactory signals (scent-marking, for example), and facial gestures communicate to other members of the species such emotional signals as fear, threats, greeting, danger, pain, hunger, courtship, and many other messages as well.

Animals often **display** when they are excited, a state that may be brought about by such situations as the presence of an outsider, a response to the display of another member of the group, or for reinforcing status relationships. The gorilla is known for its magnificent display involving such activities as hooting, throwing vegetation, and chest beating.

Displays of other primates include grunting, yawning, ground slapping, branch-shaking, head bobbing and bouncing, screams, hoots, strutting, scratching, barks, scent-marking (among prosimians), and facial gestures, such as smiling and grimacing. A display primarily communicates information that "is advantageous to the individual of the species, to the social group to which he belongs, to others of the same species, and to other species" (Buettner-Janusch, 1973, p. 307).

Dominance* **Dominance** rank, or status rank, may be measured by priority access to a desired object, such as food or sex, and also by the result of threat situations. A dominant individual is given priority, and in a confrontation is the one that usually does not give way. It is believed, although not all primatologists agree, that because dominant males compete more successfully for fertile females than do subordinate males, they have greater reproductive success. Also, dominant females, because they compete for food more successfully than subordinate females, are thus provided with more energy for offspring production and have greater reproductive success than subordinate females (Fedigan, 1983).

In many primate societies males are generally dominant over females of the same age, older or stronger individuals supplant weaker ones, and each group member must learn its rank in the hierarchy, at least within its own sex and age class. "Further, the length of time spent in the group, called 'residence' or male 'tenure,' also correlates significantly with rank, positively in the case of macaques

---

*See Fedigan, 1983, for a review of dominance theory.

Display Stereotyped behavior that serves to communicate emotional states between individuals. Display is most often associated with reproductive or agonistic behavior.

Dominance Also referred to as *dominance hierarchy* and *status* rank. The physical domination of some members of a group by other members. A hierarchy of ranked statuses sustained by hostile, or threat of hostile, behavior, which may result in greater access to resources, such as sleeping sites, food, and mates.

FIGURE 10-8 (*a*) A gorilla display; (*b*) a chimp display. The old male rocks side-to-side, swings his arms, often takes a running start, and throws objects at zoo spectators.

(*a*)

(*b*)

Consortship   Exclusive relationship of one adult male and one adult female (usually, but not always, in estrus).

Mother-infant relationship   The attachment between mother and her offspring. One of the most basic themes running through primate social relations.

. . . and negatively with the case of baboons" (Fedigan, 1983, pp. 111–112). Dominant males are sometimes responsible for protecting the troop from predators as well as for defense against other troops if that situation should arise. They may also, as in savanna baboons, act as "policemen" to break up fights among juveniles, females, and other adult males within their troop.

Dominance is adaptive because it operates to avoid conflict, obviously essential for animals living in permanent social groups. When two individuals compete for the same scarce item, the dominant one assumes priority by threat behavior. Thus dominance serves to organize social interactions; individuals know where they belong and act accordingly, avoiding chaotic, unorganized social relations. The result is a more or less smoothly functioning order of priority, which reduces endless quarrels and potentially dangerous conflicts for scarce resources.

Mother-Infant Relationship   The basic social unit among primates is the female and her infants, Adult males **consort** with females for mating purposes, but they may or may not participate as members of the social unit. Observations both in the field and in captivity suggest that this mother-offspring core provides the group with its stability.

The **mother-infant attachment**, one of the most basic themes running throughout primate social relations, begins at birth. A primate infant's first bond (in the anthropoids especially) is to its mother. After birth, the infant clings to its mother while she performs her daily activities, often without seeming regard for her offspring's success in holding on. Quite often, however, as she leaves for some activity, a mother will gather her infant protectively to her body. Unlike other social animals, in which the newborn are left in a nest or den, the clinging primate infant develops a closeness with the mother that does not end with weaning. This closeness is often maintained throughout life and is reflected in grooming behavior that continues between mother and offspring even after the children reach adulthood.

FIGURE 10-9   Primate mothers and their infants.

The crucial role played by primate mothers was clearly demonstrated by the Harlows, (1959), who raised some infant monkeys with surrogate mothers fash-

ioned from cloth and other monkeys with no mothers at all. In one experiment, infants raised with surrogate mothers retained an attachment to their cloth mother, but those raised without a mother were incapable of forming a lasting affectional tie.

In another experiment (Harlow and Harlow, 1961), monkeys raised without a mother sat passively in their cages and stared vacantly into space. Some punished themselves by seizing one of their arms with the mouth and tearing the flesh until blood flowed. Those raised with a surrogate mother acted similarly, but somewhat less dramatically. None of the males or females raised without real or surrogate mothers ever achieved any semblance of normal sexual behavior. No motherless male ever successfully copulated, and he often violently assaulted the female with whom he was paired. Females (those raised without mothers as well as those raised with cloth mothers) that were successfully impregnated and bore young, paid very little attention to their infants. A mother often brushed away her baby "as if she were brushing off flies" or crushed her infant to the floor, and these mothers rarely held their infants or protected them as normal mothers do.

The Harlows conclude: "We only know that these monkeys without normal mothering and without peer affectional relationships have behaved toward their infants in a manner completely outside the range of even the least adequate of normal mothers" (1961, p. 55).

In more recent studies, Professor Suomi of the University of Wisconsin Primate Laboratory and a student of Harlow, has confirmed the importance of the mother-infant relationship. Even brief separations from the mother have lasting effects. He further points out that peer relationships suffer if the individual does not have a good relationship with its mother (Greenberg, 1977). His review of isolation studies has led Suomi to emphasize that social isolation initiated early in life can have devastating effects on subsequent development and behavior for many spe-

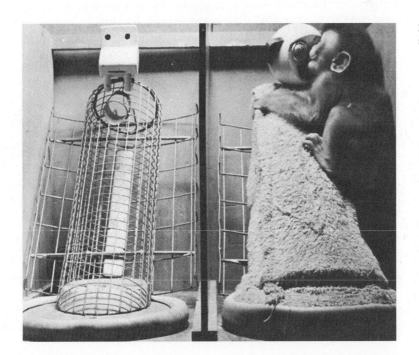

FIGURE 10-10   Wire mother and cloth mother.

Allo Combining form indicating different or other.

Nulliparous null: none, not any
parous: birth
Never having given birth.

cies of primates. The primate deprivation syndrome that results from early isolation is characterized by displays of abnormal self-directed and stereotypic behavior and by gross deficits in all aspects of social behavior (Suomi, 1982, p. 190).

Infants are mainly cared for by the mother, of course, but adult males are also known to take more than a casual interest. This phenomenon has frequently been noted among male hamadryas baboons, who sometimes "adopt" an infant. "He then carries it en route, allows it to sleep huddled against his belly at night, and prevents it from moving too far away" (Kummer, 1971, pp. 81–82). Even more dramatically in the New World, among marmosets and tamarins the males provide most of the direct infant care, carrying the infants everywhere, while only transferring them back to their mother for nursing.

What may be an extension of the mother-infant relationship has been called **allo**parent, or "aunt" behavior. This type of behavior occurs among many animal species but is most richly expressed in primates, and some researchers believe it is found among all social primates. Usually, the alloparents crowd around the newborn infant and attempt to carry, cuddle, groom, hold, or just touch it. Some species, like the common langur, are well known for their aunts, and as many as eight females may hold the infant during its first day of life. Among patas monkeys, the mother may threaten a female that touches her baby, so the interested female resorts to a subtle maneuver. "A patas female may begin to groom a mother's arm and then slowly and cautiously transfer her grooming to the infant within it" (Kummer, 1971, p. 80).

Several functions are suggested for alloparenting. If the mother dies, the infant stands a chance of being adopted by an alloparent or other individual of the group. The practice may bind together the adults of the group, since it may be more convenient for the mother to leave her infant occasionally with another female. It may also assist the training of **nulliparous** females for motherhood.

Male-Female Sexual Bond A close sexual bond between adult males and females is not common among the higher primates, although it does occur. In the one-male group, the adult male keeps his females close to him and maintains a very alert eye for any wandering adult male. Some researchers suggest that the one-male group is adaptive in arid regions where food is scarce and widely scattered, and attack by predators a constant peril. An adult male is protection for the females and offspring, and the structure of only one male to a group diminishes the consumption of scarce food resources.

Forest monkey groups, such as the black-and-white colobus, are also often composed of one-male groups. Here, food is no great problem and predators hunt by stealth. The best defense is constant vigilance by all concerned. The adult male's role, therefore, is minimal, and one male is adequate for protective and reproductive functions. And, as we shall see shortly, with only one male present, there is less competition for food, leaving more for females with dependent young.

The one-male/one-female "monogamous" or family group is characteristic of gibbons (but not great apes) and some monkeys, and can be understood in terms of adaptation to their environment. A gibbon family—one adult male, one adult female, and their offspring—controls a small patch of tropical forest, which provides enough food for a small group. Gibbons jealously protect this territory from neighbors. When a young gibbon reaches maturity, it is driven out by the adult of

FIGURE 10-11   Hamadryas one-male
groups.

the same sex, thus maintaining the small size of the group and its limited food
supply.

Role Separation between Adults and Young   Among primates, especially
the higher primates, there is a relatively long growth period spent in the protected
environment of the social group. It is during this learning stage, when the young
play and learn the skills needed in adulthood, that the brain develops the special
intelligence characteristic of primates. This learning period is spent in physical
and psychological safety because of the behavioral and psychological separation
of roles between adults and young. The young play for many hours every day,
learning many of the skills required by adults, free from anxiety because alert
adults are always present. The separation of roles between adults and young enable the young to learn and practice the social, intellectual, and physical skills they
will need as adults.

Role Separation by Sex   Perhaps one of the most interesting points to be made
about the separation of sex roles is that there is often very little separation. Except
for the protective role played by males and the childbearing and nursing role of
the mother, in many primate species both sexes perform similar functions. Females are expected to obtain their own food, as are juveniles after they are
weaned, and there is little sharing of food.

   Among terrestrial primates, there is very often a sexual dimorphism in body
size, weight, muscularity, distribution of hair on the body, and size of canines.
Usually associated with separate roles, the larger size (as in baboons and gorillas)
enables the male to play a dominant and protective role. In those species without
sexual dimorphism, the females may be highly aggressive, as in gibbons, and join
the males in defense of their territory.

Sociobiology

The sociobiological perspective has recently become widely used in primatology. In the last decade, this approach has been applied to a wide variety of animals, including nonhuman primates (see Barash, 1982, for a good general review of sociobiology). Indeed, for primatological interpretations, sociobiology holds a central position as a theoretical framework for a majority of current researchers (for example, Richard, 1985; Richard and Schulman, 1982; Smuts, 1985; Small, 1984; Hausfater and Hrdy, 1984; Ghiglieri, 1984; Pusey and Packer, 1987; Smuts, 1987; Harvey et al., 1987). Beyond the suppositions concerning nonhuman primates, some contemporary scholars even go so far as to extend this field to the interpretation of *human* primates as well.* Naturally, not all primatologists, and certainly not all anthropologists, are sociobiologists. Indeed, sociobiology has created and continues to generate a great deal of controversy.

First brought to popular attention in 1975 by Harvard zoologist E. O. Wilson, this approach can be traced to the pioneering works of R. A. Fisher (1930), J. B. S. Haldane (1932), W. D. Hamilton (1964), G. C. Williams (1966), and Robert Trivers (1971, 1972). Following publication of Wilson's monumental synthesis, vehement arguments exploded both inside and outside academia. What has caused all this furor, and what relevance does sociobiology have to understanding primates, particularly human primates?

Sociobiologists are basically classical Darwinists, postulating the evolution of behavior through operation of natural selection. Sociobiologists assume that, if any behavior has a genetic basis, its evolutionary impact will be directly measured by its effect on reproductive success. In other words, with behavioral phenotypes (just as with physical morphology), the success of genes underlying the phenotypes will be determined by their influence on reproduction. Individuals with genotypes coding for behaviors leading to higher reproductive success than other individuals will, by definition, be more fit. Consequently, they should pass on their genes at a faster rate. Sociobiologists believe genotypes have evolved in this way, producing such phenomena as sterile worker castes in bees, courtship dances in birds, and scent-marking in dogs. As a speculative model, this reasoning is all well and good. In fact, much of the theoretical way natural selection is discussed in Chapter 2 of this text utilizes terminology and concepts developed by sociobiologists.

When applied to relatively simple organisms—social insects, for example—sociobiological theory has proven of tremendous explanatory value. In fact, recent sophisticated molecular biological research with the DNA of marine snails has identified a family of genes that produce specific proteins whose combined action in turn governs the animal's egg-laying behavior (Scheller and Axel, 1984). This is of note because, for the first time, something that could be termed "complex" behavior has been traced to a specific genetic mechanism (i.e., DNA sequences that have been decoded).

Of course, neither insects nor snails are mammals (to say nothing of primates). The major dispute arises, then, when trying to postulate the actual mechanics of

---

*Some recent publications reflect this trend. See *Child Abuse and Neglect*, Gelles and Lancaster, 1987; *Parenting Across the Life Span*, Lancaster et al., 1987; *The Biology of Moral Systems*, Alexander, 1987; *Homicide*, Daly and Wilson, 1987; *Despotism and Differential Reproduction*, Betzig, 1987.

behavioral evolution in complex social animals with flexible neurological responses like primates. Which behaviors among primates have a genetic basis, and how do these behaviors influence reproductive success?

In order to answer the first question, we will have to learn considerably more about genotype/phenotype interactions in complex traits. Such an understanding is probably decades away. To answer the second question, we will need accurate data on reproductive success in primate groups similar to that shown for birds in Chapter 2 (p. 41). As of yet, such data are almost completely lacking, but it is hoped this situation will be remedied in the near future. Thus, sociobiology as an *explanation* of primate behavior remains mostly a matter of open speculation. Application of evolutionary models specifically to explain human behavior are presently even more hypothetical.

Obtaining conclusive data for primates and other mammals, we will see, is no easy matter. A good starting point, however, is framing hypotheses concerning behavioral evolution on the basis of the evidence that does exist. A good example of such a perspective is Sarah Blaffer Hrdy's (1977) explanation of infanticide among langur monkeys of India.

Langurs typically live in social groups composed of one adult male, several females, and their offspring (sometimes called a "harem"). Other males without mates associate in bachelor groups. These peripheral males occasionally attack a harem, violently overthrow the previous reproductive male, and take over the group. Often following this admittedly bloody contest, even more gruesome behavior ensues. The infants, fathered by the previous male, are attacked and killed. The adult females in the group usually try to interfere with the males' infanticidal intentions, but to little avail. In the end, most or all the infants are killed.

Why should langurs behave so? Are they not dooming their species to ultimate extinction by such destructive actions? The answer, according to sociobiologists,

FIGURE 10-12   Langur group in India.

Altruism Helping others without direct benefit to oneself.

is *not* in terms of the species. Male langurs do not know they are members of so-and-so species, nor, if they did, would they care what its future would be. Natural selection theory, as clarified by sociobiology, teaches us that individuals act to maximize their *own* reproductive success, no matter what its ultimate effect on the species.

Ostensibly, that is exactly what the male langur is doing. By killing the infants, he avoids a two to three year wait before the females come back into estrus. Once the infants are dead, the females stop lactating and become reproductively accessible to the newly arrived male. He can then inseminate them much earlier than would have been the case had he waited while the young (in which he had no genetic interest) were reared.

We might reasonably ask why the females should allow their infants to be slaughtered. Actually, females do attempt to resist infanticide, but their efforts in the face of large, aggressive, and determined males usually fail. Interestingly, it is not the infant's mother who assaults the attacking male, but other females in the group. Some writers suggest that these females are closely related (sisters of the mother, for example) and, if so, sociobiological theory provides an explanation for such seemingly **altruistic** behavior. Since individuals share genes with close relatives, they can contribute to their *own* reproductive success by aiding their relatives' offspring.

In diploid species (like langurs, humans, and all vertebrates), individuals share, on the average, ½ their genes with parents and, likewise, ½ with full siblings. For example, when a langur defends her sister's offspring, she is helping contribute genes to the next generation; genes she shares in common with her nieces and nephews (on the average she shares ¼ her genes in common with them). In this way, genes that underlie such cooperative behavior may spread in populations.

Of course, there are many possible strategies. Aiding a relative does not always completely inhibit one's own reproduction. The success of an individual's genes (that is, one's fitness in natural selection terms) is then measured as the sum of one's own offspring *plus* those of close relatives ("discounted" according to how closely they are related: ¼ for her nieces and nephews, half-siblings, or grandchildren, ⅛ for first cousins, etc.).

Langurs are, of course, not doing this consciously. As is true of the cooperative female defense efforts noted above, females are not making conscious choices as if they *knew* the alternatives. What occurs is simply that individuals who behave one way will have higher reproductive success than those individuals behaving in another way. Consequently, their genes (including any that underlie this behavior) are differentially passed onto the next generation, theoretically just another example of natural selection acting on variation.

The social pattern among common (hanuman) langurs is not extremely clear-cut, and controversy thus exists regarding the observations and interpretations of infanticide in this species. Geographically, infanticide has been seen (or logically deduced) at three field sites, but has not been seen at two others. As a result, some experts (most notably, Boggess, 1984) have argued that infanticide is *not* that common, is not adaptive, and could better be described as a "social pathology." As we will see shortly in our discussion of the limitations of sociobiological research (p. 289), controversies such as this are not easy to resolve.

Beyond langurs, however, it must be considered that infanticide is, after all, not that uncommon among primates. Infanticidal episodes have been observed (or surmised) in redtail monkeys, red colobus, blue monkeys (these three from studies at Kibale, see p. 271), savanna baboons, howler monkeys, gorillas, and chimpanzees (Struhsaker and Leyland, 1987), and have been documented in at least 84 human societies. Interestingly, in the majority of these cases (chimps and humans are exceptions), infanticide occurred in conjunction with a male transfer into a group or a change in the status (and reproductive access?) of an adult male. Moreover, in no case has it been thought that a male was attacking one of his own offspring. In both these patterns, the circumstances under which infanticide is seen conform to the expectations of the Hrdy model (what could be termed "sexual selection").

Sociobiological interpretations have also been applied to a wide range of other behaviors seen in primates. For example, the extremely large testes of male chimpanzees have been explained as an adaptation to a fairly promiscuous mating pattern—where several males successfully copulate with an estrous female (a kind of "sperm competition") (Popp and DeVore, 1979). Also, the differential ranging patterns of male and female orangutans have been viewed as the result of differing reproductive strategies between sexes and maximization of food resources (Galdikas, 1979).

MALE AND FEMALE REPRODUCTIVE STRATEGIES

The reproductive strategies of primates, especially how they differ between the sexes, has been a primary focus of sociobiological research. When we consider the tremendous degree of care required by young, growing primate offspring, it is clear that tremendous investment by at least one parent is necessary. Indeed, primates are among the most *K-selected* (i.e., high parental investment in but a few young) of all mammals (see Box 10-3). And, most especially, it is usually the mother who carries most of the burden (before, of course, as well as after birth). Primate offspring are born extremely dependent. They develop slowly (particularly constrained by brain growth), and in so doing, are exposed to expanded learning opportunities within a *social* environment.

Such an interplay between behavior and biology has promoted a feedback relationship that has led to larger brains, even slower development, and yet more chances for learning. Particularly in the large-bodied hominoids (great apes and humans) and most dramatically of all in the hominid line, this trend has been further emphasized, eventually producing the distinctively human primate. Thus, what we see in ourselves and our closest primate kin (and presumably in our more recent ancestors as well) is a strategy wherein a few "high quality," slowly maturing offspring are produced through extraordinary investment by the parent(s), usually the mother. Taken to an extreme, birth spacing (the time between live births following successful rearing or death of the previous offspring) is pushed to the limits in the great apes, with chimps giving birth only every five to six years and gorillas and orangs even more slowly than this. Consequently, a female chimp may only have opportunities for about five live births in her entire reproductive life span, and certainly not all of these are likely to survive into adulthood (a female chimp with three grown children is doing very well indeed). You will recall that Owen Lovejoy's model of early human origins (see p. 263) greatly emphasizes the reproductive limitations imposed on the highly K-selected great apes. Finding food, avoiding predators, finding mates, and especially, caring for and protecting the extremely dependent young are all difficult challenges for

BOX 10-2   CONTEMPORARY STUDIES OF BIOCULTURAL EVOLUTION

The Yanomamö; An Example of a Sociobiological Study of a Human Tribal Society

The Yanomamö are a large group of South American Indians living today mostly in Venezuela, but also in neighboring Brazil. Numbering an estimated 15,000, these tribal peoples are divided into about 200 separate villages (ranging in size from 25 up to 300 people).

Over the last twenty-five years, the Yanomamö have been visited numerous times by American cultural anthropologist Napoleon Chagnon (currently at the University of California, Santa Barbara) who has spent a total of more than four years living among this tribal society. In addition, other researchers (biologists, dentists, linguists, to name several) have been involved at various times in a large multidisciplinary effort to better document and understand the patterns of health, mortality, genetic relatedness, and the effects of acculturation on this population (similar research strategies have also been used in other parts of the world; see pp. 202 and 338 for examples).

Chagnon (1988) has recently reported some fascinating and potentially controversial data gathered over a 23-year period for 12 different villages (total current population: 1,394). As has been documented for other Yanomamö, these peoples are highly warlike, with over 30% of adult male deaths resulting from violence. Indeed, Chagnon carefully—through information obtained from informants—divides males into those who have directly participated in killing someone else (referred to by the Yanomamö as "*unokais*") as compared to those who have never killed ("non-*unokais*"). Another indication that this society is quite violent is indicated by the fact that 44% of adult men in Chagnon's sample (aged 25 or older) were *unokais*.

From his long experience among the Yanomamö as well as consistent reports from informants, Chagnon is unambiguous about the cause of most fights: sexual jealousy over women. The Yanomamö mate polygynously, with some males (particularly headmen) having several wives, while others have no mates. Thus, there is considerable potential for competition among men for wives. Chagnon believes that the vast majority of hostility either *within* or *between* villages (with raids leading to deaths, then revenge raids leading to more deaths, etc.) is caused initially by sexual jealousy.

Moreover, Chagnon has sought to explain this behavior on the basis of sociobiological principles: "But one of the most compelling aspects of Yanomamö social behavior, the feature of this society that puzzled and intrigued me most, was the constant fighting over women and sex. That behavior, more than any other, makes a great deal of sense when considered in terms of Hamilton's theory of inclusive fitness." (Chagnon, 1979, p. 87). In his more recent publication, Chagnon is even more explicit concerning causal factors: "Men who demonstrate their willingness to act violently and exact revenge for the deaths of kin may have higher marital and reproductive success." (Chagnon, 1988, p. 986).

We discuss in this chapter some of the critiques raised regarding sociobiological theory as applied to primates, human and nonhuman. Chagnon has attempted to verify his sociobiological interpretation through use of explicit and quantified data—a sound approach in any scientific endeavor (especially one that is highly controversial). Chagnon collected detailed information from informants for the 12 villages covering a period going back 50 to 60 years and including verbal documentation of 282 violent deaths. He then calculated for each age group of adult males how many wives *unokais* had vs. non-*unokais*. For the pooled samples, the results were

nonhuman primates. Moreover, among most contemporary species, males and females face and resolve these challenges by means of different strategies.

As a result of the heavy cost of carrying and caring for offspring, females especially are put under physiological stress. For the majority of nonhuman primates, females spend most of their adult lives either pregnant or lactating. Accordingly, the metabolic demands are quite high. A pregnant or lactating female primate, although perhaps only half the size of her male counterpart, may require about the same amount of calories per day. Even then, her physical resources may be

BOX 10-2

TABLE 1

Ages		UNOKAIS			NON-UNOKAIS	
	n	Number of Off-spring	Average Number of Offspring	n	Number of Offspring	Average Number of Offspring
20–24	5	5	1.00	78	14	0.18
25–30	14	22	1.57	58	50	0.86
31–40	43	122	2.83	61	123	2.02
>41	75	524	6.99	46	193	4.19
Total	137	673	4.91	243	380	1.59

Source: Chagnon, 1988, p. 989.

dramatically different; among that group who had killed, men had an average of 1.63 wives, compared to only .63 for non-*unokais*. Largely as a result of being able to attract and hold onto mates, *unokais* also had more children. (See Table 1.)

These data are at the very heart of sociobiological attempts to explain human behavior. Moreover, they were collected carefully and painstakingly over decades, keeping close track of both social kinship and probable biological relatedness (the latter not typically tracked in most ethnographic studies). But, assuredly, not everyone will be convinced. Chagnon has quite convincingly demonstrated that social and biological objectives are largely concordant, at least in the immediate (proximate) sense. But what of ultimate causation? Is complex Yanomamö (and other human) behavior influenced by certain genes that promote reproductive success? Such thorny questions are still the grist for controversy and acrimonious debate.

SOURCES

Chagnon, Napoleon. "Male Competition, Favoring Close Kin, and Village Fissioning among the Yanomamö Indians." *In* N. A. Chagnon and W. Irons (eds.), *Evolutionary Biology and Human Social Behavior*, North Scituate, MA: Duxbury Press, pp. 86–131 (1979).

Chagnon, Napoleon. "Life Histories, Blood Revenge and Warfare in a Tribal Population," *Science* **239**(1988): pp. 985–992.

drained over the long run. For example, analysis of chimpanzee skeletons from Jane Goodall's population at Gombe shows significant loss of bone and bone mineral in older females (Sumner et al., 1989).

It is not surprising, then, that considerable attention in current primatological research has been directed to the biological and social role of females. Sociobiological perspectives (with concentration on reproductive issues) have contributed to this trend (see Small, 1984). Early in the development of modern primate field studies, notably in discussions of savanna baboons, a definite male bias

BOX 10-3   **r- and K-Selection**

Differing reproductive strategies are found in various organisms, and can influence numerous aspects of biology and behavior.

r-SELECTION   A strategy in which numerous offspring are born (or hatched), and usually mature rapidly. There is little parental investment in each. Moderate to high mortality is shown. Such strategies are seen in insects and most fish.

K-SELECTION   A strategy in which only a few young are born (or hatched), and take longer to mature (*in utero*, incubation, and afterward), thus considerable parental investment is involved in each. Consequently, mortality is fairly low. Such strategies are common to birds and mammals.

Note: Neither strategy is necessarily advantageous over the other. r-selection may work well in diverse and fairly rapidly changing environments, in which young disperse widely. K-selection, conversely, may work better in fairly stable environments.

You should realize, however, that insects are by far the fastest reproducers (r-selectionists *par excellance*) among animals, and are probably the most successful animal form, if number of species, number of individuals, or biomass are taken as criteria. Even among the primarily K-selected mammals, the rodents (the most r-selected of the group) are probably the most successful.

emerged. Workers seemed especially fascinated by the dominance interactions of the adult males, and consequently paid little attention to what the females were doing. Since 1970, however, the situation has been corrected, not the least reason being that much of the crucial research was done by female primatologists.

Male-male relationships are thus now only one aspect of what is considered important in defining nonhuman primate social behavior. As Alison Richard (1985, pp. 206–207) has suggested in describing primate reproductive behavior, "The following discussion focuses upon the reproductive life of female primates, therefore, and we shall simply assume that males provide willing and able partners when called upon."

Further, as mentioned in our discussion of primate ecology (see p. 269), there may be real differences in the ways male and female primates exploit their environments. Perhaps due to the higher energy/metabolic needs of females, it has been argued (Wrangham, 1980) that they must concentrate their efforts around high-yielding food patches (e.g., particular fruiting trees). Since there is a limited number of such resources, females would tend to defend these areas against other females. However, in order to mount an effective defense, it may take more than one adult female. With whom, however, should an adult female associate? Here, too, sociobiology predicts a likely answer. In sharing resources, it would be most advantageous for an individual to bond with a close relative (e.g., a sister). In so doing, not only her own offspring, but other young in the group (potentially her nieces, nephews, etc.) are related to her and share genes. As a result, a female's inclusive fitness (see Box 10-4) is increased.

Carrying this model further, the pattern of female-female kin-based social bonding may also help explain dispersal patterns among many primates (Pusey and Packer, 1987). In most species of Old World monkeys, it is the male who transfers (usually as a young adult). The long-term social core of the group is thus composed of females, who likely share some degree of genetic relatedness. Con-

BOX 10-4 **Sociobiological Concepts and Terminology**

ALTRUISM Self-sacrificing behavior (technically costly in Darwinian fitness). On the surface, it may appear harmful to the individual as, for example, in the case of sterile worker castes in social insects, such as bees. However, through behaviors that contribute to *inclusive fitness* (see below), genotypes might actually spread (through relatives), even though some individuals may have no offspring themselves.

COST/BENEFIT ANALYSIS Borrowed from economic theory, this approach attempts to measure potential costs and benefits to individual reproductive success (or inclusive fitness) of certain behaviors. Though theoretically intriguing, in practice this is most difficult to apply.

DARWINIAN FITNESS The proportional contribution of genes (compared to other individuals) as a measure of one's *individual* reproductive success (i.e., number of successful offspring). (See p. 37.)

FITNESS Generally, a measure of reproductive success, relative to others in the group, taken as the lifetime contribution of genes to successive generations.

INCLUSIVE FITNESS The *total* contribution of genes through offspring *and* other relatives. Relatives are devalued on the basis of closeness of genetic relatedness, which prompted the British biologist J.B.S. Haldane's famous quip, "I would gladly lay down my life for two sibs or eight cousins." This phenomenon, first clearly elucidated in social insects, may provide a clue to some forms of altruism.

KIN SELECTION The process in which genes are contributed to successive generations through relatives other than offspring. In this way, *inclusive fitness* is improved.

NATURAL SELECTION The process in which some genotypes (individuals) contribute genes disproportionately to successive generations as a result of differential net reproductive success (see p. 40).

PARENTAL INVESTMENT Any behavior or contribution of a parent (gametes, energy, time, risk) to an offspring at the cost of investing in other offspring.

PROXIMATE EXPLANATION A way to explain a behavior on the basis of immediate social/ecological/physiological factors. For example, an individual baboon may leave his natal group following a dominance encounter to avoid future encounters with particular older, larger, and more dominant males.

REPRODUCTIVE VALUE The *potential* remaining reproductive output of an individual. This can be assessed at different stages of the life cycle, so that a 15-year-old baboon female has less reproductive value than an 8-year-old baboon female.

SEXUAL SELECTION The process by which certain physical traits or behavior evolve to facilitate success in competition among one sex for access to matings with the other sex. This notion was championed by Darwin. The large horns of the male mule deer or the large size and aggressive behavior in the male walrus are examples.

versely, males who transfer *into* new groups are unlikely to share much genetic relatedness with other adults.

As we noted in Box 10-1, in several primate groups only one adult male is found socially bonded to a group of females. In these cases (e.g., hamadryas baboons, patas monkeys, most groups of red colobus) at least one breeding male is required, of course, for reproductive purposes and possibly to aid in defense against predators. But why should females tolerate more than one adult male in their group? Again, sociobiological/socioecological perspectives can possibly explain the evolution of multimale societies among primates. Some resources are harder to defend, so females may, in a sense, "use" males to help aid in defense of food patches. In addition, for some animals like savanna baboons, concerted action by numerous adult males apparently is crucial in predator defense (at least, out in the open—see p. 276).

We do not wish to convey an opposite bias to the early period of modern primatology by suggesting that *males* are doing next to nothing. In all primate

FIGURE 10-13   Primate mothers with nursing infants.

societies, the interplay of behavior is extremely complex for *all* individuals. We, in fact, see a marked degree of variability among different species in male parental care, male dispersal, and ecological constraints.

We have observed that, in langurs, male and female reproductive interest may be quite different. Indeed, it has been argued that, in the long run, neither the reproduction of females *nor* males is really helped by infanticide. But in the short run, the presence of one infanticidal male in a group, potentially acting to serve his own reproductive interest, sets a whole chain of events in motion, so that other males are induced to behave similarly. Here, it is apparently the case that immediate, individual reproductive success can act to shape social determinants—even at the cost of the whole group, and perhaps even to the detriment of the *individuals* within the group as well. Glenn Hausfater, one of the leading researchers concerned with ascertaining reproductive success in primates, especially as related to infanticide, has put this relationship nicely:

> Thus, infanticide is an excellent example of a behavioral strategy that produces a short-term increase in reproductive success for some individuals of one sex but that thereby also locks adults of both sexes into patterns of behavior that ultimately result in a decreased rate of reproduction for themselves and for their population as a whole. As with so many other examples in modern behavioral ecology, the present analysis of langur infanticide supports the prevailing notion that evolution does not favor behavior that is "good for the species," but rather behavior that is good for the individual and, moreover, "good" only in the short-run. (Hausfater, 1984, p. 281)

Numerous other examples of variability of male/female strategies are known among primates. For example, in gibbons and some cebids (titis and owl monkeys) the typical social group is monogamous. Perhaps even more distinctive, in most callitrichids (marmosets and tamarins), two adult males regularly mate with one adult female (i.e., they are **polyandrous**) (Goldizen, 1987). In all of these examples, typically it is the adult male(s) who is most responsible for parental care. In chimps yet another pattern is seen. Males are the ones who are tightly bonded (presumably for organized defense against other potentially aggressive males—see p. 301), and it is the females who disperse by transferring to a new group, usually when they are young adults.

Thus, as we have said before, there is no simple relationship of biology, ecology, and behavior among primates. Nor, obviously, can simplistic evolutionary scenarios adequately account for the diversity of behavior among primates. What makes sociobiology (and its ecological correlates) so important, however, is that it provides a framework to ask *relevant* questions, thus helping shape future research. Nevertheless, sociobiological interpretation has been subject to considerable criticism by other biologists and social scientists.

Polyandrous poly: many
androus: males
Two or more males mating with one female.

PRIMATE SOCIOBIOLOGY—LIMITATIONS AND CRITIQUES

As we have seen, sociobiological interpretation has had dramatic impact on directions of current research—on reproductive strategies, male/female behavioral differences, ecological patterning, and much more.

However, sociobiologists have not been without their critics. Indeed, most primatologists who use theoretical models from sociobiology readily admit some of the current methodological shortcomings. For example, Richard and Schulman (1982, pp. 243–244), in a review of primate sociobiological research, list the following central problems for those attempting to apply this approach:

1. The lack of long-term data on the demography and social behavior of large groups of individually known animals
2. The lack of long-term, fine-grained data on the distribution of resources in time and space
3. The nearly complete absence of information on genetic relatedness through the male line
4. The difficulty in assigning reproductive and other costs and benefits to particular behaviors
5. Our almost total ignorance of the genetics of primate social behavior
6. The untestable nature, even under the best of conditions, of many sociobiological models

Some critics have gone even further to question the basic validity of sociobiology as a perspective. Eminent Harvard biologists Stephen Jay Gould and Richard Lewontin (1979) have portrayed sociobiology as a teological (circular-reasoned) pursuit. In making this point, Gould and Lewontin compare sociobiological adaptive "stories" to the wistful, naive renderings of Candide's sidekick, Dr. Pangloss (from Voltaire's classic satire *Candide*). Even in the most humiliating of circumstances, Pangloss would philosophize that, "All is for the best in the best of all possible worlds." In similar fashion, Gould and Lewontin see sociobiologists devising their scenarios to create perfectly adaptive situations.

Is natural selection indeed such a clearly self-perfecting process? Of course, no one can say for certain, since we see only a small slice of possible evolutionary strategies among living animals; but evidence does suggest that natural selection often works simply "to get by." In this way, a whole host of marginal traits and behaviors could endure for substantial periods of time. The recent lemurs of Madagascar (see p. 240) are a case in point.

Just a few hundred years ago, the island was inhabited by a host of different lemur species, but human intervention caused rapid extinction of many forms. Consequently, the survivors (like the indri) have probably moved into a variety of habitats from which competitors had once excluded them. Without such competition they now make do, but probably could not be described as particularly well-adapted.

> The lemurs alive today inhabit forests from which many species, some of them probably competitors, have vanished. It is not difficult to imagine that the surviving lemurs have expanded their life-style to include foods and perhaps whole habitats from which they were once excluded by competitors. It does not matter that they do not make very good use of these new resources, so long as they do not have to compete with more efficient animals. In short, there is no reason to suppose that the distribution, feeding habits, and social organization of lemurs today are the results of long, slow evolutionary process, each species finely tuned to make the best of its environment. More likely, what we see are animals getting by and making ecological experiments after two thousand years of rapid evolutionary change (Richard, 1985, pp. 356–358).

Of course, this is not an evolutionary situation that has had much time to reach equilibrium. But when we look at *any* modern primate, can we be assured that they are not changing (perhaps rapidly)? Are they then showing particularly functional adaptations, and if so, to which circumstances? Are they in equilibrium? Have they ever been in equilibrium? Beyond these thorny theoretical difficulties, sociobiologists must address the type of information needed to test at least limited hypotheses. Presently, however, it is the lack of long-term precise data that most bedevils attempts to make sociobiology more scientific. As Sarah Blaffer Hrdy has noted:

> In order to evolve, strategies must on average increase the reproductive fitness of those animals who enact them. Nevertheless, small sample sizes and the near-total absence of lifetime reproductive output means that at this stage it is rarely possible either to confirm or exclude most of the hypothetical strategies being proposed. Furthermore, limited funds, limited hours, and most especially the rapid destruction of tropical forests together with their primate inhabitants make it unlikely that we will ever have such data for more than a few selected groups belonging to a handful of wild species. Hence a few long term studies, such as those carried out among the Amboseli baboons will loom large in interpretation of primate evolution (1984a, p. 106).

Indeed, among wild primates, the longest-term studies concern Old World monkeys (baboons at Amboseli or Gilgil in Kenya) or chimpanzees in Tanzania (Gombe and Mahale), but still encompass barely two complete generations. Data from captive (e.g., Cayo Santiago) or heavily provisioned populations (e.g., Japanese macaques) are more complete, but are difficult to interpret, given the potentially large disruption of behavior these animals have experienced.

Since primates (especially anthropoids) are so long-lived, as Hrdy notes, it may be difficult to *ever* get the kinds of data we really need to test sociobiological models adequately. For other animals (who reproduce faster) the situation is considerably better. Most notably is a population of red deer on an island off the coast of Scotland for which detailed records were kept on reproductive success of all individuals (over 200) for 12 years (Clutton-Brock, et al., 1984).

Behavioral Data and Objectivity in Science   Perhaps an even more nagging problem than lack of long-term data is the very nature of the information itself. Primates are highly complex animals. Their behavior does not reduce down to simple discrete categories that can readily be described. Indeed, for behavioral studies it is often the case that the kinds of data collected and conclusions reached are often the product of the kinds of questions asked, the methodologies employed, and perhaps most importantly (and underlying everything else), the particular training and orientation of the observer.

We do want to make it clear that most scientists attempt to be objective and, in fact, often recognize that they have biases that must be controlled. Moreover, the great majority of scientists are honest in the presentation of research findings. In those few cases where human failings have overwhelmed scientific objectivity, the perpetrators are usually culled out by other researchers, who constantly challenge ideas and in so doing try to advance the field.

Nevertheless, when dealing with mostly subjective data—such as that on primate behavior—it is often exceedingly difficult to resolve differences of opinion without years of data accumulation and at least some agreement on basic methodologies.

As Sarah Blaffer Hrdy has courageously acknowledged concerning challenges to her interpretation of langur infanticide:

> It has struck me more than once that critics of the sexual selection model sometimes apply a double standard: The criteria for accepting negative evidence appear to be far less stringent than the criteria applied to support the sexual selection model. . . . My own writing errs in the opposite direction, a consequence of the evolutionary bias of my own world view (1984b, p. 317).
>
> When researchers noted for integrity differ so profoundly not only over interpretation of the evidence but even on the point of what is admissible as evidence, we must look for underlying causes. Inevitably, what researchers see is affected by expectations about their natural world and the way that biological and social systems "ought" to work; the resulting disagreement will not be easily resolved. Often frustrating, invariably time-consuming and inefficient, such debates remain, nevertheless, the best antidote we possess against the biases implicit in every researcher's world view (1984b, p. 319).

Primate Conservation

Probably the greatest challenge facing primatologists of the next generation is the urgent need to find ways to preserve in the wild what is left of primate species. It cannot be overstated how imminent the danger is. Without massive changes in public opinion and in the economics of countries with surviving rainforests, it will not be long before there are few primates left in the wild.

Indeed, the problem ranges far beyond primates. Habitat destruction in rainforests rushes ahead at a startling rate, swallowing huge tracts of forests and annihilating *all* those populations within them. Tragically, these very areas are among the richest biological communities known, and include more than one-half of all mammalian and bird species. Literally millions of different lifeforms are threatened.

Perhaps it would be best to outline the dimensions of the crisis. Tropical rainforests once spanned vast areas of Central and South America, Central Africa (and

FIGURE 10-14   Tropical rainforests of the world (modern distribution before recent, massive destruction).

Madagascar), and Southeast Asia (see Figure 10-14). More than 90% of living primates live in what is left of these tropical forests, and they are vanishing rapidly. No precise estimates exist, as so many countries are involved, and national governments are, understandably, reluctant to reveal such details. In any case, researchers place the current rate of destruction at 25 to 50 million acres per year (or an area the size of New York state devastated every year!) (Mittermeier, 1982). Another way to look at it is to consider that anywhere between 12.5 and 100 acres are lost every minute (Lovejoy, 1982).

Much of the motivation behind the devastation of the rainforests is, of course, economic—the short-term gains from clearing forest to create immediately available (but poor) farmland or ranchland; from use of trees for lumber and paper products; or from large-scale mining operations (with their necessary roads, digging, etc., all of which cause habitat destruction). Regionally, the loss of rainforest ranks as a national disaster for some countries. For example, the West African nation Sierra Leone had an estimated 15,000 square miles of rainforest earlier in this century. Today, only 535 square miles remain. At least 70% of this destruction has occurred since World War II (Teleki, 1986). People in the Third World are also short of fuel and most frequently use whatever firewood is obtainable. It is estimated that 1.5 billion people in the Third World are short of fuelwood (Mittermeier and Cheney, 1987).

While habitat destruction is far-and-away the leading danger to contemporary nonhuman primates, assaults against them from other directions are happening as well. Primates in many areas are hunted for food, particularly in the Americas and

BOX 10-5 **Primates in Danger***

About one-third of all living primate species live on the African continent; that is, 50 to 60 of the world total of 150 to 180 species. Although Africa is a large continent, primates inhabit a relatively small area of it, and much of it is greatly threatened from expanding agriculture and commercial lumbering.

The basic problem in Africa can easily be seen from the following:

1. Forest land is diminishing; e.g., of the 49,900 km² of forests in southern Ivory Coast in 1966, only 33,000 km² remained in 1974, a loss of 31% in only 8 years.
2. The human population rate will have increased over 3% for the 1980–1990 decade.
3. The food supply is decreasing because of environmental factors, inefficient agricultural techniques, and lack of capital resources. From 1970 to 1980, the annual increase in food production was −1.1% per capita.

As a result of the increase in population and lack of a similar increase in the rate of food production, there is agricultural pressure on forests. Where pressures on forest land are not great, monkeys and apes are often hunted for food. It is possible that by the end of the century, 13 species of very distinct local populations could be extinct if significant action is not taken to reverse the forces currently acting against them.

In 25 years another 10 species will be in danger if current trends continue. An informed guess is that in 50 years time, in the absence of major conservation action, about *half the African primate fauna* could be extinct or verging on extinction.

What can be done? Some suggestions: identify the most urgent conservation priorities; educate all involved as to the meaning, value, and practice of primate (and other resource) conservation; establish more effective wildlife reserves in forest areas; work in close collaboration with African countries; demonstrate to Africans, especially residents of rural Africa, that conservation *can* provide them with tangible benefits.

*Adapted from John Oates.

African Primates in Danger of Extinction

SPECIES/SUBSPECIES COMMON NAME	LOCATION	ESTIMATED SIZE OF REMAINING POPULATION	SPECIES/SUBSPECIES COMMON NAME	LOCATION	ESTIMATED SIZE OF REMAINING POPULATION
Barbary macaque	North Africa	23,000	Preuss's red colobus	Cameroon	8000
Tana River mangabey	Tana R., Kenya	800–1100	Bouvier's red colobus	Congo Republic	?
Sanje mangabey	Uzungwa Mts., Tanzania	1800–3000	Tana River red colobus	Tana R., Kenya	200–300
Drill	Cameroon, Fernando Po	?	Uhehe red colobus	Uzungwa Mts., Tanzania	10,000
Preuss's guenon	Cameroon, Fernando Po	?	Zanzibar red colobus	Zanzibar	1500
White-throated guenon	Southwest Nigeria	?	Mountain gorilla	Virunga Volcanoes, and Bwindi Forest	360–370
Pennant's red colobus	Fernando Po	?			

Dian Fossey—A Hero for the Twentieth Century

Despite her articles, a well-received book, and her eighteen years of dedicated work with the wild mountain gorillas, Dian Fossey, ironically, came into the full glare of media attention only after her death on December 26, 1985. She was brutally murdered in her cabin at the Karisoke Research Center, Rwanda, Africa, which she established and directed.

Dian was born in San Francisco in 1932. As a child, she loved animals, but was only allowed to keep goldfish. She later said that the first trauma of her life was the death of her pet goldfish, a trauma that foreshadowed the later tragic and brutal death of her favorite gorilla (named Digit), in 1977.

Interrupting her career as an occupational therapist, Dian borrowed $8,000 in 1963 to go on a seven-week African safari. Her purpose was to observe animals, especially gorillas. There, she met renowned anthropologist Dr. Lewis Leakey, who later sponsored her long-term study of mountain gorillas in the Virunga Volcanos, first in Zaire and then in the Parc National des Volcans in Rwanda.

Beginning in 1967, Dian achieved great success, and she came to understand gorilla behavior better than anyone else in the world. Living alone in her cabin, mostly isolated from her staff and occasional students, she became disillusioned with people who failed to share her concern for gorillas. Shortly before her death she told a reporter, "I have no friends. The more you learn about the dignity of the gorilla, the more you want to avoid people."

Increasingly over the years, Dian's concerns turned to what she termed "active conservation." She vigorously led and directed antipoaching patrols against native poachers who, with their snares for other game, posed the most severe threat to gorilla survival in the Virunga Volcanos.

While teaching briefly at Cornell University, Dian completed the book *Gorillas in the Mist*, which appeared

Dian Fossey.

in 1983. With this work, and *National Geographic* articles, public lectures, and television appearances, Dian tirelessly and effectively campaigned to educate the public to a better understanding of gorillas and their endangered plight in Africa.

For eighteen years Dian lived and worked heroically with mountain gorillas. Hopefully, she did not die in vain. The Rwandan government has indicated that not only will the research center she established be maintained, but it will be strengthened and enlarged. Perhaps in death Dian Fossey will achieve what eluded her in life: absolute protection for the mountain gorillas. In her devotion to these animals, Dian will be remembered for generations as one of the heroes of the twentieth century. Without her work, it is doubtful that mountain gorillas would have survived to the twenty-first.

Biruté M. F. Galdikas

western and central Africa. "Thousands are killed every year for the pot" (Mitter-meier, 1982). Primates are also hunted for their pelts as, for example, the skins of black-and-white colobus monkeys. It is estimated that 2 million skins of this species alone were taken by hunters, primarily for sale in the United States and Europe, just in the last decade of the nineteenth century (Mittermeier, 1982).

Insofar as the food question is concerned, the choices for local human inhab-itants are far from easy. Most tropical rainforests are located in Third World coun-tries that face current massive overpopulation and continued high growth rates. Malnutrition and undernutrition are thus major problems, and are worsening. It is sobering to consider that the horrible starvation so well-publicized in Ethiopia in the last few years is probably just the tip of the iceberg. Starvation on a massive scale will almost certainly become commonplace in Africa (and elsewhere) be-fore the end of this century.

Faced with overwhelming economic hardship, cash-poor nations seek foreign investment and an influx of capital. But what do they have to offer that will pro-duce ready cash? Their natural resources are their most immediately available commodity, so in reality their very landscapes are being chopped, packaged, and exported. This—as Sierra Leone illustrates—is only a stopgap, for in barely an in-stant resources will all be gone. In the face of such an onslaught, nonhuman pri-mates are merely pawns in a worldwide catastrophe-in-the-making.

What, then, is the status of free-ranging primates today? Of the approximately 180–190 species, 67 (one out of three) are already considered endangered, and another 26 (one out of seven) are listed as *highly* endangered. These latter could be extinct by the end of the century (Mittermeier, 1982). "And, I must emphasize that these are minimum estimates . . . Almost every time a researcher goes out to study a poorly known species, we find that it is necessary to add yet another pri-mate to the endangered list" (Mittermeier, 1982, p. 14).

There are no simple solutions. The world's booming human population, the uneven distribution of wealth among the world's peoples, and the understand-able, but short-sighted, attempts by nations to maximize income all would seem to offer little hope for turning the situation around. It is obviously already too late for many species. What will the next few decades bring, and what will our descen-dants say of us?

Summary

We have seen in Chapter 9 that, structurally, the primate order is a most diverse group. In this chapter, we have seen that *socially* as well primates are both com-plex and diverse. Indeed, the myriad demands of primate existence have pro-duced these living forms through an integrated process of *biosocial* evolution.

While the scope of this book does not allow us to touch upon all the fascinating aspects of primatological research, we have introduced some of the more dy-namic areas. In particular, we have showed that ecological challenges and how they act to influence primate social relationships is a central concern of current primatology. Another main focus of many contemporary researchers involves evolutionary explanations (through natural selection) of primate behavior. This approach, called sociobiology, is not without its drawbacks and its detractors, both within and outside primatology. Nevertheless, along with ecological consid-erations, such a perspective has allowed researchers to frame a whole array of new questions concerning primate behavior. We may never have complete answers to these questions, but we can gain useful information only by *attempting* to answer what we consider relevant questions. Such is the nature of science, particularly the science of behavior.

Beyond these methodological considerations, there are specific avenues of research that have been used to provide information on the evolution of human behavior. It is to this information that we turn in the next chapter.

Questions for Review

1. Discuss several reasons for studying nonhuman primates.
2. What features are unique to humans (or at least tend to distinguish humans from other primates)?
3. Why should primates be studied in free-ranging circumstances?
4. What are the primary methodological obstacles to studying free-ranging primates?
5. Given the methodological constraints, which primates are known best in free-ranging circumstances?
6. What major aspects of the environment are thought to influence social behavior of nonhuman primates?
7. Discuss how the study of the five species of primates in the Kibale Forest contributes to our understanding of primate socioecology.
8. What behavioral traits are common to all nonhuman primates?
9. What are the functions of grooming? Displays? Dominance?
10. Why is the mother-infant bond so crucial for primates?
11. What experimental evidence is there to argue for this strong mother-infant attachment?
12. What is the basis of sociobiology?
13. Discuss the sociobiological explanation for infanticide in langurs.
14. Give examples of how male and female nonhuman primates differ in their adaptive strategies.
15. Discuss some of the major limitations of sociobiological research.
16. Try to develop your own scenario of hominid evolution. Take into account the various sociobiological and ecological factors mentioned in this chapter.
17. What problems does artificial provisioning create?
18. Why have primatologists placed so much emphasis on socioecology in recent years?
19. Three types of nonhuman primate groups are given in Box 10-1. Can you give reasons for this variation in social organization in nonhuman primates?

Suggested Further Reading

Barash, David. *Sociobiology and Behavior*, New York: Elsevier, 1977, 1982.
A recent and authoritative review of sociobiological theory by one of the leading proponents of this approach. A student with no biological background may find parts of this work difficult to comprehend; nonetheless, the ideas are highly stimulating. The reader should be cautious, for this author makes a rather one-sided presentation.

Dawkins, Richard. *The Selfish Gene*, New York: Oxford University Press, 1976.
    Like the Barash work noted above, this book is a popularized synthesis of sociobiological theory. Very entertainingly written, it makes for enjoyable reading. Dawkins, like many other advocates of sociobiology, tends at times towards evangelism, but his final chapter is a stimulating and original contribution to our understanding of human behavior.

Ghiglieri, Michael P. *The Chimpanzees of Kibale Forest*, New York: Columbia University Press, 1984.
    A good illustration of a sociobiological and socioecological approach to the field study of primates.

Harding, Robert S., and Geza Teleki (eds.). *Omnivorous Primates*, New York: Columbia University Press, 1981.
    An edited collection of several articles concerning feeding behavior in primates (human and nonhuman). Especially emphasized is the use of nonhuman primate data to model hominid behavioral evolution.

Konner, Melvin. *The Tangled Wing*, New York: Holt, Rinehart, and Winston, 1982.
    A thoughtful and literate discussion of sociobiological principles, especially as they relate to humans.

Napier, John, and Pruh Napier. *The Natural History of the Primates*, Cambridge, Mass.: M.I.T. Press, 1985.
    An up-to-date review of the primate order, both structurally and behaviorally. Well organized and written, this work is also extremely well illustrated.

Richard, Alison. *Primates in Nature*, New York: W. H. Freeman, 1985.
    A superb synthesis of primate ecology. Discussions are organized and cogent. The bibliography is extensive and up-to-date. Highly recommended.

Small, Meredith (ed.). *Female Primates. Studies by Women Primatologists*, New York: Alan R. Liss, 1984.
    A thought-provoking collection of articles on the role of female primates in child-rearing, social relationships, ecological relationships, etc. A strong orientation running through most of the contributions is that of behavioral evolution (sociobiology).

Smuts, Barbara, D. C. Cheney, R. M. Seyforth, R. W. Wrangham, and T. T. Struhsaker, (eds.), *Primate Societies*, Chicago: University of Chicago Press, 1987.
    A superb collection of 40 articles including contributions by most of the key primate behaviorists today. Specific surveys cover more than two dozen species, and topical summaries cover aggression, infanticide, feeding, predation, and many other subjects. Highly recommended.

Wilson, E. O. *Sociobiology: The New Synthesis*, Cambridge, Mass.: Harvard University Press, 1975.
    The monumental work that provoked all the controversy concerning the validity of sociobiology. Wilson, a man of enormous knowledge, has condensed a staggering amount of data concerning the social behavior of animals (insects, birds, mammals) into this 700-page volume. Wilson's chapters on social insects, social carnivores, and primates should be of particular interest. His final chapter, "Man: From Sociobiology to Sociology," should be read critically. Highly recommended for any student interested in animal behavior.

Wilson, E. O. *On Human Nature*, Cambridge, Mass.: Harvard University Press, 1978.
    Wilson applies his sociobiological perspective to human behavior in what is bound to be a controversial book.

Note: For further primate sources, see the list of readings in Chapter 11.

Models for Human Behavior

Contents

Killer
Apes

For years, scholars and popular writers have discussed human aggression. One of the very basic questions has been (and still is, for that matter) whether human aggression is instinctive or learned, or a combination of both. This issue is significant because, if aggression is learned, it can be unlearned; or, the learning of aggression can be modified or replaced by other attitudes. If it is instinctive, then it may be necessary to develop quite different techniques in dealing with it. Many be-

lieve that a clue to the source of human aggression might be found in nonhuman primate behavior, especially that of the apes. Field studies have shown monkeys—especially baboons and macaques—to be quite aggressive, but since humans are more closely related to apes, the question of ape aggression is more relevant.

Until recently, field studies of apes have been infrequent, and those that were done were not nearly as thorough as those

that are contemporary. While much evidence remains to be obtained, the number of field studies since 1960 has increased manyfold, and data are accumulating in great quantities on chimpanzees, gorillas, and orangutans.

Dian Fossey's early reports on gorillas did not mention aggression, but in more recent accounts, Fossey writes of two kinds of gorilla aggression. One, witnessed by a student of Fossey—Peter Veit—was a violent attack by a male on a female that resulted in the female's death. The female was ill and probably would have soon perished in any event, but the male literally stomped her to death.

Fossey also reported that infanticide accounted for the deaths of 6 out of 38 infants born over a 13-year period. The killing of the infants was perpetrated by males. Fossey believes that infanticide "is the means by which a male instinctively seeks to perpetuate his own lineage by killing another male's progeny in order to breed with the victim's mother" (Fossey, 1981, p. 512). (See Sociobiology for a discussion of this theory, p. 280).

In contrast to gorillas, abundant field studies of chimpanzees show evidence of frequent aggression—including killing— among these primates. Are there killer apes—apes guilty of calculated, premeditated "murder"? The case of the male gorillas mentioned above is evidence there are. More evidence comes from chimpanzees.

For more than thirty years, beginning with Jane Goodall's study of chimpanzees in Tanzania's Gombe National Park, intensive research on chimpanzees, gorillas, and orangutans has been conducted in Africa and Borneo. Early reports from these studies led us to believe that apes were "gentle folk," kind to their children and playing out a more or less "live and let live" existence. The only animal that murdered its own kind, it seemed, was the human animal.

Beginning in 1974, Goodall and her colleagues at Gombe observed a series of at least five unprovoked (or so it seemed to the observers) brutal, savage gang attacks by males of one group against the males of another group that had splintered off several years earlier. All seven males of the splinter group were wiped out by 1977. One attack even involved an elderly female who died as a consequence of the beating. The attackers were usually young males, using their teeth, hands, and feet, although on one occasion an older male was seen throwing a rock at a prostrate victim.

Even more disturbing, perhaps, is the cannibalism that Goodall has witnessed. She reports on a mother-daughter pair of chimps that had killed and eaten possibly up to ten newborns. Another case of cannibalism in East Africa was recently reported for the chimpanzees of the Mahale Mountains. We do not know how widespread the practice is, or what its adaptive value might be.

Because of the biochemical and genetic similarity between chimpanzees and humans, chimpanzee behavior may hold clues to human origins and even present-day human behavior. The significance of the killings and the cannibalism observed among chimpanzees remains to be worked out. Meanwhile, it is distressing to find that our image of the playful, friendly chimpanzee may well be illusion rather than reality.

As Goodall observed, "It is sobering that our new awareness of chimpanzee violence compels us to acknowledge that these ape cousins of ours are even more similar to humans than we thought before."

SOURCES:

Fossey, Dian. "Imperiled Giants of the Forest," *National Geographic*, **4**: 501–522, April, 1981.

Goodall, Jane. "Chimp Killings: Is it the 'Man' in them?" *Science News*, **17**: 276, April 29, 1978.

———. *National Geographic*, **5**: 592–620, May, 1979.

———. *Through A Window*, Boston: Houghton Mifflin Co., 1990.

Hamburg, David A., and E. R. McCown. *The Great Apes*, Menlo Park, Calif.: The Benjamin/Cummings Publishing Co., 1979.

Norikashi, Kohshi. "One Observed Case of Cannibalism among Wild Chimpanzees of the Mahale Mountains," *Primates*, **23** (1):66–74, January, 1982.

Introduction

Home range The area utilized by an animal; the living area in which an animal performs its normal activities; the area the group is most familiar with, and which provides the group with food.

Most people are curious about their ancestors, and many are interested in the intriguing question of who the very first humans might have been. This proclivity is reflected in the diverse accounts of creation myths, found in just about every society in the world. In Western culture, for example, we are all familiar with the story of Adam and Eve and the garden of Eden. But this ancestral pair is only one of many. Curiosity about earliest ancestors is also a concern of scientists, especially anthropologists, and both paleoanthropologists and primatologists spend much of their research on just this question. In fact, as we saw in the last chapter, this quest is often given as a primary reason for studying nonhuman primates in their natural habitat.

In the preceding chapter, we introduced nonhuman primates and suggested that a study of their behavior might allow some of them to serve as models for our earliest hominid ancestor. In this chapter, we briefly examine the behavior of baboons and chimpanzees, the most popular primate models, to see how they fare as reasonable prototypes for our early ancestors. We will also review a few social carnivores (meat-eating animals that live in groups), since they, too, have been suggested as ancestral models. Finally, because our earliest ancestors may have been hunter/gatherers, we will describe a recent hunter/gathering society, the !Kung San,* of South Africa.

Examples of Primate Social Behavior

Baboon Social Behavior Baboons are diurnal and (with some exceptions) open-country monkeys. There are several kinds of baboons, including the common or savanna hamadryas, drill and mandrill, and gelada. Since the social behavior of each type varies, we shall describe the most widespread baboon in Africa, the savanna (*Papio cynocephalus*), which includes olive, yellow, and chacma varieties.

Savanna baboon groups range in size from under 10 to as many as 200 individuals, with a mean somewhere around 50. Usually, the sex ratio in a troop is about even, although among adults, females outnumber males.

Baboons usually sleep in trees. In the morning, they descend from their trees and drift off to the forage area, where they move slowly along for several miles. By late afternoon, they have reached the "sleeping" trees for that night. Some baboon troops return to the same sleeping trees on successive nights.

Home range varies from 1.5 to 20 square miles, with the difference in area probably associated with proximity of neighbors, concentration of food and water

---

*The diacritical mark ! indicates the proper way to sound this name. Please see footnote, p. 334.

FIGURE 11-1   Baboon eating a Thomson's gazelle.

resources, group size, and other factors. Within the home range, the group makes its daily round in the **core area**, which contains the crucial elements in the baboon world: sleeping trees, resting places, water holes, and food sources. There may be several core areas within one home range, and a troop may occasionally shift from one to the other. Home ranges of neighboring groups overlap, but convincing evidence for **territoriality** is lacking.

Baboons eat a wide variety of food. Their excellent vision, ability to climb, dig, and to cover a large area enable them to exploit many different types of food and survive in many varying habitats. They eat ripe fruit, leaves, grass seeds and blades, and other plants. They also prey on insects, as well as mammals, such as rodents, young gazelles, and small primates.

The baboons at Amboseli did not share their food, and there was fighting among adult males for the meat on an infant gazelle. After the fighting ended, other baboons waited quietly, watching the one who was eating. When he finished, they walked over and picked up the scraps.

The Pumphouse Gang, a baboon troop at Kekopey, Kenya, studied by Strum (1987), uncharacteristically developed rather sophisticated hunting techniques over a period of several years. At first their hunting was fortuitous, occasionally capturing a Thomson gazelle they happened to come across. Later, they developed systematic cooperative efforts, even to the extent of pursuing gazelles in relays. The Pumphouse Gang, like the baboons at Amboseli, do not ordinarily share food but, surprisingly, the meat available from these hunting expeditions was shared. Meat was not voluntarily distributed, but males would scoot aside and let a female friend* take some meat from the carcass. A female would even let her

Core area   An area within the home range where the group habitually sleeps, feeds, and performs routine activities. The area within the home range of greatest regular use.

Territory   The area a group defends. That part of the home range used exclusively by one group. Neighbors of the same species do not enter or else enter only on a brief foray.

---

*Smuts (1984) describes a special relationship between an adult male and female as *friendship*, and refers to them as friends (p. 305).

child join in. However, males did not share with other males, not even those who may have helped in the chase. This kind of hunting, however, was apparently an aberration, as was the sharing, and ended after a few years.

While meat eating is not uncommon among baboons, and sharing of a sort may occur, it is doubtful that meat—vertebrate meat—is an important part of the diet of most baboons, with the possible exception of adult males.

A savanna baboon troop is composed of a core of females and young males who have not yet transferred to another group, and adult males, most, perhaps all, of whom have migrated into the troop. Young, fully grown (or not quite fully grown) males normally transfer out of their natal group and emigrate to a neighboring troop. Both male and female baboons are attracted to opposite-sexed individuals from other groups. Females sometimes act in a "flirtatious" manner to attract males from another group. These actions seem to encourage male transfer.

The most likely explanation of this practice of baboon male dispersal from their natal group would be the avoidance of inbreeding (Pusey and Packer, 1987; see also p. 123). Packer (1970) points out that males transferring into a group increase the number of males, add to the competition among males, and thus, from a sociobiological point of view, those males that breed successfully are probably the most fit adult males.

Adult males are organized around a dominance hierarchy (which is one method of structuring a group), with an *alpha male* as the most dominant individual. In some cases, there may be several males in the central hierarchy. These codominants support each other in stress situations and cooperate in turning aside a threat to any one of them. The dominance hierarchy is lineal, that is, A ranks above B, B above C, and so on; however, competition is so keen among the males that rank positions change quite frequently. Adult males are dominant to all adult females, and immature males dominate females among their own-age and younger-age cohorts.

Males are very aggressive and participate in many **agonistic** encounters, especially when females are in estrus. They also frequently attack females, whom they sometimes wound severely. "With rare exceptions, males come together only to greet, fight, form alliances against other males, or compete over the same resources" (Smuts, 1984, p. 14).

Dominant males enjoy certain perquisites. They often have what is called *reproductive success*; that is, prior and more frequent access to estrous females at the time they are most likely to conceive. Dominant males may also have prior access to richer food sites, they are less harassed during mating, and they are assured of social space. However, baboon troops vary, and dominant males are not always successful in their endeavors. Female choice may be a factor, since a female may avoid the dominant male. In some cases, young adult males may challenge older males, usually at night, and take away the estrous female. Apparently, dominance is not always a bed of roses, as behavior of members of the Pumphouse Gang illustrates.

In the Pumphouse Gang troop, dominant males were the newest male transfers. Less dominant were short-term residents, and lowest-ranking males were long-time residents. The new transfers attained their dominance by being very aggressive. However, as strangers to the troop, the newcomers were suspect, and females kept their distance. Females also had male friends, and newcomers were less likely to bother a female befriended by a male, even a low-ranking male. Also, a female may "wear out" a male she does not like, using various techniques. (See p. 306.)

Matriline matri: mother
Individuals related through the mother.

Longtime resident males understood the social and complex network of the troop. Success with females required experience and skill that the newcomers had not yet learned. It would take about a year-and-a-half for an individual to become fully integrated into the group. If the newcomer did not give up before that, he would make friends, lose his dominance, and acquire skills that would help him become acceptable. After three years, he would become a longtime resident. "Low dominance and infrequent aggression ran parallel with the fact that when this type of male *did* act aggressively, such aggression was well timed, effective and a tactical feat rather than a disastrous rampage" (Strum, 1987, p. 123).

Females form the core of the social system among savanna baboons. Whereas young adult male baboons migrate to other groups, females remain in their own and rarely transfer. Thus, females in one group are related to one another through common ancestors. Furthermore, closely related females—mothers and daughters, sisters, and at times even grandmothers and granddaughters, aunts and nieces—tend to form subgroups within the larger unit. Members of the **matriline** frequently exchange friendly behaviors, such as grooming and sitting closely together. They also support one another during aggressive encounters with other troop members.

Females are also organized in a lineal dominance hierarchy, which, more stable than the males', may remain unchanged for years. Offspring acquire dominant rank just below the mother, with rank in reverse order of age. The youngest sibling has the highest rank, next youngest ranks second, etc. A high-ranking female enjoys certain advantages. She can displace a low-ranking female and take over resources, such as partially dug grass corms. She is subject to less distress interactions and, except for new mothers, is groomed more often by other females.

We have already remarked on the social significance of primate grooming, which "is the most obvious and time-consuming form of primate social behavior" (Altmann, 1980, p. 89). New mothers are groomed more often than other females, and the grooming is initiated by others, not solicited by mothers. Mothers spend most of their grooming time on their infants, juvenile offspring, and one or two associated males. However, all combinations of sex-age classes groom together, except males, who do not form grooming pairs. Females groomed males more often than vice versa, except during estrus, when males became the more frequent groomers. Generally, the amount of grooming individuals receive reflects their rank.

Grooming episodes may be as brief as a few seconds or as long as an hour, but usually last from five to ten minutes. It appears to be a pleasurable experience for all participants. The groomer lip-smacks (a friendly gesture) and "grunts softly while parting the partner's fur and gently removing dirt and ectoparasites, and the groomee tends to adopt a relaxed posture, sometimes sprawling on the ground with limbs splayed and eyes closed" (Smuts, 1984, p. 38).

Performed by both adults and young of both sexes, grooming is an important mechanism for maintaining peaceful social relationships and bonding within the baboon troop. Another way is *friendship*.* In her study of the Eburru Cliff baboons, Smuts observed a special kind of friendship occurring in a very close male/

---

*Strum notes (1987, p. 686) that this special friendship is a restraint against male aggression.

FIGURE 11-2 Primate grooming. A male patas monkey grooms a female.

female relationship. Males do not have male friends; they rarely associate with members of their own sex, nor are they ever in close proximity (except in agonistic encounters), and they almost never groom each other. For a male, only a female can be a "best" friend.

This special friendship is apparently initiated by females, probably because of their extreme vulnerability to males. Males often attacked females, and although the injuries were not always serious, a female could expect a serious injury at least once a year. Smuts observed such an attack, which could serve as a plot for a television soap opera:

> Phaedra is feeding on grass, surrounded by other baboons doing the same. Adonis, in consort with Andromeda, feeds 20 meters [65 ft.] away. He looks up at Phaedra and stares at her for a few seconds; she is unaware of his attention. Suddenly he rushes over and, with his canines, tears an 8 cm [3 in.] gash in her arm. Phaedra screams in pain and collapses on the ground. Adonis saunters back to Andromeda. (Phaedra's wound took two months to heal fully, and she did not use her arm for over 1 week.) (Smuts, 1984, p. 93).

Smuts believes the reason for the aggression was Phaedra's attacks on Andromeda, Adonis' friend. Phaedra was also a friend of Adonis and seemed annoyed by this relationship with Andromeda, who had been in consort with Adonis for over a week. Phaedra had chased Andromeda away from Adonis several times, and Adonis had run after her, which was the only way to avoid losing her to another male. On those occasions he was too busy to display aggression toward Phaedra. This time was different, and he took advantage of the situation by punishing Phaedra for her harassment of his consort partner. It worked—Phaedra was severely wounded and ceased to show aggression toward Andromeda.

The friend relationship benefits a female. By becoming a special friend of a male, a female can rely on the possibility that her friend will risk injury and come

FIGURE 11-3 Baboon troop. Note grooming, feeding, infant play, and threat display. (*a*) Dominant male, foreground, faces possible threat at the left (from a source that is out of the photograph). (*b*) Male reacts to the threat with threat display—the "yawn"; other troop members appear to pay no attention. (*c*) Threat behavior ended, members continue their activities undisturbed as gazelle wanders through.

(a)

(b)

(c)

to her aid. Also, her friend may protect her offspring from other males. To obtain these benefits, a female establishes a long-term bond with one or two males who become her friends and allies. However, there are also costs, since this relationship does not protect her from her friend's aggression.

Another form of social bonding is consortship, which differs from friendships since consortship is usually defined as the exclusive *mating* relationship of a male and an *estrous* female. About ten days after the estrous cycle begins, the female's **perineal** area begins to swell, reaching its maximum (*tumescence*) within a week or two. It remains fully swollen for a week or so and then begins to decrease (detumescence) and disappear. A female ovulates about one to four days before detumescence, and it is during these few days when conception occurs.

Once swelling begins, females are sexually receptive and solicit copulations from males. However, adult males are most interested during the peak of sexual swelling, and this is when consortships are formed. While a consortship often consists of one male and one female, Smuts reports seeing two males in consort and sometimes even three. During peak estrus, male baboons compete intensely over access to estrous females, who often change consort partners several times in one day. Peak estrus is also the time when high-status males are most successful.

It is not, by the way, entirely the male's choice that determines the partnership. A female may use several techniques to discourage a male. She may run away from him, hide, or in one way or another, refuse to be mounted. Smuts tells the story of Zizi who was in estrus and being courted by Virgil, who was very attentive and probably her current and exclusive mate.

> Zizi, however, apparently had something else in mind. She broke away from Virgil, moved rapidly through the troop, and **presented** her alluring sexual swelling to one male after another. Before Virgil caught up with her, she had managed to announce her receptive condition to several of his rivals. When Virgil tried to grab her, Zizi screamed and dashed into the bushes with Virgil in hot pursuit. I heard sounds of chasing and fighting coming from the thicket. Moments later Zizi emerged from the bushes with an older male named Cyclops. They remained together for several days, . . . [and] in Cyclop's presence, Zizi no longer approached or even glanced at other males (Smuts, 1987, p. 36).

Still another interesting bond often develops—between a male and an infant. A male (sometimes referred to as "godfather") may take a keen interest in an infant, especially if the infant's mother is friendly with the male. He may fulfill several paternal functions, such as baby-sitting, grooming, and carrying the infant, and provide reassuring contact. By overt behavior or merely his presence, the male can often serve as a buffer between mother/infant and other group members. If the male is nearby, others will approach apprehensively, cast "anxious" glances toward the adult male, and approach the mother/infant from the side opposite the male. The male sometimes threatens anyone who approaches the pair, especially if he or she pulls at the infant. This relationship often persists through the infant's third or fourth year.

A mother's male friend is not the only baboon attracted to infants. Other adults, but especially females, attempt to take hold of a new infant. This is known as allo-parenting or allomothering (see p. 278), and occurs in a number of primate groups. Ransom describes the strategy of a potential alloparent:

> An adult baboon may slowly approach the mother, showing various indications of friendly intent such as lip-smacking, narrowing of the eyes, and flattening of the ears, and embrace her in a variety of ways depending on the mother's posture and the sex of

the other adult. During this embrace the adult will touch the infant with hand or nose several times and eventually may attempt to pull it out of the mother's arms. Such attempts for the most part appear to be intended to facilitate further investigation of the infant, but others are obviously motivated by a desire to carry it off (Ransom, 1981, p. 222).

Quite frequently, the most eager allomothers are nulliparous females, but because they are inexperienced, they may harm the baby. Still, allomothering is useful to nulliparous females since it provides them with the opportunity to learn mothering.

Does this brief overview of baboon behavior support Lovejoy's hominization scenario (p. 263)? Baboons differ from Lovejoy's scheme in three significant areas:

1. *Division of labor.* Division of labor usually refers to economic activities, such as food-getting. In the case of baboons, there is no such division. Males provide food for themselves, and females forage for their own as well as their infant's, food.
2. *Monogamy.* Permanent pair bonding is another aspect of Lovejoy's scenario, and again this does not apply to savanna baboons. Consort pairs bond, as we have seen, but only when the female is in estrus. Furthermore, such bonding is of short duration and is certainly not a permanent monogamous relationship. Smut's special friendship is the bonding of a male and an *anestrous* female. While the relationship sometimes lasts through the female's pregnancy and lactation, even for years, it is not Lovejoy's permanent, food-sharing pair bond.
3. *Base camp.* There is no base camp (home base) among baboons. A base camp is a more or less permanent site where females remain, or at least remain in that vicinity. The male leaves the site in his search for food and returns to the base to share it with his female bond partner. It is true that baboons live in a territory and especially its core area(s). However, females move along with the males to another core area, or wherever the males move within the territory.

Then, too, the ecology of savanna baboons has been compared to early hominids, also considered to have been savanna primates. However, as Fedigan notes (1982, p. 312), much of African savanna may be relatively recent, formed by humans who burned and cleared forests for farming purposes. Savanna baboon behavior, therefore, may not even be specially adapted to savanna life.

Would baboon society serve as a model for the hunting-gathering society of today and the recent past? Not very well. The agonistic behavior of baboon males—among themselves as well as toward females—contrasts with the more cooperative and peaceful activities of many (probably most) hunting-gathering cultures, for example, the !Kung San (p. 334). Also, the baboon dominance hierarchies of males and females is lacking, or is much more subtle, among hunter-gatherers. Food distribution, an important economic activity among hunter-gatherers, is very restricted among baboons. It appears, then, that savanna baboons do not serve well as a model for hominization or for hunter-gatherers.

Chimpanzees (*Pan troglodytes*)*—apes that live in the forest and on the forest-savanna border—offer another possible model for early hominid behavior.

Pan troglodytes, the common chimpanzee, is the most studied, and is the species described here. The pygmy chimp (or bonobo), *Pan paniscus*, is similar in some respects, different in others.

FIGURE 11-4 Females and offspring—a closely-knit group. The female sitting at left is Flo, one of Jane Goodall's favorite chimps.

Chimpanzee Social Behavior Although chimpanzee communities vary, observers are pretty well agreed that chimpanzees are a *fusion-fission* society. Goodall describes such an organization this way:

> Fusion and fission in chimpanzee society are carried to the limits of flexibility; individuals of either sex have almost complete freedom to come and go as they wish. The membership of temporary parties is constantly changing. Adults and adolescents can and do forage, travel, and sleep quite on their own, sometimes for days at a time. This unique organization means, for one thing, that the day-to-day social experiences of a chimpanzee are far more variable than those of almost any other primate (1986, p. 147).

It is rare, adds Goodall, for a chimpanzee to see *all* the members of his or her community on the same day, and probably never two days in succession.

> He may travel one day in a large, noisy, excitable gathering; the next day, completely by himself. He may feed peacefully with a small, compatible party in the morning, then join fifteen other chimpanzees, after a successful hunt, in the late afternoon. He may be one of six males competing for the same female one week, and associate with one female, far from any other males, the next. He may spend one day at the very center of his core area and move out to a far-flung boundary on a patrol the next (p. 147).

As Goodall has clearly shown, chimpanzees form social groups whose members frequently subdivide into smaller units for feeding and other purposes, and then join up again.

Chimpanzees, compared to some other primates, are a fairly stable society. Just the reverse of baboons, chimpanzee males remain in their natal group, and females transfer in and out. It is not surprising, then, that chimpanzees are a male-bonded society with the males probably related (Fleagle, 1988). Except for male siblings, the bonds are not very tight. On the other hand, the matrilineal family, especially the mother-daughter relationship, is very strong.

A chimpanzee community varies in size from group to group and from year to year, apparently depending on habitat—thinly forested, rain forest—female birth rate, disease, available food, etc. At Ngogo in the Kibale Forest, Ghiglieri estimated the community size at 55 members; at Gombe, Goodall's records show a range between 36 and 48 over a period of almost 20 years. In a study at Kisoge, at the foot of the Mahale Mountains in East Africa, the researcher Nishida (1979) found that during a 7 year study, the size of groups varied from 21 to 34 individuals. Estimates from various other chimpanzee study sites show a range from 15 to 80.

The geographic area each adult male visits in a year (combined) is called the *community range*, and its size varies with the number of individuals in the community. The more chimps, the more food is required, and therefore the larger the area required.

In their search for food, chimpanzees, unlike most primates, do not follow a regular route. Nor do they return to the same sleeping sites each night, but construct their sleeping nests close to where they ate their last meal. Within their home range, each chimp is free to go wherever he or she pleases and to take any route to get there.

There is no overall leader; any chimp—dominant male, female, even adolescent male—can lead a small party and determine the direction it travels. It need not be the alpha male. In a consortship situation, once the male leads the female to his preferred location, the female determines the pace thereafter.

Within the community, chimpanzees spend much of their time traveling, feeding, and sleeping in *parties* (see Box 11-1), which range in size from a solitary individual to quite large groupings. Usually, the number is small, probably between 5 and 13. However, size varies with season, sex, and destination. Feeding parties, for example, tend to be larger than traveling parties, and gathering parties are the largest of all.

(a)

(b)

(c)

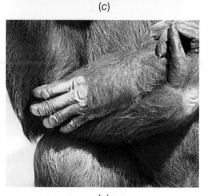

(e)

(f)

(g)

FIGURE 11-6   Chimpanzee gallery.
(a) Profile of female chimp; note especially facial prognathism and supraorbital torus.
(b) Low vault is noticeably visible in three-quarter view. (c) Prehensile dexterity is seen in the chimp's grip. (d) Chimpanzees have long fingers (but cannot straighten digits).
(e) Another view of fingers; note thumb, which is not as proportionately long to fingers as ours is. (f) Chimp and (g) Gorilla; note the differences in face and head of these two apes (chimp is female; gorilla is male).

Composition of travel parties also varies a good deal. Male chimps tend to travel with other males, probably relatives; adult females without infants prefer other females without infants and then males; females with infants travel most with juvenile females and adult females, with or without infants.

Grooming, as we have seen, is a widespread practice among primates, and is as significant in the chimpanzee society as it is in baboons. Aside from its hygienic function, it also serves social functions.

BOX 11-1   **Kinds of Parties in Chimpanzee Social Groups**

ALL-MALE PARTY Two or more adult and/or adolescent males.

FAMILY UNIT A mother and her dependents, with or without older offspring.

NURSERY UNIT Two or more family units.

MIXED PARTY One or more adult or adolescent males with one or more adult or adolescent females, with or without dependents.

SEXUAL PARTY Mixed party in which one or more of the females is in estrus.

CONSORTSHIP The exclusive mating relationship of a male and an estrous female.

GATHERING Group comprising at least half of the members of the community, including at least half of the mature males (an extra-large, mixed, usually sexual, party).

LONE INDIVIDUAL An animal who is completely alone.

Social grooming permeates virtually every aspect of chimpanzee social life, serving many functions above and beyond skin care. . . . [and] plays a vital role in regulating relationships, especially in restoring harmony in the wake of aggression (Goodall, 1986, p. 387).

Grooming often takes place when partners are in a relaxed and peaceful mood, and it is quite obvious that the groomee, as well as the groomer, enjoy the experience. Goodall recounts the story of a groomer coming across a tick or a louse:

With a quick lunge that may almost knock his client off balance, he seizes the affected part and, tooth clacking loudly, picks off the prize—which he then chews with exaggerated movements of his jaw. His companion watches the whole operation with fascination (1986, p. 388).

Grooming also occurs in tense and anxious situations. A frightened subordinate may approach a superior and groom him (or her). A female, frustrated because she has been unsuccessfully begging a male for food, may groom him perfunctorily. Grooming may be a dominant individual's response to a subordinate seeking reassurance. Two adult males in a tense situation are likely to groom each other although, if they are bitterly hostile to one another, they may not groom each other at all.

An adult female spends a great deal of time grooming her infant and other members of her family; they supply her with companionship and support. She does not spend much time grooming females who are not kin. Adult males tend to groom other males more than females, and are groomed by females more than vice versa (except during estrus, when males become the groomers).

Reciprocal or mutual grooming is characteristic of chimpanzees, but groomers do not always spend equal time at their work. After grooming for a bit, the groomer stops and waits to be groomed. Usually the groomee takes his turn, but a dominant male would groom an individual of lower rank for a shorter period of time. So would a mother groom her young offspring longer than the reverse, and nonrelated females might not reciprocate at all.

Like baboons, chimpanzee males are also organized in a dominance hierarchy, and, also like baboons, the hierarchy is not static. Changes occur when young males challenge females and then, one by one, senior males; when immigrant females compete for food with resident females; and when males compete for females in estrus.

During a stable period of status interactions—once established by aggression, observing others, or threat—each individual is aware of his/her place in the hierarchy, and aggression levels are low. But the hierarchy is subject to rapid change. The flexibility of the male dominance hierarchy may be seen in the following account from Kisoge, at the foot of the Mahale Mountains, south of Gombe. (See map, p. 317.)

> Kasonta . . . had been an alpha male for a number of years when rivalry developed between him and Sobongo, the beta male. In this ongoing conflict, the gamma male, Kamemanfu, was pivotal. At times the gamma male joined alpha against beta; at other times he reversed his position and joined beta against alpha. When the latter occurred, Kasonta, the alpha male, lost confidence and the beta male, Sobonga, became the alpha male.
>
> In 1976, Sobongo, with the help of the gamma male, was threatening Kasonta and succeeded in becoming the alpha male in June. One of the rewards of the alpha male is more frequent access to estrous females. During the months February-April, while he was still alpha, Kasonta was responsible for 85.6% of the copulations. But in months June-July, Sobongo—now the alpha male—was responsible for 87%. In May, the alpha status was unstable because gamma male Kamemanfu had switched his support to Sobongo and assisted him in attacking Kasonta. Taking advantage of the unstable situation, Kamemanfu showed the highest copulation rate.
>
> In January, 1978, Kamemanfu threw his support back to Kasonta who reassumed his alpha status. (Nishida, 1983, p. 332).

A male's ability to dominate is related to age. As a male grows through adolescence, he becomes dominant to adolescents and then adult females. As a young adult he begins to dominate the older males, and by middle age he reaches his highest rank. At this time he can dominate most, if not all, younger and older males. As he ages and his physique deteriorates, younger individuals may begin to dominate him (Bygott, 1979).

As we noted at Kisoge, a male's access to estrous females is directly related to his dominance rank. At Gombe, however, Goodall has not observed such a close relationship between status rank and reproductive success (personal communication). What seems to be important here are the tactics used by a male. These may enable a low-ranking or younger male to gain access to an estrous female, or even to lure a female away from a high-ranking male (Goodall, 1986).

Dominance and structural relationships are not as clearly defined among adult chimpanzee females. This is because some females rarely associate (their ranking is thus difficult to ascertain), and because the presence or absence of family members, such as a young or adult male or a high-ranking mother, may affect relative rank. In a hostile encounter between two females, the presence of offspring who could support her, especially young adults, would almost guarantee her success. A high-ranking mother would invariably come to a daughter's defense, if the daughter had attacked females older than herself.

When a female comes into estrus, her dominance rank rises remarkably. Young adult females have been observed threatening high-ranking females, and may even snatch food from some nonconsorting adult males. Rise in dominance rank is also related to the fact that highest ranking males often monopolize estrous females. However, this high rank among estrous females is only temporary. Linear rank hierarchy may also be present, although dominance is difficult to determine

BOX 11-2 **Stages of the Chimpanzee Life Cycle***

Infancy (0–5 years)

Birth to almost complete dependence on solid foods, usually weaned.

Childhood (5–7 years; juvenile)

Continuing close association with mother, but independent of her for transport and milk.

Early Adolescence (Ghiglieri, 1984, uses juveniles, 5–9 years)

MALES (8–12 YEARS)

Gradually increasing independence, more time spent with males, more and more aggression, beginning to try to dominate females.

FEMALES (8–10 YEARS)

Continuing closeness to mother, adolescent swellings of sex skin.

Late Adolescence (Ghiglieri uses subadult, 10–15 years)

MALES (13–15 YEARS)

Majority of time spent with adult males and estrous females; dominates adult females by end of period.

FEMALES (11–13 OR 14 YEARS)

Adolescent sterility, starting with menarche and ending when female is capable of carrying fetus to term; has regular sexual swellings, travels with males and mates, some consortships; occasional transfers (usually temporary); close ties with mother (not at all sites).

Maturity (Adult)

MALES

Young Adult (16–20 years)

Increasing integration with older males; patrols periphery of home range; attempts to raise social status.

Prime (21–26 years)

Continued vigorous attempts to raise social status.

Middle Age (27–about 33 years)

Glossy black of coat begins to change to brown; individuals still vigorous.

FEMALES (14 OR 15–ABOUT 33 YEARS)

Raising family. Female may be described as *young adult* when raising first child, *prime* for second, and *middle-aged* after third.

Old Age (about 33 years to death)

Gradual slowing down; tendency to withdraw from intensive social interaction; teeth severely worn or broken, hair thinning, back of old male scattered with gray hairs.

*Adapted from Goodall, 1986, p. 81.

---

because "physiological conditions of females make female relationships very complicated and unstable" (Nishida, 1979, p. 104). Generally speaking, older females are superior in rank to younger females. At Kisoge, for example, a past-prime female, Wantangwa, completely dominated all other females for the seven years of the group study.

Chimpanzee males are territorial, maintaining an exclusive home range by excluding alien males. This ensures the males exclusive access to their territory's breeding females, and reserves its forage resources for themselves and their offspring. Thus, "males benefit through increased individual and inclusive fitness" (Ghiglieri, 1984, p. 4). On the other hand, an estrous female maximizes her reproductive success by leaving her natal community and mating with an unrelated male. This would avoid "inbreeding depression," that is, *reduced* reproductive success. (See p. 124.)

The relationship between a chimpanzee mother and daughter is a very close one until the daughter is at least 7 years old. A newborn infant clings to the mother, holding on to her belly as she moves, and, for the first six months, the mother supports the newborn with her hand. Weaning may begin at 1 year of age and con-

Xenophobic (zeeno)
xeno: foreign
phobia: fear
Fear of foreigners, strangers, outsiders, other races, etc.

tinue until 4 or 5. For the first four years, an infant is almost completely dependent on its mother. As a juvenile (ages 5–7), a daughter is still heavily dependent on her mother, but this dependency is significantly reduced during adolescence (8–10) and disappears almost completely during the daughter's subadult stage (11–13 or 14).

A similar change occurs in the close relationship between a mother and her son when he reaches about the age of 10. The young male at this time is attracted to adult males and cycling females and, as with baboons, inbreeding with female maternal kin is avoided.

Adult or adolescent females tend to disperse and form small subgroups within the home range. They travel within small areas inside the larger home range, and, where home ranges overlap, they move back and forth between the two communities. Nevertheless, the closest bonds in a chimpanzee society are family bonds— between a mother and her offspring and between siblings. These last a lifetime, and even an adult male, after a tense event, may seek his mother's "reassurance" touch.

Sexual attraction serves as a bond among chimpanzees, but mating with an estrous female is a competitive affair, since there is always a number of males in the vicinity who are eager and willing. In addition, (at Mahale) the alpha male has prior access. A more reliable strategy is forming a consortship which, however, may take some skill, since the female must be led away from other males (but in consorting may actually mate less!).

One way of achieving his end is for the male to keep close to the female and groom her frequently. When an opportune moment arises, he may succeed in taking her away in consort. However, a female who is not interested can avoid consortship by showing her reluctance and making the association difficult for the male.

Not all consortships are necessarily with an estrous female. A consort may be a female between fertile swellings, one who is pregnant, or an adolescent who is not yet ovulating.

Chimpanzee males live in what Ghiglieri (1984) has called a **xenophobic** community. Adult males patrol the periphery of their home range, traveling silently in close compact groups. They frequently stop to look and listen, often standing bipedally to look over the tall grass, sometimes climbing a tree to scan the area for signs of chimpanzees in the adjoining home range. When they return to familiar areas, the chimps often break their remarkable silence by "an outburst of loud calling, drumming displays, and even some chasing and mild aggressive contact between individuals" (Goodall, 1986).

In their patrols, chimpanzees respond to the sight or sound of neighbors with reassurance contact behavior among themselves (Fig. 11-8), such as touching, grinning, erect hair, embracing, and mounting. If the two parties are approximately of equal size, they may approach and display until one or both groups retreat. Members of different communities seldom engage in violent agonistic behavior because only occasionally do they come close enough for face-to-face interaction. Should a patrol party encounter a single male, however, they might attack him.

While chimpanzee males rarely cross into the home range of another community, such "trespassing" can occur. Goodall (1979) tells of a community at Gombe that separated, a number of adult males and a few females moving to the southern part of their home range. Over a period of three years the original group fero-

FIGURE 11-7   Flo and Flint. Flint, at the age of eight, died of "loneliness" (depression) three weeks after the death of Flo, his mother. (Baron Hugo van Lawick, © National Geographic Society.)

BOX 11-3 **Jane Goodall—Pioneer of Chimpanzee Research**

Jane Goodall

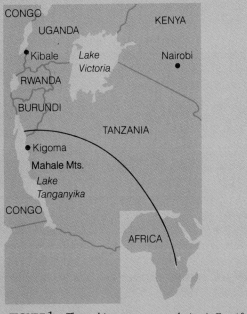

FIGURE 1   Three chimpanzee research sites in East Africa. Kigoma is Jane Goodall's area; the Mahale Mountains have been the center of research for Japanese primatologists for more than 25 years. The Kibale site, in Uganda, was studied by M. Ghiglieri.

It began in 1960 when a young Englishwoman, invited to visit a friend at a farm in Kenya, gave up her job and flew to Nairobi. Jane Goodall, who, at the early age of 8, had already decided to go to Africa and live with animals "when I grew up," could hardly pass up this opportunity to fulfill her childhood dream.

In Africa, a friend suggested to her that she get in touch with Louis Leakey, well-known anthropologist and, at that time, curator of what is now the National Museum of Natural History (back then, Jane had never heard of Dr. Leakey!). She sought him out and introduced herself. After they conversed, Leakey offered her a job at the museum. She accepted, and ultimately joined the Leakeys on their annual paleontological expeditions to Olduvai Gorge in Tanzania. Leakey was impressed with Jane's ability and dedication, and asked if she would like to study wild chimps in the Kigoma area on the shores of Lake Tanganyika (see map). Lacking what she felt to be the necessary academic background, Jane was surprised at the offer. Leakey himself, however, believed that university training might be a disadvantage in this case. What he wanted, he said, was someone "with a mind uncluttered and unbiased by theory," someone who had a sympathetic understanding of animals and a real desire for knowledge.

Jane happily accepted the position, and waited for the funding that Dr. Leakey set out to find. With monies eventually provided by the Wilkie Foundation (of the United States), Jane prepared to leave for Kigoma. She then learned that local officials objected to a young woman living alone in a jungle uninhabited by humans. Jane arranged for her mother to join her, which satisfied the government officials, and the two Englishwomen, along with a few African assistants, went on to undertake the now-famous research effort at the Gombe Stream Chimpanzee Reserve, today known as Gombe National Park.

Jane Goodall's pioneering research—now in its fourth decade—is the longest continuous study of the behavior of any wild animal species. As a result of her work, we have come to a better understanding of humans as primates, an understanding substantially broadened by anthropologists, zoologists, and other researchers from around the world who have followed in her historic footsteps.

FIGURE 11-8   Chimp reassurance behavior. (Baron Hugo van Lawick, © National Geographic Society.)

ciously attacked and killed most of the members of the southern community by forays into their home range. Goodall could not explain this behavior except for the possibility that the northern group had been prevented from using the southern part of what had once been their home range. By eliminating the southern group, this area once more became accessible to them.

Agonistic behavior occurs between adult males, reflecting a dominance-subordinance relationship, and is also directed by males against females and immature chimps. There is little agonistic behavior between adult males and infants, probably because infants are protected by the mother, although females with infants are sometimes attacked. Adult females are dominant to juveniles, but do not attack unless provoked. Adolescent males can generally intimidate young adult and adolescent females, but might be attacked by older adult females. In the rare agonistic interaction between females, the older of the two females is usually dominant.

Estrous females may be subject to attacks from resident males when they refuse to follow a male or even show reluctance. Moreover, anestrous mothers and infants may be in serious danger in meetings with strange males. In several such encounters the mothers were severely beaten, and on two occasions the infants were eaten or partially eaten (Goodall, 1986). Similar behavior is reported from Mahale. Anestrous mother Wantendele and Masudi, her son (40 months old), encountered a party of four males and several females from another community in the overlapping area of the two home ranges. When found by the observers, the mother was suffering from a bleeding head and other wounds, and Masudi had also been attacked but not seriously. The encounter lasted two hours—20 attacks directed at the mother and 3 at the son—when observers intervened to prevent the mother's death (Nishida and Hiraiwa-Hasegawa, 1985).

Unlike anestrous mothers, young nulliparous females are usually well tolerated by neighboring males. These young females move freely between their natal and neighboring communities, but the nulliparous females may be in danger from the resident females.

Another form of agonistic behavior has been observed. Between 1971 and 1984, six infant chimpanzees of both sexes were killed and/or eaten at Gombe.

Three of these were infants of stranger females and were eaten by males; the other three were infants of resident females and were eaten by a resident female, Passion, and her daughter. Cannibalism has also been reported from Uganda (Goodall, 1986). At Mahale, in 1982, Norikashi (1982) reported that a male killed an infant and consumed the flesh. Alpha or beta males killed and sometimes shared the meat of infants of mothers who had transferred in. The infants were all males; at Mahale, infants of resident mothers were never killed (Nishida and Kawanaka, 1985).

It is difficult to understand this practice unless perhaps it is to change an existing mother into a reproductive-ready female. That is, when a mother loses an infant, she shortly comes into estrus and is available for conception. (See Sociobiology, pp. 280–291, for a further discussion of infanticide.) However, in male attacks on strange females, it is the female who is the focus of the attack, not the infant, and the infant is not always killed. Further, after the attack, the males do not mate with the female, who is often seriously wounded. "Probably, we do not need to search for any causal explanation beyond the fact that the victims were all members of neighboring communities" (Goodall, 1986, p. 523). Chimpanzee males, it seems, just don't like outsiders.

Rape, as a form of agonistic behavior, is rare among chimpanzees* and appears to occur in an incest situation between maternal siblings—mother's offspring. The only rape cases Goodall reports were brother-sister encounters, which were infrequent and restricted to a few males, and one case of mother-son. In the latter case, the mother objected, and it was only after a number of attempts and many threats and even attacks, that the male succeeded. In the sibling cases, sisters usually discouraged or strenuously objected to their brother's approaches.

With fruit 60% of their diet, chimpanzees are mainly frugivorous (see p. 270). Leaves make up over 20 percent of what they eat, and almost all of the rest of their diet comes from 50 different kinds of plants. It is interesting that chimpanzees at different locations eat different kinds of food, which Goodall refers to as "cultural differences." Of course, chimps cannot eat what does not grow in their own foraging area. But chimpanzees in one region may eat food ignored in another. At Gombe, chimps feed on just about the entire oil-nut palm; Mahale chimps have never been seen eating any part of this palm. And in the Taï National Park, Ivory Coast, only the pith of the nut is eaten.

In addition to foraging for fruit and plant material, chimpanzees engage in predatory behavior. More than twenty years ago, Goodall observed chimpanzees eating animals they had killed, either by fortuitous capture or deliberate hunting (van Lawick-Goodall, 1971; Goodall, 1986). The chimpanzee animal diet, which supplements their predominant feeding pattern of fruits and leaves, consists mainly of the red colobus monkey and the anubis baboon, but they hunt other small mammals as well, such as bushpigs, red-tailed monkeys, and blue monkeys. In addition, chimps may gather various insects, fledgling birds, and birds' eggs. Their prey are medium- to small-sized mammals and birds, always smaller than themselves. In the Mahale Mountains, chimpanzees have also been observed to kill mammals, carry away the carcasses, and eat the meat.

There is some question whether chimpanzees are cooperative hunters. Busse (1978, p. 769) has pointed out that cooperative hunting might not be as efficient for chimpanzees as solitary hunting:

---

*Galdikas reports witnessing cases of rape among orangutans.

Division of labor Activities, especially food-getting, performed only by members of a particular status, such as age or sex.

Ivory Coast

• Gombe
• Mahale

FIGURE 11-9   The Taï National Park is located in the Ivory Coast rainforest in West Africa. Gombe and Mahale are located in savanna-woodland of East Africa.

The high level of observed competition for small kills supports the contention that over time individuals would obtain more meat by hunting alone than by hunting in groups. That chimpanzees do sometimes hunt in groups appears to be an incidental result of fortuitous encounters between chimpanzee groups and potential prey animals.

Nevertheless, chimpanzees on occasion hunt in groups of two or more. Goodall points out that baboons, one of the chimps' favorite hunting foods, were rarely hunted by one individual. Colobus monkeys have also been hunted cooperatively, according to Goodall (1986).

We have been discussing common chimps who inhabit a savanna-woodland area. A study of rainforest chimpanzees in the Taï National Park, Ivory Coast (Fig. 11-9) reveals significant differences from the former group. Although the forest chimps take advantage of opportunistic encounters, half of their hunting episodes are deliberately arranged. They hunt more adults than the Gombe-Mahale chimps, there is more group hunting (92.5% of all Taï hunts include at least 2 chimps), and more females participate in the hunt (Boesch and Boesch, 1989).

Like the baboons observed at Kekopey (p. 303), chimpanzees also share meat, but sharing is always solicited. Unsolicited meat sharing does not seem to be on the chimpanzee menu. Goodall observed male chimps occasionally sharing meat with other chimpanzees who begged with outstretched hands (van Lawick-Goodall, 1971). Scraps of meat left by eaters were quickly picked up by others. Some chimps attempted to take away pieces of carcass while it was being eaten by the "owner," sometimes successfully and sometimes not. Meat requesting, or begging, has several forms: by hand; peering (placing the face close to the face of the meat eater); touching the meat itself, or touching the chin and lips of the meat eater; extending the hand palm up; making "soft whimper or hoo sounds while doing any of the above" (Teleki, 1973, p. 148). Adult females, with the exception of mother-daughter pairs, rarely share meat with other females. Males are more likely to share (Goodall, 1986). Unlike meat, plant food is rarely shared by adult chimpanzees, although when sharing does occur, again it is males who do it, not females. Mothers, without solicitation, regularly share plant food with their infants, and one young adult female was observed bringing fruit to her sick mother, also unsolicited.

Another distinction between the savanna-woodland chimpanzees and the rainforest chimps is in their sharing practices. Sharing among the Taï group occurred 5.5 times more often than in Gombe, and in 31.9% of the time, the chimp holding the meat makes a movement to facilitate the individual reaching for it—a rare occurrence at Gombe (Boesch and Boesch, 1989).

Chimpanzee predatory behavior has been much discussed, and indeed it is an important chimpanzee behavior. However, meat does not make up a significant portion of the chimpanzee diet, even though they appear to enjoy the taste of it. "During the many tens of thousands of hours that field researchers have observed [all] nonhuman primates, fewer than 450 sightings of vertebrate hunting and/or feeding have been reported . . ." (Butynski, 1982, p. 423). Most of these sightings have been of chimpanzees, and although they may stalk their prey, hunt cooperatively, and share meat, these behaviors are infrequent and not well developed (Butynski, 1982).

Associated with food is an interesting aspect that might be considered a sexual **division of labor**. Hunting by males and gathering by females have, in the past, led students of hominid evolution to assign the sexual division of labor as a uniquely hominid characteristic. However, McGrew (1979) found that male and

BOX 11-4 **A Day in the Life of an Observer*** (14 October 1982)

It was a clear day with a light breeze. I began to follow Melissa and her adult daughter, Gremlin, with their two infants, Gimble and Getty. At 0905 Melissa led her family (Gimble walking, Getty riding) toward the loud calls that for some time had been heard to the east.

At 0930 the Melissa family joined two other females, Fifi and Little Bee, and their families. Gremlin displayed, running along the ground, stamping her feet, hair bristling, then pant-grunted (see Box 11-5) submissively as she approached and briefly groomed Fifi. Then began a boisterous play session with the youngsters Frodo and Tubi.

At 0957 Melissa and her party joined forces with the males and the other females. There was an eruption of pant-hoots, barks, and pant-grunts before things finally calmed down.

At 1021 the aggressive Satan charged past Melissa (who rushed out of the way, screaming) in a magnificent display. Followed by Jomeo, the two field assistants, and (presently) Goblin, Satan vanished down the slope through the tall grass.

Melissa stayed with Gremlin and adult female Miff, who was in estrus (and who became my second target). Athena, also partially swollen, was nearby. Seven adolescent males stayed back with these females. From time to time one of the young males copulated with one of the females; each time one or more of the infants interfered, running up and touching or pushing at the male concerned.

Infant Mo, age three and a half, was being weaned. Each time she tried to suckle, Miff miffed her (at least initially). Mo whimpered and then screamed loudly and insistently for minutes on end, adding to the tension in the group.

There were occasional outbursts of calling from Jomeo's direction; each time, the females and youngsters gazed intently toward the big males, often responding with pant-hoots or waa-barks.

At 1230 Jomeo moved slightly apart from the others and fed quietly; soon he rejoined the gathering as all moved on, calling and displaying. During a rest period, Miff lay stretched out on a rock while other adults groomed.

Soon the males moved again, following Satan. Miff and the females followed along in the rear. Ahead of us Jomeo and the males climbed into tall trees. Some of the females joined them; others, including Miff, moved higher still and began feeding on delicious *muhandehande* fruits. Soon the whole gathering, widely spread out, was feeding on these fruits, moving leisurely from tree to tree.

At 1318 I changed targets again and began following the two orphans, Skosha and Kristal. Pant-grunting as Satan climbed into their tree, they moved to greet him. I saw Jomeo and the young male Atlas heading north. Satan climbed down and wandered after them, and one by one the others followed. An adolescent male, Beethoven, out of sight of his superiors, performed a spectacular, hair-bristling, charging display (directed at no one, as though "practicing"), then moved on after the others.

By 1415 the only chimpanzees visible, other than my targets, were Pom and her young siblings. Pax, age four and a half, tried to get Kristal to play, but she refused. Gradually the two families drifted apart.

Later in the day (we learn from the reports of the field assistants) other females dropped out as the main party headed farther and farther north. Only two females, both of whom were in estrus and both of whom had core areas to the north of the community range, stayed with the males after 1615.

One of the things that was so striking that day was the sheer exuberance of the chimpanzees. If they had been humans, we would not hesitate to say that they were having tremendous fun. There was a good deal of noise and much play, mating, and grooming. There were wild displays with a lot of screaming, but no serious fighting. It was a carnival atmosphere.

---

*Adapted, with permission, from Goodall, 1986, pp. 150–151.

BOX 11-5 **Calls***

Made by a subordinate to a higher-ranking individual; token of respect; maintains friendly relations within community.

WAA-BARK Loud, sharp sound, given in a variety of agonistic contexts.

LIP SMACKING, TOOTH CLACKING Frequently accompanies social grooming.

PANT-HOOTS Most commonly heard call of adult individuals; serves to identify caller; given upon arrival at a new food source, when two parties meet, after return from patrol, during social excitement, during feeding, and during nesting in the evening.

*Adapted after Goodall, 1986.

female chimpanzees do not ingest the same kind of food. An analysis of a ten-month collection of fecal samples of chimpanzees at Gombe showed "a marked sex difference in insect eating: 45 of 81 (56%) female fecal samples contained at least one type of insect remains. Only 31 of 113 (27%) male fecal samples did so" (McGrew, 1979, p. 448). Fecal remains also showed that, in thirteen out of fourteen cases, it was the males who had eaten birds and mammals. It would appear from these data that, although males eat insects (especially termites), the bulk of insects are sought and eaten by females, but vertebrates are the domain of males.

Behavior associated with food seems especially pertinent in this discussion. We have seen that males share meat with friends and relatives (when solicited), and males also, on occasion, share plant food with both sexes. Mothers often share food (unsolicited) with their infants, and daughters have been seen sharing, again unsolicited, with mothers.

As mentioned, male chimps are occasional predators, and although much of their meat is obtained fortuitously, they deliberately pursue prey, perhaps even cooperatively. What is more significant is that obtaining meat

> often involves primarily male groups roaming relatively great distances and acting cooperatively when the appropriate situation fortuitously arises—in short, *hunting*. On the other hand, female chimpanzees (predominantly) obtain ants and termites by prolonged, systematic, and repetitive manipulative sequences . . . accumulating a meal of many small units that are usually concentrated at a few known permanent sources—in short, gathering (McGrew, 1979, p. 450).

This sex difference might be considered as the basis for the hominid division of labor of female-gatherer and male-hunter that at some point developed in hominid evolution.

Cultural Behavior

Another trait that makes chimpanzees attractive as models for our hominid ancestors may be called *cultural behavior*. Cultural behavior is learned behavior. We have already pointed out that all mammals are capable of learning, and among mammals, primates are the most capable. Among nonhuman primates, chimpanzees excel in the degree to which they make use of learned behavior. An outstanding example of learned behavior is chimpanzee tool manufacturing.

More than twenty-five years ago Goodall (1965) observed what has become the best-known example of nonhuman primate toolmaking: termite fishing (Fig. 11-10). The chimpanzee inserts and probes in subterranean mounds or nests of termites with pieces of bark, vine, grass blades, or twigs. When the termites seize the probe, the chimp then withdraws the tool and eats the attached termites with its lips and teeth. Chimpanzees modify some of these objects, such as twigs, by removing the leaves—in effect manufacturing a stick from the natural material, a twig. Indeed, chimpanzees show the greatest frequency and diversity of tool-using behavior of any nonhuman animal. They drag or roll branches, fallen trees, stones, cans, and camp furniture while displaying. They have been observed throwing rocks at a bushpig during predation, throwing objects "overhead," "sidearm," and "underhand" (Beck, 1980), and even using a twig as a toothpick. They can, to some extent, modify objects to a "regular and set pattern," and have been observed preparing objects for later use at an out-of-sight location (Goodall, 1986). For example, a chimp will select a piece of vine, bark, twig, or palm frond and modify it by removing leaves or any extraneous material. She then modifies it further by reducing it to a certain length—not too long or too short—and may make several of these for future use. Chimps have also been seen making these tools even before the termite or ant mounds are in sight. The tools have thus been made to "a regular and set pattern," an ability once believed to be unique to humans.

Chimps also make sponges from a handful of leaves, chew them for a moment, and then push them into the hollow of a tree where water has accumulated. The liquid is then sucked from this homemade sponge. Leaves are also used to dab at wounds on their bottoms, and sometimes, when a chimp has diarrhea, leaves serve as toilet paper.

At Bossou, Guinea (Africa), observers Sugiyama and Koman (1979) watched chimpanzees crack nuts with what they call a pebble tool. The striking stone weighed from 17 to 30 lb., and the platform stone on which the nut was placed weighed about 35 lb.:

> A chimpanzee who crouched in front of the platform stone chose a dry palm-seed, placed it in the cavity of the platform stone, gripped the handle side of the pebble tool, lifted it up to a height of 5-20 cm, and then struck the palm-seed.... When a palm-seed was broken, the chimpanzee removed the white ovule with his fingers and ate it in about 1 minute (Sugiyama and Koman, 1979, p. 515).

The authors believe this nut-cracking behavior "is highly suggestive of early man's stone-tool culture," and perhaps it is. However, it is important to note that neither the hammer stone nor the platform stone was deliberately manufactured.* Beck (1980) points out that many animals use unmodified objects as tools, but only apes—mainly chimpanzees—deliberately manufacture tools for specific purposes.

Another humanlike activity is object manipulation. Chimpanzees manipulate objects for many purposes. They throw stones, vegetation, sticks, and feces (as visitors to zoos have learned to their sorrow). They also play extensively with objects, and they use leaves for cleaning the body. Chimpanzee toolmaking and object manipulation suggest that the *potential* for toolmaking is deeply rooted in the primate past.

---

*Observers of nonhuman primates rarely distinguish *natural objects used as tools* from *modified objects deliberately manufactured* for specific purposes. The term "tool" is usually employed in both cases.

(a)

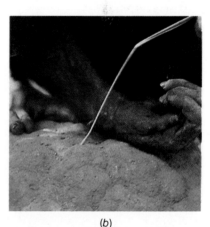

(b)

FIGURE 11-10 (a) Chimp termiting. (b) Closeup of chimp hands while termiting. Dexterity of chimp can be seen in ability to manipulate stem.

BOX 11-6 **Imo, the Inventive Macaque**

Like chimpanzees, Japanese macaques (a variety of Old World monkey) have also demonstrated a capacity for "cultural" behavior. In 1952, Japanese scientists embarked upon a provisioning procedure in which they supplied food at various places in Japan for groups of monkeys living in those areas.

Japanese monkeys have not been observed making tools, but one of them "invented" at least two methods of preparing food for eating. In 1952, sweet potatoes, a food new to the monkeys, were made available by scattering on the beach. The following year Imo, a young female, was observed using one hand to brush the sand off the sweet potatoes and the other hand to dip the potatoes in the water of a brook. The invention was picked up by juveniles through playmate relationships and was passed from juveniles to mothers, who then passed it on to their children. Within ten years, 90% of all troop members were washing sweet potatoes, except adults older than twelve years and infants less than one year.

Another invention, again by the "genius" Imo, was wheat washing. Wheat was distributed to the Koshima Island troop by scattering it on the sand, from which the

FIGURE 2 Japanese macaques. Japanese scientists established feeding centers and studied macaques as they came into the centers to feed. *(a)* In a tree nest; *(b)* at the feeding center; *(c)* eating at an old shrine.

(a)

(b)   (c)

BOX 11-6

monkeys could pick out single grains. Imo introduced the practice of scooping up sand and wheat, carrying a handful to the edge of the sea, and tossing the mixture onto the water. The sand sank, and Imo then skimmed the wheat grains off the surface and ate them! This practice also spread through the troop much as the sweet-potato washing habit: first juveniles, then adults—especially mothers—along family lines (Kawamura, 1959).

Although Japanese macaques display ingenuity in their invention and use of objects, chimpanzees must be considered more seriously than the macaques (and even the baboons) as a model for human behavior. We have described chimp toolmaking, object manipulation, and what has been called "cultural differences" in the kinds of foods eaten. These achievements of chimpanzees may seem remarkable, but an even more surprising achievement—not only of chimpanzees, but also gorillas and orangutans—is the successful learning and use of language. Until recently, language was believed to be one human attribute that distinguished humans from all other animals. Recent work with apes may change our thinking.

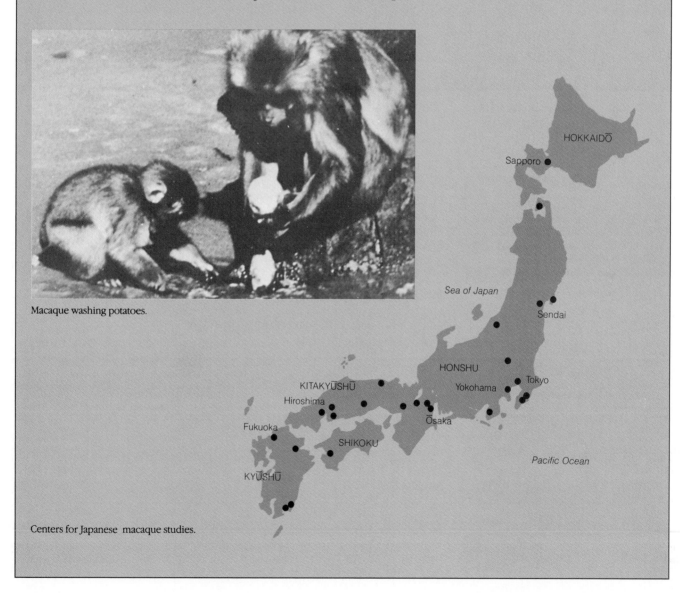

Macaque washing potatoes.

Centers for Japanese macaque studies.

FIGURE 11-11a Chimpanzee facial gestures. Chimpanzees are the most facially expressive of all nonhuman primates. (From *In the Shadow of Man*, by Jane van Lawick-Goodall. Copyright © 1971 by Hugo and Jane van Lawick-Goodall. Redrawn with permission of Houghton Mifflin Company.)

FIGURE 11-11b Jesabel, a 6-year-old chimp signing "drink."

Language and Communication

The question, "Do nonhuman primates really have language?" may be unanswerable. However, if we ask, "Can the great apes—chimps, gorillas, orangs—communicate with (what is agreed to be) language, that is, *American Sign Language* (ASL)?" then the answer certainly appears to be, "Yes." All three types of great apes have learned and have used sign language.

While many people were skeptical about the capability of nonhuman primates to acquire this ability, reports from psychologists who work with apes, especially chimps, leave little doubt that these apes learn to read signs and to use them to communicate with their trainers, with companions in their own group, and even to sign to themselves. More notable is their ability to pass the signs on to other members of their species.

Communication is common behavior among animals, from the smell and antenna signals of insects to the symbols of humans. Gestural and vocal signals have been observed among primates by a variety of investigators. Jane Goodall (1968a, 1971, 1986) documented numerous such signals among chimpanzees. She notes facial expressions, such as play-face and several grins, and vocal signals, including various kinds of hoots and grunts (Fig. 11-11). Expressions such as these are communication (see Box 11-5), of course, but can they be considered language?

Language, as distinct from communication, has been considered a uniquely human achievement, but work with captive apes has raised doubts about that supposition. Language has been defined in ways that would include insect communication on the one hand, or exclude everything except human speech on the other. Instead of debating the definition of language, we shall summarize some of the communication experiments with apes.

Probably the best-known chimpanzee that learned sign language is named Washoe, a subject in a project at the University of Nevada (Reno), in the home of her "foster" parents, Allen and Beatrix Gardner. The method the Gardners used involved treating Washoe just as if she were a child being raised by ordinary parents. The Gardners taught her signs just the way parents would teach deaf infants. In a bit over three years, Washoe had acquired at least 132 signs. "She asked for goods and services, and she also asked questions about the world of objects and events around her" (Gardner et al., 1989, p. 6).

Several months after Washoe's second child died, Roger Fouts* (who had taken over the training of Washoe) obtained a baby male chimp—Loulis—and introduced him to Washoe. Within twenty-four hours Washoe had begun to take care of Loulis as if he were her own child. Loulis acquired his signing skills from Washoe and from other chimps in the group Fouts was working with. Loulis learned just by watching Washoe, and eight days after he arrived, he began to imitate her signs. Washoe also deliberately taught signs to Loulis. Teaching him to sit ". . . Washoe placed a small plastic chair in front of Loulis, and then signed CHAIR/SIT to him several times in succession, watching him closely throughout" (Fouts, 1989, p. 290).

---

*Fouts was at the University of Oklahoma at this time. He later moved to Central Washington University and took along Washoe, Loulis, and another female chimp, Moja, whom he had acquired from the Gardners. At Central Washington, Fouts added two more chimps, Tatu and Dar, and has continued work with these five chimpanzees.

BOX 11-7 **Primate Communication**

Apes have shown considerable skill and intelligence in learning and using signs under human direction. In their natural habitat, nonhuman primates are also capable of communicating via signals.

> Chimpanzees have a rich repertoire of sounds, postures, and facial expressions which function as signals during interactions between individuals . . . indicating physiological state, emotional mood, social rank and so on, [which] facilitate the exchange of information among community members (Goodall, 1986, pp. 114–115).

Nishida (1987, p. 171) agrees and adds that chimpanzees

> have complicated systems of gestural and vocal communication, such as kissing, embracing, and touching, used for greeting, appeasement, reassurance, and display. These behaviors are performed in the context of reunions, dominance interactions, reconciliations, excitement, fear, pleasure, and grief.

> Boehm (1989a, 1989b), in his field study of vocal communication among wild chimpanzees, notes that long-distance calls are used to maintain spacing between territorial groups. Also, both the common chimp and bonobos, who often split and regroup, seldom remain together for long in large, compact groups. The changing subgroups communicate quite frequently at long distance on a purely vocal basis, chiefly through pant-hoots.

A research design, suggests Boehm, may be implemented to investigate whether chimps deliberately communicate vocally to another individual about something that is *out of sight or in the past or future*. If so, this would be *symbolic communication*, a capability humans have religiously considered to be uniquely their own.

It has also been reported that vervets, an African monkey, communicate in a *semantic* manner; that is, they use "signals to refer to objects in the external world" (Seyfarth et al., 1980a, p. 801, and 1980b). Vervets, for example, have calls that communicate danger separately for eagles, leopards, and snakes. Monkeys, hearing the calls, respond in different ways. For an eagle call, they look up and run into dense bush; if on the ground, they respond to a leopard call by running up into the trees; and snake alarms cause them to look down at the ground around them.

While these activities are, of course, a form of communication and apparently a more sophisticated form than that of other animals (except humans), calls cannot be considered language. As for captive apes—chimps, gorillas, and orangs—it is beginning to appear that the concept of language is more applicable.

There have been other chimpanzee training experiments. The chimp Sara, for instance, was taught by Professor David Premack to recognize plastic chips as symbols for various objects. The chips did not resemble the objects they represented; for example, the chip that represented an apple was not round and red. Another chimp, Lana, worked with chips attached to keys on a specially built typewriter connected to a computer. After six months, Lana recognized symbols for 30 words and was able to ask for food and answer questions through the machine (Rumbaugh, 1977).

Rumbaugh and colleagues, using a slightly different method for two other chimps, believe these two chimps capable of functional symbolic communication (1982, p. 379). Savage-Rumbaugh (1989) successfully used lexigrams, or graphics—drawings and figures—for her communication project. Two bonobo chimps were taught to point to, or touch, a lexigram that served as a symbol for a word. Touching a lexigram served as the equivalent of speaking that word.

Dr. Francine Patterson, who taught ASL to Koko, a female gorilla, claims that Koko uses more than 500 signs; that Michael, an adult male, has a considerable sign vocabulary; and that the two gorillas communicate with each other via signs.

Questions have been raised about this type of experimental work. Do the apes really understand the signs they learn? Are they merely imitating their trainers? Do they learn that a symbol is a name for an object, or that executing that symbol will produce that object? There are also questions about their use of grammar, especially when they combine more than just a few "words" to communicate.

In any event, psychologists in charge of these projects have become convinced that apes are capable of employing signs to communicate with their companions and with humans. Many of the experiments were conducted meticulously and the evidence is convincing. From an evolutionary point of view, these experiments may suggest clues to the origins of human language. One practical result has been the development of successful techniques to help mentally disadvantaged children to express themselves (Rumbaugh et al., 1982). Another result might be considered to be the revelation that defining hominids is not as simple as it once seemed to be.

Summary of Nonhuman Primate Models

There is much to be said in favor of using chimpanzees instead of other primates as models for the behavior of our earliest ancestors. We have already noted that the close molecular similarity of chimpanzees and humans indicates their divergence to be the most recent of the primates. The chimpanzee diet is more varied and includes different kinds of plants and small animals. Sexual behavior is also more varied and includes interaction not only when females are in estrus but also in consortship. Group aggression, while not common among apes, has been seen in chimps. Chimpanzees deliberately hunt and sometimes do so in groups. Sharing is fairly common and in some situations is unsolicited. Which ape is the most intelligent is arguable (how would they be tested?) but the chimpanzee's ability to learn and use signs and symbols is striking. Chimpanzees in the wild are noted for making tools to obtain food, the only apes to do so. These behaviors are similar to humans, and some of them were once believed to be restricted to humans.

If we assume that our earliest ancestors were hunter-gatherers, chimpanzees do not fare as well. Consortship is not a permanent relationship; the home range is not the human home base. The mother-daughter bond is not a complete family, chimpanzee hunting is mainly fortuitous, and meat "sharing" is rarely voluntary. It is assumed that hunter-gatherers placed more emphasis on meat than do chimpanzees. Also, we assume that the early hominids hunted game larger than themselves, which chimps do not do. It is also assumed that early hominids lived in a savannah environment to which they adapted; chimpanzees are essentially adapted to a forest environment. The social organization of chimpanzees—resident males and migrating females—is not a common pattern among humans.*

In trying to find a model for our earliest ancestor, we run into a number of obstacles. The main problem is that we do not have the archeological evidence to inform us of their behavior. The oldest hominids so far discovered, *australopithecines*, (discussed in Chapter 14), are dated at less than 4 mya. We know very little if anything about hominids that preceded them. It is not until about 2.5 mya that sites contain adequate evidence needed for reconstructing behavior, and by that time the earliest hominids no longer existed. It is very difficult to find a realistic model for hominids without evidence of what their life was like.

Studying nonhuman primates, however, is not an empty exercise. Potts (1987) suggests several reasons for continuing such studies: (1) from such studies, testable hypotheses may be developed about hominid evolution by comparing living nonhuman primates and particular species of early hominids; (2) such studies also give scientists beginning and end points for hominid behavioral evolution; and (3) these studies may show the ecological and social conditions in which early hominid adaptive behavior occurred.

Social Carnivores

Our closest relatives, the apes, are forest animals and are mainly vegetarians. Unlike apes, our early ancestors were presumably savanna dwellers and probably ate more meat. Early on, they most likely hunted small game and scavenged larger animals; however, when they did hunt, it probably was mostly in groups. To learn more about the origins of human social systems, it may be useful to look at other savanna dwellers and group hunters, the social carnivores: lions, wolves, and wild dogs. It should be noted that social carnivores and early hominids adapted in

---

*Patrilocal residence—women leave home, camp, and so forth, to join their husband's household—is widespread among modern humans, and bears a superficial resemblance to the chimpanzee practice of migrating females. Both behaviors may prevent inbreeding, but the human situation is much more complex and has a significant economic factor lacking in the chimpanzee community.

FIGURE 11-13   Lioness and cub at play.

somewhat analogous ways to a similar ecological situation. Phylogenetically, hominids are more homologous, of course, with primates, not with social carnivores.

Lions   Like chimps, a pride of lions is loosely organized, but like baboons, adult females and their young are the core of the pride. Males are dominant to females, and females have their own dominance ranking. Females lead the pride in their movement across the savanna, with males either attaching themselves to the pride or tagging on behind. Most of the hunting is done by females, either singly or communally. After the kill, males move in to eat before females are permitted to participate.

The close mother-infant relationship so typical of primates is not found among lions. Mothering ranges between care and neglect, and abandoning cubs is not uncommon. Mothers do not bring meat to their cubs, but after they have eaten, mothers may bring cubs to the leftovers, if any. The continuing relationship between mother and offspring, marked among chimpanzees, is absent in lions.

The social structure of the lion pride, although loosely organized, nevertheless provides them with superior hunting techniques, enabling them to catch large herbivores in open terrain. Operating as a group, lions are much more successful in hunting than solitary lions.

Wolves   Social carnivore behavior more similar to hominid adaptations may be seen in wolves. A wolf pack and a modern* human hunter-gatherer band maintain

---

*Recent hunting-gathering bands most likely do not structure their societies as did early hunting-gathering groups. One of the points of developing models is to suggest what that early social structure might have been.

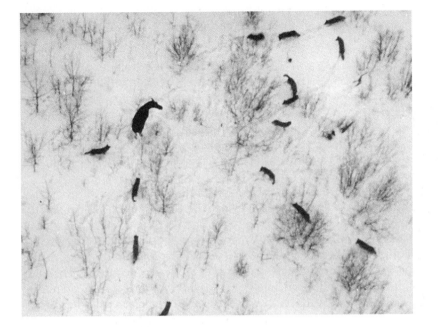

FIGURE 11-14   Wolves attacking moose.

an optimal size of the group in relation to the availability of food in regions with similar ecological characteristics. Both groups tend to control births socially, both live well below the carrying capacity of the environment, and both groups hunt cooperatively.

Food sharing exists between young and old, and rituals control much aggression within both the pack and band. In both groups, allegiance appears to be maintained through rituals involving "dancing" and "music." During food scarcity, both groups tend to split up and rejoin during abundance (Fox, 1978).

A pack of wolves is formed when a mated pair leaves its parental group to produce a litter of its own. Occasionally, several families may combine to form a large pack of 7 to 10 adults of both sexes. Wolves are territorial and avoid using an area through which another pack has recently traveled—probably indicated by urine-marking.

Care of young pups is basically a function of the mother who suckles them; however, there is great interest in the pups shown by all adult pack members. Weaning takes place at six to eight weeks, and pups eat food regurgitated by the mother or other members of the pack. When the pack hunts, the mother, or another adult, remains with the pups, and pack members bring back food for all.

Kortlandt makes the interesting suggestion that wolves (we would include wild dogs also) developed their cooperative hunting techniques as a result of hunting animals larger than themselves. Early hominids, he goes on, evolved similar cooperative hunting techniques since they, too, hunted game larger than themselves. Furthermore, the teamwork techniques of wolves required considerable extension of their social communication system. Kortlandt believes a similar evolutionary trend must have occurred among early hominids, but because the largely "instinctive social communication system" in hominids is poorer, they achieved an alternative evolutionary solution by extending their primarily "*noninstinctive* communication patterns," that is, speech (Kortlandt, 1965, p. 321).

Wild Dogs Wild dogs of Africa form very amiable and closely interacting groups, which average 9 to 10 members. Schaller (1972) reports that since the young tend to remain with the adults even after the birth of a new litter, it is very likely that a pack is composed of related individuals. Most observers do not believe a dominance hierarchy exists among wild dogs, but van Lawick (1970) is certain he observed dominance and submissive behavior. Unlike wolves, no territoriality exists among wild dogs. Ranges overlap considerably without agonistic behavior between the packs.

Care of pups is a function of all pack members, but the mother retains certain prerogatives. She suckles the young, and when the den is moved, it is her task to move the pups.

Both males and females hunt, but if there are small pups, usually the mother and possibly one or two others remain at the den as guards. When they return, the hunters share the kill by regurgitating meat to all who remained in the den. Wild dogs hunt more successfully than lions or wolves and Schaller estimates a remarkable 89% success rate. For this reason, as well as their fierceness when attacking, they have been called "the super beasts of prey" (Wilson, 1975).

Studying social carnivores is instructive because they inhabit an ecological niche probably similar to that occupied by early hominids. And, like social carnivores, early hominids also sought meat, either by hunting or by scavenging. It is possible, as Schaller suggests, "that some of the same selective forces which had an influence on the social [carnivores] also had an effect on hominid societies" (1972, p. 378). Since the carnivore group is superior to the solitary hunter in its success rate, there may, at some point, have been selection pressures in hominids for such cooperative methods as group hunting and encircling the prey. Living in groups makes division of labor possible as seen in the case of wild dogs, where the mother guards the den while others hunt. We can conjecture that fairly early on hominids also divided their labor, shared food, and may have occupied a home base.

FIGURE 11-15   Pack of wild dogs attacking zebra.

Hunting and Gathering Societies

We have reviewed two kinds of social animals, nonhuman primates and social carnivores, in order to gain some understanding of ourselves and our origins. Contemporary humans in an industrialized or agricultural community live far removed from ancient humans and, from an adaptive viewpoint, cannot easily be compared to nonhuman social mammals. However, there are peoples living at the present time in remote areas of the world who have maintained a way of life, that may be to some extent at least, similar to that of early hominids. A review of these people, whom anthropologists classify as hunter-gatherers (or, as some prefer, gatherer-hunters), may give some idea of how hominids lived 1 or 2 mya. We do not claim that contemporary hunter-gatherers live exactly as those of ancient times, but studying the contemporary versions may be as close a picture as we can get of the way of life of our early ancestors.

In the last few years, anthropologists have discussed at length the food-getting practices of early hominids—Did early hominids hunt to obtain meat or did they scavenge meat from the kills of nonhuman predators? Evidence is accumulating that appears to favor scavenging, but a definitive conclusion has not yet been reached. A recent study suggests that australopithecines may have hunted sporadically, but carnivory (or hunting to a biologically significant degree) was first practiced by *H. erectus* about 1.5 mya (Shipman and Walker, 1989).

If we wish to use a human model that might suggest the lifestyle of ancient hominids, there apparently is no choice but to use a hunting-gathering society. If australopithecines did in fact do some hunting, then we might find suggestive clues to that effect in a recent hunter-gathering society. It should also be noted that hunter-gatherers in recent times live in different environments and had to adapt to the ecology of the environment they inhabit.

Typically, modern hunter-gatherers live in small nomadic or seminomadic bands composed of loosely integrated families. They usually lack the more organized forms of kinship, such as clans and lineages. There are no specialized economic, religious, or political groups since the family itself is the organization that undertakes all these roles. Depending on the season and availability of food, the size of the band expands and contracts. Bands move from one area to another within their home range according to the availability of resources in different places at different times. The food resources used by the band are communal property, and all families have equal rights to them. To protect their resources, band members may defend their territory against encroachment by strangers (Service, 1966, p. 22).

A band is not a closed group; people constantly come and go, separating when food is scarce and regrouping for collective hunts, sharing a water hole, or participating in an important ceremony. Should conflicts arise, individuals may leave their band and seek to join another.

Men do most of the hunting and women the gathering, usually in small groups, but all share their food with other members of the band. Since hunter-gatherers exercise little or no control over the plants and animals upon which they depend, they have to accommodate themselves to seasonal and annual fluctuations in resources spread over wide areas.

As an example of a hunting-gathering society, let us take a brief look at the !Kung San of the Kalahari Desert in South Africa.

FIGURE 11-16   Map of San area.

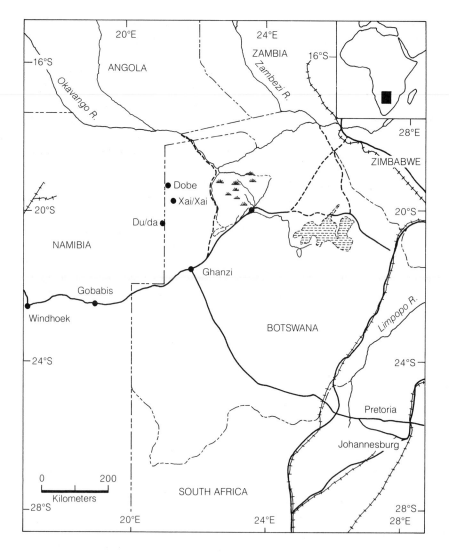

!KUNG SAN*

During the past twenty-five years, San culture has altered dramatically as outside influences have introduced new ideas, new material things, new values, etc. (See Yellen, 1985, for a brief report on Dobe San culture change.) The following description of the !Kung San, as a hunting-gathering society, is written in the present tense, as is customary in anthropology, even though they no longer live this way.

The !Kung San of the Dobe live on the border of Namibia and Botswana on the northern fringe of the Kalahari Desert of southwest Africa. This area of hot, wet summers (October to May) and cool, dry winters (May to October) is a sparsely populated sand plain across which the hunting-gathering !Kung San occupy approximately 7,000 square miles. Within this area are 10 permanent water holes occupied by approximately 500 San. Some non-San people live here, also.

---

*The diacritical mark "!" indicates a click (something like the clucking sound made to a horse), which is part of the San phonetic system. Anthropologists have discarded the term "Bushmen" for these foragers living in the Kalahari and now refer to them as San, of which the !Kung are one group. Material on the !Kung is derived from Yellen (1977) and especially Lee (1984).

At the water holes, the !Kung live in camps or villages* of from 10 to 30 individuals. The type of village varies with the season. In the dry (summer) season, the village is fairly large. It is comprised of from 8 to 15 huts and 20 to 50 people, is located near a permanent water source, and is occupied for 3 to 6 months. In the rainy season, the village, from 3 to 20 huts, is located near a seasonal water and food source and is occupied for 3 weeks to 3 months. In the spring and fall the camp is temporary, rarely occupied for more than 2 or 3 weeks, and no huts are built.

Until recently, each !Kung group moved every season, building and abandoning 3 to 6 villages each year. Eventually, these abandoned villages became buried in sand, and were converted into archeological sites. ". . . !Kung village sites of the 1960s strongly resemble the village sites of prehistoric foragers 100 to 500 or more years old . . ." (Lee, 1984, p. 33). A !Kung camp consists of kinspeople and affines (inlaws) who have found that they can live and work well together. Brothers, for example, may live together or apart, as may fathers and sons. The composition of the camp changes from day to day and month to month because the !Kung enjoy visiting. Each year about 30% of the population makes a permanent residential shift from one camp to another. There is a visiting network among camps, and during a given lifetime an individual may live for varying amounts of time at many different water holes. However, establishing residence with a camp does not require relinquishing a claim to any other camp.

What gives the camp its stability is its core, which is composed of related older people, usually siblings and cousins. Generally, the core is considered to be the water hole owners. Surrounding each water hole is land that contains food resources. This forms the basic subsistence area for the residing group. The water hole and the land immediately around it is "owned" by the *k'ausi*, the core of related people, and the ownership is passed from generation to generation as long as the descendants continue to live there.

A camp is built up over time by the addition of in-marrying spouses of the core siblings. A brother brings in his wife, and a sister may bring in her husband. These in-laws then bring in *their* siblings so that the camp has a relative—parent, child, sibling, or spouse—with links to the core group.

Settling at a water hole, the !Kung arrange their huts in a circle, with the entrances facing center. The huts are generally occupied by nuclear families, with husband, wife, and immature children sharing a single hut and hearth. Young, unmarried adults of the same sex usually live together in a separate hut, whereas widowers and co-wives have huts of their own.

People living at a water hole—residents and visitors—all share the available resources. Members of a camp, of course, have access to the resources, and, if the sharing breaks down, it ceases to be a camp. Visitors also share, and it is understood that the residents at some future time will pay a return visit to their visitors' camp and share the resources there. A fairly complex system of obligations apply between hosts and visitors.

!Kung men are excellent hunters and devote a great deal of time and effort to their pursuit of game. While snaring game is practiced, most of the hunting consists of pursuing game either singly or in twos or threes. Known to the !Kung are some 262 species of animals, of which about 80 are eaten. Although women do not hunt, men may gather when meat is scarce, and the food thus obtained accounted for 22% of all gathered food.

---

*Lee uses the words "camp" and "village" interchangeably.

FIGURE 11-17   A !Kung San camp.

When a large animal is killed, it is feasting time, and great cauldrons of meat are cooked round-the-clock. People gather from far and wide, and meat is distributed to all. The sharing is made according to a set of rules, with great care, and the arranging and rearranging of the pieces may continue for an hour to ensure that each recipient is given the right proportion. Improper meat distribution can cause bitter wrangling among close relatives. Excellent distribution will be fondly recalled for months.

As in most foraging societies, women do the gathering (see p. 233). As a matter of fact, the foundation of !Kung subsistence depends on the 105 species of edible wild plants found in their area, especially the remarkable mongongo nut, which

FIGURE 11-18   A !Kung family works at home.

provides up to half the !Kung vegetable diet. The wide variety of vegetable food available to the !Kung provides a cushion against changing environmental conditions.

In his fieldwork, Dr. Lee investigated the question of how hard the !Kung San worked. He found that over a four-week period, the overall work week was 2.4 days of work per adult. During the month of this study, at least, the people appeared to spend less than half their days obtaining food. They enjoyed more leisure time than members of many agricultural and industrial societies. And this was during the dry season of a year of serious drought! On the days the Dobe people were not hunting or gathering, they were either at the water hole entertaining visitors, or themselves visiting other camps.

It is interesting to note that the men worked longer hours obtaining food than the women.* Men worked an average of 12 out of 28 days (providing about 45% of the food), while women worked about 9 (providing about 55% of the food), a work schedule that contradicts the view that women are the workhorses of a foraging society. A day of gathering by the women produced about 68% more calories on the average than a day of hunting. Women, it seems, devote fewer days to primary subsistence activities, but produce more calories than the men.

At one time, it was believed that hunter-gatherers lived a hand-to-mouth existence, ever on the brink of starvation. The !Kung, with a modest subsistence effort of 2.4 workdays per week, produced an adequate diet *and* a surplus. What makes this way of life possible, Lee believes, is sharing:

> If I had to point to one single feature that makes this way of life possible, I would focus on *sharing*. Each !Kung is not an island unto himself or herself; each is part of a collective. It is a small, rudimentary collective, and at times a fragile one, but it is a collective nonetheless. What I mean is that the living group pools the resources that are brought into camp so that everyone receives an equitable share. The !Kung and people like them don't do this out of nobility of soul or because they are made of better stuff

FIGURE 11-19 !Kung hunter returns to camp.

---

*This report has been criticized since it does not include such food preparation as fetching water, getting wood for a fire, and cooking food.

FIGURE 11-20 Carrying her child, a !Kung woman gathers.

A large-scale research program dealing with the San of the Kalahari Desert in South Africa was started in 1963 at the University of California, Berkeley, by Irven DeVore and Richard Lee. It continued at Harvard as the Harvard Kalahari Project and then branched out to other institutions. The membership of the Project expanded to more than a dozen long- and short-term investigators who have produced many articles and books in the past 20 years. The thrust of the research has been to gather ecological and demographic data and also to provide material from an evolutionary perspective. The Project aroused a great deal of interest, and the San people of the Kalahari became a center of study for many scientists.

Among the findings of the Project are those of Lee who concluded that the San cannot serve as a proxy of early hominids, and that modern foragers* are different from each other and from ancient ones. Nevertheless, Lee believes it may be possible to discern the *principles* underlying foraging behavior, which can then be applied to more dynamic models of ancient and modern foraging societies. Lee also found that:

1. The San food supply is sufficient for their needs, a situation they reached by using only the simplest of tools

*The terms hunting-gathering and foraging are used interchangeably herein.

2. The San maintain the flexibility to adapt to changing ecological circumstances, which is more important in a hunting/gathering group structure than maintaining exclusive rights to land
3. Sharing is an integral part of !Kung life

Another member of the Project was Nancy Howell who focused on the demography of the !Kung. This included various aspects of population, such as the age structure, causes of sickness and death, birth and mortality rates, population size and growth rates, fertility performance of !Kung men and women, and population perspectives of kinship.

Howell predicted that !Kung mortality will decrease and fertility will not increase, resulting in a 40% population increase by the year 2000 (in the 30 years from 1970). The population will be younger, and the dependency burden of children and old people on productive adults will be greater. Also, as the population increases, it places a strain on Botswana, the country they live in, to provide medical, educational, and other services. She suggests the authorities offer birth control services.

John Yellen, an archeologist, studied !Kung behavior that could be applied to past and future archeological field work. For example, he found there was no direct correlation between a specific activity and where it occurs. That is, it is not possible to say that spear manufacture, for instance, is restricted to certain locations, an

than we are. In fact, they often gripe about sharing. They do it because it works for them and it enhances their survival. Without this core of sharing, life for the !Kung would be harder and infinitely less pleasant (Lee, 1984, p. 55).*

In summary, the !Kung San possess what is central to a foraging economy: sexual division of labor; simple technology; collective, nonexclusive ownership of land and resources; and widespread food sharing within and among local groups according to the principle of generalized reciprocity.

Attempting to reconstruct the situation in which early hominids evolved is speculative since so little evidence is available, especially for specific events. Evidence from social carnivores, especially wild dogs and wolves, points up the utility of cooperative hunting, which may be at least one of the reasons for their success. Additionally, reproductive success is enhanced by their home base, where

*For a delightful Christmas story, as well as a cautionary and morality tale, see Lee's account of his Christmas gift of an ox to the !Kung. It can be found in the Appendix of Lee's short monograph, *The Dobe !Kung* (see Suggested Further Readings) and is titled "Eating Christmas in Nu Kalahari."

BOX 11-8

assumption often made by archeologists. He also found that hunting-gathering societies subdivide themselves into nuclear family units. He suggests that archeologists, by analyzing a large number of sites, may be able to establish the date the nuclear family appeared.

As we mentioned, the Harvard Kalahari Project aroused much interest among anthropologists, some of whom (sometimes referred to as "revisionists") have criticized the work of the Project scientists. The revisionists claim that Project anthropologists, as well as traditional anthropologists, created a scenario of foraging societies that runs something like this: Autonomous groups remained isolated from neighboring farmers and pastoralists. They lived in independent, self-contained entities, and they were subject to no other group, thereby retaining a lifestyle that changed very little for thousands of years. Furthermore, even if they traded with other societies, as many did, their culture was not significantly affected.

Revisionists, on the other hand, emphasize the dependence of hunting-gathering societies on a trading network. They are not, and apparently never have been, completely isolated. Rather, they are the products of evolutionary processes involving not only other foragers, but farming societies and complex socio-political systems as well. Revisionists also suggest that foragers have remained foragers because it is to the advantage of the

more complex societies—who have the means of control—to keep them that way.

Hunting-gathering revisionism is relatively new, and it remains to be seen whether their hypotheses can be tested successfully.

SOURCES:

Headland, T. M. and L. A. Reid. "Hunter-Gatherers and Their Neighbors from Prehistory to the Present," *Current Anthropology*, 30(February, 1989):43–66.

Howell, Nancy. *The Demography of the Dobe !Kung*, New York: Academic Press, 1979.

Lee, R. B. *The Dobe !Kung*, New York: Holt, Rinehart and Winston, 1984.

Lee, R. B. and I. DeVore (eds.). *Man the Hunter*, Chicago: Aldine Publishing Co., 1968.

Solway, J. S. and R. B. Lee. "Foragers, Genuine or Spurious?" *Current Anthropology*, 31(April 1990):109–146.

Yellen, John E. *Archaeological Approaches to the Past*, New York: Academic Press, 1977.

the young are guarded from intruders and fed by returning hunters. Whether cooperative hunting is found among baboons and chimpanzees is presently not entirely certain, but, in any case, it is not the prevalent mode of obtaining meat.* Furthermore, meat is not as important in their diet as is vegetable matter.

!Kung San are cooperative hunters. They share both meat and vegetables according to an organized and formal plan, use a home base, pair bond, and the sexes divide their labor. A few of these characteristics, such as sharing and division of labor (and perhaps cooperative hunting) may be practiced by nonhuman primates, but to a very limited degree.

On the other hand—like all contemporary *Homo sapiens*—San people have a fully modern human brain. As such, they have highly elaborated capabilities for abstract thought, symbolic language, complex toolmaking, and so forth. They thus

---

*It will be recalled there was considerable group hunting among the rain forest Taï chimpanzees.

are not strictly comparable to early hominids, whose brain sizes were much smaller, and who probably did not possess full language.

Moreover, the !Kung San were "disrupted" by outside civilization well before the first systematic anthropological studies were carried out (in the early 1950s). As a result, they now use metal knives and arrowheads (the bow and arrow itself is probably a fairly recent import), wear cotton clothing, and employ many other introduced items. How much all of this has influenced their culture (from our point of view, specifically their ecological strategies) is difficult to say. Certainly the !Kung San (or, for that matter, any contemporary hunting-gathering group) do not have the same relationship with their environments that would have been true even a few generations ago.

Sadly, the degree of outside influence disrupting the traditional !Kung San culture has recently become overwhelming. Much of the wild game on which they had depended is either decimated or partially off-limits on protected game preserves. Pressure by governments (in South Africa and Botswana), as well as economic pressures to obtain cash resources, have led many San to settle on reservations. Here, many have become exposed for the first time to alcohol, tobacco, transistor radios, infant formula, and other modern items (Kolata, 1981).

Conclusion: Fact and Fiction of Human Behavioral Evolution

As we have seen, no single behavioral model is adequate for reconstructing early hominid beginnings. They are all flawed in one way or another. What we must do, consequently, is to *select* those aspects from each model we think are most useful.

Certainly, early hominids were social. Moreover, we know that by at least 4 mya they were exploiting open environments and were adapted for bipedalism (although perhaps not completely—we'll discuss this in further detail in Chapter 14). By at least 2.5 mya, there were hominids using stone tools, exploiting some meat resources, and perhaps carrying these and other items back to a central place. As we will see in Chapter 13, this meat exploitation initially was limited mostly to small animals and probably the scavenging of larger kills brought down by other predators. Probably, by 1 mya, our ancestors were at least occasionally going after very large animals.

Thus, the models provided by social carnivores, savanna baboons, and modern hunter-gatherers have something to tell us about how socially organized animals cope in a savanna environment. Moreover, from social carnivores (analogously) and from hunter-gatherers (homologously), we can glean some clues regarding the advantages of group hunting, food sharing, and base camps.

In addition, chimpanzees offer further insight concerning incipient tool use, concerning parental strategies for raising slowly developing offspring, and concerning complex communication (this especially from captive chimps who have been taught American Sign Language).

Beyond these generalizations, the record allows little in the way of more specific statements. Lovejoy points out that early hominids were bipedal *before* they began to systematically use stone implements. From this, he assumes that the earliest hominids were adapted for carrying something else other than tools—

and suggests it was food. Moreover, the food was carried by males back to central places and shared with females to whom they were monogamously paired.

As we have indicated, hominids certainly were bipedal early on, and at a stage where as yet no definite stone tools have been recovered. It is quite possible— even probable—that these hominids did have tools made of perishable materials (wood, bone, fiber) perhaps even before bipedalism evolved. It is also possible that early hominids did have marked sexual division of labor, monogamous pairs, concealed ovulation, and increased male parental investment. However, there is no way to know for certain.

In reading accounts of human behavioral evolution, particularly those aimed at the general public,* we caution you to keep these concerns in mind. In so doing, it will be more possible to separate the hard evidence from speculation, and you can then draw your own conclusions.

Summary

Since humans are primates and evolved from primates, anthropologists believe that the study of nonhuman primate behavior may offer insights into hominid origins and further the understanding of human behavior.

As an interpretive and organizational aid, we have presented the model of human behavioral origins proposed by Owen Lovejoy. In his model, Lovejoy emphasizes several key differences between human and nonhuman primates. These are helpful in highlighting how our primate cousins can be used to better understand human evolution. In addition, Lovejoy speculates about the sequence of certain behavioral innovations among our earliest hominid ancestors. We disagree with the implications of this, but controversies of this nature are helpful in demonstrating how various models can be used to illuminate our evolutionary history.

Baboon and chimpanzee social behavior, as specific examples of nonhuman primates, are described in some detail. Cultural behavior of chimpanzees (e.g., tool manufacture and object manipulation) is discussed. Tool manufacture is important in considering chimps as a model for human evolution. Even more important may be the chimpanzee ability to communicate using American Sign Language.

With their more flexible social structure, ability to make tools, unsolicited food sharing, matrifocal emphasis, and the learned communication skills of captive chimps, chimpanzees serve as a better model of human evolution than baboons. However, since behavior of our earliest ancestors is unknown, it is difficult to confidently assign the role of model to any nonhuman primate.

Social carnivores—lions, wolves, and wild dogs—are introduced to see whether we can find similar adaptive strategies in savanna (or savannalike) living carnivores. Wolves and wild dogs show several similarities.

Finally, we describe the social life of a recent hunting-gathering society, the !Kung San, as a reflection of the kind of adaptation that might have characterized early hominids. (There is no intention of classifying !Kung San as early hominids. Obviously, they are anatomically modern humans with a culture far, far removed from hominid life 4 mya.)

---

*For example, Morris (1967); Ardrey (1966, 1976); Tiger and Fox (1974); and Morgan (1972).

Questions for Review

1. List several reasons for studying nonhuman primate behavior.
2. What behavioral traits are common to all nonhuman primates?
3. Describe the primate social group.
4. What are the functions of grooming? displays? dominance?
5. Why is the mother-infant relationship an important one for primates?
6. Compare baboon and chimpanzee social behavior. What is the relationship between the social behavior and group structure of these primates?
7. Are baboons or chimpanzees better models for hominid behavior? Why?
8. Discuss the learning achievements of chimpanzees.
9. Chimpanzees have been taught to communicate symbolically; why is this significant?
10. Is using a hunting-gathering society as a model for early hominid behavior justified? Explain.
11. Discuss the preceding question from an adaptation point of view.
12. Describe the different adaptations of lions and wild dogs to a savanna ecological niche.
13. How does the study of social carnivores contribute to our understanding of hominid evolution?
14. What are the similarities in the adaptations of social carnivores and !Kung San?

Suggested Further Reading

Fossey, Dian. *Gorillas in the Mist*, Boston: Houghton Mifflin Co., 1983.
   A personal account of Dr. Fossey's life while studying gorillas. She gives an intimate view of how gorillas behave and her relationship with them. Recommended.
Goodall, Jane. *In the Shadow of Man*, Boston: Houghton Mifflin Co., 1971.
   An interesting and personal account of the author's remarkable study of chimpanzees at the Gombe Stream Reserve. A book that should be read by anyone interested in animals, especially primates.
———. *The Chimpanzees of Gombe*, Cambridge: The Belknap Press of Harvard University Press, 1986.
   The most comprehensive book yet written on chimps, and probably answers everything you want to know about them—and more. Well-written, with excellent photos, charts, tables, and intimate accounts of Goodall's experiences.
———. *Through A Window*, Boston: Houghton Mifflin Co., 1990.
   A thoroughly interesting story of Jane Goodall's thirty years of work with chimpanzees in the Gombe National Park. As in her first book, *In The Shadow of Man*, Goodall writes here without technical jargon. She discusses several individual chimps, sex relations, kinship relations, and goes into the problems of diminishing areas for chimpanzees in Africa and the research involving chimps in medical labs.
Gardner, R. Allen, Beatrix T. Gardner, and Thomas E. Van Cantfort (Eds.). *Teaching Sign Language to Chimpanzees*, Albany: State University of New York Press, 1989.
   A valuable volume of interesting articles by specialists in teaching sign language to chimpanzees. The Gardners are renown for their methodology in teaching sign language.
Jolly, Alison. *The Evolution of Primate Behavior*, New York: The Macmillan Co., 1972, 1985.
   Various aspects of primate behavior are seen from an evolutionary perspective. Well-written and comprehensive; valuable to a student with some background in anthropology and psychology.

Kavanaugh, Michael. *A Complete Guide to Monkeys, Apes and Other Primates*, London: Jonathan Cape Limited, 1983.

While one might quibble with the word "complete" in the title of the book (which has only 224 pages), many prosimians, monkeys, and apes are described. There are many colored photographs, a good table of contents, and an index. This book is excellent for a ready reference and is written in an easily read style.

Kummer, Hans. *Primate Societies*, Chicago: Aldine Atherton, Inc., 1971.

A small and useful book on primates and their ecological adaptations. Suitable for a beginning student.

Lee, Richard B. *The Dobe !Kung*, New York: Holt, Rinehart and Winston, 1984.

One of the case studies in the Holt series. Written by one of the best-known scholars of the !Kung San. Lee's small book is a brief ethnographic record of the Dobe !Kung and, like the other case books, is written especially for students.

Marshall, Lorna J. *The !Kung of Nyae Nyae*, Cambridge, Mass.: Harvard University Press, 1976.

A comprehensive account of a San group by the anthropologist who headed a family expedition to the Kalahari Desert in the early 1950s. Recommended for students.

Mech, L. David. *The Wolf*, New York: Natural History Press, 1970.

Authoritative review of North American wolves written by a scientist who studies wolves in the field. Readable.

Napier, J. R., and P. N. Napier. *The Natural History of the Primates*, London: British Museum (Natural History), 1985.

Excellent quick reference and overview of primates with excellent photos.

Napier, Prue. *Monkeys and Apes*, New York: Grosset and Dunlap, Inc., 1972.

A Bantam Nature paperback. An excellent reference and introduction to monkeys and apes. Illustrations are outstanding. Highly recommended. An excellent book to take to the zoo for background information on primates.

Schaller, George B. *The Serengeti Lion*, Chicago: The University of Chicago Press, 1972.

The author, who first studied gorillas, turns to lions and has written another readable book. Also included are wild dogs, leopards, cheetahs, hyenas, and jackals.

Smuts, Barbara E. *Sex and Friendship in Baboons*, New York: Aldine Publishing Co., 1985.

A fascinating look at how baboons make friends and what they do about it.

Strum, Shirley C. *Almost Human*, New York: Random House, 1987.

An intimate account of a primatologist's study of baboons in Africa. Dr. Strum tells of her reactions to, and close involvement with, the Pumphouse Gang, a troop of baboons that she studied for more than ten years. A good read that takes you "backstage" with the trials and successes of a primatologist.

Terrace, H. S. *Nim*, New York: Alfred A. Knopf, 1979.

Raising a chimp and teaching it to sign, the author questions whether chimps really learn language. Written in an easy and readable style.

Waal, Frans De. *Peacemaking Among Primates*, Cambridge: Harvard University Press, 1989.

An interesting view of aggression and control of aggression among chimpanzees at Arnhem Zoo in the Netherlands. The author has had years of field work in Africa, observing chimpanzees in their natural habitat. He makes the point that chimpanzees are not often aggressive and there appears to be a balanced behavior with aggression occurring only under great pressure.

Washburn, S. L., and Ruth Moore. *Ape into Human* (2nd Ed.), Boston: Little, Brown & Co., 1980.

An expert on primate behavior and early hominid evolution and a first-rate science writer have coauthored a fascinating little book on human evolution. Highly recommended.

Primate Evolution

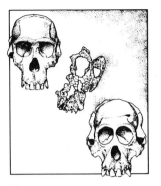

Contents

Is There
a Bigfoot?

Ancient legends tell of Sasquatch, a strange, hairy, bipedal creature prowling the wilds of North America. In fact, Sasquatches, abominable snowmen, and other such creatures have been reported from at least 100 separate areas of the world. In North America, they have been reported most often from British Columbia, Washington, Oregon, and northern California. Various unexplained beasts, however, have also been "seen" from Alaska to Mexico and from the Pacific Coast to northern Michigan. Tales of these creatures, which are usually called *Bigfoot*, are today even further embellished as sightings, footprints, hair fragments, feces, and even photographs have been collected. Are we dealing with fact or fiction?

If Bigfoot lives, what could it be? Reports are consistent, detailing a very large (eight to twelve foot), upright animal. Its size, hair, and location (in the cold Northwest) all imply a mammal. Its body shape and locomotion further limit the possibilities. Possibly it is a bear, but the gait and footprints are not right. What is left then? A hominoid of some sort?

Is this possible? In any objective pursuit of knowledge we must admit that *anything* is possible, but some things are highly improbable. What kinds of hominoids are native to the New World? The only definite remains of indigenous hominoids in North, Central, or South America are those of *Homo sapiens* (and these are relatively recent—in the last 20,000 years or so).

If Bigfoot is a hominoid, where did it come from? The closest fossil primate matching the dimensions of the fleeting Sasquatches is *Gigantopithecus*. Remains of this extinct hominoid are well known from the Old World during the Pleistocene, but none has ever been found in the New World. Such a big animal has exceedingly large teeth, which generally have a fairly good chance of being preserved. From China alone there are more than 1,000 *Gigantopithecus* teeth, and this giant hominoid has not roamed the forests of China for half a million years. It seems very strange indeed. If *Gigantopithecus* (or one of its supposed descendants) is still living, why have we not found any bones or teeth of this form? If such a large animal has existed for tens of thousands of years, where is the hard evidence?

What about the hundreds of sightings? Could they all have been faked? Probably not. Many of these people, no doubt, saw *something*. Perhaps often they were bears; the imagination can greatly influence our objectivity when primed with romantic tales of mythical beasts. What about footprints, photos, hairs, and fecal material? The prints (at least many of them) could have been faked, and so too with the photos (the primary evidence—a 16-mm film taken in northern California in 1967). Such a circumstance would suggest an elaborate, deliberate hoax, not a happy conclusion, but entirely possible (as you will see with Piltdown). The hairs and fecal material are from some animal, perhaps one already known, perhaps one yet to be discovered. The possibility exists that there are large terrestrial mammals in remote areas of North America unknown to science. Bigfoot may be such an animal.

However, of all the possibilities, the suggestion that this creature is a hominoid is about the least likely imaginable.

The conclusion that Bigfoot is an archaic hominoid is therefore both unlikely and far from conclusively established. But it is not *completely* impossible. Perhaps descendant populations of gigantopithecines migrated from China (through thousands of miles of environments exceedingly inhospitable to such a forest-adapted form), ending up in the American Northwest. In so doing, perhaps they left nary a trace all along the way. Furthering our improbable conjectures, perhaps they have existed in North America for at least 500,000 years, without leaving a single fossil remnant. Finally, perhaps they still exist today, but deliberately conceal themselves and meticulously dispose of their dead.

All of this, of course, assumes these are intelligent beasts deliberately avoiding contact with humans. They might as well be extraterrestrials on an espionage trip to earth. Once you leave the realm of science, you had better be ready to buckle into your spaceship!

SOURCES

Napier, John. *Bigfoot; the Yeti and Sasquatch in Myth and Reality*, London: Jonathan Cape, 1972.

Sanderson, Ivan T. *Abominable Snowmen: Legend Come to Life*, New York: Chilton Co., 1961.

Shuman, James B. "Is There an American Abominable Snowman?," *Reader's Digest*, January 1969, pp. 179–186.

CHAPTER 12

Introduction

In Chapters 8, 9, 10 and 11, you were introduced to the time scale of evolution, placental mammals, and particularly the primate order. We now turn to the fossil history of primates over the last 70 million years. With what you now know of primate anatomy (teeth, limbs, etc.) and social behavior, you will be able to "flesh out" the bones and teeth that comprise the evolutionary record of primate origins. In this way, the ecological adaptations and evolutionary relationships of these fossil forms to each other (and to contemporary primates) will become more meaningful. Please note that when we look at primate evolution, we are looking at our own evolution as well.

Time Scale

A brief review of the geological time scale will be helpful in understanding primate evolution during the Cenozoic.

Before discussing the fossil primates, we should caution that the formal taxonomic names for the various families and genera are horrendous to pronounce and even harder to remember. Unfortunately, there is no other adequate way to discuss the material. We must make reference to the standard nomenclature. As an aid, we suggest you refer to the marginal notes, pronunciation guide, and glossary for those names considered most significant.

ERA	EPOCH	APPROXIMATE BEGINNING (mya)
Cenozoic	Pleistocene	1.8
	Pliocene	5
	Miocene	22.5 (25)
	Oligocene	37 (35)
	Eocene	53
	Paleocene	65
Mesozoic	Cretaceous	135

Earliest Primates

The first radiation of the primate order has its roots in the beginnings of the explosive adaptive radiation of placental mammals in general. Therefore, it is not surprising that the earliest suggestions of primates in the fossil record are difficult

Purgatorius (Purg-a-tore′-ee-us)

Plesiadapis (Please-ee-a-dap′-iss)

to discern from early members of other placental mammal groups, particularly the insectivores.

The earliest discovered traces suggesting the beginnings of our order come from the late Cretaceous and early Paleocene in the Dakota area of North America. Known from several teeth and jaw specimens, this fossil form, called **Purgatorius**, exhibits the primate tendency towards a bulbous cusp pattern in the molar teeth compared to the sharper cusps seen in insectivores. Such a dental pattern apparently indicates that early primates were adapting to fruit and leaf-eating diets (Szalay, 1968), or perhaps a diet also including insects exploited in an arboreal niche (Van Valen and Sloan, 1965). Reconstructions indicate that the dental formula is still that of a generalized primitive mammal: 3-1-4-3 (Szalay and Delson, 1979). All that can be said now of this still fragmentary and mysterious animal, *Purgatorius*, is that if it was a primate, it was quite "primitive," which is not surprising considering its early date and still close ties with primitive placental mammals.

Paleocene Primates (65 my–53 my)

During the Paleocene, the first clearly recognizable primates begin to diversify. In fact, these forms are extremely diverse, with as many as 6 families and numbering more than 25 genera and 75 species (Fleagle, 1988).

One of the most widely distributed and best represented of these early primates is **Plesiadapis**, found in both North America and Europe. First known from the late Paleocene, the time range of *Plesiadapis* extends up into the early Eocene. This animal, known from several skulls plus several parts of the limb skeleton, has an estimated size range varying widely between that of a squirrel and a house cat. While these animals show definite primate tendencies, such as dependence on vision (though not completely binocular) and flexible wrists and ankles (though still probably with claws), they retain numerous primitive characteristics, such as lack of a postorbital bar, which serves to form a bony division between the orbit and the braincase. In addition, *Plesiadapis* and the majority of other Paleocene primates display unusual (compared to modern primates) specializations of their front teeth, which are large and procumbent (angled forward) and also show other dental oddities.

Given these dental specializations, the possibility that any of the Paleocene forms thus far discovered are direct ancestors of later primates seems unlikely. This poses no insurmountable theoretical problem, for we must keep in mind that our meager discoveries represent only a tiny sample of the already diverse kinds of primates living at this time.

The overall anatomical plan of all these early forms could be described as prosimian or even "protoprosimian," for they are certainly more primitive than any living primate. In fact, they are more similar in evolutionary grade to the living tree shrews, which give a fairly good model of some Paleocene primates (see p. 239).

You must note, however, that Paleocene forms are highly diverse, numbering more than twice as many as the living prosimians. While most are quite small mammals (some exceedingly so), a few apparently attained fairly good size, perhaps as large as a guenon (i.e., about 11 pounds).

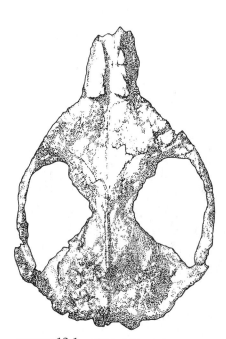

FIGURE 12-1 *Pleisiadapis* cranium.

Ancient Landscapes and Early Primate Evolution

The distribution and the eventual fate of early primate forms is understandable only within the context of the environments in which these animals lived. First and foremost, we must remember that 60 mya land masses were not arranged as they are today. As we discussed on p. 215, the continents have "drifted" to their present position, carried along on the shifting plates of the earth's surface.

In the late Mezozoic, the huge conglomerate land mass called Pangea began to break up into northern and southern continents. To the north, North America, Europe, and Asia were joined into Laurasia; to the south, Africa, South America, Australia, India, and Antarctica formed Gondwanaland (see Fig. 12-3a). Throughout the Mesozoic, the two basic land masses continued to move, with Gondwanaland breaking up into the southern continents. In the north, the continents also were separating, but North America and Europe continued to be connected through Greenland and would remain close to each other for several millions of years. As we will see, this "northern connection" had a very significant influence on the geographic distribution of early primates. In fact, North America and Europe remained in close proximity until mid-Eocene times (*circa* 45 mya) (see Fig. 12-3b).

What makes all this geologic activity relevant to primate (and other paleontological) studies is that land-living animals could cross over land bridges, but were effectively cut off by water barriers. Thus, we see species of *Plesiadapis* in *both* North America and Europe. As far as primates go, then, from their earliest beginnings (65 mya+) up until 40 mya they were mostly limited to North America and Europe (between which some migration was still possible). With further continental movements, the "New World" and "Old World" became completely separated and thereby influenced the evolutionary histories of primates still living today (see p. 250).

As the continents moved, climatic conditions changed dramatically. In the Mesozoic and into the Paleocene, the continental masses were clustered closer to the equator, and as Laurasia in particular moved north, its climate cooled.

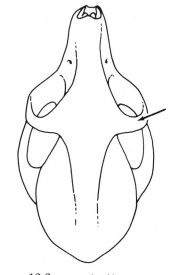

FIGURE 12-2   Postorbital bar.

FIGURE 12-3   Continental drift. Changes in position of the continental plates from Late Paleozoic to Late Eocene. (*a*) The position of the continents during the Mesozoic (*c.* 125 mya). Pangea is breaking up into a northern land mass (Laurasia) and a southern land mass (Gondwanaland). (*b*) The position of the continents during much of the Paleocene and Eocene (up to *c.* 45 mya).

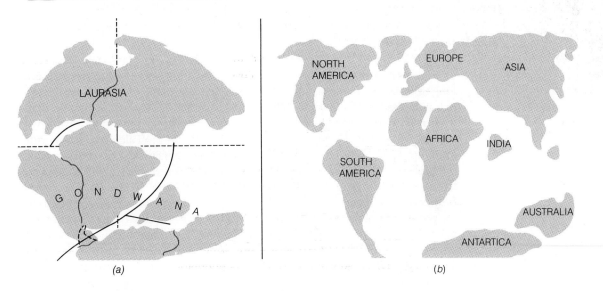

(a)

(b)

Moreover, the fragmenting of the land masses and the consequent altering of marine flow patterns (less exchange between northern and southern seas) caused the climate to cool even further.

Finally, these climatic shifts also heavily affected plant communities. Rather than the primitive, mostly tropical flora characteristic of the Mesozoic (ferns, cycads, etc.), what we see emerging in the Cenozoic is the rapid radiation of the seed plants (including flowering plants, deciduous trees, grasses, etc.). Indeed, many of these plants are frequently pollinated by insects. As insects thus became more abundant, so did the animals who fed on them—including early primates. The world was never to be the same again.

Clearly, then, it is extremely important to interpret primate evolution within the context of the earth's changing environments.

Eocene Primates (53 my–37 my)

The first primates of modern aspect appear during the Eocene. These can now clearly be called prosimians and closely resemble the loris/lemur evolutionary grade. Primate diversification accelerates during this epoch, with 4 new families and more than 60 genera represented during the 16-million-year span of the Eocene.

The Eocene may be characterized as the heyday of prosimians, who attained their widest geographic distribution and broadest adaptive radiation during this period. Indeed, almost four times as many genera are found in the Eocene than are known for the whole world today (16 living genera, with 10 of these confined to Madagascar).

The most diversified and best-known Eocene primates are members of the lemurlike Adapidae, which includes some 10 genera. The four best known of these are:

Cantius	North America and Europe
Adapis (Ad'-a-piss)	Europe
Notharctus (Noth-ark'-tus)	North America
Smilodectes (Smi-lo-dek'-teese)	North America

Some of these animals have been known from fossil evidence for a remarkably long time. In fact, the initial discovery of *Adapis* was made in France in 1821 and first described by Cuvier himself.

As mentioned, all these animals are fairly lemurlike in general adaptive level and show distinctive primate tendencies not seen in the Paleocene forms. For example, they all now have a complete postorbital bar (Fig. 12-2), larger, rounder braincases, nails instead of claws, and the eyes are rotated forward, allowing overlapping fields of perception and thus binocular vision. In the limb skeleton, further developments in prehensility are suggested, and some evidence points to the presence of an opposable large toe. In all these respects, we see the typical primate adaptive strategies allowing exploitation of an arboreal environment. Whereas these forms resemble lemurs in overall anatomical plan, they do not show the same specializations seen in contemporary lorises and lemurs, such as development of the dental comb (see p. 241).

The separate evolution of the Malagasy lemurs may date to late Eocene times, but since this island was already isolated by a deep channel from mainland Africa, they apparently reached their island sanctuary by unintentionally floating over on drifting debris.

The other major group of Eocene prosimians is the family Omomyidae, known from numerous specimens of jaws and teeth. Omomyids are the most widely distributed of known Eocene prosimians, with discoveries in North Africa and Europe, and a few specimens from Asia as well.

The earlier members of the family are somewhat more generalized than the later ones and may form an ancestral basis for all later anthropoids, New World monkeys, Old World monkeys, apes, and hominids. Additionally, some of the omomyids from the late Eocene of Europe have been suggested as closely related to the tarsier. However, many of the similarities noted are apparently superficial ones, not necessarily indicating any unique (i.e., shared-derived) relationship (Fleagle, 1988). Nevertheless, at least one feature, the position of the olfactory bulb, links these Eocene forms with later haplorhines (see p. 243). Also of interest is the fact that, when we enter later epochs, there are forms quite clearly sharing tarsier-like affinities, from the Oligocene of Egypt and from the Miocene in Thailand.

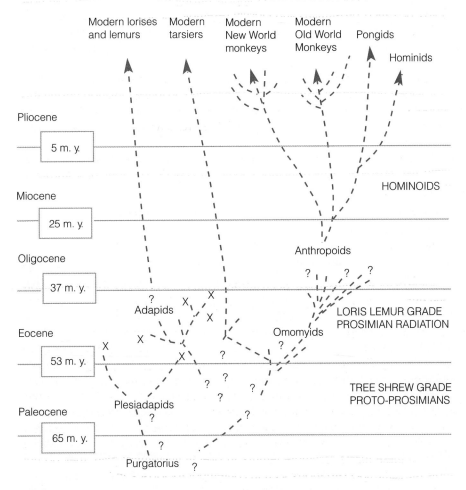

FIGURE 12-4   Summary, early primate evolution.

New World Monkeys

The center of action for primate evolution after the close of the Eocene is confined largely to the Old World, for only on the continents of Africa and Eurasia can we trace the evolutionary development of apes and hominids.

However, the New World, while geographically separated from the Old World, was not completely devoid of anthropoid stock, for here the ceboids evolved in their own right.

Any discussion of ceboid evolution and its relation to Old World anthropoid developments must consider crucial geological events, particularly continental drift. In the late Eocene and early Oligocene, South America was an island continent separate from North America and Africa.

In such a geological context, the introduction of monkeys into South America poses a certain problem. Some authorities have postulated that, because the open water distance between South America and Africa was still not very great, monkeys, originating in Africa, could then have rafted to the New World (Gavan, 1977; Ciochon and Chiarelli, 1980).

In any case, that Old and New World primates share any evolutionary history since at least the early Oligocene (37–35 mya) is unlikely. There is no trace of any ancestor of our lineage anywhere in the New World following this time until fully modern *Homo sapiens* walked into the New World during the late Pleistocene.

While primate fossils abound in the Western Hemisphere (particularly North America) during the early Cenozoic, the record is extremely sparse later on. For the entire span of Oligocene to late Pleistocene, we have only a few bits and pieces, a jaw fragment from Bolivia, a nearly complete skull from Texas, several specimens from southern Argentina, and a few other small fragments from Colombia and Jamaica. Together, all the evidence comprises barely a dozen individuals. Thus, tracing the evolutionary heritage of New World monkeys with any degree of certainty is a difficult task.

Old World Anthropoids

The focus of our attention will henceforth exclusively be the Old World (Europe, Asia, Africa), for this area is where our ancestors have lived for the past 35 million years. This evolutionary and geographic fact is reflected in the grouping of Old World anthropoids (Old World monkeys, apes, and humans) into a common infraorder (Catarrhini) as opposed to the infraorder for New World monkeys (Platyrrhini).

Oligocene (37 my–22.5 my) 35mya

It is apparent that during this epoch a great deal of evolutionary action was taking place; by the end of the Oligocene, Old World monkeys and hominoids were probably evolving along their separate evolutionary pathways. No doubt, diverse species of anthropoids were adapting to varied ecological niches in Africa and probably Asia and Europe as well. Unfortunately, the fossil record for the entire period is limited to only one locality in Egypt, 60 miles southwest of Cairo. This site, called the *Fayum*, is today an extremely arid region 100 miles inland, but, in Oligocene times, it was located close to the Mediterranean shore and was traversed by meandering streams crisscrossing through areas of tropical rain forest. The extremely rich fossil-bearing beds were laid down during the early Oligocene, between 37 and 31 mya.

Much of the Fayum fossil material is quite fragmentary. Consequently, evolutionary interpretations are not as unambiguous as we would like. Given the nature of the material, the classification of the fossils into recognized genera and species (always a difficult task; see p. 369) is somewhat disputed. The leading researcher of the Fayum fossil primates, E. L. Simons of Duke University, has recognized seven different genera from the Fayum, six anthropoids and one prosimian (Simons, 1985). In addition, the new tarsier-like fossil previously mentioned would add yet another form to this impressive tally (Fleagle, 1988). Altogether, an estimated 1,000 specimens have been recovered from the remarkably productive Fayum area. The three best known of these genera are discussed below.

***Apidium* (Two Species)**   A well-known 30-million-year-old fossil animal from the Fayum is **Apidium**, represented by about 80 jaws or partial dentitions and over 100 postcranial elements. This animal, about the size of a squirrel, had several anthropoidlike features, but also shows quite unusual aspects in its teeth. *Apidium*'s dental formula (see p. 245) is 2-1-3-3 which, as you can easily see, reveals an extra premolar not found in any contemporary Old World anthropoid. For that matter, extremely few fossil anthropoids in the Old World have this extra premolar. Some researchers suggest, therefore, that this genus and its close relatives (together called the parapithecids) may lie near or even *before* the divergence of Old and New World anthropoids. As noted, *Apidium* is represented by a large array of specimens, both dental and from the limb skeleton. The teeth suggest a diet composed of fruits and perhaps some seeds. In addition, preserved remains of the limbs indicate that this creature was a small arboreal quadruped, adept at leaping and springing.

Propliopithecus* (Two Species)   Among the first fossils found at the Fayum, an incomplete *Propliopithecus* mandible was recovered in 1907. Unfortunately, since detailed geological and paleontological methods were not yet developed, the precise geological position of this form is not known.

Morphologically, this fossil is a quite generalized Old World anthropoid, displaying a 2-1-2-3 dental formula. In most every relevant respect, this early *Propliopithecus* form is quite primitive, not showing particular derived tendencies in any direction. Both species appear small to medium in size (8 to 13 pounds) and were most likely fruit-eaters. To date, only this one specimen represents this *Propliopithecus (haeckeli)* species.

The second *Propliopithecus* species is considerably better known, with several new specimens discovered at the Fayum between 1977 and 1979. Geologically, this species (*P. chirobates*) comes from the upper beds and is, therefore, probably later in time than the isolated *haeckeli* specimen. Consequently, it is not surpris-

Apidium   (A-pid'-ee-um)

FIGURE 12-5   Location of the Fayum, an Oligocene primate site in Egypt.

---

*Some primatologists have suggested a third species of *Propliopithecus (P. markgrafi)* at the Fayum (Fleagle and Kay, 1983). This species, however, is also known from only a single specimen.

Primitive   A character state of an organism that is inherited from an ancestor (before a divergence) when comparing with another lineage.

Derived   Character state found only in particular lineages—and thus indicative of forms *after* a divergence.

Catarrhine   The group (infraorder) comprising all Old World anthropoids, living and extinct.

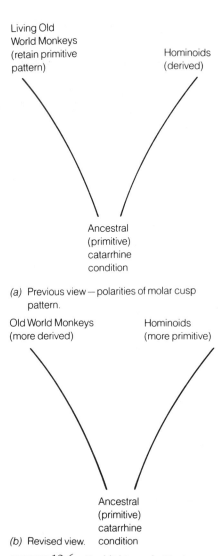

(a) Previous view—polarities of molar cusp pattern.

(b) Revised view.

FIGURE 12-6   Establishing polarities in character states among Old World anthropoids, an example.

ing that *chirobates* is more derived in several anatomical features. Still, this form is a remarkably primitive Old World anthropoid. Considerably more evolutionary change would be required to transform this animal into anything distinctively recognizable as either an ape or a monkey.

Earlier interpretations of fragmentary remains of this fossil suggested affinities with gibbons (Simons initially proposed a separate genus rank, "Aeolopithecus"). However, more complete recent discoveries have shown that such an evolutionary relationship is not likely (Kay et al., 1981).

Aegyptopithecus   The most complete and probably evolutionarily most significant fossil from the Fayum is *Aegyptopithecus* which is known from several well-preserved crania of different-aged individuals as well as numerous jaw fragments and several limb bones (most of which have been found quite recently). The largest of the Fayum anthropoids, *Aegyptopithecus* is roughly the size of a modern howler monkey, 13 to 18 pounds (Fleagle, 1983). *Aegyptopithecus* is important because, better than any other fossil, it bridges the gap between the Eocene prosimians on the one hand and the Miocene hominoids on the other.

With a dental formula of 2-1-2-3, *Aegyptopithecus* shows the familiar Old World anthropoid pattern. More detailed aspects of the dentition possibly align this Oligocene form with the Miocene hominoids (which we shall discuss shortly), but the evolutionary affinities are not presently well established. In most respects, the dentition is primitive for an Old World anthropoid, without specifically derived features in either the hominoid or Old World monkey direction. Recently, there has been a change in interpreting Old World monkey dental evolution. It was previously believed that the dental patterns (particularly, the molar cusp pattern) seen in Old World monkeys were the more **primitive** and, conversely, those seen in hominoids were more **derived** from the ancestral **catarrhine** condition. Reevaluation of the fossil materials now suggests that, if anything, the Old World monkey pattern is more derived, and the hominoid cusp arrangement is the more primitive. (See Fig. 12-6.)

The establishment of the "polarities" of primitive/derived characteristics is crucial to making sound evolutionary interpretations. However, the trajectories of evolutionary change are not always easy to ascertain. The determination of the ancestral catarrhine molar cusp pattern is only one example. In the subsequent section on Miocene hominoids, we will encounter several further dilemmas in sorting out such issues.

Even more primitive than the teeth of *Aegyptopithecus* is the skull, which is small and resembles the skull of a monkey in some details. Brain size and relative proportions can be reconstructed from internal casts of the crania thus far discovered (see Fig. 12-7). It appears that the brain was somewhat intermediate between that of prosimians and anthropoids. The visual cortex was large compared to prosimians, with concomitant reduction of the olfactory bulbs, but the frontal lobes were not especially expanded. Even considering the relative small size of this animal, the brain—estimated at only 30 to 40 cm³ (Radinsky, 1973)—was by no means large.

Evidence from the limb skeleton also revealed nothing particularly distinctive. From analysis of limb proportions and muscle insertions, primatologist John Fleagle (1983) has concluded that *Aegyptopithecus* was a short-limbed, heavily muscled, slow-moving, arboreal quadruped.

Further detailed study of *Aegyptopithecus'* anatomy has even allowed primatologists to speculate about the social behavior of this ancient primate. For instance, dental remains from different individuals vary greatly in canine size. This fact implies male/female differences (sexual dimorphism), were apparently quite marked. Comparisons with living primates further suggest that males may have been competing for females and that the mating pattern was probably polygynous.

All in all, *Aegyptopithecus* presents somewhat of a paleontological enigma. In most respects, it is quite primitive as an Old World anthropoid, and could thus be potentially an ancestor for *both* Old World monkeys and hominoids. There are some slight yet suggestive clues in the teeth that have led some researchers (most notably, E. L. Simons) to already place *Aegyptopithecus* on the hominoid line. Primarily because of the primitive aspects of this creature, other researchers (e.g., Fleagle and Kay, 1983) are not as convinced.

There remains, then, the problem of how to classify *Aegyptopithecus*. Even though they recognize that this fossil may well have lived before the major evolutionary split between Old World monkeys and hominoids (see Fig. 12-4), John Fleagle and Richard Kay still opt to call *Aegyptopithecus* a hominoid. Accordingly, they recognize that the superfamily Hominoidea then becomes what they term a "wastebasket" category (i.e., it is used for convenience, but does not reflect phylogenetic reality). This is one solution, although it will not satisfy all researchers. Perhaps, for the moment, it would be best to regard *Aegyptopithecus* (as well as the other Fayum anthropoids) as "primitive catarrhines," without referring them to particular superfamilies.

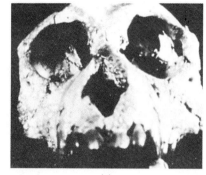

(a)

(b)

FIGURE 12-7 *Aegyptopithecus* skull from the Fayum, Egypt. Oligocene, *circa* 33 mya, discovered in 1966. (*a*) Front view; (*b*) side view.

Early Fossil Anthropoids: Summary

The spectacular array of fossils from the Fayum in the period between 35 my and 33 my demonstrates that anthropoids were radiating along several evolutionary lines. As with the earlier primate fossil material from the Paleocene and Eocene, the fragmentary nature of the Oligocene fossil assemblage makes precise reconstruction of these evolutionary lines risky.

TABLE 12-1 **Inferred General Paleobiological Aspects of Oligocene Primates**

	WEIGHT RANGE	SUBSTRATUM	LOCOMOTION	DIET
Apidium	850–1,600 gm (2–3 lb)	arboreal	quadruped	fruit 2:1:3:3 seeds
Propliopithecus	4,000–5,700 gm (8½–9 lb)	arboreal	quadruped	fruit
Aegyptopithecus	6,700 gm (15 lb) Size of howler monkey	arboreal	quadruped	fruit 30–40 cm³ some leaves?
(After Fleagle, 1988)				

Given the primitive nature of these fossil forms, it is wise, for the present, not to conclude specifically how these animals relate to later primates. In earlier primatological studies (as well as earlier editions of this book), such conclusions were indeed made, but reanalysis of the fossil material from the perspective of primitive/derived evolutionary modifications has cast serious doubt on many of these interpretations. The new interpretations, however, are still far from certain. As we have mentioned, untangling the polarity of primitive versus derived evolutionary states is a most difficult task. What many paleontologists would dearly like to establish is a clear link between these Oligocene fossils (particularly *Propliopithecus* and *Aegyptopithecus*) and the unambiguously hominoid forms of the Miocene. Unfortunately, as the following quote argues, this is not yet possible:

> In light of current knowledge about the very primitive dental, cranial, and skeletal morphology of the *Oligocene* hominoids, *Propliopithecus* and *Aegyptopithecus*, there is no reason to believe that any single group of extant hominoids (either hylobatids, hominids, or pongids) can be traced back to an Oligocene divergence (Fleagle and Kay, 1983, p. 190).

As you may recall from the Oligocene fossil anthropoid forms just discussed, *Apidium* (and its parapithecid relatives) may be near or even before the split of Old and New World anthropoids. Such a circumstance actually accords quite well with an *African* origin for New World anthropoids and their reaching South America presumably early in the Oligocene (see p. 250). *Aegyptopithecus* (and its relatives, including *Propliopithecus*) are seen by most as preceding the major split in catarrhine (Old World anthropoid) evolution; that is, the divergence of Old World monkeys from the ancestral stock of all hominoids. It would appear, then, based upon this circumstantial evidence, that this most major of Old World anthropoid evolutionary splits occurred late in the Oligocene or very early in the Miocene.

Hominoids: Large/Small; African/Asian; Fossil/Modern

Before we discuss the complex history of hominoid evolution, a brief review of their basic evolutionary relationships is in order. While currently not very diverse at all, the living hominoids (which comprise only 6 genera and 14 species) do serve as a model for most of the major radiations that also existed in the past. Based on size, the two major subgroupings are termed *small-bodied* and *large-bodied*; small-bodied varieties comprise the gibbon and siamang, and would also include all their ancestors and related sidebranches back to the time they split from the other major hominoid branch, the large-bodied forms. (See Fig. 12-8.)

Today, included among the large-bodied hominoids varieties are four different genera: *Pongo* (the orang), *Gorilla, Pan* (chimps and bonobos), and *Homo*. In turn, these four forms can be subdivided into two major subgroups: Asian large-bodied (the orang) and African large-bodied (gorillas, chimps, and humans). Again, these subgroup designations can be used to denote their respective lineages back to the time when they split from one another.

We can attempt to understand the diversity (and, admittedly, confusing complexity) of the fossil record by reconstructing the fragments and by projecting our conclusions forward to later forms, most especially those species living today. Or,

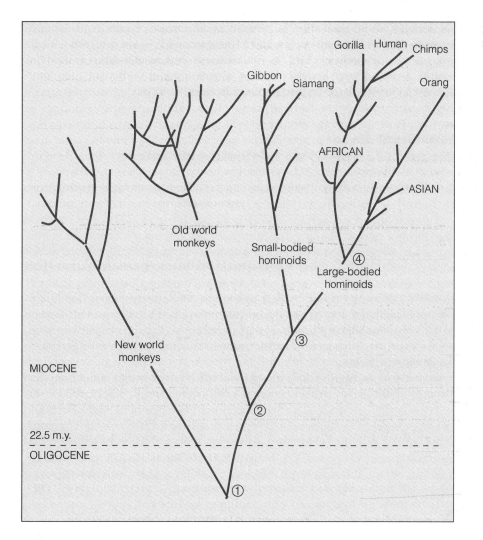

FIGURE 12-8   Major branches in Old World anthropoid evolution.

on the other hand, we can use the living forms and infer referentially (backward); in so doing, we attempt to highlight the major adaptive radiations that occurred in the past. For example, the increasing refinement of biochemical data obtained from contemporary primates discussed in Chapter 9 (see pp. 254–256) is a major advance in the use of such referential models.

One serious drawback exists, however, if we limit ourselves *strictly* to these referential models. Of all the primates that have ever existed, only a small proportion are still living today. As we saw for the Eocene, there were many more varieties of prosimians than survive today. Moreover, as we will see in the Miocene (discussed subsequently), hominoid forms were far more abundant during that epoch than the few survivors still existing. We thus must be very careful not to limit our interpretations to simple models derived from living forms only. Finally, we should not expect all fossil forms to be directly or even particularly closely related to extant varieties. Indeed, we should expect the opposite; i.e., most extinct varieties vanish without leaving descendants.

Nevertheless, in combining fossil interpretations (from functional anatomy and ecology) and referential models (especially biochemical data), most primate evolutionists would agree that there have been four major "events" (or evolutionary splits) in anthropoid evolution: (1) between Old World and New World anthropoids; (2) between Old World monkeys and hominoids; (3) between small-bodied and large-bodied forms of hominoids; and (4) between the Asian and African lines of large-bodied hominoids. (See Fig. 12-8.)

Miocene (22.5 my–5 my)—Hominoids Aplenty

If the Eocene was the age of prosimians and the Oligocene the time of great diversity for early anthropoids, the Miocene was certainly the epoch of hominoids.

A great abundance of hominoid fossil material has been found in the Old World from the time period 22–7 my. The remarkable evolutionary success represented by this adaptive radiation is shown in the geographic range already established for hominoids during this period. Miocene hominoid fossils have been discovered in France, Austria, Spain, Czechoslovakia, Greece, Hungary, China, India, Pakistan, Turkey, Saudi Arabia, Egypt, Uganda, and Kenya. While several intriguing discoveries potentially relating to gibbon evolution have been discovered at Miocene sites, the vast majority of this hominoid material relates to large-bodied forms. Unless we state otherwise, all further discussion of Miocene hominoids refers only to large-bodied varieties.

Interpretations of this vast array of fossil material (now including more than 500 individuals, and perhaps as many as 1,000) were greatly complicated for several decades due to inadequate appreciation of the range of biological variation that a single genus or species could represent. As a result, the taxonomic naming of the various fossil finds became a terrible muddle, with close to 30 genera and over 100 species proposed. The biological implications of such taxonomic enthusiasm were unfortunately not seriously considered. In such an atmosphere, it

FIGURE 12-9   Miocene hominoid distribution—fossils thus far discovered.

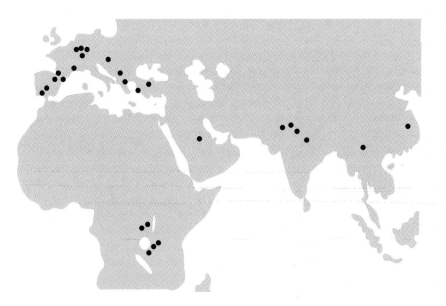

was possible for two genera to be named—one with only upper jaws represented, the other with only lower jaws, each matching the other!

It is not difficult to understand why such confusion arose if we consider that discoveries of these fossils spanned more than 100 years (the earliest find came from France in 1856) and took place on three continents. Not until the early 1960s did scientists systematically study *all* the material, the result being a considerable simplification of the earlier confusion. As a result of this research, E. L. Simons and David Pilbeam "lumped" the vast majority of Miocene forms into only two genera: one presumably quite "pongidlike" and the other "hominidlike." In just the last few years, however, a tremendous amount of new data has come to light from both new field discoveries and finds in museum collections of previously unrecognized material. Consequently, it is now apparent that the Simons-Pilbeam simplification went too far. Hominoid evolutionary radiation during the Miocene produced a whole array of diverse organisms, many of which have no living descendants (and thus no clear analog among living higher primates).

As these new discoveries are analyzed, many of the perplexing problems concerning Miocene hominoids should be solved. For the moment, it is possible to make only general interpretive statements regarding Miocene hominoid adaptive patterns.

PALEOGEOGRAPHY AND MIOCENE HOMINOID EVOLUTION

As they were to early primate evolution (see p. 349), the factors of changing geography and climates (at work as well in the Miocene) are also crucial to interpretations of the later stages of primate evolution. The Oligocene revealed a proliferation of early Old World anthropoid forms from one area in North Africa. In the Early Miocene, the evidence is also restricted to Africa, with fossils coming from rich sites in the eastern part of the continent (Kenya and Uganda). It would thus appear, on the basis of current evidence, that hominoids originated in Africa and experienced a successful adaptive radiation there before dispersing to other parts of the Old World.

The hominoids would maintain this exclusive African foothold for some time. The earliest of these East African hominoid fossils is more than 20 my old, and later fossil finds extend the time range up to at least 14 mya. For most of this period, East Africa is thought to have been more heavily forested, with much less woodlands and grasslands (savannas) than exist today (Pickford, 1983).

As in the earlier Cenozoic, the shifting of the earth's plates during the Miocene played a vital role in primate evolution. Before about 16 mya, Africa was cut off from Eurasia; consequently, once hominoids had originated there in the Early Miocene, they were isolated. However, around 16 mya the African plate "docked" with Eurasia (Bernor, 1983) through the Arabian Peninsula, a contact that was to revolutionize mammalian faunas of the later Miocene. Many forms, such as proboscideans, giraffoids, and pigs, that originated in Africa now migrated into Eurasia (van Couvering and van Couvering, 1976). Apparently, among these mid-Miocene intercontinental pioneers were some hominoids. Since they had evolved in the mainly tropical setting of equatorial Africa, most of the earlier hominoids probably remained primarily arboreal. Accordingly, it has been suggested that a relatively continuous forest would have been necessary across the Afro-Arabian-Eurasian land bridge.

Ecological changes were, however, already afoot in Africa. By 16 mya, the environment was getting drier, with less tropical rainforest and, conversely, more open woodland/bushland and savanna areas emerging (Bernor, 1983; Pickford, 1983). In other words, the environments in East Africa were being transformed more into their contemporary form. With the opportunities thus presented, some African hominoids were almost certainly radiating into these more open niches about 16 to 17 mya. Part of this adaptation probably involved exploitation of different foods and more ground-living than practiced by the arboreal ancestors of these hominoids. Some partly terrestrial, more woodland or mosaic environment-adapted hominoids were probably thus on the scene and fully capable of migrating into Eurasia, even through areas that were not continuously forested.

The environments throughout the Old World were, of course, to alter even more. Later in the Miocene, some of these environmental shifts would further influence hominoid evolution and may have played a part in the origin of our particular evolutionary lineage, the hominids. More on this later.

MIOCENE HOMINOIDS—CHANGING VIEWS AND TERMINOLOGY

So, throughout the Miocene, environmental and geographic factors imposed constraints on hominoids as well as opened new opportunities to them. Over a time span of close to 15 my, hominoids in the middle two-thirds of the Miocene were successful indeed. Once they migrated into Eurasia, they dispersed rapidly and diversified into a variety of species. After 14 mya, we have evidence of widely distributed hominoids from Pakistan, India, Turkey, Greece, Hungary, China, and Western Europe. Much of this material has only recently been uncovered and is incredibly abundant. For example, from Lufeng in southern China alone, 5 partial skulls and more than 1,000 teeth have been found in the past 15 years (Wu and Oxnard, 1983). The other areas have also yielded many paleontological treasures in recent years. Moreover, recent searches of museum collections in East Africa, as well as resurveys of fossil sites, have uncovered yet more fossils (Walker and Teeford, 1989).

Given this quantity of new information, it is not surprising that heretofore existing theories of early hominoid evolution have been reevaluated. In fact, it would not be unfair to describe the last few years as a "revolution" in paleontological views of Miocene hominoid evolution. With a great deal of this recent fossil material still unanalyzed, all the answers are not presently at hand. In fact, the more fossils found, the more complicated the situation seems to become. In order to simplify matters, we will organize the fossil material primarily on the basis of geography and secondarily on the basis of chronology. Moreover, we will suggest only tentative evolutionary relationships in most cases, as this is the best that can be currently concluded.

EAST AFRICAN FORMS (23–14 mya)

A wealth of early hominoid fossils has come from the deep and rich stratigraphic layers of Kenya and Uganda. These diverse forms are presently classified within at least 2 separate families, including perhaps 9 different genera (Fleagle, 1988). Indeed, important and mostly new finds (from the 1980s) have been uncovered, suggesting as many as 3 further hominoid genera in an as-yet-undetermined (and possibly a third) family. In other words, over the 9-million-year period for which we have evidence, as many as 12 different hominoid genera have been sampled from East Africa, with the potential for yet more as the fossil sample accumulates.

Most of the newer material has yet to be described completely, and relationships among specimens are uncertain. The best samples and thus best-known forms are those of the genus *Proconsul* (belonging to the proconsulid family). From the full array of proconsulid remains (mostly dental pieces), considerable variation is apparent. Body size estimates range from that of a small monkey (about 10 lb) to as large as a female gorilla (about 150 lb). Environmental niches were probably also quite varied, for some species were apparently confined to dense rainforests, while others potentially exploited more open woodlands. Some researchers have also suggested considerable diversity of locomotory behaviors, including perhaps some forms that were at least partly terrestrial (Fleagle, 1988). Indeed, when on the ground, some of these proconsulids may even have occasionally adopted a bipedal stance (Pilbeam, 1988).

The dentition of all the proconsulid forms is, however, quite uniform, showing the typical Old World anthropoid pattern of 2-1-2-3. Moreover, these forms all display broad upper central incisors and large sexually dimorphic canines. In the molars, the enamel is fairly thick (i.e., high cusps), but the softer dentine below penetrates well into these cusps, so that the enamel wore through fairly quickly with use (Kelly and Pilbeam, 1986). We can get some idea of diet from these teeth, which suggest that most forms were probably fruit-eaters.

From those well-preserved pieces of crania (representing currently only one species), brain size estimates are at least as large or larger than contemporary Old World monkeys (although probably not as large as contemporary hominoids; note, however, that *relative* brain size compared to body size is the crucial feature—a tricky estimate indeed for incomplete fossilized fragments). The surface features of the brain do not apparently show the derived characteristics of living large-bodied hominoids (Falk, 1983), and, in fact, show many primitive hominoid features similar to that seen in gibbon brains (Pilbeam, 1988).

A full understanding of the evolutionary relationships of the East African hominoids has not yet been attained. Indeed, in many cases, the classification still remains a muddle. For example, one fossil (discovered in the 1950s) from Rusinga Island in Kenya has been renamed and reassigned to different evolutionary groups at least six times. Just as paleoanthropologists begin to think that the situation is becoming better defined, new fossil discoveries muddy the waters still further. Some of this new material may date as early as 18–17 mya, but most of it is in the range 16–14 mya. Thus, for the most part, these finds are *later* than the proconsulids just discussed. It is not so surprising, then, to find that *Proconsul* is a more primitive hominoid (i.e., less derived). In fact, many primate evolutionists (Andrews, 1985; Pilbeam, 1988) would place *Proconsul* before the split of small- and large-bodied hominoids (as shown in Fig. 12-11). Therefore, while *Proconsul* may *not* actually have been the last common ancestor of gibbons as well as all large-bodied hominoids (including us), something resembling it may well have been.

FIGURE 12-10 *Proconsul africanus* skull. Discovered by Mary Leakey in 1948. (From early Miocene deposits on Rusinga Island, Kenya.)

EUROPEAN FORMS (13–11 mya)

Although they are the first of the Miocene hominoids to have been discovered, the European varieties still remain enigmatic. Very few fossils have been discovered,

FIGURE 12-11   The probable evolutionary
placement of the East African proconsulids
before the split of small- and large-bodied
hominoids.

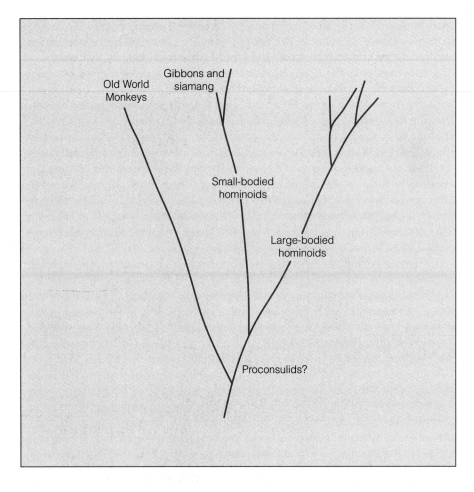

Old World
Monkeys

Gibbons and
siamang

Small-bodied
hominoids

Large-bodied
hominoids

Proconsulids?

and what has been found consists almost entirely of jaws and lower dentitions. Among the only features that distinguishes this varied lot of specimens from France, Spain, Austria (and maybe Hungary, too) is that the molar teeth are thin-enameled (i.e., the dentine penetrates far into the cusps). Most researchers would place all these forms into the genus *Dryopithecus*.

Western Europe

Discovery of similar forms from the Rudabanya Mountains in Hungary during the 1970s have complicated matters further. Initially thought to be similar to the thick-enameled varieties from southern and southwestern Asia (see below), the Hungarian fossils are now placed closer to *Dryopithecus* from western Europe. Nevertheless, many researchers still believe the Rudabanya fossils are probably a distinct genus (*Rudapithecus*) (Kelly and Pilbeam, 1986). It seems unlikely that these *Dryopithecus*-group fossils are related closely to any living hominoid.

SOUTH/SOUTHWEST ASIAN FORMS (?16–7 mya)

Three sites from Turkey have yielded fragmentary fossil hominoid remains dating to the early Middle Miocene (16–14 mya). As we noted on page 359, following "docking" of the Arabian plate with East Africa about 16 mya, land routes became available for animal migration from Africa into Eurasia. It would thus seem, from these Turkish remains, that hominoids quickly took advantage of this route and reached Eurasia by 16 mya. Most researchers would assign these remains to the genus *Sivapithecus*.

Far more complete samples of *Sivapithecus* have been recovered from southern Asia, in the Siwalik Hills of India and Pakistan. Most dramatically, over the last 15 years, paleoanthropologists led by David Pilbeam of Harvard University have recovered numerous excellent specimens from the Potwar Plateau of Pakistan. Included in this superb Pakistani collection is a multitude of mandibles (15 in all, some of which are nearly intact), many postcranial remains, and a partial cranium, including most of the face (Pilbeam, 1982).

Sivapithecus from Turkey and Pakistan was probably a good-sized hominoid, ranging in size from 70–150 lb. It probably inhabited a mostly arboreal niche, and its locomotion was "apelike," at least in the sense that *Sivapithecus* most likely displayed some suspensory abilities (Pilbeam, 1988).

Sivapithecus differs morphologically from *Proconsul* or *Dryopithecus* in its dentition and facial anatomy. The front teeth, especially the upper central incisors are often quite large, while the canine is fairly good-sized (low-crowned and robust). There are, however, large discrepancies in canine size among *Sivapithecus* individuals, partly because some species were larger overall, but also because there was considerable variation (sexual dimorphism) within the same species. In diet, like most other hominoids, *Sivapithecus* was probably a fruit-eater.

The first lower premolar is also quite variable in shape. Usually it is fairly sectorial in shape; that is, it shows the shearing surface typical of most catarrhines (consequently, this is probably the primitive condition). The most distinctive aspect of *Sivapithecus* dentition is seen in the back tooth row, where molars are large, flat-wearing, and thick-enameled (with dentine not penetrating far into cusps).

The thickness of the enamel cap has played a significant role in recent interpretations of Miocene hominoid evolution. Among living hominoids, relative to body size, humans have by far the thickest enamel caps. Gorillas and chimps have thin enamel, but orangs could be described as moderately thick (Ward and Pilbeam, 1983). Thick, in fact very thick, enamel is also seen in early hominids (in the time period 4–1 mya). As we have seen in *Proconsul* and *Dryopithecus*, their enamel thickness itself varies, but dentine usually penetrates into the cusps, so that the enamel wears through during use.

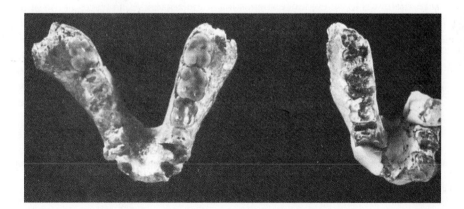

FIGURE 12-12 Two *Sivapithecus* mandibles from the Potwar Plateau, Pakistan. Discovered in 1976 and 1977. Approximate age, 9 million years.

FIGURE 12-13   Comparison of *Sivapithecus* cranium (center) with modern chimpanzee (left) and orangutan (right). The *Sivapithecus* fossil is specimen GSP 15000 from the Potwar Plateau, Pakistan, *circa* 8 mya. (*a*) lateral view; (*b*) frontal view.

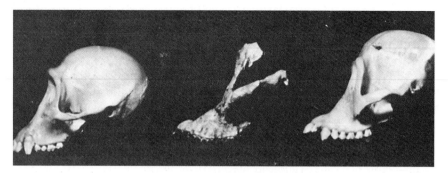

(a)

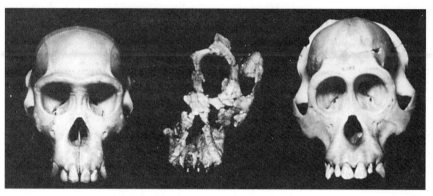

(b)

Probably, the most characteristic anatomical aspects of *Sivapithecus* are seen in the face, especially the area immediately below the nose (Ward and Kimbel, 1983). Facial remains of *Sivapithecus* from Pakistan and Turkey have concave profiles and projecting incisors (and, overall, remarkably resemble the modern orang). In particular, the partial cranium discovered in 1980 at the Potwar Plateau (Pakistan, *circa* 8 mya) and published two years later (Pilbeam, 1982) bears striking similarities to the orangutan. (See Fig. 12-13.) The published description of this specimen, with illustrations similar to those shown here, had a tremendous impact on paleoanthropology. As we have seen (p. 256), biochemical evidence demonstrates the distinctiveness of the orang from the African apes and humans; here, then, was fossil evidence suggesting some ancient Asian traces of the orang lineage. As a result, the views of biochemists and paleoanthropologists agree more closely (pp. 366–367).

It must be noted, however, that, except for the face and jaw, *Sivapithecus* is *not* like an orangutan. In fact, especially in the post-cranium (i.e., all skeletal parts except the head) *Sivapithecus* is distinctively *unlike* an orang, or any other known hominoid, for that matter. In most respects, then, *Sivapithecus* could be described as *highly derived* (Pilbeam, 1986).

Many earlier fossil-based interpretations of Miocene evolutionary affinities had, of course, to be reevaluated. As we hinted at the beginning of our discussion of Miocene hominoids (p. 359), in the 1960s E. L. Simons and David Pilbeam suggested a Middle Miocene hominoid as the first hominid (that is, clearly diverged on our particular line and separate from that leading to any extant ape). According to this view, this early hominid was "*Ramapithecus*"—known at that time mostly from India, with some bits from East Africa.

We have already illustrated some of the dramatic new discoveries of the 1970s and early 1980s. As a consequence of these new discoveries, the earlier suggestion that "*Ramapithecus*" was a definite hominid was seriously questioned and has now been rejected altogether. One primary advocate of this revised view is David Pilbeam (1977; 1982; 1986), an initial architect of the earlier widely accepted theory. Pilbeam, who has led the highly successful paleoanthropological project at the Potwar Plateau, has been swayed by the new fossils recovered there and elsewhere. These more complete specimens (like that shown in Fig. 12-13) are dentally very similar to what had been called "*Ramapithecus*." Researchers now simply lump "*Ramapithecus*" with *Sivapithecus*.

In summary, then, the fossil remains of *Sivapithecus* from Turkey and India/ Pakistan are the most clearly derived large-bodied hominoids we have from the whole Miocene. While some forms (e.g., *Proconsul*) are seemingly quite primitive and others (*Dryopithecus*) are derived in directions quite unlike any living form, *Sivapithecus* has several derived features of the face, linking it evolutionarily with the orang. The separation of the Asian large-bodied hominoid line from the African stock (leading ultimately to gorillas, chimps, and humans) thus occurred at least 12 mya (Pilbeam, 1988). (See Fig. 12-14.)

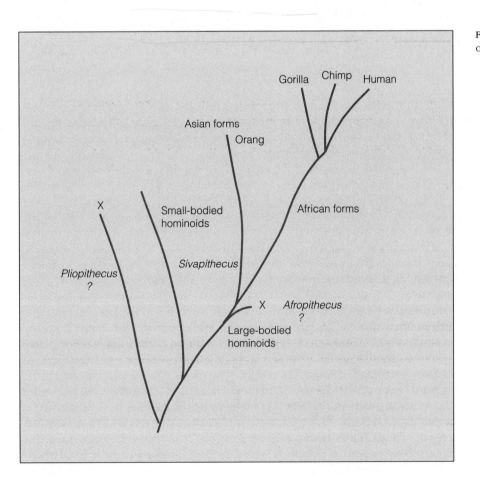

FIGURE 12-14   Evolutionary relationships of hominoids.

BOX 12-1 **Timing the Hominid-Pongid Split**

One of the most fundamental of all questions in human evolution is: When did the hominid line originate? Or, to put it another way: When did we last share a common ancestry with our closest living relatives, the pongids?

Scientists have taken different perspectives in attempting to answer this question. The traditional approach of paleontology is still the most common. Recent years have produced considerably more paleontological sophistication through a vast new array of fossil material, more precise chronometric dating, and more rigorous interpretation of primitive-derived characteristics. Still, the fossil record remains incomplete, and significant gaps exist for some of the most crucial intervals. So the question still persists: How old is the hominid line?

Data drawn from a completely different perspective have also been applied to this problem. Popularized by Vincent Sarich and Allan Wilson of the University of California, Berkeley (1967), this perspective utilizes comparisons of living animals. By calibrating the overall immunological reactions of proteins from different species, by sequencing the amino acids within proteins, or by doing DNA hybridization (see pp. 254–256), living species can be compared to each other.

Certainly, such data are immensely valuable in demonstrating *relative* genetic distances among contemporary organisms (as we discussed in Chapter 9). However, proponents of this view go considerably further and postulate that biochemical distance can be used directly to calculate evolutionary distance. In other words, a "molecular clock" is thought to provide unambiguous divergence dates for a host of evolutionary lineages, including hominids/pongids (Sarich, 1971).

Several hotly disputed assumptions are required, however, to perform this feat. Most importantly, the rate of molecular evolution must be constant over time. Such regularity could be accomplished if mutations were strictly *neutral* (see p. 104) or if selection pressures remained constant. Since environmental changes are decidedly not constant through time, the latter assumption is not valid. As for the first point, while neutral mutations certainly do occur (and perhaps do so quite frequently), many researchers are not convinced that most mutations are neutral (e.g., see Livingstone, 1980). Moreover, even if mutation was mostly neutral, major evolutionary shifts may still be quite nongradual in tempo—given the suggested punctuated mode of change (see p. 107).

Another possible complicating factor concerns generation length. Those species that reproduce in shorter periods of time should (according to strict application of the molecular clock) show, for the same period of time, greater amounts of molecular evolution than more slowly reproducing forms (Vogel, et al., 1976). Given the variation in generation lengths, it is not justifiable to make strict linear reconstruction for divergence times among prosimians, monkeys, and hominoids.

In fact, recently collected molecular data (in which DNA sequences are *directly* compared) indicate that the molecular clock does not run constantly with time. Rather, there is a marked *slowdown* in molecular divergence rate among primates, and most especially among the hominoids. Such a phenomenon is thought to be a function of greater generation length among higher primates when compared to other mammals (Li and Tanimura, 1987).

OTHER MIOCENE HOMINOIDS

Pliopithecus Another interesting but still not well-understood hominoid is *Pliopithecus*, from the Middle and Late Miocene of Europe. Since this is a fairly small hominoid (estimated at 11–16 lb; Fleagle, 1988), for several years primatologists suggested *Pliopithecus* was a gibbon ancestor. Moreover, dental features were also thought to mirror gibbon morphology. However, these similarities are superficial at best. In those respects in which *Pliopithecus* resembles contemporary small-bodied hominoids, the features are all primitive for hominoids in general. In fact, for most relevant anatomical details, *Pliopithecus* is a remarkably primitive hominoid (in fact, at least as primitive as *Proconsul*). This is surprising, given its relatively late date and Eurasian distribution (where hominoids are generally more derived than their African cousins). It may be that

BOX 12-1

Another problem is that there is no certain indicator of molecular evolutionary rates; different proteins yield significantly different rates of evolution and thus greatly influence inferences about divergence times (Corruccini et al., 1980). In fact, the *greatest* margin of error would occur in attempting to calculate relatively recent evolutionary events—for example, the hominid-pongid split.

Analysis of amino acid sequences of proteins by another group of biochemists (at Wayne State University in Detroit) has confirmed that, indeed, rates of molecular evolution are not constant, but are rather characterized by periods of acceleration and *deacceleration* (the latter being particularly true in the last few million years). Thus, these researchers conclude: "For proteins demonstrating striking shifts in rates of amino acid substitutions over time, it is not possible to calculate accurate divergence dates within Anthropoidea using the molecular clock approach. Our analysis of amino acid sequence data of several proteins by the clock model yields divergence dates, particularly within the Hominoidea, that are far too recent in view of well-established fossil evidence" (Goodman et al., 1983, p. 68).

As a result of such criticisms of the "clock," some paleontologists have been skeptical of its claimed applications. For example, Milford Wolpoff (of the University of Michigan) argues that, "Probably the best way to summarize the very disparate points raised is that the 'clock' simply *should not* work" (Wolpoff, 1983a, p. 661).

Naturally, not everyone takes so negative a view of the clock approach. Vincent Sarich continues to believe firmly in its basic accuracy (when applied correctly) and, justifiably, feels vindicated by recent recalibrations of theories derived from fossil evidence, which bring them closer to the biochemically derived hypotheses.

The fossils themselves are not going to provide the whole answer. The paleontological record is usually too incomplete to provide clearcut ancestor-descendant associations. More fossils will always help, of course, but the way we think about them (i.e., the questions we raise about them) is also crucial in framing workable theories.

The biochemical perspective has been important in that it has articulated key issues for evolutionary consideration (for example, the place of the orang in relation to other large-bodied hominoids). The interplay between the paleontological and biochemical perspectives has thus been most productive. In fact, these viewpoints agree more now on several aspects of hominoid evolution than they did just a few years ago. The greatest furor has been raised from overly strong claims for the unique validity of either approach. We have shown in this chapter that more fossil evidence *and* more controlled analyses have forced previous views to be reconsidered. Moreover, it is equally unfair to portray the clock approach as a complete answer. As one of the leading advocates of this method has stated, "The clock is one of an approximate, not metronomically perfect nature" (Cronin, 1983, p. 116).

Pliopithecus is a long-surviving descendant of an Early Miocene, very primitive ancestor, one that antedated the radiation of major hominoid lineages. (See Fig. 12-14.)

Greece ("Ouranopithecus," 12–11 mya)   From the Ravin de la Pluie near Salonika, Greece, have come several hominoid specimens (mostly mandibles, but also a partial face) discovered in the 1970s. Because the molar teeth have thick enamel, researchers initially grouped these finds with *Sivapithecus*. However, recent analysis of the critical facial anatomy (Kelly and Pilbeam, 1986) has shown that the Greek finds are not similar to *Sivapithecus* (or the orang), but their molar morphology also makes them unlike *Dryopithecus*. The evolutionary relationships of this Greek hominoid thus still remain a mystery.

Lufeng, Yunnan Province, Southern China (8–7 mya)   As we mentioned earlier, the recent discoveries from the Lufeng site in southern China have been remarkable, now totaling over 1,000 specimens (including several crania, mostly crushed mandibles, and hundreds of isolated teeth). Since the fossil collection is so large, and since the crania are in need of much restoration, most of the material has yet to be fully described. Therefore, conclusions regarding this most important fossil collection must remain highly tentative. Indeed, there is still argument concerning how many genera are represented among the Lufeng hominoids, with some experts favoring two, while others see only one genus. Ongoing interpretation of the vast dental remains has led some researchers (Kelly and Pilbeam, 1986) to suggest that *only* one species may be represented. If so, this would be an extremely variable species, most likely reflecting extreme sexual dimorphism. In fact, such a degree of sexual dimorphism (at least dentally) would exceed that seen even in the modern orang (i.e., males more than twice the size of females). We have discussed in Chapter 10 (see pp. 288–289) the differing reproductive strategies displayed by contemporary male and female primates. It thus becomes interesting to speculate about the social structure of these apparently highly dimorphic Miocene forms. (Note: *Most* Miocene hominoids from East Africa, Europe, and Asia seem to display marked sexual dimorphism.)

Like the Greek fossils discussed in the preceding section, the evolutionary relationships of the Chinese specimens are unclear. They also do not show the shared derived features of the *Sivapithecus*-orang lineage. Determining exactly where they fit thus remains a major challenge for primate evolutionists.

Other East African Hominoids (18–14 mya)   As we discussed on page 360, some fossil material (much of it quite recently discovered) is dated generally later than the proconsulids and does not comfortably fit within the same evolutionary grouping. Most notably have been new finds from northern Kenya at Kalodirr and Buluk. One form, called *Afropithecus*, from Kalodirr is a very large hominoid with hints from the dentition of a possible link specifically with African large-bodied hominoids (Fig. 12-14). Buluk is more tantalizing yet. With a quite early provisional date of 17–18 mya, a thick-enameled hominoid shows some resemblances to *Sivapithecus* from Asia (Leakey and Leakey, 1986). It is possible, then, that this lineage has diverged early in the Miocene of Africa and only later migrated to Eurasia, where some descendants apparently formed the ancestral basis for the orang line.

In order to combine all the suggested branching points discussed over the last several pages, we summarize together these suggested evolutionary relationships in Fig. 12-15. The placement and number of question marks indicate continued uncertainty. In other words, treat most of the suggested relationships (all those other than *Sivapithecus*-orang) as highly tentative.

The Meaning of Genus and Species

Our discussion of fossil primates has introduced a multitude of cumbersome taxonomic names. We should pause at this point and reasonably ask: Why use so many names like *Proconsul*, *Dryopithecus*, and *Sivapithecus*? What does such naming mean in evolutionary terms?

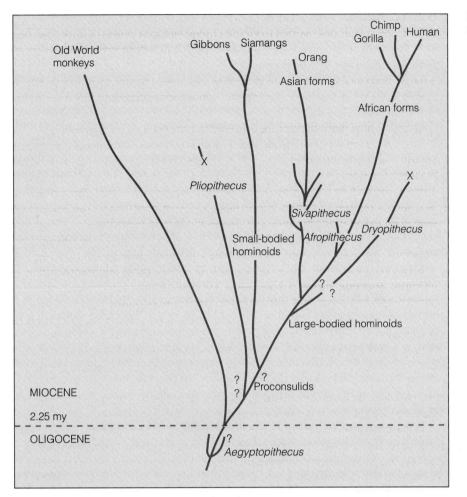

FIGURE 12-15 Summary of evolutionary relationships, Miocene hominoids.

Our goal when applying genus, species, or other taxonomic labels to groups of organisms is to make meaningful biological statements about the variation that is present. When looking at populations of living or long extinct animals, we are assuredly going to see the presence of variation. This situation is true of *any* sexually reproducing organism due to the factors of recombination (as independent assortment and crossing-over—see Chapter 3). As a result of recombination, each individual organism is a unique combination of genetic material, and this uniqueness is usually reflected to some extent in the phenotype. In addition to such *individual variation*, we see other kinds of systematic variation in all biological populations. *Age changes* certainly act to alter overall body size, as well as shape, in many animals. One pertinent example for fossil hominoid studies is the great change in number, size, and shape of teeth from deciduous (milk) teeth (only twenty present) to the permanent dentition (thirty-two present). It obviously would be a great error to assign two different fossil hominoids to different species *solely* on the basis of age-dependent dental criteria. If one were represented only by milk teeth and the other only by permanent teeth, they easily could be differently aged individuals of the *same* population.

Intraspecific Within one species.

Interspecific Between two or more species.

Variation due to sex also plays an important role in influencing differences among individuals observed in biological populations. Differences in structural traits between males and females of the same population are called *sexual dimorphism*, and we have seen that great variation does exist between the sexes in some primates (for example, gorillas and baboons) in such elements as overall body size and canine size. As we have seen when looking at body size differences, as well as differences in tooth size, among the same species of *Sivapithecus*, a reasonable assumption is that what we are really viewing is simply the variations between males and females of the *same* species.

Keeping in mind all the types of variation present within interbreeding groups of organisms, the minimum biological category we would like to define in fossil primate samples is the *species*. As previously defined in Chapter 4, the species is biologically described as a group of interbreeding or potentially interbreeding organisms that are reproductively isolated from other such groups. In modern organisms, this concept is theoretically testable by observations of reproductive behavior. In animals long dead, such testing is obviously impossible. Therefore, in order to get a handle on the interpretation of variation seen in fossil groups like the Miocene hominoids, we must refer to living animals.

We know without doubt that variation is present. The question is: What is its biological significance? Two immediate choices occur: Either the variation is accounted for by individual, age, and sex differences seen within every biological species—**intraspecific**—or the variation present represents differences between reproductively isolated groups—**interspecific**. How do we judge between the alternatives intra- or interspecific? We clearly must refer to already defined groups where we can observe reproductive behavior—in other words, contemporary species.

If the amount of morphological variation observed in fossil samples is comparable with that seen today *within species of closely related forms*, then we should not "split" our sample into more than one species. We must, however, be careful in choosing our modern analogs, for rates of morphological evolution vary widely among different groups of mammals. In interpreting past primates, we do best when comparing them with well-known species of modern primates.

Our evolutionary interpretations of the vast array of variable Miocene hominoids is greatly simplified by adhering to relevant biological criteria:

1. First we must look at *all* relevant material. We are not justified in splitting fossil groups into several species on the basis of only presumed differences in the sample (Simons' and Pilbeam's contribution was a major step in rectifying this situation for Miocene hominoids).

2. We must statistically reconstruct the variation observed in our often very small fossil *samples* to realistic dimensions of actual biological *populations*. Every piece of every bone found is part of an individual, who in turn was part of a variable interbreeding population of organisms.

3. We then refer to known dimensions of variation in closely related groups of living primates, keeping in mind expected effects of age, sexual dimorphism, and individual variation.

4. Our next step is to extrapolate the results to the fossil sample and make the judgment: How many species are represented?

5. Since fossil forms are widely scattered in time, we also must place the different species within a firm chronology.

6. Finally, we would like to make interpretations (at least, educated guesses) concerning which forms are related to other forms. To do this, we must pay strict attention to primitive as opposed to derived characteristics.

Following the above steps will greatly reduce the kind of useless confusion that has characterized hominoid studies for so long. We do not, however, wish to convey the impression that the biological interpretation of fossils into taxonomic categories is simple and unambiguous. Far from it! Many complexities must be recognized. Even in living groups, sharp lines between populations representing only one species and populations representing two or more species are difficult to draw. For example, a chain of interbreeding subspecies in gulls exchange genes at overlapping boundaries. However, at the terminal ends of the chain, two subspecies (species?) live side-by-side along the coasts of Europe with little or no hybridization (Fig. 12-16). In practice, isolating exactly where species boundaries begin and end is exceptionally difficult, especially in a dynamic situation like that represented by gulls.

In contexts dealing with extinct species, the uncertainties are even greater. In addition to the overlapping patterns of variation *over space*, variation also occurs *through time*. In other words, even more variation will be seen in such **paleo-species**, since individuals may be separated by thousands or even millions of years. Applying strict Linnaean taxonomy to such a situation presents an unavoid-

Paleospecies A group of organisms from different periods classified within the same species.

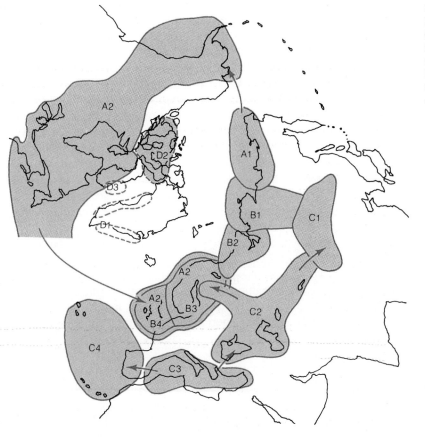

FIGURE 12-16 Circular overlap in gulls. A, B, C are subspecies of *Larus argentatus*. D (*L. glaucoides*) is a separate species. All along the chain subspecies interbreed (C1 with C2; C3 with C4, etc.) but at the terminal ends A2 lives side-by-side with B3 and B4 and does *not* interbreed. Where does one then draw species designations?

Monophyletic mono: one
phyletic: line of evolutionary descent

Cladistics The school of evolutionary biology that seeks to make hypotheses through interpreting patterns of primitive/derived characteristics.

able dilemma. Standard Linnaean classification, designed to take account of the variation present at any given time, describes a static situation. However, when dealing with paleospecies we are often involved in great spans of time and thus with much additional variation.

Where do we establish meaningful species boundaries in such a dynamic situation? Often, our task is made easier because of the incompleteness of the fossil record. Quite frequently, fossil samples are separated by great gaps of time (as between A and C in Figure 12-17) and the morphological differences may therefore also be clearcut. In such a case, we feel quite comfortable calling these different species. But what about fossil populations (B, for example) that are intermediate in both time and morphology? This question has no easy answer. Any taxonomic designation in such a continuously evolving lineage is by necessity going to be arbitrary.

Such a line, which has no speciation events (see p. 105), is referred to as **monophyletic**. For such a lineage, many evolutionary biologists see no point in making separate species designations—that is, the entire line is seen as a single paleospecies (Eldredge and Cracraft, 1980). Many biologists believe, in fact, that long, gradual transformations of this type are not the rule, but that branching (i.e., speciation) is much more typical of evolutionary change. (Once again, the view of the punctuationalists—see p. 107).

Moreover, it is imperative in evolutionary interpretation to understand ancestor-descendant relationships. Most paleontologists have traditionally made anatomical comparisons and then immediately constructed evolutionary trees (also called *phylogenies*). Recently, another perspective has been advanced. In this approach, a detailed interpretation of primitive versus derived states must first be explicitly stated. Only then can patterns of relationships be shown.

These are best interpreted in the form of a *cladogram* (a set of relationships shown as a hypothesis). In fact, usually several cladograms can be constructed from the same set of data. Those that are seen as most economically explaining the patterns of derived characteristics are then provisionally accepted, while less adequate ones are rejected. Such a perspective has been termed **cladistics**, and has injected a good deal more objectivity into paleontology (Eldredge and Cracraft, 1980). It must be pointed out, however, that not all paleontologists have accepted this approach. A basic assumption of cladistic analysis is that trait *patterns* are developed as the result of ancestor-descendant relationships and, conversely, that parallelism and convergence (see p. 225) have little import. In primate evolution, this assumption may not hold true; an analysis of morphological features in lemurs and lorises showed that 80% of the traits studied displayed some parallelism (Walker et al., 1981).

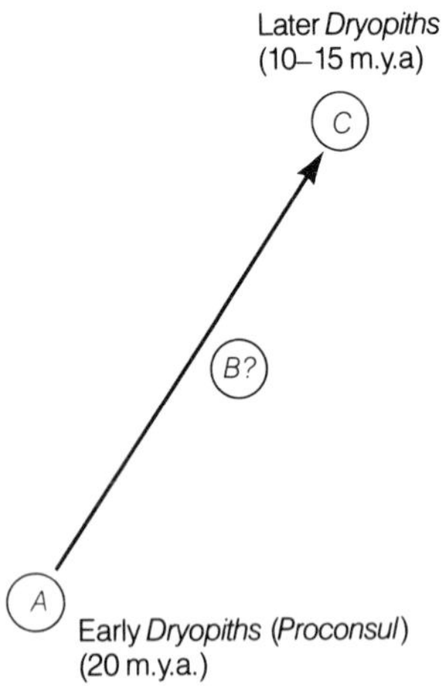

The next level of formal taxonomic classification, the *genus*, presents another problem. In order to have more than one genus, we obviously must have at least two species (reproductively isolated groups), and, in addition, the species must differ in a basic way. A genus is therefore defined as a group of species composed of members more closely related to each other than they are to species from another genus.

Grouping contemporary species together into genera is largely a subjective procedure wherein degree of relatedness becomes a strictly relative judgment. One possible test for contemporary animals is to check for results of hybridization between individuals of different species—rare in nature but quite common in captivity. If two normally separate species interbreed and produce live, though

Later *Dryopiths*
(10–15 m.y.a)

C

B?

A

Early *Dryopiths* (*Proconsul*)
(20 m.y.a.)

FIGURE 12-17 Evolution in a continuing evolving lineage. Where does one designate the different species?

not necessarily fertile, offspring, this process shows genetically that they are not too distant and that they probably should be classified into a single genus. Well-known examples of such interspecific crosses within one genus are horses with donkeys (*Equus caballus* × *Equus asinus*) or lions with tigers (*Panthera leo* × *Panthera tigris*). In both these cases, the close morphological and evolutionary similarities between these species are confirmed by their occasional ability to produce live hybrids.

As mentioned, we cannot perform breeding experiments with animals that are extinct, but another definition of genus becomes highly relevant. Species that are members of one genus share the same broad adaptive zone or, in Sewall Wright's terminology (Mayr, 1962), a similar "adaptive plateau." What this represents is a general ecological life style more basic than the particular ecological niches characteristic of species. This ecological definition of genus can be an immense aid in interpreting fossil primates. Teeth are the most often preserved parts, and they are usually excellent general ecological indicators. Therefore, if among the Miocene hominoids some animals appear to inhabit different adaptive/ecological zones (for example *Proconsul* vs. *Sivapithecus*), we are justified in postulating more than one genus present.

Operationally, then, categorization at the genus level becomes the most practical biological interpretation of fragmentary extinct forms. While species differences necessarily were also present (probably in great complexity), these are usually too intricate to recognize in incomplete material.

As a final comment, we should point out that classification by genus is also not always a clearcut business. Indeed, the argument among primate biologists over whether the chimp and gorilla represent one genus (*Pan troglodytes, Pan gorilla*) or two different genera (*Pan troglodytes, Gorilla gorilla*) demonstrate that even with living, breathing animals the choices are not always clear. Or, for that matter, some researchers—pointing to the very close *genetic* similarities between humans and chimps—would place these in the same genus (*Homo sapiens, Homo troglodytes*). When it gets this close to home, it gets even more difficult to be objective!

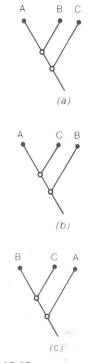

FIGURE 12-18   Cladograms. Three alternative statements representing ancestral-descendant relationships among three taxa. (*a*) C diverges earliest, with A and B sharing a more recent common ancestor; (*b*) B diverges earliest, with A and C sharing a more recent common ancestor; (*c*) A diverges earliest, with B and C sharing a more recent common ancestor.

Summary

In this chapter, we have traced the evolutionary history of our primate origins between 70 and 10 mya. Beginning in the late Cretaceous, the earliest primate ancestors are probably little more than arboreally adapted insectivores. In the Paleocene, we begin to see more definite primate trends in such animals as *Plesiadapis*, but there are still numerous "primitive" characteristics present in these forms. In the following epoch, the Eocene, we begin to see an abundant diversification of primates of modern aspect. During this epoch, the lemurlike adapids begin their evolutionary radiation. Early anthropoid origins may also date to sometime in the late Eocene. In addition, Old and New World primates apparently shared their last common ancestry in the Eocene or early Oligocene and have gone their separate ways ever since.

In the Old World, the Oligocene reveals a large number of possible early anthropoid ancestors at the Fayum. By and large, all these are primitive Old World anthropoids, and none of the modern lineages (Old World monkeys, gibbons, large-bodied hominoids) can definitely be traced into the Oligocene.

The Miocene reveals an incredibly abundant and highly complex array of hominoid forms, mostly those of large-bodied varieties. More than 10 different genera and probably dozens of species are represented in those remains discovered in East Africa, Asia, and Europe. Some early forms from Kenya and Uganda (the proconsulids) are more primitive than the majority of hominoids from Eurasia. While again there is little firm evidence tying these fossil forms to extant apes or ourselves, some tentative evidence suggests that *Sivapithecus* is closely related to the ancestors of the orang. Where, then, are the ancestors of the African apes or, even more relevantly, of ourselves? In the next five chapters, we will seek to answer this question.

Questions for Review

1. Why is it difficult to distinguish the earliest members of the primate order from other placental mammals? If you found a nearly complete skeleton of an early Paleocene mammal, what structural traits might lead you to believe it was a primate?
2. Compare the fossil primates of the Paleocene and Eocene with living members of the primate order.
3. If you (as an expert physical anthropologist) were brought remains of a fossil hominoid from South America purported to be 30 million years old, why might you be skeptical?
4. What kinds of primates were evolving at the Fayum in Oligocene times? What is meant by saying they are primitive catarrhines?
5. Compare and contrast the anatomical features of proconsulids with *Sivapithecus*.
6. How did the shifting of the earth's plates, as well as climatic changes, affect hominoid evolution in the Miocene?
7. What is meant by "small-bodied" hominoid compared to "large-bodied" hominoid?
8. If two fossil groups are classified as *Sivapithecus indicus* and *Sivapithecus sivalensis*, at what taxonomic level is the distinction being made? What are the biological implications of such a classification?
9. If two fossil groups are classified as *Dryopithecus* and *Sivapithecus*, at what taxonomic level is this distinction? What are the biological implications?

Suggested Further Reading

Buettner-Janusch, John. *Physical Anthropology: A Perspective* (Chapter 7), New York: John Wiley and Sons, 1973.
  A comprehensive and understandable review of primate evolution covered succinctly in thirty pages.
Ciochon, Russell L. and Robert S. Corrunici (eds.). *New Interpretations of Ape and Human Ancestry*, New York: Plenum Press, 1983.
  An extremely comprehensive, up-to-date series of thirty articles on hominoid evolution, including reviews of chromosomal, biochemical, paleoenvironmental, and fossil evi-

dence (the latter mostly covering recent Miocene discoveries, but also a couple of good analyses of Oligocene material). The vast majority of contributions are well done; the summary article by Russell Ciochon is especially recommended.

Clark, W. E. Le Gros. *History of the Primates*, Chicago: The University of Chicago Press, 1965.
   Although now out of date, still an excellent source for background information on grades of primate evolution. This work is particularly strong on comparative anatomy. Excellent illustrations.

Fleagle, John. *Primate Adaptation and Evolution*, New York: Academic Press, 1988.
   A superior, up-to-date discussion of primate evolution. Superbly illustrated with excellent bibliography. Highly recommended for anyone who seriously wants to pursue topics in primate evolution.

Gavan, James. *Paleoanthropology and Primate Evolution*, Dubuque, Iowa: Wm. C. Brown Co., 1977.
   A recent although fairly superficial treatment of primate evolution. Makes for an excellent introduction to the topic by showing the relationships between living and fossil primates.

Simons, E. L. "Ramapithecus," *Scientific American*, **236**:28–35, 1977.
   An up-to-date review of the crucial new evidence for hominid origins written in *Scientific American* style for the educated layman.

———. *Primate Evolution*, New York: Macmillan, 1972.
   A detailed treatment of the historical and anatomical facts of primate evolution. Excellent introductory chapters cover the geological and theoretical foundations of primate paleontology. Written by the leading expert on this topic, this book is recommended only for those students with a desire to learn a good deal about this complex field. Many excellent illustrations and photographs will prove useful for the introductory student.

Szalay, Frederick S. and Eric Delson. *Evolutionary History of the Primates*, New York: Academic Press, 1979.
   A compendium of primate taxonomy, morphology, and evolutionary interpretation. Excellent photos and drawings provide a detailed look at comparative primate anatomy. Recommended for the advanced student. Introductory students should, however, skim this book to gain a better appreciation of the quantity and quality of fossil primate data.

Paleoanthropology

Contents

Archeology and Science Fiction

Has our evolution, both cultural and biological, been systematically and deliberately tampered with by beings from other worlds? Popularized by Erich von Däniken in a series of fantastically successful books (1968, 1970, 1973), this bizarre theory has been further promulgated in movies and television. Is it possible?

Scientific inquiry cannot "prove" *anything* impossible, but it can attempt to demonstrate what is probable. Von Däniken is correct in asserting that, given the vast number of stars (and planets) in the universe, there is a high probability of intelligent life out there *somewhere*. Of all these life forms, however, how many are capable of efficient interstellar travel (necessitating speeds approaching that of light)? Furthermore, even if some life forms possessed this technology, where would they look for other intelligent life? If they randomly sampled all "inhabitable" planets in the universe, their probability of finding us would be low indeed. Perhaps, however, they are watching or listening for signs. They might assume, as we have, that an intelligent life form with even a modest degree of technological sophistication could produce radio waves. In the hope of hearing such an intergalactic message, we have recently turned our own ears to the heavens.

If creatures "out there" have done likewise, they may *eventually* hear our radio signals. However, we have been producing such communications for only the last sixty years or so (and these radio waves have only traveled about sixty light years). Special frequency signals aimed specifically at distant worlds have only been initiated in the last few years. Consequently, on the basis of simple logical deduction, it would seem unlikely that we have even been detected, to say nothing of actually playing host to extraterrestrial travelers.

Remember, however, that whereas such a postulation is exceedingly improbable, it is not completely impossible. What, then, of evidence?

Von Däniken has audaciously postulated that extraterrestrial beings have visited earth dozens of times. Nor did they *just* visit; they helped construct huge monuments (presumably to themselves —what a being capable of building spaceships would see in a stone edifice is a mystery). They even assisted with the writing of tablets and making of maps, and let themselves become deified by the masses of humble *H. sapiens* in the bargain.

Surely mysteries abound in the archeological record, which is incomplete and, thus, far from perfect. However, that fact does not justify postulating the unlikely, the bizarre, or the ridiculous when a much more probable (but admittedly, less exciting) explanation is easily found. Indeed, much of von Däniken's primary "hard" evidence has been debunked. The huge pyramids of Egypt and Mesoamerica, the mysterious geometric designs of Nazca, Peru, and the formidable stone monuments of Easter Island have all been demonstrated as *human* achievements using relatively simple technological principles and good old-fashioned human labor.

If, in 100,000 years, future generations of archeologists were to excavate some of the "wonders" of our world, they would (in the absence of written records) be struck by the seeming incongruities and mysteries. The incredible Gothic cathedrals of Europe, built during a period of economic and political disorganization, would appear a giant paradox. Did space beings build them? Or, even closer to home, the massive vaults excavated into the Rockies housing the genealogical records of the Mormon Church might also confuse and befuddle our descendants. Yet, the architects and engineers in Utah clearly did not require or receive extraterrestrial assistance in constructing this marvel.

Human beings routinely achieve the incredible, the fantastic, the inexplicable, and they do it on their own. After all, the New York Mets did win the World Series back in 1969!

SOURCES:

von Däniken, Erich. *Chariots of the Gods?*, New York: G. P. Putnam's Sons, 1968.
———. *Gods from Outer Space*, New York: G. P. Putnam's Sons, 1970.
———. *Gold of the Gods*, New York: G. P. Putnam's Sons, 1973.

CHAPTER 13

Introduction

In the last four chapters, we have seen how humans are classed as primates, both structurally and behaviorally, and how our evolutionary history coincides with that of other primates. However, we are a unique kind of primate, and our ancestors have been adapted to a particular kind of life-style for several million years. Some kind of large-bodied hominoid may have begun this process more than 10 mya, but, beginning about 5 mya, evidence from Africa reveals much more definite hominid relationships. The hominid nature of these remains is revealed by more than the morphological structure of teeth and bones; we know these animals are hominids also because of the way they behaved—emphasizing once again the *biocultural* nature of human evolution. In this chapter, we will discuss the methods scientists use to explore the secrets of early hominid behavior. We will then demonstrate these through the example of the best-known early hominid site in the world: Olduvai Gorge in East Africa.

Definition of Hominid

If any Miocene hominoid fossils represent the earliest stages of hominid diversification, our definition of them as hominid must then primarily be a *dental* one. Teeth and jaws are most of what we have of these Miocene forms. However, dentition is not the only way to describe the special attributes of our particular evolutionary radiation and is certainly not the most distinctive of its later stages. Modern humans and our hominid ancestors are distinguished from our closest living relatives (the great apes) by more obvious features than proportionate tooth and jaw size. For example, various scientists have pointed to other hominid characteristics, such as large brain size, bipedal locomotion, and toolmaking behavior, as being most significant in defining what makes a hominid a hominid (as opposed to a pongid, a cercopithecoid, or anything else for that matter). This last definition—humans as toolmakers—is the one that we wish to discuss in this chapter. The important structural attributes of the hominid brain, teeth, and locomotory apparatus will be discussed in the next chapter, where we investigate early hominid anatomical adaptations in greater detail.

BIOCULTURAL EVOLUTION: HUMANS AS TOOLMAKERS

Although other primates do occasionally make tools (see Chapter 11), only hominids depend on culture for their survival. We and our close hominid ancestors alone have the ability to "impose arbitrary form on the environment" (Holloway, 1969). For example, chimps who use termite sticks have a direct and immediate relationship with the raw material and purpose of the tool. Such is not the case in most human cultural behavior, which usually involves several steps often quite arbitrarily removed from a direct environmental context.

We are defining culture primarily as a mental process. The human mind—presumably the minds of our hominid ancestors as well—has the unique capacity to *create* symbols. When a chimp sees water, it probably sees only the immediate environmental setting plus any learned experiences that are directly associated. Humans, however, can introduce all kinds of additional meanings, such as "holy water," physically identical to all other water but with symbolic value. A chimp can see water and know from experience it is wet, drinkable, etc. However, the chimp is almost certainly not capable of grasping the superimposed, arbitrary ideas invented and understood only by humans. (We are being somewhat cautious here in noting claims of what a chimpanzee can and cannot do. The history of anthropology is littered with the wreakage of overly dogmatic assertions of just this kind!)

Obviously, we cannot "get inside the head" of a chimpanzee to know exactly what it is or is not thinking. The assumptions we have made are derived from behavioral observations in natural habitats, as well as results of learning experiments. However, as discussed in Chapter 11, among scientists there is still considerable dispute concerning the behavioral capacities of chimpanzees; the assumptions expressed here reflect the views of the authors. Humans, of course, also have the capacity to manipulate their environments in infinitely more complex ways than other animals. The simple human invention of a watertight container, such as a hollowed-out gourd or an ostrich egg, is several orders of magnitude more complex than chimp or macaque "cultural" behavior.

Culture as a complex adaptive strategy has become central to human evolution and has acted as a potent selective force to mold our anatomical form over the last several million years. In the archeological record, early cultural behavior is seen in the preserved remains of stone implements, traces of a uniquely human activity. "The shaping of stone according to even the simplest plan is beyond the behavior of any ape or monkey" (Washburn, 1971, p. 105).

Thus, when we find stone tools made to a standardized pattern, we know we have found a behavior indicator of a hominid, and *only* hominid, adaptation. We are justified, then, in defining hominids as habitual toolmakers, *culturally dependent* animals, distinct in this respect from all other primates.

FIGURE 13-1   Early stone tools. Traces of hominid behavior, from Olduvai Gorge, East Africa, about 1.6 mya.

The Strategy of Paleoanthropology

In order to understand human evolution adequately, we obviously need a broad base of information. The task of recovering and interpreting all the clues left by early hominids is the work of the paleoanthropologist. Paleoanthropology is defined as "the science of the study of ancient humans." As such, it is a diverse *multidisciplinary* pursuit seeking to reconstruct every possible bit of information concerning the dating, structure, behavior, and ecology of our hominid ancestors. In just the last few years, the study of early humans has marshalled the specialized skills of many diverse kinds of scientists. Included primarily in this growing and exciting adventure are the geologist, archeologist, physical anthropologist, and paleoecologist (see Table 13-1).

TABLE 13-1   **Subdisciplines of Paleoanthropology**

PHYSICAL SCIENCES	BIOLOGICAL SCIENCES	SOCIAL SCIENCES
Geology	Physical Anthropology	Archeology
Stratigraphy	Ecology	Cultural Anthropology
Petrology	Paleontology	Ethnography
(rocks, minerals)	(fossil animals)	Psychology
Pedology	Palynology	Ethnoarcheology
(soils)	(fossil pollen)	
Geophysics	Primatology	
Chemistry		
Geomorphology		
Taphonomy*		

*Taphonomy (taphos: dead) is the study of how bones and other materials come to be buried in the earth and preserved as fossils. A taphonomist studies such phenomena as the processes of sedimentation, action of streams, preservation properties of bone, and carnivore disturbance factors.

—study of man

The geologist, usually working with an anthropologist (often an archeologist), does the initial survey work in order to locate potential early hominid sites. Many sophisticated techniques can aid in this search, including aerial and satellite photography. Paleontologists may also be involved in this early search, for they can help find fossil beds containing faunal remains; where conditions are favorable for the bone preservation of such specimens as ancient pigs and elephants, conditions may also be favorable for the preservation of hominid remains. In addition, paleontologists can (through comparison with known faunal areas) give quick estimates of the approximate age of fossil sites without having to wait for the more expensive and time-consuming chronometric analyses. In this way, fossil beds of the "right" geologic ages (that is, where hominid finds are most likely) can be isolated.

Once potential areas of early hominid sites have been located, much more extensive surveying begins. At this point, the archeologist takes over in the search for hominid "traces." We do not necessarily have to find remains of early hominids themselves to know they consistently occupied a particular area. Behavioral clues, or **artifacts**, also inform us directly and unambiguously about early hominid occupation. Modifying rocks according to a consistent plan, or simply carrying them around from one place to another (over fairly long distances), are behaviors characteristic of no other animal but a hominid. Therefore, when we see such behavioral evidence at a site, we know absolutely that hominids were present.

No doubt, early hominids sometimes utilized implements of wood or bone, and probably began doing so several million years ago (6–4 mya?). It is not altogether clear, however, just how many of these potential tools were available without *first* processing them with stone. Naturally pointed pieces of wood could probably have been utilized as digging sticks or perhaps for puncturing an ostrich egg (to make a watertight container). Beyond this, it probably would have been quite difficult to make much use of wood resources without some modification; yet, how could this have been done without something harder with which to cut, scrape, or sharpen (i.e., stone tools)? Bone is even more intractable and would

Artifacts Traces of hominid behavior; very old ones are usually of stone.

Paleoecological paleo: old
ecological: environmental setting
The study of ancient environments.

Pedologist pedon: ground, soil

Petrologist petr: rock

seem also to have been "off-limits" to hominids without some stone implement to crush, cut, etc. Probably the only bone sources available were splinters left behind at kills by large carnivores. This all remains, of course, speculative, since *direct* evidence is not available. Unfortunately, these organic materials usually are not preserved, and we thus know little about such early tool-using behavior.

On the other hand, our ancestors at some point showed a veritable fascination with stones, for these provided not only easily accessible and transportable weights (to hold down objects, such as skins and windbreaks) but also the most durable and sharpest cutting edges available at that time. Luckily for us, stone is almost indestructible, and early hominid sites are virtually strewn with thousands of stone artifacts. The earliest artifact site now documented is from the Omo region of Ethiopia, dating from at least 2.4 mya. Another contender for the "earliest" stone assemblage is from the Hadar area, farther to the north in Ethiopia—dated 2.0–2.5 mya.

If an area is clearly demonstrated as a hominid site, much more concentrated research will then begin. We should point out that a more mundane but very significant aspect of paleoanthropology not shown in Table 13-1 is the financial one. Just the initial survey work in usually remote areas takes many thousands of dollars, and mounting a concentrated research project takes several hundred thousand dollars. Therefore, for such work to go on, massive financial support is required from governmental agencies and/or private donations. A significant amount of the paleoanthropologist's efforts and time are necessarily devoted to writing grant proposals or to speaking on the lecture circuit to raise the required funds for this work.

Once the financial hurdle has been cleared, a coordinated research project can commence. Usually headed by an archeologist or physical anthropologist, the field crew will continue to survey and map the target area in great detail. In addition, they will begin to search carefully for bones and artifacts eroding out of the soil, take pollen and soil samples for ecological analysis, and carefully recover rock samples for chronometric dating. If, in this early stage of exploration, the field crew finds a fossil hominid, they will feel very lucky indeed. The international press usually considers human fossils the most exciting kind of discovery, a situation that produces wide publicity, often working to assure future financial support. More likely, the crew will accumulate much information on geological setting, ecological data, particularly faunal remains, and, with some luck, archeological traces (hominid artifacts).

After long and arduous research in the field, even more time-consuming and detailed analysis is required back in the laboratory. The archeologist must clean, sort, label, and identify all the artifacts, and the paleontologist must do the same for all faunal remains. The kinds of animals present, whether forest browsers, woodland species, or open-country forms, will greatly help in reconstructing the local **paleoecological** settings in which early hominids lived. In addition, analysis of pollen remains by a palynologist will further aid in a detailed environmental reconstruction. All of these paleoecological analyses can assist in reconstructing the diet of early humans (see p. 401). Many complex kinds of contributions go into assembling and interpreting the relevant data in such analyses (see Table 13-2).

More information will be provided by analysis of soil samples by a **pedologist**, and rock and mineral samples by a **petrologist**. A geomorphologist may also be asked to reconstruct the sequence of past geologic events, including volcanics,

paleontologist - study of fossils of ancient animals

TABLE 13-2 **Elements of Hominid Paleoecology**

Physical Environment:

Altitude	Mean wind speed
Temperature	Degree of wind gusting
Rainfall	Mean cloud cover
Relative humidity	Surface water availability
Insulation	Surface water salinity
Soil:	
Development	
Physical composition	
Chemical composition	
Tree and shrub density	Habitat selectivity
Shade cover	Herbaceous basal cover
Degree of clumping of woody plants	Grass and forb height

Diet:

Content:	Metabolic energy requirements
Animal	Energy intake
Vegetable	Digestibility
Soil (geophagy)	Time of feeding
Manner obtained	Season of feeding
Manner eaten	
Drinking	

Population:

Numbers	Mortality
Weights	Birth spacing
Growth	Sexual maturity
Natality	

Intraspecific Relations:

Grouping	Division of labor
Group interaction	Distances between group sleeping sites
Sexual relations	Grooming
Dominance interactions	

Interspecific Relations:

Cooperation with other species	Prey
Competition with other species	Predators
Tolerance of other species	

Other Behavior:

Extent of daily movement	Group activity at various times of the day:
Tool use and manufacture:	Feeding intensively and/or moving rapidly
material, source, use	Feeding leisurely and/or resting
Sleeping place	Resting
Vocalizations	
Diurnality/nocturnality	

Source: Reprinted by permission of the Kroeber Anthropological Society from Kroeber Anthropological Society Papers No. 50, ed., Noel T. Boaz and John E. Cronin (Berkeley: Kroeber Anthropological Society, 1977), p. 56, © 1977 by the Kroeber Anthropological Society.

mountain building, earth movements, such as faulting, and changes in the orientation of the earth's magnetic pole.

As work progresses in later field seasons with more laboratory analyses, even more experts from other scientific specialties may be consulted. If a hominid bone or tooth is eventually recovered, a physical anthropologist will clean it, reconstruct it if necessary, describe it in minute anatomical detail, and attempt to relate it to other fossil hominid finds. The archeologist may decide that a particularly well-preserved location or the site of a hominid discovery calls for precise archeological excavation. In order to recover and record all relevant information in such an undertaking, thousands of work-hours are required to excavate even a relatively small area (a few dozen square feet). An extensively detailed *microstratigraphic analysis* may also be useful in re-creating the precise conditions of sedimentation, thus calling for the specialized skills of a taphonomist (see Table 13-1).

In the concluding stages of interpretation, the paleoanthropologist will draw together the following essentials:

1. *Dating*
geological
paleontological — bones of ancient animals
geophysical

2. *Paleoecology*
paleontology
palynology
geomorphology

3. *Archeological traces of behavior*

4. *Anatomical evidence from hominid remains*

From all this information, the paleoanthropologist will try to "flesh out" the kind of animal that may have been our direct ancestor, or at least a very close relative. In this final analysis, still further comparative scientific information may be needed. Primatologists may assist here by showing the detailed relationships between the structure and behavior of humans and that of contemporary nonhuman primates (see Chapters 9 through 11). Cultural anthropologists may contribute ethnographic information concerning the varied nature of human behavior, particularly ecological adaptation of those groups exploiting roughly similar environmental settings as those found at our hominid site (for example, the San or Australian aborigines—see p. 333). Ethnoarcheologists can assist further by demonstrating how observed behavioral patterns (as implement manufacture and meat eating) actually end up in the ground as artifacts. Finally, neuroanatomists, psychologists, and linguists may aid physical anthropologists in the reconstruction of physiological/behavioral information suggested by the fossil hominid remains, such as brain dimensions and their relationship to language capacities.

The end result of years of research by dozens of scientists will (we hope) produce a more complete and accurate understanding of human evolution—how we came to be the way we are. Both biological and cultural aspects of our ancestors pertain to this investigation, each process developing in relation to the other.

Paleoanthropology in Action—Olduvai Gorge

Several paleoanthropological projects of the scope discussed above are now in progress in diverse places around the globe. The most important of these include: David Pilbeam's work in the Miocene beds of the Potwar Plateau of western Pakistan (*circa* 13–7 mya); Don Johanson's project in the Hadar area of Ethiopia (*circa* 3.7–1.6 mya); a now completed research project along the Omo River of southern Ethiopia (*circa* 4–1.5 mya) directed by F. Clark Howell (both the Howell and Johanson projects have sometimes been forced to cease work due to warfare in Ethiopia); Richard Leakey's fantastically successful research near Lake Turkana (formerly Rudolf) in northern Kenya (*circa* 2.5–1.5 mya); and Mary Leakey's famous investigations at Olduvai Gorge in northern Tanzania (*circa* 1.85 mya–present). Mary Leakey retired from active fieldwork in the mid-1980s. Current research at Olduvai is being coordinated by the Institute of Human Origins in Berkeley, California (see Appendix C), in cooperation with Tanzanian scholars.

Of all these early hominid localities, the one that has yielded the finest quality and greatest abundance of paleoanthropological information concerning the behavior of early hominids has been Olduvai Gorge.

First "discovered" in the early twentieth century by a German butterfly collector, Olduvai was soon thereafter scientifically surveyed and its wealth of paleontological evidence recognized. In 1931, Louis Leakey made his first trip to Olduvai Gorge and almost immediately realized its significance for studying early humans. Since 1935, when she first worked there up to her retirement, Mary Leakey directed the archeological excavations at Olduvai.

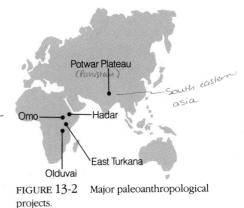

FIGURE 13-2 Major paleoanthropological projects.

FIGURE 13-3 Olduvai Gorge. A sketch map showing positions of the major sites and geologic localities.

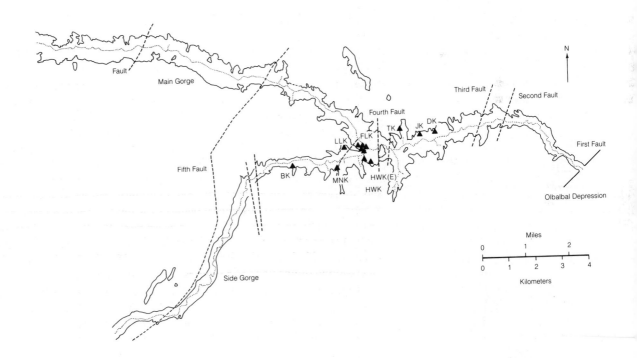

Louis S. B. Leakey 1903–1972

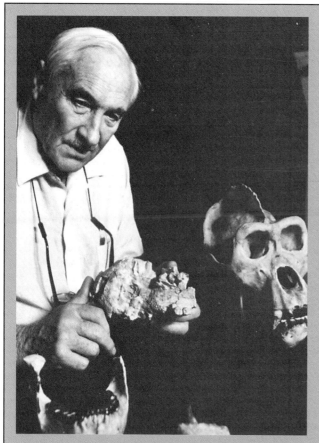

Louis Leakey displaying casts of fossil hominid discoveries from East Africa. To the right is the skull of a male gorilla.

Called the "Charles Darwin of prehistory," Louis Leakey was truly a man for all seasons. Blessed with a superior intellect and an almost insatiable curiosity, Leakey untiringly quested after knowledge, which to him included everything there was to know about everything. His interests encompassed not just prehistory, archeology, and paleontology but modern African wildlife, African peoples, languages, and customs. He once stalked, killed, and butchered a gazelle with just his bare hands and stone tools he had fashioned himself. He had previously attempted to use only his teeth and hands to dismember dead animals, but found it impossible, leading him to the conclusion that early hominids also *must* have used stone tools for butchering. Leakey also was a leading authority on handwriting, a skill he put to good use as the chief of British military intelligence for Africa during World War II.

The child of British missionary parents, Louis was born in a Kikuyu village in 1903—probably one of the first white children born in East Africa. His upbringing was to be as much African as European, and he was actually initiated into the Kikuyu tribe. Sworn to a sacred oath of silence, Louis never revealed the secret rites of initiation, even to his wife Mary.

Following his early training in the African bush, Louis was dispatched to England for a more formal education, eventually receiving his degree from Cambridge. His consuming interest, however, was focused on Africa, where he returned to begin exploration of prehistoric sites—leading his first expedition in 1926 at the age of 23! In 1931, Leakey made his first trip to Olduvai Gorge with the German paleontologist Hans Reck. Louis liked to relate years later how he found the first stone tool in context at Olduvai within an hour of his arrival there!

In the next forty years, the fantastic discoveries at Olduvai by Louis and his archeologist wife, Mary, as well as their extensive work at other sites all around the Rift Valley, were to make them famous to professional and layman alike.

However, perhaps Louis' greatest contribution was not the many discoveries he made himself, but his ability to stimulate and involve others. The definitive research on all the great apes was initiated by Louis Leakey, who personally recruited Jane Goodall to work with chimpanzees, Dian Fossey to investigate the mountain gorilla, and Biruté Galdikas to learn the secrets of the orang. Louis' greatest legacy is probably that all these projects continue today.* And, of course, the family tradition continues with Mary's work at Olduvai and their son Richard's work at Turkana, Kenya.

---

*The research goes forward on the mountain gorillas, despite the tragic death of Dian Fossey in 1985.

Located in the Serengeti Plain of northern Tanzania, Olduvai is a steep-sided valley resembling a miniature version of the Grand Canyon. Indeed, the geological processes that formed the gorge are similar to what happened in the formation of the Grand Canyon. Following millions of years of steady accumulation of several hundred feet of geological strata (including volcanic, lake, and river deposits), faulting occurred 70,000 years ago to the east of Olduvai. As a result, a gradient was established, causing a rapidly flowing river to cut through the previously laid strata, eventually forming a gorge 300 feet deep—similar to the way the Colorado River cut the Grand Canyon.

Olduvai today is a deep ravine cut into an almost mile high grassland plateau of East Africa, and extends more than 25 miles in total length. In fact, if one were to include all the side gulleys and ravines, the area of exposures would total more than seventy miles with potentially hundreds of early hominid sites. Climatically, the semiarid pattern of present-day Olduvai is believed to be similar to most of the past environments preserved there over the last 2 my. The surrounding countryside is a grassland savanna broken occasionally by scrub bushes and acacia trees. It is a noteworthy fact that this environment presently (as well as in the past) supports a vast number of large mammals (as zebra, wildebeest, and gazelle), representing an enormous supply of "meat on the hoof."

Geographically, Olduvai is located on the western edge of the eastern branch of the Great Rift Valley of Africa. The geological processes associated with the formation of the Rift Valley makes Olduvai (and the other East African sites) extremely important to paleoanthropological investigation. Three results of geological rifting are most significant:

1. Faulting, or earth movement, exposes geological beds near the surface that are normally hidden by hundreds of feet of accumulated overburden
2. Active volcanic processes cause rapid sedimentation and thus often yield excellent preservation of bone and artifacts that normally would be scattered by carnivore activity and erosion forces
3. Volcanic activity provides a wealth of radiometrically datable material

FIGURE 13-4 Aerial view of Olduvai Gorge. Volcanic highlands are visible to the south.

The results of these geological factors at Olduvai are the superb preservation of ancient hominids and their behavioral patterns in datable contexts, all of which are readily accessible.

The greatest contribution Olduvai has made to paleoanthropological research is the establishment of an extremely well-documented and correlated *sequence* of geological, paleontological, archeological, and hominid remains over the last two million years. At the very foundation of all paleoanthropological research is a well-established geological picture. At Olduvai, the geological and paleogeographic situation is known in minute detail. Olduvai is today a geologist's delight, containing sediments in some places 350 feet thick accumulated from lava flows (basalts), tuffs (windblown or waterlain fine deposits from nearby volcanoes), sandstones, claystones, and limestone conglomerates, all neatly stratified. A hominid site can therefore be accurately dated relative to other sites in the Olduvai Gorge by cross-correlating known marker beds. The stratigraphic sequence at Olduvai is broken down into four major beds (Beds I–IV), with other, more recent, beds usually referred to by specific local place names. Moreover, careful recording of the precise context of gelogical samples also provides the basis for accurate radiometric dating.

Paleontological evidence of fossilized animal bones also has come from Olduvai in great abundance. More than 150 species of extinct animals have been recognized, including fish, turtle, crocodile, pig, giraffe, horse, and many birds, rodents, and antelopes. Careful analysis of such remains has yielded voluminous information concerning the ecological conditions of early human habitats. In addition, precise analysis of bones directly associated with artifacts can sometimes tell us about the diets and hunting capabilities of early hominids. (There are some reservations, however—see Box 13-1, p. 398.)

The archeological sequence is also well documented over the last 2 my. Beginning at the earliest hominid site in Bed I (1.85 mya), there is already a well-developed stone tool kit, including chopping tools as well as some small flake tools (Leakey, 1971). Such a tool industry is called *Oldowan* (after Olduvai) and continues into Bed II with some small modifications, after which it is called *Developed Oldowan*. In addition, around 1.6 mya, the first appearance of a new tool kit, the *Acheulian*, occurs in the Olduvai archeological record. This industry is characterized by large bifacial (that is, flaked on both sides) tools commonly known as hand-axes and cleavers. For several hundred thousand years, Acheulian and Developed Oldowan are *both* found side-by-side at Olduvai, and the relationship between these parallel tool kits remains to be determined.

Finally, remains of several fossilized hominids have been found at Olduvai, ranging in time from the earliest occupation levels (*circa* 1.85 mya) to fairly recent *Homo sapiens*. Of the more than forty individuals represented, many are quite fragmentary, but a few (including four skulls and a nearly complete foot) are excellently preserved. While the center of hominid discoveries has now shifted to other areas of East Africa, it was the initial discovery by Mary Leakey of the *Zinjanthropus* skull at Olduvai in July, 1959, that focused the world's attention on this remarkably rich area. "Zinj" provides an excellent example of how financial ramifications directly result from hominid bone discoveries. Prior to 1959, the Leakeys had worked sporadically at Olduvai on a financial shoestring, making marvelous paleontological and archeological discoveries. Yet, there was little support available for much needed large-scale excavations. However, following the discovery of "Zinj," the National Geographic Society funded the Leakeys' research, and

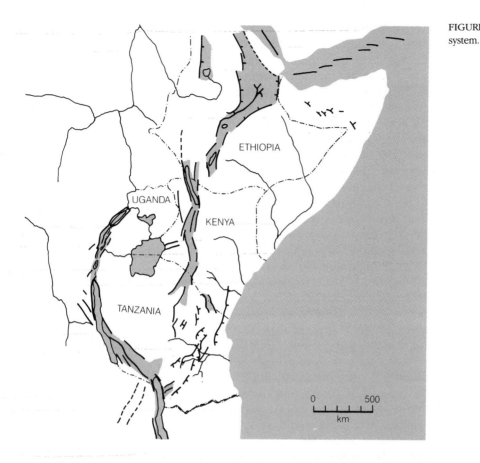

FIGURE 13-5 The East African Rift Valley system.

within the next year, more than twice as much dirt was excavated than during the previous thirty! Ongoing work at Olduvai has yielded yet further hominid discoveries. In 1987, a partial skeleton was found by researchers from the Institute of Human Origins.

Chronometric chrono: time
metric: measure
A dating technique that gives an estimate in actual numbers of years.

Dating Methods

As we have discussed, one of the key essentials of paleoanthropology is putting sites and fossils into a chronological framework. In other words, we want to know how old they are. How, then, do we date sites—or, more precisely, the geological strata in which sites are found? The question is both reasonable and important, so let us examine the dating techniques used by paleontologists, geologists, paleoanthropologists, and archeologists.

Scientists use two kinds of dating for this purpose—relative and **chronometric** (also known as *absolute dating*). Relative dating methods tell you that something is older, or younger, than something else, but not how much. If, for example, a skull were found at a depth of fifty feet, and another skull at seventy feet at the same site, we usually assume the skull discovered at seventy feet is older. We may not know the date (in years) of either one, but we would know that one is older

Stratigraphy Sequential layering of deposits.

(or younger) than the other. Whereas this may not satisfy our curiosity about the actual number of years involved, it would give some idea of the evolutionary changes in skull morphology (structure), especially if a number of skulls at different levels were found and compared.

This method of relative dating is called **stratigraphy** and was one of the first techniques to be used by scholars working with the vast period of geologic time. Stratigraphy is based upon the law of superposition, which states that a lower stratum (layer) is older than a higher stratum. Given the fact that much of the earth's crust has been laid down by layer after layer of sedimentary rock, like the layers of a cake, stratigraphy has been a valuable aid in reconstructing the history of earth and life on it.

Stratigraphic dating does, however, have a number of problems connected with it. Earth disturbances, such as volcanic activity, river activity, and faulting (earthquakes), among others, may shift about strata of rock or the objects in them, and the chronology of the material may be difficult or even impossible to reconstruct. Furthermore, the elapsed time period represented by a particular stratum is not possible to determine with much accuracy.

Another method of relative dating is *fluorine analysis*, which applies only to bones (Oakley, 1963). Bones in the earth are exposed to the seepage of groundwater, usually containing fluorine. The longer bones lie in the earth, the more fluorine they incorporate during the fossilization process. Therefore, bones deposited at the same time in the same location should contain the same amount of fluorine. The use of this technique by Professor Oakley of the British Museum in the early 1950s exposed the Piltdown (England) hoax by demonstrating that the human skull was considerably older than the jaw found with it (Weiner, 1955). Lying in the same location, the jaw and skull should have absorbed approximately the same quantity of fluorine. But the skull contained significantly more than the jaw, which meant that it (the skull) had lain in the ground a good deal longer than the jaw. It was unlikely that the skull had met an untimely demise while the jaw

FIGURE 13-6 View of the Main Gorge at Olduvai. Note the clear sequence of geological beds. The discontinuity to the right is a major fault line.

Mary Leakey 1913–

Mary Leakey, one of the leading prehistorians of this century, spent most of her professional life living in the shadow of her famous husband. But to a considerable degree, Louis' fame is directly attributable to Mary. Justly known for his extensive fieldwork in Miocene sites along the shores of Lake Victoria in Kenya, Louis is quite often associated with important hominoid discoveries. However, it was Mary who, in 1948, found the best-preserved dryopith skull ever discovered.

The names Louis Leakey and Olduvai Gorge are almost synonymous, but here, too, it was Mary who made the most significant single discovery—the "Zinj" skull in 1959. Mary had always been the supervisor of archeological work at Olduvai while Louis was busily engaged in traveling, lecturing, or tending to the National Museum in Nairobi.

Mary Leakey did not come upon her archeological career by chance. A direct descendant of John Frere (who because of his discoveries in 1797, is called the father of Paleolithic archeology), Mary always had a compelling interest in prehistory. Her talent to illustrate stone tools provided her entry into African prehistory, and was the reason for her introduction to Louis in 1933. Throughout her career, she has done all the tool illustrations for her publications, and has set an extremely high standard of excellence for all would-be illustrators of Paleolithic implements.

A committed, hard-driving woman of almost inexhaustible energy, Mary conducted work at Olduvai, where she spent most of the year. Busily engaged seven

Mary Leakey at the site of the "Zinj" find on the thirteenth anniversary of its discovery.

days a week, she supervised ongoing excavations, as well as working on the monumental publications detailing the fieldwork already done.

Since Louis' death in 1972, Mary, to some degree, has had to assume the role of traveling lecturer and fund raiser. Today, she lives outside Nairobi, where she energetically continues her research and writing.

lingered on for thousands of years. The discrepancy of fluorine content led Oakley and others to a closer examination of the bones, and they found that the jaw was not that of a hominid at all but of a young adult orangutan! (See p. 408.)

Unfortunately, fluorine is useful only with bones found at the same location. Because the amount of fluorine in groundwater is based upon the local river system and local conditions, it varies from place to place. Also, some groundwater may not contain any fluorine. For these reasons, comparing bones from different localities by fluorine analysis is impossible.

In both these methods—stratigraphy and fluorine analysis—the age of the rock stratum and the objects in it is difficult to calculate. To determine the absolute number of years of age, scientists have developed a variety of chronometric techniques based on the phenomenon of radioactive decay. The theory is quite simple: Certain radioactive isotopes of elements are unstable, disintegrate, and form an isotopic variation of another element. Since the rate of disintegration follows a

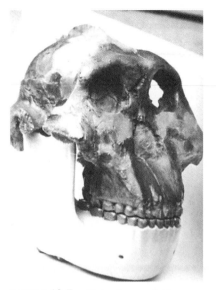

FIGURE 13-7 *Zinjanthropus* skull. Discovered by Mary Leakey at Olduvai Gorge in 1959. The skull and reconstructed jaw depicted here are casts at the National Museums of Kenya, Nairobi.

definite mathematical pattern, the radioactive material forms an accurate geological time clock. By measuring the amount of disintegration in a particular sample, the number of years it took for the amount of decay is then known. Chronometric techniques have been used for dating the immense age of the earth as well as artifacts less than a thousand years old. Several techniques have been employed for a number of years and are now quite well known.

Uranium 238 (^{238}U) decays to form lead with a half-life of 4.5 billion years. That is, one-half of the original amount of ^{238}U is lost in 4.5 billion years and through various processes becomes lead. Therefore, if a chunk of rock is measured and one-half of the uranium has been converted to lead, the age of that piece of rock is 4.5 billion years. In another 4.5 billion years, half the remaining ^{238}U would have decayed. The isotope ^{238}U has proven a useful tool in dating the age of the formation of the earth.

Another chronometric technique involves potassium 40 (^{40}K)—which produces argon 40 (^{40}Ar)—with a half-life of 1.3 billion years. Known as the K/Ar, or potassium-argon method, this procedure has been extensively used by paleoanthropologists in dating materials in the 1 to 5 million year range, especially in East Africa. Organic material, such as bone, cannot be measured, but the rock matrix in which the bone is found can be. K/Ar was used to date the deposit containing the Zinjanthropus skull (it actually dated a volcanic layer above the fossil).

Rocks that provide the best samples for K/Ar are those heated to an extremely high temperature, such as that generated by volcanic activity. When the rock is in a molten state, argon 40, a gas, is driven off. As the rock cools and solidifies, potassium (^{40}K) continues to break down to ^{40}Ar, but now the gas is physically trapped in the cooled rock. In order to obtain the date of the rock, it is reheated and the escaping gas measured. Potassium-argon has been used for dating very old events, such as the age of the earth, as well as those less than 100,000 years old (Dalrymple, 1972).

A well-known chronometric method popular with archeologists is carbon 14 (^{14}C), with a half-life of 5,730 years. It has been used to date material from less than 1,000 years to as much as 75,000 years,* although the probability of error rises rapidly after 40,000 years. The ^{14}C technique is based upon the following natural processes: Cosmic radiation enters the earth's atmosphere, producing neutrons, which react with nitrogen to produce a radioactive isotope of carbon, ^{14}C. As the ^{14}C is diffused around the earth with the earth's rotation, it mixes with carbon 12 (^{12}C) and is absorbed by plants in their life processes. It is then transferred to herbivorous animals that feed on plants and to carnivores that feed on herbivores. Thus, ^{14}C and ^{12}C are found in all living forms at a fixed ratio. When an organism dies, it no longer absorbs ^{14}C, which then decays at a constant rate to nitrogen 14 (^{14}N) and a beta particle. It takes 5,730 years for half the amount of ^{14}C to become ^{14}N.

Let us say that charcoal, the remains of a campfire, is found at an archeological site and measured for the ^{14}C:^{12}C ratio. Suppose the findings show only 25% of the original ^{14}C remains as indicated by the ^{14}C:^{12}C ratio. Since it takes 5,730 years for half the ^{14}C atoms to become ^{14}N, and another 5,730 years for half the remaining ^{14}C

*Grootes' studies (1978) suggest 75,000 years. A more recent technique using ^{14}C is being worked out at the University of California's Lawrence Berkeley Lab and at the University of Rochester. Scientists involved in the project believe it will extend the dating to 100,000 years with "no trouble" (Thomsen, 1978). This technique using a cyclotron ("atom smasher") requires a much smaller sample—"as little as one thousandth of a gram"—than the conventional method.

Discovery of Zinjanthropus July 17, 1959

That morning I woke with a headache and a slight fever. Reluctantly I agreed to spend the day in camp.

With one of us out of commission, it was even more vital for the other to continue the work, for our precious seven-week season was running out. So Mary departed for the diggings with Sally and Toots [two of their dalmatians] in the Land-Rover, and I settled back to a restless day off.

Some time later—perhaps I dozed off—I heard the Land-Rover coming up fast to camp. I had a momentary vision of Mary stung by one of our hundreds of resident scorpions or bitten by a snake that had slipped past the dogs.

The Land-Rover rattled to a stop, and I heard Mary's voice calling over and over: "I've got him! I've got him! I've got him!"

Still groggy from the headache, I couldn't make her out.

"Got what? Are you hurt?" I asked.

"Him, the man! *Our* man," Mary said. "The one we've been looking for [for 23 years]. Come quick, I've found his teeth!"

Magically, the headache departed. I somehow fumbled into my work clothes while Mary waited.

As we bounced down the trail in the car, she described the dramatic moment of discovery. She had been searching the slope where I had found the first Oldowan tools in 1931, when suddenly her eye caught a piece of bone lodged in a rock slide. Instantly, she recognized it as part of a skull—almost certainly not that of an animal.

Her glance wandered higher, and there in the rock were two immense teeth, side by side. This time there was no question: They were undeniably human. Carefully, she marked the spot with a cairn of stones, rushed to the Land-Rover, and sped back to camp with the news.

The gorge trail ended half a mile from the site, and we left the car at a dead run. Mary led the way to the cairn, and we knelt to examine the treasure.

I saw at once that she was right. The teeth were premolars, and they had belonged to a human. I was sure they were larger than anything similar ever found, nearly twice the width of modern man's.

I turned to look at Mary, and we almost cried with sheer joy, each seized by that terrific emotion that comes rarely in life. After all our hoping and hardship and sacrifice, at last we had reached our goal—we had discovered the world's earliest known human.

From: "Finding the World's Earliest Man," by L.S.B. Leakey, *National Geographic Magazine*, 118(September 1960):431. Reprinted with permission of the publisher.

---

to become ^{14}N, the sample must be about 11,460 years old. Half the remaining ^{14}C will become ^{14}N in the next 5,730 years, leaving 12.5% of the original amount. This process continues, and as you can see, there would be very little ^{14}C left after 40,000 years, when measuring becomes difficult.

Other absolute dating techniques that do not involve radioactive elements are *dendrochronology*, or dating by tree rings, especially developed for the American Southwest, and *varve chronology* (annual glacial deposit), particularly useful for the late Pleistocene and the post-Pleistocene in northern Europe. Although neither of the techniques has a direct bearing on dating early human fossils, they are both ingenious dating methods with important regional applications.

We should stress that none of these methods is precise, and that each method is beset with problems that must be carefully considered during laboratory measurement and in the collection of material to be measured. Because the methods are imprecise, approximate dates are given as probability statements with a plus or minus factor. For example, a date given as $1.75 \pm .2$ my should be read as a 67% chance that the actual date lies somewhere between 1.55 and 1.95 my.

There are, then, two ways in which the question of age may be answered. We can say that a particular fossil is x number of years old, a date determined usually either by K/Ar or ^{14}C chronometric dating techniques. Or, we can say that fossil X lived before or after fossil Y, a relative dating technique.

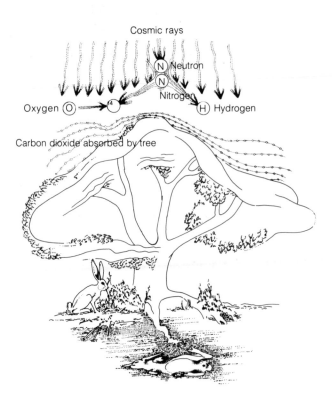

FIGURE 13-8 Carbon-14 dating. Cosmic rays bombard the upper atmosphere, producing neutrons. When these collide with nitrogen, small amounts of ^{14}C are produced. The ^{14}C combines with oxygen to form carbon dioxide. The carbon dioxide containing ^{14}C is absorbed by plants, and eventually animals feeding on the plants add ^{14}C to their bodies. When the plant or animal dies, it ceases to absorb ^{14}C and the ^{14}C changes back to nitrogen at a regular rate.

Cosmic rays

N Neutron

N

Nitrogen

Oxygen O → 14 → H Hydrogen

Carbon dioxide absorbed by tree

DATING METHODS AT OLDUVAI

Olduvai has proven a rich and varied source for numerous dating techniques, and as a result it has some of the best-documented chronology for any hominid site in the Lower or Middle Pleistocene.

Potassium-argon dating had its birth as a paleoanthropological tool in the early 1960s with its application to the dating of the "Zinj" site at Olduvai. To everyone's amazement, including Louis Leakey's, the chronometric age was determined at more than 1.75 my—more than twice the age depth previously assumed for the *whole* Pleistocene. As a result of this one monumental date (Leakey et al., 1961), the entire history of the Pleistocene and our corresponding interpretations of hominid evolution had to be rewritten.

Potassium-argon (K/Ar) is an extremely valuable tool for dating early hominid sites and has been widely used in areas containing suitable volcanic deposits (mainly in East Africa). At Olduvai, K/Ar has given several reliable dates of the underlying basalt and several tuffs in Bed I, including the one associated with the "Zinj" find (now dated at 1.79 ± .03 mya). When dating relatively recent samples (from the perspective of a half-life of 1.3 billion years for K/Ar, *all* paleoanthropological material is relatively recent), the amount of radiogenic argon is going to be exceedingly small. Experimental errors in measurement can therefore occur as well as the thorny problem of distinguishing the atmospheric argon normally clinging to the outside of the sample from the radiogenic argon. In addition, the initial sample may have been contaminated or argon leakage may have occurred while it lay buried.

Due to the potential sources of error, K/Ar dating must be cross-checked using other independent methods. Once again, the sediments at Olduvai (particularly in

Bed I) provide some of the best examples of the use of many of these other dating techniques.

Fission-track dating is one of the most important techniques for cross-checking K/Ar determinations. The key to fission-track dating is that ^{238}uranium (^{238}U) decays regularly by spontaneous fission so that, by counting the fraction of uranium atoms that have fissioned (shown as microscopic tracks caused by explosive fission of ^{238}U nuclei), we can ascertain the age of a mineral or natural glass sample (Fleischer and Hart, 1972). One of the earliest applications of this technique was on volcanic pumice from Bed I at Olduvai, giving a date of 2.30 ($\pm$ .28) mya—in good accord with K/Ar dates.

Another important means of cross-checking dates is called **paleomagnetism**. This technique is based on the constantly shifting nature of the earth's magnetic pole. Of course, as anyone knows, the earth's magnetic pole is now oriented in a northerly direction, but this situation has not always been so. In fact, the orientation and intensity of the geomagnetic field have undergone numerous documented changes in the last few million years. From our present ethnocentric point of view, we call a northern orientation "normal" and a southern one "reversed."

Paleomagnetism Dating method based on shifting magnetic poles.

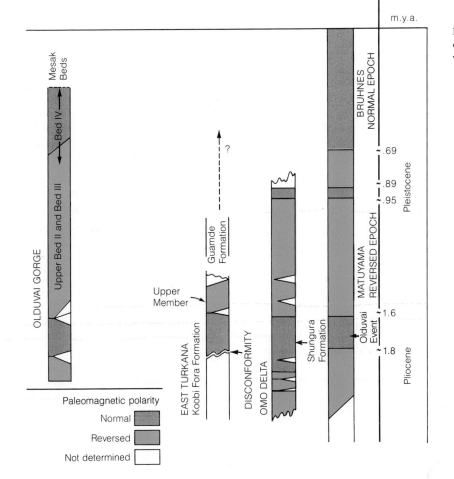

FIGURE 13-9 Paleomagnetic sequences correlated for major East African sites—Olduvai, East Turkana, Omo. (After Isaac, 1975.)

Major epochs of geomagnetic time are:

Normal
0.7 mya
Reversed
2.5 mya
Normal
3.4 mya
Reversed
'
'
'
'
?

Paleomagnetic dating is accomplished by carefully taking samples of sediments that contain magnetically charged particles. Since these particles maintain the magnetic orientation they had when they were consolidated into rock (many thousands or millions of years ago), we have a kind of "fossil compass." Then the

FIGURE 13-10 Partial biostratrigraphic sequence of pigs. Used to correlate East African sites. (After White and Harris, 1977.)

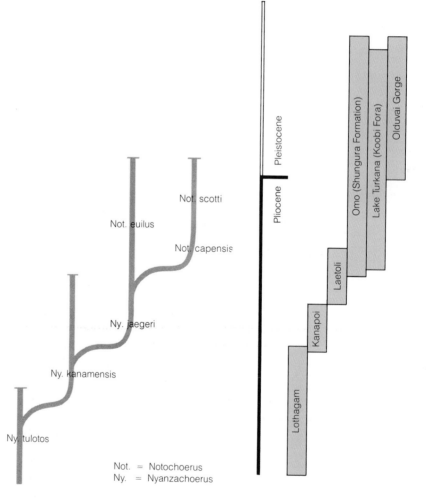

Not. scotti

Not. euilus

Not. capensis

Ny. jaegeri

Ny. kanamensis

Ny. tulotos

Not. = Notochoerus
Ny. = Nyanzachoerus

Lothagam

Kanapoi

Laetoli

Omo (Shungura Formation)

Lake Turkana (Koobi Fora)

Olduvai Gorge

Pliocene

Pleistocene

paleomagnetic *sequence* is compared against the K/Ar dates to check if they agree. Some complications can arise, for during an epoch a relatively long period of time can occur where the geomagnetic orientation is the opposite of what is expected. For example, during the reversed epoch between 2.5–0.7 mya (Matuyama Epoch) there was a time period called an *event*, lasting about 160,000 years, where orientations were normal. As this phenomenon was first conclusively demonstrated at Olduvai, it is appropriately called the *Olduvai Event*.

However, once these oscillations in the geomagnetic pole are well worked out, the sequence of paleomagnetic orientations can provide a valuable cross-check for K/Ar and fission-track age determinations.

A final dating technique employed in the Lower Pleistocene beds at Olduvai and other East African sites is based in the regular evolutionary changes in well-known groups of mammals. This technique, called *faunal correlation* or **biostratigraphy**, provides yet another means of cross-checking the other methods. Animals that have been widely used in biostratigraphical analysis in East Africa and South Africa are fossil pigs (suids), elephants (proboscids), antelope (bovids), rodents, and carnivores. From areas where dates are known (by K/Ar, for instance) approximate ages can be extrapolated to other less well-known areas by noting which genera and species are present.

All these methods, potassium-argon, fission-track, paleomagnetism, and biostratigraphy have been used in dating Beds I and II at Olduvai. So many different dating techniques are necessary because no single one is perfectly reliable by itself. Sampling error, contamination, and experimental errors can all introduce ambiguities into our so-called "absolute" dates. However, the sources of error are different for each technique, and therefore cross-checking between several independent methods is the most certain way of authenticating the chronology for early hominid sites.

Biostratigraphy Dating method based on evolutionary changes within an evolving lineage.

Excavations at Olduvai

Because the vertical cut of the Olduvai Gorge provides a ready cross-section of 2 my of earth history, sites can be excavated by digging "straight-in" rather than finding them by having first to remove tons of overlying dirt. In fact, sites are usually discovered by merely walking the exposures and observing what bones, stones, etc. are eroding out.

Several dozen hominid sites (at a minimum, they are bone and tool scatters) have been surveyed at Olduvai, and Mary Leakey has extensively excavated close to twenty of these. An incredible amount of paleoanthropological information has come from these excavated areas, data which can be generally grouped into three broad categories depending on implied function:

1. *Butchering sites*. Areas containing one or only a few individuals of a single species of large mammal associated with a scatter of archeological traces. An elephant butchering site and another containing a *Deinotherium* (a large extinct relative of the elephant) have been found at levels approximately 1.7 mya. Both sites contain only a single animal, and it is impossible to ascertain whether the hominids actually killed these animals or exploited them (presumably for meat resources) after they were already dead. A third butchering site dated at approximately 1.2 mya shows much more consistent and efficient

BOX 13-1 **Are the Sites at Olduvai Really "Sites"?**

The generally agreed-upon interpretation of the bone refuse and stone tools discovered at Olduvai has been that most, if not all, of these materials are the result of hominid activities. Recently, however, a comprehensive reanalysis of the bone remains from Olduvai localities has challenged this view (Binford, 1981; 1983). Archeologist Lewis Binford criticizes those drawn too quickly to the conclusion that these bone scatters are the remnants of hominid behavior patterns while simultaneously ignoring the possibility of other explanations. For example, he forcefully states:

> All the facts gleaned from the deposits interpreted as living sites have served as the basis for making up "just-so stories" about our hominid past. No attention has been given to the possibility that many of the facts may well be referable to the behavior of nonhominids (Binford, 1981, p. 251).

From specifics concerning the kinds of animals present, which body parts were found, and the differences in preservation among these skeletal elements, Binford concluded that much of what is preserved could be explained by carnivore activity. This conclusion was reinforced by certain details observed by Binford himself in Alaska—details on animal kills, scavenging, the transportation of elements, and preservation as the result of wolf and dog behaviors. Binford describes his approach thus:

I took as 'known,' then, the structure of bone assemblages produced in various settings by animal predators and scavengers; and as 'unknown' the bone deposits excavated by the Leakeys at Olduvai Gorge. Using mathematical and statistical techniques I considered to what degree the finds from Olduvai Gorge could be accounted for in terms of the results of predator behavior and how much was 'left over' (Binford, 1983, pp. 56–57).

In using this uniquely explicit approach, Binford arrived at quite different conclusions from those previously suggested by other archeologists:

> For instance, the very idea of a site or living floor assumes conditions in the past for which there is no demonstration. In fact, it assumes the very "knowledge" we would like to obtain from the archeological remains. Site and living floor identifications presuppose that concentrations and aggregations of archeological and other materials are only produced by man. Are there not other conditions of deposition that could result in aggregations of considerable density found on old land surfaces? The answer must be a resounding yes.

And, later, he concludes:

> It seems to me that one major conclusion is justified from the foregoing analysis: The large, highly publicized sites as currently analyzed carry little specific information about

FIGURE 13-11   Excavations in progress at Olduvai. This site is more than one million years old. It was located when a hominid ulna (arm bone) was found eroding out of the side of the gorge.

BOX 13-1

hominid behavior . . . arguments about base camps, hominid hunting, sharing of food, and so forth are certainly premature and most likely wildly inaccurate (Binford, 1981, pp. 281–282).

Binford is not arguing that *all* of the remains found at Olduvai have resulted from nonhominid activity. In fact, he recognized that "residual material" was consistently found on surfaces with high tool concentrations "which could *not* be explained by what we know about African animals" (Binford, 1983).

Support for the idea that at least some of the bone refuse were utilized by early hominids has come from a totally different perspective. Recently, researchers have analyzed (both macroscopically and microscopically) the cutmarks left on fossilized bones. By experimenting with modern materials, they have further been able to delineate clearly the differences between marks left by stone tools as opposed to those left by animal teeth (or other factors) (Bunn, 1981; Potts and Shipman, 1981). Analysis of bones from several early localities at Olduvai showed unambiguously that these specimens were utilized by hominids, who left telltale cutmarks from stone tool usage. The sites thus far investigated reveal a somewhat haphazard cutting and chopping, apparently unrelated to deliberate disarticulation. It has thus been concluded (Shipman, 1983) that hominids scavenged

carcasses (probably of carnivore kills) and did *not* hunt large animals themselves. Materials found at later sites (postdating 1 mya), on the other hand, do show deliberate disarticulation, indicating a more systematic hunting pattern, with presumably meat transport and food-sharing as well (Shipman, 1983).

If early hominids (close to 2 mya) were not hunting consistently, what did they obtain from scavenging the kills of other animals? One obvious answer is, whatever meat was left behind. However, the positioning of the cutmarks suggests that early hominids were often hacking at nonmeat-bearing portions of the skeletons. Perhaps they were simply after bone marrow, a substance not really being exploited by other predators (Binford, 1981).

The picture that emerges, then, of what hominids were doing at Olduvai around 1.8 mya hardly suggests consistent big game hunting. In Binford's words:

> . . . this is evidence of man eating a little bit of bone marrow, a food source that must have represented an infinitesimally small component of his total diet. The signs seem clear. Earliest man, far from appearing as a mighty hunter of beasts, seems to have been the most marginal of scavengers (Binford, 1983, p. 59).

exploitation of large mammals by this time. Remains of 24 *Pelorovis* (a giant extinct relative of the buffalo, with horn spans more than ten feet across!), have been found here, and Louis Leakey suggested they were driven into a swamp by a band of hominids and then systematically slaughtered (Leakey, 1971).

2. *Quarry sites*. Areas where early hominids extracted their stone resources and initially fashioned their tools. At such sites, thousands of small stone fragments are found of only one type of rock usually associated with no or very little bone refuse. At Olduvai, a 1.6 my–1.7 my old area was apparently a chert factory site, where hominids came repeatedly to quarry this material.

3. *Living sites*. Also called campsites. General purpose areas where hominids ate, slept, and put the finishing touches on their tools. The accumulation of living debris, including broken bones of many animals of several different species and many broken stones (some complete tools, some waste flakes) is a basic human pattern. As the late Glynn Isaac noted, "The fact that discarded artifacts tend to be concentrated in restricted areas is itself highly suggestive. It seems likely that such patches of material reflect the organization of movement around a camp or home base, with recurrent dispersal and reuniting of the group at the chosen locality. Among living primates this pattern in its full ex-

BOX 13-2   **Olduvai Site Names**

The naming of sites at Olduvai is a marvelous wonder concocted from fascinating combinations of the English alphabet. Sites are designated with such shorthand abbreviations as FLK, MNK, LLK, etc. The "K" stands for Korongo, Swahili for gully (Olduvai is made up of dozens of side gullies). The first initial(s) is usually, though not always, that of the individual who made an important discovery at that locality. For example, FLK stands for Frida Leakey Korongo (Louis' first wife), MNK is Mary Nicol Korongo (Mary Leakey's maiden name), and LLK is

Louis Leakey Korongo (where Louis found a hominid cranium in 1961). When more than one site is found in the same gully, those discovered later are given directional orientations relative to the initial site. For example, FLK is the main site name where "Zinj" was found in 1959. FLK N (that is, "FLK North," where the elephant and *Deinotherium* butchering sites occur at slightly different levels) is just north of the main site, and FLK NN ("FLK North North," the location of yet another important hominid discovery) is just a bit farther north up the gully.

Context   The environmental setting where an archeological trace is found.

Association   What an archeological trace is found with.

pression is distinctive of man. The coincidence of bone and food refuse with the artifacts strongly implies that meat was carried back—presumably for sharing" (Isaac, 1976, pp. 27–28). (See Box 13-1 for a different interpretation.)

Several "campsites" have been excavated at Olduvai, including one that is over 1.8 my old (DK I—see Box 13-2). This site has a circle of large stones forming what may have been the base for a windbreak or, as Mary Leakey, who dug the site, has suggested, may have been the foundation for a primitive structure. Without the meticulous excavation and recording of modern archeological techniques, the presence of such an archeological feature would never have been recognized. This point requires further emphasis. Many people assume archeologists derive their information simply from analysis of objects (stone tools, gold statues, or whatever). However, it is the **context** and **association** of objects (that is, precisely where the objects are found and what is found associated with them) that

FIGURE 13-12   A living floor at Olduvai from a site approximately 1.6 mya.

give archeologists the data they require to understand the behavioral patterns of ancient human populations. Once pot hunters or looters pilfer a site, proper archeological interpretation is never again possible.

Other possible living sites at Olduvai include the large occupation area at the "Zinj" site (FLK = 1.75 mya) and a very thin (perhaps occupied just a few days) **living floor** (HWK East = 1.7 mya). Preservation of occupational debris along one relatively narrow horizon is what is meant by a living floor, and the extraordinary conditions at Olduvai have preserved probably some of the bones and stones almost exactly as the hominids and other animals left them more than 1 mya.

Another kind of living site is MNK (Lower Middle Bed II = 1.6 mya) where occupational debris is scattered through more than six feet of earth, suggesting hominids periodically reoccupied this area—perhaps seasonally.

The detailed excavations of all these different hominid occupation areas are of tremendous importance, since the dispersal pattern of the remains of ancient human behavior can yield great insight into the biocultural evolution of humankind.

Living floor A narrow horizon of archeological remains; corresponds to brief period of occupation.

ARTIFACTS

While context, association, and ecological information are of paramount interest to the prehistoric archeologist, detailed analysis of the stone artifacts themselves can yield much additional information about the behavior of early hominids. Mary Leakey has been the pioneer in the study of Plio-Pleistocene African artifacts, and her classification system and description of some of the artifacts found at Olduvai are discussed in Box 13-3.

Diet of Early Hominids

Paleoanthropological research is concerned with more than the recovery and recording of bones and artifacts. What we are trying to obtain is a reconstruction of the kind of animal our ancestor was. Paleoanthropology must therefore be centrally concerned with interpretation of the behavioral patterns of early hominid populations.

One of the most important questions we would like to answer about early hominid behavior is: What did they eat? Scattered broken bone debris associated with artifacts *may* provide direct evidence concerning one important aspect of early human dietary behavior. However, we must not forget that modern analogs like the San of South Africa clearly show us that vegetable foods, which usually leave little trace in the archeological record, probably made up a large part (even a majority) of the caloric intake of early hominids. As Glynn Isaac noted, reconstructing dietary behavior is like navigating around an iceberg—four-fifths of what is of interest is not visible (Isaac, 1971, p. 280).

Postulated diets available to hominids 1–2 mya with use of only a simple digging stick as a tool include: berries, fruits, nuts, buds, shoots, shallow-growing roots and tubers, most terrestrial and smaller aquatic reptiles, eggs and nesting birds, some fish, molluscs, insects, and all smaller mammals (Bartholomew and Birdsell, 1953).

BOX 13-3   **Classification of Artifacts**

Stone artifacts, depending on context, shape, flake scars, and inferred function, fall into four broad categories:

1. *Manuports*. Rocks that are not modified but are found out of their natural context; that is, rocks that have been manually carried, a definite hominid behavior. The stone circle at DK I perhaps consisted of manuports, and much of the occupational debris at MNK is made up of unmodified manuports. Their functions remain unknown.

2. *Utilized material*. Stones used to modify other stones but not used as tools themselves. Under this category, Mary Leakey includes hammerstones and anvils.

3. *Debitage*. Very small flakes, either waste material struck off while making tools or perhaps used themselves as very small cutting implements.

4. *Tools*. A broad category of intentionally modified stones that have been shaped according to a preset, consistent pattern. Mary Leakey classifies the stone tools found at Olduvai primarily on the basis of shape and size. As yet no definite conclusions on their functions have been reached. Tools are thus classed as spheroids, discoids, polyhedrons, bifaces, etc. Occasionally, function is inferred with such terms as chopper, scraper, burin, and awl.

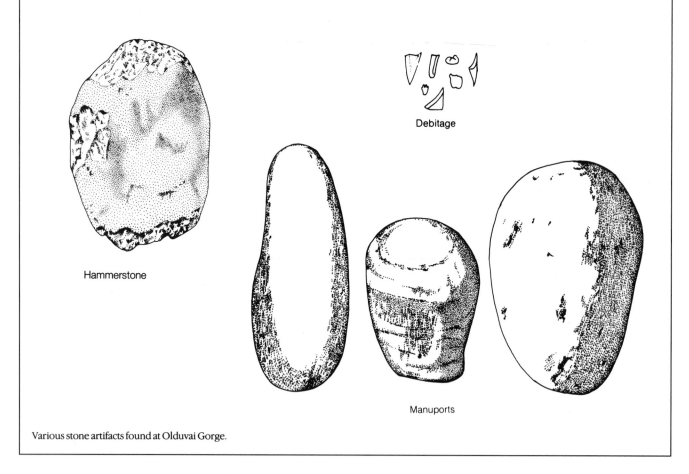

Debitage

Hammerstone

Manuports

Various stone artifacts found at Olduvai Gorge.

BOX 13-3

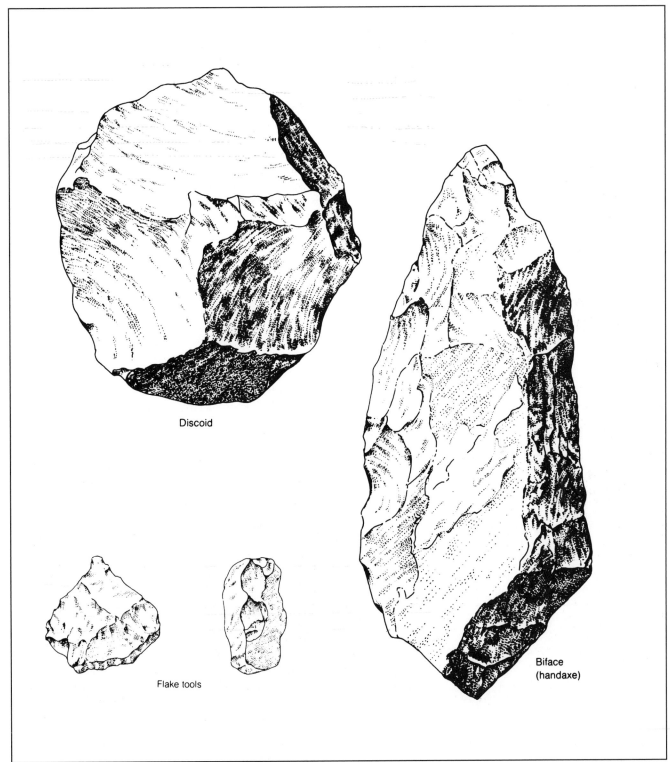

Discoid

Flake tools

Biface
(handaxe)

Olduvai has shown that the range of postulated meat resources was possibly exploited in Beds I and II (1.85–1.0 mya). Fossils of turtles, rodents, fish, birds, pigs, horses, and small antelopes are all fairly common at many Olduvai sites. Of course, exactly how much of these remains was eaten—as opposed to having just "dropped dead" there or having been preyed upon by other animals—is still undetermined (see Box 13-1). Evidence for fish eating has also come from a comparably aged site in southern Ethiopia (the Omo), where fish bones have been found in human coprolites (fossilized feces).

Moreover, as the elephant and *Deinotherium* butchering sites indicate, occasional exploitation of large mammals also occurred more than 1.5 mya. By 1 mya, some hunting of large mammals apparently provided important meat resources, as inferred by the *Pelorovis* butchering site.

Thanks to the extraordinary dedication of Louis and Mary Leakey, just one relatively small area of northern Tanzania has provided a continuous record of the development of hominids and their behavior for almost 2 my. Without Olduvai we would know much less than we do about the emergence of human culture prior to 1 mya. Moreover, Olduvai may have further secrets to reveal. Ongoing field research there has resumed under the direction of Don Johanson, Tim White, and Jerry Eck.

Summary

The biocultural nature of human evolution requires that any meaningful study of human origins examine both biological and cultural information. The multidisciplinary approach of paleoanthropology is designed to bring together varied scientific specializations in order to reconstruct the anatomy, behavior, and environments of early hominids. Such a task is centered around the skills of the geologist, paleontologist, paleoecologist, archeologist, and physical anthropologist.

Much of what we know about the origins of human culture between 1 and 2 mya comes from archeological excavations by Mary Leakey at Olduvai Gorge in East Africa. Olduvai's well-documented stratigraphic sequence, its superior preservation of remains (often as living floors), and the varied dating techniques possible there have made it an information bonanza for paleoanthropologists. Excavated sites have yielded a wealth of bones of fossil animals, as well as artifact traces of hominid behavior. Ecological reconstructions of habitat and dietary preferences are thereby possible and inform us in great detail concerning crucial evolutionary processes affecting early hominid populations.

In the next two chapters, we will survey the fossil hominid evidence in South and East Africa that inform us directly about human origins during the Plio-Pleistocene.

Questions for Review

1. Why are cultural remains so important in interpretating human evolution?
2. How are early hominid sites found, and what kind of specialist is involved in the excavation and analysis of paleoanthropological data?
3. What kinds of paleoanthropological information have been found at Olduvai Gorge? Why is this particular locality so rich in material?

4. What kinds of dating techniques have been used to date early hominid sites at Olduvai? Why is more than one technique necessary for accurate dating?

5. Why are context and association so important in the interpretation of archeological remains?

6. What different activities can be inferred from the different kinds of sites at Olduvai? Discuss alternative views in the interpretation of these "sites."

7. How do we infer what early hominids were eating? Give a brief list of the kinds of food that were probably exploited.

Suggested Further Reading

Binford, Lewis R. *Bones. Ancient Men and Modern Myths*, New York: Academic Press, 1981.
A technical but highly stimulating discussion of how archeological inference is made. Binford applies an "ethnoarcheological" approach in which cultural behavioral evidence from the present is used to reconstruct the past. In particular, he draws upon his observations of Eskimos—their use of animal resources and the predatory scavenging behavior of wolves and dogs. Using this approach, Binford attempts to interpret the archeological sites at Olduvai, but comes to a *much* different conclusion than that reached by Isaac, Johanson, and the Leakeys (see references below).

Bishop, W. W. and J. A. Miller (eds.). *Calibration of Hominoid Evolution*, Edinburgh: Scottish Academic Press, 1972.
A most authoritative though highly technical series of articles on all the major dating techniques now employed at early hominid sites.

Butzer, Karl. *Environment and Archeology: An Ecological Approach* (2nd Ed.), Chicago: Aldine-Atherton, 1971.
An excellent advanced review of the paleoecological approach to understanding hominid evolution.

Campbell, Bernard. *Humankind Emerging* (5th Ed.), Boston: Scott, Foresman/Little, Brown, 1988.
A general introduction to human evolution with particular emphasis on the discoveries and excavations of fossil hominids. Summarized from the Time-Life series, this book contains many excellent illustrations.

Chard, Chester. *Man in Prehistory* (2nd Ed.), New York: McGraw-Hill, 1975.
An excellent introduction to prehistoric archeology with discussion of archeological methods, dating techniques, and a review of culture history.

Cole, Sonia. *Leakey's Luck*, New York: Harcourt, Brace, Jovanovich, 1975.
An entertaining account of the life of Louis Leakey with a fine summary of his and his family's discoveries, particularly those at Olduvai.

Gowlett, John. *Ascent to Civilization*, New York: Alfred A. Knopf, 1984.
Essentially a history of archeological finds, this book also includes basic human evolutionary text. Beautifully illustrated, with many fine drawings, maps, and charts. The text is for the general public. Highly recommended—a quality work.

Isaac, Glynn and E. R. McCown (eds.). *Human Origins: Louis Leakey and the East African Evidence*, Reading, Massachussetts: W. A. Benjamin Inc., 1976.
This work contains several excellent not overly technical articles on the geological setting, archeological evidence, and fossil hominids from East Africa.

Johanson, Donald and Maitland Edey. *Lucy, The Beginnings of Humankind*, New York: Simon and Schuster, 1981.
A popularized account of the discoveries at Hadar and other Plio-Pleistocene African sites. Much of the romance, controversies, strong personalities, and financial problems of paleoanthropological research is detailed. Highly recommended for the introductory student.

Johanson, Donald C. and James Shreeve. *Lucy's Child. The Discovery of a Human Ancestor*, New York: Wm. Morrow & Co., 1989.

A highly personalized account of paleoanthropological work by one of the leading researchers. Johanson discusses his background and puts forward his own view of the "prime movers" of human evolution.

Klein, Richard G. *The Human Career*, Chicago: University of Chicago Press, 1989.

In addition to an excellent discussion of archeological remains, this book contains an excellent, authoritative, and up-to-date summary of hominid fossil evolution.

Leakey, M. D. *Olduvai Gorge* (Vol. 3), *Excavations in Beds I and II 1960–1963*, Cambridge: Cambridge University Press, 1971.

A detailed analysis of the archeological evidence from Olduvai covering the time range 1.85–1.0 mya. Many excellent illustrations drawn by Mary Leakey beautifully depict a wide range of stone artifacts.

———. *My Search for Early Man*, London: Collins, 1979.

A personal account of many of the discoveries and excavation techniques practiced at Olduvai. Also contains useful discussions of geology, dating techniques, and artifact analysis.

———. *Disclosing the Past. An Autobiography.* Garden City, N.Y.: Doubleday, 1984.

More autobiographical than the above book, this account offers a very personal view of the personalities, challenges, and hardships of paleoanthropological research.

Leakey, Richard E. and Roger Lewin. *People of the Lake*, New York: Anchor/Doubleday, 1978.

A popularized account of human evolution, emphasizing the exciting discoveries in East Africa. Written by one of the leading paleoanthropologists of the day, this work presents an argument for the nonaggressive nature of human evolution.

Reader, John. *Missing Links. The Hunt for Earliest Man*, Boston: Little, Brown and Company, 1981.

A recent account of paleoanthropology from a historical perspective, tracing discoveries of fossil hominids over the last century. Useful as a reference for all the remaining chapters of this text. Beautifully illustrated; highly recommended.

Willis, Delta. *The Fossil Gang: Behind the Scenes in the Search for Human Origins*, New York: Viking, 1989.

A chatty description of the personalities and difficulties in paleoanthropology. Written by a nonexpert, this book provides an "outside" view of the excitement and pettiness found in paleoanthropology.

Plio-Pleistocene Hominids

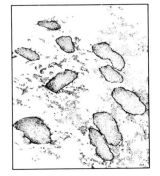

Contents

The Piltdown Caper: Who Dunnit?

FIGURE 1   The Piltdown skull.

When first announced to the world in 1912, *Eoanthropus dawsoni* ("Dawson's Dawn Man") created an anthropological sensation. Found during 1911 in Sussex in the south of England by Charles Dawson, a lawyer and amateur geologist/antiquarian, this "fossil" was to confuse, bewilder, and befuddle two generations of anthropologists. "Piltdown man," as he popularly came to be called, was comprised of a fragmented skull and parts of a lower jaw. The enigma of the fossil from the very beginning was the combination of a large *sapiens*-like skull (initially estimated at 1,070 cm³, but later shown to be more like 1,400 cm³) with an apelike lower jaw.

Most tantalizing of all, Piltdown was apparently extremely ancient, associated with long extinct fauna, such as mastodon, hippo, and rhino, all suggesting a date of early Pleistocene. A puzzling feature was the presence of these early fossils mixed in with clearly late Pleistocene fauna. The prevailing consensus, however, was that Piltdown was indeed ancient, "the earliest known representative of man in Western Europe."

Despite its seeming incongruities, Piltdown was eagerly accepted by British scientists, including Keith, Elliot Smith, and Smith Woodward (all later knighted). What made the fossil such a delectable treat was that it confirmed just what had been expected, a combination of *modern* ape and *modern* human characteristics— a true "missing link." We, of course, now know that no ancestral fossil form is a fifty-fifty compromise between modern ones, but represents its own unique adaptation. In addition to mistaken enthusiasm for a missing link, the fossil also represented a "true" man as opposed to the obviously primitive beasts (Java man, Neandertals) found elsewhere. Such a fervently biased desire to find an "ancient modern" in the human lineage has obscured evolutionary studies for decades and still causes confusion in some circles.

While generally accepted in England, experts in France, Germany, and the United States felt uneasy about Piltdown. Many critics, however, were silenced when a second fragmentary find was announced in 1917 (actually found in 1915) in an area two miles away from the original site. The matter stood in limbo for years, with some scientists as enthusiastic supporters of the Piltdown man and others remaining uneasy doubters. The uneasiness continued to fester as more hominid material accumulated in Java, China, and particularly the australopithecines in South Africa. None of these hominids showed the peculiar combination of a human cranium with an apelike jaw seen in Piltdown, but actually indicated the reverse pattern.

The final proof of the true nature of the Dawn Man came in the early 1950s, when British scientists began an intensive reexamination of the Piltdown material. In particular, fluorine analysis (see Chapter 13) performed by Kenneth Oakley showed both the skull and jaw were relatively recent. Later, more extensive tests showed the jaw to be younger than the skull and *very* recent in date. Now a much more critical eye was turned to all the material. The teeth, looking initially as though they had been worn down flat in the typical hominid fashion, were apparently ape teeth filed down deliberately to give that impression. The mixed bag of fauna was apparently acquired from all manner of places (a fossil elephant came from Tunisia in North Africa!), and the jaw was deliberately stained with chromate to match the older fossils in color. Finally, some "tools" found at Piltdown also met the hand of a forger, for the bone implements showed modifications that apparently could only have been made by a metal knife.

The "fossil" itself was probably purchased from local dealers. The skull probably came from a moderately ancient grave (a few thousand years old), and the jaw was a specially broken, filed, and stained mandible of a fairly recently deceased adolescent orang! The evidence was indisputable: a deliberate hoax. But who did it?

Just about everyone connected with the "crime" has, at one time or another, been implicated—beginning with Piltdown's discoverer: Charles Dawson. Yet, Dawson was an amateur, and, thus, may have lacked the expertise to carry out the admittedly crafty job of anatomical modification.

In addition, at various times, suspicions have been cast towards neuroanatomist Sir Grafton Elliot Smith, geologist

W. J. Sollas, and, French philosopher and archaeologist, Father Pierre Teilhard de Chardin.

One individual who had largely escaped suspicion was Sir Arthur Keith. At the time of the Piltdown discovery, he was a "rising star" in the field of anatomy in England. Later, and throughout much of the first half of this century, he would be the preeminent English scholar of human evolution. Recently, grave suspicions have even been leveled at Sir Arthur. Frank Spencer in his new book, *Piltdown: A Scientific Forgery*, notes that Keith probably had the most to gain from the whole affair. Perhaps so, but he probably also had the most to lose. One seemingly damning new piece of evidence is presented by Spencer: In 1912, in the *British Medical Journal* Keith anonymously authored a contribution containing details that at that time were still "secret." Spencer concludes that Keith was the likely mastermind behind the whole forgery and probably used Dawson as a willing accomplice.

Still, there is not an ironclad case against Keith, Dawson, or any of the other "principals." In this kind of uncertain (and suspicious) atmosphere, yet another intriguing possibility has been raised:

. . . there was another interested figure who haunted the Piltdown site during excavation, a doctor who knew human anatomy and chemistry, someone interested in geology and archeology, and an avid collector of fossils. He was a man who loved hoaxes, adventure and danger; a writer gifted at manipulating complex plots; and perhaps most important of all, one who bore a grudge against the British science establishment. He was none other than the creator of

FIGURE 2   The Piltdown committee. The individuals central to the "discovery" and interpretation of the Piltdown "fossil." Back row, standing, left to right: Mr. F. O. Barlow (maker of the casts), Prof. G. Elliot Smith (anatomist), Mr. C. Dawson ("discoverer"), Dr. A. Smith Woodward (zoologist). Front row, seated: Dr. A. S. Underwood (dental expert), Prof. A. Keith (anatomist), Mr. W. P. Pycraft (zoologist), Sir Ray Lankester (zoologist). From the painting by John Cook.

Sherlock Holmes, Sir Arthur Conan Doyle (Winslow and Meyer, 1983, p. 34).

Doyle, as a medical doctor, certainly possessed the anatomical knowhow to craft the forgery. His other avocations—chemistry, geology, and especially, anthropology—also would have been useful to him *if* he were the forger.

In a remarkable piece of detective work (worthy of the master sleuth Sherlock Holmes himself), John Winslow has assembled a convincing array of *circumstantial* evidence against Doyle who, first of all, is the only suspect that can be shown to have had ready access to all the elements of the forgery. He was friendly with collectors or dealers who easily

could have provided him with the cranium, the orang jaw, and the stone tools. As far as the animal fossils are concerned, Doyle also could have acquired many of the local (English) fossils from collector friends, but some of the odd bits obviously are from elsewhere (most likely, Malta and Tunisia). And, interestingly enough, Doyle had traveled to Malta a few years before Piltdown came to light, and may have been in Tunisia as well. At the very least, he was closely acquainted with people who had been to this part of North Africa.

But what of motive? As rich and as successful a figure as Doyle would seem an unlikely candidate for such a ruse. Winslow, however, has also found some clues that suggest Sir Arthur *may* indeed have had a motive.

Doyle was a longtime spiritualist who believed firmly in the occult and in extrasensory powers. He bore little patience with scientific critics of such views, whom he regarded as closed-minded. In particular, he had a special rival, Edward Ray Lankester, one of the most renowned evolutionists of the early twentieth century. Perhaps, as Winslow speculates, Doyle invented the whole scheme as a farce to embarrass the scientific establishment and, most especially, Lankester.

"So the case against Doyle is made. Besides the necessary skill, contacts, knowledge, and opportunity to qualify as the hoaxer, Doyle also had sufficient motive and an inviting target, Lankester" (Winslow and Meyer, 1983, p. 42).

Fascinating as it all is, we may never know whether the creator of Sherlock Holmes was also the Piltdown forger. Seventy years after the crime, the trail has grown stone cold—the forger covered his tracks very well indeed!

SOURCES:

Spencer, Frank. *Piltdown: A Scientific Forgery*, New York: Oxford University Press, 1990.

Weiner, J. W. *The Piltdown Forgery*, London: Oxford University Press, 1955.

Winslow, John Hathaway and Alfred Meyer. "The Perpetrator at Piltdown," *Science '83*, September, 1983, pp. 33–43.

CHAPTER 14

Introduction

We have seen in the last two chapters that hominids can be defined on the basis of dental adaptations and/or toolmaking behavior. In this chapter, we will review a series of remarkable discoveries in East and South Africa that persuaded paleoanthropologists to radically reassess their theories on human evolution.

Early Hominids in the Plio-Pleistocene

The beginnings of hominid differentiation almost certainly have their roots in the late Miocene (*circa* 5–10 mya). Sometime during the period between 8 and 4 mya, hominids began to adapt more fully to their peculiar ground-living niche, and evolutionary evidence from this period would be most illuminating. However, scant information is presently available concerning the course of hominid evolution during this significant 4-million-year gap. But beginning around 4 mya, the fossil record picks up considerably. We now have a wealth of fossil hominid material from the Pliocene and the earliest stages of the Pleistocene (5–1 mya), and this whole span is usually referred to as the Plio-Pleistocene.

The East African Rift Valley

Stretching along a more than 1,200-mile trough extending through Ethiopia, Kenya, and Tanzania from the Red Sea in the north to the Serengeti Plain in the south is the eastern branch of the Great Rift Valley of Africa. This massive geological feature has been associated with active mountain building, faulting, and vulcanism over the last several million years.

Because of these gigantic earth movements, earlier sediments (normally buried under hundreds of feet of earth and rock) are literally thrown to the surface, where they become exposed to the trained eye of the paleoanthropologist. Such earth movements have exposed Miocene beds at sites in Kenya, along the shores of Lake Victoria, where abundant remains of early fossil hominoids have been found. In addition, Plio-Pleistocene sediments are also exposed all along the Rift Valley, and paleoanthropologists in recent years have made the most of this unique opportunity.

More than just exposing normally hidden deposits, rifting has stimulated volcanic activity, which in turn has provided a valuable means of chronometrically dating many sites in East Africa. Unlike the sites in South Africa (see pp. 421–428), those along the Rift Valley are *datable* and have thus yielded much crucial information concerning the precise chronology of early hominid evolution.

FIGURE 14-1   East African Plio-Pleistocene hominid sites and the rift system.

East African Hominid Sites

The site that focused attention on East Africa as a potential paleoanthropological gold mine was Olduvai Gorge in northern Tanzania. As discussed in great detail in Chapter 13, this site has offered unique opportunities because of the remarkable preservation of geological, paleontological, and archeological records. Following Mary Leakey's discovery of "Zinj," a robust australopithecine, in 1959 (and the subsequent dating of its find site at 1.75 mya by the K/Ar method), numerous other areas in East Africa have been surveyed and several intensively explored. We will briefly review the geological and chronological background of these important sites beginning with the earliest.

EARLIEST TRACES

For the period preceding 4 mya only very fragmentary remains possibly attributable to the Hominidae have been found. The earliest of these fossils comes from the Lake Baringo region of central Kenya and the Lake Turkana Basin of northernmost Kenya.

In the Lake Baringo region possible hominid fossils have been found within the following geological areas:

1. Ngorora Formation (age approximately 9 my–13 my)—one partial upper molar. Not much can be said about this tooth, except that it is "hominoidlike."
2. Lukeino Formation (age approximately 5.1 my–6.3 my)—one lower molar. While some authorities believe this tooth has "distinct hominid resemblances" (Howell, 1978), detailed metrical analysis indicates this tooth is clearly primitive as a hominoid and not derived as a hominid (Corruccini and McHenry, 1980).

FIGURE 14-2   Early hominid localities in East Africa: The Baringo and Turkana Basins.

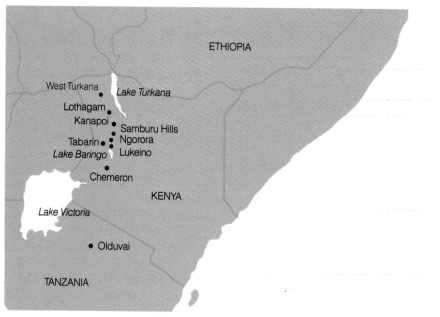

3. Chemeron Formation (age approximately 4 my), but perhaps as late as 1.5 mya—one isolated temporal bone from the side of a skull (see Appendix A). While not yet completely described, this bone appears quite hominidlike and has been provisionally referred to genus *Australopithecus* (Howell, 1978).
4. Tabarin (4–5 my)—a site west of Lake Baringo, where a partial hominid lower jaw was found in February 1984. The find—a small fragment containing two molar teeth—has not yet been described.

Abundant fossil-bearing beds spanning the period 10–4 mya are now known in the Lake Baringo area. Further explorations in this region may well contribute to filling that currently vexing gap in hominoid prehistory between 8 and 4 mya.

Samburu Hills   To the north and west of Lake Baringo, some other early and potentially highly productive fossil-bearing beds have recently been explored. In the Samburu Hills of north-central Kenya, a team led by Hidemi Ishida of Osaka University discovered a partial hominoid jaw in August 1982. Consisting of the left half of an upper jaw with five teeth in place, this find has been *very* provisionally estimated at 8 million years old. Detailed descriptions are not yet available, but are eagerly awaited by paleoanthropologists.

Lothagam (Loth'-a-gum)   Located on the southwest side of Lake Turkana in northern Kenya, this site was first explored by a Harvard University team in the middle 1960s. No radiometric dates exist for this site, but faunal correlation suggests a date of around 5.5 mya. While surveying the area in 1967, the Harvard team found one hominoid fossil, the back portion of a mandible with one molar in place. Although this specimen is too fragmentary for any firm decision to be based on it, it is certainly a hominoid and *may* be an early primitive hominid (White, 1986). Caution must be used in making phylogenetic judgments for any of these fragmentary late Miocene discoveries. As we go back ever closer to the hominid-African pongid divergence (see pp. 366–367), the distinguishing characteristics become more difficult to nail down—especially when dental remains are all that we have.

Kanapoi (Kan'-a-poy)   Located close to Lothagam on the southwest side of Lake Turkana, Kanapoi was also surveyed by members of the Harvard University research project. In 1965, they found one hominid bone at this site, the lower end of an upper arm bone, or humerus.

Dating of Kanapoi, also by means of faunal correlation, gives a date of approximately 4 mya. Like Lothagam, the hominid material is too fragmentary to allow much elaboration, except to note that it appears hominid. Also like Lothagam, surface surveys at Kanapoi revealed no archeological traces.

LAETOLI (LYE'-TOLL-EE)

Thirty miles south of Olduvai Gorge in northern Tanzania lie beds considerably older than those exposed at the Gorge. While Laetoli was first surveyed back in the 1930s, intensive work did not begin there until 1974, when Mary Leakey decided to reinvestigate the area. With numerous volcanic sediments in the vicinity, accurate K/Ar testing is possible and provides a date of 3.50–3.75 mya for this site.

Since systematic fossil recovery began at Laetoli in 1974, twenty-three fossil hominid individuals have been found, consisting almost exclusively of jaws and teeth with fragmentary postcranial remains of one immature individual (Johanson and White, 1979; White, 1980).

In February, 1978, Mary Leakey announced a remarkable discovery at Laetoli: fossilized footprints embossed into an ancient volcanic tuff more than 3.5 mya! Literally thousands of footprints have been found at this remarkable site, representing more than twenty different taxa (Pliocene elephants, horses, pigs, giraffes, antelopes, hyenas, and an abundance of hares). Several hominid footprints have also been found, including a trail more than 75 feet long, made by at least two—and perhaps three—individuals (Leakey and Hay, 1979). (See Fig. 14-3.)

Such discoveries of well-preserved hominid footprints are extremely important in furthering our understanding of human evolution. For the first time we can make *definite* statements regarding locomotory pattern and stature of early hominids. Initial analysis of these Pliocene footprints compared to modern humans suggests a stature of about 4 feet, 9 inches for the larger individual and 4 feet 1 inch for the smaller individual, who made the trail seen in Fig. 14-3 (White,

FIGURE 14-3   Laetoli hominid footprint trail, northern Tanzania. The trail on the left was made by one individual; the one on the right seems to have been formed by two individuals, the second stepping in the footprints of the first.

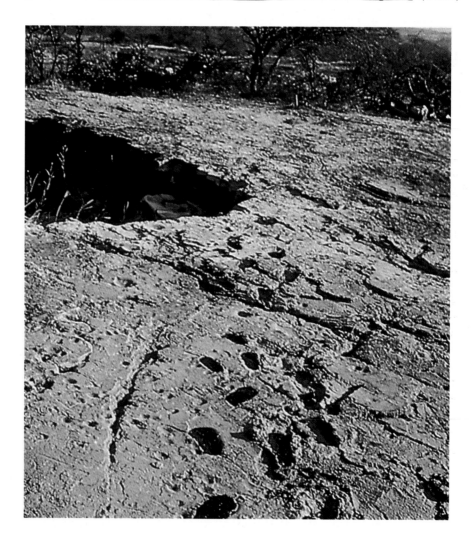

1980). Studies of these impression patterns clearly show that the mode of locomotion of these hominids was fully bipedal, and, further, *very* similar to modern humans (Day and Wickens, 1980). As we will discuss shortly, the development of bipedal locomotion is *the* most important defining characteristic of early hominid evolution. Some researchers, however, have concluded that these early hominids were not bipedal in quite the same way that modern humans are. From detailed comparisons with modern humans, estimates of step length, cadence, and speed of walking have been ascertained, indicating that the Laetoli hominids moved in a "strolling" fashion with a rather short stride (Chateris et al., 1981).

HADAR (HA-DAR') (AFAR TRIANGLE)

Potentially one of the most exciting areas for future research in East Africa is the Afar Triangle of northeastern Ethiopia, where the Red Sea, Rift Valley, and Gulf of Aden all intersect. A joint American-French team led by Don Johanson and the French geologist Maurice Taieb began intensive field work in this area in 1973. Concentrating on a 42 km² area in the central Afar called the Hadar, paleoanthropologists have found remarkably well-preserved geological beds 400–460 feet thick. Initial K/Ar dating has suggested an age of up to 3.6 mya for the older hominid fossils and 2.5 mya for the upper artifactual-bearing beds (Johanson and Edey, 1981). These dates must be considered provisional until systematically corroborated by other laboratories and other dating techniques (Curtis, 1981).

Some of the chronology at the Hadar appears clearcut. For example, there is general agreement that the Lucy skeleton (see below) is about 3 million years old. Analysis of the older beds, however, has led to some ambiguity regarding their precise dating. Study of one of the volcanic tuffs at Hadar has suggested a correlation (i.e., the result of the same volcanic eruption) with well-defined tuffs at Omo in southern Ethiopia and East Lake Turkana in northern Kenya (see below for discussion of these areas). On the basis of this chemical fingerprinting of tuffs (Brown, 1982), the paleomagnetic data, and biostratigraphic interpretations (Boaz et al., 1982), some researchers have concluded the 3.6 million year date for the earlier beds at Hadar is too old; accordingly, they suggest a basal date for the hominid-bearing levels of around 3.2–3.3 mya.

However, opinion still varies. The proposed correlation of the volcanic tuffs across northeastern Africa is not accepted by all researchers (e.g., Aronson et al., 1983). Moreover, the biostratigraphy is also subject to differing interpretations (White, 1983).

A 300,000 to 400,000 year discrepancy may not seem all that important, but it is a most significant time period (10% of the total *known* time range of hominids). To form a consistent theory of exactly what was going on in the Plio-Pleistocene, we need precise chronological controls.

The chronologies, however, often take years of study to sort out. Most crucially, cross-correlations between different dating techniques (K/Ar, biostratigraphy, paleomagnetism, fission-track) must be determined. As we will see presently, it took several years of this kind of cross-checking to establish the chronology of the important hominid locality of East Lake Turkana in northern Kenya.

Due to the excellent preservation conditions in the once-lakeside environment at Hadar, an extraordinary collection of fossilized bones has been discovered— 6,000 specimens in the first two field seasons alone! Among the fossil remains, at

FIGURE 14-4 Hadar deposits, northeastern Ethiopia.

least 36 hominid individuals (up to a maximum of as many as 65) have been discovered (Johanson and Taieb, 1980).

Two extraordinary discoveries at Hadar are most noteworthy. In 1974, a partial skeleton called "Lucy" was found eroding out of a hillside. This fossil is scientifically designated as Afar Locality (AL) 288-1, but is usually just called Lucy (after a popular Beatles' song, "Lucy in the Sky with Diamonds"). Representing almost 40% of a skeleton, this is one of the two most complete individuals from anywhere in the world for the entire period before about 100,000 years ago.*

The second find, a phenomenal discovery, came to light in 1975 at AL 333. Johanson and his amazed crew found dozens of hominid bones scattered along a hillside. These bones represented at least 13 individuals including 4 infants. Possibly members of one social unit, this group has been argued to have all died at about the same time, thus representing a "catastrophic" assemblage (White and Johanson, 1989). However, the precise deposition of the site has not been completely explained, so this assertion must be viewed as quite tentative. (In geological time, an "instant" could represent many decades or centuries). Considerable cultural material has been found in the Hadar area—mostly washed into stream channels, but some stone tools recently have been reported in context at a site dated at 2.5 mya, potentially making the findings the oldest cultural evidence yet discovered. Most unfortunately, political unrest and sporadic warfare in Ethiopia forced a halt to further investigations at the Hadar in 1977. As the situation settled somewhat, hopes for further fieldwork were rekindled. In fact, initial survey work in the Afar Triangle (Middle Awash Valley) in 1981 uncovered from two separate localities fragments of a hominid femur and cranium (dated provisionally, 4 mya) (Johanson, 1989). Plans were thus made for full-scale investigations in 1982, but Ethiopian authorities initiated a temporary moratorium on research that, for the moment, has stalled all efforts. As a result, the key researchers (Don Johanson and Tim White) are concentrating their current efforts at Olduvai (from where Mary Leakey has retired).†

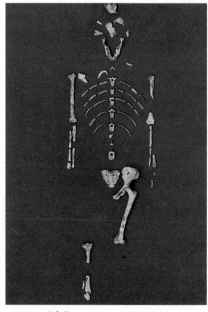

FIGURE 14-5 "Lucy," a partial hominid skeleton. Discovered at the Hadar in 1974.

*The other is a recently discovered *H. erectus* skeleton from west of Lake Turkana, Kenya.

†Researchers from the I.H.O. (led by Tim White and Desmond Clark) returned again to Ethiopia in the fall of 1990.

OMO (OH'-MOH)

The thickest and most continuous Plio-Pleistocene sequence in East Africa comes from the Omo River basin in southern Ethiopia just north of Lake Turkana. This site was also worked jointly by French and American scientists with F. Clark Howell of the University of California, Berkeley, leading the American team.

Total deposits at the Omo are more than one-half mile thick, and the area surveyed extends over more than 200 km². These exceedingly thick sediments are composed largely of lake and river deposits, but more than 100 volcanic ash deposits have also been recognized. These ash deposits provide an excellent basis for accurate K/Ar determinations. This dating technique, supported by paleomagnetic and biostratigraphic results, has placed the hominid-bearing levels at the Omo between 2.9 and 1.0 mya.

A fantastically rich paleontological sample, more than 40,000 mammal specimens alone, has been collected at the Omo. This site, with its well-documented chronology and huge paleontological series, has become the basis for extrapolation for other East African and some South African sites.

Several cultural remains have come to light in the Omo area dating from around 2 mya. Most of this cultural material consists of fragments of flakes struck from stone pebbles and chunks. Only one primary site, where archeological traces retain their original context, has been excavated, and it has revealed a large quantity of these rather crude-looking flakes. What hominids were doing at this location 2 mya is still a mystery. Apparently, it was not quite like the artifact concentrations found at Olduvai, since no animal bones were found with the tools.

Hominid discoveries at the Omo come from 87 different localities and include more than 200 teeth, 9 lower jaws, 4 partial or fragmentary skulls, and a complete ulna (a lower-arm bone).

EAST LAKE TURKANA (TUR-CAN'-AH)

Richard Leakey, the second oldest son of Louis and Mary Leakey, has greatly benefited from the fossil-hunting training given him by his parents. In fact, in the huge, remote, arid area encompassing more than 400 square miles on the eastern side of Lake Turkana,* he and his field crew have found more than twice as many hominid remains since 1968 as his parents found at Olduvai in more than forty years of searching.

Geologically, the situation at East Lake Turkana is exceedingly complex, with deep sections of lake and river deposits crisscrossed by the effects of **tectonic movements**, stream action, and volcanic activity. While the latter is useful in providing material for radiometric dating, the geological complexities have made the precise chronology of the area a matter of dispute.

The later sediments have been securely dated at 1.3–1.6 mya, and consensus on this part of the chronology has existed for several years. However, there has been considerable dispute regarding the earlier levels, particularly a key volcanic bed called the KBS **tuff**.

---

*Lake Turkana was formerly called Lake Rudolf, and the naming of specimens reflects the earlier name: KNM-ER 406 = Kenya National Museum—East Rudolf specimen #406.

Tectonic movement Movements of the earth—for example, along fault lines, during mountain building, and so forth.

Tuff A solidified sediment of volcanic ash.

Discovery of the Hadar "Family," November to December, 1975

On November 1, I set out for the new area with photographer David Brill and a visiting scientist, Dr. Becky Sigmon.

Climbing into my Land Rover, David asked, "When do we find our next hominid?"

"Today," I replied.

In less than an hour, anthropology student John Kolar spotted an arm-bone fragment. From some distance away, Mike Bush, a medical student, shouted that he had found something just breaking the ground surface. It was the very first day on survey for Mike.

"Hominid teeth?" he asked, when we ran to him. There was no doubt.

We called that spot Afar Locality 333 and scheduled full excavation for the next day.

Morning found me at 333, lying on my side so that I could wield a dental pick to excavate the upper-jaw fragment Mike had found. Michèle Cavillon of our motion-picture crew called to me to look at some bones higher up the hill.

Two bone fragments lay side by side—one a partial femur and the other a fragmentary heel bone. Both were hominid.

Carefully, we started scouring the hillside. Two more leg bones—fibulae—showed up, but each from the same side. The same side? That could only indicate two individuals.

Then from high on the slope came a cry, "Look at the proximal femur—it's complete!" Turning I saw, outlined against the blue sky, the top end of a thigh bone. Even from a distance I could tell that it was not Lucy-size; it was much larger. Slowly I groped up the hillside and held the femur.

Mike wanted to come look but was distracted by finding two fragments composing a nearly complete lower jaw. The entire hillside was dotted with the bones of what were evidently at least two individuals.

We held a strategy meeting. Maurice established that the bones we found on the surface had originally been buried several yards up the slope. Mike chose a crew of seven workers to survey carefully every inch of the area and collect all bone material, sifting even the loose soil.

Time was of the essence. Rainstorms during the months of our absence could wash away fragments that would be lost forever down the ravines. I felt I was moving through a dream: Each day produced more remains.

The picture became tangled. Another upper jaw of an adult came to light. The wear pattern on the lower jaw we'd found did not match either of the uppers. At least three individuals had to be represented. More mandible fragments appeared that could not be definitely fitted to either upper jaw. Extraordinary! We had evidence of perhaps as many as five adults of the genus *Homo*.*

Apart from teeth and jaws, we recovered scores of hand and foot bones, leg bones, vertebrae, ribs, even a partial adult skull. A baby tooth turned up, suggesting the presence of a sixth hominid at the site. Then a nearly complete lower jaw of a baby appeared, as well as an almost intact palate with baby teeth. Not heavily worn, the teeth suggested that their possessor was only about 3 years old.

So we had evidence of young adults, old adults, and children—an entire assemblage of early hominids. All of them at one place. Nothing like this had ever been found!

SOURCE:

"Ethiopia Yields First 'Family' of Early Man" by Donald C. Johanson, *National Geographic Magazine*, Vol. 150, pp. 790–811, December 1976. Reprinted with permission of the publisher.

---

*Johanson and his colleagues later assigned all this material to *Australopithecus afarensis* (see p. 431).

FIGURE 14-6 Excavations in progress. East Lake Turkana, northern Kenya.

Initially, conventional K/Ar was attempted, but frequent contamination of samples made results unreliable. Thus, a modification of this procedure* was performed, giving estimates of about 2.6 mya. Later, on the basis of fission-track results and paleomagnetic interpretations, this date was moved down to 2.4 mya.

Since, as we pointed out in Chapter 13, there are built-in errors in each of these different dating techniques, several methods must be used for cross-checking. Analysis of the faunal components at Turkana associated with the KBS tuff did not correlate with the 2.4 my age when compared to fossil materials from the Omo and Olduvai, but, in fact, suggested a date 600,000 years later. Further radiometric tests (using conventional K/Ar) corroborated these findings, and yet further analyses confirmed them: Most of the rich hominid-bearing levels at Turkana are around 1.8 million years old. In addition, there are beds considerably older, which thus far have produced a few fragments of *very* early hominids, dating back to 3.3 my (Kimbel, 1988).

Once again, then, as in our example of the dating at Hadar (see p. 415), the cross-correlation of different techniques is crucial to establishing a firm chronology for these ancient fossil sites. The sampling, testing, evaluation, comparison, and reconsideration of the Turkana dating materials took more than ten years before general agreement was reached.

As noted, numerous hominids have been discovered at East Lake Turkana in the last decade. The current total exceeds 150 hominid specimens, probably representing at least 100 individuals, and this fine sample includes several complete skulls, many jaws, and an assortment of post-cranial bones.

Next to Olduvai, Turkana has yielded the most information concerning the behavior of early hominids. More than twenty archeological sites have been discov-

---

*This technique is called the ⁴⁰Ar/³⁹Ar stepheating method and measures the steady decay of the ³⁹Ar isotope to that of ⁴⁰Ar.

TABLE 14-1   **Summary of East African Hominid Discoveries**

SITE NAME	LOCATION	AGE (MYA)	HOMINIDS
Olduvai	N. Tanzania	1.85–1	48 specimens; australopithecines; early *Homo*
Turkana	N. Kenya (eastern side of Lake Turkana)	1.9–1.3	More than 150 specimens; many australopithecines; several early *Homo*
	West side of Lake Turkana	2.5–1.6	1 cranium (australopithecine) 1 nearly complete skeleton (*Homo erectus*)
Omo	S. Ethiopia	2.9–1	215 specimens; several dozen individuals? australopithecines; some early *Homo*
Hadar	N.E. Ethiopia	?3.7–2.6	Minimum of 36 individuals (maximum of 65); early australopithecine (*A. afarensis*)
Laetoli	N. Tanzania	3.77–3.59	24 hominids; early australopithecine (*A. afarensis*)
Kanapoi	N. Kenya (S.W. Lake Turkana)	4	1 hominid = australopithecine??
Lothagam	N. Kenya (S.W. Lake Turkana)	5.5	1 hominid = ?

ered, and excavation or testing has been done at ten localities. Two sites are of particular interest and are both directly associated with the KBS tuff (age, therefore, 1.8 mya). One is a combination of stone artifacts with the broken bones of several species, whereas the other is the "butchering" site of an extinct form of hippopotamus. The stone tools from these earlier sediments at Turkana are in many ways reminiscent of the Oldowan industry in Bed I at Olduvai (with which they are contemporaneous).

West Lake Turkana

Across the lake from the fossil beds discussed above are other deposits that recently have yielded new and very exciting discoveries. In 1984, on the west side of Lake Turkana, a nearly complete skeleton of a 1.6 my *Homo erectus* child was found (see p. 488), and the following year a well-preserved skull, 2.5 my old, was also found. This latter discovery, the black skull, is a most important discovery and has caused a major reevaluation of Plio-Pleistocene hominid evolution (see p. 436).

OLDUVAI GORGE

The reader should by now be well acquainted with this remarkable site in northern Tanzania, particularly with its clear geological and chronological contribu-

BOX 14-1 **Hominid Origins**

"In each great region of the world the living mammals are closely related to the extinct species of the same region. It is, therefore, probable that Africa was formerly inhabited by extinct apes closely allied to the gorilla and chimpanzee, and as these two species are now man's nearest allies, it is somewhat more probable that our early progenitors lived on the African continent than elsewhere."

SOURCE:

Charles Darwin. *The Descent of Man*, 1871.

tions. Hominid discoveries from Olduvai now total about 50 individuals ranging in time from 1.85 mya to Upper Pleistocene times less than 50,000 years ago.

Endocast An endocast is a solid (in this case, rock) impression of the inside of the skull showing the size, shape, and some details of the surface of the brain.

South Africa: Earliest Discoveries

The first quarter of this century saw the discipline of paleoanthropology in its scientific infancy. Informed opinion considered the likely origins of the human family to be in Asia, where fossil forms of a primitive kind of *Homo* had been found in Indonesia in the 1890s. Europe was also considered a center of hominid evolutionary action, for spectacular discoveries there of early populations of *Homo sapiens* (including the famous Neandertals) and millions of stone tools had come to light, particularly in the early decades of this century.

Few knowledgeable scholars would have given much credence to Darwin's prediction (see Box 14-1) that the most likely place to find early relatives of humans would be on the continent of Africa. It was in such an atmosphere of preconceived biases that the discoveries of a young Australian-born anatomist were to jolt the foundations of the scientific community in the 1920s. **Raymond Dart** arrived in South Africa in 1923 at the age of 30 to take up a teaching position in anatomy at the University of Witwatersrand in Johannesburg. Fresh from his evolution-oriented training in England under some of the leading scholars of the day (especially, Sir Grafton Elliot Smith), Dart had developed a keen interest in human evolution. Consequently, he was well prepared when startling new evidence began to appear at his very doorstep.

The first clue came in 1924 when one of Dart's students saw an interesting baboon skull on the mantelpiece while having dinner at the home of the director of the Northern Lime Company, a commercial quarrying firm. The skull, that of a large baboon, had come from a place called Taung about 200 miles southwest of Johannesburg. When Dart saw the skull, he quickly recognized it as an extinct form and asked that any other interesting fossil material found be sent to him for his inspection.

Soon thereafter he received two boxloads of fossils and immediately recognized something that was quite unusual, a natural **endocast** of the inside of the braincase of a higher primate, but certainly no baboon. The endocast fit into another limestone block containing the fossilized front portion of skull, face, and lower jaw. However, these were difficult to see clearly, for the bone was hardened into a cemented limestone matrix called *breccia*. Dart patiently chiseled away for

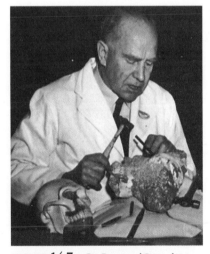

FIGURE 14-7 Dr. Raymond Dart, shown working in his laboratory.

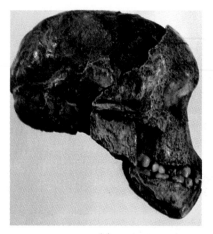

(a)

(b)

FIGURE 14-8   (a) The Taung child discovered in 1924. The endocast is in back with the fossilized bone mandible and face in front; (b) Taung. Location of the initial australopithecine discovery.

weeks, later describing the task: "No diamond cutter ever worked more lovingly or with such care on a priceless jewel—nor, I am sure, with such inadequate tools. But on the seventy-third day, December 23, the rock parted. I could view the face from the front, although the right side was still imbedded. . . . What emerged was a baby's face, an infant with a full set of milk teeth and its permanent molars just in the process of erupting. I doubt if there was any parent prouder of his offspring than I was of my Taung baby on that Christmas" (Dart, 1959, p. 10).

As indicated by the formation and eruption of teeth, the Taung child was probably about 3–4 years of age at death. Interestingly, the rate of development of this and many other Plio-Pleistocene hominids, was more like that of apes than modern *Homo* (Shipman, 1987; Bromage and Dean, 1985). Dart's initial impression that this form was a hominoid was confirmed when he could observe the face and teeth more clearly. However, as it turned out, it took considerably more effort before the teeth could be seen completely, since Dart worked four years just to separate the upper and lower jaws.

But Dart was convinced long before he had an unimpeded view of the dentition that this discovery was a remarkable one, an early hominoid from South Africa. The question was, what kind of hominoid? Dart realized it was extremely improbable that this specimen could have been a forest ape, for South Africa has had a relatively dry climate for many millions of years. Even though the climate at Taung was not as arid as was previously believed (Butzer, 1974), it was an unlikely place to find an ape!

If not an ape, then, what was it? Features of the skull and teeth of this small child held clues that Dart seized upon almost immediately. The entrance of the spinal column into the brain (the *foramen magnum* at the base of the skull) was further forward in the Taung child than in modern great apes, though not as much as in modern humans. From this fact Dart concluded that the head was balanced *above* the spine, indicating erect posture. In addition, the slant of the forehead was not as receding as in apes, the milk canines were exceedingly small, and the newly erupted first molars were large, broad teeth. In all these respects, the Taung fossil looked more like a hominid than a pongid. There was, however, a disturbing feature that was to confuse and befuddle many scientists for several years: the brain was quite small. Recent studies have estimated the Taung child's brain size at approximately 405 cm³, which translates to a fully adult size of only 440 cm³, not very large when compared to modern great apes, as the following tabulation (Tobias, 1971; 1983) shows:

	RANGE (CM³)	MEAN (CM³)
Chimpanzee	282–500	394
Gorilla	340–752	506
Orang	276–540	411

As the tabulation indicates, the estimated cranial capacity for the Taung fossil falls within the range of all the modern great apes, and gorillas actually *average* about 10% greater. It must, however, be remembered that gorillas are very large animals, whereas the Taung child represents a population whose average adult size may have been less than sixty pounds. Since brain size is partially correlated with body size, comparing such differently sized animals cannot be justified. A more meaningful contrast would be with the bonobo (*Pan paniscus*), whose body weight is comparable. Bonobos have adult cranial capacities averaging 356

Raymond Dart and the Discovery of the Taung Child, November, 1924

On his return Young told me that at Taungs he had met an old miner, Mr. M. de Bruyn, who for many years had taken a keen interest in preserving fossils. Only the previous week he had brought quite a number of stone blocks containing bone fragments to Mr. Spiers' office. When Young mentioned my interest to Mr. Spiers, Spiers gave instructions for them to be boxed and railed to me.

I waited anxiously for their arrival, reasoning that if fossilized baboon skulls were such a common feature at Taungs many other, more interesting specimens might be found there. Of course, the packages turned up at the most inappropriate time.

I was standing by the window of my dressing room cursing softly while struggling into an unaccustomed stiff-winged collar when I noticed two men wearing the uniform of the South African Railways staggering along the driveway of our home in Johannesburg with two large wooden boxes.

My Virginia-born wife Dora, who was also donning her most formal outfit, had noticed the men with the boxes and rushed in to me in something of a panic.

"I suppose those are the fossils you've been expecting," she said. "Why on earth did they have to arrive today of all days?" She fixed me with a business-like eye. "Now Raymond," she pleaded, "the guests will start arriving shortly and you can't go delving in all that rubble until the wedding's over and everybody has left. I know how important the fossils are to you, but please leave them until tomorrow."

At the time, however, this seemed of little importance when I considered the exciting anthropological bits and pieces that the boxes from Taungs might contain. As soon as my wife had left to complete her dressing I tore the hated collar off and dashed out to take delivery of the boxes which meanwhile obstructed the entrance to the *stoep*. I was too excited to wait until my African servants carried them to the garage, and ordered them to leave the crates under the pergola while I went in search of some tools to open them.

(Later on that momentous day, my wife told me that she had twice remonstrated with me but had been ignored. I had no recollection of any interruptions.)

I wrenched the lid off the first box and my reaction was one of extreme disappointment. In the rocks I could make out traces of fossilized eggshells and turtle shells and a few fragmentary pieces of isolated bone, none of which looked to be of much interest.

Impatiently I wrestled with the lid of the second box, still hopeful but half-expecting it to be a replica of its mate. At most I anticipated baboon skulls, little guessing that from this crate was to emerge a face that would look out on the world after an age-long sleep of nearly a million years.

As soon as I removed the lid a thrill of excitement shot through me. On the very top of the rock heap was what was undoubtedly an endocranial cast or mold of the interior of the skull. Had it been only the fossilized brain cast of any species of ape it would have ranked as a great discovery, for such a thing had never before been reported. But I knew at a glance that what lay in my hands was no ordinary anthropoidal brain. Here in lime-consolidated sand was the replica of a brain three times as large as that of a baboon and considerably bigger than that of any adult chimpanzee. The startling image of the convolutions and furrows of the brain and the blood vessels of the skull was plainly visible.

I stood in the shade holding the brain as greedily as any miser hugs his gold, my mind racing ahead. Here, I was certain, was one of the most significant finds ever made in the history of anthropology.

SOURCE:

Adventures with the Missing Link by Raymond Dart, 1959. Reprinted with permission of the author.

cm³ for males and 329 cm³ for females, and thus the Taung child versus a *comparably sized* pongid displays a 25% increase in cranial capacity.

Despite the relatively small size of the brain, Dart saw that it was no pongid. Details preserved on the endocast seemed to indicate that the association areas of the parietal lobes were relatively larger than in any known pongid. However, recent reexamination of the Taung specimen has shown that the sulcal (folding) pattern is actually quite pongidlike (Falk, 1980; 1983).

We must emphasize that attempts to discern the precise position of the "bumps and folds" in ancient endocasts is no easy feat. The science of "paleoneurology" is thus often marked by sharp differences of opinion. Consequently, it is not surprising that the other leading researcher in this field, Ralph Halloway (1981), disagrees with the conclusion by Falk (just cited) and suggests, alternatively, that the Taung endocast has a more hominidlike sulcal pattern.

Realizing the immense importance of his findings, Dart promptly reported them in the British scientific weekly *Nature* on February 7, 1925. A bold venture, since Dart, only 32, was presumptuously proposing a whole new view of human evolution! The small-brained Taung child was christened by Dart **Australopithecus africanus** (southern ape of Africa), which he saw as a kind of halfway "missing link" between modern apes and humans. The concept of a single "missing link" between modern apes and humans was a fallacious one, but Dart correctly emphasized the hominidlike features of the fossil.

A storm of both popular and scholarly protest greeted Dart's article, for it ran directly counter to prevailing opinion. Despite the numerous hominid fossils already discovered, widespread popular skepticism of evolution still prevailed. The year 1925 was, after all, the year of the Scopes "monkey trial" in Tennessee. The biggest fly in the ointment to the leading human evolutionists of the day—Arthur Keith and Grafton Elliot Smith—was the small size of the brain compared to the relatively large proportions of the face and jaws. At that time, anthropologists generally assumed that the primary functional adaptation distinguishing the human family was an immense increase in brain size, and that dental and locomotory modifications came later. This view was seemingly confirmed by the Piltdown dis-

FIGURE 14-9　A bonobo. A modern pongid probably similar in body size to many of the australopithecines.

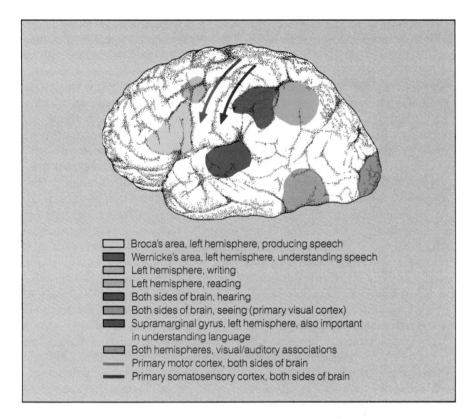

FIGURE 14-10 The human brain. Schematic diagram of surface showing major functional areas and surface features.

Broca's area, left hemisphere, producing speech
Wernicke's area, left hemisphere, understanding speech
Left hemisphere, writing
Left hemisphere, reading
Both sides of brain, hearing
Both sides of brain, seeing (primary visual cortex)
Supramarginal gyrus, left hemisphere, also important in understanding language
Both hemispheres, visual/auditory associations
Primary motor cortex, both sides of brain
Primary somatosensory cortex, both sides of brain

covery in 1911, which displayed the combination of a large brain (estimated at 1,400 cm³, well within the range of modern man) with an ape-like jaw (see pp. 408–410). Keith even went so far as to postulate a "Cerebral Rubicon" of 750 cm³ below which—by definition—no hominid could fall. Most scientists in the 1920s thus regarded this little Taung child as an interesting aberrant form of ape.

Hence, Dart's theories were received with indifference, disbelief, and scorn, often extremely caustic. Dart realized more complete remains were needed. The skeptical world would not accept the evidence of one fragmentary, immature individual no matter how highly suggestive the clues. Clearly, more fossil evidence was required, particularly more complete crania of adults. Not an experienced fossil hunter himself, Dart sought further assistance in the search for more **australopithecines** (the colloquial name referring to the members of genus *Australopithecus*). The designation "*Australopithecus*" will be used repeatedly throughout this chapter to refer to a variety of different species. However, in all contexts we will use it to denote a hominid that is bipedal, small-brained, and large-toothed. In this sense, we use it similarly to Dart's original description and interpretation.

Australopithecine (os-tral-oh-pith′-e-seen)

South African Hominids Aplenty

Soon after publication of his controversial theories, Dart found a strong ally in **Dr. Robert Broom**. A Scottish physician and part-time paleontologist, Broom's credentials as a fossil hunter had been established earlier with his highly successful paleontological work on early mammallike reptiles in South Africa.

FIGURE 14-11 Dr. Robert Broom. Shown with one of his paleontological discoveries from South Africa. This photo was taken earlier in Dr. Broom's career; it would be almost thirty years later before he would even begin his search for australopithecines.

Sterkfontein (Sterk'-fon-tane)

Kromdraai (Kromm'-dry)

Swartkrans (Swart-kranz)

Makapansgat (Mak-ah-pans'-gat)

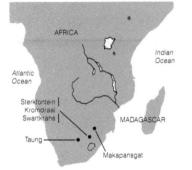

FIGURE 14-12 Australopithecine sites in South Africa.

Although interested, Broom was unable to participate actively in the search for additional australopithecines because of prior commitments and did not seriously undertake explorations until 1936. However, soon thereafter he met with incredible success. From two of Dart's students, Broom learned of another commercial limeworks site, called **Sterkfontein**, not far from Johannesburg. Here, as at Taung, the quarrying involved blasting out large sections with dynamite, leaving piles of debris that often contained fossilized remains. Accordingly, Broom asked the quarry manager to keep his eyes open for fossils, and when Broom returned to the site in August 1936, the manager asked, "Is this what you are looking for?" Indeed, it was, for Broom held in his hand the endocast of an adult australopithecine—exactly what he had set out to find! Looking further over the scattered debris, Broom was able to find most of the rest of the skull of the same individual.

Such remarkable success, just a few months after beginning his search, was not the end of Broom's luck, for his magical touch was to continue unabated for several more years. In 1938, he learned from a young schoolboy of another australopithecine site at **Kromdraai** about one mile from Sterkfontein, and, following World War II (1948), he found yet another australopithecine site, **Swartkrans**, in the same vicinity. A final australopithecine site, **Makapansgat**, was excavated in 1947 by Raymond Dart, who returned to the fossil-discovering bandwagon after an absence of over twenty years.

Numerous extremely important discoveries came from these additional sites, discoveries that would eventually swing the tide of intellectual thought to the views Dart expressed back in 1925. Particularly important was a nearly perfect skull and a nearly complete pelvis, both found at Sterkfontein in 1947. As the number of discoveries accumulated, it became increasingly difficult to simply write them off as aberrant apes.

Although Robert Broom was an absolute wizard at finding fossils, his interpretations of them were clouded by an irresistible urge to give each new discovery a different taxonomic label. Consequently, in addition to Dart's *A. africanus* from Taung, a disconcertingly large number of other names have been used at various times for the South African australopithecines (see Table 14-2). The problem with all this taxonomic splitting was a lack of appreciation for the relevant biological principles underlying such elaborate interpretations (see Chapter 12 for a discussion of the meaning of taxonomic statements).

By 1949, at least thirty individuals were represented from the five South African sites. That year represents an important turning point, since it marks the visit to South Africa and the resulting "conversion" of W. E. Le Gros Clark. As one of the leading human evolutionists of the day, Sir Wilfrid Le Gros Clark's unequivocal

TABLE 14-2 **Taxonomic Labels Applied to South African Hominids**

	SITE	DISCOVERED AND NAMED BY
Australopithecus africanus	Taung	Dart
Plesianthropus transvaalensis	Sterkfontein	Broom
Paranthropus robustus	Kromdraai	Broom
Paranthropus crassidens	Swartkrans	Broom
Australopithecus prometheus	Makapansgat	Dart
Telanthropus capensis	Swartkrans	Broom

Dr. Broom and the Discovery of the Kromdraai Ape-Man

On the forenoon of Wednesday, June 8, 1938, when I met Barlow, he said, "I've something nice for you this morning"; and he held out part of a fine palate with the first molar-tooth in position. I said, "Yes, it's quite nice. I'll give you a couple of pounds for it." He was delighted; so I wrote out a cheque, and put the specimen in my pocket. He did not seem quite willing to say where or how he had obtained it; and I did not press the matter. The specimen clearly belonged to a large ape-man, and was apparently different from the Sterkfontein being.

I was again at Sterkfontein on Saturday, when I knew Barlow would be away. I showed the specimen to the native boys in the quarry; but none of them had ever seen it before. I felt sure it had not come from the quarry, as the matrix was different. On Tuesday forenoon I was again at Sterkfontein, when I insisted on Barlow telling me how he had got the specimen. I pointed out that two teeth had been freshly broken off, and that they might be lying where the specimen had been obtained. He apologized for having misled me; and told me it was a school-boy, Gert Terblanche, who acted as a guide in the caves on Sundays, who had picked it up and given it to him. I found where Gert lived, about two miles away; but Barlow said he was sure to be away at school. Still, I set out for his home. There I met Gert's mother and sister. They told me that the place where the specimen was picked up was near the top of a hill about half a mile away, and the sister agreed to take me up to the place. She and her mother also told me that Gert had four beautiful teeth at school with him.

The sister took us up the hill, and I picked up some fragments of the skull, and a couple of teeth; but she said she was sure Gert had some other nice pieces hidden away. Of course, I had to go to school to hunt up Gert.

The road to the school was a very bad one, and we had to leave the car, and walk about a mile over rough ground. When we got there, it was about half-past twelve, and it was play time. I found the headmaster, and told him that I wanted to see Gert Terblanche in connection with some teeth he had picked up. Gert was soon found, and drew from the pocket of his trousers four of the most wonderful teeth ever seen in the world's history. These I promptly purchased from Gert, and transferred to my pocket. I had the palate with me, and I found that two of the teeth were the second pre-molar and second molar, and that they fitted on to the palate. The two others were teeth of the other side. Gert told me about the piece he had hidden away. As the school did not break up till two o'clock, I suggested to the principal that I should give a lecture to the teachers and children about caves, how they were formed, and how bones got into them. He was delighted. So it was arranged; and I lectured to four teachers and about 120 children for over an hour, with blackboard illustrations, till it was nearly two o'clock. When I finished, the principal broke up the school, and Gert came home with me. He took us up to the hill, and brought out from his hiding place a beautiful lower jaw with two teeth in position. All the fragments that I could find at the spot I picked up.

SOURCE:

Finding the Missing Link by Robert Broom (2nd Ed.), 1951. By permission of C. A. Watts/Pitman Publishing Ltd., London.

support of the australopithecines as small-brained early hominids was to have wide impact. But the tides of wisdom had begun to turn even before this. Writing in 1947, **Sir Arthur Keith** courageously admitted his earlier mistake:

"When Professor Dart of the University of Witwatersrand, Johannesburg, announced in *Nature* the discovery of a juvenile *Australopithecus* and claimed for it human kinship, I was one of those who took the point of view that when the adult was discovered, it would prove to be nearer akin to the living African anthropoids—the gorilla and chimpanzee. . . . I am now convinced of the evidence submitted by Dr. Robert Broom that Professor Dart was right and I was wrong. The Australopithecinae [formal designation of the australopithecines as a subfamily of the hominids] are in or near the line which culminated in the human form" (Keith in Le Gros Clark, 1967, p. 38).

Mosaic evolution Rate of evolution in one functional system varies from other systems.

Innominate The fused half-portion of a pelvis; contains three bones—the ilium, ischium, and pubis (also called the *os coxa*).

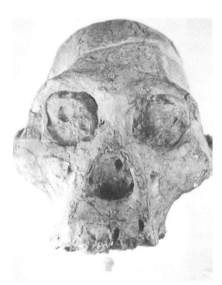

FIGURE 14-13 A gracile australopithecine skull from Sterkfontein (Sts. 5). This specimen is the best preserved gracile skull yet found in South Africa. Discovered in 1947.

FIGURE 14-14 Sir Arthur Keith.

With the exposé of the Piltdown forgery in the early 1950s, the path was completely cleared for the nearly unanimous recognition of the australopithecines as early hominids. With this acceptance also came the necessary recognition that hominid brains had their greatest expansion *after* earlier changes in teeth and locomotory systems. In other words, the rates of evolution in one functional system of the body vary from other systems, thus displaying the **mosaic** nature of human **evolution**.

Even today, the evidence from South Africa continues to accumulate. The search in recent years has continued at Sterkfontein, Kromdraai, Swartkrans, and Makapansgat. An important portion of pelvis was found at Swartkrans in 1970, and a partial skull was found at Sterkfontein (west pit) in 1976. Indeed, discoveries are now coming faster than ever. In the last few years alone more than 150 *new* specimens have come to light at Sterkfontein. In addition, several important new discoveries have been made at Swartkrans. A truly remarkable feast of early hominids, the total number of remains from South Africa exceeds 1,500 (counting all teeth as separate items), and the number of individuals is now more than 200.

From an evolutionary point of view, the most meaningful remains are those from the australopithecine pelvis, which now includes portions of nine **innominates** (Figs. 14-16, 14-17). Remains of the pelvis are so important because, better than any other area of the body, this structure displays the unique requirements of a bipedal animal, such as modern humans *and* our hominid forebears. (For anatomical comparisons, see Appendix A.)

Hominids on Their Feet

As we discussed in Chapter 9, there is a general tendency in all primates for erect body posture and some bipedalism. However, of all living primates, efficient bipedalism as the primary form of locomotion is seen *only* in hominids. Functionally, the human mode of locomotion is most clearly shown in our striding gait, where weight is alternately placed on a single fully extended hindlimb. This specialized form of locomotion has developed to a point where energy levels are used to near peak efficiency. Such is not the case in nonhuman primates, who move bipedally with hips and knees bent and maintain balance in a clumsy and inefficient manner.

From a survey of our close primate relatives, it is apparent that, while still in the trees, our ancestors were adapted to a fair amount of upper body erectness. Prosimians, monkeys, and apes all spend considerable time sitting erect while feeding, grooming, or sleeping. Presumably, our early ancestors also displayed similar behavior. What caused these forms to come to the ground and embark on the unique way of life that would eventually lead to humans is still a mystery. Perhaps natural selection favored some Miocene hominoid coming occasionally to the ground to forage for food on the forest floor and forest fringe. In any case, once it was on the ground and away from the immediate safety offered by trees, bipedal locomotion became a tremendous advantage.

First of all, bipedal locomotion freed the hands for carrying objects and for making and using tools. Such early cultural developments then had an even more positive effect on speeding the development of yet more efficient bipedalism—once again emphasizing the dual role of biocultural evolution. In addition, in the bipedal stance, animals have a wider view of the surrounding countryside, and, in open terrain, early spotting of predators (particularly the large cats, such as lions, leopards, and saber tooths) would be of critical importance. We know that modern ground-living primates, such as the savanna baboon and chimpanzee, will occasionally adopt this posture to "look around" when out in open country. Certainly, bipedal walking is an efficient means of covering long distances, and when large game hunting came into play (several million years after the initial adaptation to ground-living), further refinements in the locomotory complex may have been favored. Finally, it has been suggested that bipedalism was initially most adaptive for carrying—particularly food brought by provisioning males to females and young (Lovejoy, 1981). (See pp. 262–264.) Exactly what initiated the process is difficult to say, but all these factors probably played a role in the adaptation of hominids to their special niche through a special form of locomotion.

Our mode of locomotion is indeed extraordinary, involving as it does a unique kind of activity in which "the body, step by step, teeters on the edge of catastrophe" (Napier, 1967, p. 56). The problem is to maintain balance on the "stance" leg while the "swing" leg is off the ground. In fact, during normal walking, both feet are simultaneously on the ground only about 25% of the time, and, as speed of locomotion increases, this figure becomes even smaller.

In order to maintain a stable center of balance in this complex form of locomotion, many drastic structural/functional alterations are demanded in the basic primate quadrupedal pattern. Functionally, the foot must be altered to act as a stable

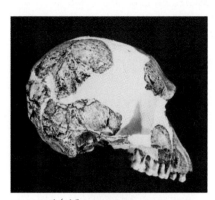

FIGURE 14-15   A partial hominid skull from Sterkfontein (Stw. 53). Discovered during excavations in 1976.

FIGURE 14-16   The human pelvis. Various elements shown on a modern skeleton.

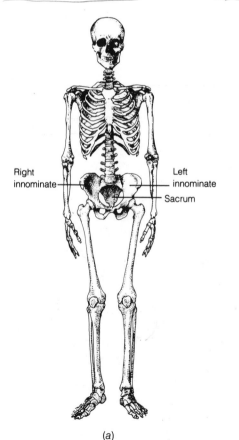

Right innominate

Left innominate

Sacrum

(a)

(b)

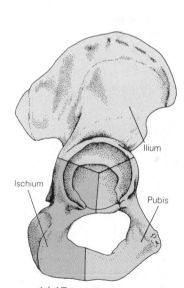

Ilium

Ischium

Pubis

FIGURE 14-17   The human innominate. Composed of three bones (right side shown).

support instead of a grasping limb. When we walk, our foot is used like a prop, landing on the heel and pushing off on the toes, particularly the big toe. In addition, the leg must be elongated to increase the length of the stride and lower the center of gravity. The lower limb must also be remodeled to allow full extension of the knee and to allow the legs to be kept close together during walking, thereby maintaining the center of support directly under the body. Finally, significant changes must occur in the pelvis to permit stable weight transmission from the upper body to the legs and to maintain balance through pelvic rotation and altered proportions and orientations of several key muscles.

The major structural changes that are required for bipedalism are all seen in the australopithecines in East and South Africa. In the pelvis, the blade (ilium—upper bone of the pelvis) is shortened top to bottom, which permits more stable weight support in the erect position by lowering the center of gravity. In addition, the pelvis is bent backwards and downwards, thus altering the position of the muscles that attach along the bone. Most importantly, the gluteus medius (glue-tee'-us meed'-ee-us) now becomes a very large muscle acting to stablize the trunk and keep it from slumping to the unsupported side while the body is supported on one leg. The gluteus maximus (glue-tee'-us max'-a-mus) also becomes important as an extensor—pulls the thigh back—during running, jumping, and climbing. (See Appendix A.)

Other structural changes shown by australopithecine postcranial evidence further confirm the morphological pattern seen in the pelvis. As we just discussed, the remarkable footprints from Laetoli show unequivocally a bipedal adaptation. In addition, the vertebral column, known from beautifully preserved specimens from Sterkfontein, as well as from Lucy, show the same forward curvature as in modern hominids, bringing the center of support forward and allowing rotation of the bottom of the vertebral column (sacrum) below, thereby getting it out of the way of the birth canal. In addition, the lower limb is elongated and is apparently proportionately about as long as in modern humans. Fossil evidence of a knee fragment from Sterkfontein and pieces from East Africa also shows that full exten-

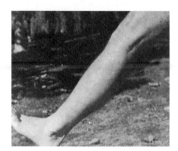

FIGURE 14-18   The knee in full extension.

FIGURE 14-19   Innominates. (*a*) *Homo sapiens*; (*b*) australopithecine (Sts. 14); (*c*) chimpanzee. Note especially the length and breadth of the iliac blade.

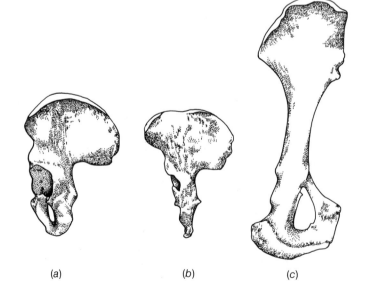

(a)   (b)   (c)

sion of this joint was possible, thus allowing the leg to be completely straightened, as when a field goal kicker follows through.

Structural evidence for the foot is not abundant in South Africa, but there is an ankle bone from Kromdraai and a few pieces recently discovered at Swartkrans. These foot bones show mixed patterns and probably belonged to an animal that was a well-adapted biped but still retained considerable climbing ability. More complete evidence for evolutionary changes in the foot skeleton comes from Olduvai Gorge in East Africa, where a nearly complete hominid foot is preserved, and from the Hadar in Ethiopia, where numerous foot elements have been recovered. As in the ankle bone from Kromdraai, the East African fossils suggest a well-adapted bipedal gait. The arches are developed and the big toe is pulled in next to the other toes, but some differences in the ankle also imply that considerable flexibility was possible (for climbing?). As we will see below, some researchers have recently concluded that the early forms of australopithecine (and perhaps early *Homo* as well) probably spent considerable time in the trees. Moreover, they may not have been as efficient bipeds as has previously been suggested (see p. 434).

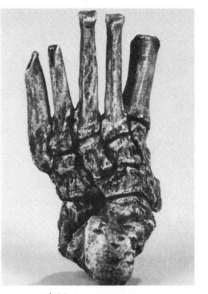

FIGURE 14-20   A nearly complete hominid foot (OH 8). From Olduvai Gorge, East Africa.

Plio-Pleistocene Hominids

From the time period between 4 and 1 mya, East and South African sites have thus far yielded close to 500 hominid individuals. This huge collection of material (much of it in well-dated contexts) has allowed paleoanthropologists to formulate (and reformulate) their interpretations of human evolution. At present, it appears that at least four groups (which we will refer to as "sets") of hominids are distinguishable in Africa during the Plio-Pleistocene. The first of these sets was distinctly earlier and more primitive, while the others appear somewhat later with at least two lineages surviving beyond 2 mya and living contemporaneously for over one million years.

SET I. EARLY PRIMITIVE AUSTRALOPITHECINES (*A. AFARENSIS*)

Prior to 4 mya the fossil hominid (or "hominoid") remains from East Africa (which is all there is anywhere) are extremely scrappy, represented by only two molars, one cranial bone, two fragmentary jaws, and one arm bone (see pp. 412–413). The best that can be said about this material is that it is hominoid, and in some cases, "hominidlike."

It is not until 4–3 mya that we get the first *definite* collection of hominid fossils. These crucial remains come primarily from two East African sites explored within the last twenty years: Laetoli in northern Tanzania and Hadar in northeastern Ethiopia. From these two sites together several hundred hominid specimens have been recovered, representing a minimum of 60 individuals and perhaps close to 100. In addition, there are of course those fascinating hominid footprints from Laetoli. Finally, there are a few bits and pieces also from this same time period and probably belonging to the same group from East Turkana (Lower Beds) and from the Omo.

FIGURE 14-21   A nearly complete cranium from Swartkrans (Sk. 48). The best preserved skull of a robust australopithecine from South Africa.

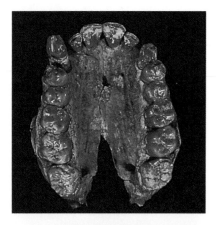

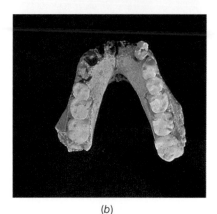

(b)

FIGURE 14-22   Jaws of *Australopithecus afarensis*. (*a*) Maxilla, AL-200-1a, from Hadar, Ethiopia. (Note the parallel tooth rows and large canines.); (*b*) mandible, L. H. 4, from Laetoli, Tanzania. This fossil is the type specimen for the new species, *Australopithecus afarensis*.

FIGURE 14-23   Comparison of hominoid crania. (*a*) human; (*b*) *Australopithecus afarensis* composite cranium assembled from three individuals—AL 333-45, 200-1a, and 400-1a; (*c*) Chimpanzee.

Interpretation of fossil hominids is a laborious and highly technical undertaking. Finding the fossils is only the first step. They then have to be cleaned (often of intractable matrix), measured, described, reconstructed, and then measured again. It is thus not surprising that, although the first hominid specimens were recovered from Hadar and Laetoli in 1973 and 1974 respectively, their taxonomic affinity was not published until 1978 (Johanson et al., 1978); a systematic reappraisal of *all* hominids from the Plio-Pleistocene appeared soon thereafter in early 1979 (Johanson and White, 1979), and comprehensive descriptions were published in April, 1982, in the *American Journal of Physical Anthropology*.

Certainly, the announcement of a new species always raises considerable professional and public interest. The proposal of *A. afarensis* by Johanson and his colleagues was no exception. Predictably, not all the reaction was favorable. In science, this is a healthy attitude; hypotheses *always* need to be scrutinized and tested against further evidence.

What exactly is *A. afarensis*? Without question, it is more primitive than any of the australopithecine material from South Africa or East Africa (discussed subsequently). In fact, *A. afarensis* is the most primitive of any definitely hominid group thus far found anywhere. By "primitive," we mean that *A. afarensis* is less evolved in any particular direction than is seen in later species of *Australopithecus* or *Homo*. That is to say, *A. afarensis* shares more primitive features with other early hominoids (such as *Dryopithecus*, *Sivapithecus*, etc.) and with living pongids than is true of later hominids, who display more derived characteristics.

For example, the teeth are quite primitive. The canines are often large, pointed teeth that slightly overlap; the first lower premolar is semisectorial, and the tooth rows are parallel or even posteriorly convergent (see Fig. 14-22*a*).

The pieces of crania that are preserved also display several primitive hominoid characteristics, including a compound sagittal/nuchal crest in the back (see Fig. 14-23), as well as several primitive features of the cranial base (involving the tubular appearance of the external ear canal, pneumatization, which is air pockets within the bone, and an open-appearing articulation for the lower jaw). Cranial capacity estimates for *afarensis* show a mixed pattern when compared to later

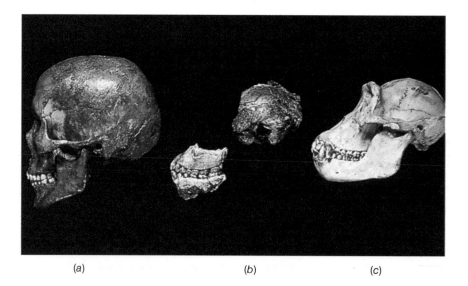

(a)   (b)   (c) hominids. A provisional estimate for the one partially complete cranium (see Fig. 14-23*b*)—apparently a large individual—gives a figure of 500 cm³, but another, even more fragmentary, cranium is apparently quite a bit smaller and has been estimated at about 375 cm³ (Holloway, 1983). Thus, for some individuals (males?), *afarensis* is well within the range of other australopithecine species, but others (females?) may be significantly smaller. However, a detailed depiction of cranial size for *A. afarensis* as a species is not possible at this time—this part of the skeleton is unfortunately too poorly represented. One thing is clear: *A. afarensis* had a small brain, probably averaging for the whole species not much over 420 cm³.

A host of postcranial pieces have been found at Hadar (mostly from the partial skeleton "Lucy," and from individuals at AL 333). Initial impressions suggest that the upper limbs are long relative to the lower ones (also a primitive hominoid condition). In addition, the wrist, hand, and foot bones show several differences from modern humans (Susman et al., 1985). Stature can now be confidently estimated: *A. afarensis* was a short hominid. From her partial skeleton, Lucy is figured to be only 3.5–4 feet tall. However, Lucy—as demonstrated by her pelvis—was a female, and at Hadar and Laetoli, there is evidence of larger individuals as well. The most economical hypothesis explaining this variation is that *A. afarensis* was quite sexually dimorphic—the larger individuals are male and the smaller ones such as Lucy are female. Estimates of male stature can be approximated from the larger footprints at Laetoli, inferring a height of about 5 feet.

If we accept this interpretation, *A. afarensis* was a very sexually dimorphic form. In fact, for overall body size, this species may have been as dimorphic as *any* living primate (i.e., as much as gorillas, orangs, or baboons). The elaborate behavioral reconstruction proposed by Lovejoy (1981) (see pp. 262–264), is based upon a *lack* of dimorphism in this species. Lovejoy points particularly to the relatively small degree of canine dimorphism between presumed males and females, but, even here, there are some reasonably good-sized differences apparent. Indeed, in the original description of *A. afarensis* (Johanson et al., 1978), a feature noted to define this form was "strong variation in canine size."

Beyond the claimed lack of canine size dimorphism, there are even more serious problems with the Lovejoy model. In those few nonhuman primates that are monogamous (e.g., gibbons) there is clearly little body size dimorphism. Yet, in *A. afarensis*, males may be twice as big as females, and thus rival or even exceed (see below) the amount of dimorphism in the most dimorphic of living primates. Clearly, these highly dimorphic primates are uniformly polygynous, and many less dimorphic species of monkeys also follow mostly polygynous mating strategies.

In conclusion, the evidence presented arguing for sexual dimorphism within *A. afarensis* could hardly be used to infer monogamous mating patterns. Indeed, it could be quite forcefully used to argue against it!

Behavioral debates such as these are certainly stimulating, but what is most interesting about *A. afarensis* is the distinctive physical morphology it displays. In a majority of dental and cranial features *A. afarensis* is clearly more primitive than are later hominids. This should not come as too great a surprise, since *afarensis* is 1 my older than most other East African finds and perhaps .5–.7 my older than the oldest South African hominid. In fact, from the neck up, *A. afarensis* is so primitive, that without any evidence from the limb skeleton, one would be hard-pressed to call it a hominid at all (although the back teeth are large and heavily enameled, unlike pongids). In the teeth particularly, *A. afarensis* is in some ways reminiscent of Miocene hominoids (e.g., *Sivapithecus*) (Greenfield, 1979).

FIGURE 14-24 *Australopithecus afarensis* reconstructed cranium—using evidence from several individuals and filling in portions for which no fossil data exist.

What then makes *A. afarensis* a hominid? The answer is revealed by its manner of locomotion. From the abundant limb bones recovered from Hadar and those beautiful footprints from Laetoli we know unequivocally that *afarensis* walked bipedally when progressing on the ground. Whether Lucy and her contemporaries still spent considerable time in the trees, and just how efficiently they walked, have recently become topics of major dispute.

Locomotion of Australopithecus afarensis A recent comprehensive analysis of the postcranial anatomy of *A. afarensis* by Jack Stern and Randall Susman of the State University of New York at Stony Brook has challenged the view that this early hominid walked bipedally, much as you or me (Stern and Susman, 1983). Their interpretation is based upon many parts of the skeleton (limbs, hands, feet, pelvis, etc.), which they have compared with other hominids (fossil and modern), as well as with great apes.

Such features as long, curved fingers and toes, long upper limbs but short lower limbs (Jungers, 1982; Susman et al., 1985), the positioning of the hip and knee joints, and pelvic orientation, have led these researchers to two conclusions: (1) *A. afarensis* was capable of efficient climbing and probably spent considerable time in the trees (sleeping, feeding, escaping from predators, etc.); and (2) while on the ground, *A. afarensis* was a biped, but walked with a much less efficient bent-hip, bent-knee gait than that seen in modern humans.

As might be expected, these conclusions themselves have also been challenged. While pointing out some slight differences from modern humans in postcranial anatomy, Owen Lovejoy (1988) and his associates (e.g., Latimer, 1984) see nothing that suggests these hominids were arboreal or, conversely, that precluded them from being *very* efficient bipeds. Moreover, Lucy's "little legs" may not really be that small, considering her small body size (although her arms were apparently quite long) (Wolpoff, 1983b).

Other researchers have also noted differences between the postcranium of *A. afarensis* and later hominids. Interestingly, however, in many respects the hand and pelvis of *A. afarensis* are extremely similar to some later australopithecines from South Africa (Suzman, 1982; McHenry, 1983).

From all this debate, little has yet emerged in the way of consensus, except that all agree the *A. afarensis* did exhibit some kind of bipedal locomotion while on the ground. In searching for some middle ground between the opposing viewpoints, several researchers have suggested that *A. afarensis* could have been quite at home in the trees *as well as* being an efficient terrestrial biped (Wolpoff, 1983; McHenry, 1983). As one physical anthropologist has recently put it:

> One could imagine these diminutive early hominids making maximum use of *both* terrestrial and arboreal resources in spite of their commitment to exclusive bipedalism when on the ground. The contention of a mixed arboreal and terrestrial behavioural repertoire would make adaptive sense of the Hadar australopithecine forelimb, hand, and foot morphology without contradicting the evidence of the pelvis. (Wolpoff, 1983, p. 451).

Challenges to Australopithecus afarensis Following the formal naming of *Australopithecus afarensis* in 1978 (Johanson et al., 1978) and its systematic interpretation a year later (Johanson and White, 1979), some questions have been raised concerning the status of this fossil hominid. In general, these challenges have taken two forms:

1. Is there more than one taxon represented at Hadar and Laetoli?
2. Can *afarensis* simply be included as an earlier member of the later South African hominid *A. africanus* (i.e., the same species as at Taung, Sterkfontein, and Makapansgat)?

Regarding the first question of possible multiple taxa (i.e., more than one species) at Hadar and Laetoli, some of the initial analyses by the primary researchers at Hadar did indeed suggest this possibility (Johanson and Taieb, 1976). Once *all* the Hadar material was evaluated, as well as comparisons made with the Laetoli fossils, this view was rejected (in favor of simply grouping all the fossils into one obviously variable, sexually dimorphic species).

Not all paleoanthropologists, however, are convinced of this latter interpretation. Two French paleoanthropologists, Brigette Senut and Christine Tardieu of the University of Paris, have suggested from analyses of postcranial remains (especially the elbow and knee) that, along with a primitive australopithecine, early members of genus *Homo may* also have been present at Hadar and Laetoli (Senut, 1981; Senut and Tardieu, 1985).

For some researchers, then, there is good reason to think more than one species has been sampled at Hadar—and perhaps at Laetoli as well. However, these claims have yet to be substantiated. Moreover, on the basis of detailed dental comparisons (White et al., 1981), there appears to be no reason to "split" the samples into different taxa. Accordingly, *A. afarensis* is seen as a quite variable and most certainly sexually dimorphic form. As we have pointed out in Chapter 12, it is most prudent to assume a minimum number of species to be represented by any given fossil sample, unless *conclusive* evidence can be presented to suggest otherwise. For the present, anyway, most paleoanthropologists are provisionally regarding *all* the Hadar and Laetoli fossils as part of one species.

Equally troublesome, is the second question concerning the status of *A. afarensis*: Is it part of *A. africanus*? Phillip Tobias, the world's leading authority on the morphology of *A. africanus* in South Africa, believes that "the Laetoli and Hadar hominids cannot be distinguished at specific level from *A. africanus*" (Tobias, 1980, p. 1).

This assertion is also entirely possible, and, on the basis of Tobias's familiarity with the South African material, it requires serious consideration. Of all the other hominids to which *A. afarensis* could be compared, it is morphologically and chronologically closest to *A. africanus*. Yet, there are still some important differences in the face, cranial vault, mandible, and teeth, all of which consistently show *A. afarensis* to be more primitive than *A. africanus* (or, for that matter, any other known hominid) (White et al., 1981; Kimbel et al., 1985). More detailed comparisons will have to be done, but, given the overall primitive morphology of at least some of these early fossil hominids from Hadar and Laetoli, they are presently best considered within their own species, *A. afarensis*, and thus separate from *A. africanus*.

SET II. LATER AUSTRALOPITHECINES—"ROBUST" FORMS
(*A. AETHIOPICUS*, *A. BOISEI*, A. ROBUSTUS)

Following 2.5 mya, later (and more derived) representatives of *Australopithecus* are found in both South and East Africa. Among them is a distinctive group that has

TABLE 14-3   Estimated Body Weights for _Australopithecus_ Species

	AVERAGE WEIGHT[1]		AVERAGE WEIGHT[2]		RANGE[2]	
	lb	kg	lb	kg	lb	kg
A. afarensis	111.6	50.6	112.4	51.0	67.0–149.2	30.4–67.7
A. africanus	100.3	45.5	101.4	46.0	72.8–127.0	33.0–57.6
A. robustus	105.2	47.7	108.0	49.0	81.8–126.8	37.1–57.5
A. boisei	101.6	46.1	108.5	49.2	72.8–152.8	33.0–69.3

[1]After McHenry, 1988.
[2]After Jungers, 1988.

popularly been known for some time as "robust" australopithecines. By "robust" it had generally been meant that these forms—when compared to other australopithecines—were larger in body size. However, recent, more controlled studies (Jungers, 1988; McHenry, 1988) have shown that all the species of _Australopithecus_ overlapped considerably in body size. Table 14-3 displays the average and estimated ranges of body weights for the four species of australopithecines for which adequate postcranial material has thus far been found. As can be seen, none of the species varies much from the others in _average_ weight, but all show dramatic intraspecific variation—presumably due to marked sexual dimorphism.

As a result of these new weight estimates, many researchers have either dropped the use of the term "robust" (along with its opposite, "gracile") or present it in quotation marks to emphasize its conditional application. We believe the term "robust" can be used in this latter sense, as it still emphasizes important differences in the scaling of craniodental traits. In other words, even if they are not larger overall, robust forms are clearly robust in the skull and dentition.

The earliest representative of this robust group (i.e., clade) comes from Northern Kenya on the west side of Lake Turkana. A complete cranium (WT-17,000—"the black skull") was unearthed there in 1985 and has proven to be a most important discovery. This skull, with a cranial capacity of only 410 cm³, has the smallest definitely ascertained brain volume of any hominid yet found. In addition, the form has other primitive traits, quite reminiscent of _A. afarensis_. For example, there is a compound crest in the back of the skull, the upper face projects considerably, the upper dental row converges in back, and the cranial base is extensively pneumatized (Kimbel, et al., 1988).

What makes the black skull so fascinating, however, is that mixed with this array of distinctively primitive traits are a host of derived ones linking it to other members of the robust group (including a broad face, a very large palate, and a large area for the back teeth). This mosaic of features neatly places skull 17,000 between earlier _afarensis_ on the one hand and the later robust species on the other.

Around 2 mya different varieties of even more derived members of the robust lineage are on the scene in both East and South Africa. In East Africa, as well-documented by finds at Olduvai and East Turkana, robust australopithecines have relatively small cranial capacities (ranging from 510–530 cm³) and very large, broad faces with massive back teeth and lower jaws. The first find of a recognized Plio-Pleistocene hominid in East Africa, in fact, was of a nearly complete robust australopithecine cranium, discovered in 1959 by Mary Leakey at Olduvai Gorge

FIGURE 14-25   The "black skull" WT-17,000, discovered at West Lake Turkana in 1985. This specimen is provisionally assigned to _Australopithecus aethiopicus._

(see p. 393). As a result of Louis Leakey's original naming of the fossil (as "Zinjanthropus"), this find is still popularly referred to as "Zinj." However, it and its other conspecifics in East Africa are now usually placed in the species, *A. boisei.*

In addition, there are also numerous finds of robust australopithecines in South Africa from sites at Kromdraai and most especially at Swartkrans. Like their East African cousins (*A. boisei*), the South African robust forms also have small cranial capacities (the only measurable specimen equals 530 cm³), large broad faces, and very large premolars and molars (although not as massive as in East Africa). Owing to the differences in dental proportions, as well as important differences in facial architecture (Rak, 1983), most researchers now agree there is a species-level difference between the East African robust variety (*A. boisei*) on the one hand and the South African group (*A. robustus*) on the other.

Despite these differences, all members of the robust lineage appear to be specialized for a diet made up of hard food items, such as seeds, nuts, and bark. For many years, paleoanthropologists (e.g., Robinson, 1972) had speculated that robust australopithecines concentrated their diet on more heavy vegetable foods than is seen in the diet of other early hominids. Recent research that included the examining of microscopic polishes and scratches on the teeth (Kay and Grine, 1988) has confirmed this view.

Another assumption that has persisted for many years concerns the toolmaking capabilities of robust forms. Put bluntly, most anthropologists did not think robust forms had much of a capacity here—at least not insofar as stone tools go. However, new evidence of hand bones from Swartkrans in South Africa has led Randall Susman (1988) to conclude otherwise. He suggests that robust australopithecines (*A. robustus*) found at this site had fine manipulative abilities, and thus could well have been the maker of the Oldowan tools also discovered at Swartkrans (see p. 401 for a discussion of stone tool industries). However, in addition to robust australopithecines at Swartkrans, another hominid (*Homo*) is also represented (albeit in small numbers). So precisely *who* was responsible for the stone tools we find at Swartkrans (or in East Africa at Olduvai, East Turkana, etc.) is still largely a matter of conjecture (Klein, 1989).

SET III. LATER AUSTRALOPITHECINES—"GRACILE" FORMS (*A. AFRICANUS*)

Another variety of australopithecine (also small-brained, but not as large-toothed as the robust varieties) is known from Africa. However, while the robust lineage is represented in both East and South Africa, the more lightly built (gracile) form is known only from the southern part of the continent.

First named *A. africanus* by Dart for the single individual at Taung (see p. 421), this australopithecine is also found at Makapansgat and, especially, at Sterkfontein.

Traditionally, it has been thought that there was a significant variation in body size between "gracile" and "robust" forms. As we showed in Table 14-3, there is not much difference in body size between "robust" and "gracile" australopithecines. In fact, most of the differences between the two forms are found in the face and dentition.

The face structure of the graciles is more lightly built and somewhat dish-shaped compared to the more vertical configuration seen in robust specimens. In robust individuals, a raised ridge along the midline of the skull, called a **sagittal crest**, is occasionally observed. Indeed, at Sterkfontein among the larger individ-

Sagittal crest Raised ridge along the midline of the skull where the temporal muscle (used to move the jaw) attaches.

Taxon (pl. Taxa) A population (or group of populations) that is judged to be sufficiently distinct and is assigned to a separate category (such as genus or species).

uals (males?) a hint of a sagittal crest is also seen. This structure provides additional attachment area for the large temporal muscle, which is the primary muscle operating the massive jaw below. Such a structure is also seen in some modern apes, especially male gorillas and orangs; however, in most australopithecines, the temporal muscle acts most efficiently on the back of the mouth and is therefore not functionally equivalent to the front tooth emphasis seen in pongids (see Fig. 14-26).

The most distinctive difference observed between gracile and robust australopithecines is in the dentition. Compared to modern humans, they both have relatively large teeth, which are, however, definitely hominid in pattern. In fact, more emphasis is on the typical back-tooth grinding complex among these early forms than the forms of today; therefore, if anything, australopithecines are "hyperhominid"! Robust forms emphasize this trend to an extreme degree, showing deep jaws and much-enlarged back teeth, particularly the molars, severely crowding the front teeth (incisors and canines) together. Conversely, the graciles have proportionately larger front teeth compared to the size of their back teeth. This contrast is seen most clearly in the relative sizes of the canine compared to the first premolar: in robust individuals, the first premolar is clearly a much larger tooth than the small canine (about twice as large) whereas, in gracile specimens, it only averages about 20% larger than the fairly goodsized canine (Howells, 1973).

These differences in the relative proportions of the teeth and jaws best define a gracile, as compared to a robust, form. In fact, most of the differences in skull shape we have discussed can be directly attributed to contrasting jaw function in the two forms. Both the sagittal crest and broad vertical face of the robust form are related to the muscles and biomechanical requirements of the extremely large-tooth-chewing adaptation of this animal.

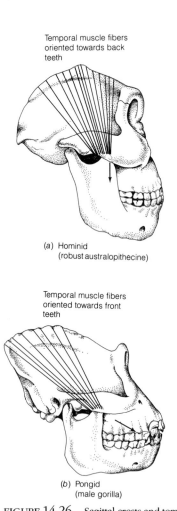

Temporal muscle fibers oriented towards back teeth

(a) Hominid (robust australopithecine)

Temporal muscle fibers oriented towards front teeth

(b) Pongid (male gorilla)

FIGURE 14-26 Sagittal crests and temporal muscle orientations. Hominid compared to pongid.

SET IV. EARLY *HOMO*

The first hint that another hominid was living contemporaneously in Africa with robust australopithecines came at Olduvai Gorge in the early 1960s. Louis Leakey named a new form of hominid *Homo habilis* on the basis of remains, some a little older than "Zinj," others somewhat more recent (Leakey et al., 1964). Unfortunately, the remains at Olduvai attributable to this **taxon** are all either fragmentary or distorted in one way or another. The initial *habilis* material included a fragmentary skull with a distorted juvenile mandible (OH 7) and a partial skull with a complete upper and lower dentition (OH 13), called "Cinderella" by the Leakeys. A third *habilis* specimen, a severely fragmented skull, discovered after being trampled by local Masai cattle (OH 16), is known popularly as "Olduvai George." A final *habilis* skull, found in 1968, is a nearly complete cranium (OH 24) that was severely crushed. It thus required extensive restoration. This fossil, thought to be female, is called "Twiggy."

The *habilis* material at Olduvai ranges in time from 1.85 mya for the earliest to about 1.6 mya for the latest. Due to the fragmentary nature of the fossil remains, interpretations have been difficult and much disputed. The most immediately obvious feature distinguishing the *habilis* material from the australopithecines is cranial size. For all the measurable *habilis* skulls, the estimated average cranial capacity is 631 cm³ compared to 520 cm³ for all measurable robust australopithecines and 442 cm³ for graciles (McHenry, 1988). *Habilis*, therefore, shows an increase in cranial size of 21 and 43%, respectively, over both forms of australopithecine.

In their initial description of *habilis*, Leakey and his associates also pointed to differences from australopithecines in cranial shape and in tooth proportions (larger front teeth relative to back teeth and narrower premolars).

The naming of this fossil material as *Homo habilis* (handy man) was meaningful from two perspectives. First of all, Leakey inferred that members of this group were the early Olduvai toolmakers. If true, how do we account for a robust australopithecine like "Zinj" lying in the middle of the largest excavated area known at Olduvai? What was he doing there? Leakey has suggested he was the remains of a *habilis* meal! Excepting those instances where cutmarks are left behind (see pp. 398–399), we must point out again that there is no clear way archeologically to establish the validity of such a claim. However, the debate over this assertion serves to demonstrate that cultural factors as well as physical morphology must be considered in the interpretation of hominids as biocultural organisms. Secondly, and most significantly, by calling this group *Homo*, Leakey was arguing for at least *two separate branches* of hominid evolution in the Plio-Pleistocene. Clearly only one could be on the main branch eventually leading to *Homo sapiens*. By labeling this new group *Homo* in opposition to *Australopithecus*, Leakey was guessing he had found our ancestors.

Since the initial evidence was so fragmentary, most paleoanthropologists were reluctant to accept *habilis* as a valid taxon distinct from *all* australopithecines. Differences from the hyperrobust East African variety (*A. boisei*) were certainly apparent; the difficulties arose in trying to distinguish *habilis* from *A. africanus*, particularly for dental traits that considerably overlap. Moreover, ambiguous dating of the South African forms made it difficult to interpret the relationship between *A. africanus* and *habilis*.

Later discoveries, especially from Lake Turkana, of better-preserved fossil material have shed further light on early *Homo* in the Plio-Pleistocene. The most important of this additional *habilis* material is a nearly complete cranium (ER 1470) discovered at East Lake Turkana in 1972. With a cranial capacity of 775 cm³, this individual is well outside the known range for australopithecines and actually overlaps the lower boundary for *Homo erectus*. In addition, the shape of the skull vault and face are in many respects unlike that of australopithecines. However, the face

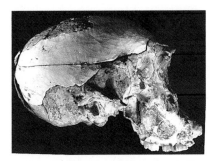

FIGURE 14-27   A nearly complete skull (OH 24, "Twiggy") from Olduvai Gorge. Initially assigned to "*H. habilis*."

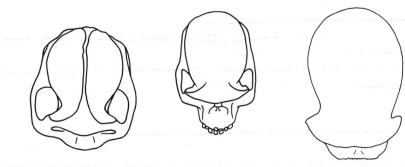

(a)
Robust
australopithecine

(b)
Gracile
australopithecine

(c)
Early Homo

FIGURE 14-28   Skull profiles (seen from above).

FIGURE 14-29 The Kenyan team at East Lake Turkana. Kamoya Kimeu (driving) is the most successful fossil hunter in East Africa. He is responsible for dozens of important discoveries.

is still quite robust (Walker, 1976), and the fragments of tooth crowns that are preserved indicate the back teeth in this individual were quite large.

Additional discoveries at Turkana also strongly suggest the presence of a hominid lineage contemporaneous with and separate from australopithecines. Another skull discovered in 1972 (ER 1590) is similar to 1470 and may even be larger! Moreover, several mandibles, including two nearly complete specimens (ER 820 and 992), have tooth proportions (relatively larger front teeth) characteristic of our genus. Finally, several postcranial remains discovered at Turkana show a taller, more gracile group than that inferred for robust australopithecines. The dating of all this crucial early *Homo* material from Turkana is tied to the dating of the KBS tuff. As we discussed on page 419, the dating of this key bed has recently been established at around 1.8 mya. Thus, the earliest *Homo* materials at Turkana *and* Olduvai are contemporaneous (i.e., 1.8–2.0 mya).

Other Plio-Pleistocene sites also have revealed possible early members of the genus *Homo*. From the Omo in southern Ethiopia, scattered remains of a few teeth and small cranial fragments are similar in pattern to other comparable early *Homo* material.

In addition, early members of the genus *Homo* have also been found in South Africa, there, too, apparently living contemporaneously with australopithecines. At both Sterkfontein (member 5) and Swartkrans, fragmentary remains have been recognized (actually discovered some time ago). In fact, Ron Clarke (1985) has shown that the key fossil of *Homo* from Sterkfontein (Stw-53) is nearly identical to the OH 24 *habilis* skull from Olduvai.

However, a problem with both OH-24 and Stw-53 is that, while most experts are agreed that they belong in the genus *Homo*, there is considerable disagreement whether they should be included in the species *habilis*. In addition, a newly discovered very partial skeleton from Olduvai Gorge (OH-62) is extremely small-statured (less than 4 feet, probably) and has several primitive aspects in its limb proportions (Johanson et al., 1987). (See p. 455.)

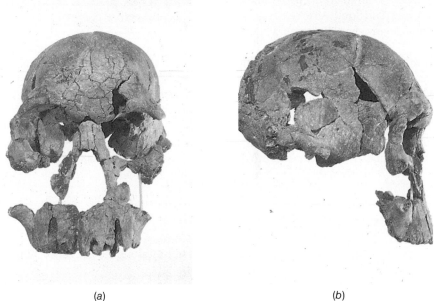

(a)   (b)

Even more troublesome are two crania from East Turkana (ER-1805 and ER-1813), which do not fit very neatly into the same species with individuals such as ER-1470. Some experts contend that *all* of these individuals can be included within a broad intraspecific umbrella, including most especially a presumed high degree of sexual dimorphism. Others (Lieberman et al., 1988) are not as convinced (see p. 456), and would thus argue for at least two species of early *Homo* (*habilis* and sp. indet., which signifies "species indeterminate").

On the basis of evidence from Olduvai and particularly from Lake Turkana we can reasonably postulate that one or more species of early *Homo* was present in East Africa by *at least* 2 mya, developing in parallel with at least one line (*A. boisei*) of australopithecines. These two hominid lines lived contemporaneously for a minimum of 1 million years, after which the australopithecine lineage apparently disappears forever. At the same time, most probably the *habilis* line was emerging into a later form, *Homo erectus*, which, in turn, developed into *H. sapiens*.

In the next chapter, we will take up in detail several alternative theories dealing with evolutionary relationships of these fossil hominids in the Plio-Pleistocene.

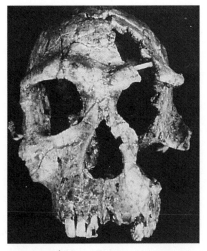

FIGURE 14-31   A nearly complete cranium (ER 1813) discovered at East Lake Turkana, 1973.

Summary

In East and South Africa during the better part of this century, a vast collection of early hominids has been gathered, a collection totaling more than 500 individuals (and thousands of fossil specimens). While considerable evolution occurs during the Plio-Pleistocene (approximately 3 million years are covered in this chapter), all forms are clearly hominid, as shown by their bipedal adaptation. The time range for this hominid material extends back to nearly 4 million years in East Africa, with the earliest and most primitive hominid now recognized—*Australopithecus afarensis*.

Later hominids of a robust lineage are known in East Africa (*A. aethiopicus*; *A. boisei*) and South Africa (*A. robustus*). These groups seem to come on the scene about 2.5 mya and disappear around 1 mya.

In addition, a smaller-toothed (but not necessarily smaller-bodied) "gracile" form is known exclusively from South Africa, beginning at a time range estimated at around 2.5 mya. However, owing to the geologic complexity, dating control in South Africa is *much* more tenuous than in East Africa. Thus we cannot be certain of any of these dates for South African hominids.

Finally, best known again in East Africa (but also found in South Africa), a larger-brained and smaller-toothed variety is also present around 2 mya. This species, called *Homo habilis*, is thought by most paleoanthropologists to lie closer to our ancestry than the later varieties of australopithecines.

Questions for Review

1. In East Africa all the early hominid sites are found along the Rift Valley. Why is this significant?
2. Compare the various East African Plio-Pleistocene sites for the kinds of cultural information uncovered.
3. How does the dating problem of the KBS tuff at Lake Turkana illustrate the necessity for cross-correlation of several dating techniques?
4. Why was Raymond Dart's announcement of a small-brained bipedal hominoid greeted with such skepticism in 1925?
5. What led Dart to suggest the Taung child was *not* an ape?
6. What was Robert Broom's contribution to revealing the hominid nature of the South African australopithecines?
7. (a) Why is postcranial evidence (particularly the lower limb) so crucial in showing the australopithecines as definite hominids? (b) What particular aspects of the australopithecine pelvis and lower limb are hominidlike?
8. What hominid sites have yielded remains of *A. afarensis*? In what ways is the fossil material more primitive than that for other hominids from South and East Africa?
9. What kinds of robust australopithecines have been found in East Africa? How do they compare with South African australopithecines?
10. Why are some Plio-Pleistocene hominids from East Africa called "early *Homo*" (or *H. habilis*)? What does this imply for the evolutionary relationships of the australopithecines?
11. What did Louis Leakey mean by using the specific name "habilis" for a fossil hominid from Olduvai?

Suggested Further Reading

Brace, C. L., Harry Nelson, and Noel Korn. *Atlas of Fossil Man* (2nd Ed.), New York: Holt, Rinehart and Winston, 1979.
A handy reference to the fossil hominid evidence with line drawings of fossil primates and hominids listed in chronological order. Brief descriptions of the details of discoveries and dating are most useful.

Campbell, Bernard. *Human Evolution*, Chicago: Aldine Publishing Co., 1985.
A fairly advanced survey of human evolution from a functional point of view covering developments of the limb skeleton, dentition, etc. Highly recommended for the student who wishes to explore the evolution of hominid adaptive systems at a slightly higher level than presented here.

Clark, W. E. Le Gros. *Man-Apes or Ape-Men?*, New York: Holt, Rinehart, and Winston, 1967.
A fairly detailed discussion of the cranial, dental, and postcranial anatomy of the australopithecines. This work also contains some entertaining introductory chapters outlining the discoveries made by Dart and Broom.

Kennedy, G. E. *Paleoanthropology*, New York: McGraw-Hill, 1980.
A thorough introduction to the study of fossil hominids particularly and, more generally, all fossil primates. Excellent discussion of the functional trends in hominid evolution. Written for upper-division courses, but suitable as a reference book—for all remaining chapters covered in this text.

Klein, Richard G. *The Human Career. Human Biological and Cultural Origins*, Chicago: University of Chicago Press, 1989.
An excellent overview of human evolution. Authoritative and well-written. Highly recommended.

Larsen, Clark Spencer and Robert M. Matter. *Human Origins. The Fossil Record*, Prospect Heights, Il.: Waveland Press, 1985.
An excellently illustrated atlas of major fossil hominid specimens; the book is organized chronologically, beginning with Miocene forms and going up through modern *sapiens*. All the major Plio-Pleistocene finds known at the time of publication are shown.

Lewin, Roger. *Human Evolution. An Illustrated Introduction* (2nd Ed.), Boston: Blackwell Scientific Publications, 1989.
A short, topical discussion of major historical and adaptive themes in human evolution. Coverage is less technical than this textbook. Format is stimulating and up-to-date.

Poirier, Frank. *Fossil Evidence. The Human Evolutionary Journey*, St. Louis: C. V. Mosby Co., 1977.
An excellent comprehensive review of hominid evolution for the moderately advanced student. This work also contains strong introductory chapters on comparative primate studies and primate paleontology. A detailed discussion of Plio-Pleistocene hominids with a comprehensive bibliography should prove most helpful for additional source material relating to this chapter.

Robinson, J. T. *Early Hominid Posture and Locomotion*, Chicago: University of Chicago Press, 1972.
Written by one of the primary participants in the discoveries of South African australopithecines, this work offers an advanced review of the functional development of bipedal locomotion.

Wolpoff, Milford H. *Paleoanthropology*, New York: Alfred A. Knopf, 1980.
Like the Kennedy text with the same title, this is a fairly technical overview of fossil hominids designed for upper-division students. Useful as a reference for all remaining topics in this text.

For more comprehensive and technical readings, see:

Coppens, Yves, F. Clark Howell, Glynn Isaac, and R.E.F. Leakey. *Earliest Man and Environments in the Lake Rudolf Basin*, Chicago: University of Chicago Press, 1975.
Highly technical discussion of geology, paleontology, and hominid evolution at East Turkana and the Omo basin. Reviews hominid discoveries in detail through 1974 at these sites. Contains several excellent photos of hominid discoveries.

Delson, Eric (ed.). *Ancestors: The Hard Evidence*, New York: Alan R. Liss, 1985.
An excellent collection of articles, concentrating on recent issues in human evolution. This book resulted from the "Ancestors" exhibit in New York in 1985. Topics also relate to Oligocene and Miocene forms (see Chapter 12).

Grine, Frederick E. (ed.). *Evolutionary History of the "Robust" Australopithecines*, New York: Aldine de Gruyler, 1988.
An up-to-date and stimulating review of one group of australopithecines. Contains contributions by all the leading workers in the field.

Isaac, G. and E. R. McCown. *Human Origins. Louis Leakey and the East African Evidence*, Menlo Park, California: W. A. Benjamin Inc., 1976.
A collection of articles on the archeology, geology, and hominids of East Africa. Especially recommended are articles on East Turkana by R. Leakey and G. Isaac, and review article on hominid evolution in the Plio-Pleistocene by P. Tobias.

Leakey, Richard E. and Roger Lewin. *Origins*, New York: E. P. Dutton, 1977.
A comprehensive review of human evolution with particular emphasis on Plio-Pleistocene discoveries in East Africa. Traces primate and hominid developments up to fairly recent time and concludes with a discussion of the nature and evolution of human aggression. Highly recommended for all students.

Tobias, Phillip V. (ed.). *Hominid Evolution. Past, Present, and Future*, New York: Alan R. Liss, 1985.
A collection of articles on hominid evolution, particularly emphasizing discoveries in Africa. Also covered are issues relating to later stages of human evolution (Chapters 16 and 17, this text). This book resulted from a conference in South Africa commemorating the 60th anniversary of the Taung discovery.

Walker, Alan and R.E.F. Leakey. "The Hominids of East Turkana," *Scientific American*, 239(1978):54–66.
A superb overview of the huge East Turkana collection. Walker and Leakey present somewhat more conservative interpretations than suggested earlier (by R. Leakey).

For the ultimate in hominid descriptive analysis, see:

Tobias, P. V. *Olduvai Gorge* (Vol. II), *The Cranial and Maxillary Dentition of Australopithecus (Zinjanthropus) Boisei*, Cambridge: Cambridge University Press, 1967.
An incredibly thorough description of one hominid discovery (OH 5) with minute analysis of every conceivable microanatomic feature. Excellent concluding chapter contains good synthesis of Plio-Pleistocene hominids known at time of publication.

Johanson, Donald C. et al. "Pliocene Hominid Fossils from Hadar, Ethiopia," *American Journal of Physical Anthropology*, 57(4), 1982.
The entire issue, comprising 11 articles and almost 350 pages of text, is devoted to describing the hominids from Hadar in minute detail. Articles include contributions on stratigraphy and chronology, the Lucy skeleton, cranial remains, mandibles, dental remains, dental root morphology, axial skeletal remains (ribs, vertebrae), upper limbs, hands, lower limbs, and feet.

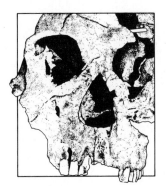

Plio-Pleistocene Hominids: Organization and Interpretation

Contents

Man, the Hunter
Woman, the Gatherer

Anthropologists have long been concerned with the behavioral evolution of our species. Accompanying changes in anatomy (locomotion, dentition, brain size and shape) were changes in mating patterns, social structure, cultural innovations, and, eventually, language. In fact, changes in these behavioral complexes are what mostly *explain* the concomitant adaptations in human biological structure.

We are, then, vitally interested in the behavioral adaptations of our early hominid ancestors. In seeking to reconstruct the behavioral patterns of these early hominids, anthropologists use inferences drawn from modern primates, social carnivores, and hunting-gathering people (see Chapter 11). In addition, they derive information directly from the paleoanthropological record (see Chapter 13).

Despite numerous detailed and serious attempts at such behavioral reconstructions, the conclusions must largely remain speculative. In point of fact, behavior does not fossilize. Accordingly, researchers must rely considerably upon their imaginations in creating scenarios of early hominid behavioral evolution. In such an atmosphere, biases often emerge; these biased renditions, in turn, stimulate heated debates and alternative scenarios —often as narrow as those being attacked.

Probably no topic has stimulated more controversy (or has been more riddled with implicit biases) than the debate concerning origins of hominid sex-role differences. Did early hominid males have characteristically different behavioral adaptations than their female counterparts? Did one sex dominate the frontier of early hominid cultural innovation? And if one sex did lead the way, which one?

A now well-known rendition of early hominid behavioral development was popularized in the 1960s and 1970s. According to this "man, the hunter" theory, the hunting of large animals by males was the central stimulus of hominid behavioral evolution. According to such widely read works as Desmond Morris' *The Naked Ape* (1967) and several books by Robert Ardrey (including *The Hunting Hypothesis*, 1976), early apish-looking forms *became* hominids as a result of a hunting way of life. As Ardrey states, "Man is man, and not a chimpanzee, because for millions upon millions of evolving years we killed for a living" (1976, p. 10).

In this reconstruction, the hunting of large, dangerous mammals by cooperating groups of males fostered the development of intelligence, language, tools, and bipedalism. Increased intelligence accompanied by the development of weapons is also blamed in this scenario for the roots of human aggressiveness, murder, and warfare.

This "man, the hunter" scenario further suggests that while the males are leading the vanguard in hominid evolution, females remain mostly sedentary, tied to the home base by the burden of dependent young. Females may have contributed some wild plant foods to the group's subsistence, but this is not seen as a particularly challenging (and certainly not a very noble) endeavor. In this situation of marked division of labor, sexual relationships quickly changed. Males, constantly away from the home base (and thus away from the females too), could not keep a watchful eye over their mates. In order to better ensure fidelity (and to reduce the risk of cuckoldry), monogamy came into being. In this way, a male would be assured that the young in which he in-

vested were his own. This important factor of male-female bonding as a product of differential foraging patterns has more recently been forcefully restated by Owen Lovejoy (1981). (See p. 263.)

From the female's point of view, it would be beneficial to maintain a close bond with a provisioning male. Consequently, she would want to appear "attractive," and thus, through time, the female breasts and buttocks would become more conspicuous. Besides rearing their young and being attractive sex objects, females were useful to males in another way. Groups of male hunters living in the same area might occasionally come into potentially dangerous competition for the same resources. As a means of solidifying political ties between groups, the males would thus routinely exchange females (by giving or "selling" their daughters to neighboring bands).

Thus, in a single stroke, this complex of features accounts for human intelligence, sexual practices, and political organization.

As might be expected, such a male-centered scenario did not go unchallenged. Ignoring females or relegating them to a definitely inferior role in human behavioral evolution drew sharp criticism from several quarters. As one anthropologist noted:

So, while the males were out hunting, developing all their skills, learning to cooperate, inventing language, inventing art, creating tools and weapons, the poor dependent females were sitting back at the home base having one child after another and waiting for the males to bring home the bacon. While this reconstruction is certainly ingenious, it gives one the decided impression that only half the species—the male half—did any evolving. In addition to containing a number of logical gaps, the argument becomes somewhat doubtful in the light of modern knowledge of genetics and primate behavior (Slocum, 1975, p. 42).

In fact, such a rigid rendering of our ancestors' behavior does not stand up to critical examination. Hunting is never defined rigorously. Does it include only large, terrestrial mammals? What of smaller mammals, sea mammals, fish, and birds? In numerous documented human societies, females actively participate in exploiting these latter resources.

Moreover, nonhuman primates do not conform to predictions derived from the "man, the hunter" model. For example, among chimpanzees, females do most of the toolmaking, not the males. Finally, in most nonhuman primates (most mammals, for that matter), it is the females—not the males—who choose with whom to mate.

Granting that the hunting hypothesis does not work, what alternatives have been proposed? As a reaction to male-centered views, Elaine Morgan (1972) advanced the "aquatic hypothesis." In this rendition, females are seen as the pioneers of hominid evolution. But rather than having the dramatic changes of hominid evolution occur on the savanna, Morgan has them take place on the seashore. As females lead the way to bipedal locomotion, cultural innovation, and intellectual development, the poor males are seen as splashing pitifully behind.

Unfortunately, this theory has less to back it up than the hunting hypothesis. Not a shred (even a watery one) of evidence has ever been discovered in the contexts predicted by the aquatic theory.

Little is accomplished by such unsubstantiated overzealous speculation. Chauvinism—whether male or female—does not elucidate our origins and only obscures the evolutionary processes that operated on the *whole* species.

Can nothing then be concluded about differential male-female sex roles? While the pattern is not as rigid as the hunting hypothesis advocates would have us believe, in the vast majority of human societies hunting of large, terrestrial mammals is almost always a male activity. In fact, a comprehensive cross-cultural survey shows that of 179 societies, males do the hunting exclusively in 166, both sexes participate in 13, and in *no* group is hunting done exclusively by females (Murdock, 1965).

In addition, as we noted in Chapter 11, there is some incipient division of labor in foraging patterns among chimpanzees. Females tend to concentrate more on termiting, while hunting (though it is only occasional) is done mostly by males. Early hominids, expanding upon such a subsistence base, eventually adapted a greater sexual division of labor than found in any other primate. Two points, however, must be kept in mind. First, both the gathering of wild plant foods and the hunting of animals would have been indispensable components of the diet. Consequently, *both* males and females always played a significant role. Secondly, the strategies must always have been somewhat flexible. With a shifting, usually unpredictable resource base, nothing else would have worked. As a result, males probably always did a considerable amount of gathering and in most foraging societies still do. Moreover, females—while not usually engaged in the stalking and killing of large prey—nonetheless contribute signifi-

cantly to meat acquisition. Once large animals have been killed, there still remain the arduous tasks of butchering and transport back to the home base. In many societies, women and men participate equally in these activities.

A balanced view of human behavioral evolution must avoid simplistic and overly rigid scenarios. As recently stated by a researcher concerned with reconstructing early hominid behavior:

Both *sexes must have been able to care for young, protect themselves from predators, make and use tools, and freely move about the environment in order to exploit available resources widely distributed through space and time. It is this range of behaviors—the overall behavioral flexibility of both sexes—that may have been the* primary *ingredient of early hominids' success in the savanna environment (Zihlman, 1981, p. 97).*

SOURCES:

Ardrey, Robert. *The Hunting Hypothesis*, New York: Atheneum, 1976.

Dahlberg, Frances (ed.). *Woman the Gatherer*, New Haven: Yale University Press, 1981.

Lovejoy, C. Owen. "The Origin of Man," *Science*, 211(1981):341–350.

Morgan, Elaine. *The Descent of Woman*, New York: Stein and Day, 1972.

Morris, Desmond. *The Naked Ape*, New York: McGraw-Hill, 1967.

Murdock, G. P. *Culture and Society*, Pittsburgh: University of Pittsburgh Press, 1965.

Slocum, Sally. "Woman the Gatherer: Male Bias in Anthropology," In: *Toward an Anthropology of Women*, R. R. Reiter, ed., New York: Monthly Review Press, pp. 36–50, 1975.

Zihlman, Adrienne L. "Women as Shapers of the Human Adaptation," In: *Woman the Gatherer*, op. cit., pp. 75–120, 1981.

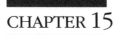

CHAPTER 15

Introduction

We have seen in the last chapter that a vast and complex array of early hominid material has been discovered in South and East Africa. In just the past few years, particularly in the eastern part of the continent, a great number of new discoveries have been made. We now have Plio-Pleistocene hominid collections totaling close to 200 individuals from South Africa and probably more than 300 from East Africa. Given the size and often fragmentary nature of the sample, along with the fact that a good deal of it is so recently discovered, we should not be surprised that many complications arise when it comes to interpretation. In addition, both popular enthusiasm and the strong personalities often connected with fossil hominid discoveries have generated even more confusion.

In this chapter, we will look at several *theories* that attempt to organize the huge amount of Plio-Pleistocene hominid material. We ask you to remember that these are only theories and must remain so, given the incomplete nature of the fossil record. Even considering the seemingly very large number of fossils there is a *great* deal of time over which they were distributed. If we estimate about 500 total individuals from all African sites recovered thus far for the period 4–1 mya, we still are sampling just one individual for every 6,000 years! Until much of the new material from East Africa has been properly analyzed and detailed reports published, we cannot form even reasonably secure hypotheses without extreme difficulty. At the present time, only a few East African hominids have been thoroughly studied; all the rest are thus far described in preliminary reports.

It will no doubt appear that many opposing and conflicting theories attempt to describe exactly what is going on in human evolution during the crucial period between 5 and 1 mya. And, indeed, there are many theories. Hominid fossils are intriguing to both scientists and nonscientists, for some of these ancient bones and teeth are probably those of our direct ancestors. Equally intriguing, some of these fossils are representatives of populations of our close relatives that apparently met with extinction. We would like to know how these animals lived, what kinds of adaptations (physical and cultural) they displayed, and why some continued to evolve while others died out.

Geology and Dating Problems in South Africa

While, as we saw in the last two chapters that the geological and archeological context in East Africa is oftentimes straightforward, the five South African australopithecine sites are much more complex geologically. All were discovered by commercial quarrying activity, which greatly disrupted the geological picture and, in the case of Taung, completely destroyed the site.

The australopithecine remains are found with thousands of other fossilized bones embedded in limestone cliffs, caves, fissures, and sinkholes. The limestone was built by millions of generations of shells of marine organisms during the Pre-Cambrian—more than 2 billion years ago—when South Africa was submerged under a shallow sea. Once deposited, the limestones were cut through by percolating ground water from below and rain water from above, forming a maze of caves and fissures often connected to the surface by narrow shafts. Through these vertical shafts and horizontal cave openings, bones either fell or were carried in, where they conglomerated with sand, pebbles, and soil into a cementlike matrix called *breccia*.

As the cave fissures filled in, they were constantly subjected to further erosion forces from above and below, so that caves would be partially filled, then closed to the surface for a considerable time, and reopened again to commence accumulation thousands of years later. All this activity yields an incredibly complex geological situation that can only be worked out after the most detailed kind of paleoecological analysis.

Since bones accumulated in these caves and fissures largely by accidental processes, it seems likely that none of the South African australopithecine sites are *primary* hominid localities. In other words, unlike East Africa, these are not areas where hominids organized activities, scavenged food, etc.

Just how did all the fossilized bone accumulate and, most particularly, what were the australopithecines doing there? In the case of Swartkrans, Sterkfontein, and Kromdraai, the bones probably accumulated through the combined activities of carnivorous leopards, sabre-toothed cats, and hyenas. However, the unexpectedly high proportion of primate (baboon and hominid) remains suggests that these localities were the location (or very near the location) of primate sleeping sites, thus providing ready prey for the predators (Brain, 1981).

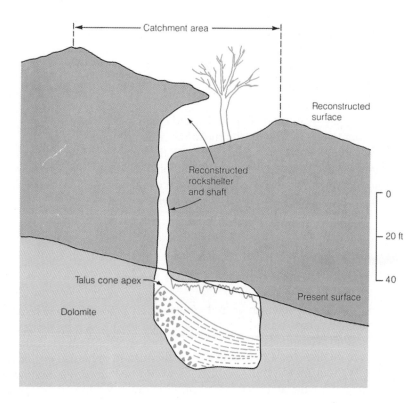

FIGURE 15-1 Swartkrans, geological section. The upper (reconstructed) part has been removed by erosion since the accumulation of the fossil-bearing deposit. (After Brain, 1970).

Osteodontokeratic osteo: bone
dento: tooth
keratic: horn

Raymond Dart argued enthusiastically for an alternative explanation, suggesting the australopithecines camping at Makapansgat regularly used bone, tooth, and horn remains as tools, which he has grandly called the **osteodontokeratic** culture complex. Analogies with modern Hottentot food habits indicate the bone accumulation at Makapansgat may be accounted for simply by hominid and carnivore eating practices. Recent paleoecological work at Makapansgat has thrown Dart's assertions into even greater doubt. Apparently, remains accumulated here primarily in a similar fashion to Sterkfontein and Swartkrans—through a narrow shaft entrance. Therefore, large animals could have entered but not departed the deep subterranean cavern. Makapansgat, like Sterkfontein and Swartkrans, probably also represents the accumulated debris of carnivore activity (perhaps hyenas) outside the cave entrance.

So little is left of the final site, Taung, that accurate paleoanthropological reconstructions are not feasible.

Due to the complex geological picture, as well as lack of appropriate material such as volcanics for chronometric techniques, dating the South African australopithecine sites has posed tremendous problems. Without chronometric dating, the best that can be done is to correlate the faunal sequences in South Africa with areas such as East Africa where dates are better known (this approach is called "biostratigraphy"—see p. 397). Faunal sequencing of this sort on pigs, bovids such as antelopes, and Old World monkeys has provided the following tenuous chronology:

LOCATION	AGE
	1 my
Swartkrans	
Kromdraai	
	2 my
Sterkfontein/Taung	
Makapansgat	3 my

Attempts at paleomagnetic dating (see p. 395) suggest an age of 3.3–2.8 mya for Makapansgat (Brock et al., 1977), thus pushing the estimates to the extreme limits of those provided by biostratigraphy. In fact, some researchers believe the paleomagnetic results are ambiguous and continue to "put their money" on the biostratigraphic data, especially those dates determined by analysis of pig and monkey fossils. From such considerations, they place the South African australopithecine sites as much as one-half million years later (i.e., for Makapansgat, around 2.5 mya) (White et al., 1981). This is crucial, since it places *all* the South African hominids after *Australopithecus afarensis* in East Africa.

Interpretations: What Does It All Mean?

By this time, it may seem anthropologists have an almost perverse fascination in finding small scraps buried in the ground and then assigning them confusing numbers and taxonomic labels impossible to remember. We must realize that the collection of all the basic fossil data is the foundation of human evolutionary research. Without fossils, our speculations would be completely hollow. Several large, ongoing paleoanthropological projects discussed in Chapter 13 are now

BOX 15-1
A Visit to the Plio-Pleistocene: East Lake Turkana, Late One Afternoon

If an observer could be transported back through time and climb a tree in the area where the Koobi Fora Formation was accumulating, what would he see?

As the upper branches are reached, the climber would find himself in a ribbon of woodland winding out through open areas. A kilometer or so away to the west would be seen the swampy shores of the lake, teeming with birds, basking crocodiles, and *Euthecodons*. Here and there are schools of hippos. Looking east, in the distance some ten or twelve kilometers away lie low, rolling hills covered with savanna vegetation. From the hills, fingers of trees and bush extend fanwise out into the deltaic plains. These would include groves of large *Acacia*, *Celtis*, and *Ficus* trees along the watercourses, fringed by shrubs and bushes. Troops of colobus move in the tree tops, while lower down are some mangabey. Scattered through the bush, the observer might see small groups of waterbuck, impala, and kudu, while out in the open areas beyond, would be herds of alcelaphine antelope and some gazelle (*Megalotragus* and *Antidorcas*). Among the undergrowth little groups of *Mesochoerus* pigs rootle, munching herbiage.

Peering down through the branches of the tree, the climber would see below the clean sandy bed of a watercourse, dry here, but with a tidemark of grass and twigs caught in the fringing bushes and showing the passage of seasonal floods. Some distance away down the channel is a small residual pool.

Out beyond the bushes can be seen large open floodplains, covered with grasses and rushes, partly dry at those seasons of the year when the lake is low and when the river is not in spate. Far across the plains, a group of four or five men approach; although they are too far off for the perception of detail, the observer feels confident that they are men because they are striding along, fully upright, and in their hands they carry staves.

To continue the reconstruction in a more purely imaginative vein: as the men approach, the observer becomes aware of other primates below him. A group of creatures has been reclining on the sand in the shade of a tree while some youngsters play around them. As the men approach, these creatures rise and it becomes apparent that they too are bipedal. They seem to be female, and they whoop excitedly as some of the young run out to meet the arriving party, which can now be seen to consist mainly of males. The two groups come together in the shade of the tree, and there is excited calling, gesturing, and greeting contacts. Now the observer can see them better, perhaps he begins to wonder about calling them men; they are upright and formed like men, but they are rather small, and when in groups they do not seem to engage in articulate speech. There are a wealth of vocal and gestural signals in their interaction, but no sustained sequential sound patterns.

The object being carried is the carcass of an impala, and the group congregates around this in high excitement; there is some pushing and shoving and flashes of temper and threat. Then one of the largest males takes two objects from a heap at the foot of the tree. There are sharp clacking sounds as he squats down and bangs these together repeatedly. The other creatures scramble around picking up the small sharp chips that have been detached from the stones. When there is a small scatter of flakes on the ground at his feet, the stone worker drops the two chunks, sorts through the fragments and selects two or three pieces. Turning back to the carcass, this leading male starts to make incisions. First the belly is slit open and the entrails pulled out; the guts are set on one side, but there is excited squabbling over the liver, lungs, and kidneys; these are torn apart, some individuals grab pieces and run to the periphery of the group. Then the creatures return to the carcass; one male severs skin, muscle, and sinew so as to disengage them from the trunk, while some others pull at limbs. Each adult male finishes up with a segment of the carcass and withdraws to a corner of the clearing, with one or two females and juveniles congregating around him. They sit chewing and cutting at the meat, with morsels changing hands at intervals. Two adolescent males sit at the periphery with a part of the intestines. They squeeze out the dung and chew at the entrails. One of the males gets up, stretches his arms, scratches under his armpits and then sits down. He leans against the tree, gives a loud belch and pats his belly. . . . *End of scenario.*

SOURCE:

"The Activities of Early Hominids" by Glynn Ll. Isaac. In *Human Origins. Louis Leakey and the East African Evidence*, G. Isaac and E. R. McCown, eds. The Benjamin/Cummings Publishing Company, Inc. © 1976. Reprinted with permission of the publisher.

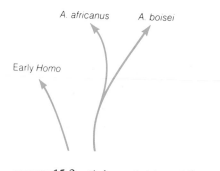

FIGURE 15-2   Phylogenetic interpretation. Early *H. habilis* genetically distinct from australopithecines.

collecting additional data in an attempt to answer some of the more perplexing questions about our evolutionary history.

The numbering of specimens, which may at times seem somewhat confusing, is an attempt to keep the designations neutral and to make reference to each individual fossil as clear as possible. The formal naming of finds as *Australopithecus*, *Homo habilis*, *Homo erectus*, etc., should come much later, since it involves a lengthy series of complex interpretations. The assigning of generic and specific names to fossil finds is more than just a game, although some paleoanthropologists have acted as if it were just that. When we attach a particular label, such as *A. boisei*, to a particular fossil, we should be fully aware of the biological implications of such an interpretation (see p. 368).

Even more basic to our understanding of human evolution, the use of taxonomic nomenclature involves interpretations of fossil relationships. For example, two fossils such as "Zinj" and ER 406 are both usually called *A. boisei*. What we are saying here is they are both members of one *interbreeding* species. These two fossils can now be compared with others, like Sts. 5 from Sterkfontein, which are usually called *A. africanus*. What we are implying now is that "Zinj" and ER 406 are more closely related to each other than *either* is to Sts. 5. Furthermore, that Sts. 5 (*africanus*) populations were incapable of successfully interbreeding with *boisei* populations is a direct biological inference of this nomenclature.

We can carry the level of interpretation even further. For example, fossils such as ER 1470 are called early *Homo (Homo habilis)*. We are now making a genus-level distinction, and two basic biological implications are involved:

1. *A. africanus* (Sts. 5) and *A. boisei* ("Zinj" and ER 406) are more closely related to each other than either is to ER 1470.
2. The distinction between the groups reflects a basic difference in adaptive level (see Chapter 12).

From the time that fossil sites are first located to the eventual interpretation of hominid evolutionary events, several steps are necessary. Ideally, they should follow a logical order, for if interpretations are made too hastily, they confuse important issues for many years. A reasonable sequence is:

1. Selection and surveying of sites
2. Excavation of sites; recovery of fossil hominids
3. Designating individual finds with specimen numbers for clear reference
4. Detailed study and description of fossils
5. Comparison with other fossil material—in chronological framework if possible
6. Comparison of fossil variation with known ranges of variation in closely related groups of living primates
7. Assigning taxonomic names to fossil material

The task of interpretation is still not complete, for what we really want to know in the long run is what happened to the populations represented by the fossil remains. Indeed, in looking at the fossil hominid record, we are looking for our ancestors. In the process of eventually determining those populations that are our most likely antecedents, we may conclude some hominids are on evolutionary side branches. If this conclusion is accurate, they necessarily must have eventually become extinct. It is both interesting and relevant to us as hominids to try to find out what caused some earlier members of our family to continue evolving while others died out.

Glynn Isaac, 1937–1985

In October, 1985, African prehistory and research into the evolution of early human culture was deprived of its acknowledged leader by the untimely and unexpected death of Glynn Isaac.

Born in Cape Town, Glynn was educated at the University there and at Cambridge, England, where he obtained his Ph.D. His training in both the natural sciences (geology and zoology) and archaeology had a profound effect on his subsequent achievements, and enabled him to create a link between disciplines that had a major influence on the remarkable advances in early man studies over the twenty-odd years of his active research.

After leaving Cambridge, he became Warden of Prehistoric Sites in Kenya and, later (1963–1965), Deputy Director of the Centre for Prehistory and Palaeontology at the Natiaonal Museum of Kenya, where he benefitted greatly from his close association with Louis and Mary Leakey.

In 1966, he joined the Anthropology Faculty at the University of California, Berkeley. He was a moving force in the creation of a highly innovative program in early man studies, and many of his students, black and white, are now in the forefront of early hominid cultural research in Africa. His understanding of Africa's ecology and human behavior led him to initiate a series of field studies using comparable, present-day analogs as clues to past patterns, thereby making it possible to narrow down alternative explanations of the archaeological record. In 1983, he accepted an appointment as Professor of Archaeology at Harvard and continued his work on early man research from there.

Glynn wrote or co-edited seven books and sixty-seven scientific papers, many of them advocating revolutionary new methods of investigation and interpretation of very early hominid cultural remains. With a keen intelligence, he was a highly stimulating teacher with boundless, communicable enthusiasm and essential kindliness, which inspired respect and affection in those who came in contact with him, and many of his students in the field are now actively following his new, wider approach to interpreting the record of human cultural evolution.

Glynn's attitude to his subject was holistic and open, and he showed us clearly that the only possibility for future advance in early man studies is by continued dialogue between the disciplines, a dialogue which, in gratitude, his friends and students must now carry on.

J. Desmond Clark

Continuing Uncertainties—Taxonomic Issues

As previously discussed, paleoanthropologists are crucially concerned with making biological interpretations of variation found in the hominid fossil record. Most especially, researchers endeavor to assign extinct forms to particular genera and species. We saw that, for the diverse array of Miocene hominoids, the evolutionary picture is exceptionally complex. As new finds accumulate, there persists continued uncertainty even as to family assignment, to say nothing of genus and species!

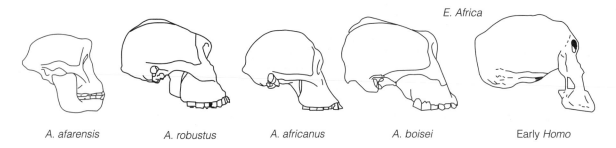

E. Africa

A. afarensis   A. robustus   A. africanus   A. boisei   Early Homo

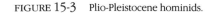

FIGURE 15-3   Plio-Pleistocene hominids.

For the Plio-Pleistocene, the situation is considerably clearer. First of all, there is a larger fossil sample from a more restricted geographic area (South and East Africa) and from a more concentrated time period (spanning 3 million years, from 4–1 mya). Secondly, more complete specimens exist (for example, "Lucy"), and we thus have good evidence for most parts of the body. Accordingly, there is considerable consensus on several basic aspects of evolutionary development during the Plio-Pleistocene. First of all, researchers agree unanimously that these forms are hominids (members of the family Hominidae). Secondly, and as support for the first point, all these forms are seen as well-adapted bipeds, committed at least in part to a terrestrial niche. Whether those early hominids were "well-adapted" bipeds has been disputed. (See p. 434.) Moreover, researchers agree as to genus-level assignments for most of the forms (although some disagreement exists regarding how to group the robust australopithecines).

As for species-level designations, little consensus can be found. Indeed, as new fossils have been discovered (for example, WT-17,000 and OH 62), the picture seems to muddy further. Once again, we are faced with a complex evolutionary process. In attempts to deal with it, we impose varying degrees of simplicity. In so doing, we hope to understand evolutionary developments more clearly—not just for introductory students, but also for professional paleoanthropologists and textbook authors! Nevertheless, evolution is not necessarily a simple process, and thus disputes and disagreements are bound to arise, especially in making such fine-tuned interpretations as species-level designations.

We discuss below some ongoing topics of interest and occasional disagreement among paleoanthropologists dealing with Plio-Pleistocene hominids. You should realize, however, that such continued debate is at the heart of scientific endeavor; indeed, it provides a major stimulus for further research.

Here, we raise questions regarding four areas of taxonomic interpretation. In general, there is still reasonably strong agreement on these points, and we follow the current consensus as reflected in recent publications (Fleagle, 1988; Grine, 1988a; Klein, 1989).

(1) How many species are there at Hadar and Laetoli (i.e., is *Australopithecus afarensis* one species)?

As we discussed on p. 435, some paleoanthropologists think that what has been described as a single species (especially regarding the large Hadar sample), actually represents at least two separate species (taxa). However, it is clear that all australopithecines were highly variable, and thus the pattern seen at Hadar might well represent a single, highly dimorphic species. Most scholars accept this interpretation, and it is best, for the moment, to follow this more conservative view. As a matter of good paleontological practice, it is desirable not to overly "split" fossil samples until compelling evidence is presented.

(2) How many genera of australopithecines are there?

Several years ago a plethora of generic terms was suggested by Robert Broom and others (see p. 426). However, in the 1960s and 1970s, most researchers agreed to "lump" all these forms into *Australopithecus*. With the discovery of early members of genus *Homo* in the 1960s (and its general recognition in the 1970s), most researchers also recognized the presence of our genus in the Plio-Pleistocene as well.

In the last five years an increasing tendency has arisen to resplit some of the australopithecines. With the recognition that the robust group (*aethiopicus, boisei,* and *robustus*) form a distinct evolutionary lineage (a clade), many researchers (Howell, 1988; Grine, 1988) have argued that the generic term, "Paranthropus" should be used to set these robust forms apart from *Australopithecus* (now used in the strict sense). We thus would have *Paranthropus aethiopicus, Paranthropus boisei,* and *Paranthropus robustus* as contrasted to *Australopithecus afarensis* and *Australopithecus africanus.*

We agree that there are adequate grounds to make a genus-level distinction, given the evolutionary distinctiveness of the robust clade as well as its apparent adaptive uniqueness (as recently further confirmed by microwear studies of teeth). However, for *closely related taxa,* such as we are dealing with here, making this type of interpretation is largely arbitrary. (See discussion, pp. 368–373). As the single genus *Australopithecus* has been used for three decades in the wider sense (to include all robust forms), and as it simplifies terminology, we follow the current consensus and continue the traditional usage—*Australopithecus* for all small-brained, large-toothed Plio-Pleistocene hominids (including all five recognized species: *A. afarensis, A. aethiopicus, A. africanus, A. robustus,* and *A. boisei*).

(3) For the South African robust australopithecines, how many species existed?

As we have discussed in the last chapter, there are robust australopithecines from two sites in South Africa, Kromdraai and Swartkrans. Owing to subtle differences in morphology, some researchers (Howell, 1988; Grine, 1988b) make a species distinction between Kromdraai [*A.* (Paranthropus) *robustus*] on the one hand and Swartkrans [*A.* (Paranthropus) *crassidens*] on the other. Moreover, even though the dating of these sites is equivocal (see above), it appears Kromdraai is slightly older than Swartkrans. Thus, these researchers also speculate that *robustus* may have evolved into *crassidens.*

It must be admitted, however, that the differences among these forms are small, and making such subtle interpretations is bound to generate disagreements. For the present, most scholars remain comfortable in treating all the South African robusts as one species.

(4) How many species of early *Homo* existed?

Here is another species-level type of interpretation that is unlikely soon to be resolved. Yet, as it strikes closer to home (i.e., our own genus) than the issue above for robust australopithecines, the current debate is generating more heat.

Whether we find resolution or not, the *form* of the conflicting views is instructive. Of course, the key issue is evaluating variation as *intra-* or *inter*specific. Those who would view all the nonaustralopithecine African hominids (*circa* 2.5–1.6 mya) as one species point out that all Plio-Pleistocene hominid species show extreme intra-specific variation. Much of this variation is assumed to reflect dramatic sexual dimorphism. These scholars are thus reasonably comfortable in referring to all this material as *Homo habilis.* Other researchers, however, see too

Phylogeny A schematic representation showing ancestor-descendant relationships, usually in a chronological framework.

much variation to accept just one species, even a very dimorphic one. Systematic comparison with the most dimorphic living primate (gorillas) show that what is called *H. habilis* differ amongst themselves more than do male and female gorillas. Consequently, we have an added complication: Must we now construct *yet another species of early* Homo *in addition to habilis*? Several researchers (for example, Lieberman et al., 1987) believe there is no other alternative, but do not as yet agree on a new name (and refer to it as "*Homo*, species indeterminate"). The recent discovery of the fragmentary partial skeleton at Olduvai Gorge does not help resolve the issue, but actually may cloud it further. This specimen is a very small individual, and thus presumably a female. How much sexual dimorphism did *H. habilis* display? Were males (on average) two to three times as large as females? We do not know the answers to these questions; but their framing in biological terms as intra- versus interspecific variation and the use of contemporary primate models demonstrate the basis for ongoing discussion.

Another problem with the so-called "early *Homo*" fossil sample is that it overlaps in time with the earliest appearance of *Homo erectus* (discussed in Chapter 16). As a result, several specimens of what has been labeled "early *Homo*" (or *H. habilis*) may actually belong to *H. erectus*. At about 1.6 mya, *H. erectus* apparently replaced earlier members of genus *Homo* quite rapidly. At sites (especially East Turkana and Swartkrans) where fragmentary traces of this process are evident, it poses a major challenge to distinguish exactly what is "*habilis*" and what is "*erectus*."

Putting It All Together

The interpretation of our paleontologic past in terms of which fossils are related to other fossils and how they are all related to us is usually shown diagrammatically in the form of a **phylogeny**. Such a diagram is a family tree of fossil evolution. This kind of interpretation is the eventual goal of evolutionary studies, but it is the final goal, only after adequate data are available to understand what is going on.

Whereas hominid fossil evidence has accumulated in great abundance, the fact that so much of the material has been discovered so recently makes any firm judgments concerning the route of human evolution premature. However, paleoanthropologists are certainly not deterred from making their "best guesses," and thus diverse speculative theories have abounded in recent years. The vast majority of more than 300 fossils from East Africa is still in the descriptive and early analytical stages. At this time, the construction of phylogenies of human evolution is analogous to building a house with only a partial blueprint. We are not even sure how many rooms there are! Until the existing fossil evidence has been adequately studied, to say nothing about possible new finds, speculative theories must be viewed with a critical eye.

In the following pages, we will present several phylogenies representing different and opposing views of hominid evolution. We suggest you do not attempt to memorize them, for they *all* could be out of date by the time you read this book. It will prove more profitable to look at each one and assess the biological implications involved. Also, note which groups are on the main line of human evolution leading to *Homo sapiens* and which are placed on extinct side branches.

Interpreting the Interpretations

In Fig. 15-4 we present several alternative phylogenies explaining early hominid evolution. All these schemes postdate 1979, with the first inclusion of *A. afarensis* as the most likely common ancestor of all later hominids (Johanson and White, 1979). Since the early 1980s, most paleoanthropologists have accepted this view. One exception is shown in Phylogeny B (after Senut and Tardieu, 1985), but this position—based upon the premise that *afarensis* is actually more than one species—has not been generally supported (see p. 435).

We have not included evolutionary schemes prior to 1979, as they do not account for the crucial discoveries at Hadar and Laetoli of *Australopithecus afarensis*. These now-outdated models frequently postulated *A. africanus* as the common ancestor of later *Australopithecus* (robust varieties) and early *Homo*. In modified form this view is still continued in some respects. (See Phylogeny C.)

Indeed, probably the most intractable problem for interpretation of early hominid evolution involves what to do with *A. africanus*. Carefully look at the different evolutionary reconstructions to see how various researchers deal with this still complicated issue.

Conclusions/Summary

After two chapters detailing hominid evolution in the Plio-Pleistocene, many students probably feel frustrated by what must seem to be endlessly changing and conflicting interpretations. However, after 75 years of discoveries of early hominids in Africa, there are several general points upon which most researchers agree:

1. *A. afarensis* is the earliest definite hominid.
2. *A. afarensis* as defined probably represents only one species.
3. *A. afarensis* is probably ancestral to all later hominids (or is very closely related to the species that is).
4. *A. aethiopicus* is ancestral solely to the "robust" group (clade), linking it with earlier *afarensis* as well as with one (or both) later robust species.
5. *A. africanus* is not related uniquely to *A. robustus* (a view depicted in Fig. 15-4, Phylogeny A, but now rejected by its original proposers; also shown in Phylogeny E).
6. All robust australopithecines are extinct by 1 mya (or shortly thereafter).
7. All australopithecine species (presumably *H. habilis* as well) were highly variable, showing extreme sexual dimorphism.
8. Since there is so much intraspecific variation, on average there was not much difference in body size among australopithecine species.
9. *A. africanus* was probably not the last common ancestor of the robust lineage *and* genus *Homo* (i.e., Phylogeny C is probably not entirely correct).
10. All forms (*Australopithecus* and early *Homo*) were relatively large-brained compared to comparably sized apes, but *afarensis* and *africanus* not especially so (most marked in *Homo*).
11. All forms (including some members of early *Homo*) had large back teeth.
12. There was substantial parallelism in physical traits among early hominid lineages.

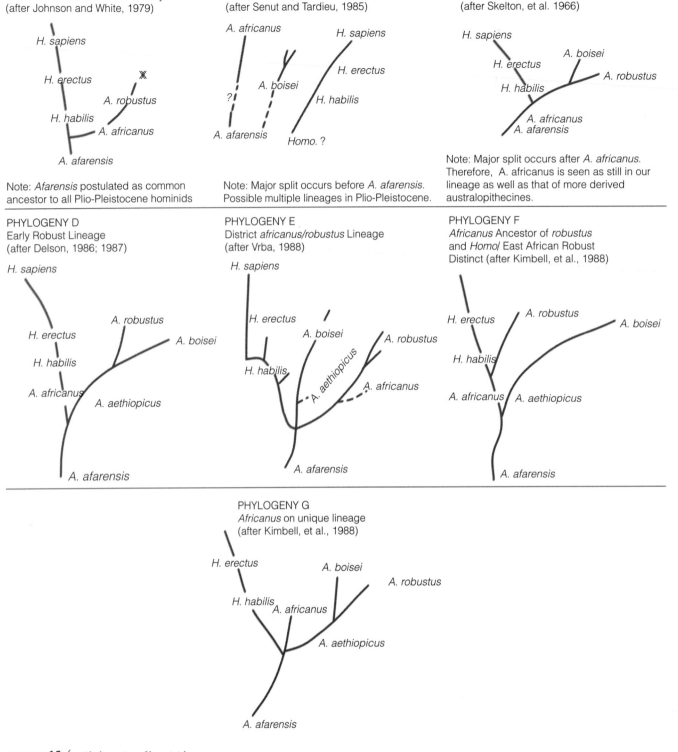

PHYLOGENY A.
Afarensis Comon Ancestor Theory
(after Johnson and White, 1979)

Note: *Afarensis* postulated as common ancestor to all Plio-Pleistocene hominids

PHYLOGENY B
Multiple Lineage Early Divergence
(after Senut and Tardieu, 1985)

Note: Major split occurs before *A. afarensis*. Possible multiple lineages in Plio-Pleistocene.

PHYLOGENY C
Africanus Comon Ancestor Theory
(after Skelton, et al. 1966)

Note: Major split occurs after *A. africanus*. Therefore, A. africanus is seen as still in our lineage as well as that of more derived australopithecines.

PHYLOGENY D
Early Robust Lineage
(after Delson, 1986; 1987)

PHYLOGENY E
District *africanus/robustus* Lineage
(after Vrba, 1988)

PHYLOGENY F
Africanus Ancestor of *robustus*
and *Homo*/ East African Robust
Distinct (after Kimbell, et al., 1988)

PHYLOGENY G
Africanus on unique lineage
(after Kimbell, et al., 1988)

FIGURE 15-4   Phylogenies of hominid evolution.

13. Given the current state of knowledge, there are several equally supportable phylogenies. In fact, in a recent publication, three leading researchers (Bill Kimbel, Tim White, and Don Johanson, 1988) make this point; moreover, they note that of four possible phylogenetic reconstructions (resembling, in Figure 15-4, Phylogenies D, E, F, and G), they have not reached agreement among themselves as to which is the most likely.

Thus, as points 1 through 12 make clear, we have come a long way in reaching an understanding of Plio-Pleistocene hominid evolution. Nevertheless, a truly complete understanding is not at hand. Such is the stuff of science!

Questions for Review

1. What kinds of dating techniques have been used in South Africa?
2. Why is the dating control better in East Africa than in South Africa?
3. Discuss the first thing you would do if you found an early hominid and were responsible for its formal description and publication. What would you include in your publication?
4. Discuss two current disputes regarding taxonomic issues concerning early hominids. Try to give support for alternative positions.
5. Why would one use the taxonomic term *Paranthropus* in contrast to *Australopithecus*?
6. What is a phylogeny? Construct one of early hominids 4–1 mya. Make sure you can describe what conclusions your scheme makes. Also, it would be good if you could defend it!
7. Discuss at least two alternative ways that *A. africanus* is currently incorporated into phylogenetic schemes.

Suggested Further Reading

In the previous three chapters, several general and a few highly technical books on hominid evolution have been suggested for further study. Here, we list several readers on physical anthropology containing collections of articles by noted anthropologists. These books are excellent sources for gaining an appreciation of the original literature and the conflicting views and personalities in this rapidly growing field.

Brace, C. L., and James Metress (eds.). *Man in Evolutionary Perspective*, New York: John Wiley and Sons, 1973.
  Articles cover topics on evolutionary principles, modern primate behavior, and hominid evolution. Contributions by Brace and Wolpoff give good synthesis of single species hypothesis.
Ciochon, Russell L., and John G. Fleagle (eds.). *Primate Evolution and Human Origins*, Menlo Park, Calif.: Benjamin Cummings, 1985.
  A very complete sampling of the literature on early primate evolution (i.e., topic of Chapter 12) and some very good topical selections on hominid evolution (including articles by Johanson and White and Lovejoy).

Dolhinow, Phyllis, and Vincent Sarich (eds.). *Background for Man*, Boston: Little, Brown and Co., 1971.

A stimulating series of articles reflecting widely different views of hominid evolution. The contribution by Sarich on the molecular technique of reconstructing evolutionary history is a particularly good summary of this approach. Articles by J. T. Robinson and F. Clark Howell reflect the more traditional paleontological approach.

Howell, F. Clark, and F. Bourliere (eds.). *African Ecology and Human Evolution*, Chicago: Aldine Publishing Co., 1963.

Although this work largely precedes the explosion of paleoanthropological data from East Africa, it has several excellent examples of paleontological and paleoecological studies.

Howells, W. W. (ed.). *Ideas on Human Evolution*, New York: Atheneum, 1967.

Contains several articles interesting from an historical perspective, particularly three contributions by J. T. Robinson.

Katz, S. H. (ed.). *Biological Anthropology*, San Francisco: W. H. Freeman and Co., 1975.

Several superior *Scientific American* contributions on bipedal locomotion, early primates, and primate behavior. Excellent introduction to first section places hominid discoveries into historical framework. Superior illustrations throughout.

Kennedy, W. J. (ed.). *Adventures in Anthropology*, St. Paul, Minn.: West Publishing Co., 1977.

A reasonably up-to-date group of articles on primate evolution, modern primate behavior and hominid evolutionary studies. This collection is particularly recommended for its strong emphasis on biocultural evolution.

Korn, Noel (ed.). *Human Evolution* (4th Ed.), New York: Holt, Rinehart and Winston, 1978.

Good collection of articles on principles of evolution and interpretations of the hominid fossil record. Some interesting articles on the use of modern primates in reconstructing early hominid behavior as well as Glynn Isaac's article on paleoanthropology are worth looking at.

Scientific American. *Human Ancestors* (Introduction by Glynn Isaac and Richard Leakey), San Francisco: W. H. Freeman and Co., 1979.

While many of the contributions in this short volume are now dated, they provide an excellent background to the history of several still active paleoanthropological controversies. Recent excellent articles include those contributed by E. L. Simons (*Ramapithecus*), Alan Walker and Richard Leakey (summary of fossil hominids from Lake Turkana), and Larry Keeley (a provocative discussion of experimental inference regarding the use of stone tools).

Washburn, S. L. (ed.). *The Social Life of Early Man*, Chicago: Aldine Publishing Co., 1961.

Although now out of date, this work contains many intriguing articles dealing with reconstruction of social behavior of early hominids.

——— (ed.). *Classification and Human Evolution*, Chicago: Aldine Publishing Co., 1963.

This work contains several excellent contributions dealing with hominoid evolution and the theoretical bases of classification.

Washburn, S. L., and Phyllis Dolhinow (eds.). *Perspectives on Human Evolution*, New York: Holt, Rinehart and Winston, 1968–1976.

A four-volume series dealing with human evolution largely from the perspective of modern primate studies.

Homo Erectus

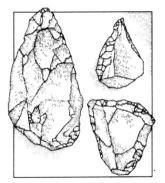

Contents

Seeking the Peking Bones

In the summer of 1941, war between the United States and Japan appeared inevitable to the officials at the Cenozoic Research Laboratory of Peking Union Medical College. To prevent the priceless Peking Man bones from falling into the hands of the Japanese, already in Peking, the officials packed them into boxes and shipped them to a warehouse at Camp Holcomb, a Marine Corps base not far from Peking. The marines, scheduled to leave China on December 8 aboard the S.S. *President Harrison*, were to take the bones with them on their return to the United States.

On December 7, 1941, Pearl Harbor was attacked, and war declared against Japan. Instead of leaving, the marines were arrested by the Japanese and interned for the duration of the war. What happened to the bones has remained a deep mystery ever since.

One account is that in the fall of 1941, Col. Ashurst, Commander of the Marine Corps Headquarters at Camp Holcomb, ordered the boxes of bones sent to Lt. Wm. E. Foley, a Marine Corps physician, who was to take the boxes with him aboard the *President Harrison*. When he received the boxes, Dr. Foley, realizing arrest and internment were imminent, distributed them to institutions and reliable Chinese friends in Tientsin, a city near Camp Holcomb. Dr. Foley has steadfastly refused ever since to divulge the names of these Chinese friends without guarantees for their safety from the Chinese government. Since he did not open the boxes when they arrived, it is not known for certain whether they even contained the bones.

In 1972, more than twenty-five years after the war ended, another chapter unfolded in the case of the missing bones. Mr. Christopher Janus, an American businessman, became interested in locating the bones after a visit to China and offered a reward of $5,000 for information leading to their recovery. Soon afterward, in New York, Janus received a telephone call from a woman who claimed her husband, a former marine now deceased, had left her a footlocker of what he believed were stolen Peking Man bones. Janus requested a meeting, which the so-called "mystery woman" insisted be held on the observation deck high atop the Empire State Building. At the meeting, the woman, who refused to give her name, showed a photograph of the footlocker's contents to Janus, who later checked the photo with Dr. Harry Shapiro, a physical anthropologist at the American Museum of Natural History. Shapiro, long interested in Peking Man and the missing bones, thought a skull in the photograph resembled that of Peking Man, and with that assurance Janus opened negotiations with the mystery woman's lawyer. The woman wanted $500,000 and guarantees that the United States government would not prosecute for possession of stolen property or confiscate the bones. Later, when these conditions were met, she raised her price to $700,000 and demanded a letter from the Chinese government stating they would not prosecute. The Chinese did not reply to the request for such a letter, and negotiations were never resumed.

Many rumors of the bones' location came to Mr. Janus, who eagerly investigated a number of them. He heard they were in Taiwan; they were not, but while there he increased the reward to $150,000. He also heard they were in Hong Kong—they were not; in Bangkok—not there, either. He was told they were in Burma, Tokyo, and Manila; but by this time he thought it was a waste of time and money to follow up these leads. Since then, 1975, Janus has not reported any further activity, and in November, 1977, withdrew his offer of reward.

The fate of the Peking bones remains unknown. The New York mystery woman might have a skull; Dr. Foley's friends in China may have all the bones; the bones might have been found in the Camp Holcomb warehouse by Japanese soldiers who, not realizing what they had, destroyed or abandoned them. They may have found their way to Burma, Bangkok, or—though very unlikely—the United States. Whoever has them—if anyone—is not telling.

The New York Times reported (May 11, 1980) that a former marine, Roger Ames, telephoned from his hospital bed in Dallas and told Janus the following story:

While on guard duty the night before Pearl Harbor he saw two marine officers, carrying a footlocker and shovels, dig a hole and bury the footlocker.

Urged on by the ex-marine's message, Janus decided to resume his investigation of the missing bones. However, to this point, no further leads have emerged.

SOURCES:

Janus, Christopher G. with William Brashler. *The Search for Peking Man*, New York: Macmillan Publishing Co., Inc., 1975.
The New York Times, Sunday, May 11, 1980.
Shapiro, Harry L. "The Strange, Unfinished Saga of Peking Man," *Natural History*, **80**:8 (No. 9), 1971.
———. *Peking Man*, New York: Simon and Schuster, 1974.

CHAPTER 16

Introduction

In the preceding several chapters, we introduced an early grade (see Box 16-1) of hominid evolution, the australopithecines of the Plio-Pleistocene. We discussed at some length the confusion surrounding them, confusion brought about by the various interpretations of the number of australopithecine species or lineages. Furthermore, recent discoveries, such as the "black skull," have added to the complexities of human evolution in the Plio-Pleistocene. These problems, discussed in Chapter 15, become even more complicated with the *H. erectus* (KNM-ER WT 15,000) find at Lake Turkana, discussed in this chapter, a contemporary of both australopithecines and *H. habilis*.

H. erectus, the next grade of hominid evolution, originated in Africa and enlarged their habitat by expanding into Asia, apparently bypassing Europe. As one might expect, they were taller, larger-brained, more culture-dependent, and more skillful toolmakers than their predecessors. Unlike australopithecines, who lived in much of the Pliocene and early Pleistocene, *H. erectus* evolved in the

FIGURE 16-1   A partial listing of *Homo erectus* sites. *H. erectus* inhabited areas of Europe, Africa, and Asia, a much wider distribution than australopithecines.

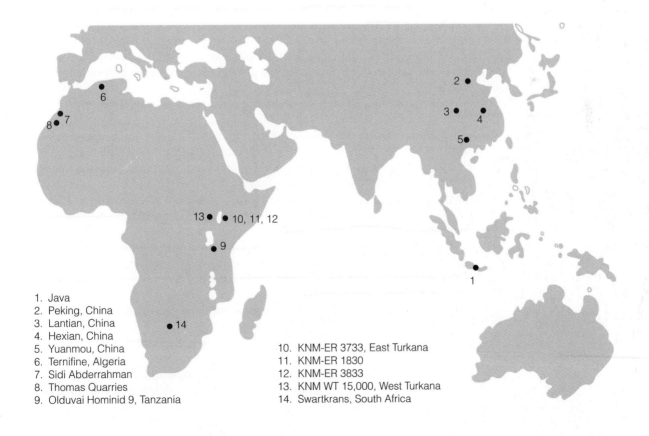

1. Java
2. Peking, China
3. Lantian, China
4. Hexian, China
5. Yuanmou, China
6. Ternifine, Algeria
7. Sidi Abderrahman
8. Thomas Quarries
9. Olduvai Hominid 9, Tanzania

10. KNM-ER 3733, East Turkana
11. KNM-ER 1830
12. KNM-ER 3833
13. KNM WT 15,000, West Turkana
14. Swartkrans, South Africa

BOX 16-1   **Grades of Human Evolution**

1. *Australopithecus**
2. *Homo erectus*
3. *Homo sapiens* (including archaic *sapiens*, Neandertals, and modern populations)

*Contemporaneous with some australopithecines is the hominid *Homo habilis*. We include in Grade 1 (*Australopithecus*), most especially the more primitive form *A. afarensis* and *A. africanus*. *Homo habilis* can be seen as transitional between Grades 1 and 2.

Interstadial   *Stadial* (from stadium): period
The periods of partial retreats during a major
glaciation.

Lower Pleistocene and lived well into the Middle Pleistocene. In our discussion of *H. erectus*, therefore, we must necessarily refer to the Pleistocene, its climate, biosphere, geological events, and dates.

The Pleistocene (1.8 mya–10,000 ya)

During much of the Pleistocene (also known as the Age of Glaciers), large areas of the northern hemisphere were covered with enormous masses of ice, which advanced and retreated as the temperature fell and rose. Until recently, European (Alpine) glaciers were considered to be four in number—Günz, Mindel, Riss, and Würm. In reconstructing the history of the Pleistocene, scholars attempted to work out the dates of these glacial advances. Then they further attempted to develop the hominid history of Europe and Asia by correlating hominid fossil bones and artifacts found in association with animals indicative of the glacial advances or retreats. For example, if human bones were found with those of a warm-weather animal, the researchers assumed that this was an interglacial or **interstadial** period. This procedure may appear straightforward enough, but one of the problems, especially in Europe, was that the glaciers have not been chronometrically dated.

At one time, the Plio-Pleistocene boundary was defined by the appearance of certain mammals believed to identify the beginning of the Pleistocene. Since the appearance of these mammals—modern cow, modern horse, Indian elephant—occurs at different times on different continents, this criterion could not be used on a worldwide basis. What was needed was an event that occurred everywhere on earth at the same time, and just such an event has been found in the reversal of the earth's magnetic field (Dalrymple, 1972). The study of such reversals is called *paleomagnetism* and is used to cross-check other dating techniques (see pp. 395–397).

We have known for a long time that the earth's magnetic field has frequently been reversed. During the reversal period, what we consider to be the North Pole became the South Pole, and a compass needle would have pointed south instead of north as it does now. Earth scientists have now succeeded in dating these reversals, which are worldwide events. The reversals now serve as markers to correlate geophysical activity in different parts of the world.

Although differences of opinion exist concerning the boundary between the Middle and Upper (or Late) Pleistocene, we shall use the widely accepted figure of 125,000 years, correlated with the beginning of the Riss-Würm interglacial. Figure 16-3 correlates Pleistocene, Alpine glacial periods, cultural divisions, and hominid sites.

	ALPINE GLACIAL SEQUENCE
10,000	
40,000	WÜRM
75,000 100,000 125,000	Riss-Würm
175,000 200,000 225,000	RISS
265,000 300,000	Mindel-Riss
380,000 400,000	MINDEL
435,000	Günz-Mindel
	GÜNZ
500,000	

FIGURE 16-2 Glacial sequence. With the exception of the Würm, dates for glacial and interglacial periods have not been well worked out yet.

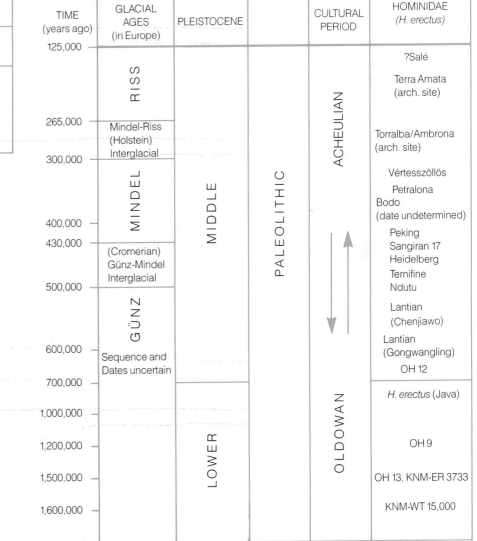

FIGURE 16-3 Lower and Middle Pleistocene (not to scale). Many dates are best estimates.

Sulcus (sul'kuss) groove, furrow

Nuchal nape
Refers to the nape of the neck area.

Alveolar (al-vee'-lar)
Tooth-bearing portion of upper or lower jaw.

Masseter Chewing

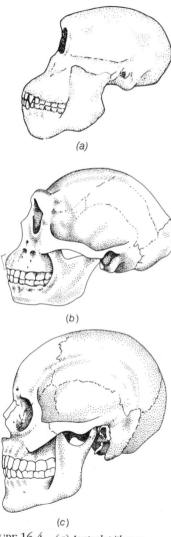

(a)

(b)

(c)

FIGURE 16-4 (a) *Australopithecus (afarensis);* (b) *H. erectus* (Peking); (c) *H. sapiens* (anatomically modern). Note the changes in prognathism, ascending ramus, slope of foreheads, vault height, and development of occiput. (Not to scale.)

The Pleistocene, which lasted almost 2 million years, was an important time in hominid evolutionary history: *Homo erectus* appears. From their brain size and tools, we can clearly see that this form, using culture as their strategy of adaptation, should be called human. By the time the Pleistocene terminated, modern humans had already appeared, dependence on culture as the human way of life had dramatically increased, and domestication of plants and animals—one of the great cultural revolutions of human history—was either about to commence or had just been invented. With this background of the time span in which *H. erectus* evolved and developed, let us examine more closely the hominid to whom we owe so much.

Homo Erectus

We have already observed that *H. erectus* was taller, larger-brained, and more dependent on culture than australopithecines. These are general statements. It will therefore be necessary to discuss the characteristics of *H. erectus* in more detail. Since we are dealing with the evolution of hominids from something resembling an australopithecine stage to the modern stage, what we shall see in the modifications of hominids, for the most part, are relative changes. That is, *H. erectus* is taller than australopithecines, but shorter* than *H. sapiens*; larger-brained than australopithecines, but smaller-brained than *H. sapiens*, etc. *Homo erectus*, in many physical and cultural characteristics, is intermediate between the australopithecine and *sapiens* stages.

The cranial capacity of *H. erectus* ranges widely from 775 to 1225 cm³, with a mean of 1020 cm³. In terms of averages, this would make the skull of *H. erectus* roughly twice the size of australopithecines, 50% larger than *H. habilis*, and 75% as large as *H. sapiens*.

When we look at the skull of *H. erectus* in profile (p. 468), several characteristics are immediately apparent. Overhanging the orbits is a pronounced bony ledge, the supraorbital torus, and, just behind it, is a marked depression known as supraorbital **sulcus**. The forehead recedes instead of rising sharply as it does in modern humans, and the long, low skull is reminiscent of a deflated football. The nasal spine shows some projection. (See Box 16-3.) At the end of the skull is the occiput, a bone forming the back and part of the base of the skull. The occipital bone angles sharply down and forward, unlike the rounded profile of *H. sapiens*. The rear end of the skull profile also points up a ridge of bone for the attachment of neck muscles that hold up the head. Protruding beyond the occiput is an extension of bone called a **nuchal** torus.

Returning to the front of the profile, we see the **alveolar** prognathism, receding chin, and teeth similar to but slightly larger than modern populations. Such traits reflect heavy chewing, and there is, indeed, a number of indications of well-developed **masseter** muscles. Heavy muscles require bony attachments, and these can be seen in the ridges on the mandible, the "buttresses on the facial skele-

---

*A find (KNM-WT 15000) of a 12-year-old *H. erectus* boy suggests *erectus* may have been as tall (perhaps taller) than *H. sapiens*.

BOX 16-2 **The Adaptive *H. erectus* Nose**

Nature, it seems, did a "nose job" on *H. erectus*. Instead of the flat, nonprojecting australopithecine nose that resembles the ape structure, the *erectus* nose—indicated on skulls by a more protruding skeletal nasal spine—is more external or projecting. And the nostrils probably faced downward, as they do in *H. sapiens*. This was not a cosmetic change or a passive result of reduction in the size of the face and teeth. Nor is this a *sapiens* nose, but there was a definite trend in a sapient direction. According to Franciscus and Trinkaus,* it was an adaptation to new environmental conditions.

Australopithecines had already begun walking bipedally, an innovation that became more habitual with

*Robert G. Franciscus and Erik Trinkaus, "Nasal Morphology and the Emergence of *Homo erectus*," *American Journal of Physical Anthropology*, 75(4):517–527, 1988.

H. habilis, and one to which *erectus* became fully committed. In an arid and open African environment, where early *H. erectus* lived, daytime activities (such as seeking food) could take a great deal of energy. In this scenario, adaptation that would combat fatigue would be very useful indeed. Assuming such adaptative response to be the case, a shift in the nose structure makes sense.

As the authors explain, an external nose, by creating an angle in the nasal passageway, increases turbulence during *exhalation*. Since the temperature of the passageway is lower than that of the body core, moisture of the exhaled air would be condensed. At the next *inhalation*, the moisture left in the nasal passage would humidify the breath, thus conserving moisture by using minimal body moisture and ensuring that the lungs function at the proper relative humidity. In this way, the physiological shift would reduce fatigue and increase activity levels.

---

ton—such as the broad nasal root, the thick supraorbital torus, the thick frontal process of the zygomatic bone—and the well-marked temporal lines" (Jacob, 1975, p. 314).

From the rear, we can see an important feature that distinguishes an *H. erectus* skull: its pentagonal shape, with maximum breadth at or near the base. In later hominids, maximum breadth is higher up on the skull. (See Figs. 16-6, 16-15, and 16-21.)

Two dental traits associated with *H. erectus* are **shovel-shaped** incisors (Fig. 16-7) and **taurodontism** (Fig. 16-8). Both features may be associated with chewing. The back of the incisors resemble a tiny scoop or coal shovel. It has been suggested that this phenomenon may be an adaptive response among hunters and gatherers, where a great deal of chewing, gripping, and tearing are done with the front teeth. Taurodontism refers to an enlarged pulp cavity, an advantage among hard-chewing humans and grazing animals. In time, the pulp hardens, and more wear is possible than in ordinary teeth.

Cheek teeth, smaller than earlier hominids but larger than *H. sapiens*, are characteristic of *erectus*. This suggests a switch in diet to softer foods that could be adequately handled by the anterior teeth.

In the past, it was believed that the locomotor skeleton of *H. erectus* was practically indistinguishable from *H. sapiens*. However, more recent analyses suggest that there are a number of morphological differences. "Nonetheless, the functional locomotor capabilities appear to have been generally similar to adaptations in *H. sapiens* for habitual erect posture and efficient striding bipedal gait" (Howell, 1978).

Diastema (dye-a-stee′-ma) Gap; space. (See Fig. 16-8.)

Shoveling Raised ridges of enamel on the tongue (lingual) side of the incisors.

Taurodontism taurus: bull dont: tooth A condition in which molar pulp cavities are enlarged; found in cattle, from whence the name. (See Fig. 16-9.)

FIGURE 16-5 *H. erectus* (Peking Man). From this view, the supraorbital torus, low vault of the skull, nuchal torus, and angled occiput can be clearly seen.

BOX 16-3 **Vocabulary**

ALVEOLAR PROGNATHISM Forward projection of the maxilla

ASCENDING RAMUS Rear upright portion of the mandible

CALLOTE or **CALVA** Uppermost portion of the braincase

CALVARIUM The skull minus the face and mandible

CERVICAL Pertaining to the neck, as in cervical vertebrae

CLAVICLE Collar bone

CONDYLE A rounded protuberance of bone which articulates (forms a joint, moves against) with another bone. The ball in a ball and socket joint (humerus and femur)

CORONAL SUTURE The suture running transversely across the skull joining the frontal and parietal bones

CRANIUM The complete skull; bones of the head, face, and mandible

FEMUR Thigh bone

FIBULA The narrow long bone on the outside of the lower leg (see tibia)

FRONTAL BONE The front bone of the skull including the forehead

HUMERUS Upper arm bone

LAMBDOID SUTURE The transverse suture at the back of the top of the skull joining the parietal and occipital bones

MAGHREB An area in Northwest Africa

MANDIBLE Lower jaw

MAXILLA Upper jaw

OCCIPUT, OCCIPITAL BONE The rear bone of the skull

PALEOLITHIC (Paleo: old; lithic: stone) Old Stone Age. The culture period preceding food-producing (farming, herding)

PARIETAL The right and left side bones on top of the skull; joined by the sagittal suture

PLATYCEPHALY (platy: flat; cephaly: head) Flatheadedness as opposed to dome shape of anatomically modern human beings

SAGITTAL SUTURE The suture joining the left and right parietals; bounded by coronal suture in front and lambdoidal suture behind

SCAPULA Shoulder blade

SUPRAORBITAL TORUS (supra: above; orbital: eye opening; torus: ridge) Ridge above the orbits on a skull, very pronounced in *H. erectus*, Neandertals, and some australopithecines

SUPRAORBITAL SULCUS A depression or groove separating the supraorbital torus from the receding forehead

TIBIA The large long bone of the lower leg; the shin (see fibula)

ZYGOMATIC ARCH The bony arch below the orbit

ZYGOMATIC BONE Outer portion of orbit forming parts of its floor, and the cheekbone

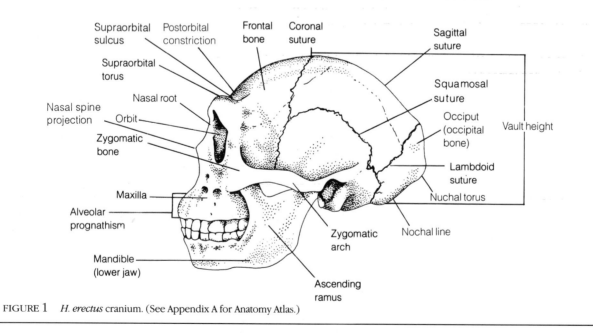

FIGURE 1 *H. erectus* cranium. (See Appendix A for Anatomy Atlas.)

Asia

JAVA

Scientific discoveries are normally the result of careful planning, hard work, and thorough knowledge of the subject. In addition, they are frequently tales of luck, adventure, and heartbreak, which brings us to the story of **Eugene Dubois**, a Dutch anatomist.

Dubois was the first scientist to deliberately design a research plan that would take him from the lab to where the fossil bones were buried, or might be buried. Up until this time, embryology and comparative anatomy were considered the proper method of studying humans and their ancestry, and the research was done in the laboratory. Dubois changed all this.

The latter half of the nineteenth century was a period of intellectual excitement. In England, Darwin's *Origin of Species* (published in 1859) provoked scientists and educated laymen to take opposing sides, often with great emotion. In Germany, for example, the well-known zoologist Ernst Haeckel eagerly supported Darwin's statement that humans descended from apes and even suggested the name for the missing transitional link between the two: *Pithecanthropus alalus*, "the ape man without speech." He was criticized by Rudolf Virchow, one of Europe's most famous scientists and Haeckel's one-time zoology professor, who publicly and scornfully disagreed with these speculations. In 1856, a strange skull had been recovered near Dusseldorf, Germany. This specimen is what we today recognize as a Neandertal skull, but, when a description of it was published, scientific opinion was again divided and feelings ran high. "The opinions and counteropinions about the Neandertal skull and other odd skulls, jaws, and bones that turned up in Europe kept science and the keenly interested lay public in something of an uproar for many years" (Moore, 1961, p. 235).

This stimulating intellectual climate surrounded the youthful Eugene Dubois, born in Holland in 1858, a year before Darwin's *Origin* and two years after the discovery of the Neandertal skull. At the age of 19, Dubois left home and enrolled in the University of Amsterdam. Disregarding his father's wishes that he become a pharmacist, he decided instead to prepare for a medical degree. He soon lost interest in becoming a practicing physician and turned to his real interest, natural

FIGURE 16-6   *H. erectus* (Peking Man). Note that the widest part of the skull is toward the bottom, giving the skull a pentagonal form.

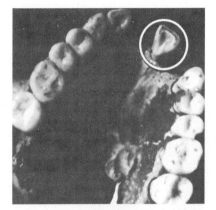

FIGURE 16-7   Shovel-shaped incisors.

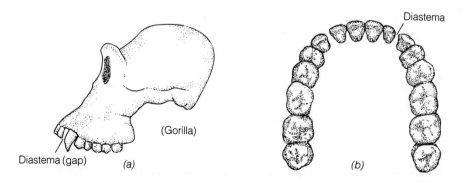

Diastema

(Gorilla)

Diastema (gap)   *(a)*

(b)

FIGURE 16-8   Diastema (*a*) in a male gorilla; (*b*) in an early Java upper jaw. Diastema occurs between the canine and lateral incisor. The gap makes it possible for the canines to overlap and the jaws to close.

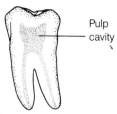

Pulp cavity

Taurodont
(Peking Man,
Heidelberg, and
some modern
populations)

Cynodaunt
(modern
Europeans)

FIGURE 16-10   Eugene Dubois.

science. Dubois was an outstanding student, and in 1881 was offered and accepted the position of assistant to his anatomy professor.

For six years Dubois worked at his research and teaching. He abruptly decided, while writing up a major research project, to leave the university and sail to southeast Asia in search of human ancestors! Why did he suddenly throw aside his job and travel to a far off place to take up a search for fossils, something no one before him had ever done? Some suggest that he was bored with lab work and loathed teaching. Later in life, he himself said he did it to primarily find the "missing link," a quest he had dreamed of as a child and had never forgotten.

Why the Dutch East Indies? Several reasons: (1) Darwin had written that a likely place to find human ancestors were the African tropics, where our close relatives—the chimpanzees and gorillas—lived, and the Dutch East Indies are tropical; (2) the islands were a Dutch possession, which facilitated getting there and working there; (3) obtaining research funds, always a serious consideration, was easier given Dutch administration. It is true that chimpanzees and gorillas did *not* live in southeast Asia, but gibbons certainly did, and Dubois believed there was a close kinship between gibbons and humans. Also, only a few years earlier, a partial "chimpanzee" jaw had been found in the Siwalk Hills, and other fossil anthropoid remains had been recovered from India and other southeast Asia locations. To Dubois, his choice of place must have seemed quite sound.

Like other scientists before him, Dubois applied to the Royal Dutch Indies Army for the post of medical officer, and he was accepted. He arrived in Sumatra on December 11, 1887 to take his appointment at a hospital.

Arranging his duties so that he had opportunity to explore the caves in the area, Dubois went to work immediately and soon unearthed a variety of animal bones, including orang, gibbon, rhino, tapir, elephant, deer, cattle, and pig. On the basis of this success, Dubois was awarded funds for continuing research in Sumatra, as well as in Java. Unfortunately, his previous success was not repeated, and Dubois believed that his chances would improve on Java, where a human skull had been found a year earlier at Wadjak.

Dubois started working in Java in June, 1890, and tried his luck by exploring numerous caves. The results were disappointing, which led Dubois to try open sites, hoping for better results. He found the banks of the Solo River to be the most productive area and concentrated his work there, near the town of Trinil. (See map, Fig. 16-11.)

The actual digging, with the help of laborers, was directed by two corporals from the engineering corps. Dubois did not establish his headquarters at the site but regularly visited the digs, keeping in close written contact with his two assistants, who sent him the material they found.

FIGURE 16-11   The Indonesian area.

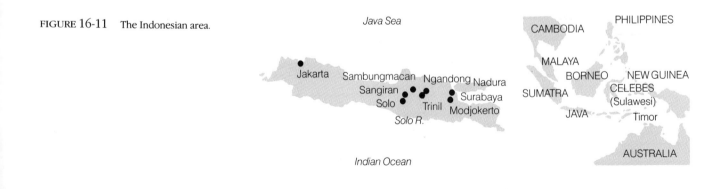

In October, 1891, the military engineers unearthed a skullcap that was to become famous around the world. Dubois named it *Pithecanthropus erectus*—erect apeman. (The name was ultimately changed to *Homo erectus erectus*.) It is now well known simply as the Java Man. Digging stopped for the rainy season and, soon after, work was resumed the following year. A femur was recovered about fifteen yards upstream in what Dubois claimed was the same level as the skullcap. When he examined it, Dubois discerned at once that it resembled a human femur that belonged to an individual who possessed an upright posture. He assumed that the skullcap (with a cranial capacity of over 900 cm³) and the femur belonged to the same individual.

After studying these discoveries for a few years, Dubois startled the world in 1894 with a paper sensationally entitled "*Pithecanthropus erectus*, a Human Transitional Form from Java." The name *Pithecanthropus* had been suggested some years before by Haeckel as the species for the transitional form between ape and human, and Dubois used this suggestion, perhaps to gain Haeckel's support. Haeckel did come to support Dubois, but the majority of scientists, including Virchow, strongly and often nastily, objected to Dubois' claims.

The opposition advanced many arguments against Dubois' claim: The skullcap was that of an ape; the femur so modern it could not possibly belong with the skull; the skull was human and probably belonged to a microcephalic idiot; Dubois' estimate of the cranial capacity was unreliable; the femur and skull were found too far apart to belong to the same individual; the skull was that of a Neandertal; the date suggested by Dubois, Upper Miocene or Early Pleistocene, was questionable, etc., etc.

Dubois returned to Europe in 1895 and countered the criticism by elaborating the points briefly covered in his paper. He also brought along the fossil material itself, which gave scientists an opportunity to directly examine the evidence. As a result, many opponents became more sympathetic to his views, although Virchow remained adamant in his opposition.

However, to this day, questions about the finds remain: Does the femur really belong with the skullcap? Did Dubois' absence from the dig create excavation problems? Did the corporals dig through several layers, thus mixing the faunal remains?

Despite the still-unsettled questions, there is general acceptance that Dubois was correct in identifying the specimen as belonging to a new species, that the cranial capacity was about right, that *Pithecanthropus erectus*, or *H. erectus* as we call the species today, is the ancestor of *H. sapiens*, and that bipedalism preceded the enlargement of the brain.

Dubois set aside working up a complete description of *Pithecanthropus*, but he was not idle. He turned to a study of the relationships between brain and body weight and published several papers on his findings, which he later applied to *Pithecanthropus*. (Gould discusses this research in *Natural History*, April, 1990, pp. 12–24.)

By 1930, the controversy had faded, especially in light of important new discoveries near Peking, China, in the late 1920s (discussed shortly). These finds clearly demonstrated that Peking Man was human, an early form no doubt, but human nevertheless. Resemblances between the Peking skulls and Dubois' *Pithecanthropus* were obvious, and scientists pointed out that the Java form was not an apeman, as Dubois contended, but a true human.

One might expect that Dubois would welcome Peking Man and the support it provided for the human status of *Pithecanthropus*, but Dubois would have none of

(a)

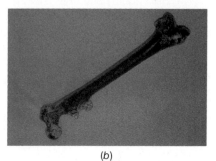

(b)

FIGURE 16-12   Skullcap (*Pithecanthropus* I, found by Eugene Dubois). Femur, also found by Dubois, led him to name this form *Pithecanthropus erectus*, now known as *H. erectus*. The abnormal spur of bone on the femur is known as an *exostosis*. It has no bearing on the identification of the femur.

BOX 16-4

Portion of a Complete Definition of *Homo erectus*

Homo erectus (Dubois) 1894 A species (extinct) of the genus *Homo*, known from Eurasia and Africa, distinguished by very substantial enlargement of the brain size, mean (1,020 cc) nearly twice that of large *Australopithecus* species and substantially above that of antecedent species of genus *Homo*; endocranial cast with essentially (modern) human fissuration pattern; generally low, flattened frontal region and prominent frontal keel; expanded (unilaterally) inferior frontal region, with wide separation from anterior temporal lobe; expanded precentral cortical area; exposed anterior insular area, in whole or part related to substantial development of Sylvian crest; lack of approximation between temporal lobe and cerebellum; absolutely and relatively narrow temporal lobe, tapering anteromedially, with poorly expanded inferior temporal area, salient superior temporal area, and posteriorly expanded posterior part of middle temporal convolution, expanded (unilaterally) inferior parietal region (supramarginal area); cerebellum with ipsilateral asymmetry, and cerebrum largely symmetrical, but with contralateral asymmetry expressed particularly in parieto-occipital and inferior frontal regions.

Cranial length greater than *Australopithecus*; vault bones of substantial to massive thickness, as expressed in outer and inner tables, cranial suture closure apparently earlier than in *H. sapiens*, and with coronal preceding sagittal suture closure; maximum breadth of vault at or toward the cranial base, usually coincident with biauricular breadth, with lesser bitemporal and biparietal dimensions; substantial postorbital constriction; low to more moderately arched vault, with low receding frontal (with or without notable frontal tuberosity), longitudinally flattened parietal, and occipital with marked to substantial angulation between upper (squama) and lower (nuchal) scales; usually distinct sagittal thickening, especially in bregmatic area, often associated with marked parasagittal depression; parietal smaller, more rectangular and transversely more curved than in *H. sapiens*, usually with sub-. . . .

F. Clark Howell, "Hominidae." In: V. J. Maglio and H.B.S. Cooke (eds.). *Evolution of African Mammals*, Cambridge: Harvard University Press, 1978.

it. He considered his fossil a *transitional*, not a human, form. He refused to recognize any connection between Peking and Java and described Peking "as a degenerate Neanderthaler" (von Koenigswald, 1956, p. 55). He also refused to accept placing *Pithecanthropus* in the same species with von Koenigswald's Java finds. Dubois maintained his belief that his famous fossil was a transitional form, a position he held until his death in 1940.

The story of *Homo erectus* does not, of course, end with the death of Dr. Dubois. Others, notably a younger paleontologist born in Germany, G. H. R. von Koenigswald, took up the search for ancient humans in Java in the 1930s.

Before reviewing the bone material found in Java, we should take note of a problem that paleoanthropologists and other scientists have faced in working out Java prehistoric chronology.

The stratigraphy of Javanese soil presents an especially complex structure. Geologists have attempted to arrange an orderly stratigraphic scheme that would enable paleoanthropologists to attach dates to the hominid fossils they excavate. Unfortunately, this has been a troublesome task, and geologists have given different age ranges for the same stratum. Furthermore, it has been difficult to order the faunal stages, and many scientists believe the old scheme of Djetis (Lower Pleistocene), Trinil (Middle Pleistocene), and Ngandong (Upper Pleistocene) to be inadequate. One of the reasons for this is that the key animals used to identify the Djetis stage are also found in the Trinil. Therefore, we shall use a faunal sequence recently proposed (de Vos, 1985, p. 216) even though it has not yet been widely accepted:

Faunal Stages

Ngandong

Kedung Brubus

Trinil H.K.

Trinil H.K. (or Ci Saat)

Ci Saat

By the Middle Pleistocene (Kabuh Formation; Trinil H.K., faunal stage) in Java, *H. erectus* had changed. Among some hominids, these changes were not great, but they do reflect a trend. There was a slight increase in the height of the vault (see craniograms in Figs. 16-15 and 16-16), and the diastema and projecting canine had disappeared. The small brain, below 1000 cm³, continues, as we see, in the skull Dubois discovered, as well as in some others. However, if the faunal stages recently suggested are correct, there is a significant increase in the brain size of *H. erectus* in the following Kedung Brubus faunal stage. *(Upper Pleistocene)*

Skulls S12 and S17 from Sangiran, and Sambungmacan from the nearby site of the same name, represent a break from the earlier smaller-brained hominids of the Middle Pleistocene. The cranial capacity of these three skulls are all over 1000 cm³, and are quite similar in many respects to the more advanced skulls from Ngandong—*H. soloensis* (see Table 16-1, Figs. 16-15 and 16-16), who may have lived more than a half million years later, in the Upper Pleistocene. The similarities may be seen in the "general size and shape of the skull, the skull contours in all views, the supraorbital torus, the ear region, the occipital torus and the nuchal area, and the cranial base" (Jacob, 1976, p. 86).

Because of some of the physical traits listed in the preceding paragraph, it is clear that Solo is related to *H. erectus*, and especially to Sangiran 17 and Sambungmacan. But there are also affinities to *H. sapiens*. Some students of Java hominids have referred to this Ngandong hominid as a Neandertal, others to *H. sapiens soloensis*, or a transitional form between *erectus* and *sapiens*, and still others as a late *H. erectus*. One contemporary author writes that "on strictly morphological grounds [Solo] might best be assigned to *H. erectus*" (Klein, 1989, p. 247). Nevertheless, a strong case could be made for placing these three fossils in an archaic *sapiens* category, since it appears they have developed beyond classic *H. erectus* anatomy. This development can be seen especially in their larger cranial capacity.

We can say little about the hominid way of life in Java. Very few artifacts have been found and those that have come mainly from river terraces, not from primary sites. ". . . on Java there is still not a single site where artifacts can be associated with *H. erectus erectus* (Bartstra, 1982, p. 319).

PEKING (BEIJING)

The story of Peking Man* is another saga filled with excitement, hard work, luck, and misfortune. It began in 1911, when J. Gunnar Andersson, a Swedish geologist,

---

*Although Beijing is the correct spelling for Peking and will be used in this text for the provence and city, there is a growing consensus among anthropologists that Peking remain the spelling for Peking man.

(a)

(b)

FIGURE 16-13   (*a*) Lateral view of Solo skull; (*b*) rear view of Solo skull.

AGE[1] (in millions)	MAGNETO[2] STRATIGRAPHY	PLEISTOCENE[3]	GEOLOGIC[4] FORMATION	FAUNAL[5] STRATA	JAVA[6] HOMINIDS	REMARKS
	BRUNHES	UPPER	NOTOPURO (Pohjajar)	NGANDONG	*H. soloensis*	Solo man (usually considered upper Pleistocene)
.51	(normal)	MIDDLE	Upper KABUH (Bapang)	KEDUNG BRUBUS	*H. modjokertensis* (Perning 1)	deVos places *H. Modiokertensis* in either the Kedung Brubus or Ngandong faunal level.
.73						
.78 .83	YAMA		Middle		S12, S17 Sambungmacan	Jacob dates Sambungmacan at 800,000 y.a.
.90			Lower Formation	TRINIL H.K.	Trinil 2 / S6, S2	Trinil 2 (*P. erectus* found by Dubois.) / S6 = *Meganthropus palaeojavanicus*
1.0						
Jaramillo .90 .97				TRINIL H.K.	S4	P4 = *P. robustus*
1.16	MATU	LOWER	PUCANGAN (sangiran)	C1 STAAT		
1.4 1.5					S5, S9	*P dubius* — oldest Java hominid
Olduvai 1.69 1.81	(reversal)		FORMATION			
2.0						

FIGURE 16-14   *H. erectus* correlations, Java.*

1. Dates are tentative. There is much confusion with dates because of Java stratigraphic uncomformities.

2. Olduvai and Jaramillo normal events may not necessarily apply to the Java paleomagnetic scheme.

3. Some scholars equate Lower, Middle, and Upper Pleistocene with, respectively, Puncangan, Kabuh, and Notopuro Formations.

4. A recent report proposes the Sangiran geologic strata be renamed as indicated in parentheses.

5. The faunal sequence is taken from de Vos (1985) who follows Sondaar (1984).

6. This chart is an attempt to correlate Java hominids with several kinds of dating methods. The chart is intended to give some chronological perspective to the Java hominid finds. More work on the stratigraphy of Java is needed before the problem of Java hominid dates can be resolved.

*The chart is not to scale; correlations are suggestive.

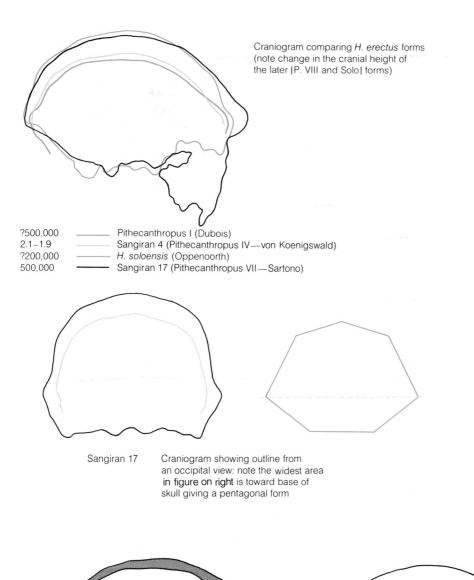

FIGURE 16-15   Craniograms.

Craniogram comparing *H. erectus* forms
(note change in the cranial height of
the later [P. VIII and Solo] forms)

?500,000	———	Pithecanthropus I (Dubois)
2.1–1.9	··········	Sangiran 4 (Pithecanthropus IV—von Koenigswald)
?200,000	———	*H. soloensis* (Oppenoorth)
500,000	——	Sangiran 17 (Pithecanthropus VII—Sartono)

Sangiran 17   Craniogram showing outline from
an occipital view: note the widest area
in figure on right is toward base of
skull giving a pentagonal form

FIGURE 16-16   Craniograms.

Peking man
Pithecanthropus I, Sangiran 2, 3, 4, 12
Sangiran 17

——— Sangiran 4 (robustus)

TABLE 16-1 **Java Hominidae (*H. erectus*)***

PLEISTOCENE	AGE YEARS, GEOLOGIC FORMATION, AND FAUNAL STRATA	DESIGNATION AND OTHER NAMES	SITE	MATERIAL	CRANIAL CAPACITY (CM³)	DISCOVERED BY	YEAR DISCOVERED
Upper ?Middle	Estimated 300,000– 100,000 Notopuro Ngandong	*H. soloensis* Ngandong Man Solo Man	Ngandong	skull bones, tibia At least 12 individuals	Range: 1150– 1300	C. ter Haar von Koenigswald	1931–1933
Middle or Upper	Kabuh Ngandong or Kedung Brubus	*H. modjokertensis*- Perning 1	Perning	Infant calvarium	650	von Koenigswald	1936
Middle	800,000 Kabuh Kedung Brubus	S12† P7	Sangiran	skull cap	1004	Sartono	1965
Middle	800,000 Kabuh Kedung Brubus	S17 P8	Sangiran	cranium	Estimated 1059, 1125	Sartono	1969
Middle	Kabuh ?Kedung Brubus	Sambungmacan 1	Sambungmacan	skull cap	1035	Jacob	1973
Middle	800,000– 900,000 Kabuh Trinil H.K.	Tr2	Trinil	skull cap	Estimates: 850–940	Dubois	1891
Middle	900,000 Kabuh Trinil H.K.	S2	Sangiran	skull cap	Estimates: 775–813	von Koenigswald	1937
Middle	900,000+ Kabuh Trinil H.K.	S6 *Meganthropus paleojavanicus*	Sangiran	partial right mandible		von Koenigswald	1941
Lower	1,000,000 + Pucangan Trinil H.K. or Ci Saat	S4 *P. robustus*	Sangiran	calvarial fragments	900	von Koeningswald	1938/1939
Lower	1,000,000 Pucangan Trinil H.K. or Ci Saat	S5, S9 *P. dubius*	Sangiran	right mandibles		S9 Sartono S5 von Koenigswald	1960 1939

*Lower and Middle Pleistocene (not to scale).
†S = Sangiran; P = "Pithecanthropus."

BOX 16-5   **Finding Peking Man**

Working the Zhoukoudian cave site for several summers, Dr. Otto Zdansky took the material he excavated back to Sweden. After carefully cleaning and preparing the material, he wrote, in 1926, to J. Gunnar Andersson, the Swedish geologist in charge back in China. Dr. Zdansky mentioned that he had found a premolar and molar, which he cautiously identified as belonging to a creature resembling *Homo sp.* Andersson, not nearly so cautious, jubilantly exclaimed, "The man I predicted has been found." (Andersson, 1934, p. 103).

With this encouraging news, Dr. Birgir Bohlin of Sweden was appointed to organize a concentrated effort to excavate the Zhoukoudian cave. Work began in April, 1927, two days before the season ended. Dr. Bohlin found a hominid tooth, which he immediately took to Dr. Davidson Black, anatomist at the Peking Union Medical College, and the man responsible for the study of hominid material recovered from the cave.

After carefully examining the tooth, Dr. Black decided it belonged to the same species as the two teeth found by Dr. Zdansky. He thus set up a new genus, *Sinanthropus*, with the species name *pekinensis*. It was an exciting discovery, and *Sinanthropus pekinensis*, which we know today as *H. erectus pekinensis*, immediately acquired worldwide fame. Shortly thereafter, Dr. Black went on leave to visit America and Europe:

He had a large gold watch chain made for him in Peking with a small receptacle hanging from it, into which the tooth exactly fitted. In this way, he travelled about the world with his precious fossil, showing it to colleagues and asking their opinion (von Koenigswald, 1956, p. 45).

accepted an appointment as adviser to the Chinese government to arrange a survey of its coalfields and ore resources. In his investigations, Andersson became interested in the mammals of Tertiary and Pleistocene deposits, and he and his colleagues collected many specimens. Europeans had known for a long time that "dragon bones" (such as the *Gigantopithecus* teeth mentioned in Chapter 12), so important to the Chinese for their healing and aphrodisiac powers, were actually mammal bones. In 1917, the Geological Survey of China resolved to find the sites where these dragon bones were collected by local inhabitants and sold to apothecary shops. In 1921, Andersson and a few other scientists were investigating a place called Chicken Bone Hill near the village of Zhoukoudian, about 30 miles southwest of Beijing. While laying plans to excavate the hill, they were approached by a local resident who told the scientists that much larger and better dragon bones could be obtained not far away.

The new discovery lay in an abandoned quarry 500 feet west of the railway station at Zhoukoudian. The villager showed them a fissure in the limestone wall, and in a few minutes they found the jaw of a pig, which indicated that the site was a more important one than Chicken Bone Hill. "That evening we went home with rosy dreams of great discoveries" (Andersson, 1934, pp. 97–98).

Dr. Birgir Bohlin (see Box 16-5) resumed working the site in 1928, and recovered more than a score of teeth, as well as parts of skulls of both young and adult individuals, but a complete skull evaded his efforts. A young Chinese geologist, W. C. Pei, took over the direction of the excavation in 1929, and concentrated in what is called the lower cave. On December 1 of that year, he began digging out the sediment in one branch of the lower cave, and at 4 P.M. of the following day,

FIGURE 16-18   Dr. Davidson Black.

found one of the most remarkable fossil skulls to be recovered up to that time. One of the Chinese workers tells the story:

> We had got down about 30 metres deep.... It was there the skull-cap was sighted, half of it embedded in loose earth, the other in hard clay. The sun had almost set.... The team debated whether to take it out right away or to wait until the next day when they could see better. The agonizing suspense of a whole day was felt to be too much to bear, so they decided to go on (Jia, 1975, pp. 12–13).

Pei brought the skull to Dr. Davidson Black (see Box 16-5), but because it was embedded in hard limestone, it took Black four months of hard, steady work to free it from its tough matrix. The result was worth the labor since the skull, that of a juvenile, was thick, low, and relatively small, but in Black's mind there was no doubt it belonged to an early hominid. The response to this discovery, quite unlike that which greeted Dubois almost 40 years earlier, was immediate and enthusiastically favorable. Peking Man, as it is known, became one of the more famous of fossil human skulls.

Work at Locality 1, as this part of the Zhoukoudian cave is known, continued. Dr. Black maintained a killing schedule, working at night so he would not be interrupted at his desk. His health was not robust, and he probably should not have remained in Beijing's harsh climate. As von Koenigswald related it:

> He tried to stick it out but it was too much for him. When his secretary entered his room on March 15, 1934, she found him slumped over his desk, dead from a heart attack, with the beloved skull of Peking Man in his hand (von Koenigswald, 1956, p. 48).

Dr. Franz Weidenreich, distinguished anatomist and well known for his work on European fossil hominids, succeeded Black. Weidenreich left his native Germany because of the academic repression and vicious "racial" policies of the Nazi regime. He was a visiting professor of anatomy at the University of Chicago when he was appointed, in 1935, to be visiting professor of anatomy at the Peking Union Medical College, and honorary director of the Cenozoic Research Laboratory, Geological Survey of China. Excavations at Zhoukoudian ended in 1937, with Japan's invasion of China, but the Cenozoic Research Laboratory continued.

BOX 16-6   **Subspecies**

Populations of a species are often designated by a sub-specific term. Here are three examples of *H. erectus* populations with their subspecific designations.	*H. erectus erectus* *H. erectus pekinensis* *H. erectus heidelbergensis*	Java China, Zhoukoudian Germany, Mauer

As relations between the United States and Japan deteriorated, Weidenreich decided he had better remove the fossil material from Beijing to prevent it from falling into the hands of the Japanese. Weidenreich left China in 1941, taking beautifully prepared casts, photographs, and drawings of the Peking material with him. After he left, the bones were packed in November, and arrangements made for the U.S. Marine Corps to take the bones with them when they left Beijing to return to the United States. The bones never reached the United States and have never been found. No one to this day knows what happened to them, and their location remains a mystery (see p. 462).

Zhoukoudian Material   According to a recent account (Wu and Lin, 1983), the total fossil remains of *H. erectus* unearthed at the Zhoukoudian cave amount to:

    6   complete or almost complete skulls

  12   skull fragments

  15   pieces of mandibles

157   teeth

    3   humerus fragments

    7   femur fragments

    1   clavicle

    1   tibia fragment

    1   lunate (wrist) bone

(and over 100,000 artifacts)

These belong to upwards of 40 male and female adults and children. This is a respectable amount of evidence, the most and the best of any *H. erectus* specimens, and (with the meticulous work by Dr. Weidenreich) has led to a good overall picture of the northern Chinese *H. erectus*.

Dating caves is not always a simple matter; in some cases, the roof of the cave has fallen in and not only is the stratigraphy disturbed, but fossil bones may have been washed into the cave. After a five-year comprehensive investigation of the Zhoukoudian site by more than 120 Chinese scientists from the Institute of Vertebrate Palaeontology and Palaeoanthropology (IVPP),* the researchers came to the

---

*The Institute (IVPP) was established in 1949. Several hundred scientists—paleoanthropologists, archeologists, geologists, biologists, botanists, palynologists and others—work at the Institute. Since its inception, there has been an extraordinary amount of paleoanthropological work accomplished throughout China.

Keel   The slight ridge where the skull peaks on *H. erectus*—along the sagittal crest (resembling the keel of a boat).

FIGURE 16-19   Dr. Franz Weidenreich.

Keeled

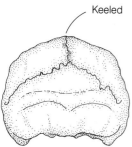

H. erectus
(a)

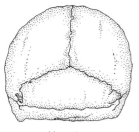

H. sapiens
(b)

FIGURE 16-20   (*a*) The keeled skull of *H. erectus*; (*b*) the skull of *H. sapiens* which does not show keeling.

following conclusions about dates in the Zhoukoudian caves: There were three cultural stages beginning 460,000 ya and ending 230,000 ya, when the people were forced out as the cave filled with rubble and sediment. These Middle Pleistocene dates place this Chinese *erectus* considerably later than their conspecifics in Java, a time lapse that probably explains why the Zhoukoudian population had moved a bit further along the hominid trail than most of their Javanese relatives.

That Beijing and Java hominids are related is clearly demonstrated by a comparison of the bones. The postcranial material is very similar, except that Peking's leg bones suggest they may have been shorter.

Peking, like Java, possesses the typical *erectus* fore and aft bulges—the supraorbital torus in front and the nuchal torus behind; the skull is **keeled** by a sagittal ridge, the face protrudes in alveolar prognathism, the incisors are shoveled, and molars contain large pulp cavities. Again, like the Java forms, the skull is vintage *H. erectus*, showing its greatest breadth near the bottom. These similarities were recognized long ago by Black and Weidenreich; at one time, in fact, it was suggested that Peking's nomen be changed from *Sinanthropus* to *Pithecanthropus pekinensis*. However, the similarities of European and African Middle Pleistocene forms to those of Asia, and the resemblance of all these to the genus *Homo*, persuaded taxonomists that the correct name was *Homo erectus*.

What mainly distinguishes Chinese from Java hominids is cranial capacity. Java hominids average 900 cm³; Chinese hominids average 1088 cm³. The difference might be due to the more recent age of the Chinese fossils. As the craniogram illustrates (Fig. 16-16), the larger Peking skull is reflected by a higher vault of the skull, a higher forehead, and a longer and broader cranium. What accounts for the larger brain? Possibly, Peking represents a later period in the evolution of *Homo erectus*. With greater dependence on culture and selective pressures associated with that dependence, brain size assuredly increased. It is probably no accident that Beijing *erectus* (460,000–230,000 years ago in China) and Sangiran 17 (500,000 years ago in Java), both late in Asiatic *H. erectus* evolution, are relatively "large-brained."

More than 100,000 artifacts were recovered from this site that was occupied for almost 250,000 years, which, according to the Chinese (Wu and Lin, 1983, p. 86), "is one of the sites with the longest history of habitation by man or his ancestors. . . ." The occupation of the site has been divided into three cultural stages:

Earliest stage (460,000–420,000 ya)*   The tools were large, close to a pound in weight, and made of soft stone, such as sandstone.

Middle Stage (370,000–350,000 ya)   Tools become smaller and lighter (under a pound) and these smaller tools comprise 68% of the total; the large tools make up only 12%.

Final Stage (300,000–230,000 ya)   Tools are still smaller, and the tool materials were of better quality. The coarse quartz of the earlier periods was replaced by a finer quartz, sandstone tools had almost disappeared, and flint tools increased as much as 30%.

The early tools were crude and shapeless but become more refined over time, and, toward the top of Locality 1, there are some finely made tools. Common tools at the site are choppers and chopping tools, but retouched flakes were fashioned

---

*These dates should be considered tentative until more precise chronometric techniques are available.

TABLE 16-2   *H. erectus* **Fossils of China**

DESIGNATION	SITE	AGE[a] PLEISTOCENE YEARS	MATERIAL	CRANIAL CAPACITY (CM³)	YEAR FOUND	REMARKS
Jinniushan	Jinnu Mt., near Yingou	280,000	Incomplete skeleton, including calvarium	1400	1984	Lu: Most complete *H. erectus* ever found. May be *sapiens*.
Hexian	Longtandong Cave, Anhui	Middle 280–240,000	calvarium, skull frag., mandible frag, isolated teeth	1025	1980/81	First skull found in southern or southwest China.
Peking Man	Zhoukoudian Cave, Beijing	Middle 460–230,000[b]	5 adult crania, skull frags., facial bones, isolated teeth, 40+ individuals	1015–1225; avg: 1088	1927– ongoing	Most famous fossils in China and some of the most famous in the world.
Yunxi	Bailongdong Cave, Hubei	Middle ?500,000	isolated teeth		1975	
Yunxian	Longgudong Cave, Hubei	Middle ?500,000	isolated teeth		1976–82	
Yuanmou	Shangnabang	Middle 600–500,000	upper central incisors		1965	
Lantian	Chenjiawo, Lantian	Middle 650,000	mandible		1963	Old female.
Lantian	Gongwangling, Lantian	Middle 800–750,000	calvarium, facial bones	780	1964	Female over 30. Oldest *erectus* found so far in China.

Sources: Wu and Dong (1985); Lisowski (1984); Pope (1984); *Atlas of Primitive Man in China* (1980).

[a]These are best estimates—authorities differ.

[b]In a recent study of dating methods used in China, Aigner (1986) questions the long duration attributed to Zhoukoudian Locality I. She believes it is "mid-Middle Pleistocene," can be equated with the Holstein interglacial of Europe, and did not last more than 100,000 years.

into scrapers, points, burins, and awls. Handaxes, found in abundance in Europe and Africa, are absent from Zhoukoudian.

Stone was not the only material selected by Zhoukoudian hominids; they also utilized bone and horn. Found in the cave were antler fragments, which had been hacked into pieces. Antler roots might have served as hammers and the sharp tines as digging sticks. Many skulls of sika and thick-jaw deer minus facial bones as well as antlers and crania bases leaving only the brain case were also found. Jia suggests that since the skulls show evidence of repeated whittling and over 100 specimens were discovered, all similarly shaped, "it is reasonable to infer they served as 'drinking bowls.'" He goes on to conjecture that the brain cases of the Beijing fossils "retain similar characteristics and probably served the same purpose" (Jia, 1975, p. 31).

The way of life at Zhoukoudian has traditionally been described as that of a hunter who killed deer, horses, and other animals, gathered fruits, berries, ostrich

TABLE 16-3   **Zhoukoudian Material (Middle Pleistocene)**

| MATERIAL | DISCOVERED | | CULTURAL MATERIAL |
	Year	By	
Premolar, molar	1923	O. Zdansky	Choppers, scrapers, points, hammerstones, anvils, worked deer skulls (?drinking cups), bone "knives," traces of fire—ash layers, charred stone and wood.
Molar	1927	B. Bohlin	
Teeth and skull fragments	1927–28	B. Bohlin	
Skullcap	1929	W. C. Pei	
Portions of skulls, mandibles, teeth, limbs, 6 complete calva, 9 skull fragments, 6 pieces of facial bone, 15 mandibles, 152 teeth, 7 fragmented limb bones; 45 persons represented.	1929–37	W. C. Pei, D. Black, F. Weidenreich	
1 calvarium, 5 teeth, 1 mandible	1960s	Pei and others	
Locality 13 (one-half mile from Peking Cave) older than Locality 1; no human skeletal material.			Some stone tools and traces of fire.
Locality 15 (225 feet from Peking Cave) more recent than Locality 1; no human skeletal material.			Stone implements and traces of fire.

eggs, and perhaps killed and ate other Zhoukoudian individuals, although their practice of cannibalism is doubted by many scholars.

The evidence for this description comes from the many bones—human and nonhuman—found in the cave. The quantity of nonhuman bones in the cave suggests hunting. Some of the bones appear to have been burned, suggesting cooking skills. Skulls consisting mainly of brain cases and lacking facial and basal bones suggest (a) the use of brain cases as drinking bowls (Jia, 1975, p. 31); or (b) mutilation of the skull, including human skulls, in order to remove the brain for eating; or (c) using the skull as some sort of trophy or possibly in some ritualistic way.

Fragments of charred ostrich eggshells, the copious deposits of hackberry seeds unearthed in the cave, and the flourishing plant growth surrounding the cave, all suggest that the meat diet was supplemented by the gathering of herbs, wild fruits, tubers, and eggs. Layers of ash in the cave, over eighteen feet deep at one point, suggest fire and hearths, but whether Beijing hominids could actually *make* fire is unknown. Wu and Lin (1983) state that "Peking Man was a cave dweller, a fire user, a deer hunter, a seed gatherer and a maker of specialized tools" (p. 94). This leads them to suggest three social adaptations for the Zhoukoudian population:

1. Living in a group. Hunting large animals is "complicated, difficult, and hazardous," and cooperation of many individuals would be required; therefore, it is likely that Beijing hominids lived in a group when they began to hunt deer. (See pp. 446–447 for a discussion of this "hunting hypothesis.")

2. **Sexual division of labor.** Because of women's physiological constraints, it would be difficult for them to engage in hunting activities, which would then be left to the men. "The pattern of male hunters and female gatherers, which is common in hunting-and-gathering societies today, may have already been established" (p. 94).

3. **Education.** Tools during the more than 200,000 years that Peking *erectus* lived in Zhoukoudian became more sophisticated. This "suggests that the earliest practice of education may have taken place in Peking Man's cave" (p. 94). Each generation could not have developed new technological skills without having learned existing ones taught by the older generation.

Could the Zhoukoudian *erectus* speak? Their hunting and technological skills would suggest they possessed some kind of symbolic communication. If the skull was, in fact, used as a symbol as we have speculated, then symbolic communication is even more suggestive. However, this is a subject on which there is little agreement. Some anthropologists argue that the tools used by *H. erectus* assumes speech capability; others study the evolution of the skull and how the brain (e.g., Broca's area) was affected, and conclude speech began quite early in hominid evolution (Falk, 1987). Still others believe that speech did not originate until the Upper Paleolithic, or at least cannot be proved until then (Davidson and Noble, 1989). At this point, we agree with Falk when she says, "Unfortunately, what it is going to take to *settle* the debate about when language originated in hominids is a time machine. Until one becomes available, we can only speculate about this fascinating and important question" (1989, p. 141).

Did they wear clothing? Perhaps, since they manufactured awls, and one of the bone tools may be a needle. How long did they live? Studies of the fossil remains reveal that almost 40% of the bones belong to individuals under the age of 14, and 2.6% are estimated in the 50–60 age group (Jia, 1975, p. 43).

This picture of Zhoukoudian life has recently been challenged by archeologist Lewis Binford and colleagues (Binford and Ho, 1985; Binford and Stone, 1986a; Binford and Stone, 1986b).* Binford and his colleagues reject Beijing *erectus* as hunters and believe the evidence clearly points to them being scavengers. The controversy of early hominids as hunter or scavenger has engaged the attention of paleoanthropologists, taphonomists, archeologists, and other scientists, and the matter is not yet settled. Binford and his colleagues also do not believe that Beijing hominids were clearly associated with fire, except in the later phases of occupation (about 250,000 years ago).

Many anthropologists disagree with these conclusions, criticizing the methods of Binford and his supporters, the short time spent examining the specimens at Zhoukoudian, the relatively small (and probably atypical) sample of bones available at the time of their visit to the cave, their interpretation of the evidence, and their interpretation of the work of other anthropologists (see Bunn and Kroll, 1987, pp. 199–201). The evidence, at the present time, supports *H. erectus* as hunter and very likely as scavenger as well.

---

*Binford and Stone (1986) visited a number of hominid sites in China, spending several days at Zhoukoudian.

Cutmarks Marks made by predators' teeth as they gnaw on bones, or by humans as they cut into a carcass with a stone tool. It is possible to distinguish between the animal-inflicted cutmarks and tool-inflicted cutmarks.

(a)

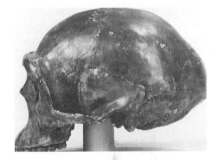

(b)

(c)

FIGURE 16-21 Peking Man (reconstructed cranium). (*a*) Frontal view; (*b*) lateral view; (*c*) rear view. The widest part of the skull is toward the bottom. The keeled effect can be seen in (*a*) and (*c*).

BOX 16-7 **The Making of Fire**

Reports of controlled fire used earlier than about 400,000 ya have come from sites in Africa, Asia, and Europe. It has been generally supposed that *H. erectus* (and, perhaps, even australopithecines) not only used fire for warmth, protection against predators, and cooking, but deliberately started them. Sillen and Brain (1990) are quite sure that *H. erectus* (about 1.6 mya) was responsible for the burnt bones found in the Swartkrans, South Africa, cave. Gowlett (1989) maintains his position that it is entirely possible, or certainly reasonable, that *H. erectus* deliberately ignited fire at Chesowanja, Kenya, about 1.4 mya. Until Binford's critique, almost everyone believed there was a long history of deliberate fire control at Zhoukoudien, beginning about one-half million years ago. Chinese archeologists are quite certain there is evidence of controlled fires in a number of sites in China.

The problem with determining the date of the origin of hominid fire-making is that any date earlier than about 400,000 is looked upon with scepticism by more than a few scientists who ask, *What is the evidence?* In a comprehensive review of the data dealing with early fire dates, James (1989) insists that the only positive evidence of such a fire is the presence of a hearth. He defines a hearth as

a circular or elliptical feature about 0.5 to 1.0 m* in diameter and 5 to 30 cm* deep that often contains charcoal, ash, burned soil, fire-cracked rock, and *possibly* charred bone and other organic matter (p. 20).

Hearths dating back more than 400,000 ya are hard to come by. They were believed to be present at Zhoukoudien but, as we have seen, Binford and others have criticized the evidence. There are those who believe that burnt bones (under certain conditions), artifacts, and faunal remains at a site may reasonably be considered a controlled-fire situation. Unfortunately, the possibility exists that bones and (even burnt) faunal remains may have been naturally burned by brush fires or lightning. Peters points out that

We have yet to accumulate a data base detailed and reliable enough to specify what we would in fact expect to see in the prehistoric record as evidence of natural vs. hominid-controlled fire without built features.† (1989, p. 18).

James believes (and we agree) there must be rigid tests and experiments to determine whether burnt material found at sites, especially earlier than 400,000 ya, indicates natural or deliberately ignited fires.

---

*m = meter; cm = centimeter
†Such as a buildup of ashes.

Peking is the best-known hominid fossil from China, and more work has been done at Zhoukoudian than at any other Chinese site—in fact, there is more material from this cave than from all the other Chinese sites combined. Nevertheless, there are other hominids worth noting. (See Table 16-2.)

Lantian   In 1963, at the village of Chenjiawo, about six miles northwest of Lantian in central China, investigators found an almost complete mandible, with several teeth, of an old woman. The mandible is quite similar to those from Zhoukoudian (Wu and Dong, 1985). However, this site has been dated at about 650,000 years and, if the dating is correct, would be older than Zhoukoudian.

The following year a partial cranium of a female over 30 years of age was discovered at Gongwangling, about 12 miles east of Lantian. A recent report gives a paleomagnetic date of 1.5–1.1 mya (others give a date of about 750,000 ya) for the fossil-bearing stratum in which the cranium was found (Zhou and Qing, 1989, p. 4). If the dating is correct, Gongwangling is considerably older than Peking; in fact, it would be the oldest Chinese fossil hominid. This correlates with the extraordinarily thick bones and small cranial capacity of 780 cm³. Wu (1980) believes it resembles the earliest robust specimen from Java.

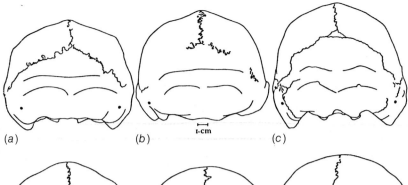

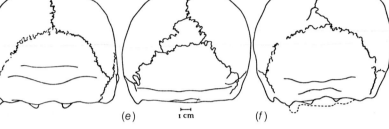

(a)   (b)   (c)

(d)   (e)   (f)

FIGURE 16-22   Views of: (a) *Homo erectus erectus* and (b) *Homo erectus pekinensis*; (c) the Solo XI skull; (d) the Rhodesian skull; (e) the Saccopastore skull; and (f) the skull of the Neandertal from La Chapelle-aux-Saints. Note the pentagonal shape of skulls in upper row compared to those of the Neandertal and Rhodesian skulls at widest point in the lower row. (From Weidenreich, 1951.) (See Chapter 17 for discussion of (d)–(f)

FIGURE 16-23   Tools used by Peking Man.

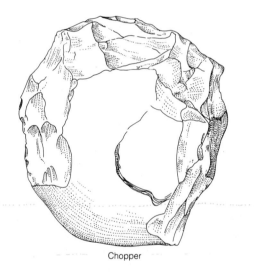

Chopper

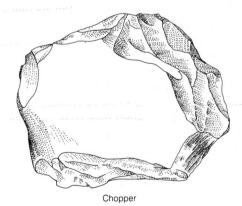

Chopper

Pointed tool

Discoidal scrapper

Broken bone (note deep incision made in the bone)

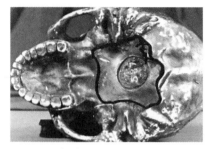

FIGURE 16-24   Cannibalism at Zhoukou-dian? The area around the foramen magnum appears to have been cut away—in order to remove the brain. Or was the base of the skull gnawed away by hyenas?

FIGURE 16-25   Lantian. A partial female cranium. This specimen may be older than Beijing fossils.

FIGURE 16-26   Fossil and archeological sites of *H. erectus* in China.

Hexian   In 1980, at Longtandong Cave in Anhui Province in eastern China, an IVPP team recovered the remains of several individuals. One of the specimens is a well-preserved cranium lacking much of its base. A mandibular fragment and four isolated teeth were also found. Additional remains were excavated the following year, including an incomplete skull cap and five isolated teeth.

The Hexian cranium resembles Peking, in that it has a cranial capacity of about 1025 cm³. Dated at less than 200,000 ya, it is not surprising that Hexian displays several advanced features lacking in the Zhoukoudian hominids. The postorbital constriction, for example, is not as pronounced, and certain temporal and occipital characteristics are "best compared with the later forms of *H. erectus* at Zhoukoudian such as are exemplified by Skull V from Locality 1" (Wu and Dong, 1985, p. 87).

Yuanmou   In 1965, two teeth, an upper right and a left central incisor, were discovered in Yuanmou County, northern Yunnan. The teeth resemble those of Locality 1, Zhoukoudian, except that these incisors appear to have two indentations that appear to be shoveled. At first, the teeth were dated at 1.7 mya, but further data show them to be in the 600,000–500,000 ya range.

We do not wish to leave the impression that Zhoukoudian Cave provides the only evidence for the way early humans lived in China. There is, in fact, a number of archeological sites considered to be as early as Zhoukoudian, and even earlier.

Early paleolithic stone tools have been found in such widely separated provinces as Hebei, Guizhou, Shanxi, Lantian, Beijing, Yunnan, and Liaoning (see map, Fig. 16-26). At present, there is little reason to believe that *H. erectus* culture in these provinces will differ much from Zhoukoudian.

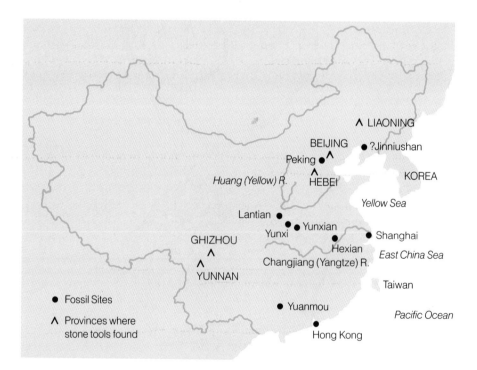

Traces of fire have been claimed for several of these sites as well as dates of a million or more years. However, serious questions have been raised about the dates (Aigner, 1981, 1986), and Binford (p. 483) has expressed doubts about the evidence for fire. With the rate of present research in China, more acceptable statements about the early life of *H. erectus* may be forthcoming in the next few years.

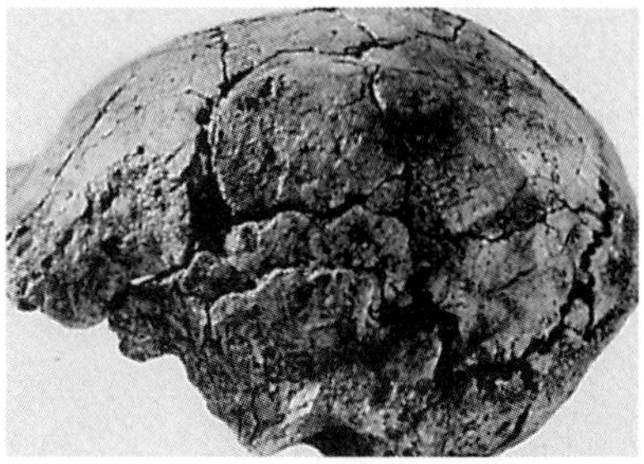

East Africa

Since 1959, with the discovery of "Zinj," East Africa has become the El Dorado of the search for ancient humans. A prodigious quantity of fossil hominid remains, many of them australopithecines, has been recovered, but an increasing number of *Homo* specimens have been excavated in recent years.

The remains of *H. erectus* have come from three East African areas: Olduvai Gorge, Tanzania; Lake Turkana, Kenya; and Bodo in Ethiopia. (See map, p. 488.)

OLDUVAI

As far back as 1960, Dr. Louis Leakey unearthed a skull at Olduvai (OH 9) that he identified as *H. erectus*. The skull of OH 9 from Upper Bed II has a massive cranium; it is faceless and has the largest cranial capacity (1067 cm³) of all the early *H. erectus* specimens. Dated at 1.2–1.1 my, this is indeed a large skull for that time period. The browridge is huge, the largest known for any hominid in both thickness and projection, but the vault walls are thin.

Also from Olduvai, from Bed IV of the Middle Pleistocene (dated at 0.83–0.62 my), comes a partial skull, OH 12, probably a female. It resembles OH 9, although the cranial capacity is considerably smaller—700–800 cm³. The small size may be due to sexual dimorphism; however, it is puzzling that a skull with similar morphology, and perhaps as much as a million years younger, should have 30% less cranial capacity.

LAKE TURKANA

Some 400 miles north of Olduvai Gorge, on the northern boundary of Kenya, is the finger lake—Lake Turkana. Excavated by Richard Leakey and colleagues since 1969, the eastern shore of the lake has been a virtual gold mine for australopithecines, *Homo habilis*, and a few *H. erectus* fossil remains.

Remains of several fossils were found at Koobi Fora, on the east side of Lake Turkana. Designated as KNM-ER 3733, 3883, and 1808, they have been dated from about 1.8 to 1.0 mya. They are considerably older than the *H. erectus* from Olduvai and their cranial capacity is significantly smaller (see Table 16-4).

In August of 1984, Kamoya Kimeu (see Fig. 14-29) with his uncanny knack for finding fossils, lived up to his reputation by discovering a small piece of skull near Richard Leakey's base camp on the west side of Lake Turkana. Leakey and his colleague, Alan Walker of Johns Hopkins University, excavated the site known as Nariokotome, in 1984 and then again in 1985.

FIGURE 16-27   The Hexian skull (lateral view). Similar to Peking Man, but note modified postorbital construction; occipital area does not appear as robust.

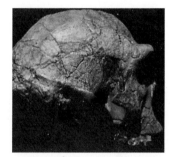

FIGURE 16-28   OH 9.

FIGURE 16-29   ER 3733.

FIGURE 16-30   *H. erectus* sites in East Africa.

The dig was a smashing success. The workers unearthed the most complete *H. erectus* yet found. Known properly as KNM-WT 15000,* the all but complete skeleton includes facial bones and most of the postcranial bones, a rare event indeed for *erectus*, since these bones are scarce at *H. erectus* sites. The completeness of the skeleton should help resolve some of the riddles associated with *H. erectus*. (See Fig. 16-32.)

Another remarkable feature of the find is its age. Its dating is based on the chronometric dates of the geologic formation in which the site is located and is set at about 1.6 million years. The fossil is that of a boy about 12 years of age and 5 feet 5 inches tall. Had he grown to maturity, his height, it is estimated, may have been 6 feet, taller than *H. erectus* was heretofore thought to be. Tentatively, the cranial capacity of WT15k** is estimated at 900 cm³, intermediate between OH 12 and OH 9. The postcranial bones appear to be quite similar, though not identical, to those of modern humans.

South Africa

In the late 1940s and 1950s at Swartkrans (see p. 426) Broom, Robinson, and others found fossil remains including a well-preserved mandible (SK 15), cranial parts, and fragments of other bones. These were assigned to *Telanthropus capen-*

FIGURE 16-31   Lake Turkana. Site of WT 15000.

---

*WT is the symbol for West Turkana; i.e., the west side of the lake. The east side of the lake is symboled as ER, East Rudolf, the former name of the lake (see p. 417).

**k is a symbol often used to indicate one thousand; 15k, therefore, indicates 15000.

TABLE 16-4 *H. erectus*, East Africa

SITE/AGE	DESIGNATION	MATERIAL	CRANIAL CAPACITY (CM³)	DISCOVERED[a] (DATE)	REMARKS
Olduvai[a]					
Tanzania					
Bed IV	OH 23	Mandible fragments		1968	
	OH 2	2 vault fragments		1935	
	OH 12	Cranial fragments		1962	
	OH 22	Right half of mandible		1968	
	OH 28	Pelvic bone, femur shaft		1970	
Bed III	OH 51	Left side of mandible		1974	
1.2 my	OH 9	Calvarium	1067	1960	Discovered by Louis Leakey
Lake Turkana[b]					
Koobi Fora, Turkana, Kenya					
1.65 my	KNM-ER 3883	Braincase, some facial bones	800	1974	
1.5–1.4 my	KNM-ER 730	Mandible lacking right side		1970–1980	
1.7 my	KNM-ER 1808	Skeletal and cranial elements		1973	
1.5 my	KNM-ER 3733	Well-preserved crania	850	1974	Discovered by B. Ngeneo, R. Leakey
West Turkana					
Nariokotome					
1.6 my	KNM-WT 15000	Almost complete skeleton	1200	1984	Most complete *erectus* yet found. Discovered by K. Kimieu, R. Leakey, Alan Walker

[a]Louis Leakey and Mary Leakey were directors of excavations at Olduvai when these finds were made.

[b]Richard Leakey is director of excavations at Lake Turkana.

sis, but later changed to *Homo* without a species designation. *Erectus* has been suggested (Brain, 1981, Sillen and Brain, 1990), but this has not yet been widely accepted.

North Africa

With evidence from China and Java, it appears clear that *H. erectus*, with superior tools and weapons and presumably greater intelligence than his predecessors, had expanded his habitat. The earliest evidence, 1.8 my, for *H. erectus* comes from

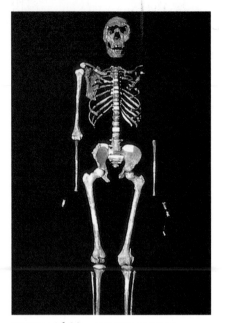

FIGURE 16-32   KMW-WT 15000. The most complete and oldest *H. erectus* yet found.

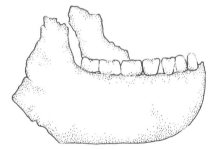

FIGURE 16-33   Ternifine mandible (Tighenif).

East Africa, and 500,000 to 400,000 years later (if the dating is correct) from Java. It is not surprising, therefore, that *H. erectus* migrations would have taken them to northwest Africa as well.

North African remains, almost all mandibles or mandible fragments, have been found in Algeria, at Ternifine (now Tighenif), and Morocco, at Sidi Abderrahman and Thomas Quarries. The three Ternifine mandibles and skull fragment, dated at roughly 700,000 ya are more archaic than the younger Moroccan material dated at about 500,000 ya.

In North Africa, then, we find a *H. erectus* population living from early Middle Pleistocene times (*circa* 700,000 ya) to about 500,000 ya. Unfortunately, there are no limb bones—only one cranium, and a few mandibles and teeth to help in classification or comparison with finds from other areas.

African forms considered to be members of *H. erectus* have been undergoing careful studies in the past few years, and many questions have been raised. There are those who believe the differences between the African forms and those from East Asia are great enough so that both cannot be placed in the same taxon. On the other hand, others see them as related, and one scholar finds, given the great distance between Africa and East Asia, that it is "surprising . . . that even greater distinctions are not apparent" (Rightmire, 1984, p. 96).

Europe

Until recently, a half dozen or so European fossil remains were considered to be *H. erectus*. However, many paleoanthropologists are persuaded that the fossils are not *H. erectus*. That is to say, *H. erectus* never made it to Europe. This may seem strange since we find *erectus* in northwest Africa, just across the Strait of Gibraltar. It would appear that *H. erectus*, in his emigration from Africa about 1.0 mya crossed over to the Near East and continued due east to eastern Asia. As we have seen, the trek continued until it reached Beijing to the north and Java to the south.

The fossils in Europe once assigned to *H. erectus* all display derived traits that associate them with *sapiens*. Not anatomically modern, to be sure, but a mosaic of primitive and late traits that mark them as archaic *sapiens*. It is a toss up whether we should deal with them in this chapter or the next, but the tendency in recent years is to place them among the *sapiens*, and we shall follow the trend. You will find these enigmatic fossils discussed in Chapter 17.

Human Emergence: *Australopithecus* to *Homo erectus*

EVOLUTION OF *H. ERECTUS*

Surveying hominid events of the Lower and Middle Pleistocene, we see the disappearance of australopithecines and early *Homo* (*H. habilis*) and the appearance of *H. erectus* populations, who expand their habitat beyond African boundaries. As we examine *H. erectus*, we find a number of changes that mark human evolution in several directions: *physical, technological, and social.*

FIGURE 16-34 *Homo erectus* in North Africa.

Physical   From the physical point of view, *H. erectus* is already notably similar to modern populations. The *erectus* femur/pelvis complex may be somewhat different from our own (Day, 1984; Kennedy, 1983), but if it were possible to observe *H. erectus* walking away from us, it is unlikely that we would observe a stride noticeably different from those around us. An *erectus* individual would not slouch forward and walk with bent knees. The stride would compare with ours; the arms would not be especially long, nor would they swing from side to side instead of front to back; and the legs would not be proportionately short. We would also note *erectus*' stature (recall that the recent find of a 12-year-old boy in West Turkana suggests an adult male height of 6 feet). This would have made *H. erectus* a walker far superior to australopithecines and *habilis*.

However, when we examine the skull, obvious differences emerge. The vault of the skull is low, not domelike as our own, and the forehead slopes back instead of up. A heavy ridge of bone over the eye is a feature remarkably different, as is the prominent projection in the tooth area of the face, and the receding chin. Although not the projecting nose of *H. sapiens*, the *erectus* nose was starting to change in that direction. At the back of the skull, the occipital bone angles sharply forward, and the widest part of the skull is much lower than it is in later hominids.

Changes in the skull, such as the heavy ridges of bone front and back, may have been due to the change in diet that emphasized chewing meat instead of softer plant foods. The brain was also evolving into one that was larger and more complex, a most important change in *erectus* evolution. This growth also had an effect on the contours of the skull.

Technological   Scholars have noted the remarkable stasis of the physical and cultural characteristics of *Homo erectus* populations, which seemed to change so little in the more than a million years of their existence. However, there were some changes; the brain of later *erectus* was larger, the nose more protrusive, the body not as robust, and there were modifications in their stone technology.

Growth of the brain especially enabled *H. erectus* to develop a more sophisticated tool kit. The important change in this kit was a core worked on both sides, called a *biface* (known widely as a handaxe, see Fig. 16-35). The biface has a flatter core than, and is a change from, the roundish earlier Oldowan pebble tool. The change enabled the stoneknapper to carefully shape the edges straighter and more sharply into a more efficient implement. This Acheulian stone tool became standardized as the basic *erectus* all-purpose tool, with some modification, for

FIGURE 16-35   Acheulian biface ("handaxe").

FIGURE 16-36 Small tools of Acheulian industry. (*a*) Side scraper; (*b*) point; (*c*) end scraper; (*d*) burin.

FIGURE 16-37 Acheulian cleaver.

more than a million years. It served to cut, scrape, pound, dig, and more—a most useful tool that has been found in Europe, Africa, and Asia.

Like their species elsewhere, *H. erectus* in China manufactured choppers and chopping tools as their core tools, and like other *erectus* toolmakers, fashioned scrapers and other small tools (see Fig. 16-36), but they did not manufacture bifaces (handaxes).

In the early days, toolmakers employed a stone hammer (simply an ovoid-shaped stone about the size of an egg or a bit larger) to percuss flakes from the core, thus leaving deep scars. Later, they put to use other materials such as wood and bone. They learned to use these new materials in the manufacture of softer hammers, which gave them more control over the flaking. These left shallow scars, sharper edges, and a more symmetrical form that appears to us to be esthetically more pleasing. Toward the end of the Acheulian industry, toolmakers blocked out a core with stone hammers, and then switched to wood or bone for refining the edges. This produced more elegant appearing and pear-shaped implements.

Also introduced by *H. erectus* was the cleaver (Fig. 16-37). Instead of coming to a point, like the handaxe, one end of the cleaver was blunted, giving the appearance of a modern axe head. It was probably used in the butchering—chopping and breaking the bones—of large animals.

Evidence of butchering is widespread in *H. erectus* sites and, in the past, has been associated with hunting. However, this assumption has been challenged, especially by archeologists (p. 483) who believe the evidence does not prove the hunting hypothesis, but believe instead that *erectus* was primarily a scavenger. However, the evidence does not yet prove the scavenger hypothesis either, and for the time being we shall discuss *H. erectus* as a hunter and scavenger.

Social One of the fascinating qualities of *H. erectus* was a penchant for travel. From the relatively close confines of East Africa, *erectus* became a world traveler, and by the time *H. sapiens* appears, 1 million years later, *H. erectus* had trekked to vast points of the earth. Moving north from East Africa, *erectus* could have chosen

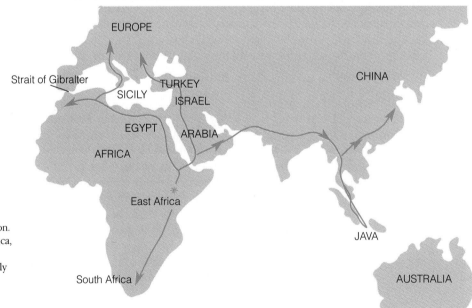

FIGURE 16-38 The *H. erectus* expansion. Assuming *H. erectus* originated in East Africa, the map illustrates emigration routes to northwest Africa, eastern Asia, and probably South Africa.

several directions. One was eastward over the land bridge that joined East Africa at that time to the Arabian Peninsula. Land bridges were exposed in many areas of the world during glacial times, when so much ocean water was locked up in the glacial ice.

The life of hunters/scavengers is nomadic and the woodland and savanna that covered the southern tier of Asia bordering the Indian Ocean, from East Africa to Southeast Asia, would have been an excellent environment for *H. erectus*, similar to the econiche of his African ancestors. As the population grew, small groups budded off the band and moved farther ahead to find their own hunting area. This process, repeated again and again, led *erectus* east to India and, with mountains to the north, through the southern route across the Sunda shelf (Fig. 16-39) to Java, arriving there several hundred thousand years later.

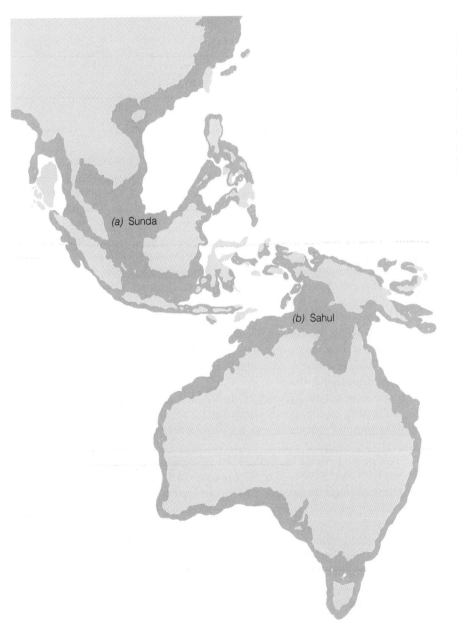

(a) Sunda

(b) Sahul

FIGURE 16-39   Sunda and Sahul. (The names given to the continental shelves of Southeast Asia and Australia.) (*a*) The Sunda shelf is a land mass that, during glacial times, formed a bridge joining the Asian continent to what are now separate islands. The map clearly shows that *H. erectus* could have walked on land from the continent to Java. (*b*) The Sahul shelf of Australia is separated from Sunda by a group of islands known as Wallacea (named for A. R. Wallace, p. 25), which was not crossed by humans until the time of *H. sapiens sapiens*.

TABLE 16-5   *Homo erectus* Sites*

Asia	
Java	Trinil, Modjokerto, Sangiran, Sambungmacan
China	Zhoukoudian, Lantian, Hexian, Yuanmou

Africa	
North Africa	Ternifine, Algeria
	Rabat, Morocco
	Salé, Morocco
	Casablanca, Morocco
East Africa	Olduvai Gorge, Tanzania
	East Turkana, Kenya
	West Turkana, Kenya
South Africa	Swartkrans

*This is not a complete listing.

Once in Java, it would have been impossible to take a further step, since there was no land bridge that joined Australia to Java. However, it would have been possible to push north through Malaysia, Thailand, skirt the northern mountains, and travel east to southern China, where Lantian *erectus* lived 700,000 to 800,000 ya or perhaps as much as 1.0 mya.

Why did *H. erectus* leave home? We will never know for certain, but there were climatic and geographic changes that may have been responsible. It was a time of heavy precipitation, which fell as snow in the Northern Hemisphere and created the great glaciers of Europe and North America. In tropical areas, heavy rainfall produced rivers, lakes, and new grasslands. With additional food sources available, a population increase may have led splinter groups to seek their own areas.

If the new groups succeeded, eventually other small groups may have budded off these, and so the process continued as *erectus* moved farther and farther away from their ancestral home, ultimately reaching Java and China to the east, and northwest Africa to the west.

We have now covered *H. erectus* in Africa and Asia. We have also discussed some of the physical changes that occurred in the evolution of *H. erectus* from the preceding hominid species. Can we account for at least some of these physical and cultural changes?

It has been suggested that meat became a regular and dependable (rather than opportunistic) part of the diet, replacing some of the more difficult-to-chew plant foods that had been dietary staples. Technological changes may have provided tools used for pounding and chopping meat to make it softer and easier to chew.

The change in diet, from tough foods to meat and softer foods, produced further changes in the skull. The load on posterior teeth decreased, making for smaller back teeth, and the load on front teeth increased, resulting in their somewhat larger size. In addition, muscles operating the jaw and the forces operating on the skull developed front and back buttressing; i.e., the supraorbital torus and the nuchal torus that provide reinforcement for the chewing and neck muscles. It is difficult to prove this scenario, but it does explain some of the changes in the *H. erectus* period.

When we look back at the evolution of *H. erectus*, we realize how significant were this early human's achievements toward *hominization*. It was *H. erectus* who increased in body size with more efficient bipedalism; who embraced culture wholeheartedly as a strategy of adaptation; whose brain was reshaped and increased in size to within *sapiens* range; who became a more efficient scavenger and likely hunter with greater dependence on meat (which in turn reduced jaw and posterior teeth size); who apparently established more or less permanent living sites, probably some sort of social organization, such as family and band; and who may have used fire extensively. In short, it was *H. erectus*, committed to bipedalism and a cultural way of life, who transformed hominid evolution to human evolution.

Summary

Homo erectus, representing the second grade of human evolution, lived from about 1.6 mya to about 200,000 ya, a period of almost 1.5 million years. The first finds were made by Dubois in Java, and later discoveries have come from China and Africa.

Differences from australopithecines are notable in *H. erectus*' larger and reproportioned brain, taller stature, and changes in facial structure and skull buttressing. The long period of *erectus* existence was marked by a remarkably uniform technology over space and time, probably due to the limitations of their brain, which was still considerably smaller than the *sapiens* brain. Nevertheless, *H. erectus* introduced more sophisticated tools and probably new or deliberately altered food using the new tools and perhaps fire. They were also able to move into different environments and successfully adapt to new conditions.

Apparently originating in East Africa, *H. erectus* migrated in several directions: south and northwest Africa, and then east to Java and China. The evidence from China, especially Zhoukoudian, supports an *erectus* way of life that included hunting and the controlling of fire, but note that there is not complete agreement about this.

It is generally assumed that *H. erectus* evolved to *H. sapiens* since many fossils, such as Ngandong, (and others discussed in the next chapter) display both *erectus* and *sapiens* features. There remain questions about *H. erectus* behavior (e.g., Did they hunt?), about evolution to *H. sapiens* (e.g., Was it gradual or rapid?), about *sapiens*'s ancestor (Was it *erectus* or a different species?). The search for answers continues.

Questions for Review

1. Describe the Pleistocene in terms of (a) temperature and (b) the dating of fossil hominids.
2. Why is paleomagnetism more useful than other methods in dating the earth's history?

TABLE 16-6 **Fossil Briefs**

FOSSIL	DATE FOUND	SITE	DATING
Ngandong *(Homo soloensis)*	1931 by W.F.F. Oppenoorth, a mining engineer	In the Ngandong Beds, Solo River Valley, Java	Estimates: Late middle Pleistocene; early Upper Pleistocene.
Java erectus *(Homo erectus erectus)*	1891. Two military engineers working under Eugene Dubois unearthed a skullcap. A femur was discovered the following year. Whether the femur belongs to the skullcap is still being debated.	On the banks of the Solo River, Central Java, near the town of Trinil.	The finds are believed to belong in the Kabuh formation, Middle Pleistocene, about 500,000 ya. The geology is complex and the fossil dating approximate.
Beijing erectus *(Homo erectus pekinensis)*	Under the supervision of W. C. Pei, an adolescent calvaria (skull minus face and jaws)—skull III—was discovered in 1929. Earlier finds of teeth and skull parts were found by Andersson, Zdansky, and Bohlin.	Locality 1 in the lower cave near the town of Zhoukoudian, 25 miles southeast of Beijing.	The original find has been dated at 450,000 ya to 400,000 ya. The site was probably occupied until 230,000 ya.
Hexian	1980 by IUPP palaeontologist Huang Wanbo and others. More remains were found in 1981.	Longtandong Cave, Hexian County, Anhui Province.	280–240,000 ya
Lantian	A field team from the Institute of Vertebrate Palaeontology in Beijing found Lantian fossils in 1963 and 1964.	1963: Chenjiawo (about 6 miles northwest of Lantian in central China). 1964: Gongwangling (about 12 miles east of Lantian).	Chanjiawo is now dated at 650,000 ya. There are three different paleo-magnetic dates given the older Gongwangling: 800–750,000 ya; 1.0 mya; and 1.5 mya. The latest date is probably the most accurate.
KNM-WT 15000	August, 1984, by Kamoya Kimeu under the direction of Richard Leakey, National Museums of Kenya.	South bank of the Nariokotome River on the west side of Lake Turkana.	Found in lake sediments immediately above Okote Tuff, which has been dated at 1.6 mya. The date for KNM-WT 15000 has been placed at 1.6 mya.

MATERIAL	TRAITS	ASSOCIATED FINDS	CRANIAL CAPACITY (cm³)
A total of 15 calvariae or skull fragments (male and female) and 2 tibiae.	Bones of skulls are thick, supraorbital torus separated at center, sloping forehead, and prominent occipital torus. Occipital area displays some early *sapiens* features and the sidewalls of the skull tend to turn in, resembling a *sapiens* characteristic.	A few stone implements, stone balls. Many mammalian bones of deer; also bones of pig, rhinoceros, and hippopatamus.	1150–1300
Skullcap and femur are the significant finds.	Skullcap. Thick bones, heavy supraorbital torus, postorbital constriction, saggital keel.	No artifacts were discovered.	900–940 (estimate)
Skulls, skull parts, mandibles, and parts of the skeleton.	Supraorbital torus, nuchal torus, postorbital constriction, saggital keel, alveolar prognathism, shoveled upper incisors, greatest breadth toward the bottom of the skull, flat skull vault. Mandibles are Chinese, robust, and with multiple mental foramina.	Many artifacts: choppers and chopping tools, scrapers, points, burins, and awls. Bone horn were also utilized as material for tools, the presence of hearths and ash have been questioned, as has the use and control of fire.	1089 (average)
1980: Calvaria, mandibular fragment, 4 teeth. 1981: frontal bone, parietal fragment, 5 teeth. (Remains represent several individuals)	Low cranial vault, flattened frontal bones, developed supraorbital torus, saggital crest, angulated occiput, and maximum cranial breadth low on the skull. Postorbital constriction is not as pronounced as early Zhoukoudian and several other advanced features suggest comparison with later skulls from Zhoukoudian, such as Skull V. Considering the late date of Hexian, the advanced features and large cranial capacity is not surprising.	Artifacts made of bone and hearth. Mammalian fauna of 47 species.	1025
Chenjiawo consists of a well-preserved mandible with several teeth of an old woman. Gongwangling consists of a calvarium (skull minus the jaw) of a female over 30 years of age.	The mandible resembles mandibles from Zhoukoudian; Gongwangling resembles the earlier Java specimens.	Chopping tools, cores, and flakes were found at both sites. Mammalian fauna were also found at both sites.	778 for Gongwangling.
An almost complete skeleton of a young male. On the basis of the dentition and unfused state of the epiphyses (they fuse at 18–20 years), the age is given at about 12.	Skull is larger than KNM-ER 3733 of about the same time period, suggesting sexual dimorphism; skull bone is thick, mandible is chinless. Stature based on long bones is 5 feet 7 inches and estimated at 6 feet at maturity. Bones are basic *H. erectus*.	No artifacts. Fish bones associated with the skeleton; mammal bones found at nearby sites.	1200

3. Describe *H. erectus*. How is *H. erectus* anatomically different from australo-pithecines? From *H. sapiens*?
4. As you look at the rear view of the *H. erectus* skull, what do you see as a significant feature? Explain.
5. What are the significant features of the cultural life of *H. erectus*?
6. What was the intellectual climate in Europe in the latter half of the nineteenth century, especially concerning human evolution?
7. Why was there so much opposition to Dubois' interpretation of the hominid fossils he found in Java?
8. Why do you think Peking *erectus* was enthusiastically accepted whereas Java Man was not?
9. What questions are still being asked about Dubois' finds? Explain.
10. What new ideas did Dubois suggest about human evolution?
11. Why did Dubois reject placing Java Man and Peking Man into one species, *Homo erectus*?
12. How does the Peking *erectus* physically differ from the Java *erectus*? How do you account for these differences?
13. Describe Peking *erectus*' way of life as suggested in the text. What objections have been made about this?
14. How do Binford's views differ from the more traditional views?
15. *Homo erectus* is called the first human. Why?
16. What is the *H. erectus* evidence from Africa, and what questions of human evolution does the evidence raise?
17. Summarize the evolutionary events (physical and cultural) of the Middle Pleistocene.
18. As a lad of 12, what *erectus* features does KNM-WT 15000 already display?
19. Cite as many reasons as you can why KNM-WT 15000 is important.
20. Can you suggest any reasons why the earliest remains of *H. erectus* have come from East Africa?
21. *H. erectus* migrated to various points in Africa and vast distances to east Asia. What does this tell you about this species?
22. What kind of stone tools have been found at *erectus* sites.
23. How and for what functions were these tools used?
24. Why do we "owe so much" to *H. erectus*?

Suggested Further Reading

Bordes, François. *The Old Stone Age*, New York: McGraw-Hill Book Co., 1968.
   A thorough account of the culture of the Old Stone Age or Paleolithic based mainly on stone tools. Many excellent drawings clearly illustrate the kinds of stone tools used by Paleolithic people.
Brace, C. Loring, Harry Nelson, and Noel Korn. *Atlas of Human Evolution* (2nd Ed.), New York: Holt, Rinehart and Winston, Inc., 1979.
   Essentially a manual of illustrations of fossil hominids carefully drawn under the supervision of Professor Brace. Background material given for each fossil illustrated.
Gowlett, John. *Ascent to Civilization.* New York: Alfred A. Knopf, 1984.
   Dr. Gowlett has written an easy-to-read account of human evolution with beautiful photographs, maps, charts, and drawings. There are several chapters on *H. erectus*, but the entire book is worth examination. Highly recommended for quick overview of human evolution.

Howell, F. Clark. *Early Man* (Life Nature Library), New York: Time, Inc., 1965.

    Many fine photographs and illustrations. Written under the direction of one of the leading scholars on fossil hominids. This volume includes a discussion of Torralba/Ambrona with illustrations.

Leakey, Richard E., and Roger Lewin. *Origins*, New York: E. P. Dutton, 1977.

    This work is well written and contains beautiful photographs and line drawings. Richard Leakey, son of Louis and Mary Leakey, and his co-author have written an excellent book on ancient hominids and their culture. It will serve the student well as a reference work and is an interesting book to read in the bargain.

Lewin, Roger. *Human Evolution; An Illustrated Introduction*, Boston: Blackwell Publications, 1989.

    Lewin has brought an earlier edition up to date. The subtitle explains the book, which includes a discussion of evolution, human fossils, and culture. There is also useful discussion of mtDNA.

Reader, John. *Missing Links*, London: Penguin Books, 1988.

    A first edition brought up to date. The book is well written and includes well-known fossils, one to a chapter. There is also a discussion of mtDNA. Recommended.

Shapiro, Harry L. *Peking Man*, New York: Simon and Schuster, 1975.

    Dr. Shapiro has been associated with the study of Peking Man for many years in his position as chairman of the Department of Anthropology at The American Museum of Natural History. In this book, he writes in detail of the discovery of Peking Man and the disappearance of the original material. A scientific whodunit.

White, Edmund, and Dale Brown. *The First Men* (The Emergence of Man Series, Time-Life Books), New York: Time, Inc., 1973.

    A fascinating review of *Homo erectus* with excellent illustrations and photos. Very helpful for understanding *Homo erectus*.

Von Koenigswald, G.H.R. *Meeting Prehistoric Man*, New York: Harper & Brothers, 1956.

    Written for the layman by one of the foremost discoverers of fossil hominids in Java. Although not up to date, it is well worth reading for its authentic data on Java finds.

Homo Sapiens

Contents

The Nature
of Science

A surprising number of people are interested in their ancestry, and in recent years personal geneology research has become a popular pastime. People have made special trips abroad to examine church records and gravestones, hoping to find clues to centuries-old ancestors. Paleoanthropologists are also interested in ancestry, but their concern is with thousands, not hundreds, of years. Anthropological interest in modern human origins is more than a hundred years old and probably constitutes the foremost paleoanthropological research effort of the past decade.

In the last century, the search for our "roots" consisted of a two-hypothesis investigation by the monogenists and polygenists (p. 186). Today, there are three hypotheses that deal with the origin of modern humans. They are known as: (1) multiple regional or local continuity; (2) single origin, displacement, or recent African evolution; and (3) Afro-European *sapiens* or Out-of-Africa. The last hypothesis is, to some extent, a combination of the first two. (See Smith et al., 1989.)

Instead of introducing these hypotheses, which are discussed in the chapter, we pose this question: Scientists have been researching the problem of modern human origins for more than a hundred years, why is it taking such a long time to settle the matter? The answer can be found in the nature of the scientific method.

When a scientist presents a hypothesis, it is carefully studied by other scientists who are specialists in the same field. It is an obligation of qualified scientists to attempt to falsify the hypothesis—that is, to point out any errors that might be in it. If no errors are found, the hypothesis is on

its way to becoming a theory. However, if errors *are* found—and they often are—then the hypothesis must be modified in some way that will make it more acceptable. The scientist may rework the hypothesis by correcting errors, adding new evidence, or changing interpretations. The hypothesis is then again presented and the process repeated. This may go on for years (especially if the subject is an important concern of the discipline) with the hypothesis, ideally, becoming more and more valid.

It is possible that other scientists in the same field may present competitive hypotheses. This may resolve the matter, or the process may become more complicated as other professionals in the field line up on one side or the other. In the case of modern human origins, there are three hypotheses to choose from, one or none of which may become acceptable, and there are reasons why a consensus has not been reached. First of all, there is the relative paucity and condition of bones. For some sites there are no bones beyond a couple of teeth or fragments of skull, and sometimes no bones at all. Secondly, there is the matter of dating the osteological and archeological material. Dating techniques have certainly improved in the past 50 years, but radiometric dating systems are not always trustworthy and sometimes even contradict one another. Without the evidence of bones, trying to arrive at something as complex as the origin of moderns is like building a wooden house without wood. And working without dates is like working without a house plan—no one knows where the bedrooms, bath, or kitchen belong. Thirdly, there is the question of interpreting the evidence. Given their vary-

ing experiences and insights, it is not surprising that scholars do not always agree. In fact, that they do not agree is an important factor in the falsification process and maintains the momentum toward reaching a valid statement. Ideally, as more evidence is found, the number of disagreements should diminish and, ultimately, a consensus reached.

Unfortunately, the circumstances surrounding the recovery of material thousands and hundreds of thousands of years old (not to mention millions of years for *H. erectus* and *Australopithecus*) are such that we will never really have enough evidence or accurate dating to develop a precise date and account of the origin of anatomically moderns. Developing a consensual hypothesis may never occur, at least in the foreseeable future, and it certainly will not be an easy assignment in any case.

The aim of science is to present as valid a statement about nature as can be made. If such a statement is not acceptable to a consensus of qualified scientists, then the statement remains in a hypothetical limbo. The process we have described is a necessary and valuable quality of the scientific method. If it appears to be taking an unnecessarily long time to resolve the question of modern human origins, then clearly the hypotheses that have been offered over so many years are faulty.

It would be gratifying, of course, if paleoanthropologists could agree on *one* hypothesis for modern human origins, but the nature of science thwarts such an effort. Too many gaps in the evidence, too many conflicting dates, and too many missing bones are formidable obstacles to simple answers.

CHAPTER 17

Introduction

In the preceding chapter we noted that *H. erectus* was present in Africa more than 1.5 mya. A million years later, give or take a few hundred thousand years, *H. erectus* could also be found in Java and China. We also noted that *erectus* fossils have not been found in Europe. Nevertheless, it is quite likely that *H. erectus* migrated to Europe (several routes could easily have provided access) since a number of fossils have been found in Europe, as well as in Africa, China, and probably Java, that display both *erectus* and *sapiens* features.

These forms, for the most part, fall into the latter half of the Middle Pleistocene, from about 400 to 130 kya* and are often referred to as archaic *sapiens*, early *sapiens*, or transitional forms. The term *sapiens* is applied since the appearance of *sapiens* traits suggests an evolutionary trend toward the *sapiens* stage. Since it appears they are evolving toward anatomically modern human beings,† but have not yet attained that stage of grace, we shall list them as archaic *sapiens*. To organize the material covering these several hundred thousand years, we shall divide the archaic *sapiens* into early archaic and Neandertals.

In this chapter, then, we shall examine the course of human evolution in the Middle Pleistocene and Upper Pleistocene.‡ The chapter is divided into two parts: archaic *sapiens* and *H. sapiens* (anatomically moderns). This scheme is somewhat simplistic given the problems of classifying evolving hominids, but it will serve as an adequate device for dealing with the emergence of the *H. sapiens* grade of human evolution.

Archaic Forms: Archaic *sapiens*

Early archaics made some advances toward the *sapiens* stage. These advances beyond *H. erectus* are reflected in brain expansion; increased parietal breadth (the basal portion of the skull is no longer the widest area) and, therefore, the rear view of the skull is no longer pentagonal; decrease in size of molars and increase in size of anterior teeth; and general decrease in cranial and postcranial robusticity.

Archaic *sapiens* are found on the three continents of Africa, Asia, and Europe. In Europe, the well-known Neandertals are included in this category. (Neandertals are not found anywhere except Europe and western Asia.) In our discussion, we shall start with the archaic *sapiens* of Africa.

---

*kya = thousand years ago. The symbol k is commonly used to stand for thousand.

†Anatomically modern will be abbreviated as a.m.

‡Included in this chapter are well-known fossils or those that help explain human evolution of the late Middle and Upper Pleistocene. A complete listing is not intended.

BOX 17-1

Comparison of *Homo sapiens sapiens* and *H. erectus*

Homo sapiens differs from *H. erectus* in a number of characteristics.* In *H. sapiens sapiens*:

1. The skull is larger with a 1350 cm³ mean cranial capacity
2. Muscular ridges in the cranium are not strongly marked
3. The forehead is rounded and vertical
4. The supraorbital ridges are not well developed and do not form a continuous and uninterrupted torus

5. The occipital region is rounded and the nuchal area is relatively small
6. Mastoid process is prominent and of a pyramidal shape
7. The calvaria is of maximum width, usually in the parietal region
8. Jaws and teeth are relatively small
9. Maxilla has concave surface including a canine fossa
10. The chin is distinct
11. Limb bones are relatively slender and slight

*For a fuller definition see Howell, 1978, p. 201ff.

FIGURE 17-1   Sites of archaic *sapiens*, including Neandertals.

AFRICA

In Africa, change toward the *sapiens* grade can be seen at several sites. One of the best known is Broken Hill (Kabwe).* Found in a shallow Broken Hill mine shaft, at Kabwe, Zambia, South Africa, were a complete cranium and other cranial and postcranial material belonging to several individuals.

*See Box 17-5 for details of some of the fossils discussed in this chapter.

Mixture of older and later traits can be seen in this fossil material. The skull's massive supraorbital torus (one of the largest of any hominid), low vault, and prominent occipital torus recall those of *H. erectus*. On the other hand, the occipital is less angulated, the vault bones thinner, and the cranial base essentially modern. A cranial capacity of 1280 cm³ is significantly beyond the *erectus* average of 1000 cm³. A surprising aspect of Broken Hill's dentition is that most of its teeth suffered from a modern problem: cavities. This is especially odd since caries in fossil teeth are rare because sugar was not used until the advent of agriculture, about 15 kya. Dating estimates of Broken Hill have ranged throughout the Middle Pleistocene and Upper Pleistocene, but recent estimates have given dates in the neighborhood of 130 kya.

Resembling Broken Hill in some features is Elandsfontein from South Africa. Elandsfontein is dated at later Middle Pleistocene (Fig. 17-4).

Discovered in 1976 in northeast Ethiopia, in the general area where Lucy was found (see Chapter 14), is an incomplete cranium (Bodo) dating from the Middle Pleistocene. Like Broken Hill, to which it has been compared, the skull displays a mixture of *H. erectus* and more modern features. Bodo's classification is also murky. It has been called *H. erectus* and also archaic *sapiens*; i.e., transitional between *H. erectus* and a.m. humans.

There are several interesting points associated with Bodo. Some evidence suggests that animals were butchered at the site. Acheulian tools (see Fig. 17-5c) are associated with several hippopotamus skeletons, and cutmarks are found on the human skull (Conroy et al., 1978).

White (1986) examined the skull and counted 17 cutmark areas. These are located in the interorbital area, on the supraorbital torus, cheek bones, and on the posterior parietals. White believes this argues "for a patterned intentional defleshing of this specimen by a hominid(s) with (a) stone tool(s)" (White, 1986, p. 508). That is to say, Bodo was scalped, and this is the earliest solid evidence for deliberate defleshing (see Fig. 17-6, *a* and *b*).

Three other crania plus four more from Elandsfontein (Saldanha), Florisbad from South Africa, Laetoli near Olduvai Gorge, and Eliye Springs from West Turkana also show a combination of *erectus* and *sapiens* characteristics (p. 506), and they are mentioned as being similar to Broken Hill. These similarities may signify a phylogenetic relationship of hominids from East and South Africa. It is also possible that several populations were evolving in a somewhat similar way from *H. erectus* to a.m. humans.

We should point out that the evolutionary path of these hominids did not take a Neandertal turn. It seems there were no Neandertals in Africa. Nor were there any in the Far East.

ASIA

China   Like their counterparts in Europe and Africa, Chinese archaic *sapiens* also display both older and later characters. Chinese paleoanthropologists believe that archaic *sapiens* traits, such as sagittal keeling, flattened nasal bones, shovel-shaped incisors, and others, are shared with *H. erectus*, especially those from Zhoukoudian. They also point out that some of these features can be found in modern *H. sapiens* in China today, indicating substantial phylogenetic continuity. That is to say, a.m. Chinese evolved separately from other *H. sapiens* in Europe or Africa.

FIGURE 17-2   Sites of African archaic *sapiens*.

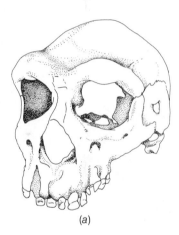

(a)

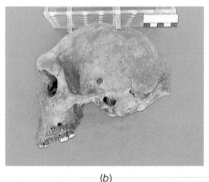

(b)

FIGURE 17-3   (*a*) Broken Hill (Rhodesian Man), Kabwe. Note very heavy supraorbital torus; (*b*) photograph of original.

Examples of Later African Archaic Sapiens

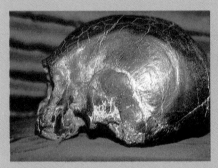

Eliye Springs, West Turkana, Kenya, East Africa

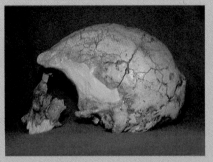

Laetoli 18, south of Olduvai Gorge, Tanzania, East Africa

Florisbad, Orange Free State, South Africa

African archaic *sapiens* who are approaching modern *sapiens*. Can you distinguish archaic from modern traits?

Map of late archaics.

That such regional evolution occurred in many areas of the world or, alternatively, that a.m. migrants from Africa displaced local populations is the subject of a major ongoing debate in paleoanthropology. This will be discussed later in the chapter.

Dali, with the most complete skull of the late Middle or early Upper Pleistocene fossils in China, displays *erectus* and *sapiens* traits and is clearly classified as archaic *sapiens* despite its relatively small cranial capacity of 1120 cm³. Changyang fragments, Ixujiayao material, the partial skull from Maba, and the almost complete skeleton from Jinniushan (Yingkou), with a surprising cranial capacity of

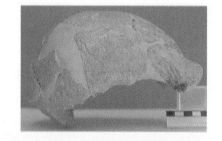

FIGURE 17-4 Elandsfontein, South Africa.

(a)

FIGURE 17-5 A Middle Pleistocene butchering site at Olorgesaile, Kenya, excavated by Louis Leakey who had the catwalk [(a) and (b)] built for observers. (c) is a closeup view of the Acheulian tools, mainly handaxes, found at the site. Acheulian tools were also found at the Bodo site.

(c)

(b)

FIGURE 17-6 (*a*) Bodo. An early archaic *sapiens* from Africa. (*b*) View from above. Note the cutmarks on the floor of the eye orbit and on the cheekbones. (Courtesy of Tim White)

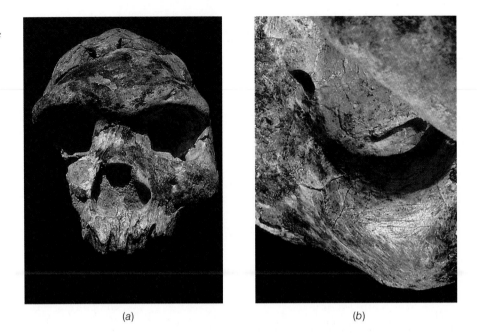

(a) (b)

FIGURE 17-7 Sites of Chinese archaic *sapiens*.

1335 cm³ (Lu, 1989, p. 2), also reflect earlier and later traits and are placed in the same category as Dali.

According to present dating, Chinese archaic *sapiens* lived from about 260 kya to 100 kya. Studies of the specimens continue, including the dating, which ranges from late Middle Pleistocene to early Upper Pleistocene. The evolutionary sequence will be clearer when the fossil dates are more secure. Nevertheless, what we observed in Africa, the apparent evolution from *H. erectus* to archaic *sapiens*, with a mosaic of *erectus* and *sapiens* traits, was also the case in China.

India In 1982 a partial skull (Fig. 17-10) was discovered in the Narmada Valley, near Hathnora, Madyha Pradesh, Central India. Associated with the fossil were Acheulian handaxes, cleavers, flakes, and choppers. It was originally identified as *H. erectus*. However, a more recent examination by K.A.R. Kennedy suggests there are more *H. sapiens* than *erectus* traits, and Narmada should be considered an archaic *sapiens*. Kennedy assigns a late Middle or early Upper Pleistocene age, which would place this specimen in the 100 kya range (Kennedy, 1990, p. 249).

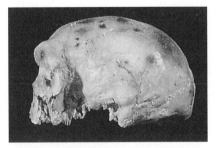

FIGURE 17-8 Dali. A good example of Chinese archaic *sapiens*.

FIGURE 17-9 Maba. Once identified as *H. erectus*, but is now considered an archaic *sapiens*.

For a number of years, Professor Otto Schoetensack, a Heidelberg University paleontologist, had been observing the commercial operations at a sandpit near the village of Mauer, six miles southeast of the university town. Because of the Tertiary and Pleistocene strata, Schoetensack had arranged with the owner of the sandpit that all bones uncovered in the ancient strata during the operation be donated to the University. The sandpit had yielded hundreds of mammalian bones, but for twenty years Schoentensack waited in vain for a human fossil. It was not until October 21, 1907, that Herr Rosch, the sandpit owner, sent a thrilling message to the patient professor:

> For twenty years you have been making efforts to find traces of primitive men in my sandpit in order to prove human be-

ings lived in this district at the same time as the mammoth. Yesterday we came across this proof. Sixty-five feet below ground level at the bottom of my sandpit the lower jawbone of a prehistoric man was found, in a very good state of preservation (in Wendt, 1963, p. 442).

Schoetensack named the jaw *Homo heidelbergensis*, which raised the hackles of many European scientists who were either still opposed to the idea of evolution or did not believe the Mauer jaw belonged to the genus *Homo*. However, the furor lacked the passionate spirit of Dubois' time and may have helped justify Dubois' views.

EUROPE

Various attempts have been made to organize European archaic *sapiens* of the Middle and early Upper Pleistocene. Because in many cases definite dates or adequate remains (or both) are lacking, it is difficult to be certain which fossils belong where in the evolutionary sequence. *H. erectus* may once have roamed the fields of Europe, but there are no fossils that unequivocally prove it. What we find in Europe are fossils, such as those in Africa and China, whose features resemble both *erectus* and *sapiens*. Among some of these archaic European *sapiens* there are features resembling those of Neandertals, which leads to the possibility that some of these forms were the ancestors of Neandertals.

It may be possible to divide the fossils of the Middle Pleistocene into two groups (see Table 17-1): an older one that tends to be morphologically closer to

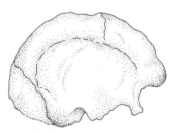

FIGURE 17-10   Outline of Narmada partial cranium.

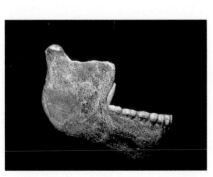

(a)

(b)

FIGURE 17-11   (*a*) Cast of Mauer; (*b*) map of Mauer site, near Heidelberg.

FIGURE 17-12   Map of European early archaic *sapiens*.

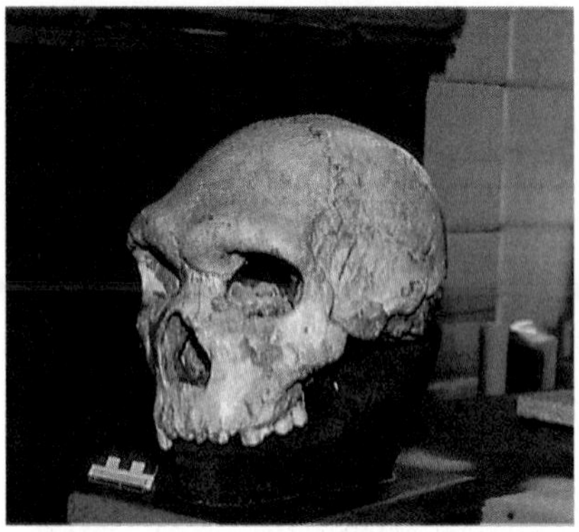

FIGURE 17-13   The Petralona skull.

TABLE 17-1   **Archaic *Sapiens***

NAME	LOCATION	DATE (ky)	CRANIAL CAPACITY (CM³)
Earlier archaics			
Arago	France	about 400	1050–1150
Atapuerca	Spain	350–200	—
Bilzingsleben	Germany	425–200	—
Mauer	Germany	500+	—
Petralona	Greece	?500	1320
Vérteszöllös	Hungary	?210–160	larger than *erectus*
Later archaics			
Biache	France	200–160	1200
La Chaise	France	200–150	—
Montmaurin	France	190–130	—
Steinheim	Germany	300–250	1100–1200 (?female)
Swanscombe	England	300	1325 (estimate)

Fieldwork at Arago cave near the village of Tautavel (close to the Spanish border in southeastern France) began in 1964 under the supervision of the husband and wife team, Henry and Marie-Antoinette de Lumley (de Lumley and de Lumley, 1973). A second glaciation (Mindel) date has been suggested, perhaps 400 kya.

In their excavation of the site, the de Lumleys disclosed more than 20 occupation levels, each separated by 2 to 7 feet of sterile sand. More than 100,000 Acheulian artifacts have been recovered from the site. Over 50 cranial and postcranial remains of at least 4 adults and 3 children have been recovered. A partial cranium, mostly face and frontal bone (Fig. 17-15) is apparently that of a young male. Like other archaic fossils, Arago displays a mosaic of *erectus* and archaic *sapiens* characters.

H. erectus; and a later group that shares derived features with Neandertals. However, the morphological differences between the two groups are not always clear-cut.

Earlier archaic *sapiens'* resemblances to *H. erectus* may be seen in the robusticity of the mandible, mandible without a chin, thick cranial bones, thick occipital bone, pronounced occipital torus, heavy supraorbital torus, receding frontal bone, marked alveolar prognathism, greatest parietal breadth near base of skull, and larger teeth. They would, of course, have one or more *sapiens* characteristics. Later archaics also possess some *erectus* characteristics, but they would also have one or more of the following traits: larger cranial capacity, occipital bun or indications of one, more rounded occipital, nonprojecting middle facial region, parietal expansion, and small teeth.

The later group, essentially from the latter half of the Middle Pleistocene, overlaps to some extent with the older group. From an evolutionary point of view, this later group may have evolved from the earlier one and, displaying traits unique to Neandertals, may, in turn, have given rise to the Neandertals.

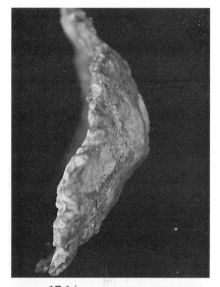

FIGURE 17-14   Vértesszöllös. The occipital was first described as modern but restudy identifies it as archaic *sapiens*.

Middle Pleistocene Evolution

Like the *erectus/sapiens* mix in Africa and China, the fossils from Europe exhibit this mosaic of traits from both species. However, it is important to note that the fossils from each continent differ; that is, the mosaic Chinese forms are not the same as those from Africa or Europe. Some European fossils, assumed to be earlier, are more robust and possess more *erectus* than *sapiens* features. The later Middle Pleistocene European fossils appear to be evolving toward Neandertals, but the uncertainty of dates prevents a clear scenario of the Middle Pleistocene evolutionary sequence.

The physical changes from *H. erectus* are not extraordinary. Bones remain thick, the supraorbital torus continues to be prominent, and vault height shows little increase. There is, however, a definite increase in brain size and a change in the shape of the skull from pentagonal to globular as seen in a rear view. There is also

FIGURE 17-15   Bilzingsleben. The frontal fragment has been identified as archaic *sapiens*.

FIGURE 17-16   Partial Arago skull.

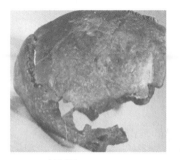

FIGURE 17-17   Cast of Swanscombe skull, England.

(a)

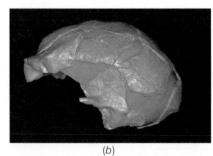

(b)

FIGURE 17-18   (a) Fontechevade II fragment, France. View of left side. The forehead is at the left. (b) Ehringsdorf, Germany. Both Fontechevade and Ehringsdorf have been suggested as possible ancestors of Neandertals. (Courtesy of Fred Smith)

a trend, especially with the later Middle Pleistocene forms, toward less occipital angulation. It is interesting to note that, in Europe, the changes move toward a Neandertal *sapiens* style, but in Africa and Asia, toward modern *sapiens*.

The lack of classic *H. erectus* remains in Europe is also interesting. There has been more digging and searching for fossils in Europe than anywhere in the world. If the bones are there, it seems plausible to expect they would have been found by now. Is it possible that *H. erectus* began their evolution toward *sapiens* before their arrival in Europe?

Middle Pleistocene Culture

The Acheulian technology of *H. erectus* persevered in the Middle Pleistocene with relatively little change until near the end of the period, when it became slightly more sophisticated. The handaxe, absent in China in the Lower Pleistocene, remains absent in the Middle Pleistocene, and choppers and chopping tools continue to be the basic tools. Bone, a very useful tool material, went practically unused by archaic *sapiens*. Flake tools similar to those of the earlier era persisted, perhaps in greater variety. Archaic *sapiens* in Africa and Europe invented a method—the Levallois technique—for predetermining flake size and shape (Klein, 1989, p. 253). This was no mean feat and suggests that the cognitive ability of late archaic *sapiens* had improved.

Archaic *sapiens* continued to live both in caves and open-air sites, and may have increased their use of caves. Did archaic *H. sapiens* control fire? Klein (1989, p. 255) suggests they did. He writes that there was a "concentration of burnt bones in depressions 50–60 cm across at Vértesszöllös . . ." and "fossil hearths have also been identified at Bilzingsleben and in several French caves that were probably occupied by early *H. sapiens*. . . ." Chinese archeologists insist that many Middle Pleistocene sites in China contain evidence of human-controlled fire. However, not everyone is convinced. (See p. 483.)

That archaic *sapiens* built temporary shelters is revealed by collections of bones, stones, and artifacts at sites where archaic *sapiens* erected shelters. Here, they manufactured artifacts and exploited the area for food. The stones may have been used to support the sides of the shelter. (See subsequent section on Terra Amata.)

FIGURE 17-19   Archaic *sapiens* sites—Swanscombe and Steinheim.

In the Lazaret cave in the city of Nice, southern France, a shelter about 36 feet by 11 feet was built against the cave wall, and skins probably hung over a framework of poles as walls for the shelter. The base was supported by rocks and large bones, and inside the shelter were two hearths. The hearth charcoal suggests they used slow-burning oak and boxwood, which produced embers easy to rekindle. Very little stone waste was found inside the shelter, suggesting they manufactured tools outside, where there was more light.

Archeological evidence clearly alludes to the utilization of many different food sources, such as fruits, vegetables, seeds, nuts, bird eggs, and so forth, each in its own season. Marine life was also exploited. From Lazaret and Orgnac (southern France) comes evidence of freshwater fishing for trout, perch, and carp. Another account of life in Middle Pleistocene France is taken from the reconstruction of Terra Amata by archeologists Henry and Marie-Antoinette de Lumley (1969) and Villa (1983).

Terra Amata   In the heart of the city of Nice, in southern France on the opulent French Riviera, stands the imposing Chateau de Rosemont, once the residence of the king of Yugoslavia and since converted into a museum of paleontology. In October of 1965, during foundation work for the construction of luxury apartments, bulldozers cut into the sloping grounds of the Chateau near an alley named Terra Amata (beloved land). As the bulldozers continued their excavation, closely monitored by de Lumley, a sandy deposit was exposed containing paleolithic implements.

De Lumley, immediately realizing the significance of the discovery, persuaded the builders to halt operations temporarily, and with the assistance of the French Ministry of Culture, mounted a major archeological salvage dig. De Lumley, his wife Marie-Antoinette, and a crew spent 40,000 hours excavating deposits 70 feet deep. They uncovered separate living floors, removed 270 cubic yards of fill using only trowels and brushes and found 35,000 objects, which were recorded on 1,200 charts. Casts were made of 108 square yards of living floor and 9,000 photographs recorded the progress of the work.

Below the surface at Terra Amata is a series of strata indicating advances of Würm, Riss, and Mindel glacial and interglacial periods. The site included three beaches, and it was the most recent beach, about 300,000 years old,* that contained evidence of human habitation. The climate at this time, toward the end of the Mindel, was colder and more humid than now. Pine trees covered the hills behind the beach and fresh water was available from a nearby stream.

Archaic *sapiens* not only selected a beautiful spot for their brief visits, but also built shelters to protect themselves against the prevailing northwest wind. The shelters were huts, shaped in an elongated oval, ranging from 26 to 49 feet in length and from 13 to nearly 30 feet in width. The evidence comes from a series of stakes-holes† averaging about three inches in diameter and driven into the sand to form the walls of the hut. To brace the walls, there was a line of stones, paralleling the stake imprints, and the sand shows imprints of stones as much as a foot in diameter, with some even stacked one on another.

(a)

(b)

FIGURE 17-20   Cast of Steinheim skull. (*a*) Basal view, showing how the foramen magnum was enlarged, apparently for removal of the brain—for dietary or ritualistic purposes; (*b*) frontal view showing warped skull.

---

*In her study of Terra Amata, Villa (1983) gives the date of 244 kya.

†Stake holes and post holes are filled with soil, of course, but gentle probing with a trowel can usually distinguish the holes from the surrounding hard-packed soil.

FIGURE 17-21   Shelter at Terra Amata. Evidence of habitation at Terra Amata enabled de Lumley to reconstruct what a hut might have looked like. (Courtesy California Academy of Sciences.)

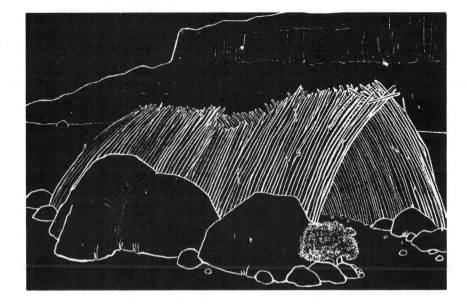

The living floor inside the huts consisted of a thick bed of organic matter and ash interrupted by imprints of holes left by posts that supported the roof. A basic feature in the center of the hut was a hearth, a foot or two in diameter, scooped out of the sand with a little wall of cobbles or pebbles built up on the northwest side of each hearth as a windscreen. The windscreen suggests that the hut was not draft free, but was a temporary structure to provide some protection against the cold and windy spring weather.

The daily activities of the Terra Amatans consisted of gathering plants, hunting small and large game in the nearby countryside, collecting sea food, and manufacturing tools. Animal bones found at the site include remains of birds, turtles, rabbits, and rodents, but the majority of bones are those of larger animals—deer, elephant, wild boar, ibex, rhinoceros, and wild ox. Like other predators, these Middle Pleistocene hunters selected the young of the species, which would have been much easier to bring down.*

The Terra Amatans also visited the beach and gathered shellfish from the Mediterranean. Found at the site are shells of oysters, mussels, and limpets. Fishbone finds indicate they did some fishing. Artifacts were mainly stone tools of Acheulian industry: chopping tools, bifaces, cleavers, several kinds of scrapers and flakes, projectile points, and pebble tools.

Inside the huts (Fig. 17-22) evidence of toolmaking can be seen in the bare patches of living floor surrounded by the leftovers of tool manufacture—stone flakes, partially chipped cores, and unworked pebbles. The bare patches are where the toolmakers sat, performing their chipping and flaking chores. Unworked stones were easily available by simply walking along the beach and picking up pebbles of flint, quartzite, limestone, or other rock.

---

*We assume here that the bones represent the result of hominid hunting. However, the assumption that bones at a site are necessarily the result of human activity has been seriously challenged. Consequently, archeologists and especially taphonomists now carefully analyze bones for evidence of hunting, scavenging, or natural accumulation.

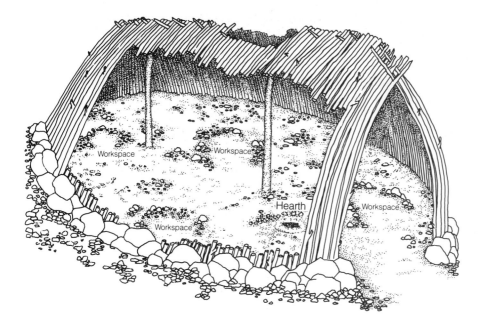

FIGURE 17-22   Cutaway of Terra Amata hut. Note the hearth, the workspaces where people sat making tools, the poles that supported the roof, and the stones at the base of the hut supporting the sides. (Adapted from de Lumley, 1969.)

The stone tools are informative. Projectile points signify a throwing weapon, probably a spear or lance (bow and arrow come much later). Scrapers were probably used with meat and chopping tools with butchering. Also, we know that Terra Amatans preferred certain kinds of tool material since the stone used for one of the tools could only have come from an area 30 miles away.

As a raw material for tools, bone was not much utilized, but one end of an elephant's leg bone was hammered into a point. Another bone point looks as if it had been hardened in fire (a technique long used for hardening the tips of spear shafts and digging sticks). Still another bone fragment is smoothed by wear, and there are others that may have served as awls and scrapers. Awls are often used for making holes in hides, which suggests that archaic *sapiens* wore some sort of skin clothing.

The huts reveal more about Terra Amata life. For one thing, the huts were hardly permanent structures. They probably fell apart after a few days, and were certainly not built to withstand a long, cold glacial winter. **Coprolites** have been analyzed and found to contain plants that shed their pollen at the end of spring and beginning of summer. This informs us that Terra Amata was visited during that period of time. De Lumley describes these brief visits:

> On arrival they set up their huts, built their hearths and windscreens, hunted for a day or two, gathered some seafood, rested by their fires, made a few tools and then departed (1969, p. 49).

That visits were short is reflected by dirt living floors, which were not compacted as they would have been after long occupation. The evidence for the early collapse of the huts can be seen from the condition of the pebbles. A freshly chipped stone tool quickly becomes bleached if it is left in the sun, but the underside, concealed from the sun's rays, retains its original coloring. Many of the pebbles found on the living floors show this kind of bleaching, indicating the huts collapsed soon after they were erected and did not protect the pebbles from weathering.

Coprolites   copr: excrement
Feces found at an archeological site; if fossilized, called **coproliths**.

As summer ended, winds covered the camp with a layer of sand that rains then packed down. By the time the hunters returned the following year, evidence of the camp was almost obliterated. The hunters again built their huts in the same place, following the outlines from the previous year, and the entire process was repeated. According to de Lumley, this occurred eleven times, since there are eleven living floors, so precisely superimposed that they represent consecutive visits, probably by many of the same individuals. Villa (1983) does not believe the occupation levels are so clearly marked. She states there is some evidence that the site was also occupied during other seasons. These visits suggest that the group was a stable one with complex institutions, perhaps family and band.

Camille Julliard, a French historian, wrote soon after the Terra Amata living floors had been exposed:

> The hearth is a place for gathering together around a fire that warms, that sheds light and gives comfort. The men here may well be nomadic hunters, but before the chase begins they need periods of preparation and afterward long moments of repose beside the hearth. The family, the tribe will arise from these customs, and I ask myself if they have not already been born.

Neandertals (125–30 kya)

Despite their apparent disappearance 40–30 kya, Neandertals continue to haunt the best laid theories of paleoanthropologists. They fit into the general scheme of

FIGURE 17-23 Upper Pleistocene. Correlation approximations. The culture periods of the Upper Paleolithic are not necessarily sequential as shown. This figure is simply meant to assist the student in organizing Upper Pleistocene data.

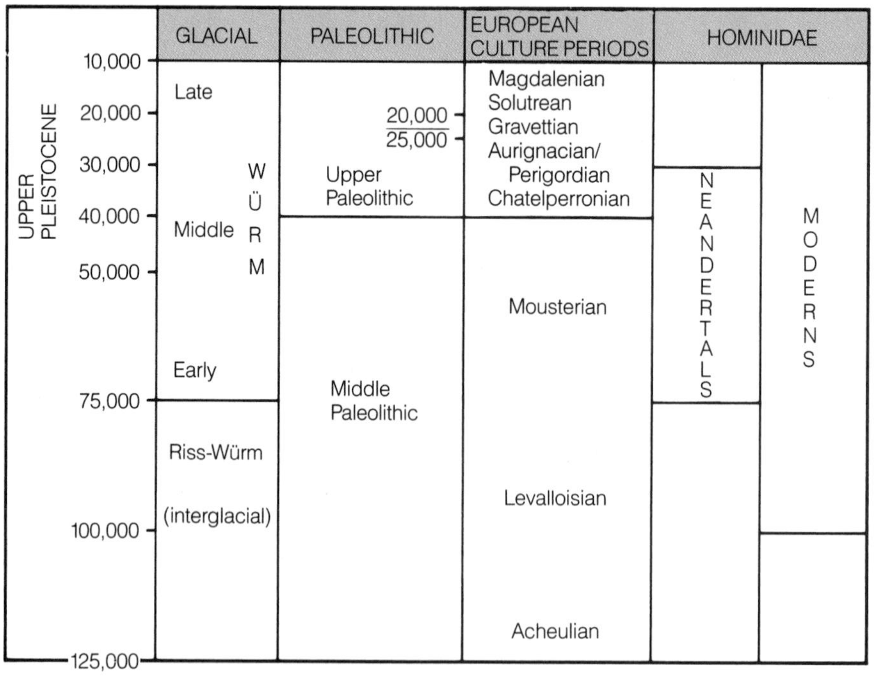
GLACIAL
PALEOLITHIC
EUROPEAN CULTURE PERIODS
HOMINIDAE
UPPER PLEISTOCENE
10,000
20,000
30,000
40,000
50,000
75,000
100,000
125,000
Late
Middle
Early
WÜRM
Riss-Würm
(interglacial)
20,000
25,000
Upper Paleolithic
Middle Paleolithic
Magdalenian
Solutrean
Gravettian
Aurignacian/
Perigordian
Chatelperronian
Mousterian
Levalloisian
Acheulian
NEANDERTALS
MODERNS

human evolution, and yet they are misfits. Classified as *H. sapiens*, they are like us and yet different. It is not an easy task to put them in their place.

Mousterian (moo-stair′-ee-en)
A cultural tradition of the Upper Pleistocene associated with Neandertals.

> Poor *Homo sapiens neanderthalensis*. Surely no other ethnic group has had so many nasty slurs and insults thrown at itself than our distant cousins of some 40,000 to 50,000 years ago (Holloway, 1985, p. 319).

These troublesome hunters are the cave man of cartoonists, walking about with bent knees, dragging a club in one hand and a woman by her hair in the other. They are described as brutish, dwarfish, apelike, and obviously of little intelligence. This image is more than somewhat exaggerated.

While cartoonists' license is not to be denied, the fact remains that Neandertals walked as upright as any of us, and, if they dragged clubs and women, there is not the slightest evidence of it. Nor are they dwarfish or apelike, and, in the light of twentieth-century human behavior, we should be careful of whom we call brutish.

As far as intelligence is concerned, Neandertals produced excellent **Mousterian** implements and, in fact, invented a new technique, the disc-core technique (Campbell, 1976, p. 328). Neandertals were also clever enough to cope with the cold weather of the glacial period. In addition to open sites, they lived in caves, wore clothing, built fires, gathered in settlements (some of which extended right up to the Arctic Ocean), hafted some of their tools, and hunted with a good deal of skill. They had to be skillful hunters in order to survive by subsisting off herds of reindeer, wooly rhinoceros, and mammoth. There was very little vegetable food available on the cold tundra.

Finally, the brain size of Neandertals is, on the average, larger than that of contemporary *H. sapiens*. The modern average is 1400 cm^3 and for Neandertals, 1520 cm^3. The larger size may be associated with the metabolic efficiency of a larger brain in cold weather. The Inuit (Eskimo) brain also averages larger (about that of Neandertals) than other present world populations.

Other physical traits set Neandertals aside as a unique population different from anatomically moderns, from their contemporaries in Africa and eastern Asia, and from their European predecessors (although later archaic *sapiens* shared some traits with them). There was, of course, physical variability in the Neandertal population, but they can be described by a characteristic morphology.

The skull is large, long, low, and bulging at the sides. At the rear of the skull, a bun protrudes, but the occiput is rounded without the *erectus* angulation. The greatest breadth of the skull is higher up on the skull. The forehead rises more vertically than *erectus*, and the browridges arch over the orbits instead of forming a straight bar (Fig. 17-25).

Compared to moderns, the Neandertal face stands out. It projects, almost as if it were pulled forward. This feature can be seen when the distance of the nose and teeth from the orbits is compared with moderns. (It would appear that Neandertals were blessed with an extraordinary large nose which, in the flesh, must have been a monumental sight.) Associated with this is lack of a chin. The anterior teeth tended to be larger, probably because of their use as tools, and the posterior teeth smaller.

Postcranially, Neandertal was very robust, barrelchested and powerfully muscled. We have stressed the differences between Neandertal and moderns, but aside from their muscularity, skull, and face, there was not a great deal of difference between "them and us."

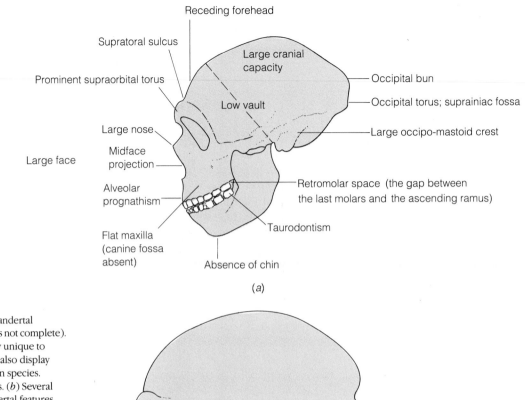

Receding forehead

Supratoral sulcus

Prominent supraorbital torus

Large cranial capacity

Low vault

Large nose

Large face

Midface projection

Alveolar prognathism

Occipital bun

Occipital torus; suprainiac fossa

Large occipo-mastoid crest

Retromolar space (the gap between the last molars and the ascending ramus)

Taurodontism

Flat maxilla (canine fossa absent)

Absence of chin

(a)

FIGURE 17-24   View of Neandertal occipital morphology (listing is not complete). Not all features are necessarily unique to Neandertal. Postcranial bones also display some differences from modern species. (a) Neandertal cranial features. (b) Several unique (automorphic) Neandertal features mentioned in text.

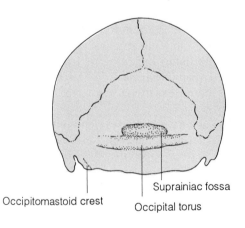

Occipital torus

Occipitomastoid crest

Mastoid crest

Occipitomastoid crest

Suprainiac fossa

Occipital torus

UPPER PLEISTOCENE

With the onset of the Riss-Würm interglacial, about 125 kya, we encounter the complex situation of the Neandertals. For some 85,000 years, Neandertals lived in Europe and western Asia, and their coming and going has raised more questions and controversies than perhaps any other hominid group.

We have traced Neandertal forebears back to the later archaic *sapiens*. But these were transitional forms, and it is not until we come to the last interglacial that we find the people we call Neandertals. Actually, very few Neandertals have been found from the interglacial. It is the Würm glacial that is considered the classic Neandertal period.

There are several basic questions to bear in mind as we examine the Neandertal event more closely. Did the anatomically modern humans of Europe evolve from Neandertals? In central Europe, for example, it is the opinion of Fred Smith, a specialist in this area, that "morphological continuity between Neandertals and the [early modern humans] is clearly documented by the available information" (1984, p. 192). Perhaps the most intriguing questions remain unanswered, and may be unanswerable: Whatever happened to the Neandertals? Did they merge with their anatomically modern contemporaries? Did they become extinct because they could not compete successfully with their modern neighbors? Did they become extinct for some other reason? Or do they still exist in some remote areas, as a Bigfoot or Yeti? (We may as well point out there is no worthwhile evidence for such survivors despite the sensational accounts that appear in the magazines at the supermarket checkstands.) In considering these and other questions, we shall start at the beginning.

NEANDERTAL BEGINNINGS

Neandertal takes its name from the Neander Valley near Düsseldorf, Germany. In 1856, workmen quarrying limestone caves in the valley blew up the entrance to one of the caves and came across fossilized bones. The owner of the quarry believed they belonged to a bear and gave them to Johann Karl Fuhlrott, teacher of natural science in the local high school. Fuhlrott knew his subject, and when he saw the bones he realized they were not the remains of a cave bear. He believed they must be those of an ancient human, something between the gorilla (first discovered a few years earlier) and *Homo sapiens*. Exactly what the bones represented became a *cause célèbre* for many years, and the fate of Neandertal Man, as the bones were named, hung in the balance for years until later finds were made.

What swung the balance in favor of accepting the Neander Valley specimen as a genuine hominid fossil were other nineteenth-century finds similar to it. What is more important, the additional fossil remains brought home the realization that a form of human different from nineteenth-century Europeans had in fact existed.

Some of these nineteenth-century finds include a skull, which no one understood, found at Gibraltar in 1848. A decade later, the Neandertal Valley find placed the Gibraltar skull in a more accurate perspective as a Neandertal. In 1866, in the La Naulette Cave, Belgium, a mandible and a few odd bones were discovered and were attributed to the same species as Neandertal. In 1880, a child's mandible from Šipka, Czechoslovakia, demonstrated that large Neandertal teeth were not

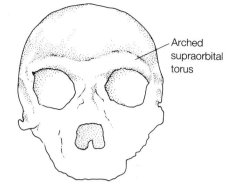

FIGURE 17-25 The arched brow ridges of Neandertal.

Arched supraorbital torus

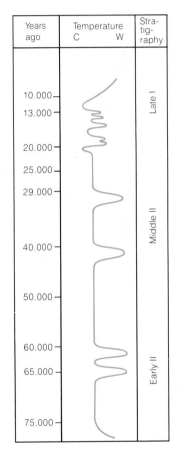

FIGURE 17-26 The Würm glaciation. During a glacial period, such as the Würm, the temperature—and the presence of ice—varies. The 65,000 years of the Würm were not simply one long cold period.

FIGURE 17-27 Map of early Neandertal discoveries.

pathological, since this young mandible possessed large and normal teeth. Whereas there were cries of pathology and abnormality, voiced especially by Virchow (see Chapter 16), most scientists were impressed by the two skeletons recovered in 1886 from a cave at Spy, near the town of Namur, Belgium. These two skeletons were carefully observed *in situ* by scientists, and the site and excavation were carefully recorded. Similarities between these remains and those of earlier Neandertals were so extensive there could be no doubt that there really was a "Neandertal Man."

In the post-Darwinian period, following the publication of *Origin* in 1859, the evolution controversy continued to rage, as we already have discussed in Chapters 2, 16, and elsewhere. Not even all scientists were persuaded that evolution was a valid concept; and more to the point, many scientists were very skeptical of the existence of hominid fossils. Cuvier's dictum, "*L'homme fossile n'existe pas*" (free translation: there is no such thing as fossil man), was still accepted by many Europeans, both laypeople and scientists. Virchow, for example, claimed to be a follower of Darwinian evolution, but was apparently unable to accept any of the hominid fossils discovered during his lifetime (he died in 1902) as honest-to-goodness hominid fossils. He described them as moderns, pathological in one way or another.

The discovery, in 1908, of La Chapelle-aux-Saints (discussed in the following section) settled the issue of the existence of fossil hominids once and for all. Unfortunately, by this time Cuvier was long since dead and, we assume, no longer in a position to change his mind. Virchow, too, had died a few years before, although the subsequent description of La Chapelle, written by Professor Marcellin Boule, seems to have been influenced by his predecessors, Cuvier and Virchow.

La Chapelle-aux-Saints One of the most important Neandertal discoveries was made in 1908 at La Chapelle-aux-Saints, near Corrèze in southwestern France. Found in a Mousterian cultural layer by three French priests, the Abbés A. and J. Bouysonnie and L. Bardon (already known for their archeological researches), was a nearly complete human skeleton. The body had been deliberately buried in

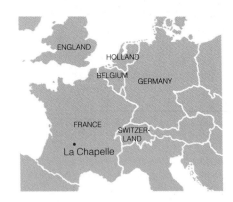

FIGURE 17-28 Map of La Chapelle site.

a shallow grave and fixed in a ritual position, a bison leg placed on its chest, and the trench filled with flint tools and broken animal bones. This attitude suggests respect toward death, and the tools included with the body may very well indicate a belief in an afterlife where such implements could be used.

The skeleton was turned over for study to a famous French paleontologist, Marcellin Boule, who published his analysis in three volumes from 1911 to 1913. It was his exhaustive, and no doubt biased, publication that set the tone for the description of prehistoric humans that survives to this day.

Why did Boule describe Neandertal as the slouching, brutish, apelike, unintelligent creature that became the staple of the cartoonist's prehistoric man? Professor Brace suggests the reason was that Boule, trained in France in the traditions of Cuvier's catastrophism, did not really believe in evolution. He could not deny, as Cuvier had, the existence of fossil humans, but he could reject the notion that Neandertals were ancestral to anatomical moderns, especially if Neandertal looked noticeably different. "With the over-emphasis of the nonmodern features of the La Chapelle-aux-Saints skeleton it became a much less likely candidate for the forefather of the succeeding Upper Paleolithic forms" (Brace, 1977, p. 219).

The skull of this male, who was at least 40 years of age, is very large, with a cranial capacity of 1620 cm³ The vault is low and long, the supraorbital ridges immense, with the typical Neandertal arched shape, and the forehead is low and retreating. Prognathism in the alveolar area is pronounced, and the face is long and projecting. At the rear of the skull, the occiput is protuberant and bun-shaped. (See Fig. 17-29.)

La Chapelle is not a typical Neandertal, but a very robust male and "evidently represents an extreme in the Neandertal range of variation" (Brace, et al., 1979, p. 117). Unfortunately, this skeleton, which Boule claimed did not even walk completely erect (he walked as erect as any other human with spinal arthritis), has been widely accepted as "Mr. Neandertal." But other Neandertals are not as extreme. Some show traits that come close to moderns. One of the mandibles found with Monte Circeo had a chin, as was the case with La Quina. La Ferrassie was not as robust as La Chapelle, and the frontal bone is less sloping and the chin less receding.

NEANDERTALS MEET MODERNS

The youngest of western European Neandertals comes from St. Cesaire, southwestern France, dated at about 37–35 kya. The bones were recovered from a bed of discarded chipped blades, handaxes, and other stone tools of a type called *Chatelperronian*, a tool industry of the Upper Paleolithic (see chart, p. 516) that is associated with Neandertals. This site is fascinating for several reasons. Anatomically modern humans were living in western Europe by about 35 kya; therefore, for perhaps several thousand years anatomically moderns and Neandertals were living "side by side!" This raises some very intriguing questions, especially, How did these two groups interact?

One group was physically shorter, more muscular, with quite a differently shaped head and could be readily distinguished from the other group. Neandertals were the muscular group with the occipital bun, without a proper chin, with less sophisticated tools, and probably less numerous than the other group. Was their relationship with the taller, more gracile group, a peaceful, cooperative one between equals, or was it violent? Did they make love or war? The evidence does

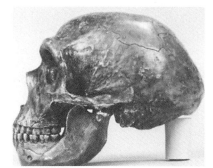

(a)

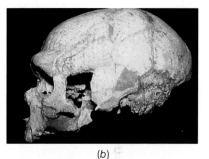

(b)

FIGURE 17-29 (a) Cast, La Chapelle-aux-Saints. Note the occipital bun, facial and alveolar prognathism, low vault, and lack of chin; (b) photo of actual calvarium.

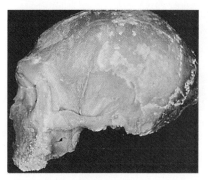

FIGURE 17-30 Monte Circeo, a more typical Neandertal. Supraorbital torus displays Neandertal traits but the occipital area is more modern.

FIGURE 17-31 Neandertal sites in France and Italy.

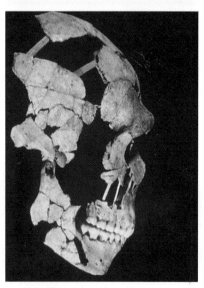

FIGURE 17-32 St. Cesaire, the "last" Neandertal.

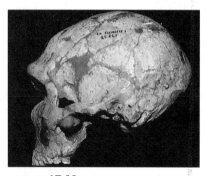

FIGURE 17-33 La Ferrassie. A more typical Neandertal. Mandible (not shown) has a chin.

not tell us, but if the history of the past several thousand years is applied, the association was violent and stratified—a superior and inferior relationship, with the superior group vanquishing the inferior as the Greeks, Persians, Romans, and more recent Europeans have demonstrated. (On the other hand, "barbaric" tribes have at times conquered the "civilized" societies, as the destruction of the Roman empire teaches us, but it seems quite clear that ultimately this was not the case with Neandertals vs. moderns.)

Whatever the quality of the relationship might be, when two groups come into contact, invariably there is a diffusion of material objects. Usually, the group with inferior tools and weapons takes on the superior ones of the other group; this borrowing is an old practice that still occurs today. Nonmaterial elements such as ideas, values, beliefs, and customs also ordinarily (although not necessarily) diffuse from the more to the less sophisticated population.

Evidence from a number of French sites (Harrold, 1989) indicates that Neandertals did indeed borrow "technological" methods and tools, such as blades, from the moderns and modified their own Mousterian tools, creating a new industry, the Chatelperronean.

However, the *concept* of diffusion does not tell us the *how* of diffusion. Did the Neandertals trade, steal, or battle for what they acquired? Did the moderns peacefully teach their technology to their neighbors? Did the two groups cooperate in hunting, exchange tall tales around a campfire, or did they fear and hunt each other with intent to kill? Did the two groups interbreed—exchange mates, for example—and over a period of time did the Neandertals become assimilated into the modern population? Or did moderns annihilate Neandertals and thereby terminate their existence?* No one knows, but it has been suggested that a difference of 2 percent mortality in the two populations (moderns lived longer than Neandertals) would have resulted in the extinction of the Neandertals in about one thousand years (Zubrow, 1989).

There is still another interesting question. Since the Neandertals borrowed technology from the moderns, how did they communicate? Was it done with some sort of sign language, or were there individuals who learned the language of the others and thus became interpreters? (For a discussion of Neandertal and language, see p. 528.)

Although western European Neandertals are the best known and considered the basic measure of Neandertal identification, there are also significant finds in Central Europe. At Krapina, Yugoslavia, there is an abundance of bones but, unfortunately, they are mostly fragments. It is believed they represent at least 20 individuals—men, women, and children. Krapina is an old site, dating back to the early Würm, about 70 kya, and the Neandertal features of the finds there, although less robust, are very similar to the western European finds. Krapina is important as a burial site, one of the oldest ones on record (Trinkaus, 1985) and it may also have been the site of a Neandertal mortuary rite.

By comparing Krapina bones with those made at a known butchering site, Russell (1987) found that cutmarks on the bones did not match those at the butchering site in kind or frequency. However, she found they did compare with human bones that had been defleshed for secondary burial. Secondary burial is an ancient human custom, practiced in recent times as well. A body that has been

---

*For a fictionalized account of the confrontation of Neandertals and a.m. humans, read Nobel prize-winner William Golding's excellent novel *The Inheritors*. Several movies have also been made on this subject. Another novel on the subject is Jean M. Auel's *Clan of the Cave Bear*.

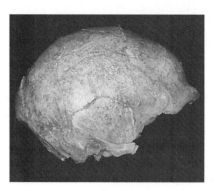

FIGURE 17-34 Spy (spee) 2. A male Neandertal from Belgium. Neandertal characteristics are clearly visible.

FIGURE 17-35 Neandertal sites. Vindija and Krapina in Yugoslavia.

buried at the time of death is exhumed at a later date, all remaining flesh is removed from the bones, and the bones are then washed and ritually reinterred. If Russell is correct and the Krapina bones underwent similar treatment, this may be evidence not only of early Neandertal intentional burial, but also of early Neandertal ritual. However, not everyone agrees with Russell's interpretation.

Another interesting site in Central Europe is Vindija,* about 30 miles from Krapina. The site is an excellent source of faunal, cultural, and hominid material in *sequence* throughout much of the Upper Pleistocene. Neandertal fossils were found in level G_3, consisting of some 35 specimens, tentatively dated at about 42 kya. Even though some of their features approach the morphology of early south-central European modern *sapiens*—reduction in size and shape of the supraorbital torus and change in shape, slight chin eminence on the mandibles, narrower nasal breadth, and perhaps the absence of occipital bunning—the overall pattern is definitely Neandertal. However, these modified Neandertal features may also be seen as an evolutionary trend toward modern *sapiens*.

Dr. Fred Smith takes the view that variation in Vindija G_3 skull features points to a trend continuing on to the later anatomically moderns of the upper levels. Does Vindija support the proposition that the origin of *H. sapiens sapiens* could have occurred here in Central Europe? As we have already mentioned, Smith does not insist upon it and suggests anatomically moderns could have come from elsewhere. But he does believe there is morphological and genetic continuity between the lower and upper levels of the cave.* (For other Central European Neandertal sites, see Table 17-2.)

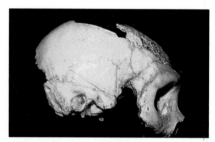

(a)

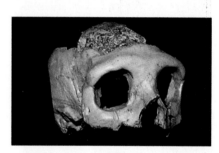

(b)

FIGURE 17-36 (*a*) Lateral view, Krapina C showing characteristic Neandertal traits; (*b*) three-quarters view.

WESTERN ASIA

Israel In addition to European Neandertals are those from southwest Asia. There are several from Israel that display some modern features and are less robust than western European Neandertals, but the overall pattern is Neandertal. The dating is not too clear for these, but they appear to be in the 60 to 70 ky range.

---

*Vindija is pronounced Vindya; the j is silent.

*For an opposing view of Vindija see Braüer, 1989, p. 137.

TABLE 17-2   **Partial List of European Neandertals***

SITE	YEAR FOUND	HUMAN REMAINS	ARCHEOLOGICAL PERIOD	DATE
Šipka, Czechoslovakia	1880	Mandibular symphysis of a child	Mousterian	Podhradem (inter-stadial, 32–28 kya)
Ochoz, Czechoslovakia	1905 1964	Adult mandible, adult molar; post-cranial fragments	Mousterian	Early Würm
Ganovce, Czechoslovakia	1926 1955	Natural endocast; cranial fragments, natural molds of postcrania	Mousterian	Riss-Würm
Subalyuk, Hungary	1932	Adult mandible and postcrania; child's cranium	Mousterian	Early Würm
Sala, Czechoslovakia	1961	Adult frontal bone	None	Upper Pleistocene
Kulna, Czechoslovakia	1965	Adult right maxilla; teeth, adult parietal fragment	Mousterian	38.6 kya 45.6 kya
Taubach, East Germany	1887	Lower first molar; lower first premolar	Middle Paleolithic	None
Wildscheuer, West Germany	1953	Cranial fragments	Mousterian	Early Würm
Salzgitter-Lebenstedt, West Germany	1956	Adult occipital and parietal	Mousterian	55.6 kya
Baco Kiro, Bulgaria	?	Very fragmentary portions	Aurignacian (?)	43.0 kya
(Above portion of table adapted from Smith, 1984, pp. 142–143.)				
Forbes Quarry, Gibraltar	1848 1928	Adult skull, child's skull fragments	Levallois-Mousterian	Early Würm
Spy, Belgium	1886	2 skeletons	Mousterian	Early Würm
Le Moustier, France	1908	Adolescent skeleton	Mousterian	Early Würm

*In addition to those included in text.

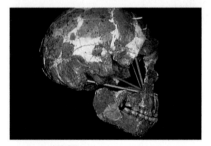

FIGURE 17-37   Tabun. Neandertal from Israel. The supraorbital torus and facial prognathism are similar to Western European Neandertals. Note the lack of occipital bunning.

In 1983, a skeleton was excavated from the Kebara cave on Mt. Carmel, where several caves have produced fossil hominids. The skeleton is incomplete—the skull and much of the lower limbs are missing. However, the pelvis is the most complete of a Neandertal so far recovered. It has been dated at about 60 ky.

The pelvis provides evidence that nullifies the suggestion that the Neandertal pelvis differed from the modern in such a way that gestation took perhaps twelve months instead of the nine required for the anatomically modern. The hyoid bone is also interesting from a language-capability point of view (see p. 528).

Iraq   A most remarkable site is Shanidar, in the Zagros Mountains of northeastern Iraq, where partial skeletons of 9 individuals—males and females (7 adults and 2 infants)—were found, 4 of them deliberately buried. These are quite typically Neandertal, although the occipital torus (Fig. 17-41) is weak, the occiput is fairly well-rounded, and an incipient chin is present on at least one of the mandibles. Several skulls look deformed, as if their foreheads had been bound when the individuals were children (Trinkaus, 1984b). Such cranial deformation is known from several areas of the world in very recent times.

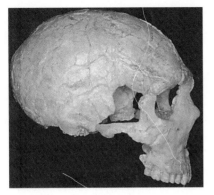

FIGURE 17-38 Amud. Neandertal from Israel. Less robust than western European Neandertals.

FIGURE 17-39 Near Eastern Neandertal sites.

LEBANON

Haifa
Tabun
Amud

Lake Kinneret
(Lake Tiberias,
Sea of Galilee)

Jerusalem

Dead
Sea

ISRAEL

(Detail of map at left)

TURKEY

Mediterranean
Sea

SYRIA

Shanidar

LEBANON

EGYPT

JORDAN

Baghdad

IRAN

IRAQ

SAUDI ARABIA

FIGURE 17-40 The Tabun cave site, located about 15 miles south of Haifa, Israel.

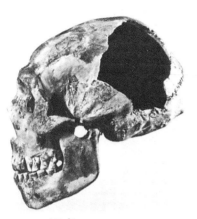

FIGURE 17-41   Shanidar 1.

One of the more interesting individuals is Shanidar 1, a male who lived to about 35 years of age, a fairly old age for his time (Trinkaus and Thompson, 1987). His stature is estimated at 5 feet, 7 inches, with a cranial capacity of 1600 cm³, quite a bit over the European Neandertal mean of 1415 cm³. The right side of his body suffered a crushing injury that affected his right arm, clavicle, scapula, and lower right limb. The injury may have been due to a rockfall, or it is possible that the atrophy of the right arm was the result of nerve injury suffered from severe damage to his left eye. It is also possible that his right arm was amputated at the elbow, which, if true, is the first evidence of deliberate human surgery (see Trinkaus, 1982, 1983; Stringer and Trinkaus, 1981).

Another individual, Shanidar 4, was deliberately buried on his left side, legs drawn up against his chest in a flexed position. Pollen analysis of the soil associated with the skeleton indicates the presence of a number of spring flowers (hyacinths, daisies, hollyhocks, and bachelor's button) that had apparently been placed on the grave at the time of death.

Neandertals must have lived dangerously, if the Shanidar evidence has been interpreted correctly. An atrophied arm, a crushing eye fracture resulting in blindness in that eye, arm and foot fractures, skull scars, and various rib injuries were found on several of the adult male skeletons. Shanidar 3 suffered a rib injury that may have been caused by a stabbing. One of his ribs was damaged by a sharp instrument that probably caused his death. If this were a deliberate stabbing, it would be the oldest known case of interpersonal violence; however, there is no way of knowing whether it was deliberate or accidental. No matter how it happened, Shanidar 3 was taken care of for at least several weeks and intentionally buried when he died (Trinkaus and Zimmerman, 1982).

Since many of the injuries were serious and the men survived for a time, some for years, it suggests that their social system was organized, that cooperation and care of the sick and disabled were an important value of their culture. Intentional burial is evidence of a special attitude toward death and perhaps a belief in a future life and the supernatural.

CENTRAL ASIA

Uzbekistan   About 1,600 miles east of Shanidar in Soviet Uzbekistan, in a cave at Teshik-Tash, we find another deliberate burial. A 9-year-old boy, with a cranial capacity of 1490 cm³, was buried in a shallow grave surrounded by five pairs of wild goat horns, suggesting a burial ritual or perhaps a religious cult. Like many other Neandertals, Teshik-Tash is a mixture of Neandertal traits (heavy brow ridges and occipital bun) and modern traits (high vault and definite signs of a chin).

Culture of Neandertals

Neandertals, who lived in the culture period known as the Middle Paleolithic, are usually associated with the Mousterian industry (although the Mousterian industry is not always associated with Neandertals), which had its roots in the second interglacial, or even the Riss glacial. In the early Würm, Mousterian culture extended

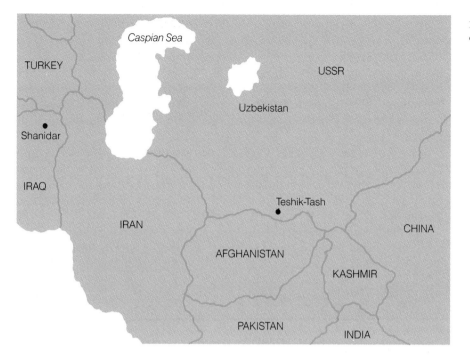

FIGURE 17-42   The site of Teskik-Tash, the easternmost Neandertal.

Nodule

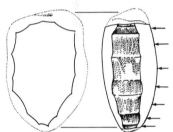

The nodule is chipped on the parameter.

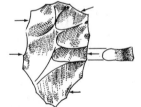

Flakes are radially removed from top surface.

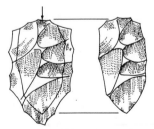

A final blow at one end removes a large flake.

FIGURE 17-43   The Levallois method.

from the Atlantic Ocean across Europe and North Africa to the Soviet Union, Israel, Iran, and as far east as Uzbekistan and, perhaps, China.

Technology   Mousterian people specialized in the production of flake tools based on the Levallois method, a prepared core technique that originated perhaps as much as 200 kya. A chunk of flint was chipped all the way round and on top, resembling a turtle in form, and then rapped on the side to produce a flake ready for use (Fig. 17-43).

Neandertals improved on the Levallois technique by inventing a variation. They trimmed the flint nodule around the edges to form a disc-shaped core. Each time they struck the edge, they produced a flake until the core became too small and was discarded. Thus, the Neandertals were able to obtain more flakes per core than their predecessors. They then trimmed (retouched) the flake into various forms such as scrapers, points, knives, and so on.

Neandertal craftspeople elaborated and diversified traditional methods, and there is some indication of development in the specialization of tools used in skin and meat preparation, hunting, woodworking, and perhaps hafting (attaching handles to tools). They may have made some use of new materials, such as antler and bone, but their specialization and innovation cannot be compared to the next culture period, the Upper Paleolithic. Nevertheless, the Neandertals advanced their technology, which tended to be similar in typology, over great geographic distances, far beyond that of *H. erectus*. It is quite likely that their modifications in technology laid the basis for the remarkable changes of the Upper Paleolithic.

Settlements   People of Mousterian culture lived in a variety of open sites, caves, and rock shelters. Living in the open on the cold tundra suggests the erection of

Convex side scraper   Point

Convergent scraper   Levallois flake

FIGURE 17-44   Mousterian tools (after Bordes).

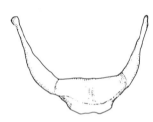

FIGURE 17-45   Hyoid bone (enlarged).

shelters, and there is some evidence of such structures, although the last glaciation must have destroyed many open sites. At the site of Moldova I, in the Ukraine region of the Soviet Union, archeologists found traces of an oval ring of mammoth bones, enclosing an area of about 26 by 16 feet, which may have been used to weigh down the skin walls of a temporary hut or tent. Inside the ring are traces of a number of hearths, hundreds of tools, thousands of waste flakes, and many bone fragments of animals probably brought home for comfortable dining around the fireplace.

Evidence for life in caves is abundant, and Mousterians must have occupied them extensively. Windbreaks of poles and skin were probably erected at the cave mouth for protection against the weather. Fire is in general use by this time, of course, and no doubt used for cooking, for warmth, and for keeping dangerous animals at bay.

How large were Neandertal settlements, and were they permanent or temporary? These questions are not yet answered, but Binford (1982) believes the settlements were short-term occupations used over and over again.

Symbolism   It has been suggested by some that although Neandertals were capable of speech (symbolic vocal language), they were limited by the physical structure of their throats. A recent discovery, the Kebara remains from Israel, included a hyoid bone (Fig. 17-45), which may be the first ever reported from a fossil hominid. Contrary to expectations, the Kebara (Neandertal) hyoid bone is very similar to moderns and, thus, a reanalysis of the Neandertal ability to speak may be required (Arensburg et al., 1989). Supporting Arensburg et al., is a report by L. E. Duchin, in a recent report of a study she made of the chimpanzee and fossil human oral cavity. She writes:

> The preliminary conclusion drawn from these calculations is that a human configuration of the anatomical region responsible for articulate speech was found in both *Homo erectus* and *H. sapiens neanderthalensis*. The interpretation of these results is that both these ancestors had the capacity to move the tongue within the oral cavity in order to successfully articulate the vowels and consonants of human speech (1990, p. 694–695).

Duchin's study will be carefully examined, and we shall see what effect it has on the continuing discussion of premodern hominid speech.

An important innovation of the Middle Paleolithic is deliberate burial. A remarkable burial occurs at the La Ferrassie (France) rock shelter. It looks like a family cemetery; the presumed parents are buried head to head and four children are interred neatly nearby. A short distance beyond, a small mound contains the bones of a newly born infant, and a bit further, under a triangular stone, is the grave of a 6-year-old child (Fig. 17-46). In the Guattari Cave, Monte Circeo (near Rome) a partially crushed skull was placed in the center of a circle of stones. There were burials at Shanidar, Kebara, and elsewhere in the Middle Paleolithic. Although a recent paper (Gargett, 1989) rejects Neandertal deliberate burial, the number of almost complete Neandertal skeletons that have been found suggests that only by intentional burial could these skeletons have survived the ravages of natural destructive events.

Some scholars believe that burials were accompanied by some sort of ritual as suggested, for example, by stones surrounding the skull in the Guattari Cave. However, this is very difficult to prove. The fact that Neandertals intentionally buried their dead tells us they may have had a more human attitude toward death

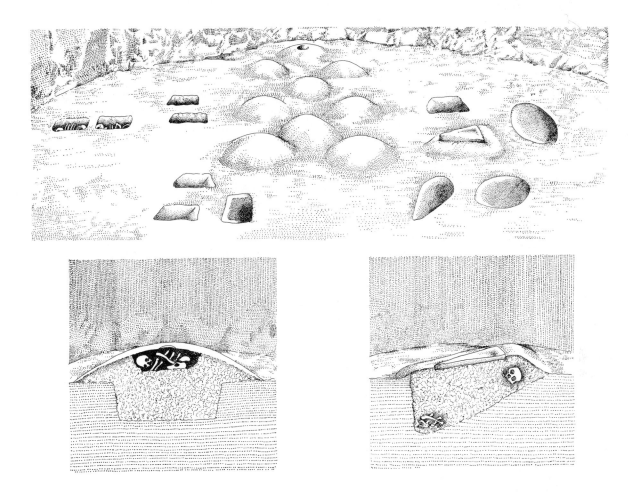

FIGURE 17-46   La Ferrassie burial.

than their predecessors, or an awareness of their distinctiveness from other living things, that they were something more than simply animals.

In our discussion of Shanidar, it was pointed out that one of the adult skeletons showed evidence of serious injuries, and that he possibly survived his wounds and suffering only because of special care given to him. It was suggested that a social structure existed with values of cooperation and concern for others, indicating a sense of compassion toward members of one's group or kin. Evidence of similar behavior can be found at other Neandertal sites.

Another innovation is a form of ornamentation or the beginnings of artistic expression. A number of items such as drilled animal teeth, drilled bone, incised bone, pierced bone, and a bear tooth with grooves have been found at Neandertal sites. Whether this can be called art or ornamentation, or whether the objects can be considered symbols is problematical. It does convey the feeling that Neandertals were moving toward a nonutilitarian use of materials. In a recent article, Marshack (1989) credits Neandertals with considerable artistic ability (including personal adornment) that influenced the brilliant art of the Upper Paleolithic.

Economy   Neandertals were successful hunters, as the abundant remains of animal bones at their sites demonstrate. As the evidence from Shanidar suggests,

FIGURE 17-47   Neandertal ritual and hunt. Neandertals are cutting up a wooly rhinoceros. The men to the left are offering pieces of meat to the rising sun. It is not known for certain whether this ritual was actually performed, but Neandertals did perform burial rituals.

they probably gathered berries, nuts, and other plants. It does not appear that they sought more exotic foods, such as seafood or birds.

It is assumed that, in the freezing weather of the fourth glacial, Neandertals must have worn clothing to survive the winters—and they may have developed methods of curing skins. But since there is no evidence of sewing equipment, the clothing was probably of simple design, like a poncho.

We know much more of European Middle Paleolithic culture than any comparable period because it has been studied longer by more scholars. In recent years, however, Africa has been a target not only of physical anthropologists, as we have seen in preceding chapters, but also of archeologists, who have added considerably to our knowledge of African Pleistocene hominid history.

One of the best-known students of African archeology is Professor J. Desmond Clark, of the University of California. We shall summarize the African Middle Paleolithic (Middle Stone Age) from one of his accounts (1982).

Culture of African Neandertals

In Africa, the Eurasian Middle Paleolithic is referred to as the Middle Stone Age (MSA) and, in many ways, it is similar to its Eurasian counterpart. The main technological industry of Africa is the Mousterian, the same industry of the Middle Paleolithic. And like its Eurasian contemporary, while the basic industry is Mousterian, regional differences are to be found.

Regional Patterning   At the beginning of the last interglacial, about 120 kya, as the climate became more temperate and sea levels rose, different ecological regions appeared. Populataions adapted to drier, warmer, and wetter conditions; the flora and fauna also changed, and people adapted the hunting, gathering, and toolmaking techniques accordingly.

Technology   The most common tool material was stone, and scrapers were the most frequently used tool. In the more humid tropics, where trees were more plentiful, wood and wood products became more important. Also, there was a greater emphasis on woodland food resources. As grains and seeds became more important in the savanna diet, hand grindstones (pestle and grinding stone) were produced.

Food Processing   Hunting strategies varied depending on the kind of game available and on the butchering and processing techniques. Adult males of aggressive species, such as buffalo, were not hunted; instead, young animals and pregnant females were exploited, since they were not as dangerous. Easier to hunt, smaller antelopes of all ages were frequent game.

Kill sites were generally located close to some natural hazard, such as a swamp, lake, cliff, or sinkhole. Game was driven into these catches, where they would be killed by the fall or drowning, or where hunters could easily dispatch the animals stuck in the muck.

It is possible that Africans in the MSA dried meat by heating it over a fire. This is evidenced by thick layers of dispersed ash and carbonized material resulting from meat repeatedly dried in the same spot during rainfalls. According to Clark (1982), it is probable that the drying of meat was one of the major developments in resource processing to take place during the Middle Stone Age.

Symbolism   We do not think of archaic *sapiens** as miners, but in a sense they were. A quarry site in Swaziland was mined for iron pigment about 44 kya. Paint was frequently used by Africans at this time—ochre-stained scrapers, a grindstone with hematite staining, and pieces of ground hematite have been recovered at various sites.

Like their Neandertal contemporaries in Eurasia, Africans buried their dead. Intentional burials have been excavated at several sites, and, at Border Cave, a burial included adults and infants, recalling the Ferrassie grave in France.

In summary, about 120 kya, the Mousterian industry was widespread in Africa. While there was a general cultural similarity throughout Africa, regional patterns were emerging as populations adapted more efficiently to particular environments. Over thousands of years, tool-and-weapon-manufacturing techniques improved, as did hunting strategies. New materials were utilized, new sources of food exploited, and the nonmaterial aspects of life can be seen in both painting and supernatural beliefs.

---

*If a.m. humans were present in Africa during all or much of the Middle Stone Age, it is difficult to know what effect, if any, they may have had on Middle Stone Age culture.

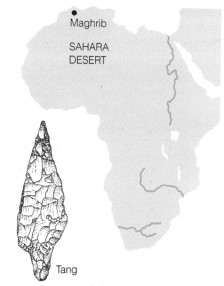

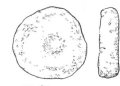

FIGURE 17-48   An example of regional technology is the fanged point found mainly in western and central Sahara.

FIGURE 17-49   Grinding stones, a savanna adaptation (Adapted from Clark, 1982).

FIGURE 17-50   Site of the Lion Cave quarry, where iron pigment was mined.

BOX 17-4

The Case of Mother Eve (The Garden of Eden Hypothesis)

Molecular biologists have developed an hypothesis postulating that anatomically moderns originated in Africa about 200 kya and then migrated out of Africa to other areas of the world about 135 kya at the earliest. Their evidence for this scenario stems from a study by Cann et al. (1987). Before venturing further, it will be useful to explain an important key in the genetic puzzle, mitochondrial DNA (mtDNA).

Mitochondria are tiny organelles found in the cell but *outside* the nucleus of the cell. They have been described as "the cell's engines" because they metabolize food and water into energy. They code for proteins needed in metabolism, a function not performed by the nucleus. Mitochondria contain a separate set of DNA from that in the nucleus, and this mtDNA is inherited *only through the mother*. (It is the nucleus of the sperm—which does not carry mitochondria—that fertilizes the ovum.) Thus, there is not the mixture of genes in mtDNA inheritance that occurs in meiotic recombination in nuclear DNA. To molecular biologists, this provides a means of tracing human ancestry (in this case, the origin of moderns) back thousands of years, solely through the female line. Male DNA is not involved.

In order to determine when and where the origin of modern humans occurred, the biologists followed a procedure already in use to determine the age of the ape-hominid divergence. It was found that primate mtDNA mutates at the rate of 2 to 4 percent every million years. If, for example, 2 primate lines separated 1 mya, each line would accumulate 2 to 4 mutations per 100 bases. Since it is unlikely that the same mutations would occur in both lines, the combined mutations would total 4 to 8. The next step is to calculate the number of mutations in the mtDNA of the present world populations, assuming a common ancestor. This could be accomplished by comparing the mtDNA of various geographic populations.

Molecular biologist Rebecca Cann gathered 147 mtDNA samples from the placentas of newborn children whose ancestors lived in Africa, Asia, Europe, Australia, and New Guinea. Each sample was cut up with restriction enzymes (see Issue, Chapter 3) into more than 300 fragments to compare similarities and differences.

The number of mutations that occurred in each sample was calculated by computer. Fourteen of the samples had essentially the same base sequences as others in the survey and were not used. This left 133 distinct types of mtDNA. The computer then constructed a tree composed of clusters of mtDNA types, based on similarities of these types.

What the tree shows, according to the investigators, is one branch composed of 7 mtDNA types, all from Africa. The remaining 126 are located on the other branch. These are clustered into related groups of mixed types, but in every cluster there is at least 1 African mtDNA type.

Homo Sapiens Sapiens (Anatomically Modern Humans)*

One of the puzzling questions being heavily debated in paleoanthropology today is the origin of modern humans. There are three hypotheses:† (1) Afro-European *sapiens*; (2) Recent African Evolution; and (3) Multiregional Evolution Model.

According to the Afro-European *sapiens* hypothesis (Brauer, 1984), an early archaic *H. sapiens* stage evolved to a later archaic *sapiens* stage, from which arose modern humans around 100 kya. Because of climatic and environmental conditions, modern humans, slowly migrating out of Africa over the years, entered Eurasia and Europe. They interbred with local populations, but the dominant feature in this process was the moderns' migration from Africa, not local evolution.

---

*Detailed descriptions of fossils are not given for anatomical moderns. Refer to Box 17-5 at the end of the chapter for data on selected fossils.

†See Smith, 1989.

BOX 17-4

In contrast, the 7 African types include no mixture from the other four areas—all the types are strictly African.

Cann et al. concluded that: (1) Since the African cluster contained only African mtDNA types and all the other clusters included at least 1 African type, the mtDNA African types in all the areas outside Africa must have come from African females who had migrated from Africa (Where else could the African types have come from?); (2) The greater diversity of African mtDNA types indicated they were older than the other types, since it would have taken more time to produce the mutations that caused the diversity; (3) If the African mtDNA were the oldest, then the origin of moderns could be traced to one African female. The researchers referred to her as "Eve."

The next step was to determine the number of years back to Eve. Calculating the number of mutations in the African branch, Cann et al. figured the date to be between 285 and 143 kya or, taking the middle figure, to be about 200 kya.* The earliest Eve's descendants could have migrated from Africa to the other areas (based on the oldest cluster on the outsider's branch) was about 135 kya.

These dates, and the assumption that moderns originated in Africa and migrated to other continents, takes us back to the argument on origin just discussed. Support-

ers of the displacement (single origin) hypothesis use the molecular evidence to support their position: anatomically moderns originated in Africa over 100 kya and then migrated to Europe and elsewhere, displacing the people living there.

Wolpoff, one of the leading advocates of the multiple origin hypothesis, counters (1989) that the fossil evidence does not conform to what he calls the "Garden of Eden (GOE) hypothesis." He also contends that the GOE hypothesis is based on displacement without gene flow between the African displacers and the local populations; i.e., no interbreeding. This seems odd indeed, given the human condition, but the GOE hypothesis justifies it by maintaining that the two populations are of different species, a claim Wolpoff completely rejects. Wolpoff also points out that the dating of African moderns is a complex business, and paleoanthropologists have not reached a consensus on the issue. Finally, Wolpoff believes the mutation rate used by Cann et al. and others, is incorrect.

The Garden of Eden hypothesis is relatively new, and it must run the gauntlet of careful scrutiny by other scientists. The GOE conclusion that modern humans originated in Africa agrees with some fossil and archeological evidence, but this evidence does not satisfy all anthropologists. And so the research continues.

---

*Other molecular dates estimate a range from 50–800 ky.

Thus, African moderns displaced local archaic populations. A similar process could have also occurred in the Far East.

The Recent African Evolution hypothesis (advocated by Stringer and Andrews, among others) resembles the preceding model, but there are important differences. Modern humans evolved in Africa perhaps as much as 200 kya. This transition occurred only in Africa, where humans appeared earlier than anywhere else. They imply that the African origin of moderns was a biological speciation event; that is, modern humans were a new species and, therefore, they could not interbreed with archaic *sapiens* (Smith, 1989). Modern humans migrated to Eurasia, Europe, and the Far East, *completely* displacing local archaic populations. There was no interbreeding, obviously, since archaics and moderns were of different species.

In both of these models, modern humans originated in Africa somewhere between 100 and 200 kya, the earliest to appear on earth. They migrated out of Africa and displaced local populations. The first model allows for interbreeding, the second does not. Advocates of both models believe that modern humans appear late in areas outside of Africa, and both models accept the mtDNA hypothesis (see Box 17-4).

Provenience The particular place something comes from; source, origin. Provenance and provenience are used interchangeably.

FIGURE 17-51   Early moderns in Africa.

(a)

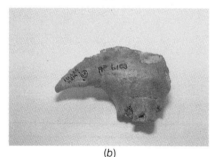

(b)

FIGURE 17-52   (a) Border Cave reconstruction reflects earlier and later traits of Early Moderns. (b) Klasies River Mouth may be one of the oldest modern humans, but dates of 100 to 300 kya have been questioned.

The third hypothesis—the Multiregional Evolution Model* (local continuity)—is substantially different from the above scenarios. The basis of this model is that evolution of regional populations in Eurasia and Africa was continuous from archaic *sapiens* to *H. sapiens sapiens*. Associated with this idea is the denial that the earliest moderns necessarily originated in Africa, that complete displacement was very unlikely, that gene flow between archaic populations was very likely, that modern humans are not a species separate from archaics, and finally, that mtDNA hypothesis is not acceptable.

Smith, one of the supporters of multiple origins, takes a more moderate view. He maintains that local continuity can be seen at the Vindija site (p. 523). However, while he thinks the evidence favoring replacement is equivocal and not as convincing as proponents suggest, their views should be seriously considered. A basic problem in this debate is the interpretation of evidence, which was noted in this chapter's Issue. In Africa, for example, the single-origin proponents accept the fossils from Klasies River Mouth and Border Cave (see Fossil Briefs) as supporting evidence for the early African dates of anatomically modern humans. The multiple-origin advocates, on the other hand, question the evidence: Klasies River Mouth fossil bones are too fragmentary, they claim, to make their modern identification certain; and, they add, the **provenience** of the Border Cave fossil bones is suspect, leaving their dating uncertain.

In the past, anatomical moderns have been associated with the Upper Paleolithic. This notion arose in Europe, where the relationship between humans and technology was first noticed in the archeological record. However, this correlation does not hold in Africa, as we have already noted. Nor is the association in Europe absolute. We must also mention that the line between the Middle Paleolithic and Upper Paleolithic cannot be clearly drawn. Nor is it a simple matter to draw a line between archaic (including Neandertals) *sapiens* and modern humans. This is true wherever we find them, since late archaic *sapiens* may exhibit modern traits, and early moderns may display archaic traits.

Paleoanthropologists make taxonomic decisions by looking at the overall configuration of the fossil find, and the more remains there are, the more valid the conclusion is apt to be. However, there are cases where the skeletal remains (especially the skull) are difficult to read. Then the decision becomes arbitrary, and the fossil may be placed in one or the other group, depending on a particular scientist's interpretation.

Another problem is dating. The proper way to determine the taxon of a fossil is by its morphology. But there are times when what appears to be an a.m. human is dated far earlier than the appearance of moderns anywhere else. Then the date may be questioned. Or, conversely, an archaic specimen may appear at what is believed to be a fairly recent date. This is why dates are often difficult to state in unequivocal terms.

Africa At the present time, it appears that the earliest moderns (Klasies River Mouth, for example) have been found in South Africa. Dates of 100 to 120 ky have been suggested. However, doubts have been raised because of fossil identification problems, questions of provenience, and differing interpretations of the evidence. It is these doubts that have led some paleoanthropologists to question whether the *earliest* moderns evolved in Africa. Other early moderns have been found in East and North Africa (see Table 17-3).

———————————————

*The most ardent advocate of this model is Wolpoff.

TABLE 17-3   **African Moderns***

NAME/COUNTRY	DATE (KYA)	MATERIAL
Dar-es-Soltan, Morocco	Uncertain	Adult young; adult calotte; teeth, limb bones, phalanges
Afalou, Algeria	12–8	Over 50 individuals; skeletons, male, female, children; blades, scrapers, burins
Kom Ombo, Egypt	13	Calvaria, adult male frontal and other cranial parts
Elmenteita, Kenya	10	Adults and juveniles: crania and cranial bones; skeletons
Lukenya Hill, Kenya	17	Adult frontal and parietal, probably male
Naivasha, Kenya	11	Adult female, over 50, cranium mandible, long bones
Lothagam Hill, Kenya	9–6	Remains of nearly 30 individuals, skeletons and various skeletal bones
Gamble's Cave, Kenya	8	Cranium; cranial bones, mandibles, limb bones; skeleton
Asselar, Mali	7	Adult male and postcranial skeleton
Taforalt, Morocco	11	Skeleton; cranium; skeleton fragments; remains of 180 adults, 6 adolescents, 97–100 children
Hmatjes River, South Africa	10.5	18 individuals of both sexes and varying ages
Wadi Halfa, Sudan	15	Mandible
Ishango, Zaire	9	Many cranial and postcranial bones
Kalemba, Zambia	15	Several crania; mandibles; vertebrae; postcranial fragments; both sexes, varying ages
Leopard's Hill, Zambia	16.7	Occipital and parietal
Mumbwa, Zambia	20	Several calvaria; cranium, mandible, limb bones

*In addition to those included in text.

The Near East   Israeli moderns possess a number of archaic traits, but their overall configuration places them in the a.m. category. Although quite robust, their skulls and postcranial bones are more gracile than archaic *sapiens*. The occiput is rounded, the vault is higher, the supraorbital torus is reduced, the chin has a definite eminence, midfacial and facial prognathism is reduced (although alveolar prognathism is accented), anterior teeth are smaller, canine fossae are present, and leg bones are more gracile.

A serious problem arises in this archaic-to-modern evolutionary sequence. Recently, a date of 90 ky was given to Israeli moderns,* but recall that Neandertal

---

*See Vallads et al. in *Nature*, 331(2 Feb 1988):614–616, and Stringer et al., in *Nature*, 338(1989):756–758.

FIGURE 17-53 (*a*) Omo I is considered to be early modern; some believe it to be archaic *sapiens*. (*b*) Jebel (or Djebel) Irhaud. An early modern said to have similarities to Neandertals. (Courtesy of Fred Smith.)

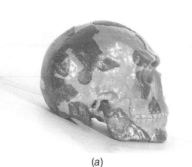

(a)

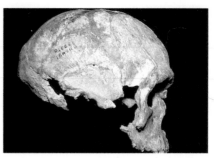

(b)

dates are 40 to 70 ky. How, then, can moderns be *older* than Neandertals? One possible answer is migration of moderns from elsewhere (Africa?) into the Near East. Another possibility is mistaken dating. The matter of dates also raises the intriguing question of overlapping modern/Neandertal residence in the same region. (See pp. 521–522.)

Central Europe Central Europe has been a source of many fossil finds, including Neandertals and anatomical moderns. At several sites, it appears that some fossils display Neandertal and modern features, which supports the local continuity (from Neandertal to modern) hypothesis. Such was the case at Vindija (p. 523).

Smith offers another example of local continuity from Mladeč (Fig. 17-58) of Czechoslovakia. One of the earlier European moderns, at about 33 ky, the Mladeč 5 skulls (2 female, 3 male), display a great deal of variation, partly due to sexual dimorphism. Although the skulls (except one of the females) possess a prominent

FIGURE 17-54 The Skhūl cave. Mt. Carmel, Israel.

(a)

(b)

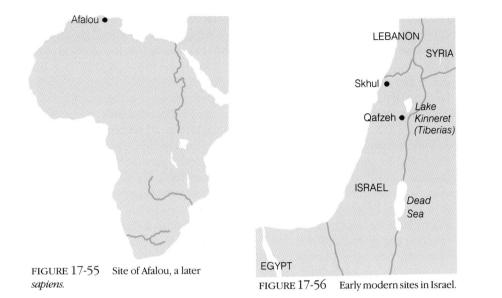

FIGURE 17-55   Site of Afalou, a later *sapiens*.

FIGURE 17-56   Early modern sites in Israel.

supraorbital torus, they are reduced from the Neandertal pattern and show a division at the approximate position of the middle of the orbit, a modern trait. Also modern is the reduction of the occipital projection, which has been called a *hemibun*. Reduced midfacial projection, a higher forehead, and postcranial elements "are clearly modern *H. sapiens* in morphology and not specifically Neandertallike in a single feature." (Smith, 1984, p. 174).

There are a number of other rather early moderns in Central Europe (Czechoslovakia, Bulgaria, Rumania, Yugoslavia, and Germany). In Central Europe we find a situation in which older moderns are more robust and display more archaic characteristics. Later moderns continue with archaic traits, but there is a definite trend toward gracilization. This trend offers support for local continuity from archaic to modern; however, there remains opposition to this model by paleoanthropologists who do not agree that *sapiens* traits in Europe were derived from Neandertals. They believe, rather, that these traits came from African migrations.

Western Europe   This area and its fossils have received the greatest paleoanthropological attention for several reasons, one of which is probably serendipity.

FIGURE 17-57   (*a*) Skhūl 5; (*b*) Qafzeh 6; (*c*) Quafzeh 9. Early moderns from Israel, dated at about 90 ky. Modified archaic traits are visible.

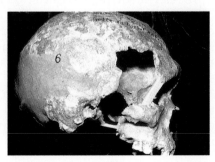

(a)

(b)

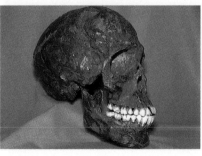

(c)

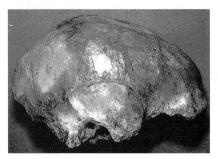

FIGURE 17-58 Mladeč 5. Possibly a transitional form—Neandertal to anatomically modern.

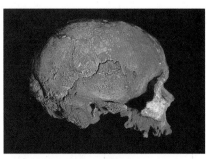

(a)

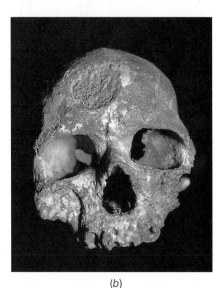

(b)

FIGURE 17-59 Cro-Magnon 1. Modern traits are quite clear. (*a*) Lateral view; (*b*) frontal view. (Courtesy of David Frayer)

Many of the scholars interested in this kind of research happened to live in western Europe, and the southern region of France happened to be a fossil gold mine; at least it seemed so for many years. Also, the idea of discovering and learning about ancient human ancestors caught the attention of the native population more so than it did peoples in other regions.

Because of this scholarly interest, a great deal of data were gathered, with little reliable information from elsewhere in the world. Consequently, theories of human evolution were based upon the western European situation. It has only been in recent years, with the advent of overwhelming evidence from other areas of the world by archeologists, paleontologists, paleobotanists, with new dating techniques, and with a great deal more money available for field research that human evolutionary theory has been seriously considered on a worldwide basis.

Best known of western European *sapiens* is unquestionably Cro-Magnon of southern France. Associated with an evolved Aurignacian industry, which is not the earliest Upper Paleolithic industry in France, Cro-Magnon cannot be considered among the earliest of France's a.m. humans. The date for Cro-Magnon is usually given as Würm III, around 25 kya. The so-called "Old Man" (Cro-Magnon 1) became the type specimen for what is known as the Cro-Magnon, or Upper Paleolithic, race of Europe. Actually, of course, there is no such race, and the old man is really not typical even of the other two male skulls that were found at the site.

The three male skulls reflect a mixture of modern and archaic traits. The old man is the most gracile of the three; one of the males has a Neandertal-like bun, and the forehead is lower and browridge more developed than the old man's. The third male has an even heavier browridge development, but the occipital lacks a bun. Most gracile, and most modern-looking is the female skull (which may be a function of sexual dimorphism).

The question of continuing, local evolution from Neandertals to anatomically moderns throughout Eurasia is far from settled. It seems unlikely that the area was divided into these isolated regions without gene flow. However, tracing such movements—considering the ever-present problems of dating, lack of fossils, fragmented condition of fossil finds, and many fossils that remain unstudied—is going to take some time.

With the retreat of the glacier and the introduction of farming and more efficient technology about 10 kya, anatomically moderns in Europe were on their way to their present physical characteristics.

Asia Most Late Pleistocene sites in China are not well dated, and it is assumed that faunal association and human morphology suggest the Late Pleistocene.

The early moderns (it is difficult to know how early) of the Late Pleistocene display a mixture of archaic and modern features (see Box 17-5). Archaic traits include the supraorbital torus and the occipital area, but the lack of facial prognathism is modern. However, the archaic traits are more gracile than the same traits of earlier *sapiens*. Also, the archaic traits are less robust than the Europeans of the same period.

Chinese paleoanthropologists see continuing evolution from archaic *sapiens* to anatomical moderns within China. In fact, they believe that a.m. humans are the end of a long evolutionary process from Chinese *H. erectus* to the present Chinese population. Wolpoff points out that the Late Pleistocene specimens provide a reasonable basis for the evolution [of present-day Chinese from early moderns]. The required changes would be a shortening and broadening of the cranium, an increase in cranial height ... a reduction in browridges, a forward expansion and size increase for the zygomatics, and a significant reduction in skeletal robustness and limb thickness (Wolpoff, 1980a, p. 322).

The earliest a.m. remains in Asia have been discovered in southern Sri Lanka and have been dated at 28,500 years (Kennedy and Deraniyagala, 1989, pp. 394–399).

Australia Indonesian islands, during glacial times, were joined to the Asian mainland, but Australia was not (see Figs. 17-62 and 16-39). Evidence shows that modern humans did some island hopping to New Guinea, New Britain, and New Ireland by 10 to 30 kya. However, in order to enter Australia, they must have developed water transport, with the right kind of boat, which apparently they did by 40 kya. The migrants entered Australia from the northeast and by about 25 kya could be found in much of the interior of Australia.

The oldest Australian fossils are from Lake Mungo, where the remains of two burials (one of them was first cremated) date to 25 kya and at least 30 kya, respectively. Their crania are rather gracile with, for example, only moderate development of the supraorbital torus. The Keilor find, more recent than these (about 15 kya) is another gracile cranium that fits in well with the Mungo forms. Dubois, who found the first *H. erectus*, also found a modern *sapiens* in Java, known as Wadjak. Similarities between Wadjak and Lake Mungo and especially Keilor have been noted by a number of researchers. These gracile specimens are quite different from the more robust Australian aborigines today.

More similar to the present aborigines are the relatively recent remains from Kow Swamp. Believed to have lived 10 kya, Kow Swamp fossils are noted for their robustness: sloping forehead, thick bones, heavy supraorbital torus, and so on. It is strange that humans living 30 kya should be more gracile than those living 20 ky later. However, since the Mungo sample numbers only 2 individuals and the variously gracile and robust Kow Swamp sample numbers over 40, it is possible there might be a similar intrapopulation variation in the Mungo sample were it as large!

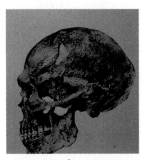

FIGURE 17-60 Předmostí 3, Czechoslovakia. An anatomical modern with a few archaic traits.

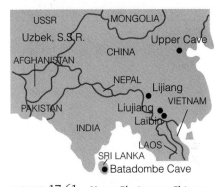

FIGURE 17-61 Upper Plesitocene Chinese and South Asian *sapiens* sites.

FIGURE 17-62 Map of several Australian *H. sapiens sapiens* sites, and one from Java.

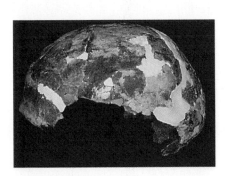

FIGURE 17-63 Mungo I, lateral view. The frontal bone reflects the gracile character of the skull. Less robust.

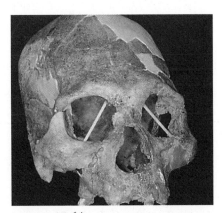

FIGURE 17-64 Kow Swamp 5. Note the greater robusticity of this skull compared with Mungo.

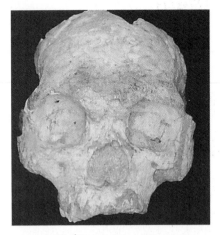

FIGURE 17-65   Wadjak. A fully modern *sapiens* from Java with resemblances to Lake Mungo. Found by Dubois.

FIGURE 17-66   The punch blade technique.

Human Achievement in the Upper Paleolithic

About 30 kya, a warming trend of several thousand years partially melted the glacial ice. The result was that much of Eurasia consisted of tundra and steppe. It was a vast area of treeless country covered with lakes and marshes and a permafrost that prevented the growth of trees but permitted the growth, in the short summers, of flowering plants, mosses, and other kinds of vegetation. The vegetation served as an enormous pasture for herbivorous animals, huge and small, and carnivorous animals that fed off the herbivores. It was a hunter's paradise, with hundreds of thousands of animals stretched across miles of tundra, from Spain through Europe and into the Russian steppes.

New tools for coping with large, and possibly dangerous, animals appeared. The last stage of the Upper Paleolithic, known as the Magdalenean, was a spectacular period of technological innovation. The spear thrower (Fig. 17-69), a wooden or bone hooked rod, extended the hunter's arm, thus enabling him to throw a spear with greater penetrating force. For catching salmon and other fish in rivers, the barbed harpoon was a clever example of the craftsperson's skill. There is also some evidence that the bow and arrow may have been used during this period. The introduction of the punch technique provided blank cores that could be fashioned into burins, for working wood, bone, and antler; into borers, for drilling holes in skins, bones, and shells; and into blades with serrated or notched edges for scraping wooden shafts into a variety of tools.

Large herds of reindeer roamed the tundra along with mammoths, bisons, horses, and a host of smaller animals that served as a bountiful source of food. It was a time of affluence, and the Magdaleneans spread out over Europe, living in caves and open-air camps, and building large shelters. Mammoth bone dwellings

Burin

FIGURE 17-67   Burin, a kind of chisel.

FIGURE 17-68   Upper Paleolithic economy. A common method of hunting used in recent times in North America. This method involves driving a herd over a cliff where they could be easily killed by the hunters. (Courtesy California Academy of Sciences.)

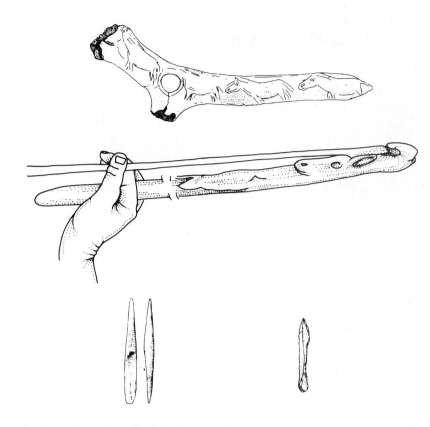

FIGURE 17-69   Magdalenian material. During this last period of the Upper Paleolithic, early human artistic expression reached its greatest height. Note the carving on the spear thrower.

with storage pits have been excavated in the Soviet Union, with evidence of social status distinctions (Soffer, 1985). It was during this period that western Europe (or perhaps Africa) achieved the highest density of population in human history up to that time.

Hunters in Europe continued an older practice of driving animals into bogs and swamps, where they could easily be dispatched and butchered. They also used the method of stampeding horses and caribou over cliffs or into canyon cul-de-sacs. Food was so abundant that it has been suggested that the extinction of some of these Pleistocene prey animals was due to overkill. It is also possible that the change of climate, as the glaciers retreated, affected vegetation and created generally unfavorable ecological conditions for those animals.

The **Upper Paleolithic** was a technological age and, in its way, can be compared to the past several hundred years in our own time of amazing invention and technology after centuries of relative quiet. It appears those living then not only invented new and specialized tools, but the increased use of, and probable experiment with, new materials and new tools, indicating an involvement in technology unknown up to that time.

In addition to their reputation as hunters, western Europeans of the Upper Paleolithic are even better known for their art. Marshack (1989) has traced Upper Paleolithic art to the Neandertal Mousterian period. He believes that the beginnings of artistic expression started with Neandertals and developed from their work to the brilliant art of the Upper Paleolithic.

Solutrean tools may be an example of this. No one is quite sure who made them or where they came from, but stoneknapping developed to the finest degree ever

Upper Paleolithic   Culture period noted for technological, artistic, and behavioral innovations. Also known for appearance of anatomically modern human beings.

FIGURE 17-70   Solutrean blade. This is the best-known work of the Solutrean tradition. Solutrean stone work is considered the best of the Upper Paleolithic.

FIGURE 17-71   Cave painting. A fine
painting of a bison bellowing.

known. Using a pressure-flaking technique, they made beautiful parallel-sided lance-heads, sensitively flaked on both surfaces, with such delicate points they can be considered works of art that never served a utilitarian purpose.

Interest in art can be seen throughout the Upper Paleolithic. Fine sculpture has been excavated in western, central, and eastern Europe, but it is in western Europe during the Upper Paleolithic's final stage that European art surpassed itself. The Magdalenean, in southern France and northern Spain, climaxed years of Upper Paleolithic fine art achievement.

Tools and tool handles often engraved with beautiful and realistic animal carvings and sculptured figurines can be found in many areas of Europe. In the Aurignacian/Perigordian stage, preceding the Magdalenean, cave wall art (see Fig. 17-71) is already in full display, and sculpture in the round is achieved with surprising grace and style. In the Lascaux Cave of southern France, immense wild bulls dominate what is called the Great Hall of Bulls, and horses, deer, and other animals adorn the walls in black, red, and yellow, drawn with remarkable skill.

Female figurines, known as Venuses, were sculpted not only in western Europe, but in central and eastern Europe, and Siberia as well. Some of these figures were realistically carved, and the faces appear to be modeled after actual women. Other figurines may seem grotesque (Fig. 17-72) with sexual characteristics exaggerated, perhaps for fertility or ritual purposes.

The age of art continues and, arguably, reaches its pinnacle in the last Upper Paleolithic stage, the Magdalenean. Although their artwork is also found in France, it is a cave at Altamira in northern Spain that is the most famous. Superb portrayals of bison in red and black, painted on walls and ceilings, taking advantage of natural bulges to give a sense of relief, fill the cave. It is a cornucopia of beautiful art whose meaning has never been satisfactorily explained. It could have been ritualistic, religious, magical, a form of visual communication, or art for the sake of its beauty.

FIGURE 17-72   Venus of Willendorf.

Ever since cave art was discovered, attempts have been made to interpret the sculptures, paintings, and other graphic material found in the caves or on rocks and tools at open-air archeological sites. One of the early explanations of Upper Paleolithic art emphasized the relationship of paintings to hunting: hunting rituals as a kind of imitative magic that would increase hunted animal populations or help hunters successfully find and kill their prey. As new hypotheses were published, their deficiencies were discussed. As these hypotheses faded others were expounded and the cycle of new hypotheses, critiques, new (or refurbished old) hypotheses, critiques, etc., continued.

Among these hypotheses, the association of religious ritual and magic is still viable because of the importance of hunting in Upper Paleolithic economy. Other ideas about these graphics have been widely discussed: the viewing of Upper Paleolithic art from a male/female perspective; the consideration of the dots and lines motif as a notational system associated with language, writing, or a calendar system (Marshack, 1972, 1976); or the dots and lines interpreted as mnemonic devices. Other explanations include why certain areas of caves were used for painting, but not other similar areas; why certain animals were painted but not others; why males were painted singly or in groups, but women only in groups; why males were painted near animals, but women never were; and why groups of animals were painted in the most resonant areas.

These hypotheses intimate certain aspects of Upper Paleolithic culture, especially in western Europe. Hunting was an activity that not only dominated hunters (presumably males) but also artists. Men and women lived "separate" lives, men forming their own groups and women theirs. Rituals, probably for success in hunting, were performed in the best acoustic areas of the cave. (Rituals could also have been a means of passing on cultural traditions to the next generation.) Another use of animal paintings may have been to indicate which animals were most usefully hunted and which were most dangerous. It is also possible that the Upper Paleolithic dots and lines on walls and tools reflect the symbols of the beginning of writing and keeping track of time. It is, of course, very difficult to prove that these cultural activities existed, but with the present hypotheses, they seem reasonable.

Most of our knowledge of the Upper Paleolithic stems from European studies. There were similar changes in other parts of the world, but they have yet to be as thoroughly examined. In Africa, microliths (thumbnail-sized stone flakes hafted to make knives, saws, etc.) and blades characterize Late Stone Age technology.

Open-air settlements, probably temporary camps for a particular purpose, such as butchering, are well known. Also common, and continuing from the Middle Stone Age, are settlements at springs, caves, and rock shelters. These constructed shelters continue to be simple windbreaks, however. Personal adornment items come into use in the Late Stone Age. Bone beads and shell and stone pendants have a wide distribution, and ochre and other coloring materials may have been used for painting the body or decorating clothing. Rock art of the Late Stone Age is known from many areas of sub-Sahara Africa.

In Australia, the coast, river, and lake areas were already inhabited. Core tools were used for procuring wood and shaping such implements as throwing sticks. More than 20 kya, Australians had begun grinding stone ax heads, the first ever made anywhere, and a few thousand years later ground stone mortars, pestles, grinders, and grinding slabs had become established. These stone tools suggest

Between the Atlantic Ocean on the west and Lake Victoria on the east, and between 4° north and 4° south of the equator, live some 150 to 200,000 Pygmies, mainly in the still heavily forested area of the Central African Republic, Zaire, and Cameroon. A research project with a major focus on Pygmy health was directed by Dr. Luligi Cavalli-Sforza, a geneticist from Stanford University, during the years 1967 to 1976. Although Pygmies in other areas were also studied, those from the Central African Republic (C.A.R.) were the center of most of the research, and it is the material on the C.A.R. Pygmies that forms the base of this case study. The team of scientists involved in the project included geneticists, anthropologists, clinicians, and nutritionists.

Pygmies are a short people with an average stature of 5 feet 2 inches for men and a weight of 105 pounds; 4 feet 7 inches and 93 pounds for women.* Their stature is 86.7% of the African average, but in head, chest, and hip measurements, they are very close to average African measurements. Pygmies have been known for about 5000 years and until recently have been forest hunters and gatherers. Many still are. There is a trend in recent years for Pygmies to permanently move into villages, and it appears to be only a matter of time before most Pygmies are acculturated into a sedentary life.

Throughout the area where Pygmies live, a reciprocal relationship had developed between Pygmies and farmers, a relationship that may go back as much as 2000 years (Cavalli-Sforza, 1986). For several months of the year, Pygmies work for the farmers and provide them with meat, mushrooms, honey, and wood for building their huts. In exchange, the villagers provide Pygmies with food (especially bananas and manioc†), iron, pottery, and clothing. The villagers believe themselves superior to the Pygmies and think of them as their property. The relationship is hereditary; that is, the children of the family who work for a farmer continue to work for the farmer's children, and so on. However, as Colin Turnbull (1965) has made clear, Pygmies are not slaves but have always retained their independence, coming and going as

they please. As a matter of fact, farmers are more economically dependent on Pygmies than vice versa.

With some variation, Pygmies typically spend about 80% of the year in the forest living in their traditional way by hunting and gathering. A camp consists of about 9 huts, with each hut ordinarily occupied by a single family, with an average of 3.4 persons per hut. The average number of persons per camp is 32.6. There are no chiefs, and each camp makes its own decisions on where and when to move on an average of every two months. Families are not tied to any one camp and move about from one camp to another, resulting in a good deal of fission/fusion. Camps are separated by about an hour's walk and several camps, forming a band, may cooperate in hunting.

The essential aim of the Pygmy project was to analyze Pygmy health. Because of the difficulties inherent in forest living, researchers performed the work of taking blood samples and examining people during the months that Pygmies lived in the villages. This way of proceeding may have skewed their findings, as working in the village and eating starchy bananas and manioc produced nutritional and other quirks in the Pygmies that apparently might not have occurred under an evidently healthier life in the forest. Following is a brief report of the results of the research project.

Examinations revealed a mild protein deficiency in the Pygmies, which was probably due to their village diet wherein they subsisted mainly on starches. Although infrequent, several cases of kwashiorkor (see p. 168) among children were found, supporting the hypothesis of insufficient protein intake. It is also possible that the heavy starch diet during this time might have been responsible for the relatively high incidence of goiters found, especially among women. The presence of goiters, known to be associated with manioc, correlated with those Pygmies who had close contact with villagers and adopted their diet.

Also possibly diet-related were the Pygmies' dental problems, such as tartar and caries, which are widespread in industrial nations as well. Tartar was not as common as caries, which were found in 27% of the Pygmy men and 18% of the Pygmy women. More prevalent still was atrophic gingivitis—a recession of the gums that can lead to the loss of teeth—that affected 62% of the women and 77% of the men. Gingivitis was also attrib-

---

*Ituri Pygmies, who live in Cameroon, are about 3 inches shorter than those in the Central African Republic.

†Manioc is a starchy root crop that resembles the sweet potato and is eaten in much the same way. It is native to Brazil and is widely grown in Africa.

uted to the kinds of food that Pygmies ate during their stay in the village.

A rather high percentage of Pygmies were afflicted with enlarged livers and spleens (the spleen filters blood and produces red blood cells when necessary)—70% had either enlarged livers or enlarged spleens or both. Researchers believe that malaria may cause enlarged spleens. Liver enlargement could be the result of numerous infections and parasites, but it might possibly be associated with malnutrition. Researchers could not discover the cause here without further laboratory work, which was not feasible in the field.

The cardiovascular systems of the Pygmy population were in pretty good shape. The average blood pressure of adults was 118 (systolic) over 68.9 (diastolic) for women and for men it was 123.3 over 20.9. Out of 168 persons examined, only 6 had high blood pressure. A mere 1.8% out of 555 subjects examined had extrasystolic arrhythmias. No valvular cardiopathy was diagnosed, perhaps because those who suffered this severe condition would not have survived for very long in the harsh rainforest environment. Systolic heart murmurs were quite frequent in about 20% of the population, but researchers could detect no reason for this relatively high occurrence.

Malaria was found to be endemic, actually hyperendemic (a frequency greater than 50%) among the children of the Pygmies of the Central African Republic. The parasite *Plasmodium falciparum*, carried by the *Anopheles* mosquito, was found in more than 50% of the children (12 years of age and under).

Intestinal protozoa were fairly common, but much more frequent were intestinal worms (helminths, nematodes, hookworms, and roundworms). Some of the worms existed in over 75% of the population. Cavalli-Sforza writes that, "The load of micro- and macroparasites must be responsible for the relatively high mortality at all ages." (1986, p. 421).

There were other parasite-caused diseases found in the Pygmy. These are:

1. *Yaws*, which produces skin lesions. This disease has virtually disappeared from most of the rest of the world due to the efficacy of treatment with penicillin. Unfortunately, penicillin is not easily available to Pygmies, so yaws are present and widespread among them. Yaws resembles (but is not) syphilis. Venereal diseases themselves are rare among Pygmies.

2. *Toxoplasmosis*, which is an infection caused by parasitic organisms that attack the central nervous system. Toxoplasmosis is found in almost 40% of Pygmies and can be fatal in infants. Cats are the ordinary source of the infection, but since Pygmies do not have cats, researchers suggest that poorly cooked meat may be responsible, or possibly forest felines.

3. *Toxocariasis*, which is a common parasite found in dogs. This condition can also infect humans. About 45% of Pygmies tested positive, and dogs—the Pygmies' only domestic animal—are the obvious source of the infection.

4. *Scabies*, which is caused by a mite. This is not a serious disease but it results in intense and annoying itching. It is common among Pygmies of all ages.

5. *Chiggers*, common in the southern United States, is also common among Pygmies. It is caused by a mite, and produces itching and sometimes small blisters or swelling.

6. *Parotid hypertrophy*, which is the swelling of the parotid glands located above the angle of the jaw. This swelling is usually associated with mumps, but if it is not diagnosed as mumps, it is considered an index of prior protein malnutrition. It was found to be frequent among Pygmies.

Researchers found that the five leading causes of death* of Pygmy adults were: diarrhea, 26.7%, probably caused by amoebic dysentery, the result of poor sanitation; witchcraft (according to Pygmies), 10.8%; old age, 8.8%; bronchitis, 7.4%; and accidents during hunting and gathering (such as falling from trees while searching for honey), 3.7%. Among children, the leading cause of death was measles at 23.1%. (The high incidence of measles was due to an epidemic that occurred during the research period.) Other causes of children's death were: diarrhea, 12.9%; convulsions, 12.9%; witchcraft, 3.2%; and malaria, 3.2%.

---

*Identification of the death-causing diseases were based on descriptions given by the Pygmies and not by researchers' diagnoses. Researchers believed Pygmy descriptions were accurate enough for identification to be valid.

An interesting finding of the project was that genetic markers (genes) reflected an admixture of 65% among C.A.R. Pygmies. This indicates considerable interbreeding between these Pygmies and non-Pygmy Africans. Some Pygmy groups showed a higher percentage, and others, a lower. The C.A.R. percentage is supported by their stature measurement, which is intermediate between Ituri Pygmies, with the lowest (almost zero percentage) and average Africans.

If the C.A.R. Pygmies admixture is 65%, shouldn't their stature be taller than it is? Cavalli-Sforza explains the short stature as an adaptation to the hot and very humid environment in which they live. Less weight produces less internal heat, which decreases the chances of heat exhaustion. Climate may also explain the width of the nose, which is greater, in absolute measurements, than the African average, and the nose becomes even wider when considered in proportion to the rest of the body. Since these features are so important for survival in the forest, Pygmies have retained them.

The results of the Pygmy study do not clearly indicate whether C.A.R. Pygmies are healthy or sick. If the enlarged spleen, enlarged liver, and the heavy load of parasites they carry are the criteria, Pygmies are very ill indeed. However, Cavalli-Sforza sums up:

. . . in spite of these problems, disease does not seem to impair in any important way the capacity of these Pygmies to

lead an incredibly active and happy life. [But he adds] Naturally, the ones we see are, in almost all cases, those who have survived conditions that kill more than 50% of Pygmies before they reach adult age. (1986, p. 421)

A final note: Cavalli-Sforza (1986, p. 422) believes Pygmies may be a model of the Upper Paleolithic. However, he also believes that Pygmies have been in contact with farmers for 2000 years. We have learned that the contact between the two groups is very close, that there is also a close economic relationship between them, that Pygmy admixture reflects interbreeding with the farmers, that Pygmies no longer use stone weapons but rather use iron and pottery implements that they acquire in their trade with the farmers, and that they are in touch with whatever ideas and material culture is found in the villages. Under these conditions, it seems quite doubtful that the ancient Pygmy culture has remained so unmodified that their present culture could serve as a model for the Upper Paleolithic.

SOURCES:

Cavalli-Sforza, Luligi Luca (ed.). *African Pygmies*, New York: Academic Press, 1986.

Turnbull, Colin M. *Wayward Servants*, Garden City: The Natural History Press, 1965.

the gathering of seeds, roots, and vegetables, and at least made possible a semi-sedentary lifestyle.

The early Australians buried their dead, and some were ceremoniously cremated and then buried, a practice maintained by aborigines through the last century. They also produced a rock art—red ochre was used to decorate artifacts, walls, and bodies of the living. Bone beads were another decorative, and perhaps, ceremonial item.

Summary of Upper Paleolithic

As we look back at the Late Pleistocene (or Upper Paleolithic), we can see it as the culmination of several million years of cultural development. Change was slow at first, but as cultural traditions and materials accumulated and the brain (and, we assume, intelligence) expanded, the rate of change quickened.

Cultural evolution continued with the appearance of early archaic *sapiens* and moved a bit faster with later archaic *sapiens*. Neandertals in Eurasia, and their contemporaries elsewhere, added ceremonial burials, rituals, technological innovations, and much more.

Building on the existing culture, Late Pleistocene populations attained sophisticated cultural and material heights in a seemingly short burst of exciting activity. In Europe

> Everything seems to have exploded during the upper paleolithic, which saw the appearance of big-game hunting on a regular mass-killing basis; of potent new weapons, including harpoons, spear-throwers, and possibly the bow and arrow; of necklaces and other body ornaments; long-distance trade; needles and "tailored" clothing; burials with grave goods, indicating people of status; and very probably basic changes in the nature of language itself. (Pfeiffer, 1987, p. 88)

Upper Paleolithic changes also occurred on other continents, but it is in the caves of western Europe where its display is most spectacular.

This dynamic age was doomed, or so it appears, with the climatic changes of about 10 kya. As the temperature slowly rose and the glaciers retreated, animal and plant species were seriously affected, and humans were thus affected as well. As traditional prey animals and easy-to-process food were depleted or disappeared altogether, other means of obtaining food were sought.

Grinding hard seeds or roots became important, and as familiarity with vegetation increased, domestication of plants and animals developed. Dependence on domestication became critical; permanent settlements, new technology, and more complex social organization appeared.

With the advent of the Upper Paleolithic, the long period of *sapiens* evolution, beginning in the latter half of the Middle Pleistocene, reaches *H. sapiens sapiens*. Starting with transitional forms between *H. erectus* and *sapiens*, (Petralona, Verteszöllös, Bilzingsleben, Arago—see Box 17-5), this mosaic of earlieer and later forms continues with later archaic *sapiens* in the latter portion of the Middle Pleistocene.

It has been suggested that since the more modern traits resemble those of Neandertals rather than fully anatomical moderns, these individuals (La Chaise, Biache, etc.) are more properly called preneandertal. That is, they were the ancestors of the Würm populations of Eurasia.

Human evolution was also proceeding in Africa and the Far East, including Indonesia and Australia. Australia has no record of *H. erectus*, and it is clear, at the present time, that it was settled by *sapiens* migrants from Indonesia and New Guinea (and other nearby islands), who evolved to the present aborigines.

Chinese human evolution begins with *H. erectus*, then to archaic *sapiens*, and finally to modern *sapiens*. This may have occurred without gene flow (as Chinese and other paleoanthropologists believe), or there may have been migrations from southeast Asia.

Africa's hominid history is much older than China's and, according to present evidence, the oldest hominids (australopithecines) are found here. Also, the oldest *H. erectus* was discovered in Africa and, if the dates and fossil designations are correct, the oldest fully moderns as well.

Finally, we would emphasize that Neandertals and all humans on earth today belong to the same species: *H. sapiens*. There are physical differences between us, of course, and for that reason Neandertals* are assigned to the subspecies *H. sa-*

---

*There are paleoanthropologists who advocate a separate species for Neandertals, such as *H. neandertalensis*.

piens neanderthalensis, and we to the subspecies *H. sapiens sapiens*. Neandertals have received a bad press for the past 75 years and are often portrayed as pathological creatures of little skill, grace, or intelligence. Actually, the differences between "us" and "them" are minor, but the overhanging brow, facial prognathism, and the absence of a chin influence our judgment. If we prefer the modern face, it is pertinent to recall the suggestion that our present face became modern because our ancestors were compelled for a variety of reasons to change the food they chewed.

The New World

By 30 kya northeast Asia was inhabited by anatomically moderns. They hunted large herbivores using stone- and bone-tipped weapons and probably domesticated dogs. Their tailored skin clothing, shelters made from animal hides, and the use of fire helped them survive in this cold and barren environment. It is very likely that this population was the ancestors of American Indians.

During the last glaciation, known in the New World as the Wisconsin, much of the northern latitudes were covered by vast sheets of ice for thousands of years at a time. Water frozen in the glaciers lowered sea levels of the world more than 300 feet. The Bering Sea floor was exposed and formed a land bridge, Beringia, about 1,300 miles wide from north to south. The land bridge served as an extension of northeast Asia to North America, and people moving into it for its available resources, eventually entered Alaska.

The newcomers settled in central Alaska, which was free from ice, and immigrants later moved into Canada and then migrated south, occupying North and

FIGURE 17-73   *H. sapiens sapiens* sites. Note that anatomically moderns inhabit all continents. Only better known fossils are listed.

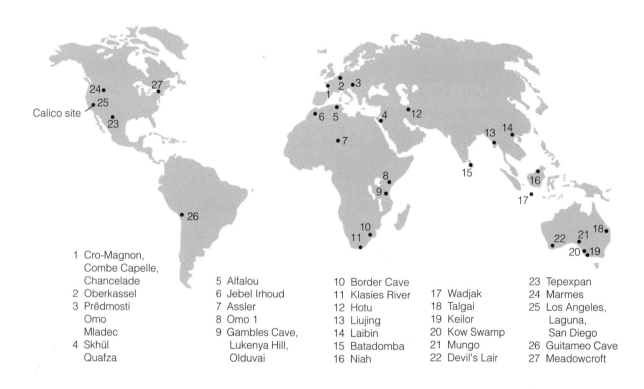

1 Cro-Magnon,
  Combe Capelle,
  Chancelade
2 Oberkassel
3 Prêdmosti
  Omo
  Mladec
4 Skhül
  Quafza

5 Alfalou
6 Jebel Irhoud
7 Assler
8 Omo 1
9 Gambles Cave,
  Lukenya Hill,
  Olduvai

10 Border Cave
11 Klasies River
12 Hotu
13 Liujing
14 Laibin
15 Batadomba
16 Niah

17 Wadjak
18 Talgai
19 Keilor
20 Kow Swamp
21 Mungo
22 Devil's Lair

23 Tepexpan
24 Marmes
25 Los Angeles,
   Laguna,
   San Diego
26 Guitameo Cave
27 Meadowcroft

FIGURE 17-74   Major types of North American Paleo-Indian projectile points: (*a*) Clovis, (*b*) Folsom, (*c*) Plano, (*d*) Dalton. (Courtesy of William Turnbaugh)

(a)   (b)   (c)   (d)

South America. The people we know as American Indians may have entered North America in one or more migrations; the number is still open to question. Recently, three migrations, correlated with linguistic, dental, and genetic data, were suggested (Greenberg et al., 1986). The date of entry into the New World is still a major archeological issue.

There are (at least) two schools of thought on the matter: (1) One believes that the hunters came across the Bering Strait *more than* 12.5 kya. Of this group, there are proponents who supports an estimate of 80–100 kya—others argue for a 30 kya date; (2) The second school, representing the traditional position, proposes a date of 12 kya because, they claim, there is *no solid evidence* beyond about 12.5 kya. Archeological evidence is abundant for the more recent date, and this evidence is quite common in western United States, where the early projectile points known as **Folsom** and **Clovis** were found.

There are a number of sites that may be older than 12 kya, such as Meadowcroft near Pittsburgh, Pennsylvania, Monte Verde in Chile, and sites in Alaska. However, many archeologists believe there are problems with these sites that preclude accepting the dates claimed by the excavators (Marshall, 1990). Archeologists have learned to be very cautious when there is any doubt about site dates, geology, stratigraphy, contamination, or anything else that is not clear about the excavation. It is entirely possible that sites older than 12.5 kya do, in fact, exist, but none has yet been accepted without reservations by most archeologists.

The earliest people of the New World, called Paleo-Indians, were big game hunters, the big game being mammoths and other large animals, which they hunted with spears or lances armed with Clovis-fluted projectile points. (They also used the atlatl which extended the distance a spear or lance could be thrown.) About 10 kya, mammoth hunters were succeeded by hunters who pursued the giant long-horned bison, employing a smaller fluted point, the Folsom. With the disappearance of the giant bison, hunters using still another type of fluted point, the **Plano**, switched their efforts to the smaller bison we know today, *Bison bison*

Clovis   Phase of North American prehistory, 12 kya to 11 kya in the West, during which short-fluted projectile points were used in hunting mammoths.

Folsom   Phase of southern Great Plains prehistory, 10 kya to 8 kya, during which long-fluted projectile points were used for bison hunting.

Fluting   Removal of large flakes in order to thin projectile point bases for hafting.

Plano   Great Plains bison-hunting culture of 8 to 7 kya, which employed narrow unfluted points.

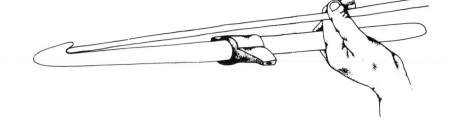

occidentalis. A popular bison-hunting method was stampeding bison into arroyo cul-de-sacs or over cliffs (Fig. 17-68).

Perhaps Paleo-Indians overhunted the large game, or perhaps the end of the Ice Age created adverse ecological conditions, but about 10 kya large game was becoming extinct. Although hunting remained an important source of food, more emphasis was being placed on foraging for a wide variety of plant food. Fish and shellfish also became a regular part of the diet. This period is known as the Archaic, and we see the development of new technologies that produced fishing gear, traps, baskets, and other containers, and composite weapons, such as harpoons and the throwing board, or atlatl (Fig. 17-75).

As in the Old World, food collection developed into food production in the New World about 9 kya, but only a few animals were domesticated. Farming became a significant food source in sections of North America, the dry highlands of Mexico, and western South America.

Summary

Archaic *sapiens*, apparently evolving from *H. erectus*, display a mosaic of *erectus* and *sapiens* characteristics. In Europe and western Asia, Neandertals appear about 125 kya. Archaic *sapiens* are also present in China and Africa and in both cases lead to a.m. humans without a Neandertal phase. Neandertals introduced technological innovations, new settlement patterns, and new methods of obtaining food. They also practiced some forms of religious ceremonies. Recent research suggests Neandertals may have been capable of articulated speech.

The date and location of the appearance of a.m. human beings is being fiercely debated at present. One side claims anatomical moderns evolved in Africa more than 100 kya and then, migrating out of Africa, displaced archaic *sapiens* in the rest of the world. The "Garden of Eden" hypothesis, which is based on molecular biology research work with mtDNA, supports this position. The other side maintains that, in various geographic regions of the world, local groups of archaic *sapiens* evolved to anatomical moderns.

In the Late Pleistocene, new technological, ritualistic, and artistic developments appear at a more rapid rate. Various forms of art are practiced on all continents, but the most sophisticated artistic achievements are seen in the caves of western Europe.

Modern humans reached Australia 40 kya or earlier, probably island-hopping from New Guinea. Entry into the New World was made by people from northeast Asia over the land bridge that is now the Bering Strait at least 12.5 kya.

All a.m. populations were hunters, but climatic changes may have altered conditions so that new sources of food were required. An emphasis on collecting plant food led to farming in many areas of the world.

Questions for Review

1. Support the argument for and against gradual human evolution.
2. What physical traits characterize archaic *sapiens* as *sapiens*?
3. Can you account for the appearance of these traits?
4. How do archaic *sapiens* differ from modern humans?
5. What physical and cultural differences do you find between earlier and later archaics?
6. Describe the culture of European archaic *sapiens*.
7. Why are Neandertals so well known to the general public?
8. What technological innovations did Neandertal introduce?
9. It has been said that La Chapelle was one of the most important Neandertal discoveries. Explain why La Chapelle does, or does not, deserve this attention.
10. Discuss the case of St. Cesaire. What problems does this fossil raise? What problems does it resolve?
11. Were Neandertals cannibals? What is the evidence?
12. Discuss the question of single source vs. multiple sources of *H. sapiens sapiens*. Give examples to support your choice.
13. Describe the Neandertal lifestyle. Why do you believe it was a (good) (poor) time to live?
14. Do you see basic differences between Neandertal and African Middle Stone Age cultures? Explain.
15. Of what theoretic significance is it if anatomical moderns *did* evolve in Africa more than 100 kya.
16. What is the "Garden of Eden" hypothesis?
17. Describe the method that was used to develop this hypothesis.
18. What arguments do the opponents of this hypothesis present?
19. Why is Australia significant in a.m. human history?
20. How does the New World fit into the history of a.m. humans?
21. In what way(s) was Upper Paleolithic inferior/superior to Middle Paleolithic culture.
22. Discuss the following statement from the text: "If we prefer the modern face, it is pertinent to recall the suggestion that our present face became modern because our ancestors were compelled for a variety of reasons to change the food they chewed."

BOX 17-5 **Fossil Briefs**

Guide to Fossil Briefs

Early Archaic *Sapiens*

Africa	Bodo
	Broken Hill
Asia	Dali
	Maba
Europe	Arago
	Bilzingsleben
	La Chaise
	Petralona
	Suard
	Steinheim
	Swanscombe
	Vértesszöllös

Later Archaics

Europe	Ehringsdorf
	Fontechevade
Neandertals	
Europe	La Chapelle-aux-Saints
	Krapina
	St. Cesaire
Israel	Tabun

Anatomically Moderns

Africa	Border Cave
	Klasies River Mouth
	Omo 1
Israel	Qafzeh
	Skhūl 5
Europe	Cro-Magnon
	Mladeč
China	Upper Cave
Australia	Kow Swamp
	Mungo

Early Archaic *Sapiens*: Africa

Bodo

Date found:	In 1976, by A. Asfaw, P. Whitehead, and C. Wood.
Site:	Bodo d'Ar, Awash River Valley, Afar, Ethiopia.
Dating:	Middle Pleistocene (more precise dating unavailable).
Material:	Incomplete skull.
Traits:	Extraordinarily thick vault bones; face is large and rugged; browridges prominent; postorbital constriction not as great as African *H. erectus*, such as Olduvai Hominid 9; flattening of frontal bone.
Comment:	Transitional form of East Africa; first evidence of scalping.

Broken Hill, also Kabwe

Date found:	June, 1921, by T. Zwigelaar, A. S. Armstrong, A. W. Whittington, and H. Hrdlička.
Site:	Broken Hill Mine, Kabwe, Zambia, South Africa.
Dating:	Various dates have been suggested; recent dates are 130 kya and late Middle Pleistocene.
Material:	Skull, parietal, maxilla, humerus, sacrum, and 2 ilia belong to 3 or 4 individuals.
Traits:	Cranium: massive browridges, retreating forehead, low vault. Prominent occipital torus, greatest width low, no canine fossa, cranial base modern; postcranial bones quite similar to modern humans; postcranial bones may not belong to skull.
Associated finds:	Quartz and chert stone tools of the African Middle Stone Age (Upper Pleistocene); fauna includes birds, reptiles, and mammals—mongoose, lion, elephant, zebra, rhino, buffalo.
Cranial capacity:	1280 cm³
Comment:	Key fossil in discussion of *sapiens* in Africa.

BOX 17-5

Early Archaic *Sapiens*: Asia

Dali

Date found:	In 1978, by S. Liu and others.
Site:	Near Jiefang village, Dali County, Shaanxi Province.
Dating:	Late Middle Pleistocene; 230–100 kya.
Material:	Well-preserved cranium of male under 30 years, with some distortion in the lower face.
Traits:	Cranium size is at upper end of *H. erectus* range; robust supraorbital torus; prominent muscular markings; cranial vault low; cranium with sagittal keeling; retreating forehead; skull height intermediate between Zhoukoudian and western archaic *sapiens*; broadest part of skull higher than *erectus*; skull thickness less than Zhoukoudian but more than European archaic *sapiens*; face does not appear prognathous.
Associated finds:	Many stone tools, mainly small scrapers of flint and quartzite. Fauna: deer, rhino, beaver, horse, ostrich.
Cranial capacity:	Estimates: 1120 cm³, 1200 cm³.
Comment:	Evidence of archaic *sapiens* in China.

Maba

Date found:	In 1958, by farm workers.
Site:	Cave on Shizi Hill, about one mile southwest of Maba village, Shaoguan County, Guangdong Province.
Dating:	Early Upper Pleistocene, 140–120 kya.
Material:	Incomplete calotte of middle-aged male.
Traits:	Modest keel on frontal bone; frontal recedes, but postorbital constriction less than *erectus*; broad nasal bones.
Associated finds:	No artifacts; fauna: tapir, rhino, pig, deer, cattle, ancient elephant.
Comment:	Originally known as Neandertal; now considered archaic *sapiens*.

Early Archaic *Sapiens*: Europe

Arago

Date found:	1964 and later by Henry de Lumley.
Site:	Cave site, Verdouble Valley, Pyrenees, near village of Tautavel, near the Spanish border in southeastern France.
Dating:	Estimated at about 400 ky.
Material:	Over 50 cranial and postcranial remains of at least 4 adults and 3 children. Most important specimens are: damaged partial cranium (Arago 21) consisting mostly of deformed face and vault and five teeth in place (Fig. 16-43); two mandibles, parietal bone, almost complete innominate, and various other cranial and postcranial fragments. Arago 21 bones are of

BOX 17-5 **Fossil Briefs, continued**

young "male" with very pronounced supraorbital torus and relatively long, flat, and narrow forehead. However, distortion of face and frontal bones makes measurement difficult. Hip bones and femur resemble *H. erectus* from Olduvai and Beijing.

Associated finds:	Tools: Most tools are Tayacian (pre-Mousterian) industry and Acheulian. Fauna: wolf, cave bear, wild boar, wild ox, deer, reindeer, ibex, rhinocerous, horse, elephant, beaver, rabbit, rodent, tortoise, and some birds.
Cranial capacity:	1050–1150 cm³ range.
Comment:	One of the larger archeological sites in France for the period in which Arago lived.

Bilzingsleben

Date found:	1972 by D. Mania and other workers from 1972 through 1977. Much of the material written up by E. Vlček.
Site:	Steinrinne, about ½ mile south of village of Bilzingsleben, about 25 miles north of Weimar, Germany.
Dating:	Most likely Mindel-Riss interglacial, about 425–200 kya, probably closer to 280 kya. Questions still remain concerning date.
Material:	Mainly pieces of one skull: glabellar fragment, frontal fragment, two parietal fragments, right upper molar; teeth from at least 2 individuals. Glabellar fragment associated with pronounced supraorbital torus. Upper molar has large pulp cavity (i.e., taurodontism).
Associated finds:	Tools: flake industry, quartzite chopping tools, antler clubs, and retouched bone implements. Interglacial fauna: straight-tusked elephant, rhino, wild horse, wild ox, deer, pig, monkey, bear, wildcat, beaver, and giant beaver. Flora also interglacial: oak, lime, maple, hazel, and firethorn.
Cranial capacity:	No estimate.
Comment:	Looks more like *erectus* than any European fossil, but date suggests archaic *sapiens*.

La Chaise

Bougeois-Delaunay

Date found:	Site discovered in 1850. Hominid remains found by A. Debenath in 1970s.
Site:	Rock shelter near village of La Chaise, a few miles west of Montbron, Charente, western France.
Dating:	Unclear. Estimates from 200–150 kya.
Material:	Remains represent 3 or 4 individuals, adults or adolescents. The skull (calotte) is very low and thick, much of the parietals and the frontal bone (supraorbital region missing) are present, also the occipital; an almost complete mandible; femur shaft.
Traits:	Occipital measurements are intermediate between Swanscombe and Neandertals—shows Neandertal morphology, as does a temporal bone. No taurodontism, but mandible morphology similar to Neandertals. Femoral shaft characteristics are similar to Neandertals.
Cranial capacity:	No estimates.
Comment:	La Chaise appears to represent a connection between earlier archaic forms (such as Swanscombe) and later archaic forms (such as Würm Neandertals).

BOX 17-5

Petralona

Date found:	1959. Villagers digging for water fell into a cave that had been sealed and unknown. A year later, a practically complete fossil hominid skull was found.
Site:	Cave near Petralona, 23 miles southwest of Thessaloniki, northeastern Greece.
Dating:	Several dating methods used, but secure date still unavailable. Estimates range from 160 to 620 ky. Some agreement that reasonable date would be around 350–500 ky.
Material:	Almost complete skull.
Traits:	Skull shows mosaic of characters resembling *H. erectus* and other later hominids. Prominent supraorbital torus, retreating forehead, skull vault low, and occipital bone protuberant. Cranial thickness and occipital morphology *erectus*-like, but parietals, temporals, and nasal morphology closely resemble later hominids.
Associated finds:	Some stone tools and bone artifacts recovered from cave; tools belong to early Mousterian culture and include quartz "balls," scrapers, and chopping tools. Bone awls and bone scrapers also found. Mammalian remains include cave bear, red deer, cave lion, horse, deer, wild ox, wild goat, wolf, hyena, and rhino.
Cranial capacity:	Estimates, 1190–1220 cm³
Comment:	Could be one of the oldest human fossils in Europe. Possibly ancestral to Neandertals.

Suard

Date found:	1870. Later excavations by P. David and A. Debenath.
Site:	West of Bougeois-Delaunay in La Chaise cave area, Charente, western France.
Dating:	Complicated: ?215–100 kya.
Material:	Incomplete calotte. Parietal and left half of frontal of young adult; adult occipital. Children's remains: frontal, mandible, and some teeth.
Traits:	All bones have affinities with Neandertal, in most cases, intermediate between *H. erectus* and Neandertal.
Cranial capacity:	1050 cm³.
Comment:	Like La Chaise, Suard presents evidence for a pre-Neandertal lineage.

Steinheim

Date found:	July 24, 1933, by Karl Sigrist, son of the owner of the gravel pit. It was removed under the direction of Fritz Berckhemer, curator of the Württembergische Naturaliensammlung.
Site:	Gravel pit at Steinheim on the Murr, twelve miles north of the city of Stuttgart, Germany.
Dating:	Mindel-Riss interglacial, about 300–250 kya. Dating still uncertain.
Material:	Calvarium (skull minus the mandible) of a young individual, dated to about 250 kya. The skull is seriously damaged on left side (see Fig. 17-3b), the damage inflicted during life. The skull was then removed from the body. The foramen magnum was enlarged to open up the base, presumably to remove the brain (see Fig. 17-3a). "Such a procedure on the dead body may have involved magical or religious activity" (Adam, 1985, p. 275).

BOX 17-5 **Fossil Briefs, continued**

Traits:	Archaic features—relatively small skull; small mastoid process, heavy supraorbital torus, broad nasal aperture. Advanced features—large frontal sinus, vertical parietals, deep nasal root, pronounced canine fossa, relatively small third molar, thin occipital bone and gracile occipital torus.
Cranial capacity:	Estimate: 1100 cm³.
Comment:	May be ancestral to Neandertal.

Swanscombe

Date found:	June, 1935, and March, 1936, by A. T. Marston; July, 1955, by Mr. and Mrs. B. O. Wymer, A. Gibson, and J. Wymer.
Site:	Barnfield pit, Swanscombe, Kent, England.
Dating:	Mindel-Riss interglacial, about 300–250 kya. Dating still uncertain.
Material:	Occipital bone, 1935; left parietal, 1936; right parietal, 1955. The 1955 right parietal is remarkable, since it was found 19 years after the left and clearly fits t he earlier parietal and occipital bones.
Traits:	Bones look modern, but parietals are exceptionally thick; occipital shows no signs of a bun but a suprainiac fossa is present; occipital condyles and orientation of foramen magnum do not significantly differ from *H. sapiens*. Unfortunately, the frontal bone and the face are missing, and whether Swanscombe would have had a supraorbital torus similar to Steinheim is still debated. The occipitals of Steinheim and Swanscombe are similar, and both individuals lived at about the same time.
Associated finds:	Numerous hand axes and flake tools of Middle Acheulian industry. Mammalian bones: wolf, lion, elephant, rhino, horse, deer, giant ox, hare, and cave bear skull.
Cranial capacity:	Estimate: 1325 cm³.
Comment:	May be ancestral to Neandertal.

Vértesszöllös

Date found:	1965 by Dr. Laslo Vertes
Site:	Near the village of Vértesszöllös, 30 miles west of Budapest, Hungary.
Dating:	Once dated at 350 ky but more recently at 185 ky.
Material:	Adult occipital bone and fragments of infant teeth.
Traits:	Thickness, breadth, and angulation of occiput are older traits, as is undivided occipital torus. Height and curvature of upper segment of occiput are modern.
Associated finds:	Numerous artifacts found including pebble tools, chopper tools, flaked tools, many of them small. Faunal remains of early Middle Pleistocene: wolf, lion, bear, wild horse, deer, hyena, and giant beaver.
Cranial capacity:	Estimated, 1115–1437 cm³.

BOX 17-5

Later Archaics: Europe

Ehringsdorf

Date found:	Collected between 1908–1925 by workers in Kämpfe's and Fischer quarries.
Site:	Ehringsdorf, near Weimar, Germany.
Dating:	Complex stratigraphy makes dating difficult; possible last interglacial; Uranium Series dating give various dates: 225 kya, 60 to 120 kya, and 115 kya. Best estimate: last interglacial.
Material:	9 individuals: several parietals, femoral shaft, cranial fragments; adult mandible, juvenile facial and postcranial fragments.
Traits:	Parietals seem advanced trait, but other material resembles classic Neandertals.
Associated finds:	Tools: mainly flint scrapers, some bifaces.
Comment:	Could be an ancestor of Neandertals. Dating problems make phylogenetic placement difficult.

Fontechevade

Date found:	1947 by Mlle. G. Henri-Martin.
Site:	Cave near Montbron, Charente, western France.
Dating:	Probably late Riss glacial.
Material:	Frontal bone fragments; partial calotte (2 individuals).
Traits:	Still debated whether bones display a.m. human traits or classic Neandertal; partial calotte more robust; several reconstructions display character of bones differently; bones may be too fragmented to determine classification.
Associated finds:	Numerous choppers, chopping tools, large end scrapers made from quartz and quartzite.
Comment:	May be an ancestor of Neandertal.

Later Archaics: Neandertals (Europe)

La Chapelle-aux-Saints

Date found:	1908 by the Abbés A. and J. Bouyssonie and L. Bardon.
Site:	In a cave near the village of La Chapelle-aux-Saints, about 25 miles southeast of Corrèze, southwest France.
Dating:	Upper Pleistocene, probably early Würm in the 50 kya range.
Material:	An almost complete skeleton of an aging male. Bones are very robust, heavy supraorbital torus, and sloping forehead. Associated with bones were evolved Mousterian tools. Also in the cave were cold weather animal bones such as woolly rhinoceros, reindeer, ibex, wild horse, and land bison.
Cranial capacity:	1620 cm³.
Comment:	The best-known Neandertal who was made famous by the detailed description of M. Boule (1908). It was this description that has been used by cartoonists to satirize Neandertals. As more Neandertals have been discovered, it became very clear that La Chapelle is not typical of this group of archaic *sapiens*.

BOX 17-5   **Fossil Briefs, continued**

Krapina

Date found:	1899–1905, by K. Gorjanovic-Kramberger.
Site:	Rock shelter on the outskirts of Krapina, 25 miles north of Zagreb, Yugoslavia.
Dating:	End of Riss-Würm Interglacial; possibly early Würm glacial.
Material:	About 800 fragments, including almost 200 isolated teeth, make up the sample; from many individuals including men, women, and children. There are 5 skulls (A, B, C, D, E) complete enough to study, but C is the only one that gives some form of cranium and face. Almost all bones of the body are represented, but all are fragmented.
Traits:	Relatively low vault, broad occiput and probably occipital bun; large face; canine fossae lacking; midface prognathism but not as much as in western European Neandertals; chin lacking; anterior teeth very large, extensive taurodontism in molars; retromolar space in mandible; postcranial bones quite similar to other Neandertals.
Associated finds:	Tools: mainly Mousterian, including points and scrapers. Fauna: rhinoceros, cave bear, wild ox, beaver, red deer, and marmot.
Cranial capacity:	1450 cm^3 (Krapina B).
Comment:	Key fossil site of Central Europe. Once classified as "progressive" Neandertal; question of cannibalism; oldest deliberate burial, perhaps.

St. Cesaire

Date found:	1979, by F. Lévèque.
Site:	Pierrot's Rock, just south of St. Cesaire, some 7 miles from Saintes, Charente-Maritime, France.
Dating:	Würm glaciation, 34–35 kya.
Material:	Right half of cranium; right half of mandible, some postcranial bones.
Traits:	Receding forehead, low cranial vault, prominent supraorbital torus, bifacial prognathism, flattened maxilla without canine fossa; mandible, chinless with large retromolar space; limb bones similar to other Neandertals.
Associated finds:	Points and backed blades of Chatelperronian (Upper Paleolithic) industry. In layers above human remains are tools attributed to the Upper Paleolithic Aurignacian industry; also in upper layers are faunal remains, especially of reindeer.
Cranial capacity:	No estimates.
Comment:	Its very late appearance raises questions of the Neandertal/a.m. human relationship.

BOX 17-5

Later Archaics: Neandertals (Israel)

Tabun

Date found:	In 1932 by T. D. McCown (Joint Expedition of the British School of Archaeology in Jerusalem and the American School of Prehistoric Research.)
Site:	Mugharet et-Tabun (Mt. Carmel), south of Haifa, Israel.
Dating:	Unclear; perhaps 50–70 ky.
Material:	Almost complete adult female skeleton; robust (probably male) mandible; miscellaneous fragments.
Traits:	Browridges large, alveolar prognathism, occiput rounded with occipital torus; no chin.
Associated finds:	Levallois-Mousterian flake tools; Acheulian hand-axes. Fauna: hippopotamus, boar, deer, wild ox, gazelle.
Cranial capacity:	1271 cm³.
Comment:	Tabun and Skhūl were history-making discoveries and raised human evolutionary questions still not settled.

Anatomically Moderns: Africa

Border Cave

Date found:	In 1940, and later, by W. E. Horton; H. B. S. Cooke, B. D. Malar, and L. H. Wells; others.
Site:	Cave near border of North KwaZula and Swaziland, southeast Africa.
Dating:	110–90 kya.
Material:	Partial male adult cranium with very little of face; two adult mandibles; partial infant skeleton in shallow grave.
Traits:	Steep forehead, no supraorbital torus; occipital rounded; features resemble anatomical moderns.
Associated finds:	All tools of Levallois type of Middle Stone Age. Fauna: hippopotamus, bushpig, warthog, cape buffalo, antelope, wildebeest, zebra, baboon, horse.
Cranial capacity:	Estimate: 1507 cm³.
Comment:	Bones may be modern but date is insecure because bones may not have come from the archeological horizon in which they were found.

Klasies River Mouth

Date found:	In 1968, by J. J. Wymer, University of Chicago Archaeological Expedition, directed by R. Singer.
Site:	Cave near Klasies River Mouth, coast of South Africa.
Dating:	120–130 kya, by oxygen isotope.
Material:	Fragment of frontal bone; facial fragments; cranial fragments; several mandibles; loose teeth.
Traits:	Low and narrow vault; one mandible with pronounced chin; other mandibles, chin weak; jaw within range of fully modern humans; supraorbital region modern.

BOX 17-5   **Fossil Briefs, continued**

Associated finds:	Middle Stone Age stone tools; mollusk remains; bird and mammal remains; burnt bones.
Cranial capacity:	No estimate.
Comment:	May be evidence of early moderns in Africa and earliest in the world. However, fragmentary condition of bones has raised doubts about identification as anatomically moderns.

Omo I

Date found:	In 1967, by The International Palaeontological Research Expedition to the Omo Valley, Kenyan team, headed by Richard Leakey.
Site:	Lower basin of the Omo River, southern Ethiopia.
Dating:	Difficult to determine; 130 kya has been suggested.
Material:	Partial skeleton, consisting of incomplete vault, mandible fragments, both maxillae, and a few teeth; postcranial remains include parts of the upper-limb area and parts of the lower limbs.
Traits:	Robust skull, rounded vault, expanded parietal region; mandible with chin; postcranial skeleton essentially *sapiens*.
Associated finds:	Fauna: Old World monkeys, elephant, rhinoceros; a few flake tools.
Cranial capacity:	No estimate.
Comment:	Another candidate for earliest modern in the world—if date and bone interpretation are correct.

Anatomically Moderns: Israel

Jebel Qafzeh (also Qafzeh)

Date found:	In 1933, by R. Neuville; later finds at various times by R. Neuville and Stekelis; B. Vandermeersch.
Site:	About 1.5 miles south of Nazareth.
Dating:	90 kya.
Material:	Remains of at least 15 individuals—adults, a child, infants. Remains include almost all parts of the body—calottes, incomplete skeletons, limbs, teeth, etc.; the Qafzeh 6 skull, a young adult male, has been reconstructed.
Traits:	Skull 6 is generally robust, with high well-founded vault; modest supraorbital torus without supratoral sulcus; occipital bone rounded without bun; maxillae large with canine fossae; alveolar prognathism but no midfacial prognathism; mandible with prominent chin; the postcranial bones are those of moderns; very few are of Neandertal character.
Associated finds:	Stone tools of Levallois-Mousterian industry, including scrapers, Levallois points, backed knives and burins of Upper Paleolithic type. Fauna: horse, rhinoceros, deer, wild ox, gazelle, and some bird remains.
Cranial capacity:	1570 cm^3.
Comment:	Along with Skhūl, these two sites may represent earliest Eurasian a.m. humans. Does this suggest migration (or gene flow) from east to west into Europe?

BOX 17-5

Skhūl 5

Date found:	In 1932, by T. D. McCown (Joint Expedition of the British School of Archaeology in Jerusalem and the American School of Prehistoric Research).
Site:	Mugharet es-Skhūl, Wadi el-Mughara, south of Haifa, Israel.
Dating:	Possibly 90 kya.
Material:	Skeletons, limb bones, mandibles, and fragments of more than 10 individuals, including adult males and females, children, and infants.
Traits:	High vault; some midfacial projection, alveolar prognathism; chin present; no occipital bun; supraorbital torus prominent but reduced from Neandertal.
Associated finds:	Tools: scrapers, Levallois flakes, cores, and burins. Fauna: hyena, hippopotamus, rhinoceros, wild ass, gazelle, several species of deer, boar, and small carnivores.
Cranial capacity:	Estimates for Skhūl 5—1450 cm³; 1518 cm³.
Comment:	Skhūl is one of the earliest Eurasian anatomical moderns. Reflects both archaic and modern traits.

Anatomically Moderns: Europe

Cro-Magnon

Date found:	In 1868, by L. Lartet.
Site:	Cro-Magnon, Les Eyzies, Dordogne, France.
Dating:	Würm glaciation, about 25 kya.
Material:	Remains of 5 skeletons, male and female and child; many other bones.
Traits:	Robust, but has all the markings of fully modern *sapiens*. Some archaic traits like browridges, but not prominent.
Associated finds:	Evolved Aurignacian industry. Fauna: bear, horse, reindeer, bison, mammoth.
Cranial capacity:	Cro-Magnon 1 (old man): 1600 cm³.
Comment:	Mainly historical. Unfortunately, the term "Cro-Magnon" has been used as the name for the "race" (or the basic "race") inhabiting Europe in the Upper Paleolithic.

Mladeč

Date found:	In 1881, and later, by J. Szombathy; Jan Knies; others.
Site:	Bocek's Cave, west of Mladeč village, Czechoslovakia.
Dating:	Würm I/II Interstadial; ?30–33 kya.
Material:	Seven skulls or partial skulls, male, female, children; many facial bones, teeth, and postcranial bones; several adult crania destroyed at end of World War II.
Traits:	Great deal of morphological variation in archaic and modern features; e.g., Mladeč 1 has moderate supraorbital torus, Mladeč 2 has none; Mladeč 1 has marked posterior cranial flattening; in Mladeč 2, the back of the cranium is higher and rounder; foreheads also vary in slope; archaic facial prognathism; bones fairly robust.

BOX 17-5 **Fossil Briefs, continued**

Associated finds:	Aurignacian stone and bone industries; fauna of warm climate.
Cranial capacity:	Average, 1557 cm³.
Comment:	One of the largest and most informative sites of central and eastern Europe. Also, some of the earliest of European fully modern humans.

Anatomically Moderns: China

Upper Cave

Date found:	In 1933 and in 1934, by W. C. Pei.
Site:	Upper Cave, Zhoukoudian.
Dating:	Late Pleistocene; 18 kya.
Material:	Three crania (1 old male, 2 young females); young male calotte; adolescent calvaria, child calvaria, infant calvaria; several mandibles; several postcranial fragments.
Traits:	Old male: vault low, forehead moderately receding; prominent supraorbital torus; zygomatics strongly angled to give face a flat look. Young female (102): frontal region may have been deliberately deformed. Middle-aged female (103): high vault; sagittal keel; broad nasal aperture.
Associated finds:	Finely crafted ornaments, bone needle. Fauna: hedgehogs, bats, hares, squirrels, leopards, horses, hyenas, foxes, pigs, cave bears; also birds and reptiles.
Cranial capacity:	Old male: 1500 cm³; young female (102): 1380 cm³.
Comment:	The first a.m. humans discovered in China. Found in the same cave—upper area—as *H. erectus*. Does this speak for local continuing evolution?

BOX 17-5

Anatomically Moderns: Australia

Kow Swamp

Date found:	In 1968, by A. G. Thorne and A. L. West.
Site:	Kow Swamp, 2 miles south of Leitchville, Victoria.
Dating:	10 kya.
Material:	Remains of over 40 burials.
Traits:	Sloping, flattened forehead; thick cranial bones; moderately large supraorbital torus. Faces broad and prognathic, not markedly different from modern Australian aborigines; Kow 1, sagittal keel; Kow 9, nuchal torus thick; overall fully modern.
Associated finds:	Mollusks; quartz artifacts.
Cranial capacity:	Not available.

Mungo

Date found:	In 1968, by J. M. Bowler; in 1969, by R. Jones and H. Allen.
Site:	Southern shore of Lake Mungo, 62 miles northeast of Mildura.
Dating:	25 kya; 30+ kya.
Material:	3 skeletons: no. 1, female; no. 2, fragmentary; no. 3, male.
Traits:	Well-rounded forehead, weak muscle attachments, weak or moderate supraorbital torus; generally very gracile; occiput somewhat archaic; less robust than modern; some resemblances to China specimens.
Associated finds:	Australian core-tool and scraper tradition. Fauna: kangaroos, wallabys; fishes, birds.
Cranial capacity:	Not available.

Suggested Further Reading

There is an immense literature, both popular and professional, dealing with Neandertals and Upper Paleolithic *sapiens* from almost every possible point of view. The following list is not intended to be either complete or comprehensive; the books listed are readable, useful, and are directly associated with chapter material.

Brace, C. Loring, Harry Nelson, and Noel Korn. *Atlas of Human Evolution* (2nd Ed.), New York: Holt, Rinehart and Winston, 1979.
    A handy reference of well-known fossil hominids. The large and careful drawings of skulls are considered to be very accurate.

Day, Michael. *Guide to Fossil Man* (4th Ed.), Chicago: The University of Chicago Press, 1986.
    A selected list of hominids arranged by geographic area. Excellent background data for each hominid with photographs. Recommended for reference.

Hogarth, Paul, and Jean-Jacques Salomon. *Prehistory*, New York: Dell Publishing Co., 1962.
    Imaginative illustrations portray the history of the Paleolithic. Interesting overview.

Kuhn, Herbert. *On the Track of Prehistoric Man*, New York: Random House, 1955.
    Popular account of Upper Paleolithic cave art.

Lewin, Roger. *Human Evolution* (2nd Ed.), Cambridge, Mass.: Blackwell Scientific Publications Inc., 1989.
    The author covers human evolution from australopithecines through moderns with many fine illustrations, charts, and maps. It is a useful adjunct to the course.

————. *In the Age of Mankind*, Washington, D.C.: Smithsonian Institution, 1988.
    Another useful book written for nonspecialists. Lewin is not always careful in his popular books, so caution is needed in reading. Beautiful photographs and artwork. Like his book *Human Evolution*, the contents of this covers more than *H. erectus* and *H. sapiens*.

Reader, John. *Missing Links: The Hunt for Earliest Man*, London: Penguin Books, 1988.
    This book, the second edition, contains a section on Neandertals and other fossils we have discussed in Chapters 12 through 17. There is a readable section on mtDNA. The book is highly recommended.

Shipman, Pat. "Old Masters," *Discover*, July, 1990, pp. 60–65.
    An interesting article by a physical anthropologist who comments on some of the explanations of Upper Paleolithic cave art.

Two
Views
of the
Future

A Personal View

Like many other scholars, physical anthropologists are often asked to comment about the future of humanity. As we have pointed out in this text, one area of anthropological research concerns the study of nonhuman primates in their natural environments. Since, today, most of these nonhuman primates live in tropical rainforests, their current predicament mirrors the overall plight of their habitats. Indeed, since most primate species are quite flexible in their ability to adapt, their conservation status is often considered to be a good *index* of what's happening with tropical forest fauna in general.

Just how well off are contemporary nonhuman primates? The answer is that they are not very well off at all. (See Chapters 9 through 11.) And, unfortunately, their sorry state reflects the deteriorating conditions displayed in tropical forests throughout the world.

The threat is not just to a few species only (in fact, there are less than 200 primate species extant in the whole world); rather, the fate of literally millions of species hangs in the balance. No one knows exactly how many species today live partly or exclusively in rainforests, but probably a majority of mammals as well as birds (at least seasonally) do so. Taking mammals, birds, reptiles, and amphibians into account, roughly 5,000 to 10,000 species are thought to be in peril. And this figure does not even include invertebrates, especially insects. From very tentative data, researchers speculate that there are perhaps 15 million insect species, of which as many as 90% live *only* in tropical forests. The animal (and plant) diversity in these ancient, fragile habitats is enormous. Here at the end of the twentieth century, we have barely a glimmer of the extraordinary biological bonanza these environments contain.

Yet, even as you read this page, several acres of rainforest are being destroyed. Every minute of every day more of these habitats are being consumed by the urgent, irrepressable appetite of one voracious species: humans. Extrapolating from current rates, experts estimate that, by the middle of the next century (well within the natural lifespans of many contemporary college-age students), there will be no tropical forests left. Long before these habitats have vanished for good, many resident species will find themselves trapped in small, isolated forest patches. Unable to range beyond these forest fragments to find food or mates, many—if not most—of these species will become extinct, perhaps long before 2050.

As bad as current projections now appear, the situation is bound to worsen. The human population continues to expand rapidly, with estimates that, instead of the 5 billion people that must now be fed, sheltered, educated, given health care, and so on, by 2050 there will be 9 billion. Indeed, in 1990 the world's population will increase by 92 million: In other words, *every year* an already taxed ecosystem is further burdened by a population *larger than that of Mexico!*

Some progress is being made, as the following section demonstrates, but one should be cautious of rosy projections implying "good news." We all, of course, would like to believe that there is still time to reverse the situation, thus providing ourselves with an excuse to continue our current environmentally destructive ways. *But there is no time.* For most lifeforms, it is now midnight. We *may* be able to save some small chunks of the "natural" world for our descendants, but we surely will not be able to reverse current trends significantly. No rational appraisal of today's ecological predicament would support such a view. An overly optimistic, unattainable dream is just as dangerous as apathy. We can best address this crisis by realizing its immensity and calmly pondering what we can and cannot do about it.

As this century draws to a close, it seems certain that further environmental deterioration is unavoidable, a trend that will create untold suffering for our fellow travellers on this planet. Nor will all this sacrifice of the earth be likely to improve the human condition. As more humans crowd the planet, diverting ever-poorer lands into agricultural use, food production efficiency will decline all the more. The danger signs are there already. In Africa, despite heroic and often desperate attempts to change the situation, per capita production has actually declined in the last decade. Statistics aside, more starvation and suffering are on the way.

If this crisis is not brought home to you by the specter of vast and wonderful habitats laid to waste, their abundant residents annihilated, with human misery intensifying, then consider this: The condition of the forests may determine the stability of the atmosphere and, perhaps, ultimately the health of the whole planet. We have all heard of the "greenhouse effect." The problem here is that the burning of fossil fuels adds carbon dioxide to the atmosphere. The increased level of carbon dioxide, along with other industrial gasses produced by humans, causes solar radiation to be trapped in the atmosphere, which leads to a general warming of the earth's surface. Carbon dioxide is primarily removed from the atmosphere (at least temporarily) by trees and green plants during photosynthesis. Consequently, the current pace of deforestation with its destruction of greenery can only make problems with the atmosphere more severe.

Each and every one of us has a stake in what happens. The kind of world we leave behind—whether enriched, at least a little, by our long and common evolutionary bequest, or irreversibly despoiled by short-term, short-sighted needs—is our choice alone.

Robert Jurmain

An Alternative View

If you have read this far, you know that our planet is now facing a critical situation with the pollution produced by our automobiles and factories, and with the loss of tropical rainforests and the clearing of temperate zone forests to feed the endless appetite of industrial nations for raw forest products, with the endangering of plant and animal species in the bargain. Unfortunately, most of the world's rainforests are located in third-world countries, which depend on these forests for much of their income. It is difficult to convince impoverished nations that they should not touch one of their few profitable resources. Nevertheless, steps *are* being taken to preserve the rainforests, which we discuss below.

The United States and other industrial nations are becoming much more conservation conscious and are enacting laws to protect the environment within their own borders. It may seem unfashionable to predict that all will end well, that our planet—its animal and plant species, the ozone layer, and the lives of future human generations—will be saved before environmental rot overtakes us. However, it is clear that citizens and governments, not only in industrial nations but in the Third World as well, are becoming aware of the danger. They have begun to institute measures (or make plans) for conservation that will improve our ecological situation.

Brazil, for example, after experiencing the world's worst loss of trees, has become acutely aware of environmental concerns. Since 1987, Brazil has taken vigorous steps to reduce the amount of deforestation within its borders. In 1990, the president of Brazil announced that troops and military aircraft would patrol the Amazon area during the dry season to prevent farmers from cutting and burning trees. Hundreds of conservation officers already participate in increased surveillance. Tax incentives that encouraged the large-scale clearing of forests have been eliminated.

Measures are also being taken in Panama. The Panamanian National Association for the Conservation of Nature has promoted ecological education in the schools, has developed programs to provide signs, trails, and workers for forest protection, and has designated more wilderness areas for preservation. The Association works closely with such organizations as The World Wildlife Fund, the Nature Conservancy, and the Smithsonian Institution. Interestingly, the Association raises half its funds from local merchants, which suggests that there is wide support in the population for environmental protection.

With little money to spend on conservation, Costa Rica has one of the world's highest deforestation rates. However, an arrangement has been developed whereby American banks holding Costa Rican loans can sell these debt accounts at a large discount (in return for which they are permitted to write the debts off their taxes as charity deductions). Conservation groups buy the accounts at discount prices and donate them to Fundacion Neotropica, a Costa Rican conservation organization. The Foundation sells the accounts and uses the income to buy land, pay workers, and perform other activities that assist in improving the environment. The Costa Rican government is trying to integrate agriculture and conservation so that the country will be ecologically sustainable.

Industrial nations are developing strategies that will reduce pollution. The Soviet Union has become aware of the world ecological crisis—from ozone depletion to deforestation and disastrous air pollution—especially since the Chernobyl disaster. According to Soviet conservationists, the crisis is convincing evidence that the world we live in is interrelated and interdependent. They support the United Nations' conservation plans and action, and they consider it necessary to develop international and legal mechanisms for protecting unique natural zones of global importance, especially the Antarctic.

The Soviets would like to see an international system established for the purpose of exchanging ecologically clean technologies that could be effectively accessed by all nations. They are also ready, they say, to open their own country to inspection. They emphasize that the right to a healthy environment must be considered a basic human right.

In Europe, member states of the European Community are debating the organization and functions of a European Environmental Protection Agency. They have suggested forming an "International Green Cross" to assist nations in ecological trouble.

Japan instituted energy-saving technology in the 1970s, and a strong conservation movement is active there. Canada is still cutting too many trees, but conservation groups are becoming more vocal. However, little action has yet been taken.

In the spring of 1990, fifty-nine countries took an unprecedented step by agreeing to stop producing chemicals that destroy the earth's protective ozone layers. The agreement requires participating nations to cease the production of chloroflurocarbons (CFCs) and halons by the end of the century. Those nations signing also agreed to lower production of methyl chloroform by 70% by the year 2000 and completely by 2005, and tetrachloride completely by the year 2000. Also in 1990, most of the industrialized world agreed to set firm targets for reducing carbon dioxide emissions. Unfortunately, the United States, the Soviet Union, and Saudi Arabia did not join in this particular agreement.

Experiments have begun in the United States to improve (actually, to revolutionize) the process of manufacturing steel. If successful, it would reduce a slow and cumbersome process of three steps to just one. Steel mills, with their coke ovens and slow manufacturing process, are among the worst air polluters.

Magazines in many countries routinely carry articles on energy problems and suggestions for reducing the use of energy. There are environmental journals devoted specifically to publishing material on the dangers of deforestation, pollution, and other such problems. They publish samples of regulations that can be adopted and they discuss planetary rights and obligations. Leaders of various nations have given speeches supporting such measures. There are many agencies that monitor agricultural and industrial emissions that lead to atmospheric pollution. Such findings are published regularly.

Many American newspapers publish, at least once a week, an "environment watch" column, and editorials are often directed at local and national pollution and other environmental problems. Television news coverage also devotes time to the environment, and a number of television specials have dealt with the problem. In elementary grades, children are given instruction on the environment, which is sometimes developed into a more formal program. In Hawaii, for example, "Willie's Remarkable Recycling Flight," a play that introduces schools to recycling, will travel to twenty Oahu schools selected as recycling collection sites. This is in addition to curbside collection of recyclable items, a practice that has been introduced in many American cities. Supermarkets, college campuses, and cities are providing receptacles or areas for depositing paper, tin cans, plastic, and glass.

Although federal and state regulations have improved conditions for animals used in research labs, there is still much to be done. Anthropologists have been especially interested in primates, and monkeys and chimpanzees have been helped, but Jane Goodall and others are not satisfied and continue their efforts. There is also the danger of extinction of African nonhuman primates, and several organizations, in conjunction with African governments, are working on this problem. There are many endangered species whose extinction appears imminent. In the United States, laws have been passed in recent years that support the preservation of endangered species; however, there are other areas of the world, unfortunately, with very little protection, or none at all, for endangered species. It seems that the worldwide concern for the environment includes scant attention to the plight of endangered species.

Ecological destruction is not going unnoticed in the world, but this is not to say that being aware of such problems have solved them. This is certainly not the case. Furthermore, there are powerful interests, both political and economic, that object to environmental regulations and do not obey them, or take measures to impede their enforcement. However, awareness of the problems has increased worldwide—among the people, and those in governing bodies, industry, and agriculture. As just pointed out, the message appears in newspapers, television, books, and is being taught in schools. With awareness comes the realization that the environment is in danger, that protective action is not only desirable but necessary. From steps already taken, and more being planned, the preservation of the environment may be considered more optimistically. We might even say, the question really is not *whether* conditions will improve, but whether they will improve in time. Let us hope so.

Harry Nelson

Atlas of Primate Skeletal Anatomy

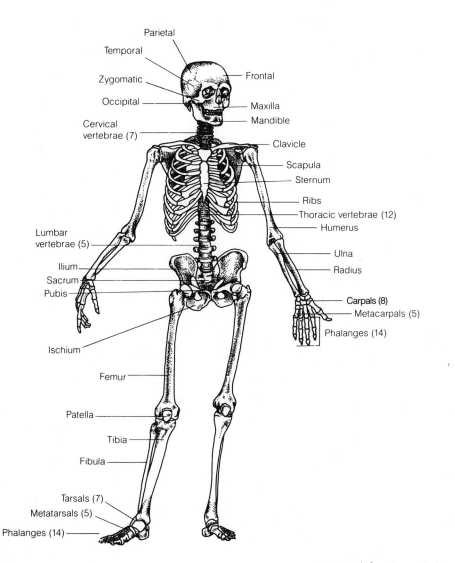

Parietal

Temporal

Zygomatic

Occipital

Frontal

Maxilla

Mandible

Cervical
vertebrae (7)

Clavicle

Scapula

Sternum

Ribs

Thoracic vertebrae (12)

Humerus

Lumbar
vertebrae (5)

Ulna

Radius

Ilium

Sacrum

Pubis

Carpals (8)

Metacarpals (5)

Phalanges (14)

Ischium

Femur

Patella

Tibia

Fibula

Tarsals (7)

Metatarsals (5)

Phalanges (14)

FIGURE A-1 Human skeleton (*Homo sapiens*)—bipedal hominid.

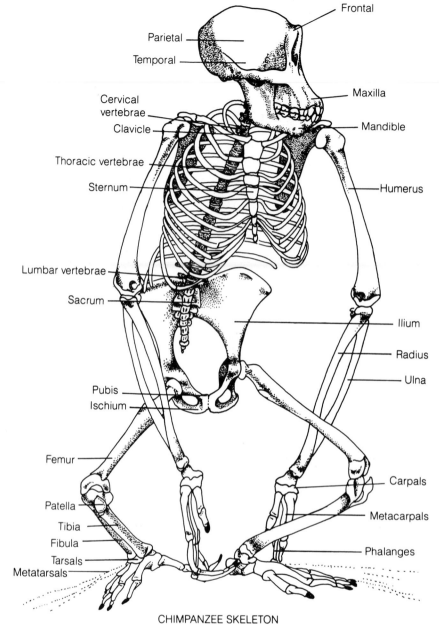

FIGURE A-2   Chimpanzee skeleton (*Pan troglodytes*) A knuckle-walking pongid.

Frontal

Parietal

Temporal

Maxilla

Cervical vertebrae

Mandible

Clavicle

Thoracic vertebrae

Sternum

Humerus

Lumbar vertebrae

Sacrum

Ilium

Radius

Ulna

Pubis

Ischium

Femur

Carpals

Patella

Metacarpals

Tibia

Fibula

Phalanges

Tarsals

Metatarsals

CHIMPANZEE SKELETON

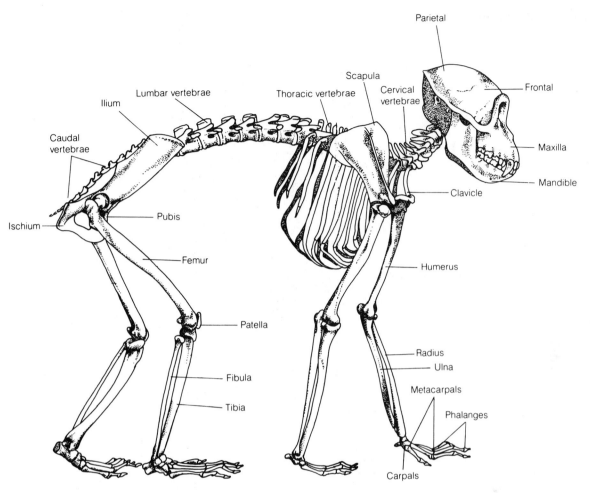

MONKEY SKELETON

FIGURE A-3 Monkey skeleton (rhesus macaque; *Macaca mulatta*)—A typical quadrupedal primate.

FIGURE A-4   Human cranium.

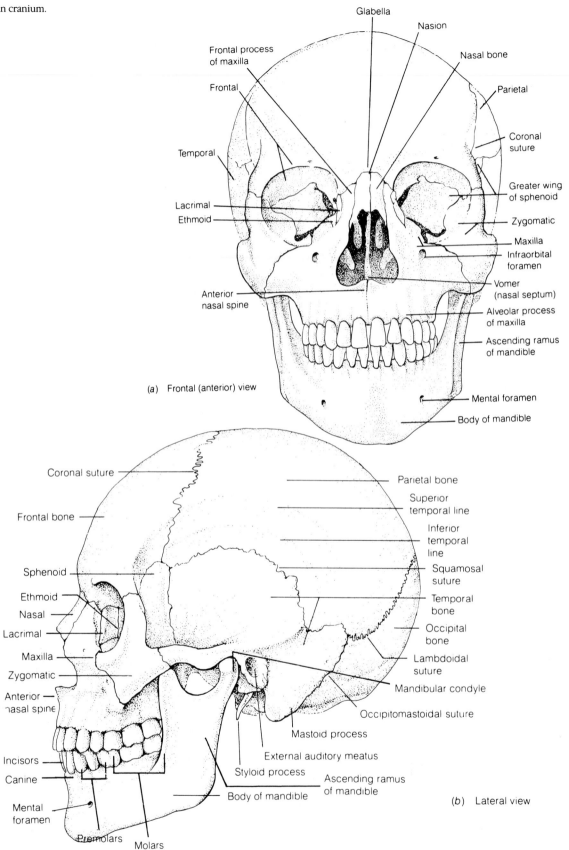

Glabella

Nasion

Nasal bone

Parietal

Frontal process
of maxilla

Coronal
suture

Frontal

Greater wing
of sphenoid

Temporal

Zygomatic

Lacrimal

Maxilla

Ethmoid

Infraorbital
foramen

Vomer
(nasal septum)

Anterior
nasal spine

Alveolar process
of maxilla

Ascending ramus
of mandible

(a)   Frontal (anterior) view

Mental foramen

Body of mandible

Coronal suture

Parietal bone

Superior
temporal line

Frontal bone

Inferior
temporal
line

Sphenoid

Squamosal
suture

Ethmoid

Temporal
bone

Nasal

Lacrimal

Occipital
bone

Maxilla

Zygomatic

Lambdoidal
suture

Anterior
nasal spine

Mandibular condyle

Occipitomastoidal suture

Incisors

Mastoid process

Canine

External auditory meatus

Styloid process

Ascending ramus
of mandible

Mental
foramen

Body of mandible

(b)   Lateral view

Premolars   Molars

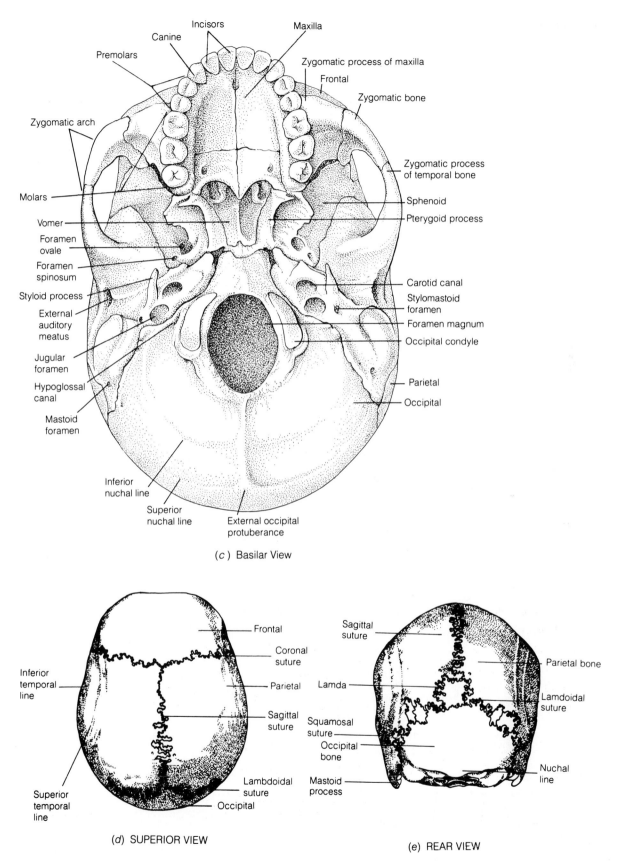

(c) Basilar View

(d) SUPERIOR VIEW

(e) REAR VIEW

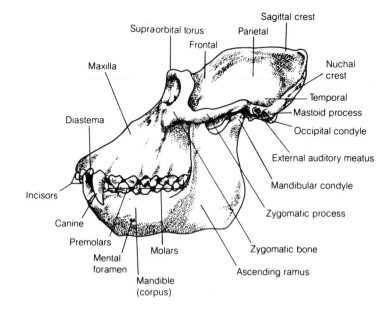

(a) MALE

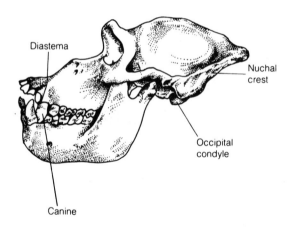

(b) FEMALE

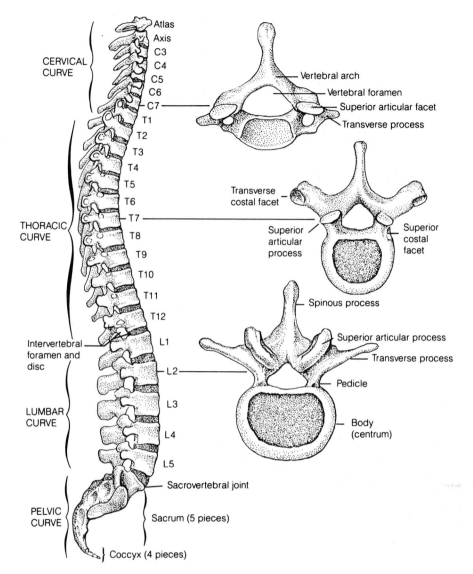

CERVICAL CURVE

Atlas
Axis
C3
C4
C5
C6
C7

Vertebral arch
Vertebral foramen
Superior articular facet
Transverse process

T1
T2
T3
T4
T5
T6
T7
T8
T9
T10
T11
T12

THORACIC CURVE

Transverse costal facet

Superior articular process

Superior costal facet

Spinous process

Superior articular process

Transverse process

Pedicle

Intervertebral foramen and disc

L1
L2
L3
L4
L5

Body (centrum)

LUMBAR CURVE

Sacrovertebral joint

PELVIC CURVE

Sacrum (5 pieces)

Coccyx (4 pieces)

Human vertebral column (lateral view) and representative views of selected cervical, thoracic, and lumbar vertebrae (superior views).

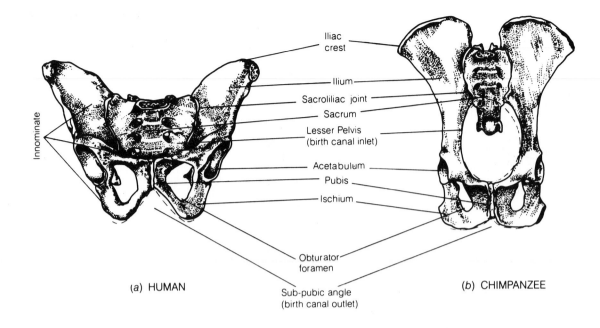

FIGURE A-7   Pelvic girdles.

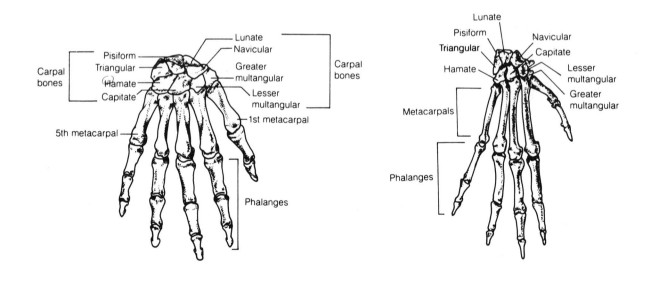

FIGURE A-8   Hand anatomy.

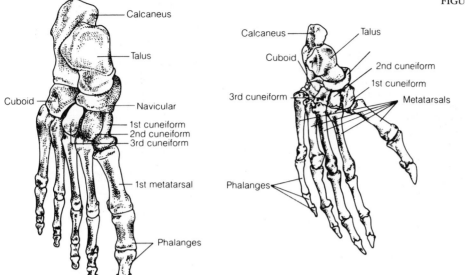

(a) Human (dorsal view)

(c) Chimpanzee

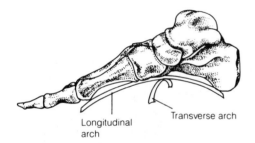

(b) Human (medial view)

Forensic Anthropology*

It is a fascinating and startling fact that there are hundreds of millions of humans buried around this planet, and often their bones come to light for one reason or another. Indeed, thousands of skeletons have been excavated and are now curated in various natural history and anthropology museums. Skeletal biologists (also called *human osteologists*) are often asked to assist in unearthing these human remains and to perform various specialized analyses on them when prehistoric or, occasionally, historic burial sites are excavated.

Many situations occur in which forensic anthropologists are called upon by the police and other law enforcement agencies to assist in identification by using their knowledge of skeletal biology. Usually, the anthropologist is called upon to provide clues as to the personal identity of a deceased individual or individuals (through analysis of partially skeletalized remains), but is also occasionally asked to perform other tasks. Some examples of these tasks are: to identify skeletal trauma, match remains from a suspected scene of a crime with the corpus delecti, sort human from nonhuman remains, and, sometimes, to either compare a photograph to a living person, or to compare two photographs to determine the identity of the persons pictured. A few case reports will better illustrate the types of problems encountered by a forensic anthropologist. These are based on actual cases, and will be resolved for you at the end of this section.

Case 1: An old plane crash was discovered in the remote mountains of Colorado, and skeletal material was still inside. How many people are represented by this skeletal material, and who were they?

Case 2: A skeleton was discovered by a farmer while plowing his fields before planting. He contacted the local sheriff, who wondered if a past homicide victim could have been buried there.

Case 3: A building has exploded because of a natural gas leak, and five people are thought to have been inside at the time of the explosion and fire. These indi-

---

*This appendix was written by Diane France and Robert Jurmain, with special thanks to George Gill for his contributions.

viduals were: a 23-year-old female and a 24-year-old female, both with no children, a 32-year-old female with three children, a 53-year-old male and a 54-year-old male. As these remains were almost completely skeletonized, how could they be identified?

Case 4:   A very old photograph that bore a striking resemblance to Abraham Lincoln was discovered in the attic of an old house. Tests could be performed by other forensic specialists (questioned documents examiners, for example) to determine the age of the photographic paper, etc., and, of course, these would aid in discounting a fraudulent claim; but the photograph could still be of the correct age and be of a person other than Lincoln.

The first three cases must begin with a determination of the species represented by the remains. If the bones are not human, the forensic anthropologist's role is usually over, but if they are human, the work has just begun. Even if the police have an idea of who is represented by these remains, the specialist usually begins the investigation with a determination of the basic features: sex, age, race, stature, skeletal pathology, and notation of idiosyncrasies that could aid in final identification (such as healed fractures, prosthetic devices, and so on).

Sexing the Skeleton

Several evolutionary factors have helped us to be able to identify sex in the human skeleton. The pelvic girdles in quadrupeds do not differ greatly between males and females of a species, but in humans the birth canal had a tendency to become smaller with bipedalism. This problem was compounded by the human newborn, whose head was relatively larger than the newborns of other animals, so throughout our evolution modifications were selected for in the female pelvic girdle relating to proportionately larger birth outlets, and these modifications aid in the determination of sex today. This sexual dimorphism (difference in morphology between the sexes) is most reliably diagnosed in the pelvic girdle, as shown below (see Figures 1 and 2).

FIGURE B-1   Male pelvic girdle.

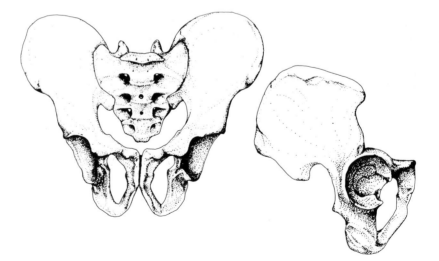

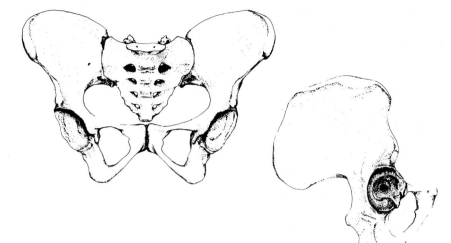

PELVIC GIRDLE	TYPICAL MALE	TYPICAL FEMALE
Subpubic angle	Less than 90 degrees	More than 90 degrees
Pubic shape	Triangular	Rectangular
Subpubic angle shape (see also Phenice, 1969)	Convex	Concave
Greater sciatic notch	Less than 68 degrees	More than 68 degrees
Sacrum	Smaller and more curved	Larger and straighter

In addition, humans display types of sexual dimorphism also common to most other animals: Males are usually larger and have more rugged areas for muscle attachments than do females of the same species. However, in order to utilize this size difference in sex determination, the researcher must be able to identify the population from which the skeleton was taken, as whole populations differ in skeletal size and robusticity. For instance, Asian Indians are much smaller and more gracile than Australian Aborigines.

After the pelvis, the cranium is the area of the skeleton most commonly used for sex determination. Some of these traits are listed below (see Figure 3).

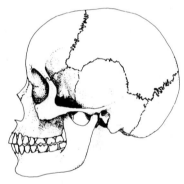

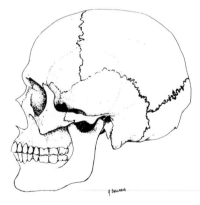

CRANIUM	TYPICAL MALE	TYPICAL FEMALE
Muscle attachment areas (mastoid process, etc.)	More pronounced	Less pronounced
Supraorbital torus (brow ridges)	More pronounced	Less pronounced
Frontal bone	Slanting	Globular
Supraorbital rim (in eye orbit)	Rounded	Sharp
Palate	Deep	Shallow

FIGURE B-3   Cranium and mandible: female (top); male (bottom).

(a) Birth: The crowns for all the deciduous (milk) teeth (shown in color) are present; no roots, however, have yet formed.

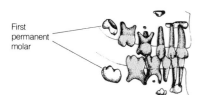

First permanent molar

(b) 2 years: All deciduous teeth (shown in color) are erupted; the first permanent molar and permanent incisors have crowns (unerupted) formed, but no roots.

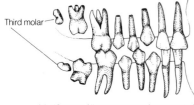

Third molar

(c) 12 years: All permanent teeth are erupted except the third molar (wisdom tooth).

FIGURE B-4   Skeletal age: dental development.

Other bones of the body also show secondary sex characteristics, but are often less reliable than those of the cranium, as heavy muscle use affects the size and ruggedness of the muscle attachments, which can then sometimes change the diagnosis of sex. Areas probably not as affected by muscle use are:

Suprascapular notch on scapula	Often present	Often absent
Femur: angle of neck to shaft	Smaller angle	Greater angle

The standards discussed here are for adult skeletons; sexing techniques for pre-adolescents are not as yet widely used.

Determination of Age

During growth, the skeleton and dentition undergo regular changes that allow the determination of age at death. The age determination in individuals under about 20 years centers on deciduous (baby) and permanent dentition eruption times, on the appearance of ossification centers, and on the fusion of the separate ends of long bones to bone shafts.

DENTAL ERUPTION

The determination of the ages at which the deciduous and permanent dentition erupts is useful in identifying age to approximately 15 years. The third molar (wisdom tooth) erupts after this time, but is so variable in age of eruption (if it erupts at all) that it is not a very reliable age indicator. (See Fig. B-4.)

BONE GROWTH

Postcranial bones are preceded by a cartilage model that is gradually replaced by bone, both in the primary growth centers (the diaphyses) and in the secondary centers (the ends of the bones, or epiphyses). The initial ossification centers are, of course, very small, and are only rarely encountered by a forensic anthropologist. The bone continues to grow until the epiphyses fuse to the diaphyses. Because this fusion occurs at different times in different bones, the age of an individual can be determined by which epiphyses have fused and which have not (see Figs. 5 and 6). The characteristic undulating appearance of the unfused surfaces of bone helps differentiate it from the mature long bone (smooth) or merely a broken end of a bone (sharp and jagged).

Females mature more quickly than males, so usually 1 to 2 years must be subtracted from the previous ages for female skeletons.

Once a person has reached physiological maturity (by the early 20s), the determination of age becomes more difficult. Several techniques are used, including the progressive, regular changes in the pubic symphyseal face (the most common technique), in the sternal ends of the ribs, in the auricular surface of the ilium, in ectocranial (outside the cranium) and endocranial (inside the cranium) suture closures, and in cellular changes determined by microscopic examination of the

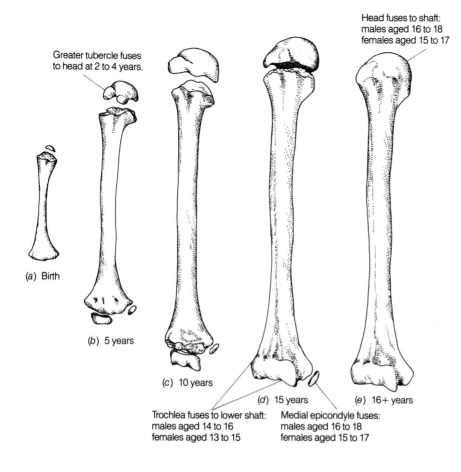

Greater tubercle fuses to head at 2 to 4 years.

Head fuses to shaft:
males aged 16 to 18
females aged 15 to 17

(a) Birth

(b) 5 years

(c) 10 years

(d) 15 years

(e) 16+ years

Trochlea fuses to lower shaft:
males aged 14 to 16
females aged 13 to 15

Medial epicondyle fuses:
males aged 16 to 18
females aged 15 to 17

FIGURE B-5   Skeletal age: epiphyseal union in the humerus. Some regions of the humerus exhibit some of the earliest fusion centers in the body, while others are among the latest to complete fusion (not until late adolescence).

cross section of various long bones. In addition, degenerative changes, including arthritis and osteoporosis, can aid in the determination of relative age, but should not be used by themselves to determine age, as injury and certain diseases can cause changes that mimic old age in bones.

Pubic Symphyseal Face: The pubic symphyseal face in the young (Fig. 8) is characterized by a billowing surface, (with ridges and furrows) such as seen on a normal epiphysis, but undergoes regular metamorphosis from age 18 onwards. Figure 9 shows a symphyseal face typical of an age in the mid-30s, with a more finely grained face and perhaps still containing remnants of the ridge and furrow system. Figure 10 is typical of an age in the early 60s, with bony outgrowths often developing on the outer rims of the symphyseal face. The first technique was developed by T. W. Todd (1920, 1921) utilizing dissection room cadavers. McKern and Stewart (1957) developed a technique using American males killed in the Korean War. Both of the samples from which these systems were derived have limitations in that the dissection room sample used by Todd is based on individuals of uncertain age (Brooks, 1985, 1986) and the Korean War Dead sample is predominantly young Caucasoid males, with few individuals over age 35.

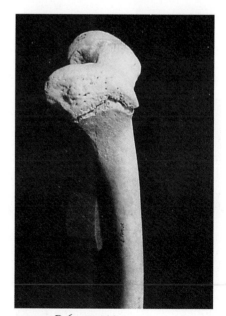

FIGURE B-6   Distal femur.

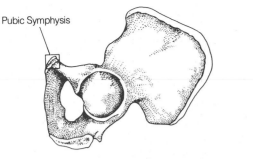

Pubic Symphysis

(a) Position of the pubic symphysis. This area of the pelvis shows systematic changes progressively throughout adult life. Two of these stages are shown in (b) and (c).

(b) Age: 21. The face of the symphysis shows the typical "billowed" appearance of a young joint; no rim present.

(c) Age: mid-50s. The face is mostly flat, with a distinct rim formed around most of the periphery.

FIGURE B-7   Skeletal age: Remodeling of the pubic symphysis.

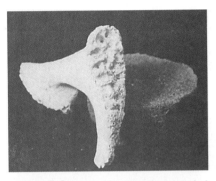

FIGURE B-8   Pubic symphysis face typical of an age in the late teens or early twenties.

FIGURE B-9   Pubic symphysis face typical of an age in the mid-thirties.

Recently a system has been developed by J. M. Suchey, D. Katz, and S. T. Brooks based on a large sample ($n = 739$) of males for whom legal documentation of age is provided by death certificates. This autopsy room sample should be more representative of the general population than past samples. The majority of the males were born either in the United States or Mexico. This sample was taken at autopsies involving homicides, suicides, accidents, or unexpected natural deaths.

Determination of Race

When an anthropologist is asked to help in the identification of a parcel of bones, part of that identification must include a statement as to probable race, because society includes race as a part of the personal identity. Racial identification is often difficult, however, as most of the morphological characteristics we use to distinguish race follow a continuum; that is, one trait is more often, but not exclusively, associated with one race. Even skin color, the most noticeable of characteristics, cannot adequately categorize all individuals, for there are dark-skinned Caucasoids and Mongoloids (disregarding the effects of tanning), and light-skinned Negroids. In fact, it can be said that for many traits, there is more variation *within* races than *between* races. (See Chapter 7.)

The races of the world have been divided in different ways in history, but many anthropologists today identify five or six basic groups: Mongoloids (including Japanese, Chinese, and North, Central, and South American Indians), Negroids (including African and American Blacks), Caucasoids (including Europeans, and other people with European ancestry, West Asians, Asian Indians, and some North American peoples), Australoids (Australian Aborigines), and Polynesians. This is not by any means a complete classification scheme, nor is it the only classification scheme used by physical anthropologists today.

The chart below lists some of the differences we usually see in the skulls of three races common to the Western Hemisphere (most of the currently important differences used in the identification of race occurs in the skulls). (See also Brues, 1977; Krogman, 1962; Stewart, 1979; Bass, 1987; and Gill, 1986).

FEATURE	NEGROID	CAUCASOID	MONGOLOID
Central incisors (cross section) (Dahlberg, 1951)	Blade	Rarely shoveled	Shoveled
Cranial shape[a]	Dolicocranic (long)	Mesocranic (medium)	Brachycranic (round)
Nasal root (top of (nasal bridge)	Wide, rounded	Narrow, pinched	Medium tented
Nasal aperture[b]	Platyrrhiny (wide)	Leptorrhiny (narrow)	Mesorrhiny (medium)
Zygomatic bone	Medium	Retreating	Projecting
External auditory meatus (ear opening)	Round	Round	Oval
Facial shape	Prognathic (lower face projects forward)	Orthognathic (lower face nonprojecting)	Medium

FIGURE B-10   Pubic symphysis face typical of an age in the early sixties.

In addition to the standard measurements, indices, and observations discussed here, further methods using skull and face measurements have been developed to aid in race determination. The most widely used of these is a *discriminant function* method (using a set of formulae), and was developed by Giles and Elliot (1962) for distinguishing Blacks, Caucasoids, and American Indians. Measurements are taken on the cranium of each adult, plugged into the formulae, and the final values plotted on a graph. It must be pointed out that, first, sex must be established (the formulae vary for males and females) and, secondly, the method is devised to answer only a limited question ("Is the cranium from a Black, from a Caucasoid, or from an American Indian?"). The discriminant function method itself helps address the first point (sex) since the technique has also been used to devise a formula for sex determination (from a few of the same measurements). The problem with this method is not so much the need to determine sex first, or the fact that it answers a limited question (since most skulls on this continent come from Blacks, Caucasoids, or American Indians), but rather it relates to its accuracy.

[a] The cranial shape is obtained from the Cranial Index, calculated from:

$$\frac{\text{Cranial breadth}}{\text{Cranial length}} \times 100$$

Up to 75 = dolicocrany
75–79.9 = mesocrany
80–84.9 = brachycrany
85 and up = hyperbrachycrany
(Bass, 1987)

[b] The nasal aperture shape is obtained from the Nasal Index:

$$\frac{\text{Nasal breadth}}{\text{Nasal height}} \times 100$$

Up to 47.9 = Leptorrhiny
48–52.9 = Mesorrhiny
53 and up = Platyrrhiny
(Bass, 1987)

Particularly regarding American Indian specimens from the western United States, the percentage of correct ascertainment is quite low (Birkby, 1966; Gill, 1986). The sexing formula has proven quite accurate, however.

A new metric method developed by Gill and Hughes (Gill et al., 1988) appears to be much more accurate in race determination than the widely used Giles-Elliot approach. With six measurements (and three indices from them), it defines the amount of projection of the mid-face (which is extreme among the sharp-featured Caucasoids). The method does require a specialized (and rather rare) caliper, but is quite reliable in sorting Caucasoids from members of all other populations (in approximately 90 percent of cases). This method is also mathematically simple, and can be performed quickly in an autopsy setting. However, it cannot address the problem of sorting Mongoloids from Blacks, since their mid-facial projections are similar.

So, even today, with many new techniques and extensive use of the computer, race determination remains a challenging and somewhat subjective area. It requires the simultaneous use of many approaches rather than any single "foolproof" method. "By definition, race is quantitative [no sharp boundaries]. Perfection can never be attained in defining or diagnosing a condition that does not even exist in absolute form" (Gill, 1986: 156).

Estimation of Stature

Formulae for stature reconstruction in unidentified individuals have been developed by measuring the long bones of deceased individuals of known stature

FIGURE B-11   Estimating stature: measuring the length of the femur.

FEMUR LENGTH	STATURE	
(mm)*	cm	inches
452	169	66
456	170	66
461	171	67
465	172	67
469	173	68

*Note: Data drawn from White males with known statures at time of death.

(Trotter and Gleser, 1952; Genoves, 1967). As is true of any statistical approximation of a population, these formulae are applied most reliably to the samples from which they are derived, though they may also be used on wider populations represented by these samples. Because these formulae were derived for each sex of various racial groups, the sex and race of the unknown individual must be known before these formulae can be reliably applied.

Resolution of the Case Studies

Case 1: Even though the remains were burned, at least two individuals were identified as the pilot and friend who had filed the initial flight plan. It had been suspected at the time of the crash that at least one more person had been aboard, but there was no evidence to support that claim.

Case 2: The skeleton was human, and was determined to be that of an American Indian male. Although often remains of this kind in these circumstances are automatically diagnosed as an archeological burial, the rapid decay rates of flesh and bone in many areas of the United States and other countries will cause the remains to look ancient in a very short time; thus, a forensic anthropologist must be alert to this possibility. In this case, however, further circumstantial evidence suggested that this was archeological, in that a projectile point was found in the tibia at the knee.

Cases of this kind are useful in disputes between American Indian groups in land and resource ownership, for, in increasing numbers, the tribal affinity of remains can be determined. Human identification in these circumstances has far-reaching ramifications.

Case 3: As noted in the introduction, the ages of two of the females and two of the males were very similar to each other, so that even with the determination of sex and age, the identity of these very fragmentary remains was not easily determined. The 32-year-old female was identified by age determination of the pubic symphysis, and by the evidence on the pelvis that she had had children. There was evidence of at least two other women aside from the 32-year-old female, but because the stature of these other women was very similar, the identification was only tentative. Completely reliable identification was not possible, and it was noted only that there was no evidence that those women were *not* present in the building. The identification of the men was similarly difficult, as they again were about the same age. In addition, though one of the men had a surgical staple in his right knee, which would ordinarily have been evidence for identification, that area of the body was not recovered for either individual. One of the men, however, was over 6 feet tall, while the other was around 5 feet 8 inches tall. Stature reconstruction using the femur, and premortem and postmortem x-rays of the pelvic region of the men were ultimately used for the identification.

Case 4: Dr. Ellis Kerley (1984) determined, by comparing many features of a known Lincoln photograph to this photograph, that this was of a person other than our sixteenth president.

Photo Superimposition

Employed when a probable identification has been made, the technique of photo superimposition has been used in many cases lately, including the famous case of the identification of the Nazi war-criminal Josef Mengele (presented at the Annual Meeting of the American Academy of Forensic Sciences in New Orleans in 1986). In this and other cases, the skull (or large portions of the skull) are superimposed onto photographs of the known individual. If enough landmarks fall on the same position on the skull *and* on the photograph, the researcher is satisfied that he has made the correct identification. (Note: this technique could also have been used to reinforce the decision made in some of the cases outlined above.)

Facial Reconstruction in Human Identification*

Facial reconstruction (also termed *facial reproduction*) is a process used when other identification procedures (including fingerprints and dental matches) have been unsuccessful. Two different methods of producing a face on the skull are employed: a portrait of the individual using clues from the bones of the face; and a more direct, three-dimensional method of applying clay to the skull (or to a plaster cast of the skull). These techniques employ both science and art: The physical anthropologist discovers the age, sex, and race of the skull, but there is no direct evidence from bone that indicates the eye color, hair color and style, lip form, or degree of wrinkling or fleshiness in the individual. Therefore, there is a great deal of subjectivity in the rendering of the finished product; an exact reproduction is not expected, only a general likeness.

The following photographs show a facial reproduction taking shape. Erasers or blocks of clay marking tissue depths (arrived at experimentally from cadavers) are commonly glued to the skull. Clay strips, graduated to the various tissue depths, then "fill in the dots" between erasers, and the face is "fleshed out." The eyes, nose, lips, and sometimes ears are then fashioned according to various guidelines, and a wig is usually added.

Figures i and j show the reproduction of a Caucasoid female, over 60 years old. The first figure shows a nearly complete reproduction, but without the effects of aging, while Figure 12j is the finished product, including the features characteristic of a woman of that age.

---

*Contributed by Diane France and Sandra C. Mays, Supervisor, Crime Laboratory Section, Wyoming State Crime Laboratory. Stages of reconstruction are from both authors; finished reconstruction by Sandra Mays.

FIGURE B-12   Facial reconstruction from a skull.

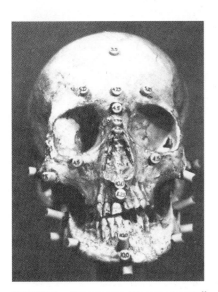

FIGURE a   Erasers precut to experimentally determined tissue depths are glued to skull.

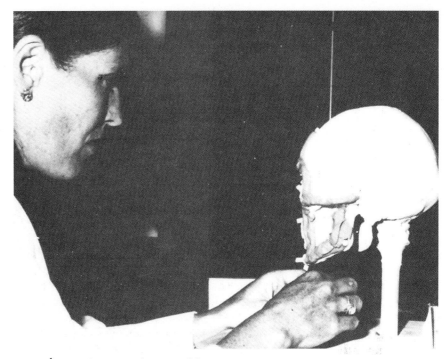

FIGURE b   Sandra Mays applies strips of clay between erasers, graduated to eraser depths.

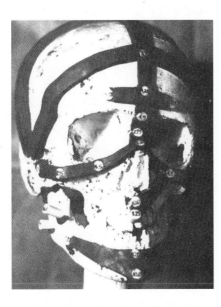

FIGURE c   Strips of clay connect erasers.

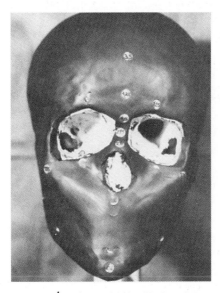

FIGURE d   Clay is added to "flesh out" the face.

FIGURE e and f   A nose and lips are added and refined.

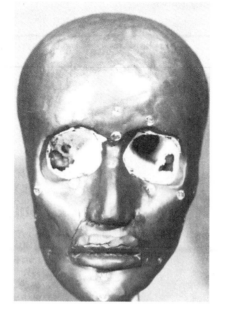

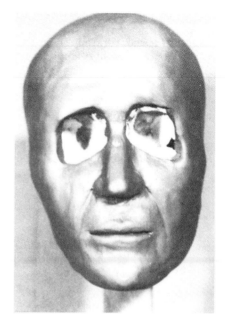

FIGURE g and h   Glass (or plastic) eyes are placed into orbits and eyelids are fashioned.

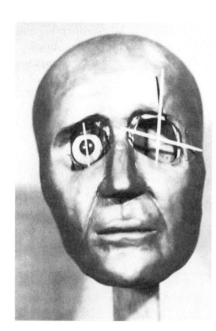

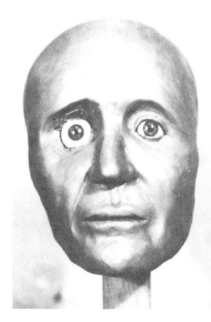

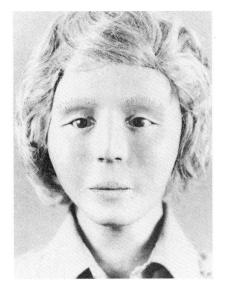 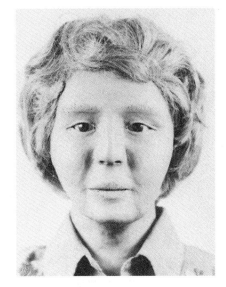

FIGURE i and j Completed reproduction. (i) Before adding aging features. (j) After "aging" the face to correspond with aging indicators ascertained from other parts of the skeleton.

Practicing Physical Anthropology

Careers in Physical Anthropology

Students who are interested in and stimulated by physical anthropology often ask, "What can one do with it?" Traditionally, the answer was straightforward: One would first have to get a Ph.D. then seek a teaching position in a two-year or four-year college. However, the number of new teaching positions has declined considerably in the last few years, while, at the same time, a steady stream of new graduates with doctorates has emerged. As a result, in the last decade, Ph.D.s in physical anthropology have actively turned to a variety of alternatives wherein they productively employ their specialized skills.

Most especially, physical anthropologists have become involved in bio-medical research, which has led to staff positions at medical and dental schools. A solid background in anatomy, as well as a broad understanding of human disease and adaptive response, are obviously good qualifications for a newly graduated physical anthropologist seeking work in this area. In research of this kind, epidemiological and bio-social models of disease are often investigated, providing excellent opportunities for some physical anthropologists.

Most openings in this field (usually advertised as fellowships) are funded by "soft money" sources, predominantly grants from federal agencies (such as the National Institutes of Health) or donations from private sources, who usually provide funds on a short-term basis (about one to three years, typically). In other words, these positions in medical or dental schools are not often permanent and must be frequently renewed through ongoing grant support. Nevertheless, numerous recent graduates have been engaged in this manner for a number of years. At the very least, opportunities like these provide excellent chances to do interesting research and to publish. They are also good places to be while awaiting openings in academia.

Physical anthropologists trained in osteology can sometimes work as forensic experts,* consulting with local coroners (medical examiners) or, occasionally, for the military.

---

*See Appendix B.

In addition, physical anthropologists now and then find employment teaching anatomy at a four-year college or teaching biology at two-year schools or at private or public secondary schools. Although most states require further certification (beyond attainment of the Ph.D.) to obtain a public school position, the need for adequately trained public-school biology teachers will continue to be pressing in the immediate future.

Other kinds of opportunities arise in various places, but actual openings are usually scant. For example, some physical anthropologists have been hired by the military to assist in the design of jet fighter cockpits or in the design and distribution of uniforms and other equipment. Also, a few jobs exist in museums and at private research foundations. Some physical anthropologists who have computer skills and enjoy applying them find employment as computer consultants at universities or in the business community.

A final word on teaching positions is in order. Some teaching jobs do come open every year. Moreover, given the demographics of current college professors, it is predicted that large numbers of retirements will take place in the mid 1990s, thus making more academic positions available. Any of you who are currently undergraduates will certainly not be in the academic job market until just about the time that more positions should be opening up. So, the situation regarding teaching is not entirely bleak.

A Degree in Physical Anthropology: What Does It Take?

From the fact that you are reading this text, we assume you are currently enrolled in an introductory anthropology course. Such a situation does not, of course, necessarily lead one to pursue anthropology further. However, if you are interested in doing so, first of all, you should consult with advisors in the anthropology department at your school or university. If you decide to pursue an anthropology undergraduate major, they can advise you on curricular and graduation requirements.

If you are already dedicated to another major, or if no formal anthropology major exists at your school, that does not preclude being accepted into an anthropology graduate program. An undergraduate anthropology major does help in gaining acceptance, but it is not mandatory in the view of many prestigeous graduate schools.

Graduate level degrees are of two kinds:

The Masters, or M.A., "Master of Arts." (At some institutions this may be an M.S., or "Master of Science.")

The Ph.D., or "Doctor of Philosophy." (Also simply called "the doctorate.")

Most master's programs are designed for completion in one to two years. If you are seriously committed to a career in physical anthropology, we recommend that the M.A. be used as a stepping-stone to the Ph.D. Some of our students have obtained the M.A. first, either because they needed to bolster their G.P.A. or because personal or financial circumstances did not make a move to a full Ph.D. program desirable immediately after graduation. It sometimes can be much easier to get accepted into a Ph.D. program after first completing a master's. Note that very few career opportunities within physical anthropology exist for those holding *only* the M.A. Thus, from a professional standpoint, the M.A. degree is a good springboard, but is not really an end in itself.

Ph.D. programs are usually designed to be completed in approximately five to seven years. If a master's is completed first, an additional time of only four years for the doctorate is entirely possible. In other words, whether an M.A. is achieved or not, you should assume a minimum of five years additional schooling/research after your undergraduate graduation in order to obtain a doctorate (which includes graduate course work, individual research, and the writing of a doctoral thesis).

Specific admission criteria vary, and graduate curricular requirements for institutions sometimes differ. You should check with advisors on your campus for their recommendations. In addition, of tremendous help is the *Guide to Departments of Anthropology*, published every year by the American Anthropological Association. For any would-be graduate applicant, this is an indispensable publication—containing all graduate (and undergraduate) programs in the U.S. and Canada. Specifically listed are the degrees offered, the entire faculty with academic specializations, and relevant addresses and phone numbers. For a copy you can write to:

American Anthropological Association
1703 New Hampshire Ave., N.W.
Washington, D.C. 20009

Research Institutions for Anthropology

The basis of any science is research. Without research, the finding of new evidence, the developing of new interpretations, and the achieving of new ideas would all be seriously affected. Vital to research is funding, because without funds, research can be sluggish, discouraging, and often impossible. When Louis Leakey was asked why so many hominid fossils were discovered after 1959 (when Zinj was found), he answered simply, "money." Zinj was such an exciting find that it inspired a number of funding institutions to support Leakey's research in Africa, which led to more finds, which in turn led to more funds, and so forth, not only to Leakey but to many paleoanthropologists.

Although there is a long history of government financial support for research, we refer here to private organizations. There are three notable institutions involved in anthropological research: The Wenner-Gren Foundation for Anthropological Research, Inc., The Leakey Foundation, and The Institute of Human Origins.

The Wenner-Gren Foundation For Anthropological Research, Inc.
1865 Broadway, New York, NY 10023, (212) 957-8780

The Wenner-Gren Foundation for Anthropological Research, Inc. was endowed in 1941 as the Viking Fund, Inc.* by Swedish industrialist Axel Leonard Wenner-Gren (1881–1861). It was his intention to dedicate the Foundation to the support of an-

---

*It was given its present name in 1951.

thropology (physical *and* cultural) that offered interdisciplinary perspectives and historical dimension. In 1951 he wrote, "I had in mind an organization that would deal not only with human evolution in general but particularly with the fields of intercultural understanding, the improvement of international and racial relations and the encouragement of world area studies." He believed that cooperation should begin with our appreciation and respect for one another's views and for the value of cultures different from one's own.

A prime goal of the Foundations is fostering communication within the broad range of behavioral and life sciences, which it pursues on an international scale. With this in mind, it promotes programs that create a climate of exchange and flow of information directed at the study of human origins, development, and variation.

In 1958, the Foundation established an international conference center at a renovated castle, donated by founder, Wenner-Gren, at Burg Wartenstein in Austria. Until 1980, important anthropology symposia were held annually at Burg Wartenstein. Some of the Symposia were: "Social Life of Early Man" (1959); "African Ecology and Human Evolution" (1961); "The Behavior of the Great Apes" (1974); "Stratigraphy and Patterns of Cultural Change in the Middle Pleistocene" (1975); and "Origins and Affinities of the First Americans" (1976).

To assist individual research, the Foundation operates a grant-in-aid program that has supported such projects as: "The elderly in Lingch'uan, Republic of China"; "Comprehensive research on aging through the study of osteoarthritis and osteoporosis in rhesus monieys"; and "Training in stable isotope geochemistry in preparation for research on role of dietary change in hominid evolution."

Foundation activities provide unique in-house resources for understanding and tracking the anthropological profession, its productivity, directions, and needs. About 1,500 inquiries regarding potential funding for specific projects and an additional 500 requests for information and advice are received annually.

In 1960, the Foundation initiated publication of *Current Anthropology*, a journal that remains one of the outstanding anthropology journals in the world. In addition to providing a forum for the exchange of ideas and information, *Current Anthropology* innovated the practice of publishing an article *along with* its solicited comments from other scholars and the author's response.

For students who wish to subscribe (there is a student rate) write *Current Anthropology*, Orlie Higgins, Circulation Manager, The University of Chicago Press, Journals Division, P.O. Box 37005, Chicago, Il 60637.

The Leakey Foundation
Foundation Center 1-7, Pasadena, CA 91125, (818) 449–0507

Dr. Louis Leakey was a frequent visitor to the United States, where he gave lectures and attended conferences. He always made California part of his visits. As an outstanding speaker and persuasive advocate of anthropological research, he inspired interested people who, in his honor, established the Leakey Foundation in 1968.

The stated purpose of the Foundation is to pursue Leakey's "vision of a multidisciplinary science—one that seeks to understand our ancestors, the ecology of their times, their cultures and traditions, as well as the behavior of our closest living relatives, the great apes." (The Foundation provides funds for studying all primates, not only hominids and apes.)

Although the Leakeys (Louis, Mary, and Richard) have confined their research efforts to Africa, the Foundation supports worldwide research. Grants have supported work in many countries of the world. The Foundation has already allocated grants totaling over 3 million dollars, and plans to fund larger projects are in place.

Leakey grants run the gamut of anthropological concern, as a few of the funded projects illustrate: "Changes in the Face of Asia: Response to Food Preparation Practices"; "Miocene Excavations at Pasalar, Turkey"; "Micromammalian Evidence for Paleoenvironmental Change"; "Reconstructing the Ranging Behavior of Early Hominids"; "Demography and Kinship in a Natural Baboon Population"; and "The Origins of Modern Human Adaptation."

In addition to its grants program, the Foundation sponsors lectures, symposia, and conferences throughout the United States. It also sponsors an education program through its Franklin Mosher Baldwin Fund, which offers support to African archeologists for field study and doctoral training in the United States. Moreover, the Foundation is involved in a cooperative venture with the Los Angeles Unified School District to encourage courses in human evolution, in which schools are provided with casts of fossil ancestors, books, and slides. Known as "Paleoproject" or "Stones and Bones," the program is being extended to the rest of the country.

The Foundation publishes a newsletter—*AnthroQuest*—four times a year. The Leakey Foundation is a public foundation and membership is open to the public. For more information write to The Leakey Foundation at the address provided in the heading of this section.

The Institute of Human Origins
2453 Ridge Road, Berkeley, CA 94709, (415) 845–0333, 845–0334

Located in Berkeley, adjacent to the University of California, the Institute of Human Origins was founded by anthropologists in 1981. This group was led by Dr. Donald C. Johanson, the well-known discoverer of Lucy, who is Director of the Institute.

A major objective of the Institute is to assist paleoanthropologists, geologists, and other investigators who are engaged in the recovery and interpretation of ancient hominid fossils. Another goal is to develop paleoanthropological resources in countries where Institute scientists are engaged in field work and to help obtain funding for the construction and support of research facilities in these countries.

The Institute sponsors, and provides support for, several African students in anthropology programs at American universities where study can lead to a doctorate degree.

A public program, consisting of a series of three lectures on topics in the area of human evolution, are presented by the Institute in the spring and fall. The series in the fall of 1987 offered lectures on *H. erectus*, Koko, and early hominids.

The Institute houses several research laboratories: an Archeology Laboratory, Paleontology Laboratory, and the Berkeley Geochronology Center for potassium-argon dating. This last is a state-of-the-art radiometric dating facility where the ages of fossil discoveries may be determined and verified.

The Institute publishes a quarterly newsletter and participates in an outreach program to public schools in northern California. Lecturers are available to schools—primarily to colleges—on subjects pertaining to human origins. Membership in the Institute is open to the public.

Geologic Time Scale

Era	Period	Time (million years)	Paleomagnetic Chronology — Epochs	Paleomagnetic Chronology — Events	Time¹	Glacial Sequence	Culture Periods² — Stage	Culture Periods² — Periods	Hominid Stages³
CENOZOIC	QUATERNARY		HOLO-CENE			Alpine Glaciation of Europe	Neo-lithic	Food production (domestication of plants/animals)	H. sapiens sapiens Anatomically modern humans (probably appeared 100,000 years ago)
		.010			10,000				
			Upper		40,000	WURM	Upper	Magdalenian Solutrean Gravettian Aurignacian Chatelperronian	
					75,000		Middle	Mousterian	Neandertals (in Europe and Near East only)
		.125			100,000	Riss-Würm			
					125,000				
			PLEISTOCENE / BRUNHES (normal)		175,000			Levalloisian	
					225,000	RISS	PALEOLITHIC		
		.250	Middle		265,000	Mindel-Riss		Clactonian	
					300,000				
					380,000	MINDEL			H. sapiens (archaic)
					400,000				
					430,000	Günz-Mindel	Lower	Acheulian	
						GÜNZ			
		.730			750,000				
		1,000		Jaramillo					
		1,250	MATU-YAMA (reversed)			Uncertain geological sequences			
		1,500	Lower						
		1,750		OLDUVAI (normal)					
		1.8							H. erectus (?) Homo sp.
	TERTIARY	2	Pliocene	Gauss (normal) Gilbert (reversed)				Oldowan	Australo-pithecines
		5						?	
		25	Miocene	Hominoidea (apelike creatures) dryopithecines flourish. Probable appearance of hominids					
		35	Oligocene	Anthropoidea and appearance of Hominoidea					
		53	Eocene	Prosimians flourish; possible appearance of anthropoidea					
		65	Paleocene	Appearance of Prosimii					

ROCKY MOUNTAIN REVOLUTION

Era	Period	Time	Description
MESOZOIC	Cretaceous	136	Appearance of placental and marsupial mammals. Dinosaurs peak and become extinct. First modern birds
	Jurassic	190	Great age of dinosaurs—flying and swimming dinosaurs. First toothed birds
	Triassic	225	Reptiles dominant. First dinosaurs. Egg-laying mammals

APPALACHIAN REVOLUTION

Era	Period	Time	Description
PALEOZOIC	Permian	280	Reptilian radiation. Mammal-like reptiles. Many old forms die out.
	Carbon-iferous	345	First reptiles. Radiation of amphibia. Modern insects evolve.
	Devonian	395	Age of fish. Amphibians—first air-breathing vertebrates. First forests
	Silurian	430	Jawed fishes appear. First air-breathing animal—scorpionlike aurypterid. Definite land plants
	Ordovi-cian	500	First fishes. Trilobites still abundant. Graptolites and corals becoming plentiful. Possible land plants
	Cambrian	570	Trilobites abundant, also brachiopods, jellyfish, worms, and other invertebrates.
PRE-CAMBRIAN			Various marine protozoa, mainly algae. Toward close of era, some evidence of invertebrates.

¹Dates are approximations.

²Except for the Oldowan, the culture periods in this column have been the most intensively studied and are all located in western Europe. Local names are given to culture periods in other areas of the world.

³Note overlap of Neandertals and anatomically moderns in Europe and the Near East. See text pp. 541, 548-551.

Glossary

Acclimatization Long-term physiological response within individuals to environmental pressure; usually takes a few weeks to a few months.

Acheulian The culture period, or stone tool industry, of the Middle and part of the Lower Pleistocene; characterized by the handaxe.

Acquired characteristics The notion developed by Lamarck that traits acquired during the lifetime of an organism could be passed on to offspring. Known as the theory of acquired characteristics.

Acrocentric chromosome A chromosome with its centromere towards one end.

Adaptation Genetic changes within populations in response to selection (environmental) pressure; usually takes many generations.

Adaptive niche The whole way of life of an organism: where it lives, what it eats, how it gets food, and so forth.

Adaptive radiation The rapid increase and spread of an evolving group of organisms which diversify and adapt to new niches.

Adenine One of the chemical bases (purines) found in both DNA and RNA.

Advanced In evolutionary terms, an organism further removed from an evolutionary divergence than a more primitive one; usually now termed "derived." *See* Primitive.

Aegyptopithecus An early hominoid form from the Oligocene; Fayum, Egypt.

Agonistic behavior Behavior actively related to fighting—aggression, conciliation, or retreat.

Allele An alternative form of a gene at the same locus (position) on a chromosome.

Allen's rule Within species of warm-blooded animals (birds and mammals) those populations living in colder environments will tend to have shorter appendages than populations in warmer areas.

Allo Combining form indicating different or other.

Allometric growth Differential patterns of growth whereby some parts of the body are disproportionately related to other parts.

Altruism Helping others without direct benefit to oneself. In natural selection terms: sacrificing your own reproductive success to help another.

Alveolar Tooth-bearing portion of the upper jaw.

Alveolar prognathism Forward projection of the maxilla (much reduced in anatomically modern humans).

Ameslan American sign language. AMESLAN is used among deaf humans and also for teaching language to some apes.

Amino acids Small molecules that are the building blocks of protein.

Amniote egg The developing reptilian embryo is surrounded by three sacs: one for food, one for waste matter, and one filled with liquid—amniotic fluid—for protection. This egg evolved with reptiles.

Analogous structures Similarities in parts of the anatomy not based on descent from a common ancestor, but based on common function (the bird wing and butterfly wing, for example).

Analogy Similarities between organisms based on common function, not due to evolutionary relationship. *See* Homology.

Anatomically modern (a.m.) *H. sapiens* (or human beings) Populations of the Upper Paleolithic who physically resemble populations of today.

Anomaly Different, irregular deviation.

Anthropoidea The suborder (of Primates) of anthropoids, including New World monkeys, Old World monkeys, and hominoids (apes and hominids).

Anthropology The study (or science) of humankind.

Anthropometry Measurement of the human body.

Anticodon A triplet of bases in tRNA which complements the triplet of bases in mRNA. The anticodon corresponds to a particular amino acid.

Arboreal Tree-living. Many prosimians and monkeys, as well as the gibbon and the orangutan, are arboreal.

Archeology The study of prehistoric culture through remains left by ancient humans.

Artifacts (archeological traces) Traces of hominid behavior. Very old artifacts are usually made of stone.

Artiodactyl Even-toed hoof (e.g., cows, pigs, camels).

Ascending ramus Rear upright portion of the mandible.

Association What an archeological trace is found with (other archeological traces, bone refuse, etc.).

Atlatl A throwing board or spearthrower.

Aurignacian A culture period (*circa* 30,000 ya) of the Upper Paleolithic; probable beginning of Upper Paleolithic art.

Australopithecine The common term for members of the genus, *Australopithecus.*

Australopithecus The extinct genus of Plio-Pleistocene hominids found in South and East Africa; usually divided into: *A. africanus* and *A. robustus* (S. Africa), and *A. aethiopicus*, *A. boisei*, and an early primitive representative, *A. afarensis* (E. Africa).

Autapomorph (-ous), -ic [adj.]) A new morphological trait unique to a group in an evolutionary lineage.

Autosome Any chromosome except a sex chromosome.

Balanced polymorphism The maintenance of two or more alleles in a population due to a selective advantage of the heterozygote.

Base One of the four chemicals attached to a sugar molecule and a phosphate to make up a nucleotide. In DNA, a base is always paired with another base.

Behavior, social The behavior of animals that live together as a group; gregariousness, sociability.

Binomial The binomial (two-term) system of classification developed by Linnaeus. Every organism is identified by two Latin names: the first word is the generic term; the second, the specific.

Biocultural An approach to the study of human beings, their evolution and behavior. The biocultural approach considers both human biology and culture.

Biological adaptation Genetic changes within populations in response to selection (environmental) pressure; usually takes many generations.

Biosphere The entire area inhabited by organisms.

Biostratigraphy Dating method based on evolutionary changes within an evolving lineage.

Bipedalism Walking on two legs as the natural means of locomotion.

Blade A parallel-sided flake at least twice as long as it is wide.

Brachiation Arm-over-arm suspensory locomotion beneath branches.

Brachycephalic Broad-headed. A skull in which the width of the skull is 80% or more of the length.

Breccia Cemented conglomerate containing limestone, sand, and bone.

Breeding isolate A population geographically and/or socially separate and, therefore, relatively easy to define.

Calva (or callote) Uppermost portion of the braincase.

Calvaria The skull minus the face and mandible.

Calvarium The skull minus the mandible.

Cambrian The first period of the Paleozoic.

Canine Usually a long and pointed (conical) tooth in front of the mouth, lateral to incisors; used for piercing and grasping.

Carbon 14 (^{14}C) dating A method of determining the age in years of an organic specimen by measuring the loss of the radioactive isotope, ^{14}C.

Carboniferous Fifth period of the Paleozoic. The first reptiles appear during this period.

Carcinogen An agent that promotes cancer.

Carnivore A meat-eating animal. Also the common name for a member of the mammalian order, Carnivora (for example, dogs, cats, bears).

Catarrhine The group (infraorder) comprising all Old World anthropoids, living and extinct.

Catastrophism The idea that there were a series of violent and sudden catastrophes which destroyed most living things. This would explain the extinction of many species. Also part of catastrophism was the belief that after each catastrophe, a new set of creations established new species. Associated with Cuvier.

Ceboidea The anthropoid superfamily of New World monkeys.

Cenozoic Era (65 mya–present) The present era; the era following the Mesozoic.

Centromere The constricted part of the chromosome to which spindle fibers are attached during mitosis and meiosis.

Cercopithecoidea The anthropoid superfamily of Old World monkeys including colobines and cercopithecines.

Cerebellum Hind portion of brain. The cerebellum is the center of unconscious control of skeletal muscles.

Cerebrum ´ The front portion of the brain; the largest portion of the brain in placental mammals.

Cervical Pertaining to the neck, as in cervical vertebrae.

Chatelperronian An early culture period (*circa* 32,000 ya) of the Upper Paleolithic; perhaps transitional between Mousterian and later Upper Paleolithic culture.

Cheek teeth Premolars and molars.

Chromosomal mutation A rearrangement of large sections of DNA (whole pieces of chromosomes) such as deletions, translocations, inversions, and duplications.

Chromosome Threadlike, gene-carrying body, consisting of 1 or 2 DNA molecules.

Chronometric dating Determining the age of a specimen in number of years. Potassium-argon, ^{14}C, ^{238}U, dendrochronology (and others) are used to obtain chronometric dates.

Cladistics The school of evolutionary biology that seeks to make evolutionary hypotheses through interpreting patterns of primitive/derived characteristics.

Cladogram A diagrammatic representation of population relationships using several genetic traits simultaneously.

Class A category of classification in the Animal (or Plant) Kingdom; a subdivision of subphylum. A class includes those animals (or plants) that have adapted to a similar way of life. Vertebrate classes are Pisces, Amphibia, Reptilia, Aves, and Mammalia.

Clavicle Collar bone.

Cline A gradual distribution of allele frequencies over space. (An isopleth, connecting points of equal value.)

Clovis A phase of North American prehistory 12 kya to 11 kya in the West. During this time short-fluted projectile points were used in hunting mammoths.

Coadaptation (genetic coadaptation) Interaction of genes at the genotypic level. Natural selection acts upon the complex product of such interactions rather than upon individual loci.

Codon A triplet of bases in mRNA that codes for a specific amino acid. The triplet is matched by another triplet of bases in tRNA.

Condyle A rounded protuberance of bone which articulates with another bone (that is, forms a joint with or moves against another bone).

Context   The environmental setting where an archeological trace is found.

Convergence (convergent evolution)   Evolution of similar adaptive traits in unrelated forms; for example, the wings of birds and wings of butterflies. *See* Parallelism.

Coprolite   Feces found at an archeological site; if fossilized, called *coprolith*.

Core   Stone reduced by flake removal.

Core area   Area, within the home range, of greatest regular use.

Coronal suture   The suture running transversely across the skull joining the frontal and parietal bones.

Cosmology   The study of the creation of the universe and the laws that govern it.

Cranium   The complete skull; bone of the head, face, and mandible.

Crepuscular   Active at twilight or dawn.

Cretaceous   Final (third) period of Mesozoic. Dinosaurs become extinct. Probable appearance of first primates.

Crossing-over   The exchange of genetic material between homologous chromosomes during meiosis.

Crossopterygians   Lobe-finned fish; probably gave rise to amphibians.

Culture   The ways humans discover, invent, and develop in order to survive. Culture is the human strategy of adaptation.

Cytoplasm   That portion of the cell lying outside the nucleus.

Cytosine   One of the chemical bases (pyrimidines) found in both DNA and RNA.

Dental arcade   The shape of the tooth row: posteriorly divergent, parallel, parabolic, etc.

Dental formula   The number of each kind of tooth present. Shown usually for one-quarter of the mouth as: Incisors; Canine; Premolars; Molars.

Devonian   Fourth period of the Paleozoic. Age of Fish. Appearance of amphibians.

Diastema   Gap, space, especially between the upper lateral incisor and canine (also seen in the lower jaw between the canine and first premolar); found in many monkeys and pongids.

Diploid number (2n)   The full complement of chromosomes—46 in humans—in a somatic cell or in a sex cell before meiosis.

Display   Stereotyped behavior that serves to communicate emotional states between individuals. Display is most often associated with reproductive or agonistic behavior.

Diurnal   Active during daylight hours.

Division of Labor   Activities performed only by members of a particular status, such as age or sex.

Dizygotic   Twins derived from two zygotes, genetically related the same as any full sibs; differences between them are caused both by the environment and genetic variation.

DNA (deoxyribonucleic acid)   A large molecule composed of adenine, guanine, cytosine, and thymine plus phosphate and sugar; DNA carries the genetic code.

Dolichocephalic   Narrow or long-headed. A skull in which the width is less than 75% of the length.

Dominance (dominance hierarchy)   The physical domination of some members of a group by other members. A hierarchy of ranked statuses sustained by hostile, or threat of hostile, behavior which results in greater access to resources such as food, sleeping sites, and mates.

Dominant   A trait determined by a dominant allele. A trait that is visible or measurable and that prevents the appearance of the recessive.

Dorsal   Pertaining to the back (toward the backbone) of an animal.

Double helix   The structure of DNA composed of a pair of matching helixes.

Dryopithecus   The genus name referring to a diverse group of extinct hominoids from the Miocene.

East Lake Turkana   A Plio-Pleistocene locality in northern Kenya which has yielded dozens of fossil hominids. Hominid-bearing levels date 1.8–1.0 mya.

Ecological niche (econiche)   Environment to which a species is adapted.

Effective breeding population   Those individuals in a population actually producing offspring; usually about one-third total population size.

Empirical   Derived from or depending on experience or experiment.

Endocast   An impression of the inside of the skull showing the size, shape, and some details of the surface of the brain.

Endogamy   Mating within the social unit (that is, the population). *See* Exogamy.

Endoskeleton   An internal bony skeleton, characteristic of vertebrates. *See* Exoskeleton.

Eocene   Second epoch of Cenozoic. Radiation of prosimians. Possible appearance of anthropoids.

Estrous cycle   An hormonally initiated cycle in female mammals correlated with ovulation. Estrus may involve observable physical and behavioral changes.

Ethnography   The study of surviving, nonliterate societies.

Eutheria   The most numerous subclass of Mammalia. Embryo and fetus of these (placental) mammals are nourished by a placenta.

Evolution   A change in allele frequency in a population from one generation to the next.

Evolutionary reversal   The reacquisition of a structure previously lost in the evolution of a life form—an extremely unlikely event.

Evolutionary trend   A set of anatomical and/or behavior traits which tend to characterize a group of evolutionarily related organisms. For example: pentadactyly, retention of complete clavicle, and stereoscopic vision among the primates.

Exogamy Mating outside the social unit (that is, the population).

Exoskeleton A hard, supporting external covering, characteristic of many invertebrates such as ants and lobsters. *See* Endoskeleton.

F_1 First filial generation; offspring resulting from a cross of homozygous dominants and homozygous recessives. All individuals resulting from such a cross are heterozygous.

F_2 Second filial generation; offspring of a cross of F_1 individuals—a mating of two heterozygous individuals (or selfing in a species where this is possible, as in the case of Mendel's peas).

Family Members of a family usually inhabit a similar environment; a category that includes genera and species.

Fayum An Oligocene fossil primate site in Egypt yielding several early anthropoid forms.

Femur Thigh bone.

Fibula The narrow long bone of the lower leg. *See* Tibia.

Fixity of species The belief that species, once created, never changed but remained fixed. This belief was firmly held by most scholars in the eighteenth century.

Fluorine dating A method of relative dating by measuring the amount of fluorine in a specimen. More fluorine indicates a greater age.

Fluting Removal of large flakes in order to thin projectal point bases for hafting.

Folsom Phase of southern Great Plains prehistory, 10 ky to 8 kya, during which long-fluted points were used for bison hunting.

Foramen magnum Opening in the base of the skull through which the spinal cord passes.

Forensic Pertaining to courts of law. In anthropology, the use of anthropology in questions of law.

Founder effect (Sewall Wright Effect) A type of genetic drift in which allele frequencies are altered in small populations which are nonrandom samples of larger populations.

Frontal bone The front bone of the skull including the forehead and the brow region over the eyes.

Gamete A haploid cell (sperm or ovum) that may combine with a haploid cell of the other sex to form a fertilized cell.

Gene That section of DNA responsible for the ultimate synthesis of a specific polypeptide chain of amino acids; that portion of DNA with a detectable function.

Gene frequency (allele frequency) A numerical indicator of the proportion of genes (alleles) in a population. *See* Hardy-Weinberg Equilibrium.

Gene pool The total complement of genes in a population.

Generalized Pertains to a trait capable of several functions. The human hand is generalized because it is used for a number of functions; the human foot is specialized and is used in a very limited way. *See* Specialized.

Genetic drift (random genetic drift) The evolutionary factor which accounts for evolutionary changes (shifts in allele frequency) due to random events. A function of population size.

Genetic screening Testing programs to ascertain individuals with genetic diseases or carriers of potentially deleterious genes.

Genotype The genetic makeup of a particular organism; an individual's "genetic formula"; the genes at one or more loci.

Genotypic proportion The relative frequency of the genotypes in a population. For a two-allele system (such as A, a), there will be three genotypes (AA, Aa, aa). Hardy-Weinberg equilibrium makes idealized predictions of these genotypes according to the formula: $p^2 + 2pq + q^2 = 1$. *See* Hardy-Weinberg Equilibrium.

Genus (pl. genera) A category of classification in the Animal (or Plant) Kingdom. Genus groups together closely related species usually inhabiting similar ecological niches; for example, *Homo, Pan, Felis, Canis*.

Geochemistry The study of the chemical composition of the earth's crust.

Geology The study of the history and structure of the earth as recorded in rocks.

Gracile Small, lightly built; used to refer to more lightly built australopithecines. *See* Robust.

Gravettian A culture period (*circa* 25,000 ya) of the Upper Paleolithic; associated with Lascaux Cave art.

Grooming, Social Cleaning the body of another by picking through the hair and fur with the fingers or teeth. Grooming is common among primates.

Guanine One of the chemical bases (purines) found both in DNA and RNA.

Günz First glacial of the Pleistocene.

Habilis A species of genus *Homo*, first applied by Louis Leakey to Plio-Pleistocene hominids from East Africa.

Hadar A Plio-Pleistocene hominid locality in northeastern Ethiopia. Hominid-bearing levels dated ?3.7–2.6 mya.

Haploid number (n) The number of chromosomes in the gamete after meiosis (23 in humans).

Haplorhini The classificatory term used to group tarsiers with monkeys, apes, and humans (either suborder or semiorder).

Hardy-Weinberg Equilibrium The mathematical relationship expressing—under ideal conditions—the predicted distribution of genes in populations; the central theorem of population genetics.

Helix A spiral or anything with a spiral form.

Helix, double The structure of DNA resembles a double helix (spiral).

Herbivore A plant-eating animal.

Heritability The relative amount of variation in a trait due to genetic causes as part of total phenotypic variation.

Heterodontism Having different teeth. Characteristic of mammals whose teeth consist of incisors, canines, premolars, and molars.

Heterozygote A cell or individual that is heterozygous. (A hybrid is heterozygous for a particular trait.)

Heterozygous Having different alleles at a given locus on a pair of homologous chromosomes.

Holistic Viewing the whole as an integrated and interdependent system. Anthropology includes as its concern all aspects of human beings—physical and behavioral.

Holocene   Second (present) epoch of Quaternary; begins with end of Pleistocene glaciation.

Holstein   Second interglacial between the Mindel and Riss glaciations.

Home range   The area utilized by an animal; the area the group is most familiar with and which provides the group with food.

Hominid   Popular form of Hominidae, the family to which humans belong. Hominids include bipedal primates such as *Australopithecus* and *Homo*.

Hominidae   The family, of the order Primates, to which humans belong.

Hominization   Process of becoming more human.

Hominoid   Abbreviated or popular form of Hominoidea, the superfamily to which hominids, pongids, and gibbons belong.

Homo   The genus to which humans belong, including *erectus* and *sapiens*.

Homodontism   Having the same teeth. Refers to the situation wherein all teeth of the mouth are similar, as in fish and reptiles.

Homoiothermy   Pertains to an organism that maintains the same temperature (mammals and birds, for example). Warm-blooded.

Homologous chromosomes   Paired chromosomes. Chromosomes that are paired during meiosis and participate in cross-over. Homologous chromosomes contain the same loci.

Homologous structures   Similarities in parts of the anatomy based upon common descent.

Homologue   Occurs in meiosis when a chromosome duplicates itself. The double-stranded chromosome is a homologue.

Homology   Similarities of organisms based on common evolutionary descent.

Homo sapiens   The species which appeared 200,000 to 300,000 years ago; includes Neandertals, other archaic forms, and anatomically modern humans.

Homo sapiens sapiens   The subspecies to which modern humans belong; anatomically modern human beings.

Homozygote   A cell or individual that is homozygous. (A purebred is homozygous for a particular trait.)

Homozygous   Having the same allele at a given locus on a pair of homologous chromosomes.

Human   A term now generally applied to *H. erectus* and *H. sapiens*.

Human evolution   Biological changes over time leading to anatomically modern human beings.

Human variation   Physical differences among humans.

Humerus   Upper arm bone.

Hybrid   Offspring of parents of mixed ancestry. A heterozygote.

Hypothesis   Unproved theory. A theory is a statement with some confirmation.

Immune response system   The production of specific antibodies in response to the introduction of specific foreign antigens into the body.

Immunity   An organism's ability to recognize and deactivate foreign antigens very quickly as a consequence of earlier (mild) exposure (for example, through vaccination).

Inbreeding   A type of nonrandom mating in which blood relatives mate more often than predicted under random mating conditions.

Incisors   Front teeth, usually spatulate in primates; used for cutting and nipping.

Independent assortment   Where gene pairs on one set of homologous chromosomes do not influence the distribution of gene pairs on other chromosomes—they separate independently from one another during meiosis and are randomly assorted in the gametes. Known as Mendel's second law.

Innominate   The fused half-portion of a pelvis; contains three bones—the ilium, ischium, and pubis (also called the os coxa).

In situ   In its original or natural position.

Interspecific variation   Variation between two separate species.

Interstadial   The period of partial retreat during a major glaciation.

Intraspecific variation   Variation within a species due to age, sexual dimorphism, individual genetic differences, or geographic separation.

Intron   Within a genetic locus, a section of DNA that is not translated.

Ischial callosities   Hardened sitting pads found on the rear ends of Old World monkeys. Also seen to some degree in chimpanzees.

Jurassic   Second period of Mesozoic. Great age of dinosaurs. First appearance of birds.

Kabuh   Middle Pleistocene geologic formation.

Kanapoi   A Plio-Pleistocene hominid site in northern Kenya. Estimated age approximately 4 mya.

Karyotype   The chromosome complement contained in a cell, especially the diagram of chromosomes arranged according to size and banding patterns of each chromosome.

KNM-ER   Kenya National Museum—East Rudolf (the former name for Lake Turkana). The prefix preceding paleontological discoveries from East Lake Turkana.

Kromdraai   A Plio-Pleistocene hominid site in South Africa yielding remains of robust australopithecines.

Lactose intolerance   Inability to digest milk (and other dairy products) after early childhood; characteristic of a majority of humans today. Lactose intolerance is due to the absence of the enzyme, lactase.

Laetoli   A Plio-Pleistocene hominid site in northern Tanzania. Dated 3.77–3.59 mya.

Lamarckism   Lamarck's ideas about evolution. *See* Acquired characteristics.

Lambdoidal suture   The horizontal or transverse suture at the back of the top of the skull joining the parietal and occipital bones.

Lemuroidea   The prosimian superfamily of lemurs, today confined to Madagascar.

Levant   Countries bordering the eastern Mediterranean.

Lineage   An evolutionary line of related forms distinct from other such lines.

Linguistics   In anthropology, the description and study of the structure and history of language and its relationship to culture.

Living floor   A narrow horizon of archeological remains. Corresponds to brief period of hominid occupation.

Locus   (pl. loci) The position of a gene on a chromosome.

Lorisoidea   The prosimian superfamily of lorises. Today all are nocturnal forms, found in Africa and southern Asia.

Lothagam   A Plio-Pleistocene hominid site in northern Kenya. Estimated age, approximately 5.5 mya.

Macroevolution   Large evolutionary changes (result of long-term major shifts in allele frequencies) produced only after many generations. *See* Microevolution.

Magdalenean   Final period of the Upper Paleolithic (*circa* 15,000 ya) (in Europe) and a time of spectacular technological growth; associated with art from Altamira Cave in Spain.

Major histocompatibility complex (MHC)   The large genetic complex (located in humans on chromosome #6) that plays a central part in immune response—recognition of foreign antigens and production of specialized cells to deactivate them.

Makapansgat   A Plio-Pleistocene hominid site in South Africa yielding remains of gracile australopithecines.

Malnutrition   A diet insufficient in quality (i.e., lacking in some essential components).

Mammals   The class of animals that nurse their young from mammary glands. Primates belong to this class.

Mandible   Lower jaw.

Marsupials   A subclass of mammals—metatheria—that bear live young; infants are nursed in the mother's pouch, Marsupium pouch.

Masseter   Chewing; refers to muscles used in the operation of the jaw—originating on the zygomatic (cheek) bones and inserting on the mandible.

Mastoid process   A triangular bone behind the ear hole on a human skull; usually more pronounced in males than females.

Matriline   Individuals related through the mother.

Maxilla   Upper jaw.

Meiosis   Cell division, consisting of two divisions, in which the total complement (diploid number) of chromosomes is reduced by half (haploid number) in the gametes (sperm in males; ova in females). Also known as reduction division.

Melanin   The biochemical compound produced by specialized cells in the basal layers of the epidermis. Melanin is very important in influencing skin pigmentation.

Mendelian trait (simple trait)   An inherited trait with a straightforward pattern, controlled by one genetic locus.

Mesozoic Era (225–65 mya)   The era following the Paleozoic. Known as the Age of Reptiles.

Metacentric chromosome   A chromosome with its centromere near the center.

Metatheria   A subclass of mammals (marsupials); infants are nursed in the mother's pouch.

Metazoa   Multicellular animals. A major division of the Animal Kingdom.

Microevolution   The small-scale evolutionary changes occurring over just a few generations and involving relatively small changes in allele frequencies. What the Hardy-Weinberg formula measures. *See* Macroevolution.

Migration   Movement of individuals (and, necessarily, genes) between populations. An evolutionary factor that may cause changes in allele frequencies.

Mindel   Second glacial of the Pleistocene.

Miocene   Fourth epoch of Cenozoic. Radiation of hominoids. Possible appearance of hominids.

Mitosis   Cell division into two daughter cells in which the chromosome complement is identical to the mother cell and to each other.

Molars   Cheek teeth, following the premolars. In anthropoids these are the last three teeth of the tooth row; used for grinding and chewing.

Molecule   Smallest portion of a substance that acts like that substance and is capable of existing independently. Several to many atoms constitute a molecule.

Mongrelization   Racial mixture.

Monogenists   Term applied to those who believe that all races derived from a single pair (Adam and Eve).

Monotreme   A subclass of mammals—prototheria—that lay eggs.

Monozygotic   Twins derived from one zygote, genetically identical. Differences between the twins are caused solely by the environment.

Mosaic evolution   Term applied when the rate of evolution in one functional system varies from other systems.

Mousterian   A culture period, or stone tool industry, of the Middle Paleolithic; usually associated with Neandertals. Characterized mainly by stone flakes.

Multivariate   Pattern for several variables assessed simultaneously.

Mutagen   An agent that mutates (alters the DNA of a cell).

Mutation   An alteration in the genetic material (DNA). The true "creative" factor in evolution. Mutation is the only way to produce new variation and is the starting point of all evolutionary change.

Natural selection   The evolutionary factor, first articulated by Charles Darwin, that causes changes in allele frequencies in populations due to differential net reproductive success of individuals. *See* Net reproductive success.

Neandertals   *H. sapiens* form different from anatomically modern human beings (*H. sapiens sapiens*); usually associated with Mousterian culture and the Middle Paleolithic.

Negative assortative mating   A type of nonrandom mating in which individuals of unlike phenotype mate more often than predicted under random mating conditions.

Neopallium or Neocortex   A covering of the cerebral hemispheres begun in reptiles, expanded in mammals, and reaching its greatest expansion in humans. Higher mental activity is concentrated in this area.

Net reproductive success The number of offspring successfully raised; the bottom line of natural selection.

Nocturnal Active during nighttime. *See* Diurnal and Crepuscular.

Nuchal Pertaining to the neck.

Nucleotide A purine or pyrimidine base attached to a sugar and a phosphate group: a subunit of DNA and RNA.

Nulliparous Never having given birth.

Nucleus A body, present in most types of cells (i.e., eukaryotes), containing chromosomes.

Occiput (occipital bone) The rear bone of the skull. The occiput also forms most of the base, including the occipital condyles and foramen magnum.

OH Olduvai Hominid. The prefix preceding hominid discoveries (numbered sequentially) from Olduvai Gorge.

Olduvai Gorge A paleoanthropological site in northern Tanzania yielding remains of Plio-Pleistocene hominids and a wealth of biocultural data.

Olfactory Smell.

Oligocene Third epoch of Cenozoic. Radiation of anthropoids.

Omnivore An animal that will eat both plants and meat.

Omo A Plio-Pleistocene hominid locality in southern Ethiopia. Hominid-bearing levels dated 2.9–1.0 mya.

Oöcyte Female sex cell; a cell that undergoes meiosis and produces an egg (ovum).

Oögenesis Division process of the female sex cell that produces ova.

Oötid A haploid cell produced by meiosis and differentiating into an ovum.

Order A category of classification in the Animal (or Plant) Kingdom. A subdivision of Class. Members of an order usually inhabit a similar environment; for example, Carnivora, Rodentia, Primates.

Ordovician The second period of the Paleozoic. First fishes appear.

Osteology The study of bones.

Ostracoderm Shell-skin or armored.

Oviparity Egg birth, characteristic of most animals.

Ovum (pl. ova) Female sex cell.

P₁ The parental generation in which homozygous dominants and recessives are crossed. Parents homozygous (pure) for smooth seeds and parents homozygous for wrinkled represent such a parental cross.

Paleoanthropology The multidisciplinary approach to the study of human biocultural evolution. Includes physical anthropology, archeology, geology, ecology, and many other disciplines.

Paleocene First epoch of Tertiary. Prosimians present.

Paleolithic Old Stone Age. The culture period that includes the beginning of culture up to approximately the end of the Pleistocene glaciation. Usually divided into Lower, Middle, and Upper.

Paleolithic, Lower The earliest period of the Paleolithic, characterized by Oldowan (pebble tools) and Acheulian (hand-axe) industries.

Paleolithic, Middle A stone flake industry associated with the Mousterian culture period and Neandertals.

Paleolithic, Upper The final stage of the Paleolithic, associated with more sophisticated culture such as cave painting, sculpting, engraving, and stone tools made from blades. Worldwide expansion of anatomically modern humans.

Paleomagnetism Dating method based on the shifting nature of the earth's geomagnetic field.

Paleontology The study of the fossils of ancient animals.

Paleopathology The study of ancient diseases.

Paleospecies A group of organisms found in paleontological contexts and usually separated by large amounts of time, thus adding to the amount of variation seen in extant groups.

Paleozoic Era (570–225 mya) The era following the Proterozoic, beginning 570 million years ago. The first era in which fossils are relatively abundant.

Palynology The analysis of pollen found in the soil of archeological excavations to determine the kinds of plants present at the ancient site.

Parallelism (parallel evolution) Evolution of similar adaptive traits in forms that were once related but then diverged, developing along similar lines. *See* Convergence.

Paranthropus The genus name sometimes used to refer to robust australopithecines and, therefore, making a generic distinction between them and gracile australopithecines (*Australopithecus*).

Parietal The right and left side bones on top of the skull, joined by the sagittal suture.

Pentadactyly Having five digits. A generalized trait of mammals and primates.

Penultimate Last but one; next to last.

Peptide A compound of two or more amino acids joined by peptide bonds. Linked peptides form polypeptides which, in turn, join to form proteins.

Perineum The area between the anus and genitalia.

Periodontal Gum and jaw.

Perissodactyl Odd-toed hoof (e.g., horse).

Permian Final period of the Paleozoic. Appearance of mammal-like reptiles.

Phenotype The observable or measurable characteristic of an organism. Smoothness in a seed is an observable phenotype. In blood groups, A, B, and O and AB are measurable phenotypes.

Phenotypic ratio The ratio of phenotypes, especially from a hybrid cross. Mendel's famous F₁ hybrid cross of peas produced a 3:1 phenotypic ratio.

Phylogeny The study of evolutionary lines of descent. A "family tree."

Phylum (pl. phyla) A primary division of the Animal (or Plant) Kingdom; for example, Arthropoda, Chordata.

Piltdown A forged "fossil" hominid from England, "discovered" in 1911. Combining a fully *sapiens* cranium with a modern pongid jaw, it served to confuse anthropologists for four decades.

Pithecanthropus Name originally given to *H. erectus* by Eugene Dubois.

Placenta Tissue connected to the uterus that nourishes the fetus and absorbs its waste. This structure is characteristic of most mammals and has given its name to that form—placental mammals.

Placental mammals (eutheria) Mammals whose embryonic development is associated with a placenta.

Platycephaly Flatheadedness, as opposed to the dome shape of the skull of anatomically modern humans.

Pleistocene Sixth epoch of the Cenozoic. *H. sapiens* becomes widespread throughout Old World. *H. sapiens sapiens* evolves toward end of Pleistocene. Ice Age.

Plesiomorph (-ous, -ic [adj.]) A character of common inheritance found in an evolving lineage; primitive traits.

Pliocene Fifth epoch of Cenozoic. Hominids definitely present.

Point mutation Change in just one base in the DNA sequence. Probably the most common kind of mutation with evolutionary impact.

Polygenic Traits controlled by two or more loci; usually such traits (for example, stature, weight, IQ) are also influenced considerably by the environment.

Polygenists Term applied to those who believe in a multiple origin of races.

Polygyny One male and two or more females in a mating relationship.

Polymorphism The situation when two or more alleles at a given genetic locus occur with frequencies greater than 1% in a population.

Polypeptide A group of peptides linked together. One or more polypeptide chains make a protein.

Population Within a species, a community of individuals where mates are usually found.

Population genetics Studies in contemporary populations through measurement of allele frequencies. *See* Hardy-Weinberg Equilibrium.

Positive assortative mating A type of nonrandom mating in which individuals of like phenotype mate more often than predicted under random mating conditions.

Postcranial The skeleton behind (below) the skull.

Postorbital bar The bony element that completes encirclement on the outside of the eye orbit—a characteristic of primates.

Potassium-argon (K/Ar) dating Determining absolute age (in years) by measuring the amounts of potassium-40 (^{40}K) and argon-40 (^{40}Ar). The greater the amount of argon that has built up, the older the specimen. Used only on rocks once heated to a very high temperature, such as that generated by volcanic activity.

Prehensility Adaptation for grasping.

Premolars Cheek teeth similar in form to the molars; situated between canines and molars. Old World anthropoids possess two premolars and New World forms normally three in each quadrant. Human premolars have two cusps, compared to four or more in molars, and are known as bicuspids.

Presenting A behavior, often indicating subordination or appeasement, in which an animal places itself on all fours and elevates its rear end toward another. During estrus a female may present for purposes of copulation.

Primates The order of mammals to which humans, apes, monkeys, and prosimians belong.

Primitive In evolutionary terms, an organism that is closer to an evolutionary divergence than a later (more derived) one. *Also see*, Plesiomorph.

Principle of independent assortment The distribution of one pair of genes does not influence the distribution of other pairs of genes.

Principle of segregation Genes occur in pairs. In the production of a gamete, the pair is separated so that each gamete contains only one of the pair.

Prosimian Common form for Prosimii; the suborder of primates, including lemurs, lorises, and tarsiers.

Protein A macromolecule, composed of one or more polypeptide chains of amino acids. Proteins are responsible for carrying out most of the cell's metabolic activities, and are thus the basic structural and functional compounds of the cell.

Protein synthesis The manufacture of a protein from the DNA to the final product. The process by which amino acids are linked (by a peptide bond) to form a polypeptide chain. The completed chain or chains form a protein.

Proterozoic A geologic era immediately preceding the Paleozoic. Not much evidence of life.

Prototheria A subclass of mammals (monotremes) that lay eggs and nurse their young.

Provenience The particular place something comes from.

Punctuated equilibrium The view that evolutionary rates are not constant, but proceed slowly (equilibria) until "punctuated" by rather sudden spurts.

Purines A class of chemical bases—adenine and guanine—found in DNA and RNA.

Pyrimidines A class of chemical bases—cytosine, thymine, uracil—found in nucleic acids.

Quadrumanual Using all four limbs for grasping during locomotion, as in the orang.

Quadrupedal (quadrupedalism) Using all four limbs as weight supports while moving. Trunk typically horizontal. The basic mammalian, and primate, form of locomotion.

Quaternary Second (present) period of Cenozoic. Period of *Homo erectus* and *Homo sapiens*.

Race Currently defined by anthropologists as a breeding population; formerly applied to a group of people who resembled each other in physical appearance. Many anthropologists do not believe the term to be a useful one when applied to humans.

Ramapithecus An extinct hominoid from the Miocene (13–9 mya) thought by some to be an early hominid. Now usually included within *Sivapithecus. See Sivapithecus.*

Recessive A trait that is not phenotypically expressed in heterozygotes. A trait that is phenotypically expressed only in the homozygous state.

Recombination The reshuffling of genetic material every generation as the result of sexual reproduction. Recombination occurs during meiosis (through crossing-over and random assortment) and provides variation for natural selection to act upon.

Ribosomes Small, spherical particles, composed of rRNA and proteins, found in the cytoplasm. The ribosome is the site of protein synthesis.

Rift Valley (Great Rift Valley) A massive (1,200 mile long) geological feature in East Africa associated with mountain building, volcanoes, faulting, etc. The results of "rifting" have provided preservation and access to several superb Plio-Pleistocene sites (Olduvai, East Lake Turkana, Hadar, etc.).

RNA (ribonucleic acid) A nucleic acid found both in the nucleus and the cytoplasm. RNA differs from DNA in that its sugar component is ribose.

> **mRNA** Messenger RNA. This RNA carries genetic information from DNA in the nucleus to the ribosomes in the cytoplasm.
>
> **rRNA** Ribosomal RNA; a major constituent of ribosomes.
>
> **tRNA** Transfer RNA. This RNA brings amino acids together to form a polypeptide chain.

Riss The third major glaciation of the Alpine system.

Robust More heavily built; used to refer to the larger-toothed australopithecines. *See* Gracile.

Sagittal crest Raised ridge along the midline of the skull where the temporal muscle (used to move the jaw) attaches.

Sagittal suture The suture joining the left and right parietals; extending the length of the skull from the coronal suture in front to lambdoidal suture behind.

Savanna A grassland with a scattering of trees, usually in the tropics or subtropics.

Scapula Shoulder blade.

Sectorial Compressed single-cusped tooth (1st lower premolar) seen in pongids (and many extinct hominoids); compared to the bicuspid form found in most hominids.

Segregation Genes exist on paired chromosomes. At meiosis, the pairs are segregated so that a gamete has only one of the pair. Mendel's first law.

Sex cells Cells that divide by meiosis and become gametes.

Sexual dimorphism Marked physical differences between adult males and females of a species. Examples: greater size of gorilla and baboon males; sagittal and occipital crest of male gorilla.

Shovel-shaped incisors (shoveling) Incisors with raised ridges of enamel on both sides of the teeth.

Sickle-cell anemia (sicklemia) A severe, usually lethal disease caused by an alteration (point mutation) in adult hemoglobin. The disease is only expressed when the mutant allele is inherited in double dose.

Sickle-cell trait An alteration (point mutation) in adult hemoglobin. This term usually refers to carrying the mutant allele in single dose (that is, a carrier).

Silurian Third period of the Paleozoic. Jawed fishes appear. First air-breathing animals.

Sinanthropus The name originally given by Davidson Black to hominid specimens from Zhoukoudian; now known as *H. erectus pekinensis*.

Sivapithecus An extinct hominoid from the Miocene (*circa* 13–7 mya) found mostly in Eurasia. Some species are probably closely related to orangs.

Sociobiology An evolutionary approach to the explanation of behavior—largely in terms of natural selection (individual reproductive success).

Solutrean A culture period (*circa* 20,000 ya) of Europe; known for its magnificent flintwork.

Somatic cells Cells that do not divide by meiosis and do not become gametes. Body cells.

Specialized A trait that evolved for a specific function is said to be specialized. The human foot is specialized, the hand generalized. *See* Generalized.

Speciation The evolutionary process that produces new species from previous ones.

Species A category of classification of the Animal (or Plant) Kingdom. A population or group of populations living in the same econiche that can, or actually do, interbreed and produce fertile offspring.

Sperm Male fertilizing fluid; semen.

Spermatid A haploid cell produced by meiosis and differentiating into a sperm cell.

Spermatocyte A cell that undergoes meiosis and produces a spermatid. A male sex cell.

Sterkfontein A Plio-Pleistocene hominid site in South Africa yielding remains of gracile australopithecines and, perhaps, early *Homo*.

Stratigraphy Sequential layering of deposits. The sequence of layers is used as a means of dating, relatively, the layers as well as the materials in the layers.

Strepsirhini The classificatory term used to group lemurs and lorises (either suborder or semiorder).

Subphylum A major division of a phylum—such as vertebrata.

Substrate The physical surface on which an animal moves or rests.

Superfamily A group of closely related families.

Supraorbital torus Ridge above the orbits on a skull. The supraorbital torus is very pronounced in *erectus*, Neandertals, and some australopithecines.

Swartkrans A Plio-Pleistocene hominid site in South Africa yielding remains of robust australopithecines and *Homo*.

Sympatric Two or more species living in the same area.

Synapomorph (-ous, -ic [adj.]) A new morphological feature, shared between two or more groups in an evolving lineage, that signifies their close and unique relationship; restricted to characters.

Taphonomy Study of how bones come to be buried in the earth and preserved as fossils.

Tarsiioidea The prosimian superfamily of tarsiers, a nocturnal form found in southern Asia.

Taung A South African Plio-Pleistocene australopithecine site. The location of the first australopithecine discovery (1924).

Taurodontism Molar with expanded pulp cavity.

Taxon A population (or group of populations) judged to be sufficiently distinct to be assigned to a separate category (such as genus or species).

Taxonomy   The science of the classification of organisms, including the principles, procedures, and rules of classification.

Tectonic movement   Movements of the earth (along fault lines, during mountain building, and so forth).

Tektite   A round, glassy body of unknown origin.

Teratogen   An agent that disrupts development.

Terrestrial   Living on the ground. Humans, gorillas, and some monkeys are terrestrial.

Territoriality   Behavior in defense of the territory of a group; establishment of exclusive right to the use of a territory. Some primates are much more territorial than others.

Territory   The area a group defends. That part of the home range used exclusively by one group. Neighbors of the same species do not enter or else enter only on a brief foray.

Tertiary   First period of the Cenozoic. Period of primate radiation. (Includes: Paleocene, Eocene, Oligocene, Miocene, and Pliocene.)

Tetrad   A structure of four DNA molecules of a pair of homologous chromosomes. Seen during meiosis.

Thymine   One of the chemical bases (pyrimidines) found in DNA, but not in RNA.

Tibia   The large long bone of the lower leg; the shin. *See* Fibula.

Tool   A natural object deliberately modified for utilitarian purposes.

Triassic   First period of Mesozoic. First dinosaurs.

Trinil fauna   Animal remains associated with the Middle Pleistocene Trinil period in Java.

Triplet   A sequence of three bases; found in mRNA and tRNA. Codes for a specific amino acid. A codon or anticodon.

Tuff   A solidified sediment of volcanic ash.

Typology, racial   Dividing humans into discrete racial types.

Undernutrition   A diet insufficient in quantity (calories) to support normal health.

Uniformitarianism   A concept maintaining that the ancient changes in the earth's surface were caused by the same physical principles acting today. The earth's crust was formed slowly and gradually. Mountains, rivers, valleys, etc., were the result of purely natural forces such as erosion by wind, water, frost, ice, and rain. Although not originated by Charles Lyell, uniformitarianism is associated with him because he popularized it.

Upper Paleolithic   A culture period noted for technological, artistic, and behavioral innovations. Also known for the widespread expansion of anatomically modern human beings.

Uracil   One of the chemical bases (pyrimidines) found in RNA, but not in DNA.

Variation (genetic)   Inherited differences between individuals. The basis of all evolutionary change.

Ventral   Toward the belly; the front of an organism (as in humans) or the undersurface of an animal that does not stand erect (as a dog).

Vertebra (pl. vertebrae)   A single bone of the spinal or vertebral column (backbone).

Viviparity   Live birth; characteristic mainly of mammals.

World view   A literal translation from the German, *Weltanschauung*. A personal or group philosophy explaining history; a way of looking at the world.

Würm   The fourth glacial in the Old World.

Xenophobic   Fear of foreigners.

Y-5 pattern (Dryopithecine Y-5)   A pattern of cusps on the molar teeth characteristic of hominoids.

Zygomatic (or zygomatic bone)   Malar or cheek bone.

Zygomatic arch   The bone along the side of the skull connecting the zygomatic and temporal bones.

Zygote   A fertilized cell formed by the union of a male gamete and a female gamete.

Bibliography

Adam, Karl Dietrich
1985   "The Chronological and Systematic Position of the Steinheim Skull." *In* Delson, q.v., 272–276.

Aigner, Jean S.
1981   *Archaeological Remains in Pleistocene China.* Munich: C. H. Beck.

———
1986   "The Age of Zhoukoudian Locality 1." *Anthropos* (Brno), **23**: 157–173.

Aigner, Jean S. and Wm. S. Laughlin
1973   "The Dating of Lantian Man and His Significance for Analyzing Trends in Human Evolution." *American Journal of Physical Anthropology,* **39**:97–110.

Alland Jr., Alexander
1971   *Human Diversity.* New York: Anchor Press/Doubleday.

Allen, J., J. Golson and R. Jones
1977   *Sunda and Sahul.* New York: Academic Press.

Altman, I.
1978   "Crowding: Historical and Contemporary Trends in Crowding Research." *In: Human Response to Crowding,* A. Baum and Y. M. Epstein (eds.), New York: John Wiley and Sons.

Altmann, Jeanne
1981   *Baboon Mothers and Infants.* Cambridge: Harvard University Press.

Altmann, Stuart A. and Jeanne Altmann
1970   *Baboon Ecology.* Chicago: University of Chicago Press.

Ames, Bruce N.
1983   Dietary Carcinogens and Anticarcinogens. *Science* **21**:1256–1264.

Amos, D. Bernard and D. D. Kostyu
1980   "HLA—A Central Immunological Agency of Man." *In: Advances in Human Genetics* (Vol. 10), H. Harris and K. Hirschhorn (eds.), New York: Plenum Press, pp. 137–208.

Andersson, J. Gunnar
1934   *Children of the Yellow Earth.* New York: Macmillan.

Andrews, P. J.
1983   "The Natural History of *Sivapithecus.*" *In*: R. Ciochon and R. Corruccini (eds.), q.v., pp. 441–463.

Andrews, Lauline
1985   "Family Group Systematics and Evolution Among Catarrhine Primates." *In*: E. Delson (ed.), q.v., pp. 14–22.

Andrews, Peter
1985   "Family Group Systematics and Evolution Among Catarrhine Primates." *In*: E. Delson (ed.), q.v., pp. 14–22.

Andrews, Peter and Elizabeth Evans
1979   "The Environment of *Ramapithecus* in Africa." *Paleobiology* **5**(1):22–30.

Andrews, Peter and Jens Lorenz Franzen (eds.)
1984   *The Early Evolution of Man.* Frankfurt A.M.: Cour. Forsch.-Inst. Seckenberg, 69.

Anthrop, Donald F.
1973   *Noise Pollution.* Lexington, Mass.: D. C. Heath & Co.

ApSimon, Helen and Julian Wilson
1986   "Tracking the Cloud from Chernobyl." *New Scientist*, July 17, 1986: pp. 42–45.

Ardrey, Robert
1976   *The Hunting Hypothesis.* New York: Atheneum.

Arens, W.
1979   *The Man-Eating Myth.* New York: Oxford University Press.

Arensburg, B., A. M. Tillier, B. Vandermeersch, et al.
1989   "A Middle Palaeolithic Human Hyoid Bone." *Nature,* **338**:758–760.

Arensburg, B., L. A. Schepartz, A. M. Tiller, et al.
1990   "A Reappraisal of the Anatomical Basis for Speech in Middle Paleolithic Hominids." *American Journal of Physical Anthropology,* **83**(2):137–146.

Aronson, J. L., R. C. Walter, and M. Taieb
1983   "Correlation of Tulu Boi Tuff at Koobi Fora with the Sidi Hakoma Tuff at Hadar." *Nature,* **306**:209–210.

Baba, M. L., L. L. Darga, and M. Goodman
1981   "Maximum Parsimony Test of the Clock Model of the Molecular Change Using Amino Acid Sequence Data." Paper presented at the Annual Meetings, American Association of Physical Anthropologists, April 1981.

Badrian, Alison and Noel Badrian
1984   "Social Organization of *Pan paniscus* in the Lomako Forest, Zaire." *In: The Pgymy Chimpanzee,* Randall L. Susman, New York: Plenum Press, 325–346.

Baker, Paul T.
1966   "Human Biological Variation as an Adaptive Response to the Environment." *Eugenics Quarterly,* **13**:81–91.

Baker, Paul T. and Michael A. Little
1976   "Environmental Adaptations and Perspectives." *In: Man in the Andes,* P. T. Baker and M. A. Little (eds.), Stroudsburg, Penn.: Dowden, Hutchinson, and Ross, Inc., pp. 405–428.

Barash, David
1982   *Sociobiology and Behavior.* 2nd Ed. New York: Elsevier.

Barnes, Deborah M.
1986   "Grim Projections for AIDS Epidemic." *Science* **232**: 1589–1590.

Bartstra, Gert-Jan
1982 "*Homo erectus erectus*: The Search for Artifacts." *Current Anthropology*, **23**(3):318–320.
Barzun, Jacques
1965 *Race: A Study in Superstition*. New York: Harper and Row.
Bass, W. M.
1987 *Human Osteology: A Laboratory and Field Manual* (3rd Ed.). Columbia, Mo.: Missouri Archaeological Society Special Publication No. 2.
Bayanov, Dmitri and Igor Bourtsev
1974 "Reply (to comments on Proshner's article)." *Current Anthropology*, **15**(4):452–456.

1976 "On Neanderthal vs. Paranthropus." *Current Anthropology*, **17**(2):312–318.
Beck, Benjamin B.
1980 *Animal Tool Behavior*. New York: Garland Publishing, Inc.
Behrensmeyer, Anna K. and Andrew P. Hill
1980 *Fossils in the Making: Vertebrate Taphonomy and Paleoecology*. Chicago: The University of Chicago Press.
Bennett, Kenneth A.
1979 *Fundamentals of Biological Anthropology*. Dubuque, Iowa: Wm. C. Brown Co. Publishers.
Benyon, A. D. and M. C. Dean
1988 "Distinct Dental Development Patterns in Early Fossil Hominids." *Nature*, **335**:509–514.
Biddiss, Michael D.
1970 *Father of Racist Ideology: The Social and Political Thought of Count Gobineau*. New York: Weybright and Talley.
Binford, Lewis R.
1981 *Bones. Ancient Men and Modern Myths*. New York: Academic Press.

1982 Comment on White's article, "Rethinking the Middle/Upper Paleolithic Transition." (*See* White, 1982)

1983 *In Pursuit of the Past*. New York: Thames and Hudson.

1985 "Ancestral Lifeways: The Faunal Record." *AnthroQuest*. Pasadena: The L.S.B. Leakey Foundation News, **32**, Summer, 1985.
Binford, Lewis R. and Chuan Kun Ho
1985 "Taphonomy at a Distance: Zhoukoudian, 'The Cave Home of Beijing Man'?" *Current Anthropology*, **26**:413–442.
Binford, Lewis R. and Nancy M. Stone.
1986a "The Chinese Paleolithic: An Outsider's View." *AnthroQuest*, Fall 1986(1):14–20.

1986b "Zhoukoudian: A Closer Look." *Current Anthropology*, **27**(5): 453–475.
Birdsell, Joseph B.
1981 *Human Evolution*. (3d Ed.), Boston: Houghton Mifflin Co.
Birkby, W. H.
1966 "An Evaluation of Race and Sex Identification from Cranial Measurements," *American Journal of Physical Anthropology*, **24**:21–28.
Black, Francis L.
1975 "Infectious Diseases in Primitive Societies." *Science*, **187**:515–518.
Boas, Franz
1938 *General Anthropology*. New York: D. C. Heath and Co.

1940 "New Evidence in Regard to the Instability of Human Types." *Reprinted In*: *Race, Language and Culture*, F. Boas (ed), New York: The Free Press, pp. 76–81.
Boaz, N. T.
1977 "Paleoecology of Early Hominidae in Africa." *Kroeber Anthropological Society Papers*, **50**:37–62.
Boaz, N. T., F. C. Howell, and M. L. McCrossin
1982 "Faunal Age of the Usno, Shungura B and Hadar Formation, Ethiopia." *Nature*, **300**:633–635.
Bodmer, Walter F.
1972 "Race and IQ: The Genetic Background." *In*: *Race and Intelligence*, Ken Richardson and David Speers (eds.), Baltimore: Penguin Books, Inc., pp. 83–113.
Bodmer, W. F. and L. L. Cavalli-Sforza
1976 *Genetics, Evolution, and Man*. San Francisco: W. H. Freeman and Company.
Boehm, Christopher
1989 "Vital Communication of Wild Chimpanzees." *AnthroQuest*, Spring:15–18.

1989 "Methods for Isolating Chimpanzee Vocal Communication." *In*: P. Heltne and L. Marquardt, q.v., pp. 38–59.
Boesch, Christopher and H. Boesch
1989 "Hunting Behavior of Wild Chimpanzees in the Tai National Park." *American Journal of Physical Anthropology*, **78**:547–573.
Bogaarts, John
1980 "Does Malnutrition Affect Fecundity? A Summary of Evidence." *Science*, **208**:564–569.
Boggess, Jane
1984 "Infant Killing and Male Reproductive Strategies in Langurs (*Presbytis entellus*)." *In*: *Infanticide*, G. Hausfater and S. Blaffer Hrdy (eds.), Hawthorne, N.Y.: Aldine de Gruyter, pp. 280–310.
Bolton, Ralph
1973 "Aggression and Hypoglycemia among the Qolla; a Study in Psychological Anthropology." *Ethnology*, **12**:227–257.

1984 "The Hypoglycemia–Aggression Hypothesis: Debate versus Research." *Current Anthropology*, **25**:1–53.
Bonner, T. I., R. Heinemann and G. J. Todardo
1980 "Evolution of DNA Sequences Has Been Retarded in Malagasy Primates." *Nature*, **286**:420–423.
Bordes, François
1968 *The Old Stone Age*. New York: McGraw-Hill Book Co.
Bowler, J. M. and A. G. Thorne (eds.)
1976 "Human Remains from Lake Mungo: Discovery and Excavation of Lake Mungo III." *In*: *The Origin of the Australians*, R. L. Kirk and A. G. Thorne (eds.), Canberra: Australian Institute of Aboriginal Studies (Humanities Press Inc., New Jersey), pp. 127–138.
Boyd, Wm. C.
1950 *Genetics and the Races of Man*. Boston: Little, Brown.
Brace, C. Loring
1964 "The Fate of the 'Classic' Neanderthals: A Consideration of Hominid Catastrophism." *Current Anthropology*, **5**:3–43.

1967 *The Stages of Human Evolution*. Englewood Cliffs, N.J.: Prentice-Hall, Inc.

1973 "Sexual Dimorphism in Human Evolution." *In*: *Man in Evolution-*

ary Perspective, C. L. Brace and J. Metress (eds.), New York: Wiley Publishing Co., pp. 238–254.

1979   "Biological Parameters and Pleistocene Hominid Lifeways." *In: Primate Ecology and Human Origins*, Irwin S. Bernstein and E. O. Smith (eds.), New York: Garland Publishing Co., pp. 263–289.

1982   "The Roots and Concepts in American Physical Anthropology. *In*: F. Spencer, q.v., pp. 11–29.

Brace, C. Loring and Frank B. Livingstone
1971   "On Creeping Jensenism," *In: Race and Intelligence*, C. L. Brace, G. R. Gamble and J. T. Bond (eds.), Anthropological Studies, No. 8, American Anthropological Association, Washington, D.C.

Brace, C. L. and Ashley Montagu
1977   *Human Evolution* (2nd Ed.). New York: Macmillan.

Brace, C. Loring, Harry Nelson and Noel Korn
1971   *Atlas of Human Evolution*. New York: Holt, Rinehart and Winston. (2nd Ed. 1979).

Braidwood, Robert J.
1975   *Prehistoric Men* (8th Ed.). Glenview, Ill.: Scott, Foresman.

Brain, C. K.
1970   "New Finds at the Swartkrans Australopithecine Site." *Nature*, **225**:1112–1119.

1975   "The Bone Assemblage from the Kromdraai Australopithecine Site." *In: Paleoanthropology: Morphology and Paleoecology*, R. Tuttle (ed.), World Anthropology Series, Chicago: Aldine, pp. 225–243.

1981   *The Hunters or the Hunted? An Introduction to African Cave Taphonomy*. Chicago: University of Chicago Press.

Bramblett, Claud A.
1976   *Patterns of Primate Behavior*. Palo Alto, Ca.: Mayfield Publishing Co.

Brauer, Gunter
1984   "A Craniological Approach to the Origin of Anatomically Modern *Homo sapiens* in Africa and Implications for the Appearance of Modern Europeans." *In*: Smith and Spencer, q.v., 327–410.

Brock, A., P. L. McFadden and T. C. Partridge
1977   "Preliminary Paleomagnetic Results from Makapansgat and Swartkrans." *Nature*, **266**:249–250.

Bromage, Timothy G. and Christopher Dean
1985   "Re-evaluation of the Age at Death of Immature Fossil Hominids." *Nature*, **317**:525–527.

Brooks, S. T.
1985   Personal Communication.

1986   "Comments on 'Known' Age at Death Series." Presented in conjunction with "Skeletal Age Standards Derived from an Extensive Multi-Racial Sample of Modern Americans," by J. Suchey and D. Katz, at the Fifty-Fifth Annual Meeting of the American Association of Physical Anthropologists, Albuquerque, New Mexico.

Brose, David and Milford H. Wolpoff
1971   "Early Upper Paleolithic Man and Late Middle Paleolithic Tools." *American Anthropologist*, **73**:1156–1194.

Brues, A. M.
1977   *People and Races*. New York: MacMillan Publishing Company.

Buettner-Janusch, John
1973   *Physical Anthropology: A Perspective*. New York: John Wiley and Sons.

Buffon, George Louis Leclerc, Compte de
1860   "*Histoire Naturelle Generale et Particuliere*." Translated by Wm. Smellie, London. *In*: Louis L. Snyder, q.v., pp. 102–103.

Bugliarello, G., A. Alexander, J. Barnes and C. Wakstein
1976   *The Impact of Noise Pollution: A Sociotechnological Introduction*. New York: Pergamon Press.

Bunn, Henry T.
1981   "Archaeological Evidence for Meat-eating by Plio-Pleistocene Hominids from Koobi Fora and Olduvai Gorge." *Nature*, **291**:574–577.

Bunn, Henry T. and Ellen M. Kroll
1987   "On Inferences from the Zhoukoudian Fauna." *Current Anthropology*, **28**(2):199–202.

Burkhardt, Richard W., Jr.
1977   *The Spirit of System: Lamarck and Evolutionary Biology*. Cambridge: Harvard University Press.

Busse, Curt D.
1978   "Do Chimpanzees Hunt Cooperatively?" *American Naturalist*, **112**:767–770.

Butynski, Thomas M.
1982   "Vertebrate Predation by Primates: A Review of Hunting Patterns." *Journal of Human Evolution*, **11**:421–430.

Butzer, Karl W.
1974   "Paleoecology of South African Australopithecines: Taung Revisited." *Current Anthropology*, **15**:367–382.

Butzer, Karl W. and Glynn L. Isaac, (eds.)
1975   *After the Australopithecines*. The Hague: Mouton Publishers and Chicago: Aldine Publishing Co.

Bygott, J. David
1979   "Agonistic Behavior, Dominance, and Social Structure in Wild Chimpanzees of the Gombe National Park." *In*: Hamburg and McCown (eds.), q.v., pp. 405–427.

Campbell, Bernard
1974   *Human Evolution*. Chicago: Aldine Publishing Co. (2nd Ed., 1985).

1976   *Humankind Emerging*. Boston: Little, Brown and Co. (4th Ed., 1984).

Cann, Rebecca L.
1987   "In Search of Eve." *The Sciences*, Sept./Oct.:30–37.

Cann, R. L., M. Stoneking and A. C. Wilson
1987   "Mitochondrial DNA and Human Evolution." *Nature*, **325**:31–36.

Carpenter, C. R.
1965   "The Howlers of Barro Colorado Island." *In*: I. DeVore, (ed.), q.v., pp. 250–291.

Cartmill, Matt
1972   "Arboreal Adaptations and the Origin of the Order Primates." *In: The Functional and Evolutionary Biology of Primates*, R. H. Tuttle (ed.), Chicago: Aldine-Atherton, pp. 97–122.

1974   "Rethinking Primate Origins." *Science*, **184**:436–443.

Cavalieri, Liebe F.
1976   "New Strains of Life—or Death." *New York Times Magazine*, **22**:8, August.

Cavalli-Sforza, L. L. and M. W. Feldman
1981   *Cultural Transmission and Evolution: A Quantitative Approach.* Princeton, N.J.: Princeton University Press.
Chalmers, Neil
1980   *Social Behaviour in Primates.* Baltimore: University Park Press.
Charteris, J., J. C. Wali, and J. W. Nottrodt
1981   "Functional Reconstruction of Gait from Pliocene Hominid Footprints at Laetoli, Northern Tanzania." *Nature,* **290**:496–498.
Chia, Lan-Po
1975   *The Cave Home of Peking Man.* Peking: Foreign Language Press.
China Pictorial
1981   "A Complete Ape-Man's Skull Unearthed at Longtan Cave." *China Pictorial,* **3**:20–21, Beijing, China, March 1981 (no author).
Chivers, David J., Bernard A. Wood and Alan Bilsborough
1984   *Food Acquisition and Processing in Primates.* New York: Plenum.
Chopra, S.R.K.
1983   "Significance of Recent Hominoid Discoveries from the Siwalik Hills of India." *In*: R. Ciochon and R. Corruccini (eds.), q.v., pp. 539–557.
Ciochon, Russel L.
1983   "Hominoid Cladistics and the Ancestry of Modern Apes and Humans. A Summary." *In*: R. Ciochon and R. Corruccini (eds.), q.v., pp. 783–843.
Ciochon, R. L. and A. B. Chiarelli (eds.)
1980   *Evolutionary Biology of the New World Monkeys and Continental Drift.* New York: Plenum Publishing Co.
Ciochon, Russel L. and Robert S. Corruccini
1983   *New Interpretations of Ape and Human Ancestry.* New York: Plenum.
Clark, J. Desmond
1981   "The Cultures of the Middle Palaeolithic/Middle Stone Age." *In*: J. Desmond Clark (ed.), *The Cambridge History of Africa I*:248–341.
Clark, W. E. LeGros
1959   *The Antecedents of Man.* New York: Quadrangle.

1967   *Man-apes or Ape-men?* New York: Holt, Rinehart and Winston.
1971   The New York Times Books (3rd Ed.).
Clarke, R. J.
1976   "New Cranium of *Homo erectus* from Lake Ndutu, Tanzania." *Nature,* **262**:485–487.

1985   "*Australopithecus* and Early *Homo* in Southern Africa." *In*: Eric Delson, q.v., pp. 171–177.
Clarke, R. J. and F. Clark Howell
1972   "Affinities of the Swartkrans 847 Hominid Cranium." *American Journal of Physical Anthropology,* **37**:319–336.
Clodd, Edward
1897   *Pioneers of Evolution from Thales to Huxley.* New York: Freeport (Reprinted 1972).
Clutton-Brock, T. H., S. D. Albon, and F. E. Guinness
1984   "Maternal Dominance, Breeding Success, and Birth Sex Ratios in Red Deer." *Nature* **308**:358–360.
Clutton-Brock, T. H., F. E. Guiness, and S. D. Albon
1982   *Red Deer Behavior and Ecology of Two Sexes.* Chicago: University of Chicago Press.
Clutton-Brock, T. H. and Paul H. Harvey
1977   "Primate Ecology and Social Organization." *Journal of Zoological Society of London,* **183**:1–39.

Cohen, I. Bernard
1985   *Revolution in Science.* Cambridge: Harvard University Press.
Coleman, William and C. Limoges (eds.)
1984   *Studies in History of Biology.* Baltimore: The Johns Hopkins University Press.
Combe, Andrew
1982   "On the Influence of Organic Size on Energy and Function, Particularly as Applied to the Organs of the External Senses and Brain." *Phrenology Journal* **4**(1826–7):181–183. *In*: N. Stepan, q.v.
Conroy, G., C. J. Jolly, D. Cramer and J. E. Kalb
1978   "Newly Discovered Fossil Hominid Skull from the Afar Depression." *Nature,* **276**:67–70.
Constable, George
1973   *The Neanderthals* (Emergence of Man Series, Time-Life Books). Waltham, Mass.: Little, Brown and Co.
Cook, J., C. B. Stringer, A. P. Currant, H. P. Schwarcz and A. G. Wintle
1982   "A Review of the Chronology of the European Middle Pleistocene Hominid Record." *Yearbook of Physical Anthropology,* **25**:19–64.
Cooke, H.B.S.
1978   "Faunal Evidence for the Biotic Setting of the Early African Hominids." *In*: *Early Hominids of Africa,* C. Jolly (ed.), New York: St. Martin's Press.
Coon, C. S., S. M. Garn and J. B. Birdsell
1950   *Races—A Study of the Problems of Race Formation in Man.* Springfield, Ill.: Charles C. Thomas.
Corruccini, R. S.
1975a   "Multivariate Analysis of *Gigantopithecus* Mandibles." *American Journal of Physical Anthropology,* **42**:167–170.

1975b   "The Interaction Between Neurocranial and Facial Shape in Hominid Evolution." *Homo,* **26**:136–139.
Corruccini, R. S. and H. M. McHenry
1980   "Cladometric Analysis of Pliocene Hominids." *Journal of Human Evolution,* **9**:209–221.
Corruccini, R. S., M. Baba, M. Goodman, R. L. Ciochon and J. E. Cronin
1980   "Non-Linear Macromolecular Evolution and the Molecular Clock." *Evolution,* **34**:1216–1219.
Count, Earl W. (ed.)
1950   *This Is Race.* New York: Henry Schuman.
Cronin, J. E.
1983   "Apes, Humans, and Molecular Clocks. A Reappraisal." *In*: R. Ciochon and R. Corruccini (eds.), q.v., pp. 115–150.
Cronin, J. E. and V. M. Sarich
1980   "Tupaiid and Archonta Phylogeny: The Macromolecular Evidence." *In*: W. P. Luckett (ed.), q.v., pp. 293–312.
Crook, J. H.
1970   "Social Organization and Environment: Aspects of Contemporary Social Ethology." *Animal Behavior,* **18**:197–209.
Curtis, Garniss
1981   "A Matter of Time: Dating Techniques and Geology of Hominid Sites." Paper delivered at the symposium, "Our Ancestors, Ourselves," Davis, Ca., May 10, 1981.
Curtis, G. H., T. Drake, R. Cerling and A. Hampel
1975   "Age of KBS Tuff in Koobi Fora Formation, East Rudolf, Kenya." *Nature,* **258**:395.

Dahlberg, A. A.
1951   "The Dentition of the American Indian." *In*: *The Physical Anthropology of the American Indian.* Viking Fund, Inc., **5**:138–176.

Dalrymple, G. B.

1972 "Geomagnetic Reversals and North American Glaciations." *In*: Calibration of Hominoid Evolution, W. W. Bishop and J. A. Miller (eds.), Edinburgh: Scottish Academic Press, pp. 303–329.

Damon, Albert

1977 *Human Biology and Ecology*. New York: W. W. Norton and Co.

Dart, Raymond

1959 *Adventures with the Missing Link*. New York: Harper and Brothers.

Darwin, Charles

1859 *On the Origin of Species*. A Facsimile of the First Edition, Cambridge, Mass.: Harvard University Press (1964).

Darwin, Francis (ed.)

1950 *The Life and Letters of Charles Darwin*. New York: Henry Schuman.

Davidson, Iain and W. Noble

1989 "The Archaeology of Perception: Traces of Depiction and Language." *Current Anthropology*, **30**:125–155.

Dawkins, Richard

1976 *The Selfish Gene*. New York: Oxford University Press.

Day, Michael

1986 *Guide to Fossil Man*. Chicago: The University of Chicago Press, 4th ed.

Day, M. H., M. D. Leakey and C. Magori

1980 "A New Fossil Hominid Skull from Nu Ngaloba Beds, Laetoli, Northern Tanzania." *Nature*, **289**:55–56.

Day, M. H. and E. H. Wickens

1980 "Laetoli Pliocene Hominid Footprints and Bipedalism." *Nature*, **286**:385–387.

DeBonis, L.

1983 "Phyletic Relationships of Miocene Hominoids and Higher Primate Classification." *In*: R. Ciochon and R. Corruccini (eds.), q.v., pp. 625–649.

Delson, Eric (ed.)

1985 *Ancestors: The Hard Evidence*. New York: Alan R. Liss, Inc.

Delson, Eric

1987 "Evolution and Palaeobiology of Robust *Australopithecus*." *Nature*, **327**:654–655.

De Luce, Judith and Hugh T. Wilder

1983 *Language in Primates*. New York: Springer-Verlag.

De Lumley, Henry

1969 "A Paleolithic Camp at Nice." *Scientific American*, May, **220**:42–50.

De Lumley, Henry and Marie-Antoinette De Lumley

1973 "Pre-Neanderthal Human Remains from Arago Cave in Southeastern France." *In*: Yearbook of Physical Anthropology 1973, **16**:162–168.

De Lumley, Henry and Arun Sonakia

1985 "Contexte Stratigraphique et Archeologique de L'Homme de la Narmada, Hathnora, Madhya Pradesh, Inde." *L'Anthropologie* (Paris), **89**(1):3–12.

De Lumley, Marie-Antoinette

1975 "Ante-Neanderthals of Western Europe." *In*: Paleoanthropology: Morphology and Paleoecology, Russel H. Tuttle (ed.), The Hague: Mouton Publishers, pp. 381–387.

De Lumley, Marie-Antoinette and Arun Sonakia

1985 "Premiere Decouverte d'un *H. erectus* sur le Continent Indien a Hathnore dans la Moyenne Vallee de la Narmada." *Anthropologie* (Paris), **89**(1):13–61.

Dene, H. T., M. Goodman and W. Prychodko

1976 "Immunodiffusion Evidence on the Phylogeny of the Primates." *In*: *Molecular Anthropology*, M. Goodman, R. E. Tashian and J. H. Tashian (eds.), New York: Plenum Press, pp. 171–195.

Dene, H., M. Goodman, W. Prychodko and G. Matsuda

1980 "Molecular Evidence for the Affinities of Tupaiidae." *In*: W. P. Luckett (ed.), q.v., pp. 269–291.

De Vos, J.

1985 "Faunal Stratigraphy and Correlation of the Indonesian Hominid Sites." *In*: Delson, q.v., pp. 215–220.

Dingle, Herbert

1959 "Copernicus and the Planets." *In*: A Short History of Science, Jean Lindsay (ed.), New York: Doubleday & Co., pp. 18–26.

Dobzhansky, Theodosius

1970 *Genetics of the Evolutionary Process*. New York: Columbia University Press.

———

1971 "Race Equality." *In*: The Biological and Social Meaning of Race, Richard H. Osborne (ed.), San Francisco: W. H. Freeman and Co., pp. 13–24.

Drake, R. E., et al.

1980 "KBS Tuff Dating and Geochronology of Tuffaceous Sediments in the Koobi Fora and Shungura Formations, East Africa." *Nature*, **283**:368–372.

Draper, Patricia

1973 "Crowding Among Hunter-Gatherers: The !Kung Bushmen." *Science*, **182**:301–303.

Duchin, Linda E.

1990 "The Evolution of Articulate Speech." *Journal of Human Evolution*, **19**:687–697.

Dumont, R. and B. Rosier

1969 *The Hungry Future*. New York: Praeger.

Dunbar, I. M.

1988 *Primate Social Systems*. Ithaca: Cornell University Press.

Dunn, Frederick L.

1968 "Epidemiological Factors: Health and Disease in Hunter-Gatherers." *In*: Man the Hunter, R. B. Lee and I. DeVore (eds.), Chicago: Aldine, pp. 221–228.

Dunn, L. C.

1951 *Race and Biology. The Race Question in Modern Science*. UNESCO.

———

1965 "Mendel, His Work, and His Place in History." *In*: Proceedings of the American Philosophical Society, Vol. 109, No. 4 (Commemoration of the publication of Gregor Mendel's pioneer experiments in genetics), August 18, Philadelphia: American Philosophical Society.

Durham, William

1981 Paper presented to the Annual Meeting of the American Anthropological Association, Washington, D.C., Dec. 1980. Reported in *Science*, **211**:40.

Eddy, J. H., Jr.

1984 "Buffon, Organic Alterations, and Man." *In*: Coleman and Limoges, Vol. 4, q.v., pp. 1–45.

Eiseley, Loren

1961 *Darwin's Century*. New York: Anchor Books.

Ekberg, Douglas R.

1979 *Intelligence and Race*. New York: Praeger.

Eldredge, Niles and Joel Cracraft

1980 *Phylogenetic Patterns and the Evolutionary Process.* New York: Columbia University Press.

Erison, Harry J.

1973 *Evolution of the Brain and Intelligence.* London: Academic Press.

Falk, Dean

1980 "A Reanalysis of the South African Australopithecine Natural Endocasts." *American Journal of Physical Anthropology*, **53**:525–539.

——— 1983 "The Taung Endocast: A Reply to Holloway." *American Journal of Physical Anthropology*, **60**:479–489.

——— 1987 "Brain Lateralization in Primates and Its Evolution in Hominids." *Yearbook of Physical Anthropology*, **30**:107–125.

——— 1989 "Comments." *Current Anthropology*, **30**:141.

Fedigan, Linda M.

1982 *Primate Paradigms.* Montreal: Eden Press.

——— 1983 "Dominance and Reproductive Success in Primates." *Yearbook of Physical Anthropology*, **26**:91–129.

Fisher, R. A.

1930 *The Genetical Theory of Natural Selection.* Oxford: Clarendon.

Fleagle, J. G.

1983 "Locomotor Adaptations of Oligocene and Miocene Hominoids and their Phyletic Implications." *In*: R. Ciochon and R. Corruccini (eds.), q.v., pp. 301–324.

——— 1988 *Primate Adaptation and Evolution.* New York: Academic Press.

Fleagle, J. G. and R. F. Kay

1983 "New Interpretations of the Phyletic Position of Oligocene Hominoids." *In*: R. Ciochon and R. Corruccini (eds.), q.v., pp. 181–210.

——— 1985 "The Paleobiology of Catarrhines." *In*: E. Delson (ed.), q.v., pp. 23–36.

Fleischer, R. C. and H. R. Hart, Jr.

1972 "Fission Track Dating, Techniques and Problems." *In*: *Calibration of Hominoid Evolution*, W. W. Bishop and J. A. Miller (eds.), Edinburgh: Scottish Academic Press, pp. 135–170.

Flynn, L. J. and G. Qi

1982 "Age of the Lufeng, China Hominoid Locality." *Nature*, **298**:746–747.

Fobes, James L. and James E. King (eds.)

1982 *Primate Behavior.* New York: Academic Press.

Fossey, Dian

1981 "The Imperiled Mountain Gorilla." *National Geographic*, **159**(4):501–523.

——— 1983 *Gorillas in the Mist.* Boston: Houghton-Mifflin.

Fouts, D. H.

1985 *Friends of Washoe.* Central Washington University, Winter.

Fouts, Roger S.

1982 *Friends of Washoe.* Central Washington University, Spring.

——— 1983 "Chimpanzee Language and Elephant Tails: A Theoretical Synthesis." *In*: Judith DeLuce and Hugh T. Wilder (eds.), q.v., pp. 63–75.

Fouts, Roger S. and Richard L. Budd

1979 "Artificial and Human Language Acquisition in the Chimpanzees." *In*: D. Hamburg and E. McCown (eds.), q.v., pp. 375–392.

Fouts, Roger S., D. H. Fouts and T. T. van Cantfort

1989 "The Infant Loulis Learns Signs from Cross-Fostered Chimpanzees." *In*: R. Gardner, et al., q.v., pp. 280–292.

Fox, Michael W.

1978 "Man, Wolf, and Dog." *In*: *Wolf and Man*, R. L. Halland and H. S. Sharp (eds.), New York: Academic Press, pp. 19–30.

Fox, Robin (ed.)

1975 *Biosocial Anthropology.* New York: John Wiley & Sons.

——— 1971 "The Cultural Animal." *In*: *Man and Beast*, John F. Eisenberg and Wm. S. Dillon (eds.), The Smithsonian Institution Press (reprinted in Yehudi A. Cohen, *Man in Adaptation, The Biosocial Background*, 2d Ed., Chicago: Aldine Publishing Co., 1974).

Francoeuer, Robert T.

1965 *Perspectives in Evolution.* Baltimore: Helicon.

Frayer, David

1973 "*Gigantopithecus* and Its Relationship to *Australopithecus*." *American Journal of Physical Anthropology*, **39**:413–426.

——— 1980 "Sexual Dimorphism and Cultural Evolution in the Late Pleistocene and Holocene of Europe." *Journal of Human Evolution*, **9**:399–415.

——— 1984 "Biological and Cultural Change in the European Late Pleistocene and Early Holocene." *In*: Smith and Spencer, q.v., 211–250.

Freedman, Jonathan L.

1975 *Crowding and Behavior.* New York: Viking Press.

Freeman, L. G.

1975 "Acheulian Sites and Stratigraphy in Iberia and the Maghreb." *In*: K. W. Butzer and G. L. Isaac (eds.), q.v., pp. 661–743.

Friedman, Milton J. and William Trager

1981 "The Biochemistry of Resistance to Malaria." *Scientific American*, **244**:154–164.

Frisancho, A. R.

1978 "Nutritional Influences on Human Growth and Maturation." *Yearbook of Physical Anthropology*, **21**:174–191.

Galdikas, Biruté M.

1979 "Orangutan Adaptation at Tanjung Puting Reserve: Mating and Ecology." *In*: *The Great Apes*, D. A. Hamburg and E. R. McCown (eds.), Menlo Park, Ca.: The Benjamin/Cummings Publishing Co., pp. 195–233.

Galdikas, B.M.F. and G. Telecki

1981 "Variation in Subsistence Activities of Male and Female Pongids: New Perspectives on the Origins of Hominid Labor Division." *Current Anthropology*, **22**:241–256.

Gantt, D. G.

1983 "The Enamel of Neogene Hominoids. Structural and Phyletic Implications." *In*: R. Ciochon and R. Corruccini (eds.), q.v., pp. 249–298.

Gardner, Beatrice T. and R. Allen Gardner

1975 "Evidence for Sentence Constituents in the Early Utterances of Child and Chimpanzee." *Journal of Experimental Psychology: General*, **104**:244–267.

Gardner, Eldon

1965 *History of Biology.* Minneapolis: Burgess Publishing Co.

Gardner, R. Allen, B. T. Gardner and T. T. van Cantfort (eds.)

1989 *Teaching Sign Language to Chimpanzees.* Albany: State University of New York Press.

Gargett, Robert H.

1989 "Grave Shortcomings." *Current Anthropology*, **30**:157–190.

Garn, Stanley M.

1969 *Human Races.* Springfield, Ill.: Charles C. Thomas.

Gavan, James

1977 *Paleoanthropology and Primate Evolution.* Dubuque, Iowa: Wm. C. Brown Co.

Gelvin, Bruce R.

1980 "Morphometric Affinities of *Gigantopithecus.*" *American Journal of Physical Anthropology,* **53**:541–568.

Gerson, Donald

1977 "Radiation in the Environment." *In: Human Biology and Ecology,* A. Damon (ed.), New York: W. W. Norton and Co., pp. 246–265.

Gighlieri, Michael P.

1984 *The Chimpanzees of Kibale Forest.* New York: Columbia University Press.

Giles, E. and O. Elliot

1962 "Race Identification from Cranial Measurements," *Journal of Forensic Sciences,* **7**:147–157.

Gill, G. W.

1986 "Craniofacial Criteria in Forensic Race Identification." *In: Forensic Osteology: Advances in the Identification of Human Remains,* K. J. Reichs (ed.), Springfield: Charles C. Thomas.

Gill, G. W., S. S. Hughes, S. M. Bennett, and B. M. Gilbert

1988 "Racial Identification from the Mid-facial Skeleton with Special Reference to American Indians and Whites," *Journal of Forensic Sciences,* **33**(1).

Gingerich, Phillip D.

1986 "Early Eocene *Cantius torresi*—Oldest Primate of Modern Aspect from North America." *Nature* **319**:319–321.

Gingerich, P. D. and A. Sahni

1979 "*Indraloris* and *Sivaladapis.* Miocene Adapid Primates from the Siwaliks of India and Pakistan." *Nature,* **279**:415–416.

Ginger, Ray

1958 *Six Days or Forever?* Boston: Beacon Press.

Glass, Bently (ed.)

1959 *Forerunners of Darwin, 1745–1859.* Baltimore: Johns Hopkins Press.

Goldizen, Anne Wison

1987 "Tamarins and Marmosets: Communal Care of Offspring." *In:* Smuts, et al., (eds.), q.v., pp. 34–43.

Goldstein, M., P. Tsarong and C. M. Beall

1983 "High Altitude Hypoxia, Culture, and Human Fecundity/Fertility: A Comparative Study." *American Anthropologist,* **85**:28–49.

Goodall, Jane

1965 "Chimpanzees of the Gombe Stream Reserve." *In: Primate Behavior,* I. DeVore (ed.), New York: Holt, Rinehart and Winston, Inc., pp. 425–473.

————

1968a "A Preliminary Report on Expressions, Movements and Communications in the Gombe Stream Chimpanzees." *In: Primates,* P. C. Jay (ed.), New York: Holt, Rinehart and Winston, pp. 313–374.

————

1968b "The Behavior of Free Living Chimpanzees in the Gombe Stream Reserve." *Animal Behavior Monographs,* **1**:(3).

————

1971 *In the Shadow of Man.* Boston: Houghton Mifflin Co.

————

1978 Public Lecture at San Jose State University. April 26.

————

1979 "Life and Death at Gombe." *National Geographic,* **155**(5):597–620.

————

1986 *The Chimpanzees of Gombe.* Cambridge: The Bellknap Press of Harvard University Press.

————

1990 *Through A Window.* Boston: Houghton Mifflin Co.

Goodall, Jane, A. Bandora, E. Bergmann, C. Busse, H. Matama, et al.

1979 "Intercommunity Interactions in the Chimpanzee Population of the Gombe National Park." *In:* D. A. Hamburg and E. R. McCown (eds.), q.v., pp. 11–53.

Goodman, M., M. L. Baba and L. L. Darga

1983 "The Bearing of Molecular Data on the Cladogenesis and Times of Divergence of Hominoid Lineages." *In:* R. Ciochon and R. Corruccini (eds.), q.v., pp. 67–86.

Goodman, Morris and Gabriel W. Lasker

1975 "Molecular Evidence as to Man's Place in Nature." *In: Primate Functional Morphology and Evolution,* R. H. Tuttle (ed.), The Hague: Mouton Publishers, pp. 71–101.

Gorcyca, Diane A., Patrick Garner and Roger Fouts

1975 "Deaf Children and Chimpanzees." Paper presented at the Speech Communication Association Convention, Houston, Texas, December.

Gossett, Thomas F.

1963 *Race, the History of an Idea in America.* Dallas: Southern Methodist University Press.

Gould, Stephen Jay

1976 "Darwin and the Captain." *Natural History,* January, **85**:32–34.

Gould, S. J. and N. Eldredge

1977 "Punctuated Equilibria: the Tempo and Mode of Evolution Reconsidered." *Paleobiology,* **3**:115–151.

Gould, S. J. and R. Lewontin

1979 "The Spandrels of San Marco and the Panglossian Paradigm: A Critique of the Adaptionist Programme." *Proceedings of the Royal Society of London,,* **205**:581–598.

Greenberg, Joel

1977 "Who Loves You?" *Science News,* **112**:139–141, August 27.

Greene, John C.

1959 *The Death of Adam.* Ames, Iowa: Iowa State University Press (Mentor Book).

————

1981 *Science, Ideology, and World View.* Berkeley: University of California Press.

Greenfield, L. O.

1979 "On the Adaptive Pattern of *Ramapithecus.*" *American Journal of Physical Anthropology,* **50**:527–548.

————

1980 "A Late Divergence Hypothesis." *American Journal of Physical Anthropology,* **52**:351–365.

————

1983 "Toward the Resolution of Discrepancies between Phenetic and Paleontological Data Bearing on the Question of Human Origins." *In:* R. Ciochon and R. Corruccini (eds.), q.v., pp. 695–703.

Grine, Frederick E. (ed.)

1988a *Evolutionary History of the "Robust" Australopithecines.* New York: Aldine de Gruyter.

1988b "New Craniodental Fossils of *Paranthropus* from the Swartkrans Formation and their Significance in "Robust" Australopithecine Evolution." *In:* Grine (ed.), q.v., pp. 223–243.

Grobstein, Clifford

1977 "The Recombinant DNA Debate." *Scientific American,* **237**:22–31, July.

Grootes, P. M.
   1978   "Carbon-14 Time Scale Extended: Comparison of Chronologies."
         Science, **200**:11–15.
Gurin, Joel
   1980   "In the Beginning." *Science 80*, **1**(5):44–51.

Haldane, J.B.S.
   1932   *The Causes of Evolution*. London: Longmans, Green (reprinted as
         paperback, Cornell University Press, 1966).
Halstead, L. B.
   1968   *The Pattern of Vertebrate Evolution*. San Francisco: W. H. Freeman
         & Co.
Hamburg, David A. and E. R. McCown (eds.)
   1979   *The Great Apes*. Menlo Park, Ca.: The Benjamin/Cummings Pub-
         lishing Co.
Hamilton, W. D.
   1964   "The Genetical Theory of Social Behavior: I and II." *Journal of
         Theoretical Biology*, **7**:1–52.
Hanna, Joel M. and Daniel A. Brown
   1979   "Human Heat Tolerance: Biological and Cultural Adaptations."
         Yearbook of Physical Anthropology, **22**:163–186.

   _____   1983   "Human Heat Tolerance. An Anthropological Perspective." *An-
         nual Reviews of Anthropology*, **12**:259–284.
Harding, Robert and Shirley C. Strum
   1976   "The Predatory Baboons of Kekopey." *Natural History Magazine*,
         85(3):46–53.
Harlow, Harry F.
   1959   "Love in Infant Monkeys." *Scientific American*, **200**:68–74.
Harlow, Harry F. and Margaret K. Harlow
   1961   "A Study of Animal Affection." *Natural History*, **70**:48–55.
Harrold, Francis R.
   1989   "Mousterian, Chatelperronian and Early Aurignacian in Western
         Europe: Continuity or Discontinuity." *In*: Mellars and Stringer,
         q.v., pp. 212–231.
Harvey, Paul H., R. D. Martin and T. H. Clutton-Brock
   1987   "Life Histories in Comparative Perspective." *In*: Smuts, et al.,
         (eds.), q.v., pp. 181–196.
Hatley, T. and J. Kappelman
   1981   "Bears, Pigs, and Pliopleistocene Hominids: A Case for the Exploi-
         tation of Belowground Food Resources." *Human Ecology*, **8**:371–
         387.
Hausfater, Glenn
   1976   "Predatory Behavior of Yellow Baboons." *Behaviour*, **56**:44–68.

   _____   1984   "Infanticide in Langurs: Strategies, Counter Strategies, and
         Parameter Values." *In*: *Infanticide*, G. Hausfater and S. Blaffer
         Hrdy, (eds.), pp. 257–281.
Hausfater, Glenn and Sarah Blaffer Hrdy (eds.)
   1984   *Infanticide. Comparative and Evolutionary Perspectives*. Haw-
         thorne, New York: Aldine de Gruyter.
Heiken, A. and M. Rasmuson
   1966   "Genetical Studies on the Rh Blood Group System." *Hereditas
         Lund*, **55**:192–212.
Heltne, Paul G. and L. A. Marguardt (eds.)
   1989   *Understanding Chimpanzees*. Cambridge: Harvard University
         Press.
Hiatt, H. H., J. D. Watson and J. A. Winsten (eds.)
   1977   *Origins of Human Cancer* (3 volumes). Cold Spring Harbor Labo-
         ratory, Cold Spring Harbor, New York.

Hiernaux, Jean
   1964   "The Concept of Race and the Taxonomy of Mankind." *In*: *The
         Concept of Race*, Ashley Montagu (ed.), New York: The Free Press,
         pp. 29–45.

   _____   1968   *La Diversité Humaine en Afrique subsahariénne*. Bruxelles: L'In-
         stitut de Sociologie, Université Libre de Bruxelles.
Hoffman, Antoni
   1989   *Arguments on Evolution: A Paleontologist's Perspective*. New
         York: Oxford University Press.
Hoffstetter, R.
   1972   "Relationships, Origins, and History of the Ceboid Monkeys and
         the Caviomorph Rodents: A Modern Reinterpretation." *In*: *Evolu-
         tionary Biology*, Th. Dobzhansky, T.M.K. Hecht and W. C. Steere
         (eds.), Vol. 6, New York: Appleton-Century-Crofts, pp. 323–347.
Holloway, Ralph L.
   1969   "Culture: A Human Domain." *Current Anthropology*, **10**:395–407.

   _____   1981   "Revisiting the South African Taung Australopithecine Endocast:
         The Position of the Lunate Sulcus as Determined by the Stereo-
         plotting Technque." *American Journal of Physical Anthropology*,
         56:43–58.

   _____   1983   "Cerebral Brain Endocast Pattern of *Australopithecus afarensis*
         Hominid." *Nature*, **303**:420–422.

   _____   1985   "The Poor Brain of *Homo sapiens neanderthalensis*: See What You
         Please." *In*: Delson, q.v., pp. 319–324.
Hooton, E. A.
   1926   "Methods of Racial Analysis." *Science*, **63**:75–81.

   _____   1946   *Up from the Apes*. New York: The Macmillan Co.
Howell, F. Clark
   1966   "Observations on the Earlier Phases of the European Lower
         Paleolithic." *American Anthropologist*, **68**(2):88–201.

   _____   1978   "Hominidae." *In*: *Evolution of African Mammals*, V. J. Maglio and
         H.B.S. Cooke (eds.), Cambridge: Harvard University Press, pp.
         154–248.

   _____   1988   "Foreword." *In*: Grine (ed.), q.v., pp. xi–xv.
Howells, W. W.
   1971   "The Meaning of Race." *In*: *The Biological and Social Meaning of
         Race*, Richard H. Osborne (ed.), San Francisco: W. H. Freeman and
         Co., pp. 3–10.

   _____   1973   *Evolution of the Genus* Homo. Reading, Mass.: Addison-Wesley.

   _____   1974   "Neanderthals: Names, Hypotheses, and Scientific Method." *Amer-
         ican Anthropologist*, **76**:24–38.

   _____   1975   "Neanderthal Man: Facts and Figures." *In*: *Paleoanthropology:
         Morphology and Paleoecology*, R. H. Tuttle (ed.), The Hague:
         Mouton Publishers, pp. 389–407.

   _____   1980   "*Homo erectus*—Who, When, Where: A Survey." *Yearbook of
         Physical Anthropology* 1980, **23**:1–23.
Hrdy, Sarah Blaffer
   1977   *The Langurs of Abu*. Cambridge, Mass.: Harvard University Press.

   _____   1984a   "Female Reproductive Strategies." *In*: *Female Primates*, M. Small
         (ed.), New York: Alan R. Liss, pp. 103–109.

1984b "Assumptions and Evidence Regarding the Sexual Selection Hypothesis: A Reply to Boggess." *In*: *Infanticide*, G. Hausfater and S. Blaffer Hrdy (eds.), q.v., pp. 315–319.

Hublin, J. J.
1985 "Human Fossils from the North African Middle Plesitocene and the Origin of *Homo sapiens*. *In*: Delson, q.v., pp. 283–288.

Hudson, Liam
1972 "The Context of the Debate." *In*: *Race and Intelligence*, K. Richardson and D. Spears (eds.), Baltimore: Penguin Books, Inc., pp. 10–16.

Iltis, Hugo
1966 *Life of Mendel*. New York: Hafner Publishing Co. (first published in Germany, 1924).

The Institute of Vertebrate Palaeontology and Paleoanthropology, Chinese Academy of Sciences
1980 *Atlas of Primitive Man in China*. Beijing: Science Press (Distributed by Van Nostrand, New York).

Isaac, G. L.
1971 "The Diet of Early Man." *World Archaeology*, **2**:278–299.

1975 "Stratigraphy and Cultural Patterns in East Africa During the Middle Ranges of Pleistocene Time." *In*: K. W. Butzer and G. L. Isaac (eds.), q.v., pp. 495–542.

1976 "Early Hominids in Action: A Commentary on the Contribution of Archeology to Understanding the Fossil Record in East Africa." *Yearbook of Physical Anthropology* 1975, **19**:19–35.

Jacob, François
1975 "Morphology and Paleoecology of Early Man in Java." *In*: *Paleoanthropology: Morphology and Paleoecology*, R. H. Tuttle (ed.), Chicago: Aldine Publishing Co., pp. 312–325.

Jacob, Teuku
1976 "Early Populations in the Indonesian Region." *In*: R. L. Kirk and A. G. Thorne (eds.), q.v., pp. 81–93.

Jacobs, Louis L. and David Pilbeam
1980 "Of Mice and Men: Fossil-Based Divergence Dates and Molecular 'Clocks.' " *Journal of Human Evolution*, **9**:551–555.

James, Steven R.
1990 "Hominid Use of Fire in the Lower and Middle Pleistocene." *Current Anthropology*, **30**:1–26.

Jarvis, J.V.M.
1981 "Eusociality in a Mammal: Cooperative Breeding in Naked Mole-Rat Colonies." *Science*, **212**:571–573.

Jaeger, Jean-Jacques
1975 "The Mammalian Faunas and Hominid Fossils of the Middle Pleistocene of the Maghreb." *In*: K. W. Butzer and G. L. Isaac (eds.), q.v., pp. 399–418.

Jelinek, Arthur J.
1982 "The Tabun Cave and Paleolithic Man in the Levant." *Science*, **216**:1369–1375.

Jensen, Arthur
1969 *Environment, Heredity, and Intelligence*. Cambridge, Mass.: Harvard Educational Review.

1974 "Kinship Correlations Reported by Sir Cyril Burt." *Behavior Genetics*, **4**:1–28.

1980 *Bias in Mental Testing*. New York: The Free Press.

Jerison, H. J.
1973 *Evolution of the Brain and Behavior*. New York: Academic Press.

Johanson, Donald C.
1989 "The Current Status of *Australopithecus*." *Hominidae*, Proceedings of the 2nd International Congress of Human Paleontology, Milan: Editoriale Jaca Book, pp. 77–96.

Johanson, Donald and Maitland Edey
1981 *Lucy: The Beginnings of Humankind*. New York: Simon and Schuster.

Johanson, Donald, F. T. Masao, G. G. Eck, et al.
1987 "New Partial Skeleton of *Homo habilis* from Olduvai Gorge, Tanzania." *Nature*, **327**:205–209.

Johanson, Donald C. and Maurice Taieb
1976 "Plio-Pleistocene Hominid Discoveries in Hadar, Ethiopia." *Nature*, **260**:293–297.

1980 "New Discoveries of Pliocene Hominids and Artifacts in Hadar." International Afar Research Expedition to Ethiopia (Fourth and Fifth Field Seasons, 1975–77). *Journal of Human Evolution*, **9**:582.

Johanson, D. C. and T. D. White
1979 "A Systematic Assessment of Early African Hominids." *Science*, **203**:321–330.

1986 Fossil Debate. Letter, *Discover* **7**:116.

Johanson, D. C., T. D. White and Yves Coppens
1978 "A New Species of the Genus *Australopithecus* (Primates: Hominidae) from the Pliocene of Eastern Africa. *Kirtlandia*," No. 28, pp. 1–14.

Johnson, A. E., Jr.
1979 "Skeletal Estimates of *Gigantopithecus* Based on a Gorilla Analogy." *Journal of Human Evolution*, **8**:585–587.

Jolly, Alison
1984 "The Puzzle of Female Feeding Priority." *In*: Meredith F. Small, q.v., pp. 197–215.

1985 *The Evolution of Primate Behavior*. (2nd Ed.), New York: Macmillan.

Jolly, C. J.
1970 "The Seed Eaters: A New Model of Hominid Differentiation Based on a Baboon Analogy." *Man*, **5**:5–26.

Jungers, W. L.
1982 "Lucy's Limbs: Skeletal Allometry and Locomotion in *Australopithecus afarensis*." *Nature*, **297**:676–678.

1988 "New Estimates of Body Size in Australopithecines." *In*: Grine (ed.), q.v., pp. 115–125.

Kamin, Leon
1974 *The Science and Politics of IQ*. New York: John Wiley & Sons.

Kan, Yuet Wai and Andrée M. Dozy
1980 "Evolution of the Hemoglobin S and C Genes in World Populations." *Science*, **209**:388–391.

Katz, D., and J. M. Suchey
1986 "Age Determination of the Male Os Pubis," *American Journal of Physical Anthropology*, **69**:427–435.

Kawamura, Syunzo
1959 "The Process of Sub-culture Propagation among Japanese Macaques." *In*: *Primate Social Behavior*, C. H. Southwick (ed.), Princeton: D. Van Nostrand Co. Inc., pp. 82–90 (originally published in the *Journal of Primatology*, **2**(1):43–60).

Kawanaka, Kanji
1982 "A Case of Inter-Unit-Group Encounter in Chimpanzees of the Mahale Mts." *Primates*, **23**(4):558–562.
Kay, John P., et al.
1981 "Normalization of Low-Density Lipoproteins Levels in Heterozygous Familial Hypercholesterolemia with a Combined Drug Regimen." *New England Journal of Medicine*, **304**:251–258.
Kay, Richard F.
1981 "The Nut-Crackers—A New Theory of the Adaptations of the Ramapithecinae." *American Journal of Physical Anthropology*, **55**:151–156.
Kay, R. F., J. G. Fleagle and E. L. Simons
1981 "A Revision of the Oligocene Apes of the Fayum Province, Egypt." *American Journal of Physical Anthropology*, **55**:293–322.
Kay, Richard and Frederick E. Grine
1988 "Tooth Morphology, Wear and Diet in *Australopithecus* and *Paranthropus*." *In*: Grine (ed.), q.v., pp. 427–447.
Kay, R. F. and E. L. Simons
1983 "A Reassessment of the Relationship Between Late Miocene and Subsequent Hominoidea." *In*: R. Ciochon and R. Corruccini (eds.), q.v., pp. 577–624.
Kelso, A. J.
1974 *Physical Anthropology* (2nd Ed.). New York: J. B. Lippincott Co.
Kelly, Mark and David Pilbeam
1986 "The Dryopithecines: Taxonomy, Comparative Anatomy, and Phylogeny of Miocene Large Hominoids." *In*: *Comparative Primate Biology*, Vol. 1, Systematics, Evolution, and Anatomy, D. R. Swindler and J. Erwin (eds.), New York: Alan R. Liss, pp. 361–411.
Kennedy, G. E.
1980a *Paleoanthropology*. New York: McGraw-Hill Book Co.

1980b "The Emergence of Modern Man." *Nature*, **284**:11–12.

1984 "The Emergence of *Homo sapiens*: The Post Cranial Evidence." *Man* (N.S.), **19**:94–110.
Kennedy, Kenneth A. R.
1990 "Narmanda Man Fossil Skull from India." Summary of paper given at meeting of American Association of Physical Anthropology. *American Journal of Physical Anthropology*, **31**:248–249.
Kennedy, Kenneth A. R. and S. U. Deraniyagala
1989 "Fossil Remains of 28,000-Year-Old Hominids from Sri Lanka." *Current Anthropology*, **30**:397–399.
Kimbel, William H.
1988 "Identification of a Partial Cranium of *Australopithecus afarensis* from the Koobi Fora Formation, Kenya." *Journal of Human Evolution*, **17**:647–656.
Kimbel, William H., Tim D. White and Donald C. Johanson
1985 "Craniodental Morphology of the Hominids from Hadar and Laetoli: Evidence of 'Paranthropus' and *Homo* in the Mid-Pliocene of Eastern Africa?" *In*: E. Delson (ed.), q.v., pp. 120–137.

1988 "Implications of KNM-WT-17000 for the Evolution of 'Robust' *Australopithecus*." *In*: Grine (ed.), q.v., pp. 259–268.
King, J. L. and T. H. Jukes
1969 "Non-Darwinian Evolution." *Science*, **164**:788–798.
Kinzey, Warren G. (ed.)
1987 *The Evolution of Human Behavior: Primate Models*. Albany: State University of New York Press.
Kirk, R. L. and A. G. Thorne
1976 *The Origin of the Australians*. Human Biology Series, N.Y. Australian Institute of Aboriginal Studies, Canberra. New Jersey: Humanities Press Inc.
Klein, R. G.
1977 "The Ecology of Early Man in Southern Africa." *Science*, **197**:115–126.
Kolata, Gina
1986 "Anthropologists Suggest Cannibalism is a Myth." *Science*, **282**:1497–2000.
Konigsson, Lars-Konig (ed.)
1980 *Current Argument on Early Men*. Oxford: Pergamon Press.
Kortland, Adriaan
1965 "A comment on 'On the Essential Morphological Basis for Human Culture.' " *Current Anthropology*, **6**:320–326.
Kraatz, Reinhart
1985 "A Review of Recent Research on Heidelberg Man, *Homo erectus heidelbergensis*." *In*: Delson, q.v., pp. 268–271.
Krogman, W. M.
1962 *The Human Skeleton in Forensic Medicine*. Springfield: C. C. Thomas.
Kummer, Hans
1971 *Primate Societies*. Chicago: Aldine-Atherton, Inc.

Lack, David
1966 *Population Studies of Birds*. Oxford: Clarendon.
Lamarck, Jean Baptiste
1809, 1984 *Zoological Philosophy*. Chicago: University of Chicago Press.
Lancaster, Jane B.
1975 *Primate Behavior and the Emergence of Human Culture*. New York: Holt, Rinehart and Winston, Inc.

1984 "Introduction." *In*: Small, q.v., pp. 1–10.
Lasker, Gabriel W.
1969 "Human Biological Adaptability: the Ecological Approach in Physical Anthropology." *Science*, **166**:1480–1486.
Latimer, Bruce
1984 "The Pedal Skeleton of *Australopithecus afarensis*." *American Journal of Physical Anthropology*, **63**:182.
Leakey, L.S.B.
1966 "*Homo habilis*, *Homo erectus*, and the Australopithecinae." *Nature*, **209**:1279–1281.
Leakey, L.S.B., J. F. Everden and G. H. Curtis
1961 "Age of Bed I, Olduvai Gorge, Tanganyika." *Nature*, **191**:478–479.
Leakey, L.S.B., P. V. Tobias and J. R. Napier
1964 "A New Species of the Genus *Homo* from Olduvai Gorge." *Nature*, **202**:7–10.
Leakey, Mary D.
1971 "Remains of *Homo erectus* and Associated Artifacts in Bed IV at Olduvai Gorge, Tanzania." *Nature*, **232**:380–383.
Leakey, M. D. and R. L. Hay
1979 "Pliocene Footprints in Laetolil Beds at Laetoli, Northern Tanzania." *Nature*, **278**:317–323.
Leakey, R.E.F.
1974 "Further Evidence of Lower Pleistocene Hominids from East Rudolf, Kenya, 1973." *Nature*, **248**:653–656.

1976 "New Hominid Fossils from the Koobi Fora Formation in Northern Kenya." *Nature*, **261**:572–574.
Leakey, R.E.F. and M. G. Leakey
1986 "A New Miocene Hominoid from Kenya." *Nature*, **324**:143–146.

Leakey, R.E.F. and Alan C. Walker

1976 "*Australopithecus, Homo erectus* and the Single Species Hypothesis." *Nature*, **261**:572–574.

───── 1985 "New Higher Primates from the Early Miocene of Buluk, Kenya." *Nature* **318**:173–175.

Lee, Richard B.

1984 *The Dobe !Kung*. New York: Holt, Rinehart and Winston.

Lerner, I. M. and W. J. Libby

1976 *Heredity, Evolution, and Society*. San Francisco: W. H. Freeman and Company.

Lewellen, Ted C.

1981 "Aggression and Hypoglycemia in the Andes: Another Look at the Evidence." *Current Anthropology*, **22**:347–361.

Lewin, Roger

1981 "Biggest Challenge Since the Double Helix." Research News, *Science*, **212**:28–32.

───── 1983 "Is the Orangutan A Living Fossil?" *Science*, **222**:1222–1223.

───── 1987 "Africa: Cradle of Modern Humans." *Science*, **237**:1292–1295.

Lewontin, R. C.

1972 "The Apportionment of Human Diversity." *In: Evolutionary Biology* (Vol. 6), Th. Dobzhansky et al. (eds.), New York: Plenum, pp. 381–398.

Li, Wen-Hsiung and Masako Tanimura

1987 "The Molecular Clock Runs More Slowly in Man than in Apes and Monkeys." *Nature* **326**:93–96.

Lieberman, Daniel, David R. Pilbeam and Bernard A. Wood

1988 "A Probalistic Approach to the Problem of Sexual Dimorphism in *Homo habilis*: A Comparison of KNM-ER-1470 and KNM-ER-1813." *Journal of Human Evolution*, **17**:503–511.

Lieberman, P. and E. S. Crelin

1971 "On the Speech of Neanderthal." *Linguistic Inquiry*, **2**:203–222.

Lindroth, Sten

1983 "The Two Faces of Linnaeus." *In: Linnaeus: The Man and His Work*, Tore Frangsmyr (ed.), Berkeley: University of California Press.

Lindsay, Jean

1959 *A Short History of Science*. New York: Doubleday & Co.

Lisowski, F. P.

1984 "Introduction." *In*: Whyte, q.v., pp. 777–786.

Little, M. A., R. Brooke Thomas, Richard B. Mazess and Paul T. Baker

1971 "Populational Differences and Developmental Changes in Extremity Temperature Responses to Cold Among Andean Indians." *Human Biology*, **43**:70–91.

Livingstone, Frank B.

1964 "On the Nonexistence of Human Races." *In: Concept of Race*, A. Montagu (ed.), New York: The Free Press, pp. 46–60.

───── 1969 "Polygenic Models for the Evolution of Human Skin Color Differences." *Human Biology*, **41**:480–493.

───── 1980 "Natural Selection and the Origin and Maintenance of Standard Genetic Marker Systems." *Yearbook of Physical Anthropology*, 1980, **23**:25–42.

Lovejoy, Arthur L.

1959 "Buffon and the Problem of Species." *In: Forerunners of Darwin, 1745–1859*, Bentley Glass (ed.), Baltimore: Johns Hopkins Press, pp. 84–113.

Lovejoy, C. Owen

1981 "The Origin of Man." *Science*, **211**:341–350.

───── 1983 Paper presented at the Institute of Human Origins Conference on the Evolution of Human Locomotion (Berkeley).

───── 1988 "Evolution of Human Walking." *Scientific American*, **259**(Nov.): 118–125.

Lovejoy, C. O., G. Kingsbury, G. Heiple and A. H. Burstein

1973 "The Gait of *Australopithecus*." *American Journal of Physical Anthropology*, **38**:757–780.

Lovejoy, Thomas E.

1982 "The Tropical Forest—Greatest Expression of Life on Earth." *In: Primates and the Tropical Forest*, Proceedings, California Institute of Technology, World Wildlife Fund—U.S., pp. 45–48.

Löwenberg, Bert James

1959 *Darwin, Wallace, and the Theory of Natural Selection*. Cambridge, Mass.: Arlington Books.

Lu, Zun'e

1987 "Cracking the Evolutionary Puzzle—Jinniushan Man." *China Pictorial*, 1987/4 [April].

───── 1989 "Mosaic Evolution of Jinniushan Archaic *Homo sapiens*." *Circum-Pacific Prehistory Conference*: 1–20 Seattle: University of Washington Press.

Luckett, W. Patrick

1980 "The Suggested Evolutionary Relationships and Classification of Tree Shrews." *In: Comparative Biology and Evolutionary Relationships of Tree Shrews*, W. P. Luckett (ed.), New York: Plenum Press, pp. 3–31.

Mai, L. L.

1983 "A Model of Chromosome Evolution and Its Bearing on Cladogenesis in the Hominoidea." *In*: R. Ciochon and R. Corruccini (eds.), q.v., pp. 87–114.

Maier, W.

1977 "Chronology and Biology of the South African Australopithecines." *Journal of Human Evolution* **8**:89–93.

Mann, Alan

1975 "Some Paleodemographic Aspects of the South African Australopithecines." *University of Pennsylvania Publications in Anthropology* (No. 1), Philadelphia.

Marschack, A.

1972 *The Roots of Civilization*. New York: McGraw-Hill Publishing Co.

───── 1989 "Evolution of the Human Capacity: The Symbolic Evidence." *Yearbook of Physical Anthropology*, **32**:1–34.

Marshall, John C.

1989 "The Descent of the Larynx." *Nature*, **338**:702–703.

Maw, B., R. L. Ciochon, and D. E. Savage

1979 "Late Eocene of Burma Yields Earliest Anthropoid Primate, *Pondaungia cotteri*." *Nature*, **282**:65–67.

Mayr, Ernst

1962 "Taxonomic Categories in Fossil Hominids." *In: Ideas on Human Evolution*, W. W. Howells (ed.), New York: Atheneum, pp. 242–256.

───── 1970 *Population, Species, and Evolution*. Cambridge: Harvard University Press.

1982   *The Growth of Biological Thought*. Cambridge: Belknap Press.

McBrearty, Sally
1990   "The Origin of Modern Humans." *Man*, **25**:129–143.

McGrew, Wm. C.
1979   "Evolutionary Implications of Sex Differences in Chimpanzee Predation and Tool Use." *In*: Hamburg and McCown (eds.), q.v., pp. 441–463.

McHenry, Henry
1975   "Fossils and the Mosaic Nature of Human Evolution." *Science*, **190**:425–431.

1982   "The Pattern of Human Evolution: Studies on Behavior, Mastication, and Encephalization." *Annual Reviews of Anthropology*, **11**:151–173.

1983   "The Capitate of *Australopithecus afarensis* and *A. africanus*." *American Journal of Physical Anthropology*, **62**:187–198.

1985   "Implications of Postcanine Megadontia for the Origin of *Homo*." *In*: E. Delson, ed., q.v., pp. 178–183.

1988   "New Estimates of Body Weight in Early Hominids and their Significance to Encephalization and Megadontia in 'Robust' Australopithecines." *In*: Grine (ed.), q.v., pp. 133–148.

McKern, T. W., and T. D. Stewart
1957   "Skeletal Age Changes in Young American Males, Technical Report EP-45." Natick, MA: U.S. Army Quartermaster Research and Development Center.

McKusick, Victor
1980   "Anatomy of the Human Genome." *Journal of Heredity*, **71**:370–391.

1988   *Mendelian Inheritance in Man* (8th Ed.). Baltimore: Johns Hopkins Press.

Mech, L. David
1966   *The Wolves of Isle Royale*. Washington, D.C.: U.S. Government Printing Office.

Mellars, Paul and C. Stringer
1990   *The Human Revolution*. Princeton: University of Princeton Press.

Mendel, Gregor
1965   "Experiments in Plant Hybridisation" (A paper read before the Natural History Society of Brünn in 1865). Cambridge: Harvard University Press.

Menosky, Joseph A.
1981   "The Gene Machine." *Science 81* (July-Aug.):38–41.

Merrick, H. V. and J. P. S. Merrick
1976   "Archeological Occurrences of Earlier Pleistocene Age from the Shungura Formation." *In*: *Earliest Man and Environments in the Lake Rudolf Basin*, Y. Coppens et al. (eds.), Chicago: University of Chicago Press, pp. 574–584.

Miles, H. Lyn
1983   "Apes and Language: The Search for Communicative Competence." *In*: J. de Luce and H. T. Wilder (eds.), q.v., pp. 43–62.

Mittermeir, Russel A.
1982   "The World's Endangered Primates: An Introduction and a Case Study—The Monkeys of Brazil's Atlantic Forests." *In*: *Primates and the Tropical Rain Forest*, Proceedings, California Institute of Technology, World Wildlife Fund—U.S., pp. 11–22.

Mittermeir, R. A. and D. Cheney
1987   "Conservation of Primates in their Habitats." *In*: Smuts, et al., (eds.), q.v., pp. 477–496.

Montagu, Ashley (ed.)
1980   *Sociobiology Examined*. New York: Oxford University Press.

Moore, Lorna G. and Judith G. Regensteiner
1983   "Adaptation to High Altitude." *Annual Reviews of Anthropology*, **12**:285–304.

Moore, R. V.
1987   "Variation in *Homo erectus* and Its Effect on Our Understanding of the Distribution of this Hominid Species." (Abstract of above paper in *American Journal of Physical Anthropology*, **72**(2):234, 1987.)

Moore, Ruth
1961   *Man, Time and Fossils*. New York: Alfred A. Knopf.

Morbeck, M. E.
1975   "*Dryopithecus africanus* Forelimb." *Journal of Human Evolution*, **4**:39–46.

1983   "Miocene Hominoid Discoveries from Rudabánya. Implications from the Postcranial Skeleton." *In*: R. Ciochon and R. Corruccini (eds.), q.v., pp. 369–404.

Morgan, Elaine
1972   *The Descent of Women*. New York: Stein and Day.

Morris, Desmond
1967   *The Naked Ape*. New York: McGraw-Hill.

Mturi, A. A.
1976   "New Hominid from Lake Ndutu, Tanzania." *Nature*, **262**:484–485.

Mueller, William H. et al.
1979   "A Multinational Andean Genetic and Health Program. VIII. Lung Function Changes with Migration between Altitudes." *American Journal of Physical Anthropology*, **51**:183–196.

Murray, R. D.
1980   "The Evolution and Functional Significance of Incest Avoidance." *Journal of Human Evolution*, **9**:173–178.

Myerowitz, Rachel and Norman D. Hogikyan
1986   "Different Mutations in Ashkenazi Jewish and Non-Jewish French Canadians with Tay-Sachs Disease." *Science*, **232**:1646–1648.

Napier, John
1967   "The Antiquity of Human Walking." *Scientific American*, **216**:56–66.

Napier, J. R. and P. H. Napier
1985   *The Natural History of the Primates*. London: British Museum (Natural History).

Napier, Prue
1977   *Chimpanzees*. New York: McGraw-Hill Book Co.

Nature
1986   "Chernobyl Report." *Nature*, **323**:26–30.

Newman, Marshall T.
1975   "Nutritional Adaptation in Man." *In*: *Physiological Anthropology*, Albert Damon (ed.), New York: Oxford University Press, pp. 210–259.

Newman, Russell W.
1970   "Why Man Is Such a Sweaty and Thirsty Naked Animal: A Speculative Review." *Human Biology*, **42**:12–27.

Newman, Russell W. and Ella H. Munro
1955   "The Relation of Climate and Body Size in U.S. Males." *American Journal of Physical Anthropology*, **13**:1–17.

Ninkovich, D. and L. H. Burcle
1978   "Absolute Age of the Base of the Hominid Bearing Beds in Eastern Java." *Nature*, **275**:306–308.

Nishida, Toshisada
1979   "The Social Structure of Chimpanzees of the Mahale Mountains."

In: *The Great Apes*, David A. Hamburg and E. R. McCown (eds.), q.v., pp. 73–121.

——— 1983 "Alloparental Behavior in Wild Chimpanzees of the Mahale Mts., Tanzania." *Folia Primatologica*, **41**:1–33.

Nishida, Toshisada and M. Hiraiwa-Hasegawa
1985 "Response to a Stranger Mother-Son Pair in the Wild Chimpanzee: A Case Report." *Primates*, **6**:1–13.

——— 1987 "Chimpanzees and Bonobos: Cooperative Relationships among Males." *In*: Smuts, et al., q.v., pp. 165–177.

Nishida, Toshisada and Kenji Kawanaka
1985 "Within-Group Cannibalism by Adult Male Chimpanzees." *Primates*, **26**(3):274–284.

Nishida, Toshisada, S. Uehara, and R. Nyundo
1979 "Predatory Behavior among Wild Chimpanzees of the Mahale Mts." *Primates*, **20**(1):1–20.

Norikashi, Kohshi
1982 "One Observed Case of Cannibalism Among Wild Chimpanzees of the Mahale Mountains." *Primates*, **23**(1):66–74.

Oakley, Kenneth
1963 "Analytical Methods of Dating Bones." *In*: *Science in Archaeology*, D. Brothwell and E. Higgs (eds.), New York: Basic Books, Inc.

Oakley, Kenneth Page, Bernard G. Campbell and Theya I. Mulleson
1977 *Catalogue of Fossil Hominids*. Part I: Africa; Part II: Europe (1971); Part III: Americas, Asia, Australia (1975). London: The British Museum (Natural History).

Olby, Robert O.
1985 *Origins of Mendelism*. (2nd Ed.), Chicago: University of Chicago Press.

Oldroyd, D. R.
1980 *Darwinian Impacts: An Introduction to the Darwinian Revolution*. Atlantic Highlands: Humanities Press.

Olson, Everett C.
1980 "Taphonomy: Its History and Role in Community Evolution." *In*: *Fossils in the Making*, K. Behrensmeyer and A. Hill (eds.), Chicago: University of Chicago Press, pp. 5–19.

Olson, Todd R.
1985 "Cranial Morphology and Systematics of the Hadar Formation Hominids and *Australopithecus africanus*." *In*: E. Delson (ed.), q.v., pp. 102–119.

Osborne, Richard (ed.)
1971 *The Biological and Social Meaning of Race*. San Francisco: W. H. Freeman Co.

Ovey, C. D. (ed.)
1964 "The Swanscombe Skull." Royal Anthropological Institute, Occasional Paper 20.

Oxnard, C. E.
1975 "The Place of the Australopithecines in Human Evolution: Grounds for Doubt?" *Nature*, **258**:389–395.

Packer, C.
1979 "Inter-Troop Transfer and Inbreeding Avoidance in *Papio Anubis*." *Animal Behaviour*, **27**:1–36.

Parker, Seymour
1976 "The Precultural Basis of the Incest Taboo: Toward a Biosocial Theory." *American Anthropologist*, **78**:285–305.

Parks, Michael
1981 "Skulls Found in China Important in the Puzzle of Man's Evolution." *San Jose Mercury News*, Sunday, May 17, 1981.

Passingham, R. E.
1982 *The Human Primate*. San Francisco: W. H. Freeman and Co.

Patterson, Francine
1983 "Why Koko (and Michael) **Can** Talk." *Gorilla*, **6**(2), June.

Pauling, Linus
1974 "The Molecular Basis of Biological Specificity." *Nature*, **248**:769–771.

Peoples, James and G. Bailey
1988 *Humanity*. St. Paul: West Publishing Co.

Peters, Charles R.
1989 "Comments." *Current Anthropology*, **30**:17–18.

Petit, Charles
1981 "Ancient Skull Raises New Storm." *San Francisco Chronicle*, September 26, 1981.

Pfeiffer, John E.
1985 *The Emergence of Man* (4th Ed.). New York: Harper and Row, Publishers.

——— 1987 "Underground Bestiary." *Natural History*, October: 84–88.

Phenice, T. W.
1969 "A Newly Developed Visual Method of Sexing the Os Pubis," *American Journal of Physical Anthropology*, **30**:297–302.

Pickford, M.
1983 "Sequence and Environments of the Lower and Middle Miocene Hominoids of Western Kenya." *In*: R. Ciochon and R. Corruccini (eds.), q.v., pp. 421–439.

Pilbeam, David
1972 *The Ascent of Man*. New York: Macmillan.

——— 1975 "Middle Pleistocene Hominids." *In*: K. W. Butzer and G. L. Isaac (eds.), q.v., pp. 809–856.

——— 1977 "Beyond the Apes: Pre-*Homo* Hominids: The Ramapithecines of Africa, Asia, and Europe." Symposium Lecture, March 5, Davis, Calif.

——— 1979 "Recent Finds and Interpretations of Miocene Hominoids." *Annual Reviews of Anthropology*, **8**:333–352.

——— 1981 "New Fossil Hominoid from Pakistan." Paper presented at the Annual Meeting, American Association of Physical Anthropologists, April, 1981.

——— 1982 "New Hominoid Skull Material From the Miocene of Pakistan." *Nature*, **295**:232–234.

——— 1986 "Distinguished Lecture: Hominoid Evolution and Hominoid Origins." *American Anthropologist*, **88**:295–312.

——— 1988 "Primate Evolution." *In*: G. A. Harrison, et al., (eds.), *Human Biology*, New York: Oxford University Press, pp. 76–103.

Pilbeam, David, G. E. Meyer, C. Badgley, et al.
1977 "New Hominoid Primates from the Siwaliks of Pakistan and Their Bearing on Hominoid Evolution." *Nature*, **270**:689–695.

Pope, G. G.
1984 "The Antiquity and Paleoenvironment of the Asian Hominidae." *In*: Whyte (ed.), q.v., pp. 822–847.

Pope, G. G. and J. E. Cronin
1984 "The Asian Hominidae." *Journal of Human Evolution*, **13**:377–396.

Popp, Joseph L. and Irven DeVore
1979 "Aggressive Competition and Social Dominance Theory." *In*: *The*

Great Apes, David A. Hamburg and E. R. McCown (eds.), q.v., pp. 317–318.

Post, Peter W., Farrington Daniels, Jr. and Robert T. Binford, Jr.
1975   "Cold Injury and the Evolution of 'White' Skin." *Human Biology*, **47**:65–80.

Potts, Richard and Pat Shipman
1981   "Cutmarks Made by Stone Tools from Olduvai Gorge, Tanzania." *Nature*, **291**:577–580.

Poulianos, Aris N.
1981   "Pre-*sapiens* Man in Greece." *Current Anthropology*, **22**(3):287–288.

Premack, David
1971   "Language in Chimpanzee?" *Science*, **172**:808–822.

Premack, David and Ann J. Premack
1983   *The Mind of an Ape*. New York: W. W. Norton & Co.

Proctor, Robert
1988   "From Anthropologie to Rassenkunde." *In*: George W. Stocking, q.v., pp. 138–179.

Proshnev, B. F.
1974   "The Troglodytidae and the Hominidae in the Taxonomy and Evolution of Higher Primates." *Current Anthropology*, **15**(4):449–450.

Pusey, Anne E. and Craig Packer
1987   "Dispersal and Philopatry." *In*: Smuts, et al. (eds.), q.v., pp. 250–266.

Quinn, Thomas C., J. M. Mann, J. W. Curran and P. Piot
1986   "AIDS in Africa: An Epidemiologic Paradigm." *Science*, **234**:955–963.

Radinsky, Leonard
1973   "*Aegyptopithecus* Endocasts: Oldest Record of a Pongid Brain." *American Journal of Physical Anthropology*, **39**:239–248.

Rak, Y.
1983   *The Australopithecine Face*. New York: Academic Press.

Ransom, Timothy W.
1981   *Beach Troop of the Gombe*. Lewisburg: Bucknell University Press.

Ray, John
1692   *The Wisdom of God Manifested in the Works of the Creation*. London: Printed for Samuel Smith at the Princes Arms in St. Paul's Church-yard.

Raza, S. Mahmoud, et al.
1983   "New Hominoid Primates from the Middle Miocene Chinji Formation, Potwar Plateau, Pakistan." *Nature*, **306**:52–54.

Repenning, Charles A. and Oldrich Fejfar
1982   "Evidence for Earlier Date of Ubeidya, Israel, Hominid Site." *Nature*, **299**:344–347.

Richard, Alison F.
1985   *Primates in Nature*. New York: W. H. Freeman and Co.

Richard, A. F. and S. R. Schulman
1982   "Sociobiology: Primate Field Studies." *Annual Reviews of Anthropology*, **11**:231–255.

Rightmire, G. P.
1976   "Relationships of Middle and Upper Pleistocene Hominids from Sub-Saharan Africa." *Nature*, **269**:238–240.

——   1979   "Cranial Remains of *Homo erectus* from Beds II and IV, Olduvai Gorge, Tanzania." *American Journal of Physical Anthropology*, **51**:99–116.

——   1983   "Lake Ndutu Cranium and Early *Homo sapiens* in Africa." *American Journal of Physical Anthropology*, **61**:245–254.

——   1985   "The Tempo of Change in the Evolution of Mid-Pleistocene *Homo*." *In*: Delson (ed.), q.v., pp. 255–264.

Roberts, D. F.
1973   *Climate and Human Variability*. An Addison-Wesley Module in Anthropology, No. 34, Reading, Mass.: Addison-Wesley.

Robinson, J. T.
1953   "Telanthropus and Its Phylogenetic Significance." *American Journal of Physical Anthropology*, **11**:445–501.

——   1972   *Early Hominid Posture and Locomotion*. Chicago: University of Chicago Press.

Rodman, Peter S. and John G. H. Canat (eds.)
1984   *Adaptations for Foraging in Nonhuman Primates*. New York: Columbia University Press.

Romer, Alfred S.
1959   *The Vertebrate Story*. Chicago: University of Chicago Press.

Rose, M. D.
1983   "Miocene Hominoid Postcranial Morphology. Monkey-like, Ape-like, Neither, or Both?" *In*: R. Ciochon and R. Corruccini (eds.), q.v., pp. 405–417.

——   1984   "Food Acquisition and the Evolution of Positional Behaviour: The Case of Bipedalism." *In*: David J. Chivers, et al., q.v., pp. 509–524.

Rose, Noel R.
1981   "Autoimmune Diseases." *Scientific American*, **244**(2):80–103.

Rose, Steven
1972   "Environmental Effects on Brain and Behavior." *In*: *Race and Intelligence*, Ken Richardson and David Speers (eds.), Baltimore: Penguin Books, Inc., pp. 128–144.

Rowell, Thelma E.
1972   *The Social Behaviour of Monkeys*. Baltimore: Penguin Books.

——   1984   "Introduction." *In*: Small, q.v., pp. 13–16.

Rudnai, Judith
1973   *The Social Life of Lions*. Wallingford, Pa.: Washington Square East.

Rumbaugh, D. M.
1977   *Language Learning by a Chimpanzee: The Lana Project*. New York: Academic Press.

Rumbaugh, Duane M., E. Sue Savage-Rumbaugh and John L. Scanlon
1982   "The Relationship Between Language in Apes and Human Beings." *In*: James E. King and James L. Fobes (eds.), q.v., pp. 361–385.

Russell, Mary D.
1987   "Mortuary Practices at the Krapina Neandertal Site." *American Journal, Physical Anthropology*, **72**:381–397.

Ryan, Alan S. and Donald C. Johanson
1989   "Anterior Dental Microwear in *Australopithecus afarensis*: Comparisons with Human and Nonhuman Primates." *Journal of Human Evolution*, **18**:235–268.

Sanders, Richard J.
1986   "Teaching Apes to Ape Language: Explaining the Imitative and Nonimitative Signing of a Chimpanzee (*Pan troglodytes*). *Journal of Comparative Psychology*, **99**(2):197–210.

Sanderson, Ivan T.
1969   "The Missing Link." *Argosy*, May, pp. 23–31.
Sarich, Vincent
1971   "A Molecular Approach to the Question of Human Origins." *In*: *Background for Man*, P. Dolhinow and V. Sarich (eds.), Boston: Little, Brown & Co., pp. 60–81.
Sarich, V. M. and A. C. Wilson
1967   "Rates of Albumen Evolution in Primates." *Proceedings, National Academy of Sciences*, **58**:142–148.
Sartono, S.
1975   "Implications Arising from *Pithecanthropus* VIII." *In*: *Paleoanthropology: Morphology and Paleoecology*, R. H. Tuttle (ed .), Chicago: Aldine Publishing Co., pp. 327–360.
Savage-Rumbaugh, Sue, et al.
1983   "Can a Chimpanzee Make a Statement." *The Journal of Experimental Psychology: General*, **112**(4):457–492.
Savage-Rumbaugh, Sue, M. A. Romski, W. D. Hopkins, et al.
1989   "Symbol Acquisition and Use by *Pan troglodytes, Pan paniscus, Homo sapiens*." *In*; Heltne and Marquardt, q.v., pp. 266–310.
Scarr, Sandra
1981   "The Effects of Family Background: A Study of Cognitive Differences among Black and White Twins." *In*: *Race, Social Class, and Individual Differences in I.Q.*, S. Scarr (ed.), Hillsdale, N.J.: Lawrence Erlbaum Associates, Inc., pp. **261–315.**
Scarr, Sandra and R. A. Weinberg
1976   "IQ Test Performances of Black Children Adopted by White Families." *In*: S. Scarr (ed.), q.v., pp. 109–159.
Schaller, George B.
1963   *The Mountain Gorilla*. Chicago: University of Chicago Press.

———
1972   *The Serengeti Lion*. Chicago: University of Chicago Press.
Scheidt, Walter
1924   "The Concept of Race in Anthropology and the Divisions into Human Races from Linnaeus to Deniker." *In*: *This Is Race*, E. W. Count (ed.), New York: Henry Schuman, pp. 354–391.
Scheller, Richard H. and Richard Axel
1984   "How Genes Control Innate Behavior." *Scientific American*, **250**:54–63.
Scopes, John T. and James Presley
1967   *Center of the Storm*. New York: Holt, Rinehart and Winston.
Schull, William J., M. Otuke and J. V. Neel.
1981   "Genetic Effects of the Atomic Bombs: A Reappraisal." *Science*, **213**:1220–1227.
Sebeok, Thomas A.
1980   *Speaking of Apes*. New York: Plenum Press.
Senut, Brigette
1981   "Humeral Outlines in Some Hominoid Primates and in Plio-Pleistocene Hominids." *American Journal of Physical Anthropology*, **56**:275–283.
Senut, Brigette and Christine Tardieu
1985   "Functional Aspects of Plio-Pleistocene Hominid Limb Bones: Implications for Taxonomy and Phylogeny." *In*: E. Delson (ed.), q.v., pp. 193–201.
Service, Elman R.
1966   *The Hunters*. Englewood Cliffs, N.J.: Prentice-Hall, Inc.
Seyfarth, Robert M., Dorothy L. Cheney and Peter Marler
1980a   "Monkey Responses to Three Different Alarm Calls." *Science*, **210**:801–803.

———
1980b   "Ververt Monkey Alarm Calls." *Animal Behavior*, **28**:1070–1094.

Shapiro, Harry
1936   *The Heritage of the* Bounty. New York: Simon and Schuster.
Shipman, P. L.
1983   "Early Hominid Lifestyle. Hunting and Gathering or Foraging and Scavenging?" Paper presented at 52nd Annual Meeting, American Association of Physical Anthropologists, Indianapolis, April, 1983.

———
1985   "The Ancestor That Wasn't." *The Sciences*, March/April:42–48.

———
1986   "Baffling Limb on the Family Tree." *Discover*, **7**:87–93.

———
1987   "An Age-Old Question: Why Did the Human Lineage Survive?" *Discover*, **8**:60–64.
Shipman, Pat and A. Walker
1989   "The Costs of Becoming a Predator." *Journal of Human Evolution*, **18**:373–392.
Sibley, Charles and Jon E. Ahlquist
1984   "The Phylogeny of the Hominoid Primates as Indicated by DNA-DNA Hybridization." *Journal of Molecular Evolution*, **20**:2–15.
Sillen, Andrew and C. K. Brain
1990   "Old Flame." *Natural History*, pp. 6–10.
Simons, E. L.
1969   "The Origin and Radiation of the Primates." *Annals of the New York Academy of Sciences*, **167**:319–331.

———
1972   *Primate Evolution*. New York: Macmillan.

———
1985   "African Origin, Characteristics and Context of Earliest Higher Primates." *In*: *Hominid Evolution: Past, Present, and Future*. P. Tobias (ed.), New York: Alan R. Liss, pp. 101–106.
Simons, E. L. and P. C. Ettel
1970   "*Gigantopithecus*." *Scientific American*, **222**:76–85.
Simpson, G. G.
1945   "The Principles of Classification and a Classification of Mammals." *Bulletin of the American Museum of Natural History*, **85**:1–350.

———
1961   *Principles of Animal Taxonomy*. New York: Columbia University Press.
Simpson, G. G., C. S. Pittendright and L. H. Tiffany
1957   *Life*. New York: Harcourt, Brace and Co., Inc.
Singer, Charles
1959   *A Short History of Scientific Ideas to 1900*. London: Oxford University Press.
Singer, R. and Wymer, J. J.
1982   *The Middle Stone Age at Klasies River Mouth in South Africa*. Chicago: The University of Chicago Press.
Skelton, R. R., H. M. McHenry and G. M. Drawhorn
1986   "Phylogenetic Analysis of Early Hominids." *Current Anthropology*, **27**:1–43; **27**:361–365.
Small, Meredith F. (ed.)
1984   *Female Primates. Studies by Women Primatologists*. Monographs in Primatology, Volume 4. New York: Alan R. Liss.
Smith, B. Holly
1986   "Dental Development in *Australopithecus* and Early *Homo*." *Nature*, **323**:327–330.
Smith, Fred H.
1982   "Upper Pleistocene Hominid Evolution in South-Central Europe." *Current Anthropology*, **23**:667–703.

1984   "Fossil Hominids from the Upper Pleistocene of Central Europe and the Origin of Modern Europeans." *In*: Smith and Spencer, q.v., pp. 187–209.

Smith, Fred H., A. B. Falsetti and S. M. Donnelly
1989 "Modern Human Origins." *Yearbook of Physical Anthropology*, **32**:35–68.

Smith, Fred H. and Frank, Spencer (eds.)
1984 *The Origins of Modern Humans.* New York: Alan R. Liss, Inc.

Smuts, Barbara
1985 *Sex and Friendship in Baboons.* Hawthorne, N.Y.: Aldine de Gruyter.

Smuts, Barbara B., Dorothy L. Cheney, Robert M. Seyfarth, et al. (eds.)
1987 *Primate Societies.* Chicago: University of Chicago Press.

Snyder, Louis L.
1962 *The Idea of Racialism.* New York: Van Nostrand Reinhold Co.

Soffer, Olga
1985 *The Upper Paleolithic of the Central Russian Plain.* New York: Academic Press.

Solecki, Ralph
1971 *Shanidar, The First Flower People.* New York: Alfred A. Knopf.

Sonakia, Arun
1985a "Skull Cap of an Early Man from the Narmada Valley Alluvium (Pleistocene) of Central India." *American Anthropologist*, **87**(3):612–616.

_____
1985b "Early *Homo* from Narmada Valley, India." *In*: E. Delson, (ed.), q.v., pp. 334–338.

Sondaar, Paul Y.
1984 "Faunal Evolution and the Mammalian Biostratigraphy of Java." *In*: Andrews and Franzen (eds.), q.v., pp. 219–235.

Speth, J. D. and D. D. Davis
1976 "Seasonal Variability in Early Hominid Predation." *Science*, **192**:441–445.

Stanyon, Roscoe and Brunetto Chiarelli
1982 "Phylogeny of the Hominoidea: The Chromosome Evidence." *Journal of Human Evolution*, **11**:493–504.

Stebbins, G. Ledyard
1982 *Darwin to DNA.* San Francisco: W. H. Freeman and Co.

Steegman, A. T. Jr.
1970 "Cold Adaptation and the Human Face." *American Journal of Physical Anthropology*, **32**:243–250.

_____
1975 "Human Adaptation to Cold." *In*: *Physiological Anthropology*, A. Damon (ed.), New York: Oxford University Press, pp. 130–166.

Stepan, Nancy
1982 *The Idea of Race in Science: Great Britain 1800–1960.* Hamden: Archon Books.

Stern, Curt
1973 *Principles of Human Genetics* (3rd Ed.). San Francisco: W. H. Freeman and Company.

Stern, Jack T. and Randall L. Susman
1983 "The Locomotor Anatomy of *Australopithecus afarensis*." *American Journal of Physical Anthropology*, **60**:279–317.

Stewart, T. D.
1979 *Essentials of Forensic Anthropology: Especially as Developed in the United States.* Springfield: C. C. Thomas.

Stocking, George W. Jr.
1968 *Race, Culture, and Evolution.* New York: The Free Press.

Stocking, George W., Jr. (ed.)
1988 *Bones, Bodies, Behavior. History of Anthropology*, Vol. 5. Madison: The University of Wisconsin Press.

Stringer, C. B. (ed.)
1981 *Aspects of Human Evolution.* London: Taylor & Francis Ltd. (Symposia of the Society for the Study of Human Biology, Vol. XXI).

_____
1982 "Towards a Solution to the Neanderthal Problem." *Journal of Human Evolution*, **11**(5):431–438.

_____
1984 "Fate of Neandertal." *Natural History.* December:6–12.

_____
1985 "Middle Pleistocene Hominid Variability and the Origin of Late Pleistocene Humans." *In*: Delson (ed.), q.v., pp. 289–295.

Stringer, Christopher B., F. Clark Howell and John K. Melentis
1979 "The Significance of the Fossil Hominid Skull from Petralona, Greece." *Journal of Archaeological Science*, **6**:235–253.

Stringer, C. B., J. J. Hublin and B. Vandermeersch
1984 "The Origin of Anatomically Modern Humans in Western Europe." *In*: Smith and Spencer, q.v., pp. 51–135.

Stringer, C. B. and E. Trinkaus
1981 "The Shanidar Neanderthal Crania." *In*: *Aspects of Human Evolution*, C. B. Stringer (ed.), London: Taylor & Francis Ltd., pp. 129–165.

Struhsaker, Thomas T. and Lysa Leland
1979 "Socioecology of Five Sympatric Monkey Species in the Kibale Forest, Uganda." *Advances in the Study of Behavior*, Vol. 9. New York: Academic Press, pp. 159–229.

_____
1987 "Colobines: Infanticide by Adult Males." *In*: Smuts, et al. (eds.), q.v., pp. 83–97.

Struhsaker, Thomas T. and John F. Oates
1975 "Comparison of the Behavior and Ecology of Red Colobus and Black-and-White Colobus Monkeys in Uganda: A Summary." *In*: *Socioecology and Psychology of Primates*, R. H. Tuttle (ed.), Chicago: Aldine Publishing Co.

Strum, Shirley C.
1981 "Processes and Products of Change at Gilgil, Kenya." *In*: *Omnivorous Primates*, R.S.O. Harding and Geza Teleki (eds.), New York: Columbia University Press.

_____
1983 "Baboon Cues for Eating Meat." *Journal of Human Evolution*, **12**:327–336.

_____
1987 "The 'Gang' Moves to a Strange New Land." *National Geographic* (Nov.):pp. 677–690.

Sugiyama, Yukimaru and Jeremy Koman
1979 "Tool-Using and -Making Behavior in Wild Chimpanzees at Bossou, Guinea." *Primates*, **20**:513–524.

Sumner, D. R., M. E. Morbeck and J. Lobick
1987 "Age-Related Bone Loss in Female Gombe Chimpanzees." *American Journal of Physical Anthropology*, **72**:259.

Suomi, Stephen J., Susan Mineka and Roberta D. DeLizio
1983 "Short- and Long-Term Effects of Repetitive Mother-Infant Separation on Social Development in Rhesus Monkeys." *Developmental Psychology*, **19**(5):710–786.

Susman, Randall L.
1988 "New Postcranial Remains from Swartkrans and their Bearing on the Functional Morphology and Behavior of *Paranthropus robustus*." *In*: Grine (ed.), q.v., pp. 149–172.

Susman, Randall L., Jack T. Stern and William L. Jungers
1985 "Locomotor Adaptations in the Hadar Hominids." *In*: E. Delson (ed.), q.v., pp. 184–192.

Suzman, I. M.
1982 "A Comparative Study of the Hadar and Sterkfontein Australopithecine Innominates." *American Journal of Physical Anthropology*, **57**:235.
Suzuki, David and Peter Knudtson
1989 *Genethics*. Cambridge: Harvard University Press.
Szalay, Frederick S.
1968 "The Beginnings of Primates." *Evolution*, **22**:19–36.
Szalay, Frederick S. and Eric Delson
1979 *Evolutionary History of the Primates*. New York: Academic Press.

Tanner, J. M.
1977 "Human Growth and Constitution." *In*: *Human Biology*, G. A. Harrison, et al. (eds.), New York: Oxford University Press, pp. 299–385.
Tanner, Nancy M.
1981 *On Becoming Human*. New York: Cambridge University Press.
Tattersall, Ian
1986 "Species Recognition in Human Paleontology." *Journal of Human Evolution*," **15**(3):165–175.
Tattersall, Ian and Niles Eldredge
1977 "Fact, Theory and Fantasy in Human Paleontology." *American Scientist*, **65**:204–211.
Tauxe, Lisa
1979 "A New Date for *Ramapithecus*." *Nature*, **282**:399–401.
Teleki, G.
1973 *The Predatory Behavior of Wild Chimpanzees*. Cranbrook, N.J.: Bucknell University Press.

1986 "Chimpanzee Conservation in Sierra Leone—A Case Study of a Continent-wide Problem." Paper presented at "Understanding Chimpanzees" Symposium, Chicago Academy of Sciences, Chicago, Nov. 7–10, 1987.
Terrace, Herbert S.
1979 *Nim*. New York: Alfred A. Knopf.

1982 "Why Koko Can't Talk." *The Sciences*, **22**(9):8–10, Columbia University.

1983 "Apes Who 'Talk': Language or Projection of Language by Their Teachers" *In*: De Luce and Wilder, q.v., pp. 19–42.
Theunissen, Bert
1985 *Eugene Dubois and the Ape-Man from Java*. Dordrecht; Boston: Kluwer Academic Publishers.
Thomsen, Dietrick E.
1978 "Radioisotope Dating with Accelerators." *Science News*, **113**:29–30, January 14.
Thorne, A. and P. Macumber
1971 "Discoveries of Late Pleistocene Man at Kow Swamp, Australia." *Nature*, **238**:316–319.
Thouveny, N. and E. Bonifay
1984 "New Chronological Data on European Plio-Pleistocene Faunas and Hominid Occupation Sites." *Nature*, **308**:355–358.
Tiger, Lionel and Robin Fox
1971 *The Imperial Animal*. New York: Holt, Rinehart and Winston.
Tobias, Phillip
1967 *Olduvai Gorge* (Vol. 2). *The Cranial and Maxillary Dentition of Australopithecus (Zinjanthropus) boisei*. Cambridge: Cambridge University Press.

1971 *The Brain in Hominid Evolution*. New York: Columbia University Press.

1972 "Early Man in Sub-Saharan Africa." *In*: *The Functional and Evolutionary Biology of the Primates*, R. Tuttle (ed.), Chicago: Aldine-Atherton, pp. 63–93.

1976 "African Hominids: Dating and Phylogeny." *In*: G. L. Isaac and E. R. McCown (eds.), q.v., pp. 377–422.

1980 "*Australopithecus afarensis* and *A. africanus*. Critique and an Alternative Hypothesis." *Palaeontologica Africana*, **23**:1–17.

1983a "Hominid Evolution in Africa." *Canadian Journal of Anthropology*, **3**:163–185.

1983b "Recent Advances in the Evolution of the Hominids with Especial Reference to Brain and Speech." Pontifical Academy of Sciences, *Scrita Varia*, **50**:85–140.
Tobias, P. V. and G.H.R. von Koenigswald
1964 "A Comparison between the Olduvai Hominines and Those of Java and Some Implications for Hominid Phylogeny." *Nature*, **204**:515–518.
Todd, T. W.
1920–21 "Age Changes in the Pubic Bone," *American Journal of Physical Anthropology*, **3**:285–334; **4**:1–70.
Tomkins, Jerry R. (ed.)
1965 *D-Days at Dayton*. Baton Rouge: Louisiana State University Press.
Trigg, Roger
1982 *The Shaping of Man. Philosophical Aspects of Sociobiology*. New York: Shocken Books.
Trinkaus, Eric
1982 "The Shanidar 3 Neandertal." *American Journal of Physical Anthropology*, **57**:37–60.

1983 *The Shanidar Neandertals*. New York: Academic Press.

1984a "Neandertal Pubic Morphology and Gestation Length." *Current Anthropology*, **25**(4):509–514.

1984b "Western Asia." *In*: Smith and Spencer, q.v., pp. 251–293.
Trinkaus, E. and W. W. Howells
1979 "The Neandertals." *Scientific American*, **241**(6):118–133.
Trinkaus, Eric and Marjorie LeMay
1982 "Occipital Bunning Among Later Pleistocene Hominids." *American Journal of Physical Anthropology*, **57**:27–35.
Trinkaus, Eric and Fred H. Smith
1985 "The Fate of the Neandertals." *In*: Delson, q.v., pp. 325–333.
Trinkaus, Eric and David D. Thompson
1987 "Femoral Diaphyseal Histomorphometric Age Determinations for the Shanidar 3, 4, 5, and 6 Neandertals and Neandertal Longevity." *American Journal of Physical Anthropology*, **72**:123–129.
Trinkaus, Eric and M. R. Zimmerman
1982 "Trauma Among the Shanidar Neandertals." *Ibid*, pp. 61–76.
Trivers, R. L.
1971 "The Evolution of Reciprocal Altruism." *Quarterly Review of Biology*, **46**:35–57.

1972 "Parental Investment and Sexual Selection." *In*: *Sexual Selection and the Descent of Man*, B. Campbell (ed.), Chicago: Aldine, pp. 136–179.

Turner, C.
1975 "The Correlation and Duration of Middle Pleistocene Interglacial Periods in Northwest Europe." *In*: K. W. Butzer and G. L. Isaac (eds.), q.v., pp. 259–308.

Tuttle, Russell H.
1985 "Ape Footprints and Laetoli Impressions: A Response to the SUNY Claims." *In*: P. Tobias (ed.), q.v., pp. 129–133.

———
1990 "Apes of the World." *American Scientist*, **78**:115–125.

Van Couvering, A. H. and J. A. Van Covering
1976 "Early Miocene Mammal Fossils From East Africa." *In*: *Human Origins*, G. Isaac and E. R. McCown (eds.), Menlo Park, Ca.: W. A. Benjamin, pp. 155–207.

Vandermeersch, B.
1981 "A Neandertal Skeleton from a Chatelperronian Level at St. Cesaire (France)." *American Journal of Physical Anthropology*, **54**:286.

———
1985 "The Origin of the Neandertals." *In*: Delson, q.v., pp. 306–309.

Van Lawick, Hugo and Jane van Lawick-Goodall
1970 *Innocent Killers*. Boston: Houghton Mifflin.

Van Lawick-Goodall, Jane
1971 *In the Shadow of Man*. Boston: Houghton Mifflin Co.

Van Valen, L. and R. E. Sloan
1965 "The Earliest Primates." *Science*, **150**:743–745.

Villa, Paola
1983 *Terra Amata and the Middle Pleistocene Archaeological Record of Southern France*. University of California Publications in Anthropology, Vol. 13. Berkeley: University of California Press.

Vleck, F.
1978 "New Discovery of *Homo erectus* in Central Europe." *Journal of Human Evolution*, **7**:239–252.

Vogel, F.
1970 "ABO Blood Groups and Disease." *American Journal of Human Genetics*, **22**:464–475.

Vogel, F., M. Kopun and R. Rathenberg
1976 "Mutation and Molecular Evolution." *In*: *Molecular Anthropology*, M. Goodman, et al. (eds.), New York: Plenum Press, pp. 13–33.

Von Koenigswald, G.H.R.
1956 *Meeting Prehistoric Man*. New York: Harper & Brothers.

Vrba, E. S.
1985 "Ecological and Adaptive Changes Associated with Early Hominid Evolution." *In*: E. Delson (ed.), q.v., pp. 63–71.

———
1988 "Late Pliocene Climatic Events and Hominid Evolution." *In*: F. Grine (ed.), q.v., pp. 405–426.

Walker, A.
1976 "Remains Attributable to *Australopithecus* from East Rudolf." *In*: *Earliest Man and Environments in the Lake Rudolf Basin*, Y. Coppens, et al. (eds.), Chicago: University of Chicago Press, pp. 484–489.

———
1981 Presentation of New Miocene Hominoid Material from East Africa. Annual Meetings, American Association of Physical Anthropologists, April, 1981.

Walker, Alan, Dean Falk, Richard Smith, and M. Pickford
1983 "The Skull of *Proconsul africanus*: Reconstruction and Cranial Capacity." *Nature*, **305**:525–527.

Walker, Alan and Richard E. F. Leakey
1978 "The Hominids of East Turkana." *Scientific American*, **239**:54–66.

Walker, A., R. E. Leakey, J. M. Harris, and F. H. Brown
1986 "2.5 Myr *Australopithecus boisei* from West of Lake Turkana, Kenya." *Nature*, **322**:517–522.

Walker, A. C. and M. Pickford
1983 "New Postcranial Fossils of *Proconsul africanus* and *Proconsul nyanzae*." *In*: R. Ciochon and R. Corruccini (eds.), q.v., pp. 325–351.

Walker, A., D. Pilbeam, and M. Cartmill
1981 "Changing Views and Interpretations of Primate Evolution." Paper presented to the Annual Meetings, American Association of Physical Anthropologists, April, 1981.

Walker, Alan and Mark Teaford
1989 "The Hunt for *Proconsul*." *Scientific American*, **260**(Jan.):76–82.

Ward, Steven and William H. Kimbel
1983 "Subnasal Alveolar Morphology and the Systematic Position of *Sivapithecus*." *American Journal of Physical Anthropology*, **61**:157–171.

Ward, S. C. and D. R. Pilbeam
1983 "Maxillofacial Morphology of Miocene Hominoids From Africa and Indo-Pakistan." *In*: R. Ciochon and R. Corruccini (eds.), q.v., pp. 211–238.

Waser, Peter M.
1987 "Interactions among Primate Species." *In*: Smuts, et al. (eds.), q.v., pp. 210–226.

Washburn, S. L.
1963 "The Study of Race." *American Anthropologist*, **65**:521–531.

Watson, J. B.
1924 *Behaviorism*. New York: W. W. Norton.

Watson, James D.
1968 *The Double Helix*. New York: Atheneum.

Weidenreich, Franz
1946 *Apes, Giants, and Man*. Chicago: University of Chicago Press.

———
1951 "Morphology of Solo Man." *Anthropological Papers of the American Museum of Natural History*, Vol. 43, No. 3.

Weiner, J. S.
1954 "Nose Shape and Climate." *American Journal of Physical Anthropology*, **12**:615–618.

———
1955 *The Piltdown Forgery*. London: Oxford University Press.

———
1977 "Human Ecology." *In*: *Human Biology*, G. A. Harrison et al. (eds.), New York: Oxford University Press, pp. 387–483.

Weiner, J. S. and B. G. Campbell
1964 "The Taxonomic Status of the Swanscombe Skull." *In*: *Royal Anthropological Institute of Great Britain and Ireland*, Occ. Paper 20, D. Ovey (ed.), pp. 175–215.

Weiss, Mark L. and Alan E. Mann
1981 *Human Biology and Behavior* (3rd Ed.). Boston: Little, Brown, and Co.

Wendt, Herbert
1963 *In Search of Adam*. New York: Collier Books.

White, Randall
1982a "Rethinking the Middle/Upper Paleolithic Transition." *Current Anthropology*, **23**:169–192.

1982b "On the Middle/Upper Paleolithic Transition: A Response to Mellars." *Current Anthropology*, **23**:358–359.

White, T. D.
1980 "Evolutionary Implications of Pliocene Hominid Footprints." *Science*, **208**:175–176.

———
1983 Comment Made at Institute of Human Origins Conference on the Evolution of Human Locomotion (Berkeley, Ca.).

———
1986a "*Australopithecus afarensis* and the Lothagam Mandible." *Anthropos*, **23**:79–90.

———
1986b "Cut Marks on the Bodo Cranium: A Case of Prehistoric Defleshing." *American Journal of Physical Anthropology*, **69**(4):503–509.

White, T. D. and J. M. Harris
1977 "Suid Evolution and Correlation of African Hominid Localities." *Science*, **198**:13–21.

White, Tim D. and Donald C. Johanson
1989 "The Hominid Composition of Afar Locality 333: Some Preliminary Observations." *Hominidae*, Proceedings of the 2nd International Congress of Human Paleontology, Milan: Editoriale Jaca Book, pp. 97–101.

White, T. D., D. C. Johanson and W. H. Kimbel
1981 "*Australopithecus Africanus*: Its Phyletic Position Reconsidered." *South African Journal of Science*, **77**:445–470.

Whyte, Robert Orr (ed.)
1984 *The Evolution of the East Asian Environment*. Centre of Asian Studies Occasional Papers and Monographs, No. 59. Hong Kong: Centre of Asian Studies, University of Hong Kong.

Willerman, L., A. F. Naylor, and N. C. Myrianthopoulos
1970 "Intellectual Development of Children from Interracial Matings." *Science*, **170**:1329–1331.

Williams, G. C.
1966 *Adaptation and Natural Selection: A Critique of Some Current Evolutionary Thought*. Princeton: Princeton University Press.

Williams, Robert C.
1985 "HLA II: The Emergence of the Molecular Model for the Major Histocompatibility Complex." *Yearbook of Physical Anthropology*, **28**:79–95.

Wilson, E. O.
1975 *Sociobiology, The New Synthesis*. Cambridge: Harvard University Press.

Wolbarsht, M. L.
1975 "Letter to the editor." *Science*, **187**:600.

Wolpoff, Milford H.
1980a *Paleoanthropology*. New York: Alfred A. Knopf.

———
1980b "Cranial Remains of Middle Pleistocene European Hominids." *Journal of Human Evolution*, **9**:339–358.

———
1983a "*Ramapithecus* and Human Origins. An Anthropologist's Perspective of Changing Interpretations." *In*: R. Ciochon and R. Corruccini (eds.), q.v., pp. 651–676.

———
1983b "Lucy's Little Legs." *Journal of Human Evolution*, **12**:443–453.

Wolpoff, Milford H. et al.
1981 "Upper Pleistocene Human Remains from Vindija Cave, Croatia, Yugoslavia." *American Journal of Physical Anthropology*, **54**:499–545.

Wolpoff, Milford, Wu Xin Chi, and Alan G. Thorne
1984 "Modern *Homo sapiens* Origins." *In*: Smith and Spencer (eds.), q.v., pp. 411–483.

Wood, B.
1976 "Remains Attributable to *Homo* in the East Rudolf Succession." *In*: *Earliest Man and Environments in the Lake Rudolf Basin*, Y. Coppens et al. (eds.), Chicago: University of Chicago Press, pp. 490–506.

Wood, Bernard
1985 "Early *Homo* in Kenya, and its Systematic Relationships." *In*: E. Delson (ed.), q.v., pp. 206–214.

Wood, C. S., G. A. Harrison, C. Dove and J. S. Weiner
1972 "Selection Feeding of *Anopheles gambiae* According to ABO Blood Group Status." *Nature*, **239**:165.

Wrangham, Richard
1980 "An Ecological Model of Female-Bonded Primate Groups." *Behavior*, **75**:262–300.

Wu, Rukang
1981 "Where Did Humankind Originate?" *China Pictoral*, No. 7, pp. 16–18.

———
1982 "Paleoanthropology in China, 1949–79." *Current Anthropology*, **23**:473–477.

Wu, Rukang and S. Lin
1983 "Peking Man." *Scientific American*, **248**(6):86–94.

Wu, Rukang and John W. Olsen (eds.)
1985 *Palaeoanthropology and Palaeolithic Archaeology in the People's Republic of China*. New York: Academic Press, Inc.

Wu, Rukang and C. E. Oxnard
1983 "Ramapithecines from China: Evidence from Tooth Dimensions." *Nature*, **306**:258–260.

Wu, Rukang and Xingren Dong
1985 "*Homo erectus* in China. *In*: Wu and Olsen, q.v., pp. 79–89.

Yellen, John E.
1977 *Archaeological Approaches to the Present*. New York: Academic Press.

Yunis, Jorge J. and Om Prakesh
1982 "The Origin of Man: A Chromosomal Pictorial Legacy." *Science*, **215**:1525–1530.

Zihlman, Adrienne L.
1985 "*Australopithecus afarensis*: Two Sexes or Two Species?" *In*: P. Tobias (ed.), q.v., pp. 213–220.

Zhou Min Zhen and Wang Yuan Quing
1989 "Paleoenvironmental Contexts of Hominid Evolution in China." *Circum-Pacific Prehistory Conference*, 2–15, Seattle: University of Washington Press.

Zubrow, Ezra
1989 "The Demographic Modeling of Neanderthal Extinction." *In*: Mellars and Stringer, q.v., pp. 212–231.

Index

Scotland. Fig. 12-7(a), (b) E. L. Simons; Fig. 12-10 The British Museum; Figs. 12-12, 12-13 David Pilbeam; Fig. 12-16 From *Populations, Species and Evolution* by Ernest Mayr, Harvard University Press. Copyright © 1963, 1970 by the President and Fellows of Harvard College.

Chapter 13: Fig. 13-1 R. Jurmain; Fig. 13-3 M. D. Leakey, *Olduvai Gorge*, Vol. III, Cambridge University Press, 1971; p. 386 David Siddon, L.S.B. Leakey Foundation; Figs. 13-4, 13-6, p. 391 R. Jurmain; Fig. 13-7 H. Nelson; Figs. 13-11, 13-12 R. Jurmain.

Chapter 14: p. 408 R. Jurmain; p. 409 The Geological Society of London, British Museum; Fig. 14-3 Peter R. Jones, Laetoli Research Project; Fig. 14-4 D. C. Johanson; Fig. 14-6 The Cleveland Museum of Natural History; Fig. 14-6 Reproduced with permission of the National Museums of Kenya. Copyright reserved; Fig. 14-7 Courtesy of Raymond Dart, photo by Alun R. Hughes; Fig. 14-8 Photo by Alun R. Hughes, reproduced by permission of Professor P. V. Robias; Fig. 14-9 Ellen Ingmanson; Fig. 14-11 The American Museum of Natural History; Fig. 14-13 Transvaal Museum, South Africa (also source of specimen); Fig. 14-14 The Bettmann Archive; Fig. 14-15 P. V. Tobias (reconstruction by Ronald J. Clark); Figs. 14-18, 14-20 H. Nelson; Fig. 14-21 Transvaal Museum, South Africa, (also source of specimen); Fig. 14-22(a), (b) H. Nelson; Fig. 14-23 The Cleveland Museum of Natural History; Fig. 14-24 Photo by T. White, reconstruction by W. H. Kimbell and T. White; Fig. 14-25 Institute of Human Origins; Fig. 14-27 Tim White; Fig.

14-29 Reproduced with permission of the National Museums of Kenya. Copyright reserved; Figs. 14-30, 14-31 Reproduced with permission of the National Museums of Kenya. Copyright reserved; courtesy of Alan Walker.

Chapter 15: p. 453 Courtesy J. D. Clark; Fig. 15-3 Reproduced with permission of the National Museums of Kenya. Copyright reserved.

Chapter 16: Figs. 16-5, 16-6, 16-7 H. Nelson; Fig. 16-10 New York Academy of Medicine Library; Fig. 16-12(a), (b) H. Nelson; Fig. 16-13 S. Sartono; Fig. 16-17 H. Nelson; Figs. 16-18, 16-19 The American Museum of Natural History; Figs. 16-21, 16-24, 16-25 H. Nelson; Fig. 16-32 Reproduced with permission of the National Museums of Kenya. Copyright reserved; courtesy of Alan Walker.

Chapter 17: Fig. 17-3 Fred Smith; Box, p. 514 H. Nelson; Fig. 17-5 Tim White; Figs. 17-8, 17-9(a) Wu Xinzhi IVPP, Beijing; Fig. 17-9(b) H. Nelson; Fig. 17-11(a) H. Nelson; Fig. 17-14, 17-15 Milford Wolpoff; Figs. 17-16, 17-17 H. de Lumley; Fig. 17-18(a), (b) Fred Smith; Fig. 17-20(a), (b) H. Nelson; Fig. 17-21 Wattis Hall of Man, California Academy of Sciences, Golden Gate Park, San Francisco; Fig. 17-29(a) H. Nelson, (b) Fred Smith; Fig. 17-30 Fred Smith; Fig. 17-32 H. Nelson; Fig. 17-33 Fred Smith; Fig. 17-34 Milford Wolpoff; Fig. 17-36(a) Fred Smith, (b) Milford Wolpoff; Figs. 17-40, 17-41 H. Nelson; Fig. 17-47 Wattis Hall of Man, California Academy of Sciences, Golden Gate Park, San Francisco; Fig. 17-52 Fred Smith; Fig. 17-53(a), (b) Milford Wolpoff; Fig. 17-54(a), (b) David Frayer; Figs. 17-57, 17-58 Fred Smith; Fig. 17-59(a), (b) David Frayer; Fig. 17-60 Fred Smith.